# THE
# COOK
# BOOK

# THE
# COOK
# BOOK

*Terence and Caroline Conran*

American Consultant: *Charlotte Turgeon*

Crown Publishers, Inc., New York

# Contents

*The Cook Book* was edited and designed by Mitchell Beazley Publishers Limited, Mill House, 87–89 Shaftesbury Avenue, London W1V 7AD

Editor **Alexandra Towle**
Associate Editor **Dian Taylor**
Art Editor **Val Hobson**
Assistant Art Editor **Ingrid Mason**
Art Assistant **Janel Minors**
Assistant Editor **Rosamond Massie**
Research **Nancy P. Anthony**
Copy Editors **Fiona Grafton, Jane Garton, Anthea Matthison**
American Consultant **Charlotte Turgeon**
American Copy Editor **Helen Scott-Harman**
Editorial Assistants **Atalanta Grant-Suttie, Amanda Lynch, Maxine Stait**
Production **Barry Baker**

Contributors **Maria Kroll, Ann Sayer**
Photographers **Clive Corless, Christine Hanscomb, Terry Trott**
Illustrators **Ingrid Jacob, Andrew Davidson, Paul Brooks**
Lettering **Flick Ekins**

**Library of Congress Cataloging in Publication Data**
Conran, Terence
   The Cook Book
   Includes index
   1. Cookery 2. Menus
I. Conran, Caroline  Joint Author
II. Title
TX715.C7583 641 80-15543
ISBN 0-517-54018-5

Printed in the United States of America by R. R. Donnelley and Sons

**HOW THE BOOK WORKS**
The four main sections chart the progress of food from the shop to the kitchen to the table. All sections are cross-referenced—for example, when reading about lobster in Part One, the reader will find, at the bottom of the relevant column, cross-references to the preparation of lobster (also in Part One), recipes including lobster (Part Two), the presentation of lobster dishes (Part Three), and the recommended specialist equipment for dealing with lobster (Part Four). This system allows the book to be used on many different levels. Novices can explore any subject in depth, while experienced cooks can easily find whatever information they require.

## PART TWO: RECIPES

## PART THREE: PRESENTATION

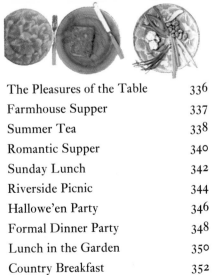

## PART FOUR: EQUIPMENT

# Introduction

This book is about food, and is intended as a reference book for cooks; but unlike most other cook books, it does not have a bias towards the terms and usages of *haute cuisine*. Quite the reverse, this is the book for home cooks who want practical information and a straightforward approach, and who like food cooked beautifully but without pretension.

It is concerned with food in all aspects—it is about raw ingredients and their preparation, and about the cooking and presentation of food. Stated so baldly it sounds a dry affair, but where food is concerned, the matter can never really be dull. Food has a marvellous sensuality about it; even the simplest raw vegetable has a vitality and beauty of its own. The colors, textures and smells of food are all stimulating to the cook, inspiring a desire to cook in the same way that a writer wants to write or a painter to paint. And, like a painter or writer, the cook never knows exactly what will emerge at the end. Predictability would be boring, but luckily good ingredients are so individual—one tomato varying from the next according to the sun, the soil, the season—that there are constant surprises to keep up interest.

Many variations can be made on each theme too. Every time a dish is cooked, there is a feeling it can be improved upon, that it can be done a little differently from the time before. But to do this, one must be intelligent and well informed; the wider the knowledge, the more interesting and successful will be the experiments. This book hopes to provide a knowledge of a vast range of different foods, so that the cook—like someone with an extensive vocabulary—can be fluent and confident. Take, for example, olive oil: when you see it in the ingredients for a recipe, you may go straight to the supermarket and buy an olive oil that has been blended to appeal to the majority, and which therefore cannot afford to have much character. But, if you first find out about olive oil and then try all the different qualities and pressings with their strong individual flavors, you will be in a much better position to judge what the true olive oil taste is like, and which particular oil would be best suited to your purpose. Whether it is oils or cheeses, this book will encourage you to learn to seek out and try individual foods sold in specialist stores or markets where the produce is not designed for mass appeal, and different foods are consequently allowed to have a character of their own.

As a matter of fact, all good food starts with the shopping—certainly living out of a freezer is convenient, but it does away with a good deal of enjoyment. The seasons and their differences are part of the experience of life. If you constantly eat frozen green peas throughout the year, where is the pleasure when the first young peas appear in the spring?

Obviously it is madness not to freeze or preserve food when it is in abundance, and would go to waste otherwise, but does it make sense to ship or fly food many thousands of miles so that we can eat it all the year through? And surely shopping for fresh food in the market is a much more inspiring and entertaining performance than burrowing in the freezer for anonymous-looking if carefully labelled frosty packages.

The recipes we have chosen for this book will provide a basis for everyday cooking. With these recipes, which for the most part are very simple, you can cook throughout the year. There are no flights of culinary fantasy, although we have included one or two grand classic dishes—*quenelles de brochet* for example, and leg of lamb stuffed with kidneys—to prove that we do not in any way reject the refined culinary arts. But we have, in the main, tried to give recipes at a level that one can live with. Nowadays, with life getting more and more complicated, it is good to be simple whenever possible—simple surroundings and simple food, with the occasional elaborate dish to please the stomach.

Simplicity does not mean dullness. There are countless tastes, flavors and experiences available to people who take the trouble to find and try them. This book is intended to help you to do so.

*Caroline Conran*
*Terence Conran*

# PART ONE

## The purchase
## and preparation of food

*Understanding and appreciating
the raw materials*

# Fish

Fish is a food of tremendous character and charm. To a cook with true feeling for raw materials, there is great satisfaction to be found in the beauty of form, the shimmering colors of scale and skin, and the distinctive flavors and textures of fish of all kinds.

It pays to look beyond the inevitable cod, haddock and sole—although these are no less good for their predictability. But the seas, rivers and lakes are filled with an extravagant variety of fish, each with its own character. It is comparatively easy to obtain a thick slice of halibut, a red snapper or eel; more of a triumph to find a silvery skinned pompano, a dolphin fish or a fresh tuna steak. Cooking becomes more of a pleasure if one can make an occasional experiment or discovery, and among fish there are endless discoveries to be made.

## Choosing fish

There is no excuse for bad fish being offered for sale any more, now that refrigerated equipment makes it easy to transport fish for long distances in a freshly caught state. What we are more likely to see in fish shops these days are fresh fish that have been in the shops too long, or fish that have been in and out of the freezer several times, thawed out and sold as "fresh." Unfortunately, the tell-tale signs of a thawed-out fish are less easy to detect than those of a stale fish. If you are not an expert, the best fish to buy are those you see in a crate, packed in ice and obviously straight from the wharf or wholesale market. These fish will have been chilled—not blast-frozen—immediately after they have been caught.

However, with frequent visits to the fish dealer it soon becomes easy to recognize the differences between good, fresh fish that have simply been chilled, stale fish and thawed-out frozen fish. Don't be afraid to sniff the fish if you are suspicious, or to ask pertinent questions. Here are the signs to look for—remembering that the fish is likely to be only marginally on the stale side rather than offensively bad.

### Fresh fish

A really fresh fish looks almost alive and ready to swim away. It gleams, it slides and slithers springily through your hands as though it would like to escape. Its color is bright, its flesh firm and rigid yet elastic to the touch, and the skin will shine with a viscous slime that is clear and evenly distributed.

**Eyes** Bright, bulging eyes with black pupils are a clear indication of freshness. The eyes of stale fish have greyish pupils with red rims, and are dull and sunken.

**Gills** These should be clean and bright red. Dirty, dark or slimy gills are a sure sign of a bad fish.

**Smell** Fresh fish smell fresh and pleasant, while quite obviously, the more offensive the odor, the staler the fish will be.

### Frozen fish

Commercially frozen fish, usually in fillets, are sold from freezers in stores and supermarkets. But there are other fish, usually sold whole, that have been frozen and thawed out, and are sometimes sold with no sign to indicate their previously frozen state. This is an unfortunate deception. Genuinely fresh fish must be eaten as soon as possible after they are caught or bought, but these thawed-out fish are usually imported and have travelled some distance. As long as you are aware of their condition, they need not be shunned —often they are the only chance you will have of tasting unusual fish from far away. To detect a badly thawed-out fish, look for a sad appearance and dull, flabby skin that has lost its natural slime and shininess. If a fish has suffered badly from freezing and thawing it will be unpleasantly watery and woolly.

### Storing fish

There is only one essential piece of advice on the storing of fresh fish—don't. If you must keep it overnight put it, well wrapped in several layers of newspaper, in the coldest part of the refrigerator (but not in the ice-making compartment). Fresh mackerel, herrings and sardines should be eaten the day they are purchased—if this is not possible, put them in the freezer overnight.

### Freezing fish

Domestic deep-freezers simply do not act fast enough to prevent large ice crystals forming in the flesh of a fish. The jagged crystals puncture the delicate tissues, resulting in the loss of texture, juices and flavor. So if you want a freezerload of fish as a standby, you would be well advised to buy commercially frozen fish, which should keep for two to three months.

There is a way to preserve a degree of texture and flavor using a domestic deep-freeze, and this is called glazing. First clean and gut the fish in the normal way, then place it, unwrapped, in a freezer set to fast freeze. When the fish is reasonably solid, dip it into cold fresh water. A thin film of ice should instantly form. Return it to the freezer immediately and, when the ice has set solid, repeat the process two or three times until the fish is completely encased in a good coating of ice, then store it in a freezer bag in the usual way.

Fish that best withstand the freezing process are those with fine-grained flesh, such as the sole and its flat relations. Salmon, and other fish with flesh that falls into flakes, can be frozen but are decidedly nicer fresh; the flesh becomes a little soft with the freezing and thawing process. The shorter the time any fish remains frozen, the better it will be.

Frozen fish should be defrosted before cooking. If cooked from frozen, the outside is overcooked before the inside has had time to thaw out, which is less than ideal.

### Saltwater fish

Fish from the sea can be roughly divided into those that have white flesh and those that are oily. Within these broad categories exist several natural culinary groups, such as the flat fish, the cod and its relatives, the sea basses and porgies, and the oily mackerels and herrings. The great ocean fish, such as tuna and swordfish, have a category of their own, and there is a section for the multitude of fish, such as red snapper and skate, that do not fall easily into categories.

French names have been given in case you wish to sample something new from a restaurant menu, before deciding whether to add it to your own repertoire.

*Fresh fish have bright, bulging eyes and skin that shines with a clear, natural slime. A fish with dull, discolored, sunken eyes and lifeless skin is well past its prime.*

### Flat fish

All flat fish are fine fleshed, white, delicate and lean, and two members of this group—turbot and Dover sole—rank in the top echelon of all sea fish.

### Dover sole (sole)

The true Dover, or Channel, sole is perhaps the cook's perfect fish, a fact reflected by its prominence on restaurant menus in England and Europe. The flesh is firm, white and delicate and keeps well (in fact sole tastes better if it is at least 24 hours old). It lends itself to almost any cooking method and is excellent with a multitude of sauces, but is at its finest simply cooked on the bone and served with butter, parsley and lemon. Only poor-quality fish need dressing up. If you order filleted Dover sole from the fish dealer, remember to take the head and bones home with you—they make the basis of an excellent fish stock.

*Buying guide:* available fresh all year in Europe. There is no true sole in American waters—although a number of flounder-like fish are labelled sole—but imported Dover sole is available in larger East Coast cities. Buy whole if serving plainly broiled or fried; in fillets if serving in a sauce. Each fish provides four good fillets. The price of Dover sole has become inordinately high, but a 7–8 oz/200–225 g sole is enough for one person, though vegetables will be needed if it is to be served plain.

*Best cooking methods:* broiled, fried or *à la meunière*, or filleted and poached in sauce.

### Flounder (*flet*)

The European flounder, or fluke, is a fish of poor reputation. It has a dark brown, distinctly rough skin and a pale belly, and little of the other flat fishes' delicacy of flavor. In America, however, the flounder family includes the excellent summer flounder (also known as fluke), the winter flounder and the grey and lemon sole. These are all quite good eating when freshly caught and are often used in recipes that call for Dover sole or turbot since they respond to the same methods of cooking.

*Buying guide:* winter months for European flounder; year round for American flounder, with the exception of fresh summer flounder. Sold whole and in fillets.

*Best cooking methods:* a good-quality thick

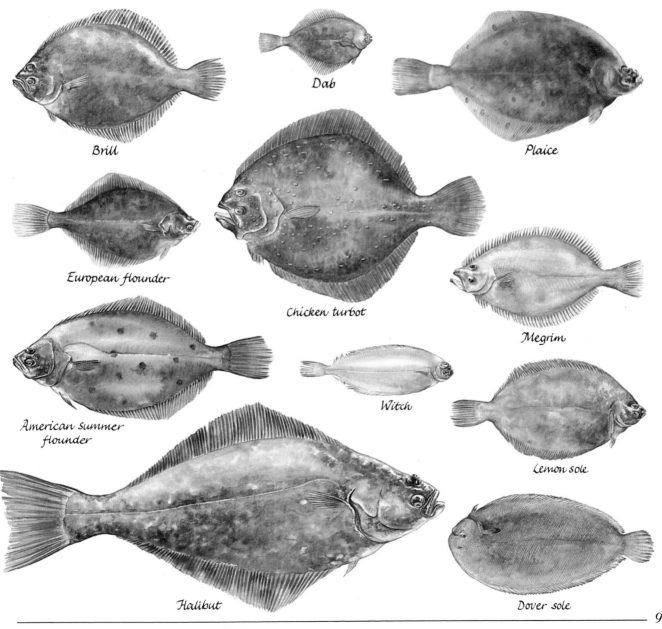

Brill

Dab

Plaice

European flounder

Chicken turbot

Megrim

American summer flounder

Witch

Lemon sole

Halibut

Dover sole

# Sea Fish

flounder can be poached like turbot; a thin one should be fried gently in butter or cooked like sole.

## Turbot (*turbot*)

Turbot is one of the finest of sea foods. Its flesh is the firmest and most delicate in flavor of all the white fish and has to be paid for dearly these days, but any opportunity to buy it should not be missed. Recognize turbot by its knobbly brown skin and awesome size: a whole fully grown specimen can weigh up to 28 lb/12 kg and makes a handsome centerpiece on the fish dealer's slab, usually white belly uppermost. In the heyday of the turbot in the nineteenth century, a huge fish could be poached whole in a turbotière designed for the purpose. These days most of us can only manage to cook chicken turbot (a young turbot weighing 2–6 lb/900 g–2.5 kg) in this way, substituting a large pan for the turbot kettle. If you can't manage a whole turbot, you can buy fillets or steaks, but remember that they take less time to cook.
*Buying guide:* available all year, sold whole, in fillets and in steaks. The flesh should be creamy white; a bluish tinge means that it is stale. Imported turbot may be found in large American cities.
*Best cooking methods:* turbot is so excellent that it suits any cooking method, but is best simply poached or broiled and served with parsley sauce, lobster sauce or hollandaise.

## Halibut (*flétan*)

A giant among flat fish, the halibut can grow up to 6 ft/2 m long and is not, in fact, particularly flat. It is a medium to darkish brown on top and pearly white underneath. It has almost as good a flavor as turbot, although it doesn't hold its succulence so well. It is, however, cheaper than turbot.
*Buying guide:* available all year. Best when small: a young halibut, called chicken halibut, weighing less than 3 lb/1.5 kg is a very good-looking lunch or dinner for 4–6 people, depending on how it is served. Larger halibut are sold in steaks, cutlets and fillets. Avoid frozen halibut, which is dull and dry.
*Best cooking methods:* poach or bake, with a good sauce—lobster, egg or parsley—or melted butter. Also good when eaten very fresh, as in a seviche.

## Lemon sole (*limande-sole*)

A delicious-sounding fish, lemon and sole being such a good combination of tastes, lemon sole in fact neither tastes of lemon nor is it a sole (it belongs to the dab and plaice family and corresponds to the American yellowtail flounder). A pleasant-looking, yellowish-brown fish, it has a fresh salt-and-iodine taste and benefits greatly from

total freshness. Soft textured but pleasant, it is best simply cooked with few additional ingredients.
*Buying guide:* available all year, sold whole or in fillets. Frozen fillets tend to be somewhat woolly.
*Best cooking methods:* use simple dab or Dover sole recipes. Filleted, egg-and-crumbed and fried, lemon sole makes a good children's lunch.

## Plaice (*plie* or *carrelet*)

Dark brown with russet spots on its upper side and white on its underside, plaice is a mainstay of every English fish and chip shop, its mild, soft flesh heavily encased in batter and deep fried. It is certainly a perfectly palatable fish when served this way, provided it is quite fresh. Gently poached in milk, it is a particularly good fish for children and invalids. American plaice can be prepared in the same ways.
*Buying guide:* available all year. Sold whole or in fillets.
*Best cooking methods:* deep fry in a good batter or in egg and bread crumbs and serve with hollandaise or tartare sauce, or poach and cover with a cheese or parsley sauce.

## Dab (*limande*)

Looking like a small flounder with rough skin, the European dab is not the most exciting of fish although its flesh is soft, fragile and easily digested. It can grow up to 12 in/30 cm long but is usually smaller. The American sand dab, or rust dab, is slightly different but prepared in the same ways.
*Buying guide:* best in autumn and winter. Sold whole or in fillets.
*Best cooking methods:* broil whole like a piece of toast, or fillet, egg-and-crumb and fry for breakfast or a light supper dish.

## Brill (*barbue*)

A very good European fish akin to turbot, brill has a mixed-tweed coloring and is smaller than its cousin. Its flesh is softer and not so gelatinous as that of brill, but it is sweet and delicate to eat.
*Buying guide:* available all year, sold whole or in fillets.
*Best cooking methods:* recipes for turbot, halibut and sole suit brill, and it is excellent in a matelote.

## Megrim (*cardine*)

A small, yellowish-grey, rather transparent fish, megrim is also known as whiff, sail-fluke, West Coast sole, white sole and lantern flounder. Not a particularly good fish, it has the advantage of being cheap and, like rock sole or dab, it makes a reasonably good contribution to fish soup.
*Buying guide:* autumn and winter, sold whole or in fillets.

*Best cooking methods:* as for lemon sole or plaice, but probably best filleted and fried with the added texture of crisp bread crumbs to help it along.

## Witch (*plie grise*)

Also known as Torbay sole, witch sole, witch flounder or pole flounder, this long, narrow, cold-water fish is shaped rather like a sole and has sandy-brown coloring. Cook it in exactly the same ways as sole, but witch is a duller fish so use a little more seasoning, herbs and spices.

## The Cod family

This large family of white-fleshed fish, including such cornerstones of the fishing industry as cod, haddock and whiting, keep their succulence best when lightly poached, fried in batter or bathed in a good light homemade sauce.

## Cod (*cabillaud*)

The cod is a handsome fish with a skin of greenish bronze dappled with yellow. It is so plentiful in northern European and American waters that it is frequently abused by cooks; too often it is overcooked until dry and grey and hidden under a blanket of sauce. When treated with care, cod proves to be very fine, but it must be very fresh to be first class. The flesh is succulent and comes in large flakes—a really fresh fish will produce a curd between the flakes, rather like salmon. The cod has an excellent roe—used in taramasalata—and its liver produces a disagreeable but effective vitamin supplement. An adult cod can weigh up to 80 lb/36 kg; small cod, or scrod, just as good, about 1½–2½ lb/700 g–1 kg.
*Buying guide:* available all year, but best in winter. Fresh cod is sold mainly as steaks and fillets. If you are able to choose a cut, pick the middle, which combines the tenderness of the tail with the flavor of the shoulder. Never buy fillets or steaks with yellow or pinkish patches on the flesh. Frozen cod, although reliable, lacks the flavor of really fresh cod, but is certainly a better buy than cod of dubious quality.
*Best cooking methods:* the flesh falls naturally into large, firm flakes and keeps its texture well. It is splendid poached and excellent in fish pies, croquettes, salads and fish cakes. Also bake, broil, fry or deep fry with good homemade sauces such as hollandaise or tartare. In Britain poached cod is traditionally served with slices of lemon and horseradish relish, but nowadays you are more likely to be offered aïoli (mayonnaise heavily flavored with garlic). In order to whiten and tenderize the flesh, it is a good idea to rub it with a cut lemon half an hour or so before cooking.

### Haddock (*églefin* or *aiglefin*)

Fresh haddock is sometimes preferred to cod, but haddock is really no better a fish. It has a fresh marine flavor, a light, firm texture and is blessed with fairly good keeping qualities. It looks like cod, but has a greyer skin, larger eyes and a marked black lateral line. Haddock is also smoked.

*Buying guide:* available all year, best in winter and early spring. Fresh haddock is usually sold in fillets.

*Best cooking methods:* deep fried and served with French fries, in fish pie (especially good mixed half and half with smoked haddock) or any method suitable for cod.

### Hake (*merluche*)

An elongated, deep-water member of the cod family, hake appears on some French menus as white salmon (*saumon blanc*), and is familiar—although probably unrecognized—all over the United States as "deep-sea fillets." Silver hake, from America's East Coast, is a particularly fine fish which also goes under the name of whiting (not to be confused with the European whiting, a lesser fish). Hake is most popular in Spain,

fried in beaten egg or in an escabeche—a cold hors d'oeuvre of fried fish in herby marinade, but it is sadly becoming an increasingly rare sight in the fish shops of northern Europe, and no opportunity should be missed to buy it though it does tend to be expensive. It has tender, flaky flesh, somewhat lighter than that of cod, with a delicate flavor. It also has the advantage of possessing comparatively few bones, which are fairly easy to remove.

*Buying guide:* fresh hake must be very fresh and is sold whole, in fillets and in steaks. It is also sold frozen, but beware of imported frozen South American hake, which is a very inferior relation and is really only fit for commercial processing.

*Best cooking methods:* deep fried in batter, pan fried, baked with pine nuts, bread crumbs and cheese, or poached and served on a bed of spinach or sorrel mixed with fresh cream.

### Whiting (*merlan*)

This is a common but unexciting European fish not found in American waters (in the United States whiting is another name for

silver hake). It is grey and white with a pointed head and backward-slanting teeth. A really fresh whiting is quite good, light and easily digestible, but a tired and travelled specimen will be dry, dull and tasteless.

*Buying guide:* available all year but best in winter. Sold whole, usually between ½ and 1 lb/225–450 g, or in fillets.

*Best cooking methods:* flake and use in fish cakes, purée for mousses and mousselines, poach and serve with a julienne of vegetables, or fry fillets covered with egg and crumbs—which will improve the texture—and serve with fresh tomato sauce.

### Pollock (*lieu noir*)

Regarded as cat food by the uninformed, this is nevertheless a useful fish whose worst feature is its coloring and the best its price. Firm textured and strong flavored, it is one of the mainstays of the ocean-fresh and deep-sea fillet markets. The off-putting greyish flesh whitens considerably during cooking, even more so if rubbed generously with lemon juice beforehand, and although pollock does not have the succulence of cod it is fine for everyday fish cakes and fish pies. Smoked and served with hot toast, it makes a passable substitute for smoked salmon pâté.

*Buying guide:* available all year, sold in fillets or steaks.

*Best cooking methods:* in well-seasoned soups, pies and fish cakes.

### Pollack (*lieu jaune*)

This European fish, also called lythe, is somewhat short on flavor and needs a little help in the form of a good sauce like hollandaise, or interesting seasoning.

*Buying guide:* available all year, best in autumn and winter. Sold whole, in fillets or steaks.

*Best cooking methods:* as for cod, but best in pies, fish cakes and fish soups.

**Some less sought-after members of the cod family:**

**Ling,** when dried, is known as lutfisk and is popular in Sweden boiled and eaten with masses of butter. The flesh of the fresh fish is well flavored and can be used in fish pies and soups of all kinds.

**Cusk** is eaten in pies and soups, and sometimes steamed with a cream sauce.

**Pouting** should be eaten very fresh indeed as its main claim to fame is that it goes bad very quickly—it is sometimes known as stinkalive. Cook like whiting.

### Bass, Bream, Porgy and Grouper

Firm and white fleshed, these fish go well with strong Mediterranean flavors—saffron, fennel, olive oil, tomatoes, white wine

Haddock

European hake

European whiting

American silver hake

Pollock

European pollack

Cod

# Sea Fish

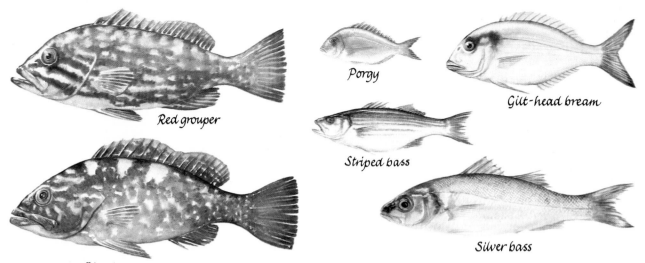

Red grouper

Porgy

Gilt-head bream

Striped bass

Mediterranean grouper

Silver bass

and garlic. They are delicious grilled whole over charcoal in the open air, or baked with olive oil and herbs.

**Bass** (*bar, loup de mer*)
Sea bass, whether one of the North American varieties—striped bass, black sea bass, rock bass—or the beautiful silver bass of the Mediterranean and warmer northern European waters, is the ideal fish for a splendid meal at home. It is just the right size for a small family and has delicately flavored milky flesh.
*Buying guide*: available all year. Sold whole or in steaks and fillets.
*Best cooking methods*: bass up to 2 lb/900 g can be grilled whole—in France they are cooked on charcoal with herbs and a handful of fennel twigs is put on the fire. Bake larger fish, and bake or poach steaks and fillets. Bass is also excellent in salads or a seviche, or, for an unusual dish, steamed on a bed of seaweed.

**Porgy or bream** (*daurade*)
Some species of sea bream are distinctly better than others: the finest is the Mediterranean gilt-head, with its gold spot on each cheek and its compact body. The red bream, the only good bream found in northern European waters, is a large fish usually sold in fillets and only recognizable by its orange-red skin. Porgies and scups, the American East Coast bream, are quite small. They all have rather coarse but juicy flesh and a pleasant taste that suits fairly strong accompanying flavors. They must be scaled —ask your fish dealer to do this for you, or cook the fish with its scales intact and carefully remove them with the skin just before serving.
*Buying guide*: available all year but best in autumn. Sold whole or in fillets.

*Best cooking methods*: season well and broil or bake in foil, or roll in cornmeal or flour and fry briskly in oil. Make two or three slashes on each side with a sharp knife if cooking whole, so that the heat may quickly penetrate the thicker parts, thus ensuring that the whole fish cooks evenly.

**Grouper** (*mérou*)
A delicacy in Mediterranean countries, grouper are not widely available in northern Europe, which is a pity because their flesh is particularly firm and well flavored. America enjoys a number of varieties—red grouper are found from Virginia down to Florida, and the Gulf has black grouper or yellowfish. In California, grouper can often be found in fillets labelled golden bass.
*Buying guide*: sold whole, weighing up to 15 lb/6 kg, and in steaks and fillets.
*Best cooking methods*: as for sea bass.

## Oily fish and small fry
Absolute freshness is essential—all oily fish are inedible when stale. The traditional accompaniments of mustard for herring and green gooseberry for mackerel counteract their natural oiliness.

**Mackerel** (*maquereau*)
The mackerel is one of the easiest of all fish to recognize—the taut, steel-blue skin, mottled on the back with blues and greens and a pattern of blackish bands, is so smooth that it looks almost enamelled. The belly is pearly white, the inside of the mouth black. If the natural markings have lost their brilliance and the fish does not positively shine up at you, do not buy it. The pink-tinted flesh is firm, richly flavored, very oily and rich in vitamins.
*Buying guide*: at their best in April, May

and June, when they are in roe. Mackerel are sold whole, usually weighing about 1 lb/450 g which will serve one person as a main course, two as a first course.
*Best cooking methods*: grill; good stuffed; soft roe can be mixed with the stuffing, but a hard roe is better baked under the fish. Also bake, or poach in white wine or roll fillets in oatmeal and fry them like herring. Sauces for mackerel, apart from gooseberry, include mustard and horseradish.

**Horse mackerel or scad** (*chinchard*)
These somewhat off-putting names, and others such as jack mackerel and round robin, belong to a group of fish regarded as poor man's mackerel—rather unfairly to the mackerel, since although horse mackerel have much in common with true mackerel they are not related. They lack the fine markings of the true mackerel and are not considered a high-quality fish, being rather coarse and bony.
*Buying guide*: available all year. Sold whole —a large one will feed two people, a small one, one person.
*Best cooking methods*: treat as mackerel, but they will not respond as well, or braise.

**Bluefish** (*tassergal*)
Familiar along America's East Coast in summer and in the warm waters around Bermuda, the bluefish can be identified by the blue-green sheen along its back. The flesh is rather soft and goes best with sharp accompanying flavors—lemon juice, capers or green gooseberries.
*Buying guide*: most seasonable in spring, summer and autumn. Usually sold whole— 2–3 lb/900 g–1.5 kg is a manageable size, but it can be up to 10 lb/4.5 kg.
*Best cooking methods*: brush with melted butter and broil (in Turkey, it is grilled on

charcoal), or bake with a little white wine and butter, or poach whole and serve with melted butter.

## Herring (*hareng*)
Once plentiful, popular and cheap, herrings are rapidly becoming less available because of overfishing. This is a pity because they are a tasty fish and rich in protein, fat, iodine and vitamins A and D. They produce a pervasive smell while cooking and need cleaning and may need deboning before cooking, but this is a simple job.
*Buying guide:* available all year but best from spring to autumn. Choose herrings that are large, firm and slippery. They are usually sold whole.
*Best cooking methods:* pat with seasoned oatmeal and fry in a little lard or butter, or score, brush with fat and broil. Never discard the roe, which is very good.

## Smelt (*éperlan*), **argentine and atherine** (*pêtre*)
Although unrelated, these bright, silvery, semi-transparent little fish are very similar in size, appearance and taste. About 7 in/ 17 cm long, they spawn in fresh water. The smelt is the superior of the three: it has a delicious scent when very fresh—some say of cucumber, others of violets—but this disappears very rapidly, so if they seem scentless when you buy them it doesn't mean that they are stale. They all need delicate handling—leave the head and tail on and clean them through the gills.
*Buying guide:* best in winter and spring, but there are good and bad smelt years so buy

smelt whenever you see them—it may be a long time before you see them again.
*Best cooking methods:* traditionally they are strung on a skewer through their heads, dipped in milk and flour and deep fried.

## Sardines (*sardines*)
Fresh sardines are a delight, but they must be fresh. They travel badly so are usually only found close to where they are caught, such as the Mediterranean coasts of France and North Africa (the true Mediterranean sardine is named after the island of Sardinia). When you do find them in fish markets, they are simplicity itself to prepare. Cut the head almost through from the backbone, pull, and as the head comes off the gut will come with it.
*Buying guide:* at their best in spring. Fresh sardines are sold whole; sizes vary so judge by eye how many you need per person. Also sold frozen—the finest are from Portugal.
*Best cooking methods:* fry in olive oil, or coat lightly with salt and olive oil and grill, preferably over charcoal. Eat them with chilled rough wine and fresh bread.

## Anchovy (*anchois*)
Seeing fresh anchovies for the first time, with their slim bodies and sparkling silvery greenish-blue skin, comes as something of a surprise when one's only previous acquaintance with this useful fish has been as canned fillets. Fresh, they can be distinguished from the sardine by their slimmer body and protruding upper jaw. To enjoy their delicate flavor at its best they should

be straight from the sea, which ideally means the Mediterranean, but some varieties do appear in northern European and North American waters.
*Buying guide:* sold whole.
*Best cooking methods:* fry or broil as sardines. Also delicious marinated in lemon juice, or boned and fried with garlic and parsley.

## Sprats (*sprats*)
These are worth some attention if only for their superabundance in European waters, which means that they are very cheap. Tiny silvery fish, they look rather like small herrings but are shorter and stouter.
*Buying guide:* a winter fish, said to be best when the weather is frosty.
*Best cooking methods:* sprats are very oily so are best when broiled, or they can be dusted with flour or oatmeal and dry fried in a pan sprinkled with salt.

## Whitebait (*blanchaille*)
The small fry or young of herrings and sprats, whitebait are the most delicious little fish. Bright, silvery and slender, they are scarcely more than $1\frac{1}{2}$ in/4–5 cm long and have for a long time been one of the summer treats of the English. Whitebait are eaten whole so there is no need to clean them— simply rinse them gently.
*Buying guide:* traditionally February to August. Allow about 4 oz/12 g per person.
*Best cooking method:* the best and only way to cook whitebait is to dip them in milk, shake them up in a bag of flour and deep fry them. They should be so crisp that they rustle as they are put on the plates.

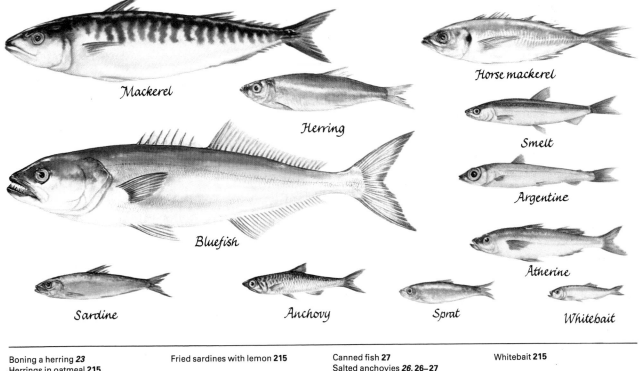

Mackerel
Horse mackerel
Herring
Smelt
Bluefish
Argentine
Atherine
Sardine
Anchovy
Sprat
Whitebait

---

# Sea Fish

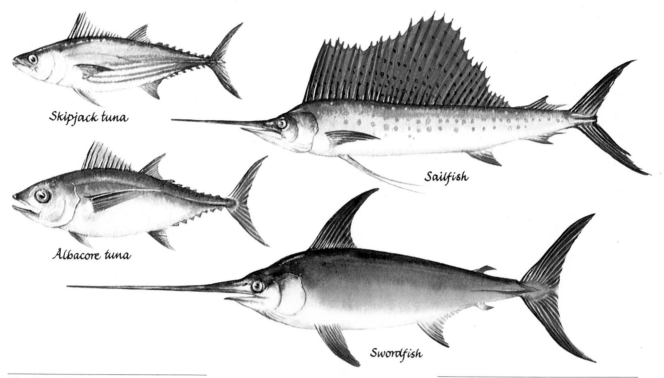

*Skipjack tuna*

*Albacore tuna*

*Sailfish*

*Swordfish*

### The Great Fish

The great ocean fish make firm, meaty eating. Their flesh is inclined to be dry, so marinate it in oil, lemon juice or white wine and herbs before cooking.

### Tuna (*thon*) and bonito (*bonite*)

Found in all the warmer waters of the world, the powerful, beautifully shaped tuna family is related to the mackerel and includes the bluefin, the albacore, the skipjack and bonito. When you see fresh tuna, don't be put off by the ugly, stained look and close-grained texture of the flesh—it improves during cooking. Much drier than canned tuna, it needs plenty of oil and seasoning. Bonito can be treated as either tuna or mackerel.

*Buying guide:* available all year. Sold in steaks and occasionally very small ones are available whole.

*Best cooking methods:* broil, or bake in slices not less than 1½ in/4 cm thick, basting often with oil, salt and pepper, or slice very quickly into small scallops, dust with flour and fry gently in butter and oil for 2–3 minutes on each side.

### Swordfish (*espadon*)

Familiar in Mediterranean waters and popular in America as "the steak of the sea," the swordfish is only a very occasional visitor to northern European waters. It makes delicious eating, but the flesh is close grained and inclined to be dry so is often marinated in wine, oil and herbs before cooking.

*Buying guide:* sold fresh in steaks; also sold frozen in countries which import it. *Best cooking methods:* broil or grill and serve with plain or herb butter, or seal in butter and then bake in a sauce. Also excellent as kebabs.

### Sailfish, spearfish and marlin (*voilier, makaire, marlin*)

Well known to American sport fishermen, these majestic fish are spectacular fighters and highly prized trophies. But if you don't want to put them on the wall, all three make very good eating.

*Buying guide:* not commercially fished, but occasionally sold as steaks in ports near the fishing grounds.

*Best cooking methods:* as for swordfish.

### Opah (*lampris*)

Whatever you call this splendid fish—sunfish or moonfish, mariposa or kingfish—you should never miss a chance to sample it. But a rare chance it will be, for it lives deep in the Atlantic, Pacific and Indian oceans and is only occasionally caught, by accident rather than design. It is thought it might exist in great numbers, but little is known about its habits, and only solitary opahs have been caught. The skin reflects blue, rose, silver and gold, and the texture of the flesh has much in common with that of the salmon.

*Buying guide:* should you ever see one for sale, ask for steaks or scallops.

*Best cooking methods:* bake, fry, broil or poach, but take care not to overcook. Serve with hollandaise.

### Assorted fish

Many fish do not fall naturally into a culinary category except that they are good to eat. For many of them their looks are not their greatest asset, but it is a pity that they should be so often passed by in favor of their better known and more comely cousins.

### Monkfish, angler fish (*lotte, baudroie*)

This fish is sometimes muddled with the angel fish, which is also known as monkfish but is a member of the shark family. Certainly there would be no confusion if the fish dealer would leave the monkfish intact, but it is usually sold headless. Despite its rather endearing ugliness, it is one of the best fish you can buy. The flesh is firm, very white and has the succulence of lobster, and its taste is more associated with shellfish than with fish. It is also called goosefish.

*Buying guide:* available all year. Ask for a good tail piece—3 lb/1.5 kg for six people. It can then be sliced or cooked whole.

*Best cooking methods:* can be treated almost as meat—it is sometimes roasted and called *gigot de mer.* It can also be poached like cod, but allow twice as long for the cooking, or split the tail in half, brush with oil and broil well on both sides. Simplest and best of all are small scallops marinated in lemon and garlic, dusted in flour, and fried in butter.

### Skate, ray (*raie*)

Only the wings of skate are eaten—they contain no real bones but strips of gelatinous cartilage from which the flesh comes off in long succulent shreds. Fresh skate is covered with a clear slime, which reappears when wiped dry, and the flesh should be pearly white, resilient and not flabby to the touch. Don't worry if there is a slight smell of ammonia, this disappears during cooking. Large skate are generally kept by the fish dealer for a day or two in chilled conditions as they are inclined to be tough when very fresh.

*Buying guide:* best in autumn and winter. Small wings are sold whole; otherwise choose a thick middle cut.

*Best cooking methods:* the classic French skate dish is *raie au beurre noir*—skate poached in court bouillon and served with browned butter. It can also be broiled, deep fried or poached. The skin is easy to remove after cooking, if the fish dealer has not done it for you: simply scrape it carefully from the thicker part towards the edge. Because of its gelatinous quality, skate makes a good fish stock or aspic.

**Red mullet** (*rouget de roche*)
The mullet families can be confusing. There are two species of fish—not related—called mullet in European waters. One is the grey mullet, the other the red mullet, by far the finer of the two species. In America the term mullet applies to fish of the grey mullet family; fish belonging to the red mullet family which inhabit American waters are known as goatfish or bellyfish.

The Mediterranean red mullet is a superb fish, deep rose with a faint golden bar along each side. The flavor is quite distinctive, something between shrimp and sole. This is the ideal fish to cook with strong Mediterranean flavors—garlic, saffron, rosemary and fennel. Its liver is often left in during cooking and provides an added richness of flavor, giving red mullet its nickname of sea woodcock.

*Buying guide:* best in summer, but if they seem to be bent sideways they have been frozen and have just thawed out. Sold whole: always ask for the liver to be left in.

*Best cooking methods:* ideal for fish terrines, mousses or pâtés. Also excellent broiled, baked or *en papillote*—red mullet is seldom cooked with water.

**Grey mullet** (*muge, mulet*)
There are several varieties of grey mullet, known variously as striped mullet, black mullet, jumping mullet and lisa, and they are too frequently neglected in favor of the more highly prized red mullet, which is in fact no relation. Grey in color, it has large thick scales and a heavy head with thick, delicate lips. The flesh is coarse and slightly soft, but the flavor is very good, particularly if heightened with fennel or Pernod. The roe is excellent and, used salted, is the proper roe for making the Greek specialty taramasalata.

*Buying guide:* available all year. Sold whole;

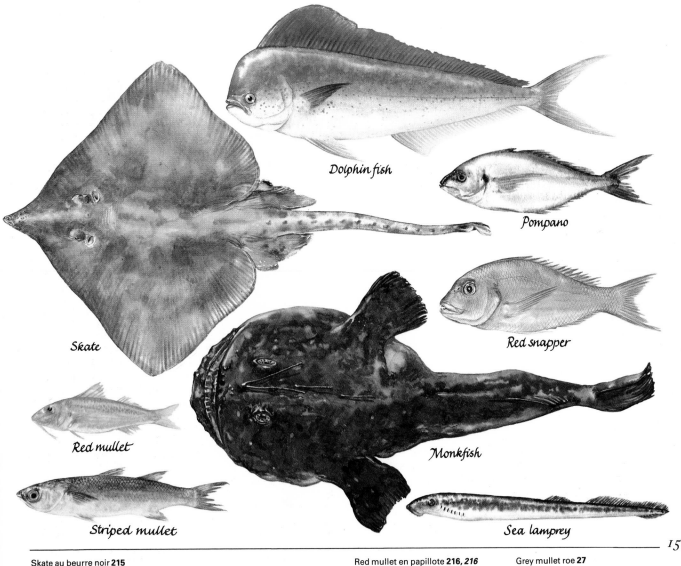

Dolphin fish

Pompano

Skate

Red snapper

Red mullet

Monkfish

Striped mullet

Sea lamprey

Skate au beurre noir **215**

Red mullet en papillote **216**, *216*

Grey mullet roe **27**
Taramasalata **221**

# Freshwater Fish

rather than wash it. Remove the gills but leave the head on—the eyes will turn quite white as the fish is cooking. The skin can be removed after cooking, if wished, in one whole piece.

*Buying guide:* available all year, fresh (hatchery) or frozen. Sold whole. Allow one trout per person, unless the trout are particularly large.

*Best cooking methods:* trout can be poached in a court bouillon, served *à la meunière*, baked, broiled or fried, or smoked in a home smoker. It can also be cooked in beer with horseradish and served with horseradish sauce, and another good, if surprising, sauce is a purée of green gooseberries. If the trout is still alive or is extremely fresh it can be cooked *au bleu* in water with vinegar in it; served with hollandaise or mousseline sauce it is well worth the trouble. In Sweden trout is boiled in a very little salt water and served with butter.

## Char (*omble*)

The arctic char of northern Europe and Canada, the char (*omble-chevalier*) of the deep lakes of the French and Swiss Alps, and the Dolly Varden, brook trout and lake trout of North America (also chars) all belong to the enormous and excellent salmon family.

The arctic char is a silver, salmon-like fish with a pink underside, which flushes deep red during spawning. It has firm, delicate flesh and makes a delicious meal. Arctic char used to be so prolific in the Lake District of northern England that potted char became a famous breakfast delicacy, but these days its numbers have lessened considerably. In France, the *omble-chevalier*, which resembles trout, is eaten throughout

the summer and is definitely worth ordering if you see it on a menu. The Dolly Varden, brook trout and lake trout are also very good table fish and deservedly popular.

*Buying guide:* the arctic char is best in early autumn; American chars are available all year. Small brook trout are sold whole, each enough for one person. Lake trout are larger, and these and arctic char can be cut into steaks, or cooked whole.

*Best cooking methods:* as for trout or salmon. Steaks can be poached for a few minutes with bay leaves and eaten cold.

## Grayling (*ombre*)

A delicious, thyme-scented fish, called by St. Ambrose the flower fish or flower of fishes, grayling should be eaten if possible as soon as it is caught because the delicate flavor is fugitive. It is a graceful fish, silver with finely marked geometric scales and a long spotted back fin. It cannot survive in even slightly polluted water and only thrives in cold, crystal-clear, turbulent rivers, often living alongside trout and eating the same food. A very fresh grayling has much in common, in taste and texture, with trout, and bears up well in comparison.

You will probably have to catch your own grayling to try one. Scale it before cooking—scald with boiling water and use a knife or a fish scaler, or try picking the scales off with your fingernails. Grayling never weigh more than 4 lb/2 kg, and are usually less than 2 lb/900 g.

*Best cooking methods:* brush with butter, flavor with thyme—especially if you find thyme near the brook where the fish was caught—and grill, broil, or fry gently in clarified unsalted butter.

## Carp (*carpe*)

One of the hardiest of all fish, the carp is known to have existed in Asia thousands of years ago and is reputed to live to a grand old age. A somewhat lumbering fish, in its natural state it lives in slow and often muddy rivers or lakes, but it can survive well in domestic ponds and is extensively farmed.

The common or king carp is covered with scales, but variants have been bred such as the crucian, mirror, spiegel and leather carp with just a few large scales that can be picked off with your fingernails, or with no scales at all. To scale a common carp, pour some boiling water over it first, but better still ask the fish dealer to scale it for you. A compact and meaty fish, carp needs to be cooked with plenty of interesting flavors.

*Buying guide:* at their best in late summer and autumn. Sold whole, usually a good size for four people.

*Best cooking methods:* stuffed and baked, or poached and served with horseradish or sorrel sauce. A baked carp can be served on a platter, surrounded by fried gudgeon if that is what the day's catch has consisted of —the small fish have just their bodies coated with eggs and crumbs, leaving their heads and tails free as if they were in a muff, and are then deep fried. Jewish recipes for carp are excellent.

## Pike (*brochet*), pickerel (*brocheton*) and muskellunge

The predatory pike is quite handsome in its way, especially the younger fish, or jack, which has bold markings on a golden brown or greenish silver background. An adult pike can weigh up to 40 lb/18 kg or more, and the flesh is white and firm. The

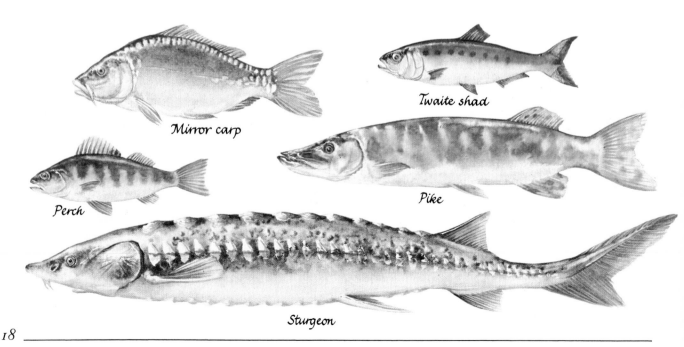

Mirror carp

Twaite shad

Perch

Pike

Sturgeon

muskellunge of northeastern and north central North America can grow even larger, but the pickerel, or young pike, of the eastern and southern states is much smaller, usually around 5 lb/2.5 kg. In France pike is much admired, and quenelles de brochet, the lightest of fish dumplings, served with a white wine sauce, is a classic dish.

The theories about cooking pike are many: it should be bled to remove the sharp, reedy taste; it should have quantities of salt forced down its throat and be left to hang overnight to dissolve the bones; it should not be washed because its natural slime keeps it tender. However, a medium-size pike is perfectly good cooked without any of these refinements. Simply scale it before cooking —pour a little boiling water over it first. Watch out for the bones when you eat it, for they are vicious and plentiful; and don't ever eat the roe, which in some cases can be poisonous.

*Buying guide:* best in autumn and early winter. If you do see pike for sale, a small, whole one is best. Large pike are usually cut into steaks.

*Best cooking methods:* pike tends to be dry and a very large one may also be tough, so steaks should be marinated before being fried or broiled. Small pike can be poached and served with *beurre blanc*, melted butter, parsley sauce or caper sauce. Best of all, you can make it into quenelles. In Scandinavia, pike is boiled and eaten with horseradish.

### Perch (*perche*), pike perch or zander (*sandre*) and yellow perch

The perch is a beautiful little fish, pale greenish-gold with a white or yellowish belly and superb coral-colored fins. The back has dangerously sharp spines and the scales are stubborn, but the fish is well worth the trouble of preparing; it is firm fleshed, delicate and light, and has a very good flavor. It is a fish that should only be eaten when it is gleamingly fresh.

Looking somewhat like a cross between pike and perch, with a bony head, thick skin and spiny dorsal fin, the European pike perch is reared, like trout, in special conditions for fast growth. Even so it is a most delicious fish with firm, white, wonderfully flavored flesh, more interesting than trout and well worth purchasing whenever you see it. The American pike perch is also known as the yellow pike perch, blue pike perch and walleyed pike.

The yellow perch, sold in many American midwestern markets, is a popular pan fish, known as "yellow ned" in many localities. It is closely related to the common perch and can be cooked in the same ways.

To prepare perch and pike perch for cooking, first carefully cut off the spines and fins with strong scissors, then bend the fish over and scrape the scales that will be raised a little from their usual flat position. The procedure is slightly easier if you hold the fish firmly by the tail with a cloth or paper towel, or you can sprinkle your hands with salt. A pair of stout scissors is also useful for opening the fish to gut it.

*Buying guide:* these fish are sold whole. Smaller fish are more delicate to eat than the large ones.

*Best cooking methods:* perch and pike perch are probably best fried slowly in clarified butter, about ten minutes on each side for a 1½ lb/700 g fish. They can also be baked, boiled or broiled. Perch *maître d'hôtel* is perch split, seasoned and broiled with a dressing of butter and chopped parsley poured over it before it is sent to the table. This is simple and good.

### Shad (*alose*)

The shad is a large migratory member of the herring family which spawns in fresh water. White fleshed and nutritious, it has a good flavor but also, unfortunately, a multitude of fine wire-like bones. The roe is particularly good—it is even classed as an aphrodisiac by more hopeful gourmets.

The allis shad, which can grow up to 2 ft/60 cm long, and the smaller twaite shad (*alose finte*) are caught in the Loire and Garonne rivers of France in the springtime, when they are full-roed. The American shad (*alose canadienne*) has been successfully transplanted from the Atlantic to the Pacific and the roes are sold frozen and canned as well as fresh.

Remove as many of the bones as possible before cooking shad, using tweezers if necessary. When the fish is cooked, cut it through in lengthwise parallel strips about 4 in/10 cm apart and remove any accessible bones before serving, moving your finger over the surface of the flesh to detect the hidden ones.

*Buying guide:* best in spring when full-roed. Usually sold whole; a 3 lb/1.5 kg shad will feed six. Ask the fish dealer to scale and possibly bone the fish when he cleans it.

*Best cooking methods:* stuff with sorrel and bake, or bake and serve on a bed of sorrel. If the roe is not cooked with the fish, it can be cooked *à la meunière* or gently baked in butter. Shad can also be filleted, with the skin left on, and gently broiled. Serve with

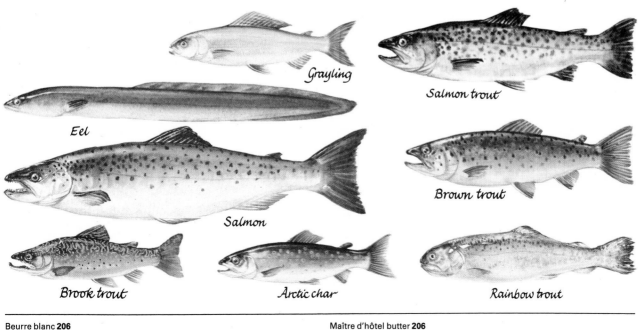

Grayling

Salmon trout

Eel

Brown trout

Salmon

Brook trout

Arctic char

Rainbow trout

fresh tomato sauce, *beurre blanc* or sorrel purée mixed with fresh cream.

## Sturgeon (*esturgeon*)

A huge and somewhat prehistoric looking creature, the sturgeon spends most of its life in the sea, but is most sought after when it comes into rivers to spawn. It can grow up to 20 ft/6 m or more and the beluga sturgeon —usually a more modest size and the source of the most expensive caviar—can live to the ripe age of 100. Sturgeon are still caught in some American and European rivers, but they are most plentiful in the Caspian Sea, using its southern rivers for spawning. The flesh is white, very firm, rich and close textured, and is frequently likened to veal. It is inclined to be dry and is improved by being steeped in a white wine marinade before it is cooked.

*Buying guide:* best in spring. Usually sold in large pieces or as steaks.

*Best cooking methods:* broil or fry in butter, like veal, or poach in white wine and serve with a creamy sauce. In France, a luxurious version is sturgeon poached in champagne. It is also very good smoked, like salmon.

## Eels and elvers (*anguilles*)

Eels have a life cycle as strange as that of any fish. The European eel is spawned in the Sargasso Sea and promptly travels up to 4,000 miles/7,000 km to find the fresh waters of its ancestors, where it will spend most of its life, only returning to the Sargasso to spawn and then die. (American, Australian and Japanese eels have spawning grounds closer to land, but still have a very long way to travel.)

By the time they reach the river mouths the larvae have grown into elvers 2–3 in/ 5–8 cm long. These little creatures, looking like transparent spaghetti, are good to eat, rather like whitebait but not as crisp. By their second winter in fresh water the elvers have become small yellow eels, which are not so good to eat. These then mature into the familiar silver eels, velvety brown on their backs and silver below, and excellent to eat—meaty, even textured, succulent and very rich.

*Buying guide:* elvers appear in the spring; eels are in season all year but are best in autumn. Try to buy live eels—they become tough and go off instantly once killed. If you flinch at the prospect of dispatching a live eel yourself, ask the fish dealer to kill and skin it for you and to chop it into pieces. Fish dealers tend to chop eels into 1 in/ 2.5 cm lengths, but ask for 3 in/8 cm pieces, which look better and are better able to keep their moisture during cooking.

*Best cooking methods:* jellied eels and "eel pie and mash" with a kind of parsley liquor or sauce have long been a specialty of London's East End, and jellied eels are an English seaside treat. You may prefer to stew your eel in red wine, wrap it in bacon and sage leaves and broil it, or sauté it with a few bay leaves and serve it with green sauce. Elvers should be washed and tossed dry in a cloth, dipped in flour, then cooked immediately in hot oil. In Spain they are served in a fried tangle with a fiery fresh tomato sauce.

## Other freshwater fish

The following freshwater fish are not commercially fished or grown in hatcheries, and are unlikely to be found in a fish market —they are trophies for the angler rather than the cook.

**Barbel** Respected by European anglers as one of the hardest freshwater fish to catch, the barbel does not make very good eating, the flesh being somewhat coarse and flannelly. It must be cleaned and soaked and rinsed and soaked again before cooking, and the roe is slightly poisonous. Cook in the same ways as catfish.

**Bass** A collective name for a large family of bony fish with spiny fins, which includes the magnificent sea bass. All make good eating. Cook small ones whole, baked and stuffed, or broiled with fennel stalks. Fillets from larger fish can be poached or served *à la meunière*.

**Bleak** A small, slim, silvery fish found in the rivers of northern Europe, which can be cooked just like whitebait.

**Bluegill** A popular fish with anglers, this dry but well-flavored member of the sunfish family is best when pan-fried. It is also known as bream and sun perch.

**Buffalo fish** A popular freshwater fish from the Great Lakes and the Mississippi Valley which makes good eating. It is often smoked, but can be prepared as for carp when fresh. Other varieties are the common buffalo, the red mouth, the prairie buffalo and the big mouth rooter.

**Burbot** This handsome golden fish is the only member of the cod family to inhabit fresh water, and it is found in Europe, Britain and the United States. Burbot has good, firm, fatty flesh and a richly flavored liver that can be sliced to release its oils and baked or poached with the fish. The fish may also be cooked in red wine, or served with a tomato, cheese and cream sauce. Burbot is best in summer.

**Catfish** So called because of the long barbels that hang about its mouth like drooping cat's whiskers, the catfish is a particularly hardy creature. It is easily transplanted from one region to another, and is a candidate for intensive fish culture. It should be skinned before cooking, and is usually deep fried as fillets and served with tartare sauce. It also makes a good basis for a fish soup that should include plenty of tomatoes, garlic, herbs and white wine.

**Chub** A fish that precisely fits the description "cotton wool stuffed with needles," chub is watery fleshed, full of small forked bones and not really worth eating. If, however, you do catch one and don't want to waste it, try stewing it, frying it or baking it in foil with herbs. It should be cooked as soon as possible after being caught as the flavor deteriorates in a very short time.

**Crappie** Known to anglers as white crappie, this is an excellent Mississippi Valley and New England freshwater fish. It is related to the delicious calico bass or black crappie and is usually fried.

**Dace** The European and American dace are completely different fish that happen to have the same name, but neither is of much culinary interest. Both may be rolled in flour and deep fried, or fried in butter (preferably over an open fire on the river bank just after they have been caught).

**Gudgeon** Found on the sandy bottom of many rivers and lakes in Britain and Europe, gudgeon are delicious little fish which can be crisply fried like whitebait, and served with lemon and chopped parsley.

**Lake herring/cisco** A whitefish found in plentiful supply in the Great Lakes, lake herring, nicknamed cisco, make good eating and can be used for trout, smelt or salmon recipes.

**Roach** A quite well-flavored British and European fish, roach sadly defies much enjoyment because it has such quantities of bones. Larger specimens (around 3 lb/ 1.5 kg) can be scored and fried in butter, or baked in white wine. The roe, which is greenish, is good, and becomes red when it is cooked.

**Sheepshead** Not to be confused with the saltwater red bream, for which sheepshead is another name, this fish is found in fresh waters of the American Middle West and southern states. It is a relative of croakers and drums, and can be either poached or pan fried when very fresh.

**Tench** This fish, which is said to be best when taken from fast-running waters in Britain, must be scaled, cleaned and soaked in cold water before cooking. The flesh is rather flaccid and has a somewhat muddy flavor, but it may be cooked in a matelote together with eel, carp and pike, or fried or baked and served with an interesting sauce that should include such strong flavors as herbs, cloves, garlic or shallots. Tench are in season between autumn and spring.

**Vendace and powan** Known collectively as whitefish, these fish, which slightly resemble salmon in appearance, are found in cool, clear lakes of northern Europe, including the lochs of Scotland and Ireland. Both fish may be treated as for grayling.

**Trimming
flat fish**

**1.** *Flat fish are
usually gutted on the
boat as soon as they
are caught, so
preparing them for
cooking is a simple
task. First, snip off
the tough upper
pectoral fin. The
fish here is a
small halibut.*

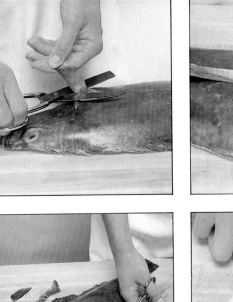

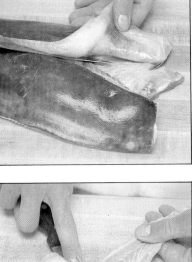

**2.** *Slice down one
side of the fish,
edging the knife
between the flesh and
the bones. For the
second fillet, slice
away the flesh from
the opposite side.
For the third and
fourth fillets, turn
the fish over and
repeat the process.*

**2.** *Trim the tail and
cut away the dorsal
and anal fins.*

**3.** *To skin the fillets,
hold each firmly by
the tail end and
work a sharp
filleting knife down
the length of the
fillet, keeping the
blade as close to the
skin as possible.*

**3.** *Cut off the head
just below the gills.*

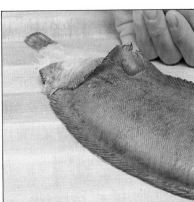

**Skinning sole**

**1.** *To skin a flat fish
that is to be cooked
whole, first make a
nick in the skin
across the tail end on
the darker side. Run
a finger up either
side of the fish
between the skin
and the flesh.*

**Filleting and
skinning flat fish**

**1.** *Make a slit down
the backbone from
top to tail.*

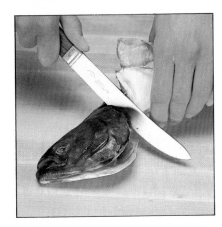

**2.** *Ease the skin
away from the flesh,
pulling towards the
head. If the skin
proves too slippery
to grip, dip your
fingers in salt. If you
want to remove the
white skin from the
reverse side, turn the
fish over and repeat
the process.*

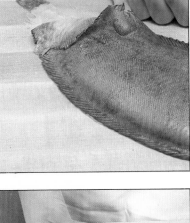

# Fish/*Cleaning and filleting*

**Scaling a round fish**
*Hold the fish by the tail. Scrape away the scales with the back of a knife, working towards the head.*

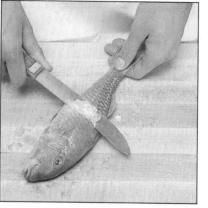

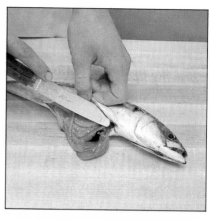

4. *Slit open the fish's belly and ease out the guts. Finally, rinse the fish thoroughly, inside and out, under cold running water.*

**Cleaning round fish**
1. *Before cooking a fish whole, it is important to remove the bitter-tasting gills. Lay the fish— in this case a mackerel—on its back and ease open the gill flaps.*

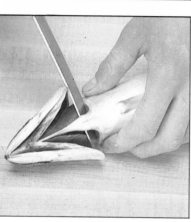

**Filleting round fish**
1. *Starting just behind the head, cut into the back of the fish, sliding the knife closely along one side of the backbone.*

2. *Push the fan of gills out from between the gill flaps, sever and discard them.*

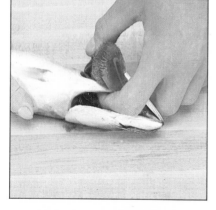

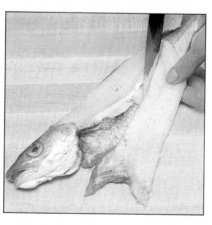

2. *Continue slicing down the length of the fish, severing the fillet just below the gills and at the tail.*

3. *Trim off all the fins with blunt-ended scissors.*

3. *Cut the second fillet from the opposite side of the backbone. Skin the fillets in the same way as illustrated for flat fish.*

**Boning a herring**

**1.** *Cut down into the head and, when the knife is almost through, ease the head away from the body, taking the guts with it.*

**2.** *Slice down the back of the fish, keeping the knife close against one side of the backbone. Do not puncture the belly. Open out the herring like a book.*

**3.** *Turn the fish flesh side down and cut away the backbone and small adjoining bones.*

**4.** *Discard the head, guts and bones. This method of boning a herring is particularly suitable when the fish is to be stuffed.*

**Cutting salmon scallops**

**1.** *Take a tail end section of fresh salmon.*

**2.** *Cut it lengthwise along each side of the backbone, starting at the tail and cutting as close to the bone as possible. Discard the backbone and skin each fillet.*

**3.** *Slice each fillet into two thin slices, using a long, sharp, flexible knife.*

**4.** *Place each slice of salmon between two pieces of dampened wax paper and gently but firmly flatten the fish into scallops, using a rolling pin or a cutlet beater.*

# Preserved Fish

Fresh fish deteriorates fast and has always been a natural subject for traditional preserving methods. Indeed, the smoking, pickling, salting and drying of fish used to be a matter of simple necessity—when fishing boats relied on the wind, and overland transport on the horse and cart, fresh sea fish was practically unknown inland. Moreover, as fish was the prescribed food for the numerous meatless days in the Christian calendar (as many as 12 a month), to preserve it, and to preserve it palatably, was a matter of great importance.

## Smoked fish

Fish must be salted before smoking. This process, which entails either soaking the fish in a brine strong enough to keep a potato afloat, or rubbing into it a generous amount of dry salt, improves both the flavor and the keeping qualities. After salting, the fish is cold- or hot-smoked. The protein content remains unchanged, calories are diminished.

To find smoked fish you like, try different varieties for they vary enormously, and regional specialties still find their way into stores. Some are pale and oak-smoked, while others are over-salted and artificially dyed in fierce hues of red or yellow.

There are several ways of improvising a smoker in your garden—all you need is a container/chimney for the smoke and a draft for the fire. If you intend to smoke a great deal, then it is worth rigging up a barrel smoker. For the less ambitious, the Scandinavian smoke-box is much less of a production, it can even be used indoors and will hot-smoke a gutted, salted fish in 10 to 20 minutes. These smoke-boxes come with sawdust to which you could add thyme, rosemary or juniper berries, whose scent will make your fish both smell and taste much more interesting.

Store-bought smoked fish will keep for about three days, or up to twenty days in a freezer. Home-smoked fish should be eaten at once. Only dried and salted fish keeps indefinitely.

## Cold-smoked fish

Cold-smoking takes place at temperatures of around 75°F/24°C, which smokes the fish but does not cook it. Products of the cold-smoking process are either eaten raw, like smoked salmon, or may require further cooking, like kippers or finnan haddie.

**Smoked salmon** The British think that salmon is best when caught in Scottish waters, Norwegians say that those caught in Norwegian waters are better still, and all agree that Canadian salmon comes third. Smoked salmon should be fresh and succulent, melting away under the knife as it is sliced. The best of all is the pale pink-gold, rather under-salted salmon. A darker red, or a deep orange color usually means dyed or overcured fish, and is not a good sign.

The traditional Scottish way of kippering salmon, as the process used to be called (kippers having merely borrowed the word), involves brining the boned sides of salmon, wiping them, drying them, oiling them and then covering them in brown sugar. Another wipe with a cloth, often soaked in whisky, another anointing with olive oil, and another whisky wipe, and then the sides are smoked over a fire of peat and oak chips.

Fresh smoked salmon is usually sliced for you in the shop, but if you can afford the outlay, a whole side works out to be slightly more economical. A side is half the whole length of the fish from shoulder to tail. Buying a whole side has the advantage of giving you both the denser, saltier, lower cuts and the fatter middle. To slice the salmon, go across the grain of the flesh—that is, cut from the shoulder towards the tail. You need an extremely sharp, long, flexible knife—one with a wavy edge is best—and a nail through the tail helps to keep the fish steady.

Scottish smoked salmon is eaten sliced transparently thin with lemon and thin brown bread and butter. Lox—as the Jewish community calls smoked salmon—is eaten with cream cheese and bagels. Royktlaks—Norwegian smoked salmon—is, of course, much used for smørbrød.

Vacuum-packed, frozen and indeed canned smoked salmon are all available. All are no more than vividly pink shadows of the fresh variety. What can be a good buy is "trimmings"—untidy scraps of fresh smoked salmon with bits of skin and bone attached. Provided they are moist and soft, they are ideal for smoked salmon mousse or any dish requiring chopped smoked salmon.

**Kippers** Split washed herrings are briefly brined, hung on "tenterhooks" to dry, and then smoked for 4–6 hours. At least that is how it should be done—a new, unattractive idea is to permeate them with a smoky taste by means of an electrical charge.

Many kippers are now dyed during brining, emerging mahogany colored after smoking. There are, however, undyed kippers to be had, notably those from the Isle of Man, which lies in the Irish Sea and has more stringent food regulations than the mainland. Delicate Loch Fyne kippers from Scotland are also worth tracking down.

Buy a fat kipper—lean kippers tend to be dry. And buy your kippers fresh and loose—frozen kippers, although they keep their texture fairly well, do not taste as good, and boil-in-the-bag fillets make very dull eating. If you think your kippers will be too salty, put them head first into a pitcher and pour boiling water over them. Leave them a few minutes, pour off the water, and then prepare in the normal way—broiled with a lump of butter for breakfast or supper, or cold in salads and pâtés for lunch.

**Finnan haddie—smoked haddock** Finnan haddie is so called because it was in the village of Findon, not far from Aberdeen in Scotland, that the method of curing this fish, giving it its distinctive pale appearance, was invented. Originally the beheaded fish were dried and cured in the smoke of seaweed. By a modernized process, finnan haddie is now produced far beyond Scotland. So are its imitations—fillets of white fish that are artificially dyed a bright, bright yellow and chemically treated to taste of smoke. It is easy to tell the true from the false: the color is a complete giveaway.

Smoked haddock is eaten hot. Broil, or poach it for a few minutes in milk or water, then simply serve it with butter, or use it to make dishes such as the creamed finnan haddie of New England, or the Anglo-Indian kedgeree, or the poached smoked haddock of Scandinavia which is served with carrots, hard-boiled eggs and butter. Scotland eats Ham and Haddie, using the palest version of the fish from the Moray Firth and frying it in the fat rendered from a few slices of smoked ham.

**Smoked halibut** Young halibut are sometimes lightly smoked. Their taste is delicate, their texture firm, and they are served in the same way as smoked haddock.

**Bloaters, harengs saur** Bloaters are inshore herrings that are lightly salted and then smoked without the gut being removed. The slight fermentation of the enzymes occurring during this process causes the fish to get bloated and develop a gamy flavor. Bloaters are silvery in appearance, and the flesh is soft and moist. They do not keep as long as kippers, and must be gutted before they are served. They are either broiled, used to make bloater paste or simply mashed to make a sandwich filling. The famous *harengs saur* of Boulogne are even more plumped up than the British bloater, as is the Swedish surströmming, a small fermented herring from the Baltic—this is not much exported, but deeply loved at home, where it is eaten with thin crisp bread or potatoes.

**Smoked sturgeon** If fresh sturgeon, with its finely grained white flesh, tastes rather like veal, smoked sturgeon resembles nothing so much as smoked turkey both in color and taste. It is, however, more delicious still, more buttery and melting in the mouth, and of course a great deal more expensive. Eat it like smoked salmon.

**Smoked roes** Fish eggs from any number of species are smoked and eaten with enjoyment. It should be added that hard roes alone are roes—soft roes are not roes at all but "milt," or sperm, and come from the male of the species. Smoked roes should be firm and moist with no signs of skin breakage. Smoked cod's roe is deliciously grainy and glutinous. Serve as a first course like pâté, or use it to make taramasalata.

**Hot-smoked fish**

Hot-smoking takes place at temperatures of about 180°F/82°C and is the method used for eel, trout, buckling and mackerel, which are smoked and lightly cooked at one and the same time. They are bought ready to eat and can also be served hot.

**Smoked trout** The best smoked trout has gone into brine as soon as it left the water. It is drawn only after it has been drained, and is then ready for smoking. Silver birchwood is said to give it the best and sweetest flavor, and a little peat and a few fir cones make it taste even better. The fish turns golden and, if left longer, to bronze. Look for springiness in a smoked trout: the flesh should be neither mushy nor dry—the fine, firm texture of a nice plump trout is as much of a pleasure as its delicate flavor. Serve smoked trout for a summer lunch or supper with lemon wedges, thin brown bread and butter, and horseradish mixed with a dash of the heaviest cream.

**Smoked mackerel** Silvery-gold smoked mackerel can be very good indeed. As it is not a very subtly flavored fish, it emerges from careful kippering tasting straight-

forwardly of itself and is, usually, firm and juicy. Best bought loose and whole, it is also available filleted and packed in heat-sealed envelopes. Avoid packs that ooze with oil: this indicates that the fish has been stored for too long or at the wrong temperature, and the flesh will be dry. Eat smoked mackerel cold with horseradish sauce or lemon.

**Bucklings** allegedly get their name from a fourteenth-century Dutchman, William Beukels, who invented this method of preserving ungutted herrings. A good fat buckling can be an almost triumphant rival of a smoked trout. It is good eaten with brown bread and butter and lemon wedges, and also good mashed to a paste. In Germany buckling is sometimes lightly broiled or gently fried with the roe left in and served with sauerkraut or scrambled eggs.

**Sprats, sild and brisling** are all small

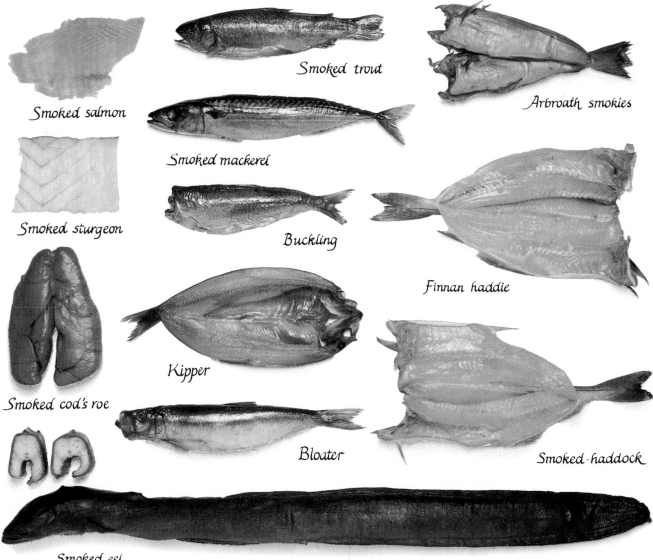

Smoked salmon

Smoked trout

Arbroath smokies

Smoked mackerel

Smoked sturgeon

Buckling

Finnan haddie

Smoked cod's roe

Kipper

Smoked haddock

Bloater

Smoked eel

# Preserved Fish

herrings which when smoked are simply served with dark bread, butter, lemon and a glass of beer. As well as being candidates for smoking they also sometimes find themselves canned as sardines.

**Arbroath smokies** These are small smoked haddock that have been beheaded and gutted but not split, and hot-smoked in the round. After brining they are placed over birch and oak smoke until they are a dark, dull copper with traces of black soot. To serve, open the fish out, remove the backbone, put butter and some freshly milled black pepper inside, close it up again and heat it gently under the broiler or in the oven. When you peel off the dark skin, you will find a golden outer crust and gradually paling flesh.

**Smoked eel** Some say that the densely textured smoked eel is even more delicious than smoked salmon. Smoked eel is very rich, oily and filling, and is usually served with pepper, lemon juice and brown bread and butter. Pinky-beige smoked eel fillets laid over a plateful of golden scrambled eggs, bordered with triangles of fried bread, make a first course that is especially delicious.

## Pickled and salted fish

The pickling process is particularly suited to oily fish, such as herrings. They are steeped in a vinegar or brine solution which halts enzyme action in the same way that cooking does.

**Gravlax** is a most delicious Swedish specialty—it is fresh raw salmon pickled with dill, sugar, salt, white peppercorns and sometimes cognac. It is eaten raw with a rather sweet mustard sauce.

**Salt herrings** are sold whole. They should be soaked for up to twelve hours, filleted and chopped for salads or bathed in sour cream for an hors d'oeuvre.

**Maatjes herrings** are the best salt herrings. They are lightly salted fat female fish with translucent, slippery flesh of a beautiful old-rose color. They need no soaking.

**Rollmops** These are herrings—boned and halved lengthwise—that have been rolled up tightly around peppercorns and slices of onion and fastened with a toothpick before being put into jars to which is added hot, spiced white wine vinegar. Eat them with black bread and unsalted butter.

**Bismarck herrings** These herrings, blue of skin and white of flesh, are first steeped in white wine vinegar. They are drawn, boned, topped, tailed and split and kept for 24 hours layered in a dish, duly seasoned and interspersed with onion rings and sometimes with a few round slices of raw carrot. Eat them with new potatoes or bathed in sour cream or a thin mayonnaise dressing.

**Soused herring, bratheringe** Many people like to souse herrings at home by steeping them in a vinegary marinade to which herbs and spices are added. Soused herring (or mackerel) can, however, be found in specialist stores, as can German *bratheringe*, which is first turned in flour and fried golden brown, and only then steeped for 24 hours in a boiled marinade.

**Anchovies** Preserved salted anchovy fillets usually come canned in oil, those in olive oil being the best. Plain salted anchovies, sold direct from a barrel or a large jar, need a brief steeping in fresh water to make them less harsh.

An anchovy is the most versatile of piquant ingredients, seasoning a great many dishes without imparting the least hint of fishiness. Anchovies are good for salsa verde, braised

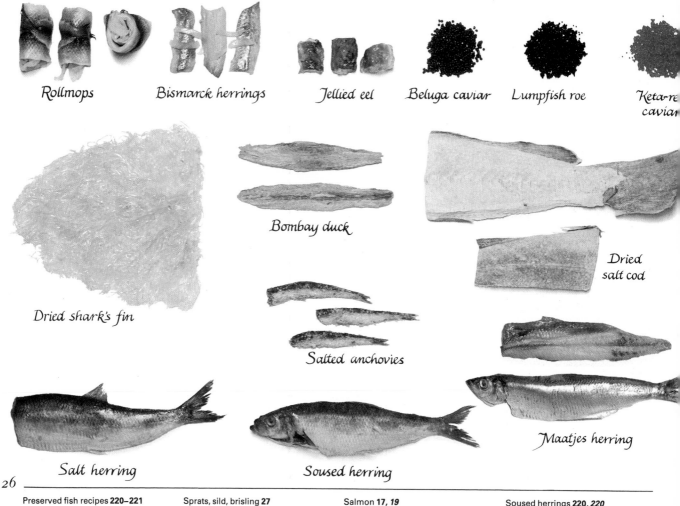

Rollmops

Bismarck herrings

Jellied eel

Beluga caviar

Lumpfish roe

Keta-re caviar

Dried shark's fin

Bombay duck

Dried salt cod

Salted anchovies

Salt herring

Soused herring

Maatjes herring

veal, stews, pizzas, and for eating with egg mayonnaise, with sliced tomatoes and in potato salad and salade niçoise.

## Dried fish

Fish that had been hung up to dry in the wind provided an almost indestructible food supply for our ancestors. This earliest method of preserving fish is the precursor of modern freeze-drying. Salting is another way to extract moisture from fish, thus discouraging decay.

**Dried cod, stockfish** Dried to a flatness and hardness resembling hide, cod and other members of its family—ling, haddock, pollock—spring back to life when they are soaked. This process may take up to two weeks, but in Scandinavia, where stockfish—air-dried Norwegian cod—is much eaten, it is now possible to buy it presoaked and even frozen. The revived fish is often eaten with yellow peas, and also appears in a fish pudding, light as a soufflé, which is served with hollandaise sauce. In Holland, Belgium and Germany, stockfish is often soaked in lime water before being cooked.

In Portugal, where bacalhau—dried salted cod—is almost a staple food, they boast that they have more than 1,000 different ways of cooking it. Some of the best recipes for dried cod are Basque, and variously involve the fish—bacalao—with garlic, oil, tomatoes, pimentos, onions and potatoes.

**Bombay duck** This is the most famous of the various Eastern dried fish. It is found in Indian delicatessens, and provides seasoning for the rice that is eaten with curry. Made from cured bommaloe fish, Bombay duck smells awful when you buy it. Toast it slowly until its edges curl and no trace of the objectionable smell remains. Then crumble it and sprinkle over cooked rice.

**Dried shark's fin** This is delicately flavored cartilage of the fin, which, when you buy it, looks like the tousled beard of Father Christmas. It requires soaking overnight, or even longer, in many changes of water, until it has become like a firm jelly. In China, shark's fin is banquet food: it goes into party soups, into rather liquid party stews and braises, and, shredded fine, into omelets. Its gelatinous properties have been likened to those of calves' feet.

## Salted roes

Into this category fall the costly caviar and its less exotic alternatives.

**Grey mullet roe** Known as tarama in Greece, the salted, dried, pressed roe of the mullet is considered a great delicacy, ranging immediately after caviar and before salmon roe. As the name suggests, it makes taramasalata—one of the "cream salads" of the Middle East. For this purpose the roe is divested of its skin, pounded with oil, lemon juice and crushed garlic, and bound with soft white bread crumbs or mashed potato, and sometimes with an egg yolk.

**Caviar** The fish that are used for commercial caviar production are the sevruga, the large osetra and the giant beluga, which has a huge roe to match. All are members of the *Acipenser* tribe, and are collectively known as sturgeon, although only the osetra rightfully bears this name. The roes are passed through finely meshed sieves to separate the eggs, which are then salted. The brining of caviar is a delicate business. The condition of the fish and the size of the eggs both have a bearing on it, and the finest grade emerges from the care of the master-tasters as malassol, meaning "slightly salted."

Caviars come in a variety of sizes and colors. Sevruga is small grained and greeny-black. Osetra, larger grained, may be golden-brown, or bottle-green, or slate-grey; it can also be pale—almost bluish-white. Beluga, the largest and the best, is grey. The closer to spawning the fish is caught, the paler the roe—and all of these, depending on their quality, make "first-grade" caviar.

First-grade caviar is sometimes pasteurized, which lengthens its shelf life. Non-pasteurized caviar is kept refrigerated at $32°F/0°C$: warmer and it goes off; colder and its flavor is ruined. The contents of an open container should be kept, covered, in the refrigerator, but should certainly be eaten within a week.

This also applies to pressed caviar—which is slightly less expensive than the malassol but is in fact the first choice of many caviar experts. It is caviar that has been poured into cheesecloth bags and drained of some of its liquid. The eggs, of course, are squashed in the process, and what emerges is a fairly solid mass, saltier than malassol, but tasting more intensely of sturgeon, since 2 lb/900 g of caviar are reduced to make 1 lb/450 g of pressed. Second-grade caviar may be saltier caviar of a single variety, or a mixture of different caviars, some of them highly superior.

To educate one's palate, one really needs to eat a lot of caviar, not with tiny special caviar spoons but by the solid mouthful. In the USSR, where large helpings of second-grade caviar are fairly unceremoniously served, it is often eaten with blinis—fat little buckwheat pancakes—and sour cream. But as a rule it is best with a little lemon, some fresh Melba toast and unsalted butter: chopped hard-boiled egg and finely chopped raw onion will eke out a small supply.

**Keta—red caviar** This is made from the roe of the salmon. It is bright orange and large grained, not so much an imitation caviar but a fresh-tasting product in its own right. It, too, is sometimes eaten with sour cream, but usually just with toast, butter and a squeeze of lemon.

**Lumpfish roe** The pink eggs of the arctic lumpfish are salted, colored black and pressed. Sold as German or Danish caviar, it is usually used to make an impression on cocktail party canapés. Alone, it is less interesting than true caviar but is a pleasant experience, served with sour cream and raw onion, and compared with the real thing, it is reasonably inexpensive.

## Canned fish

Fish is one of the few foods that stand up well to the business of canning. Canned tuna and sardines, for example, have become foods worth eating in their own right—quite different from their fresh counterparts, but good nonetheless.

**Salmon** Canned salmon comes in many grades, from the not-so-good bright red to a more acceptable pink (the darker, the oilier). It can be good and is useful in fishcakes and patties.

**Sardines** Good brands of sardines have been gently brined, correctly dried and lightly cooked in olive oil, and stored for about a year, so that the flavor of fish and oil are mingled. The sardines caught off the west coast of France are the best and the most expensive. Portuguese and Spanish sardines are less delicious but much cheaper. Eat sardines bones and all, with dark bread and butter and a squeeze of lemon, or mash them and use in sandwiches or stuffed eggs.

**Pilchards** These fish, slightly larger than sardines, are not very exciting and never as good as sardines. In order to add a little interest, packers tend to bathe them in tomato sauce before canning.

**Tuna** The best canned tuna is taken from the albacore, the king of the tunas, which alone is permitted to be described as "white meat." Other tuna varieties—skipjack, yellow fin, bluefin—are a little darker, but all make very good salads. Use canned tuna for the classic *vitello tonnato*, cold veal with a creamy tuna sauce. Buy good-quality tuna, which comes in solid pieces, packed in oil rather than water. The cheaper brands are often nothing but broken up pieces, and are only good for sandwiches.

**Jellied eels** This traditionally Cockney delicacy is difficult to find freshly cooked. But it is sold in cans, and makes a good appetizer: serve it with little bunches of watercress.

**Sprats, sild, brisling** These are Scandinavian names for young herrings. Small ones are canned and sold under all three names, though they are usually bought as stand-ins for sardines.

# Shellfish

Although overfishing and pollution have taken their toll of shellfish, there are signs that things are improving. Waters that were a hazard to the health of both shellfish and consumers have been radically cleaned up, and new farming methods are making it possible to harvest fast-growing shrimps, prawns and lobsters, for example, in large quantities.

True, the shrimps may not be the small, delicate northern ones but large Pacific varieties; the lobsters may be small and soft-shelled, and we may find oysters on the market the size of tennis balls that can only be eaten chopped like large clams and cooked, but we should be able to enjoy more abundant and possibly less costly supplies. And the delicious local varieties of shellfish are still available. Buy them from a dealer who specializes in them and can be trusted to sell them only when they are sweet and fresh.

If you are buying cooked shellfish, a quick sniff should distinguish the freshly cooked from the fading. Shrimps and prawns lose the color in their shells and become lighter as they dry up. Lobsters and crabs also lose weight—choose heavy specimens with tension in the tail or claws. If they are floppy and unresisting they are likely to be stale. If you want to cook them live, plunge them into fast-boiling salted water, seawater or court bouillon. Take care not to overcook them— all shellfish toughen and become rubbery if they are cooked for too long.

## Crab (*crabe*)

To pick the meat out of a crab is a labor of love but always worth the effort—the flavor and texture are almost equal to that of lobster, and certainly much less expensive. The large crabs with fiercesome claws found all around the British coast, the sweet spider crabs beloved of the French and the soft green-backed shore crabs which are a Venetian specialty are all delicious, especially if you can choose a female with its berry, a brilliant coral-red roe that tastes and looks superb. In America the crab really comes into its own, with an abundance of blue crabs from the Atlantic and Gulf coasts, the superbly flavored Pacific Coast crab, the Dungeness, the Florida stone crabs, the Alaska king crabs and the rock crabs found on the California and New England coasts.
*Buying guide:* alive or cooked, choose crabs that feel heavy for their size and smell fresh and sweet, with no hint of ammonia. About 1 lb/450 g of crab in the shell or $\frac{1}{4}$ lb/115 g of crab meat is usually sufficient for each person, depending on how it is prepared.
*Best cooking methods:* the best crab is the one you boil and dress yourself, eaten cold with mayonnaise and dark bread and butter. Hard-shelled crabs are also good steamed, and can be used to make a very delicious bisque. Soft-shelled crabs—crabs that have just molted their old shells—can be eaten *à la meunière*, or be broiled or deep fried.

Live crab

Small live lobster

Cooked brown shrimps

Cooked shrimps

Live crawfish

Cooked Dublin Bay prawns

Cooked crawfish

Cooked crayfish

Shellfish recipes **222–226**
Preparing shellfish **32–35**

Picking a cooked crab **32–33**

Dressed crab **222**

## Lobster (*homard*)

"There is nothing more delicious in life," said Byron, "than the fireside, a lobster salad and good conversation." With or without the embellishments, lobster is a treat for both the eye and the palate. The colors—creamy-pink flesh, speckled cream and coral shell underneath, deep old brick-red on the back; the texture—firm, delicate and luscious; and the flavor—an appetizing, elusive marine taste—are all highly desirable. And, alas, expensive.

Lobsters from colder waters are generally the finest; the best are the superb Irish and Scottish lobsters and those from Brittany, on the European side of the Atlantic, and the northern lobsters from Maine to Nova Scotia on the American side. The cock lobster is firmer-fleshed than the hen and has larger, meatier claws, but the hen has a more delicate flavor, a broader tail and the delicious coral, or roe, which turns scarlet when cooked and makes excellent lobster sauce—if you can bear to use part of this costly creature for making sauce.

*Buying guide:* fresh lobsters are available all year, but are at their best and most abundant during the summer. Choose a lobster that is heavy for its size and has both its claws—sometimes a claw is lost in a fight, and some of the best meat is in the claws. Alive, the best way to buy lobsters, the shell is dark blue or green; if already boiled, the shell should be bright red. If the lobster is pre-cooked, check that its tail springs back into a tight curl when pulled out straight. This shows that it was cooked when alive. If you are brave enough, give it a sniff underneath, too, to make sure it is quite fresh.

If you intend to cook the lobster yourself, make sure you get a lively specimen and, again, that it is a heavy one—sometimes lobsters get quite thin in captivity waiting for someone to come along and buy them. To keep a live lobster in the refrigerator, but not for more than a day or two, roll it loosely in newspaper to prevent it crawling about, enclose it in a paper bag pierced with air holes and put it in the vegetable crisper.

If called upon to face cutting a live lobster in half or in pieces before cooking, lay it on a board, stomach upwards, and cover the head and claws with a wet cloth to protect your hands. Hold it down firmly and with a strong, sharp, pointed knife make a swift incision in a head-to-tail direction at the point where the head and tail shells meet. This severs the spinal cord. Leave for a few minutes for the reflexes to cease, then cut the lobster in pieces, or split it in half lengthwise through the stomach shell and open it out flat, or cut it in half right through the hard back shell. Clean it, removing the sand sac, if any, from the head and reserving any coral and the delicious creamy tomalley or liver to use in lobster sauce. Cook the lobster immediately.

Small lobsters are usually the most tender: a 1 lb/450 g lobster will feed one person, so you may have to buy several. Large lobsters are also excellent—and work out less expensive—for salads and sauces. Cooked lobster meat, frozen or in cans, is really best forgotten or used as an ingredient in a shellfish salad. Never have anything to do with a dead, uncooked lobster—the flesh spoils very quickly.

*Best cooking methods:* the simplest are best: broiled, boiled, steamed or grilled, served with melted butter and a little lemon juice or a good mayonnaise. Keep the shells to put into fish soup or use them as a basis for lobster bisque or lobster sauce.

## Crawfish (*langouste*)

Depending on where you find it, this comparatively clawless cousin of the lobster is also known as rock lobster, spiny lobster or crayfish—which must be very confusing for the little freshwater crayfish which, in turn, is sometimes known as a crawfish. Depending, too, on where it comes from—it thrives in the warm waters of the Pacific and Mediterranean—it ranges in color from brownish-green to reddish-brown with yellow and white markings. Slightly paler than lobster when cooked, it has dense white flesh, well flavored but inclined to be coarse. The choicest meat is in the tail, and there is a lively market for frozen tails.

*Buying guide:* fresh is best, in late spring or early autumn. Choose specimens without eggs, as those with eggs are not considered to be wholesome. Otherwise, follow the same guidelines as for buying lobsters.

*Best cooking methods:* when fresh, they are best eaten simply boiled with melted butter. Anything left makes a fine salad, with mayonnaise, or a very good bisque together with some shrimps or prawns in their shells, with plenty of cream and Madeira or brandy. Otherwise, use the same recipes for crawfish as for lobster.

## Crayfish (*écrevisse*)

A sweet-fleshed miniature of the lobster, the crayfish (alias freshwater lobster, crawdad and crawfish) is the only edible freshwater shellfish. Once a great feature of country-house tables in Britain, crayfish are still relished in France and Scandinavia. To find your own, look in clear, unpolluted ponds or streams, where they may be found from June to October lurking under the banks. You can catch them by knocking out the inverted cone in the bottom of a wine bottle, baiting the bottle with meat, putting in the cork and lowering the bottle into the water. With luck, the little crayfish will crawl in. Another way is to overturn large stones, pushing a net close by to catch the crayfish as they try to escape; or simply bait a piece of string with some meat. Leave them in a bowl under cold running water for an hour before cooking them, and remove the dark thread of intestine by twisting off the middle tail fin, which will bring the intestine with it. Alternatively, put them into a bucket of water in which you have put three or four tablespoons of dried milk powder, leave them for 12 hours and the crayfish will clean themselves.

*Buying guide:* apart from the native wild crayfish, several cultivated varieties are available from good fish dealers. If you buy them fresh, make sure they are lively—they spoil very quickly once dead. Allow at least 10-12 crayfish per person, depending on your recipe.

*Best cooking methods:* boiling is best. Put some smooth stones in the bottom of a large pot of water—this will keep the heat up so that the crayfish don't suffer when they are dropped in. Bring the water, into which you have put plenty of salt and fresh dill, to a rapid boil. Drop each crayfish in separately so that the water keeps boiling all the time and cook for about five minutes, until they turn bright scarlet. Turn off the heat and let them get cold in their liquor. The French cook them *à la nage*—in a well-flavored court bouillon—and serve them in an appetizing scarlet mound with hot melted butter, or cold with mayonnaise. Crayfish are also used to make a beautiful creamy bisque, and for sauce Nantua—the most delicate of sauces, frequently served with quenelles de brochet (pike dumplings).

## Dublin Bay prawns (*langoustines*)

Whether you meet them as *langoustines* or Dublin Bay prawns, Norway lobster (their Latin name is *Nephrops norvegicus*) or Italian scampi, these pretty pinky-orange-shelled creatures with their pale claws can be treated as exceedingly large shrimps or very small lobsters, depending on which way you like to look at them. The predictability of finding them in their frozen form on the menus of bad, expensive and pretentious restaurants has led to their being passed over by many people interested in their food, but cooked with care, and not surrounded by soggy batter, they make many delicate dishes, both hot and cold.

*Buying guide:* if you are lucky enough to find them fresh, they will most likely be preboiled. Usually only the tails are sold. For four people buy 2 lb/900 g in their shells, half that amount if they are already shelled. Always available frozen.

*Best cooking methods:* if raw, cook them in

Preparing cooked lobster **32**

Lobster sauce **207**
Broiled lobster with butter **222**
Boiled lobster **222**

Crayfish cooked with dill **222**

# Shellfish

their shells in gently boiling, well-salted water for not more than ten minutes and eat them with melted butter. Overcooking makes them soggy and tasteless. Preboiled, reheat them gently for a hot dish; never re-cook them as they easily toughen. Cold, they make a very good salad with oil and vinegar dressing or mayonnaise. In Venice they are dipped in a very light eggless batter, with a few other kinds of small fish and shellfish, deep fried and served with cut lemons. They are also excellent grilled over charcoal with oil and garlic—even frozen ones are good cooked in this way.

## Shrimps and prawns (*crevettes*)

There are so many species in the shrimp family that anything more than 2–3 in/ 5–7 cm long is called in Europe a prawn, and it is the discerning French and Italians who award them the distinction of separate names. The *crevette rouge*, or *gambero rosso*, for example, is the large, expensive prawn, very strong flavored, much enjoyed by the Italians, who often eat a whole pyramid of them with a bowl of mayonnaise and a bottle of white wine. A clear, deep coral color with a violet splotch showing through the transparent shell of the head, it turns a bright pink-red when cooked.

The delicious *crevette rose*, or *gamberello*, is the common large pink prawn, at its best eaten cold with dark bread and butter and lemon juice, or with mayonnaise or in a salad. The *crevette rose du large*, or *gambero rosa*, with pretty red markings on its crested head, is one of the best of the prawns, very delicate and much appreciated in northern France, where it is simply boiled, laid on a bed of brown seaweed with ice and halved lemons and served with brown bread and butter. In the United States, where more shrimps are consumed than anywhere else in the world, classification is usually by size, from the large and luscious Gulf shrimp (10–12 make 1 lb/450 g) to the tiny cold-water specimens which need 100 or more to tip the scales.

Also delicious are the cold-water prawns of Scandinavia, with their firm meat and fresh taste. They are usually boiled in sea-water on board the trawler as soon as they are caught, which gives them a mild, sweet-ish flavor. It is these that you will often find frozen or canned.

Freshly caught and freshly boiled, *crevettes grises*, the little brown shrimps, are difficult to shell because they are so small, but perhaps it is this fiddly, companionable job that makes the reward so worth while. Much more delicate than their larger cousins, these are delicious with lemon and dark bread and butter, or potted and served with lemon and hot toast. Brown shrimps turn browner when cooked; pink shrimps are greyish-brown when caught and turn pink when they are cooked. These are also the little shrimps that are used for open sandwiches and canapés, and go into salads and seafood cocktails.

*Buying guide:* fresh prawns and shrimps should be springy with bright, crisp shells—avoid any that are soft or limp or have a smell of ammonia about them. They are almost invariably sold without their heads and they can also be bought shelled and deveined. Frozen shelled prawns or shrimps should be bought frozen—those thawed-out specimens in trays at the fish market may have been around for some time, and defrosted food always spoils much more quickly than fresh food does.

*Best cooking methods:* make an incision along the shrimp's back and remove the dark vein, then simply drop them into a large pan of boiling seawater or salted water and simmer them for a minute or two, depending on their size—don't overcook them as they lose their delicate texture and turn hard. Recooking prawns or shrimps toughens them, so they should be heated gently and for as short a time as possible when being used in a hot dish. They can be shelled and deveined before or after cooking. The larger the species, the better it lends itself to broiling, deep frying and grilling over charcoal.

## Oysters (*huitres*)

Oysters are a shellfish you either love or loathe. To some people they are the height of ecstasy, to others a cause of revulsion. Aldous Huxley said, "I suppose that when the sapid and slippery morsel—which is gone like a flash of gustatory summer lightning—glides along the palate, few people imagine that they are swallowing a piece of machinery (and going machinery too) greatly more complicated than a watch." Perhaps oyster-lovers prefer not to think about it. It is certainly hard to believe that oysters were once the food of the poor: they only became fashionable and expensive as they became scarce, and would have disappeared al-together if a French marine biologist had not discovered the ancient oyster beds at Lake Fusaro, near Naples, and learned how oysters could be artificially reared.

There are a number of varieties of oysters, some distinctly finer than others. The best European oysters include the Whitstable, Colchester and Helford, and the Belons and green Marennes from France. The less fine European species are called Portuguese oysters. In America the East Coast yields the fine Eastern or American oyster, more commonly known as the Blue Point. On the West Coast the tiny Olympia oysters and the much larger, tougher Pacific oysters, or Geigers, are found. There are stringent

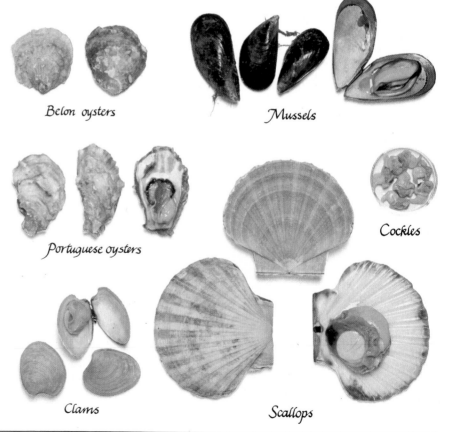

Belon oysters

Mussels

Portuguese oysters

Cockles

Clams

Scallops

regulations to keep oysters safe from pollution, but if you do have one that tastes bad, spit it out.

Oysters are best eaten raw, on the half-shell. Serve them in the deep halves of their shells, on a bed of crushed ice, and take care not to spill the liquid they contain—it has an exquisite salty, marine flavor with a hint of iodine. Accompany them with lemon wedges and, if you like, cayenne papper, Tabasco or chili sauce and dark bread and butter, and a chilled Alsace or Chablis.

*Buying guide:* best in late autumn and in winter, when they are not spawning. They can also be bought canned or frozen, but these are only for cooking. Canned smoked oysters make a good hors d'oeuvre.

*Best cooking methods:* Portuguese and Pacific oysters, which must be chopped as they are rather tough, are most often used for cooking. They are delicious in a creamy oyster stew, in steak and kidney pudding, or in a dry white wine and cheese sauce which is sprinkled with bread crumbs and browned under the broiler.

## Scallops (*coquilles St. Jacques, vanneaux*)

These are a particular favorite among shell-fish-lovers, partly because they are such a delight to eat and partly because they are beautiful and symbolic. Often represented in painting (notably Botticelli's *Venus*), the scallop is a symbol of Christianity and a badge of the pilgrim.

Europe can boast the best of the many species of scallop that abound, including the most common great scallop, the pilgrim scallop and the queen scallop. These latter, called *vanneaux* in France, are smaller than ordinary scallops, with two slightly hollow shells rather than one convex and one flat. Small and delicate, they have the texture of butter. American scallops—the large deep-sea variety and the small, tender bay scallops—are sold without their coral or roe, although in Europe this is considered to be the best part.

*Buying guide:* at their best in winter, scallops are becoming an increasingly unusual sight in fish shops and are very expensive, but fortunately you do not need many—three or four large ones per person is usually sufficient. If using queen or bay scallops, allow between 10 and 15 per person. In America they are always, and in Europe they are often, sold already shelled and cleaned, but ask the fish dealer to let you have some shells, if possible, to use as serving dishes.

*Best cooking methods:* be careful not to over-cook scallops or they will be tough—small ones only take a few seconds, large ones a minute or two at the most. They can be fried or baked in the oven in butter with parsley, garlic and lemon juice, or sautéed

and served with a little port and cream stirred in to make a sauce, or broiled with bacon on a skewer, made into a chowder, or lightly poached or steamed and served in a white wine sauce, sprinkled with bread crumbs and browned under the broiler. When served in a cream sauce they have become known simply by their French name, coquilles St. Jacques.

## Clams (*praires*)

North America is the place to appreciate clams: aficionados can distinguish between long necks and little necks, cherrystones, quahogs and razors, surf clams, butter clams and pismo clams. Clam chowder is almost a national dish and a clambake is a serious and favorite pastime, while expressions like "tight as a clam" or "happy as a clam at high tide" are frequently heard along the shore-lines. Clambakes, which involve steaming the shellfish on a bed of seaweed over heated stones, are most popular on the East Coast, especially in Maine and Massachusetts, and here too you can find stands by the side of the road where clams, gathered from the shore at low tide, are sold. These are deep fried in batter and served with tartare sauce or ketchup and salt.

In France you may be offered clovisses, palourdes, olives or praires (the best); in Italy, vongoli, tartufi di mare; in Spain, almejas, margaritas or amayuelas. In England clams are not as impossible to find as they once were and the large quahogs are sometimes available. These have hard shells and can be difficult to open. A good method is to freeze them—as the water turns to ice and expands, the clam is forced open.

*Buying guide:* available all year. Since clams vary so much in size from one variety to another, ask the clam-seller how many to allow for each person. Canned clams are also widely available.

*Best cooking methods:* the soft or long-neck varieties such as razor and Ipswich clams can be eaten raw just like oysters, and so can small hard-shell clams such as cherrystones. Larger ones like quahogs can be steamed and ground for chowder, fried in olive oil with lemon juice and parsley, broiled with butter, bread crumbs and garlic, or chopped and made into the excellent sauce for *spaghetti alla vongole*, which is also delicious made with tiny cherrystone clams.

## Mussels (*moules*)

Clumped in blue-black masses on rocks and piers or attached singly to shingle stones in estuaries, mussels have in the past quite unfairly been considered the poor man's shell-fish. Their status, however, has been improving rapidly. In America, where they

are to be found on both coasts, they are growing steadily in popularity, and in Europe, where they are extremely popular, there are mussel farms around Mediterranean coasts where the mussels are bred on long stakes in clean seawater. If you are collecting your own mussels, make sure that they are living in unpolluted water and known to be safe. Do not collect them in the heat of summer (when there is not an "r" in the month) and discard any that are even remotely damaged.

To clean mussels, put them in salted water with a sprinkling of oatmeal or flour for an hour or two so that they rid themselves of grit, then scrape the shells clean with the back of a knife and rinse thoroughly in cold water. Pull out the stringy beard and cut it off, and rinse the mussels again in a bowl of clean water. It is important to discard any that float to the surface or whose shells are damaged or open.

The French are enthusiastic about raw shellfish and will eat whole platefuls of raw mussels with lemon juice as if they were oysters. Only the thin-shelled French species can be eaten in this way, and they should be from a very pure location.

*Buying guide:* mussels are happily inexpensive. The medium-size or smaller ones are best; large mussels are not so appetizing. Always buy more mussels than you need, to allow for those you have to discard. For two people, buy a quart (about 2 lb/900 g).

*Best cooking methods:* one of the best-known recipes for mussels is the excellent moules à la marinière. They can also be used, once opened, like snails, broiled with bread crumbs, garlic, parsley and butter, or in a garlicky tomato sauce, in spaghetti sauce, seafood salad or deep fried.

## Cockles (*coques, sourdons, maillots*)

These have long been a favored shellfish in Britain, traditionally sold with winkles and whelks at the seaside and outside London pubs. Years ago, when vendors did not possess weighing scales, they measured out their pre-boiled wares in their empty pint-size beer mugs, and ever since cockles have been sold by the pint (the equivalent of about 1 lb/450 g).

*Buying guide:* at their best in the summer, cockles are usually sold boiled. At seaside stands they are accompanied by salt, pepper, vinegar and dark bread and butter.

*Best cooking methods:* eat cockles raw, or boil them in a court bouillon until their shells open. They also make a splendid soup, combined with mussels, garlic, potato, bacon and milk, and are a good addition to risottos and fritters, or they can be stewed with their juices in a thick tomato sauce and served with pasta.

**Preparing a cooked lobster**

**1.** If you wish to remove the claws and legs, simply twist them off. Dressed lobster dishes are usually presented with the claw meat already extracted.

**2.** To extract the meat from the claws and legs, crack them open, using the back of a knife or, as for crab, a hammer or nutcracker.

**3.** Splitting a lobster in half is easiest to do in two stages. First, draw a sharp knife through the head from the shoulder up towards the eyes.

**4.** Reinsert the knife and draw it in the opposite direction, cutting down to the tip of the tail and splitting the lobster completely in two.

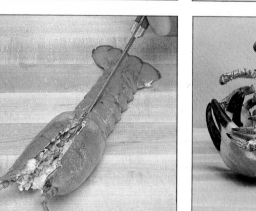

*5. Pull the halves apart to expose the flesh. This fine female lobster has an excellent red coral, and also some darker external roe, which is unusual. Both are edible and should be reserved.*

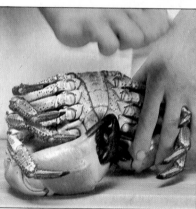

*6. Discard the white gills, which will be found in both halves in the top of the head, and the intestinal canal, which runs down the middle of the tail. As well as the coral, the creamy green tomalley, or liver, should also be reserved to make lobster sauce.*

**Picking a cooked crab**

*1. Hold the crab firmly in one hand and give its back underside a sharp thump. This should loosen the body and legs from the shell.*

*2. Stand the crab on its head and, pushing against the body with your thumbs, lever away the back end of the shell with your fingers.*

**3.** *Pull the body and the legs away from the shell.*

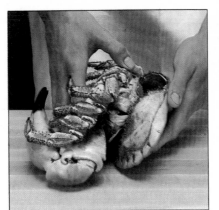

**4.** *Remove and discard the messy bundle of intestines. This will be found either in the shell or still clinging to the body. Comb it gently with a fork to remove any brown meat that is adhering to it.*

**5.** *Scoop out the brown creamy meat from inside the shell.*

**6.** *Discard the grey gills, known as dead men's fingers, which lie on either side of the body.*

**7.** *Twist off all the legs and claws. To expose the body's white meat, make two cuts, one on either side of the bony central peak. The two cuts should meet in a V shape at the peak of the body. This divides the body in three. Discard the middle bit, which contains no flesh.*

**8.** *With a skewer, dig out the white meat from the two outer pieces of the body. This requires a little time and patience if you are to avoid crushing the brittle inner shell. The meat on the plate shows how much you can expect from half the body of a large crab.*

**9.** *Crack open the claws and legs with a hammer or nutcracker and extract their meat. The meat on the plate is the amount obtained from one claw and one leg.*

**10.** *Mix together the white meat from the legs, claws and body, and serve it with the brown meat.*

**Shucking oysters**
*1. Hold the oyster steady and insert a strong, rigid knife between the two shells, just next to the hinge. The knife used here is a special oyster-shucking knife, and the oyster is an English Whitstable.*

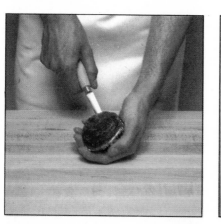

*2. Keep a firm grip on the oyster and, pushing against the hinge, twist the knife until the hinge breaks.*

*3. Open the oyster and sever the muscle that adheres to the rounded shell.*

*4. Run the knife underneath the oyster to free it from the flat shell.*

*5. Turn the oyster over to display its more attractive side, and serve it with its own marine-flavored juices in the rounded shell.*

**Preparing scallops**
*1. Lever the shells apart with the end of a strong broad-tipped knife.*

*2. Sever the scallop from the rounded shell by carefully sliding a knife underneath the adhering muscle.*

*3. Rinse the scallop under cold running water, pull away the film of membrane, or "beard," and discard it.*

4. Keep the scallop under running water and, holding back the white flesh and coral with your thumb, push away the black intestine and sever it.

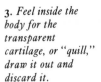

3. Feel inside the body for the transparent cartilage, or "quill," draw it out and discard it.

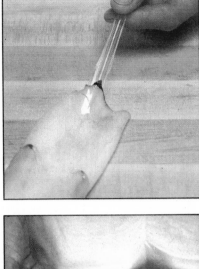

5. The cushion of muscle and the delicious orange coral are now ready to cook.

4. Wash the body thoroughly, inside and out, under cold running water and then separate the two flaps from the body. You will find that they pull away quite easily, as if held in place only by suction.

**Preparing squid**
1. Grasp the squid with one hand and with the other reach inside the body and pull the head and tentacles away.

5. Cut the tentacles from the head. If the long, narrow ink sac is present and still intact, you will find it attached to the head; remove it carefully and put it aside to use in an accompanying sauce. The remains of the head, which contain the entrails, can now be discarded.

2. Pull off and discard the body's mottled skin.

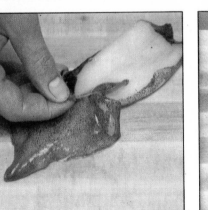

6. Cut the body into thick rings, slice the flaps in broad strips and cut the tentacles to a manageable size. The squid is now ready to cook.

# Other Seafoods, Snails and Frogs' Legs

Many creatures are so strange and so lacking in allure that they are usually, for want of a better label, called "miscellaneous." But unappetizing though they may look, with their spiny, jelly-like or leathery exteriors, some rank among the most delicious of foods and all are a challenge to the adventurous cook.

Fortunately such things as snails, frogs' legs and turtle soup are readily available canned or frozen from supermarket shelves. After all, who would want to buy a whole turtle—assuming that one would be available from the local fish dealer—simply to make turtle soup, and our kitchens certainly wouldn't be equipped to deal with the leftovers.

Some seafoods, like limpets, although perfectly edible, are not worth marketing and you will have to rely on gathering them yourself, always remembering that any living thing gathered from the sea and its shores is potentially dangerous if it comes from a polluted area, and that many varieties are simply inedible. If in any doubt about the safety of your haul, check with an environmental health officer.

## Squid, octopus and cuttlefish

The Mediterranean countries understand best how to deal with these extraordinary creatures, having eaten them in great quantities since the earliest days of civilization. They also play an important role in the cooking of China and Japan. All are at their sweetest and tenderest when small; larger specimens can be improved by soaking for several hours in a marinade of wine vinegar, sliced onion, salt and pepper.

**Squid** Familiar in Mediterranean dishes as kalamari, calmar or encornet, calamaro or calamar, squid is delicious to eat if you understand the principle that the cooking must be either very brief or very long—anything in between and your squid will be as tough as rubber. Once cleaned, the pocket can be stuffed with ground meat and the chopped legs and baked in a tomato-and-garlic-flavored sauce, or sliced in rings and fried plain or dipped first into a light batter. Larger specimens can be stewed gently with olive oil, wine and tomatoes.

It is a pleasure, in Spain, to be served with two little dishes at the same time, one holding a fragrant stew of the legs, with onions and garlic, and the other the sliced, crisply fried rings of the body. Squid can also be boiled very briefly—more than a minute or two, when they lose their pearly transparent look, will toughen them—and

then put into a seafood salad. The tiniest squid, with fragile bodies no more than 3 in/8 cm long, can be very quickly deep fried in a coating of beaten egg and flour.

**Octopus** can be very tough, and the larger it grows the tougher it gets, so it is a wise precaution, having removed the beak and head (if the fish dealer has not already done so) and turned out the contents of the body, to pound the legs and body with a mallet or a steak beater until they are soft. The octopus contains its ink within its liver and this is sometimes used to make a very strong and heavily scented gravy.

Octopus can be stewed or stuffed and baked like squid, but a large specimen will need up to two hours or more to become tender. Little ones can also be fried gently in olive oil and make a delicious salad, often eaten warm, with lemon juice, olive oil, garlic and chopped parsley.

**Cuttlefish** Often gracefully camouflaged by striped markings, the cuttlefish has a larger head than the squid and a much wider, dumpier body. Inside lies the white shell, or cuttlebone, found washed up on beaches and given to pet birds to peck at (ground, it was once used as tooth powder, jewel polish and as face powder by Roman ladies who wanted to look delicate). More tender than octopus or squid, cuttlefish can be cooked in the same ways and very small ones are delicious deep fried. They are cleaned and prepared in the same way as squid. The ink, or sepia, can be used to make a sauce in which the cuttlefish can be stewed, and goes into the Italian dish risotto nero, black rice.

## Single-shelled creatures

These all belong to the same family that includes the familar garden snail. They are all mobile, moving around on a muscular "foot," and can go into fish soups, sauces and stews, as well as being tasty snacks when simply accompanied by plenty of vinegar, pepper and dark bread and butter.

**Abalone, ormer** "Delicious ambrosia," an enthusiast wrote in the 1600s about the ormers of the Channel Islands. These white-fleshed shellfish with their curiously ear-shaped shells, the inside gleaming with pearly colors, can still be found fresh around the Channel Islands and the Breton coast at certain times of the year, and in the warm waters off California.

Fresh abalones, even little ones, need to be well beaten to make them tender. Very small abalones can then be eaten raw with a squeeze of lemon juice, larger ones are usually thinly sliced and marinated in white wine, oil, herbs and chopped shallot and then fried very briefly in butter—overcooking only toughens them. They can also be used like clams in soup or chowder.

Canned abalone is a good substitute for fresh, but dried abalone is not worth the effort of making it edible—it needs to be soaked for four days before anything can be done with it.

**Winkles or periwinkles** There is something homey and comfortable about winkles. Their little dark shells are small enough to make them completely acceptable in a way that many large snails are not. In England they are eaten with bread and butter and a pot of tea, and make a tasty snack on seaside piers, accompanied by vinegar. In France you are likely to be given a plate of *bigorneaux* with a glass of kir—cassis and white wine—in an Alsace brasserie while waiting for your pork knuckle and sauerkraut or your slice of foie gras. Whatever the circumstance, a long pin is indispensable for wheedling the little shellfish out of their shells. To cook winkles, boil them in their shells in salted water for about 10 minutes. Eat only the first part of the body—the second part is easily separated.

**Whelks** These handsome shellfish with their ribbed, deeply whorled shells are usually sold already boiled. They are eaten with vinegar and brown bread and butter, like winkles, but are a much more substantial mouthful and easier to remove from their shells. The large "foot" is the part that is usually eaten. Whelks can also be used in fish soups and stews. On the Scottish island of Iona, where whelks are a traditional part of the islanders' diet, whelk soup is made by thickening seasoned whelk stock with oatmeal and minced onion.

**Conch** The term conch—pronounced konk—is often used to include the winkle and whelk, but what is usually thought of as being the best of the family is the large Caribbean conch with the graceful spiral-shaped shell in which one seems to hear the sound of the sea. Fresh conch meat needs to be tenderized by vigorous beating and can then be stewed in a wine sauce with herbs and spices, or thinly sliced and deep fried. It also goes into chowders or can be eaten raw in a salad with a good vinaigrette.

**Limpets** Never very good unless you are very hungry, limpets are exceptionally tough—you can tell they are going to be tough by the strength of the muscle which clamps them to the rocks as soon as they are touched and makes them almost impossible to prize off. However, with persistence they can be gathered at low tide (they are rarely marketed) and eaten raw or used to flavor a soup. They can also be fried in butter with chopped parsley, pepper and vinegar, or baked for a few minutes with a little butter in each shell. The smaller ones are better boiled and eaten with vinegar, pepper and bread and butter.

**Slipper limpets** Native to North America,

these are now quite common along the southern coastlines of England. They prey on oysters, which makes them very unpopular with oyster-lovers, but are quite good to eat either cooked or raw.

## "Fruits" of the sea

Some of the most astonishing candidates for any sort of cuisine are nonetheless considered delicacies by their devotees.

**Sea urchin, oursin** A menace to the bather but a pleasure to the gourmet, the sharp-spined sea urchin is plentiful in many parts of the world and its pretty lacy patterned shell—minus the spines—is often brought home as a memento of seaside holidays. Best for eating are the green sea urchin and the black sea urchin. These can be lightly boiled and are sometimes pickled, but are best eaten fresh, raw and straight from the shell. To accomplish this the sea urchin is cut in half, ideally with a *coupe-oursin* designed for this task. This exposes the rose-colored or orange ovaries, which are simply given a drop of lemon juice and scooped out with pieces of fresh crusty bread. The crushed corals can also be used in omelets and as a garnish for fish.

**Sea anemone and tomate de mer** These inhabitants of rocky pools, enticingly waving their multitude of soft arms, are sometimes eaten in Japan, Samoa and France. The snake-locks anemones, known as *orties de mer*, are carefully gathered in France and marinated, dipped into a light batter and fried. They also go, together with a few red *tomates de mer* and a great many shellfish, into a Mediterranean soup.

**Figue de mer, violet** This very odd, leathery skinned creature is particularly relished in Provence, where it has the proper accompaniment of hot sun and a plentiful supply of white wine. Found anchored to rocks or the sea floor, siphoning water in through one spout and out of the other, it is cut in half and the yellow part inside is eaten raw.

**Bêche de mer** Also known as sea cucumber, because of its shape, and as sea slug, trepang and balatan, this warm-water creature is sliced and eaten raw in Japan with soy sauce, vinegar or mustard, and several species are smoke-dried and used in soup. In China it is known as *hoy sum* and has a reputation as an aphrodisiac. One recipe using dried *hoy sum* involves four days of preparation and yields 12 Chinese servings or 95 Western servings, which is either a miscalculation or says a great

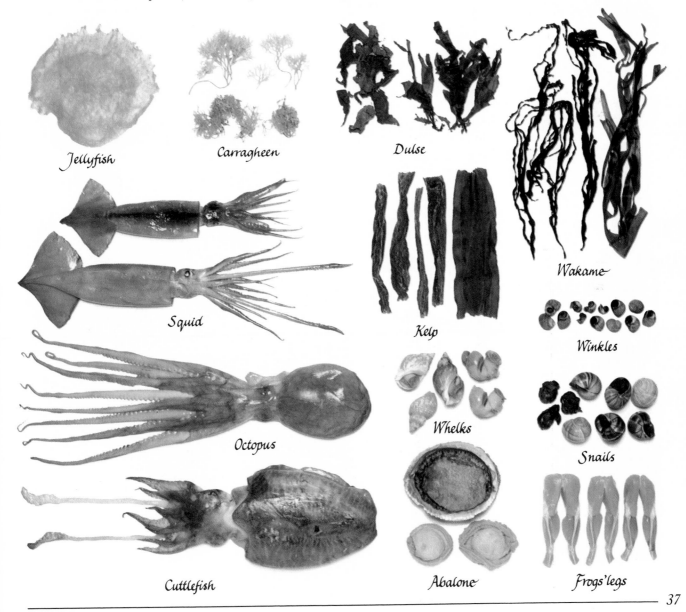

Jellyfish

Carragheen

Dulse

Wakame

Squid

Kelp

Winkles

Octopus

Whelks

Snails

Cuttlefish

Abalone

Frogs'legs

deal about the slug's lack of appeal to the Western palate.

**Jellyfish** The Chinese are great users of dried jellyfish, primarily to add texture to a meal, and slabs of dried jellyfish can usually be found in the more specialized Chinese supermarkets. If the jellyfish has been salted it will need to be washed and allowed to soak for some hours in several changes of fresh water. Once soaked, it can be cut into slivers and stir-fried with chicken, or scalded, which produces crunchy curls which are served with a sauce of sesame-seed oil, soy sauce, vinegar and sugar. In Japan jellyfish is cooked into crisp-textured strips and eaten with vinegar as a side dish.

## Samphire and seaweeds

Apart from being such a pleasure to gather, in the early months of summer when most of them are at their most luxuriant, seaweeds are a rich source of minerals as well as of intriguing textures and flavors. If you gather your own, cut the plant well above its base so that it can grow again, and always wash it thoroughly in fresh water before cooking. Most of the better-known seaweeds can be found in dried form in health food stores or oriental supermarkets and can be reconstituted by soaking.

**Samphire** Also known as sea fennel and Peter's cress, or *herbe de St. Pierre*, this green plant can be found growing on seaside cliffs. It is quite common along southern European and Mediterranean coastlines, but in England is found only in East Anglia, where it can sometimes be bought in bundles, along with the similar but unrelated marsh samphire, from the fish market. The flavor of fresh marsh samphire is salty and iodiney—like seawater but green; it is the crisp texture that is interesting.

Samphire can go fresh into salads and is often steeped in vinegar to make a delicate pickle. In East Anglia it is greatly appreciated as a vegetable, simply boiled and dipped in melted butter, then drawn through the teeth like asparagus to strip the succulent part from the thin central core.

**Laver** With its delicate taste of the sea, this reddish-purple seaweed was very popular in England in the eighteenth century. It is seldom appreciated in the West today, except in Wales, where it is enthusiastically boiled until it turns into the spinach-like purée called laver bread—although why it should be called bread is a mystery. The purée is then mixed with oatmeal, shaped into small flat cakes and fried with bacon for breakfast, or heated through with a knob of butter and the juice of an orange or lemon to make a sauce to eat with mutton. In China, laver is dried and then simmered to produce a nutritious jelly. In Japan, where it is

cultivated and called *nori*, it is pressed and dried in thin sheets, toasted lightly and wrapped around rice balls or crumbled over rice as a salty garnish.

**Carragheen, Irish moss** Although Ireland and the village of Carragheen have given it its most commonly used names, this pretty red-tinged plant is common along most northerly Atlantic shorelines. It can be used fresh or dried, when it bleaches to a creamy white, and is an important source of agar-agar, a vegetable gelatine much used in the food industry. The traditional way to make a carragheen jelly is to simmer the moss in milk or water until most of it dissolves, strain and leave it to set. The result is very nourishing, and if you don't like its faint taste of the sea it can be flavored with vanilla, honey or fruit.

**Kelp** A number of large seaweeds are popularly known as kelp and have long been used as a source of food and of medicine, being particularly rich in iodine. Much liked in Japan, where it is called *kombu*, kelp finds its way to the table as a delicate salad vegetable, a seasoning for root vegetables, a garnish for rice or fashioned into miniature baskets, deep fried and stuffed with vegetables. It is also used for making soups and stocks or can simply be cooked as a vegetable to accompany fish.

**Dulse** Another of the familiar purplish-red seaweeds, dulse is to be found growing plentifully on rocks and on larger weeds. It can be eaten raw as a salad and around the Mediterranean it sometimes goes into ragouts, but it is a very tough, rubbery plant and needs to be cooked for up to five hours. Dried, it can be chewed as a rather unconventional appetizer, without any further preparation, or used as a relish. It has a salty, fish-like flavor.

**Wakame** A rich source of minerals, this dark green seaweed is much used in Japan. The soft leaves go into salads or are cooked with other vegetables, and both leaves and stems are used in soups.

## Snails

The French, of course, are the main eaters of snails, and the snails the French prize most are the hefty specimens from the vineyards of Burgundy, where they are fed—like the snails of ancient Rome—on grape leaves until they have grown fat and luscious. The classic way to prepare snails is the Burgundian way, in which case they become *escargots à la bourguignonne*, served sizzling in their shells with great quantities of rich garlic butter and fresh crusty bread for mopping. However, as there are never enough Burgundian snails to meet the demand, the alternative is a smaller striped snail, the *petit gris*, which makes up for

its lack of size by being sweet, tasty and tender. A drawback is that the *petit gris* shells, unlike those of the Burgundian snail, may be too fragile to be used once their occupants have been removed, but this is solved by using the little ceramic pots called *godets*, easily washed and always ready to be used again. Other essentials for the dedicated enjoyment of snails are the dimpled plates called *escargotières*, which hold six or twelve snail shells or *godets*, tongs for picking up the piping hot shells and special forks which have two prongs for twisting the snails out of their shells.

The business of preparing live snails means that it is much simpler to buy snails canned, already cleaned and ready to cook, or cooked and only needing to be reheated and combined with their sauce. As a change from garlic butter, snails are very good simmered in olive oil with garlic, tomato and fresh rosemary or mint—the traditional dish to serve on Midsummer's Eve in Rome.

## Frogs' legs

Like snails, frogs' legs as a delicacy have long been associated with the French. Escoffier, the "king of chefs," is credited with making them acceptable to the English: in the 1890s for a party held by the Prince of Wales at the Savoy Hotel, London, he prepared what he called *nymphes à l'aurore*, frogs' legs poached in white wine and served cold in aspic with a little paprika to evoke the rose-gold glow of dawn. Presumably he called his frogs' legs "nymphs" out of delicacy of feeling for the English diners. When he wasn't preparing them for the Prince of Wales, Escoffier simply seasoned them with salt and pepper and sautéed them in butter, serving them with a squeeze of lemon juice and a sprinkling of parsley.

Today, those who know their frogs still go frogging in likely streams and lakes, but not all frogs are edible and what appears frozen and canned in the shops and on restaurant menus will have come from special frog farms. They are light and easily digestible, rather like chicken in flavor—in China, where frogs thrive in the paddy fields and frogs' legs are much enjoyed at banquets, they are known as "field chickens." In America frogs' legs are often big enough to be southern-fried like chicken legs, but the smaller legs are usually more tender and have a subtler flavor. But Escoffier's way with them is still the best, first blanched and skinned, and then cooked gently in oil or butter for about five minutes until golden brown and served with lemon and a sprinkling of parsley, or they can be poached in a little white wine and served hot with a creamy sauce. They can also be prepared *à la provençale*, with garlic and tomato.

# Meat

Meat is such an important part of our diet, so delicious and so expensive that it makes sense to buy it as intelligently as possible.

If you always go to a high-class butcher, possibly one who raises his own stock, certainly one who buys meat by the carcass and hangs it until it has reached the peak of juiciness and flavor, and who butchers it with finesse, you will seldom have a disappointing piece of meat. You will also be able to buy meat in greater variety, as he will be able to offer you the lesser-known cuts that can go a long way towards making your food more interesting. Because there will be little waste by way of unwanted fat, gristle and awkward bones, his prices will be high, but cooking will be a joy.

## Choosing meat

Failing such a paragon, it pays to develop your own expertise when it comes to shopping. Of course, most butchers will give friendly and sometimes disinterested advice when asked. However, at the supermarket there often is no one to turn to, and the trays of meat can look distressingly similar. Some stores do label their meat "roasting," "braising" and "stewing," and this service is spreading. But many others simply give you the name of the type and cut, sometimes adding a flag saying "prime," and leave it at that.

In America legal standards demand that meat is graded "prime," "choice," "good" and "standard," but in England the word "prime" is merely an adjective used by the butcher to describe the best meat he has.

All meat destined for the table is carefully raised: special attention is paid to the ratio of fat to lean while the herd is still on the hoof, the animals' diet is carefully supervised, and they are rested before slaughter in the cause of tenderness. The finer the herd, the more care is lavished upon them and the more delicious is their meat.

## The look of meat

At a really good store all the cuts, even the cheapest, will look appetizing. They should look silky, not wet. All boned, rolled cuts should be neatly tied, not skewered, since piercing causes a loss of moisture during cooking and may introduce bacteria into the center of the meat. Barding should be neat, complete and even. Where there are bones, these should be sawn smoothly, not jaggedly chopped, and meat should be neatly trimmed, particularly chops and steaks, with excess fat removed.

The cut surface of meat exposes the grain, or muscle fibers, which are potentially coarser and tougher in an older animal, or in parts of the anatomy, such as the leg or the neck, which have had more active use. However, the fineness or otherwise of grain is not really a reliable indicator of either eating quality or tenderness.

## Tenderness

When all pieces of meat look equally beautiful, it can be hard to distinguish between the tender and the not so tender, and many factors, apart from anatomy, contribute to this: the age and breed of the animal; the way it was handled before slaughter; the temperature to which the carcass was chilled, the way the meat is cut, and so on.

There are many schools of butchery, producing different cuts of meat not only in different countries but in different regions; in fact there are as many regional variations and names for the different cuts as there are regional recipes.

However, no matter where and how a carcass is divided, most of the best meat of each animal comes from the hindquarter and loin, and the tenderest meat of all comes from the parts that have had the least exercise. Exercise means the development of muscle fiber and of the connective tissue that holds the muscles together in bundles, and it is connective tissue that is primarily responsible for toughness.

The tender cuts with little connective tissue respond to dry heat (roasting, frying and broiling), but the others need slow cooking in moist heat (braising, stewing or boiling), which breaks down the connective tissue into gelatine.

Although commercial tenderizers are sometimes used on beef cattle this is not, fortunately, general practice. Based on papain, with its tenderizing enzymes that "digest" proteins, they may be applied to the tougher pieces by the wholesalers, leading to an upgrading of the meat, which will, however, become duller to eat. As the enzymes work on all the flesh, the tender parts as well as the tougher ones, the advantage of the breaking down of connective tissues is often balanced by a general loss in character and flavor—a decided disadvantage. Tenderized meat does not become any less fibrous—the fiber merely becomes soft as it is "digested."

There are ways of preparing tough meat in the kitchen so that it arrives at table full of flavor and juice, fit to be cut with a spoon. Try marinating it in a marinade including wine, lemon juice, vinegar, yogurt, or even pulped tomatoes. All these acids help to break down connective tissue. Oil, too, is used in many marinades to add succulence, especially in Greece and the Middle East. Of course, lengthy cooking in moist heat must follow to complete the process, but this is no disadvantage since the tougher cuts need time, above all, to develop their flavor to the full.

Pounding or cutting is another way to break up connective tissue, thus making tough meat pass for tender, but then quite a lot of flavoring—chopped onions, garlic, herbs both fresh and dried, spices, seasoning, sharp sauces and relishes—is needed to make it taste good. You can perform the cutting operation yourself with a sharp, heavy knife, chopping the surface of the meat first one way and then the other.

## Ageing

This improves the taste and tenderness of meat. Carcasses to be aged are hung in a refrigerated chamber, their moisture evaporates, and enzymes in the meat break down tendons and tough tissues. Beef should be aged for 10–14 days, lamb for no more than four days. Pork and veal are not aged, nor is kosher meat. Since ageing leads inevitably to weight loss, correctly hung meat costs more than fresh meat but is well worth the difference in price, and a butcher who supplies meat that has been correctly aged is certainly worth cultivating.

## Storage

Always unwrap meat as soon as you get it home and put it in the coldest part of the refrigerator. All cuts of meat will keep best when they are lightly covered—perfectionists use cheesecloth—and when they are not so tightly packed as to rule out the circulation of air. A loose foil wrap that allows the passage of air will do almost as well, but never put meat away wrapped in plastic as the meat will deteriorate rapidly, developing a sticky and bad-smelling film over the outside.

## Cooking processes

On the whole, it is wisest to use the correct cooking process for each cut: dry heat for the tender ones; moist for those not so tender. Broiling, frying and roasting come into the first category; braising, pot roasting, stewing and simmering into the second. Of course, delicious results can be achieved by using a superior cut for the humbler processes, but the reverse is not the case.

## Broiling

This is suitable for small, reasonably thick pieces of best quality meat from the tenderest parts of the animal. The meat, first brushed with butter or oil to prevent drying out, is seared on both sides close to the source of heat to produce color and flavor. Generally speaking, the thinner the piece of meat, the closer it should be to the heat source. It is then removed a little way from the heat to finish cooking more slowly. Salt should not be added until halfway through the process, as its moisture-retaining properties would inhibit searing and browning. Always allow broiled meat to rest for a few minutes after cooking so that it acquires an even texture. Since with this process there is little or no juice, broiled meat is often served with a sauce or a pat of herb butter.

## Frying

Good quality, flattish cuts are needed for this process. They are fried in a little hot oil or butter in a shallow pan so that the meat browns rapidly. The meat can be turned once or twice as it cooks. Do not pierce it while it cooks and keep a fairly brisk heat going under the pan or the juices will escape too fast, and the meat will boil and toughen in its own juice. Do not overheat the fat as it will burn, and burnt fat imparts an unpleasant, bitter flavor. Fried meat, like broiled meat, should rest for a few minutes after cooking.

Choose a frying pan with a good, thick base, and make sure it is the right size. Meat has a tendency to stew in its own juice in an overcrowded pan, and if the pan is too big, a large surface area of fat is exposed that could all too easily burn. A very good reason for not allowing this to happen is that the pan juices, deglazed with a little wine, water or stock, make the best possible accompaniment to fried steaks or chops.

## Roasting

Top quality meat goes into a hot oven in an open pan, so that it is browned on all sides and the outside seared. It can go straight into a dry pan, fat side down, or into a little hot fat or oil, or can be cooked on a rack in a dry pan or in a pan with a little water or wine in it. Frequent basting with hot fat helps to prevent the meat from drying out. Some people like to place all meat on a rack in the pan, so that the fat collects beneath it, but this is only essential for really fatty cuts, especially pork.

Roasting times and temperatures vary according to type of meat, cut and quality, but after the initial searing it is a good idea to lower the oven temperature so that the interior of the meat cooks slowly. However, top quality cuts will always be tender, no matter how briefly or how fast they may have been cooked. A thermometer that records the internal temperature of a piece of meat as it is roasting is a foolproof gadget for determining the exact moment when the meat is cooked to the required degree.

There are two golden rules for all cuts: do not add salt until after roasting, and let the meat sit in a warm place for at least 20 minutes after it comes out of the oven to allow the juices time to settle, making the

texture and color more even and the meat easier to carve. The exception to the no-salting rule is pork crackling, which needs to be well salted or oiled before roasting in order to crisp to perfection.

## Braising and pot roasting

Large pieces of medium quality meat respond well to these processes, either in the oven or on top of the stove.

**Braising** needs a pan with a tightly fitting lid on which the steam from the cooking meat can condense, falling back onto the meat and basting it as it cooks. The meat is browned and placed on a bed of chopped vegetables, with the possible addition of bacon or salt pork that may have been browned beforehand. Stock, water, wine, cider or beer are added—just enough to cover the vegetables. The meat is then slowly cooked in a casserole at a very moderate temperature, 325°F/170°C, until meltingly tender.

This usually takes about 30 minutes per 1 lb/450 g with 30 minutes over, but times vary according to quality. The meat is turned and basted once or twice during cooking, and seasoned halfway through. If the meat is salted at the outset, there is a danger the salt may draw out too much moisture too quickly.

You may find it better to replace the vegetables with a fresh batch towards the end of the cooking time, as the hours they have spent in the pot may well have rendered them lifeless and tasteless.

**Pot roasting** in a covered pot dispenses with the liquid, and possibly with the vegetables, relying only on the steam from the meat, which condenses on the lid and bastes the meat. Pot-roasted meat needs to be started off with a little fat in the bottom of the pan in order to brown it and to prevent its sticking and burning. Turn the meat every half hour or so during cooking so that it browns evenly. This operation is made much easier if you have previously tied the meat with trussing string into a neat and compact bundle. Pot roasting takes about the same amount of time as braising.

## Stewing

A tougher cut of meat does best when cut across the grain into smallish pieces, cooked long and slowly in a little liquid—not too much, or the meat will be boiled rather than stewed. The liquid is provided by the meat juices plus whatever is specified in the recipe. After the initial browning of the meat to give both color and flavor—usually in fat in which a few vegetables have been gently fried until golden—cooking liquid, flavoring and seasonings are added. When it is tender (which may take from 1½–3½ hours depending on the type of

meat), the gravy may be thickened. If the thickener, usually flour, has been introduced early on, the meat is usually coated with it before being browned, and care must be taken not to burn it. Stews cooked on the top of the stove will need stirring occasionally to prevent the meat from sticking to the pan.

## Boiling

Simmering in liquid is the best way to render large pieces of meat tender, but such good things as *boeuf bouilli* and all the other cuts eaten in the rich broth characteristic of the process really need at least a medium quality meat. If you want to keep most of the flavor in the meat, plunge it into unsalted boiling water, or, better still, into boiling stock. If, on the other hand, you want a rich, well-flavored broth at the expense of the meat, put the meat into salted cold water and bring it slowly to the boil.

Once the liquid has reached boiling point, turn it down to the gentlest of simmers. If meat is subjected to the intense heat of rapidly boiling water, the gelatinous connective tissue will dissolve and the meat will become tough and dry, while at a gentle simmer the connective tissues melt gradually, keeping the meat succulently moist and tender.

After the scum has been skimmed off, and has ceased to rise, salt, vegetables and herbs are added for flavoring both the meat and broth and the meat is simmered to tenderness. Allow 20 minutes per 1 lb/450 g and 20 minutes over for pieces more than 6 lb/3.5 kg in weight; 30 minutes per 1 lb/450 g plus 30 minutes over for smaller pieces. Positively all the scum must go, but while a bouillon is allowed to be cloudy, a consommé must be crystal clear, which entails a further clarifying process.

## Meat for the freezer

It is not easy to freeze meat successfully at home because it must be done very fast—faster than lies within the capacity of any domestic freezer.

Buy meat which has been blast-frozen when it is in season, and at its best and often cheapest, from one of the specialist freezer-food suppliers. From the point of view of quality it may be better still, if your butcher offers a freezing service, and many do, to choose correctly hung meat in his shop and ask him to blast-freeze it for you. Meat for freezing must be correctly aged and of high quality—inferior grades of meat will only deteriorate further, making them scarcely worth the expensive space they are taking up in your freezer. Many independent butchers have blast freezers and will sell you any quantity you require, from a

Meat recipes **236–244**
Meat preparation *52–59*
Pans and casseroles **372–375**

Meat thermometers **367**, *367*

To clarify consommé **196**

small bag of chops to half a carcass. To take up less space large pieces should be boned before freezing, and all excess fat removed.

To buy meat by the whole, half or quarter carcass seems an economical way of shopping, but only if you do not eat your way through your investment faster than you normally would, just because it is there.

### Storing meat in the freezer

Limits are placed on the storage times for meat, not because the meat will become unsafe to eat but because the quality deteriorates. Meat storage times are determined largely by the fat content, as fat eventually turns rancid even in the freezer. Pork fat turns rancid more quickly than lamb or beef fat, and the presence of salt (as in bacon or ham) makes matters worse.

Meat that has been inadequately wrapped for the freezer will develop freezer burn, which manifests itself in greyish-white or brownish patches. These are caused by dehydration on the surface, which results in changes in color, texture and flavor. The meat will be perfectly safe to eat but will taste dry and unpleasant, so be sure to wrap meat securely in something tough such as heavy-duty foil or extra-thick moisture- and vapor-proof freezer bags, and expel all the air before sealing them.

### Cooking frozen meat

All meat tastes infinitely better if properly thawed before cooking. Bone-in roasts and small cuts of meat may be cooked from frozen without risk to health, but inevitably the outside will be overdone before the inside is cooked. For frozen roasts you will need a meat thermometer to check on the internal temperature. For frozen steaks, chops, cutlets and so on, it will be necessary to start the cooking at a lower temperature and to cook for almost twice as long as usual. Boned and rolled roasts, however, must never be cooked from frozen, as the inside and outside surfaces of the meat will have been handled, and it is therefore important to destroy any bacteria which may be present by thorough cooking.

To thaw large cuts, allow 6–7 hours per 1 lb/450 g in the refrigerator, in its own wrapping. This is much the best way, as the slower the thaw, the more the juices get reabsorbed; but only about 2–3 hours per 1 lb/450 g are needed at room temperature. Cook the meat as soon as it has thawed out —while still cold to the touch. If left thawing longer than necessary, the juices have further opportunity to escape.

Steaks and chops need about 5 hours in the refrigerator to thaw properly—2–4 hours in the warmth of the kitchen, but if you are in a hurry, warm water helps as long as the package is watertight.

## APPROXIMATE MAXIMUM STORAGE TIMES FOR MEAT

| Uncooked Meat | In a Cool Place | In a Refrigerator | In a Freezer |
|---|---|---|---|
| BEEF | 2 days | 3–5 days | 12 months |
| VEAL | 2 days | 3–5 days | 12 months |
| LAMB | 2 days | 3–5 days | 9 months |
| PORK | 2 days | 2–4 days | 6 months |
| GROUND MEAT | same day | 1–2 days | 3 months |
| VARIETY MEATS | same day | 1–2 days | 2 months |
| **Cooked Meat** | | | |
| CASSEROLES With bacon | 1 day | 2 days | 3 months |
| Without bacon | 1 day | 3 days | 6 months |
| HAM | 1–2 days | 2–3 days | 2 months |
| MEAT PIES | 1 day | 1 day | 3 months |
| ROAST MEAT Sliced in sauce | 1–2 days | 2–3 days | 3 months |
| Whole roast | 1–2 days | 2–4 days | 2 months |
| PATE | 5 days | 7 days | 3 months |
| STOCK | 1 day | 2 days | a month |

Courtesy of the Meat Promotion Executive of the Meat and Livestock Commission, London

## APPROXIMATE COOKING TIMES FOR MEAT

| Meats and Cuts | Roasting | Pot Roasting/Braising | Boiling |
|---|---|---|---|
| | *Minutes per 1 lb/450 g and temperatures* | | |
| **BEEF** Tender cuts rare: | 15 + 15 over Hot | 30–40 stove top | |
| medium: | 20 Hot | 40 in a warm oven | |
| Coarser cuts | 20 Fairly hot | | 1 hour at a steady simmer |
| Boned/rolled | 30 Fairly hot | | |
| **VEAL** Thin cuts and cuts on bone | 25 + 20 over Fairly hot | | |
| Thick and boned and rolled cuts | 35 Warm | 40–50 in a warm oven | |
| **LAMB** Tender cuts | 20 Fairly hot (+ 15 over for large cuts) | Total of 2½ hours in a warm oven | 30 |
| Smaller cuts for casseroles and stews | | Total of 1½ hours in a warm oven | |
| **PORK** Small, thin cuts | 30 + 20 over Moderate | 60 stove top | |
| Thick cuts | 35 + 25 over Moderate | 60 in a warm oven | |
| Pickled cuts | | | Your butcher will advise |

# Meat/*Beef*

A beef carcass should be aged by being hung, usually for about 10–14 days, to reach its peak of flavor and tenderness, but this process results in considerable weight loss, which is reflected in the price, so expect aged beef to be expensive.

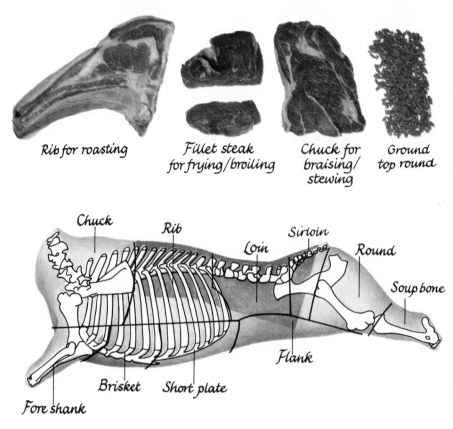

Rib for roasting    Fillet steak for frying/broiling    Chuck for braising/stewing    Ground top round

### Choosing beef

The color of lean beef varies from coral pink to a deep burgundy red. The color variations of the lean indicate the age, sex and breed of the animal, not the eating quality. Freshly cut surfaces of any piece of beef will be bright red, deepening to a brownish-red on exposure to air—thus a well-aged piece of beef will have a dark, plum-colored crust. The color of the fat will vary according to diet—grass-fed beef has yellowish fat, the fat of barley-fed beef is whiter. Something positive to look for is marbling—the lean of good roasting beef should be well endowed with flecks and streaks of fat that melt during cooking, basting the roast from within and guaranteeing tenderness.

The quality of ground beef is fairly simple to judge—it should look red. If it is pink, the proportion of fat will be too high.

As a provider of beef, the steer (a young castrated male) is the undoubted king. Different countries consider him to be at his peak at different ages—from ten months to six years old—but all agree that a steer, and perhaps a heifer (a cow that has not calved), produce the most succulent meat. Working animals, bulls and cows, are far less good.

### Cooking with beef

When beef is good and succulent, little is needed by way of added flavors. Horseradish or mustard makes a good accompaniment to roast beef, but the gravy of roast beef is nicest when the pan juices are simply reduced with a little boiling water and perhaps some red wine, and plainly seasoned with salt and pepper. Most vegetables go with beef—carrots being the traditional accompaniment to British boiled beef, cabbage is usually served with corned beef, and the Sunday roast beef comes to the table with roasted potatoes, parsnips and often a golden Yorkshire pudding.

Tastes in beef-eating have changed over the years. There was a time when beef was considered at its best when roasted to a crisp. Today more and more people are enjoying their roasts and steaks on the blue side of rare, and even raw. The Italians (never renowned as great eaters of meat) have

introduced a new delicacy—raw tenderloin cut transparently thin like smoked salmon.

**Broiling and frying** Timing depends so much on the thickness of the steak that you can only be sure whether it is done to your liking by pressing it with your finger as it cooks. If the steak feels soft and wobbly, it is very rare, or *bleu*; a little give and it will be medium rare, or *saignant*; firm, and it will be well done; if it feels hard, it will be quite spoiled.

**Roasting** The finest cuts of prime beef respond best when roasted at a high temperature, which makes them crisp on the outside, leaving them a tender rosy pink within. Overcooked beef turns leathery, even when it is meat of the very best quality. For prime cuts such as sirloin, allow 15 minutes per 1 lb/450 g and 15 minutes over at a temperature of 425°F/220°C for the larger cuts for rare meat; 20 minutes to the 1 lb/450 g for medium. The coarser cuts, such as top round, make juicier eating when roasted more slowly—allow 20 minutes per 1 lb/450 g at 375°F/190°C for thin pieces, or for cuts with the bone in, and 30 minutes per 1 lb/450 g for thick pieces, or those that are boned and rolled.

**Pot roasting and braising** Allow 30–40 minutes per 1 lb/450 g over medium heat, and 40 minutes per 1 lb/450 g in the oven at 325°F/170°C for pot roasts.

Braises need about the same time, but a great deal depends on the quality of the meat for this and for the other processes.

**Boiling** The tougher boiling cuts may need up to 1 hour per 1 lb/450 g of beef at a gentle simmer.

### The cuts

Because butchering techniques vary from country to country, and indeed from region to region, the various cuts for roasting, pot roasting, braising, stewing and boiling differ slightly all over the world. It remains true, of course, that in the case of cattle (as well as the other animals raised for the table) the very best and most expensive cuts come from the back half of the animal, and most of the very best of those from the fleshy hindquarters; but the actual names of the cuts and their shapes differ considerably, as do the direction of the grain and the way the bones are dealt with.

### Cuts for frying, broiling and roasting

These are the top quality cuts that respond best to cooking in dry heat.

**The loin** provides the tenderest meat that beef cattle or other animals have to offer. The most luxurious piece of all is the tenderloin or fillet—a strip of practically grainless flesh running inside the rib cage, parallel with the spine. Some butchers offer the tenderloin in its entirety: it may be roasted, having been larded with strips of fat to keep it moist, or enclosed in a pastry case to make *boeuf en croûte* (which is also known as beef Wellington in memory of the Duke of the same name). In this case a stuffing goes between the pastry and the meat to add moisture. The tenderloin is often cut into steaks—the thinnest part makes filets mignons; next come tournedos, which may be wrapped around with white pork fat; then come larger slices, called tenderloin or fillet steak. Next to these lies the Chateaubriand, a steak so hefty that it is considered a meal for two hungry people.

Raw ground tenderloin, spiced to taste with cayenne, Tabasco, Worcestershire sauce and capers and bound with a raw egg, makes a classic steak tartare. Cut into fine strips, tenderloin is used to make *boeuf stroganoff*.

There are many people who consider any part of the tenderloin too bland, soft and woolly, much preferring for texture and flavor rump steaks, porterhouse steaks, sirloin steaks and T-bones (which include the end of the sirloin and a piece of tenderloin), or entrecôtes (cut from the thin end of the sirloin nearest the rib cage).

The various national schools cut their steaks differently, some leaving the tenderloin to form part of larger steaks. But this does not really affect the cook, since the principle of cooking steak remains constant and the various forms of serving it differ only in the presentation. As steaks that are broiled are sealed so fast that they do not make their own juice, it is usual to send them to the table with one of the compound butters. Steaks may also be fried—usually tournedos are cooked by this process, and served on a piece of fried bread to absorb the juices that spurt when the meat is cut. Fried or broiled, steaks are much enhanced by light sauces such as a simple shallot sauce; a light sauce of egg yolks, lemon juice and parsley; a classic hollandaise or béarnaise; or even a raw relish of shallots, lemon juice and oil similar in texture to a salad dressing. Crisp French fries and a green salad are the best accompaniments.

The sirloin is part of the loin, which may be sold in a single piece for roasting, either on or off the bone, with or without the tenderloin which is then called the undercut. A sirloin, on the bone and complete with the undercut, makes a wonderful meal, so good in fact that the gourmand King Henry VIII was moved to knight it—hence Sir Loin. When two unboned sirloins have not been severed at the backbone but arrive looking like an enormous saddle, the cut is known as a baron of beef, but this noble joint is very rarely encountered except at large banquets.

In America and France the sirloin is often cut into enormous steaks, which are cooked on the bone and carved into slices at the table. In Britain steaks, with the exception of the Chateaubriand, are usually cooked in individual portions.

The rump end of loin yields roasts and beautiful juicy rump steaks for broiling and frying. There will be a few tough sinews running through the meat and these should be lifted out with a sharp knife.

**The rib** When Americans say roast beef, what comes to mind are the great standing roasts from the rib section. The English equivalent to this roast is the forerib—the traditional "Sunday joint" served with Yorkshire pudding. This piece may be bought on or off the bone, but with the bone is sweeter. Serve with roast potatoes and lightly cooked vegetables, not forgetting the horseradish sauce. The French rib roast is boned and rolled, served *au jus* (with its pan juices) accompanied by French fries and a simple green salad.

Cuts from farther down the rib cage—the short plate—are best braised or pot roasted, but they can be used for roasting. They are juicier when left on the bone but tricky to carve. The thin ribs, known also as oven busters, have a lot of fat and bone, which can be removed by the butcher. The same applies to the fatty flat ribs from the rib end of the flank.

**For stewing, pot roasting and boiling**
The cuts used for these processes are the tougher pieces that benefit from slow cooking in moist heat.

**The round** yields boneless cuts, called topside and silverside in England, from the top of the leg. Together they make the very best *boeuf bouilli*, France's classic boiled beef dish, which is eaten in its bouillon with boiled potatoes and the vegetables that were cooked alongside it; little gherkins called cornichons are often served separately. Top round (the inside leg) is a good braising and pot-roasting meat—being very lean, it usually gets a wrapping of fat. Top round can also be roasted, although it may well be rather on the dry and tough side. It remains much juicier when it is kept very rare, in which case it is also excellent cold.

Bottom round (the outside leg) is much like top round in character. Roasting is not advised, as it is slightly less tender (and slightly cheaper) than top round, but it makes nice pot roasts and good stews. Salted and spiced, bottom round makes the traditional English boiled salt beef, eaten with carrots and dumplings.

**Tip roast**, often referred to as thick flank, and called top rump in Britain, comes from the underside of the hind leg where leg meets flank. Whole, it can be roasted or pot roasted and cut into cubes it makes excellent daubes and stews like *boeuf burguignonne*. Ground, it makes good hamburgers.

**The shoulder** area of the carcass is juicy and well flavored. It is known as chuck in the United States and chuck or blade in England. Blade steak is cut from the flat of the shoulder blade. When scored across with a heavy knife to cut through all the fine connecting tissues, it can be fried like a regular steak. Chuck is excellent for stews, goulash, pies and daubes. Ground, it makes good meat loaves and meatballs.

Meat from the neck is bony. Trimmed and boned it is used for stews. On the bone it is a good addition to the stock pot.

**Brisket** is the flesh of the breast, running from between the forelegs to meet up with the forward end of the flank. It is fatty meat that needs pot roasting or braising, and is nicer when it has been marinated. It is sold on or off the bone and is very economical. It is made into corned beef, in which case it is boiled and often eaten cold, cut into very thin slices.

**Flank** meat is coarse and there is plenty of fat. The thinner end of flank is used for making stock, curries and stews. Towards the leg end, the flank becomes more tender. **Skirt** is a lean muscle from this region. In England it is used with the drier chuck for steak and kidney puddings and pies. In America this muscle is called London broil, and is first scored like the blade steak, then slowly broiled and served cut across the grain in thin strips.

**The fore shank** gives gelatinous stewing meat with a lovely flavor, but takes several hours to cook.

**The hind shank** has a lot of gristle and sinew, but tastes delicious. Slowly cooked it makes a well-flavored stew.

**Marrow**
This is a delicious fatty substance to be found inside the large bones of beef and veal. In young animals and in the shorter bones of older animals, the marrow is red; in the leg bones of older animals it is yellow, and it is this yellow marrow that is regarded as a delicacy. Beef leg bones are fairly widely available, already cut into pieces.

Marrow makes a wonderful addition to stocks, in which case the split bones are boiled along with the other ingredients to give up their goodness. If you want to use the marrow for sauces or for spreading on toast, the bones should be soaked overnight in cold water, then wrapped in foil and cooked in a fairly hot oven for 45 minutes. The marrow can then be scooped out from the center of the bones. In Victorian times, marrow on toast was very popular, the bones served wrapped in starched white napkins and the goodness scooped from inside with long narrow marrow spoons.

Veal is a neutral and versatile meat—a perfect vehicle for flavors subtle and creamy or strong and piquant.

Loin for roasting    Tenderloin, chop and scallop for frying/broiling    Neck for braising/stewing    Ground veal

### Choosing veal

Good veal comes from the same breed of cattle as good beef. There are two types of veal: the first comes from milk-fed calves or vealers slaughtered between eight and twelve weeks of age, and the second from grass-fed calves, which are between four and five months old.

Milk-fed veal should be the palest pearly pink. It should look firm and moist but never wet, and have bright, pinky-white, translucent bones. Grass-fed veal is a little darker in color, but never red. Redness is a sure sign that the animal had grown too old before slaughter. If veal has a brown or grey tinge, it means that it is stale and should be avoided. Veal has a little marbling, which should be hard to spot as the fat is practically the same color as the meat. If there is too much marbling and too much covering fat, then it means the calf has been overfed. What fat there is should look like white satin, and there shouldn't be much of it except around the kidneys.

Shoulder   Rib   Loin   Round/leg   Breast   Shank

### Cooking with veal

Because it hasn't much marbling, there is little interior lubrication while the meat is cooking, and veal can be dry unless other fat is added by way of larding or barding for roasting, or by using plenty of butter, good olive oil or bacon in sautéed, pot-roasted and stewed dishes.

The flavor of veal is unassertive, so a strongly flavored garnish is often welcome: the combination of veal and anchovies dates from the earliest times. Lemon and orange often feature in the best sauces, as does white wine and, particularly, Marsala. In Italy, a roast of veal may be studded with strips of anchovies; in Parma, they slit a leg cut of veal and introduce strips of paper-thin smoked ham. Scallops and cutlets of veal may also appear under a slice of mildly cured ham on which a generous slice of cheese is gently melting.

Onions have a special affinity with veal, not only because of their taste but because of their slippery texture—they are often put into the pan alongside a roast. As for accompaniments: any really fresh-looking vegetable is good, as is salad. Veal is pale, so dark green spinach or beans will provide a beautiful background. Potatoes, of course, go with veal in almost any form, and so do rice and noodles. Golden saffron rice is the traditional side dish for osso bucco, and a ring of snow-white rice often surrounds a blond blanquette or a fricassée of veal. (A fricassée differs from a blanquette only in the lack of cream and eggs in the sauce.) Tagliatelle is often served with veal, the slippery texture compensating for any possible dryness in the meat.

All veal bones are extremely gelatinous, and give an excellent texture to sauces and stocks: if the butcher has trimmed the meat for you, be sure to carry a few of the bones home with you and add them to the pot when braising a piece of veal, removing them before you dish up.

**Broiling and frying** Because of the lack of interior fat, the smaller cuts—chops, cutlets, scallops, medallions and the like—are more often fried than broiled.

Thin scallops should be fried quickly over a medium heat; chops should be first seared over high heat and then cooked on slowly, otherwise they will become tough and dry. Because of the high temperature of the initial cooking, chops will need to be fried in oil or in an oil and butter mixture, but scallops can be successfully fried in unsalted butter.

Veal can be rather indigestible and nasty unless it is thoroughly cooked, so wait until the juices run clear, with no tinge of pinkness, before withdrawing it from the heat.

**Roasting** Baste veal frequently if you do decide to try roasting it—pot roasting and braising are often more successful with this dry meat. Roast for 25 minutes per 1 lb/450 g and 20 minutes over at a medium temperature—about 375°F/190°C—for cuts that are thin or on the bone; 35 minutes per 1 lb/450 g at 325°F/170°C for those that are thick or cuts that have been boned and rolled or stuffed.

A hefty cut, like a leg, will preserve its succulence better if sprinkled with flour and covered with slices of bacon before it goes into the oven. The lean little roasts, such as a boned loin, should be threaded through with strips of pork fat (larded) or covered with a lattice of pork fat (barded). This extra fat will keep the meat moist.

**Pot roasting and braising** This is the best method of cooking a large piece of veal. Add some little onions, potatoes or carrots to the pot to help produce the moisture which will prevent the veal from drying out. In Italy, a good-sized carrot is sometimes inserted through the middle of the meat for the same purpose.

Allow 40–50 minutes per 1 lb/450 g at 325°F/170°C, basting the meat frequently with wine and butter.

**Stewing** should be done very gently, for well over an hour. Veal is good stewed in a flavorsome broth which is thickened and enriched at the end of the cooking time with egg yolks and cream.

**Boiling** or, more strictly speaking, poaching should be only a mere simmering: add a split calf's foot, and reduce the cooking liquid after the veal has been removed to make a beautiful aspic, having carefully skimmed off the scum which rises to the top of the pot at the beginning.

## The cuts

Like beef, cuts of veal vary according to the various butchery techniques. However, since calves are smaller than full-grown beef cattle, there is not quite so much scope for variations and not as much difference between the cuts. In fact most countries follow the economical French style of butchery for veal—and that involves trimming away all gristle and sinew most meticulously and dividing the meat neatly along the natural seams in the muscles.

### Cuts for frying, broiling and roasting

Veal needs plenty of additional fat to prevent it from drying out completely in the dry heat of these processes.

**The leg** Only the hindlegs go by this name, as the forelegs are called shanks. This large and fleshy joint is almost always divided into the hock end and the fillet end. These cuts can be roasted under a layer of bacon or, better still, braised with vegetables to keep them moist and juicy.

The round roast, or fillet end of the leg—the top slices of which go by the name of round steak or cutlets—is the equivalent of a top round of beef. A boneless round roast makes a succulent meal—it is particularly good stuffed with a moist mixture of pork fat, anchovy fillets and currants and then braised in a web of caul fat.

The most delicate leg meat is from the muscle that runs vertically along the thigh bone. In French butchery it is sold separately as the *rouelle*, but in general, leg of veal cuts tend to be sliced crosswise, containing some of each of the three muscles, which are very similar in taste. So, whether on or off the bone, a cut of center leg makes good eating. It is this bit that is used for the famous Italian dish *vitello tonnato*—always eaten cold and coated with a sauce of tuna fish pounded to an emulsion with olive oil, lemon juice and capers.

**The sirloin**, situated at the point where leg meets loin, is usually boned and rolled for slow roasting and braising.

**Scallops** It is from the fillet end of the leg that the best scallops are cut, across the grain and on the bias. Of course, many stores sell thin pink slices of fatless, trimmed veal under the name of escalopes, scallopini or scallops from other parts of a calf's anatomy,

particularly the ribs, but first-rate butchers only recognize those from the leg as the real thing. Ask the butcher to press them flat for you for extra tenderness, and when you egg-and-crumb these diaphanous slices, you get the perfect scallops *panés*. These are classically served with a slice of lemon, perhaps a rolled anchovy and possibly some chopped hard-boiled egg arranged in a circle around it, and a few scattered capers.

If you find that you have to pound the scallops yourself, do take care not to beat the life out of them—a well-cut scallop will only require a gentle flattening. If you don't possess a cutlet beater, then use a rolling pin or ease the meat into shape with the heel of your hand.

There are many, many ways to serve veal scallops. This rich diversity is in part due to the fact that the scallop is one of the mainstays of Italian cooking, and it features often in the varied cuisines of France, Germany and Austria.

In Italy, for instance, a great favorite is saltimbocca—which means literally "to jump into the mouth." This is a dish of small scallops rolled up around a stuffing of prosciutto ham and fresh sage.

Piccate, or scallopini, are tiny scallops traditionally dipped in flour and fried in butter. Ideally, they come from the same part of the leg as scallops; they are usually sautéed and served with a good sauce.

In France, veal scallops are often simply browned in butter, with the last-minute addition of a handful of finely chopped shallots or scallions.

The Germans and Austrians are of course famed for their *Weinerschnitzels*—traditionally these are dipped first into flour, then beaten egg, then bread crumbs and then briefly deep fried in hot oil.

**Loin of veal**, a lean roasting cut, contains the tenderloin, which is the equivalent of beef tenderloin. It may also contain the kidneys. But these, as well as the fillet, are often removed to be sold separately: the tenderloin to make nice little medallions that look like tournedos. The loin can be divided into chops or sold whole for roasting.

When roasting a loin, keep it very well basted with butter or bacon fat, or cook it in a covered casserole to keep it moist.

**Rib** This is the section that is divided into delicious veal chops, which should not be cut too thin. Chops should be cooked very gently after browning or they may become dry. Like scallops, which are also often cut from these parts, cutlets usually have their garnish sitting on top: a poached egg and a cross of anchovy fillets earns them the suffix Holstein; and fontina cheese, prosciutto, small white mushrooms and of course anchovies may all feature.

**The middle neck**, which forms part of the

shoulder in the United States, provides veal cutlets, which the Americans call shoulder chops, the French *cotelettes découvertes*. Smaller than chops, they are prepared in much the same way, though they are sometimes sealed in butter and enclosed in a paper case together with a farce of shallots, onion, mushrooms and parsley and baked in the oven, to be served *en papillotte*. When the cutlets are not quite severed at the base, and teased around to form a crown of veal, the onion and mushroom stuffing may go into the center. Off the bone, the meat of the middle neck is used for pies, *blanquette de veau* and goulash.

### For braising, pot roasting and boiling

Veal adapts particularly well to moist heat, absorbing both moisture and any flavorings added to the pot.

**Shoulder or oyster of veal** is a fairly lean cut suitable for slow roasting or pot roasting. It is almost always sold boned and rolled, often with stuffing, although it is vastly preferable to make one's own. For this purpose, good butchers often leave an empty pocket in the center. Boned and cubed shoulder is a prime candidate for blanquettes and fricassées—especially when mixed with the meat from the breast region. It is the traditional cut for veal Marengo, which unlike its namesake, chicken Marengo, requires no truffles, crayfish or fried eggs. A traditional veal Marengo is a simple braise made with plenty of oil, garlic, tomatoes and mushrooms.

Ground shoulder, flavored with marjoram and rosemary and bound together with egg, makes delicious meatballs—made more delicious with the addition of a sauce of white wine, cream and finely chopped shallots.

**Neck of veal or stewing veal** may be used for braised dishes as it provides meat that is suitable for long simmering. Ground, it makes good meat loaves, meatballs and stuffings, and can be used in pâtés. Ground veal, in fact, is an ingredient in many classic forcemeats for stuffing pork tenderloin, poultry and game birds.

**Breast and flank of veal** are often seen boned, and provide a vehicle for some very good stuffings. Traditionally, something green is included in these: spinach, perhaps, or peas, or pistachio nuts. Served cold, a stuffed breast of veal, simmered, gently pressed and allowed to cool in its own gelatine, makes a beautiful summer lunch. A breast is also very good hot—casseroled together with a chunk of salt pork and some large, juicy onions.

**The shank or foreleg** is a tough, sinewy but well-flavored piece of meat consisting mainly of bone, which, sawn into thick slices, makes one of the most delicious veal dishes—osso bucco.

# Meat/Lamb

First grade lamb has rosy flesh. Its bones are slender and red, the fat is white, silky and resilient. The very best lamb, meltingly tender but expensive and difficult to find, is milk-fed lamb with flesh of the palest pink which turns almost white when cooked. It is at its best at Eastertime, and is especially good when cooked in the ancient way, herb-strewn on glowing embers.

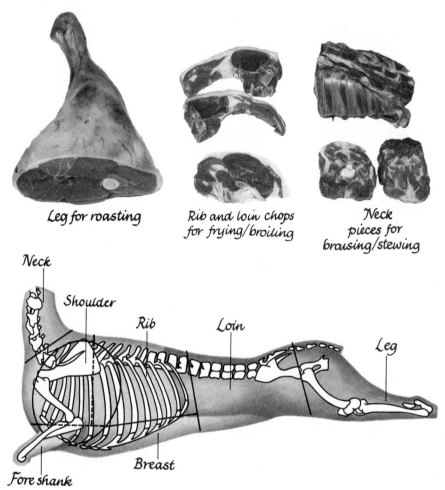

*Leg for roasting*

*Rib and loin chops for frying/broiling*

*Neck pieces for braising/stewing*

*Neck*

*Shoulder*

*Rib*

*Loin*

*Leg*

*Fore shank*

*Breast*

Spring lamb that has been weaned will be much the same size as milk-fed lamb: a whole leg may just feed four people. Summer and autumn lamb has flesh that is darker than Easter lamb. Lamb only qualifies for the name when it has been slaughtered before its first birthday. After that, it becomes hogget, then mutton.

Yearling mutton gives delicious meat; it is a little darker and a little stronger tasting than lamb. The expression "mutton dressed as lamb" arose because all too many butchers used to try deceiving their customers (and thrifty hosts their guests), but there is really no mistaking the two kinds of meat: mutton is dark red, not pink, and there should not be too much fat. Although mutton used to be as despised as lamb was admired, it is just the right sort of meat for the heftier regional dishes. Ironically, now that supplies of good lamb are quite constant—not least because this meat freezes particularly well—people who actually want to buy good old-fashioned mutton often have great difficulty in finding it.

## Choosing lamb and mutton

When buying lamb or mutton, go for the leanest piece you can see—even the fatty cuts vary greatly in their proportions of fat to lean. Avoid those with fat that looks brittle and crumbly or discolored—the most appetizing-looking pieces will make the best eating and have the most flavor.

Some of the most delicious lamb comes from sheep that have grazed on salt marshes: the *pré-salé* lamb—"pre-salted" lamb—of France's Atlantic coast is world-famous. Most lamb for the table comes from lowland farms where the sheep are fat, but some prefer the leaner lamb from the hills: Welsh lamb, small and slender-boned, is a good example of this superb meat. Hillside lamb is a touch gamier in flavor, and there are many recipes for cooking lamb like venison, using the traditional marinades and the same accompaniments: rowanberry or red currant jelly, or a compote of cranberries.

## Cooking with lamb and mutton

Lamb is basically a tender, succulent meat, so take care not to overcook it—generally, lamb should be pink and juicy inside.

**Broiling and frying** Chops and steaks of lamb, nicely trimmed, are equally good broiled or fried. The timing depends on the thickness of the pieces. Test them by pressing them with your finger during cooking: when they are becoming firm but still supple, they are done.

**Roasting** Much depends on the age of the animal and the quality of the meat.

The timing varies according to whether you like your roast rosy pink or well done. A leg of lamb should be pink within, most gourmets would agree, although not everyone shares the taste of the French, who like it rose-red in the center. The rib end, saddle and loin are best fairly rare—cook all these prime quality cuts at 375°F/190°C, allowing about 20 minutes per 1 lb/450 g and maybe 15 minutes over for larger cuts, but test by piercing: when the juice runs red, the meat is rare; rosy, it is fairly rare; and when the meat juices run clear, the meat is thoroughly cooked.

The shoulder and all boned, rolled cuts, including stuffed, rolled breasts, are better when they are well done: cook them at 325°F/170°C, allowing about 30 minutes per 1 lb/450 g.

**Pot roasting and braising** is done at an even lower temperature: 300°F/160°C, allowing about 2 hours for a leg or shoulder, 1½ hours for casseroling smaller cuts, and a lamb stew should be ready for eating after 1½ hours of cooking.

**Boiling** takes about 30 minutes per 1 lb/450 g for larger cuts of mutton, but it is best to cook them well before they are needed, since they taste nicest reheated and, since mutton for boiling tends to be rather fatty, it gives you a chance to lift off the fat, which solidifies when the dish has cooled. If there is not time to wait for this to happen, the broth can be defatted either by careful skimming, or by plunging ice cubes into the liquid and lifting out the fat when it congeals.

Because all lamb fat congeals so quickly, it is important to take your stew to the table in a preheated dish and to serve it as soon as possible on very hot plates.

## The cuts

Most large cuts of lamb can be roasted; even the fattier ones will taste good.

### Leg of lamb, or gigot

This succulent piece, simply roasted on the bone, is one of the greatest cuts of meat there is. It may be subdivided into the shank and the sirloin end. The sirloin end, in turn, makes leg steaks. Divested of all membranes, this fleshy steak, cut into cubes, makes lovely little kebabs.

The leg or gigot is also sold boned. It is usually rolled, but is sometimes left flat—in America this version is called a butterfly leg of lamb. In whatever form, this cut makes a lovely roast. Leave on the papery outer skin to ensure even cooking, and if you want to make this extra crisp, dredge it with a little flour after basting.

Serve young lamb with mint sauce and spring vegetables; autumn lamb with root vegetables. If you braise half a leg on a bed of vegetables and use cream and tarragon in the sauce, it becomes *agneau jardinière*, but what is particularly delicious and all too rarely encountered is a noble, very English, boiled leg of lamb—the shank end —served with caper or onion sauce.

In France the centerbone is sometimes removed from the sirloin end of a gigot, leaving only the shank bone in place: this makes carving easier when the meat is served.

### Center roast

Lying between the leg and the sirloin, this piece is sometimes sold as a separate cut for roasting. Often it is cut into the juiciest steaks—expensive, since each leg yields only two or three. In some schools of butchery it simply forms part of the leg itself. The two legs, center roast, sirloin and loin make a very impressive cut called a baron of lamb.

### Loin

Two joined loins make a saddle, very good for parties. This is sometimes decorated at one end with the kidneys, and a bas-relief of braided fat running its length. The single loin may be bought on the bone, but it also comes boned and rolled, often around the kidneys—slices of this are called kidney lamb chops.

The loin is often divided into chops—each with a small T-shaped bone dividing the two pieces of lean. There are a hundred ways of garnishing chops; left plain, fried or broiled, serve them pink inside with watercress and mashed potatoes. Loin chops can be boned and trimmed of any excess fat until only the eyes remain.

### The rib

This cut, which the French usually call the carré, and which is sometimes referred to as rack of lamb, lies next to the loin. If you mean to roast or braise it in the piece, ask the butcher to chine it for you, to enable you to carve neat chops after cooking. Two racks placed opposite each other, fat side out, bones in the air and interlinked like swords at a military wedding, make a good party piece called Guard of Honor. A good, moist stuffing goes in between the two pieces of meat, the same type that you would put into the center of a crown of lamb, which is made from the identical two cuts, joined at both ends. The rack, trimmed and chined and with the ribs removed, can also be neatly rolled and divided into noisettes.

Sliced, the rib end or rack gives chops that are a fraction less juicy than loin chops, but still very good. When they are "frenched"—trimmed with the elegance and care that most French butchers bestow on all the meat they handle, so that in this case the bones are pared of fat—they may come to table with a paper frill at the end, and are sometimes eaten with the fingers. The farther back the chops lie, the leaner they are; towards the front, they tend to become quite fatty.

Chops are often egg-and-crumbed. When they are served with a sauce made of vegetables, ham and herbs, all chopped finely, moistened with stock, thickened with cornstarch and flavored with red currant jelly, they become Reform cutlets—named after the London club where they are still served in this way. But elegant classic garnishes—truffles, creamed mushrooms, foie gras, asparagus tips—also find their way onto lamb chops and cutlets.

### Shoulder of lamb

Easy to cook, this makes a sweet and juicy roast. It is fattier than the leg, and harder to carve, especially when it is on the bone, but is often a more succulent meal. Boned and tied, it may be stuffed—whether it comes as a long roll or, as in France, in a kind of melon-shaped bundle also known as a ballotine, or *épaule en ballon*. The shoulder also provides blade and arm chops which are good for braising.

Shoulder, trimmed of all fat and membrane, is the cut that is often ground up, perhaps together with meat from the foreshank, for use in moussaka, stuffed peppers, grape leaves and the like. In the Middle East this cut of lamb is sometimes pounded to the consistency of an ointment: this smooth paste, which also involves burghul, is called kibbeh—it is formed into little patties which are eaten raw with onions.

### Shoulder chops

Lying underneath the shoulder blade next to the rack, shoulder chops are a decidedly fatty cut, but useful for broth, lamb stew and Lancashire hotpot (unless you make this in the traditional way, with rib chops standing upright in a deep earthenware pot).

### Neck and fore shank

Both of these cuts are very economical buys. They are used in the same way as shoulder chops, but have more bone, gristle and fat. Use them to make a good Irish stew—a dish which used once to be made with kid, but lamb is now almost always used. Because they are fatty, use plenty of potatoes to soak up the juices.

A top layer of thickly cut slices of potato benefits from the rich aromatic fat that rises as the meat cooks. A shepherd's pie, with its covering of mashed potatoes, works on the same principle, as do casseroles or haricots of lamb where dried beans act as the blotting paper. Essentially, haricot, ragout and navarin are all stews—although a *navarin printanier* only applies to a more spring-like dish, in which carrots, turnips and peas feature as vegetables. Pilafs, too, feature stewing lamb and rice.

### Breast of lamb

This thin, fatty cut tastes better when it has been slowly cooked. The breast cage makes riblets for barbecuing; the less bony parts can be boned, stuffed and rolled, or tied flat, like a sandwich, with the stuffing in the middle. Boneless breast can be simmered, cooled, cut into squares, egg-and-crumbed and fried; these morsels are called epigrams, a charming name and a good dish.

---

### Kid

When it comes to athletic lamb from craggy hillsides with no pasture to speak of, the meat is not notable for its succulence. This is where kid, better adapted to such regions, is much preferred to lamb.

Cooked in oil and wine with garlic, wreathed in rosemary or myrtle, young kid, creamy white and tender, makes the festive dishes in such places as Corsica and Sardinia, while lamb is for every day. Saudi Arabia, too, feasts on kid: rubbed with coriander, ginger and onion juice, stuffed with rice, dried fruits and nuts, and served with clouds of rice and hard-boiled eggs. Lamb can, of course, be substituted—as far as recipes go, the two kinds of meat are interchangeable. But as the taste of kid is bland, it needs plenty of flavoring.

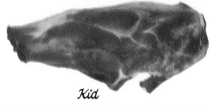

*Kid*

# Meat/Pork

Prime, fresh pork should be a lovely pearly pink, fine textured, and with visible fat that is dense and milk-white. There is a good deal of intramuscular fat in any piece of pork. Even a suckling pig, slaughtered at about three weeks old, makes a rich, filling meal, although it has hardly had time to grow stout.

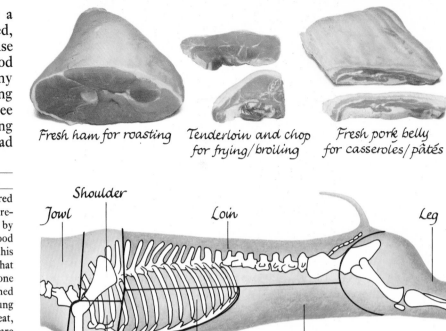

*Fresh ham for roasting*

*Tenderloin and chop for frying/broiling*

*Fresh pork belly for casseroles/pâtés*

Jowl · Shoulder · Loin · Leg

Hock · Picnic shoulder · Spare ribs · Belly

## Choosing pork

In the case of meat from animals slaughtered between four and six months—called, respectively, young pigs and mature hogs by the trade—make sure that there is a good proportion of lean meat to fat, and this applies even more to porkers, which is what pigs are called between six months and one year. By this time, the meat has darkened to rose-pink and the bones, pinkish in young animals, are white. Deep rose-colored meat, white brittle bones and rough skin are signs of a porker's unduly advanced age; red meat with a dried-up look is not worth bothering with. If you notice brown or yellowish stains on the skin, if the meat looks wet and slippery rather than damp, the meat will be of poor quality, and if there is any kind of smell, the meat is stale.

## Cooking with pork

Although all cuts of pork taste rich, not all of them are liberally lubricated from within. The leg, for example, does not have much in the way of intramuscular fat, so meat from this part of the animal may appear to be on the dry side, and to remain as juicy as possible should be slowly cooked.

All cuts of pork without exception need to be well cooked—partly because raw pork may contain microscopic parasites which are killed only when the meat reaches an internal temperature of about 140°F/60°C, and, just as important, because underdone pork tastes very unpleasant.

The humbler cuts of pork are cooked and served with plenty of fat on the meat, and so the best accompaniments are mealy—beans, dried peas and lentils, which will absorb some of the fat.

Chestnuts have the same effect, and in Spain and Portugal potatoes are added to braised or stewed fatty pork dishes about half an hour before serving to soak up the fat that has risen to the top of the pot.

The more expensive, less fatty cuts of pork —leg and loin—are more often served with fruit or vegetables that provide a contrast to the rich, dense meat. Apples are probably the best-known accompaniment, while in Tours, cutlets or fillet steaks of pork are

cooked with prunes. In Denmark prunes are used to stuff a loin roast, and a mixture of soaked, dried fruit is used in Poland. In the Rhineland, the mealy and fruity elements are combined in a dish called Heaven and Earth—a mixture of puréed potatoes and apples.

For moistening purposes, beer, wine and stock are occasionally used, but cider is the liquid most associated with pork.

By way of herbs, pork takes kindly to the warm flavor of fennel and caraway seeds, as well as to the bitter flavor of sage. Some people in England still make their own sage and onion stuffing for their Sunday roast of pork—much nicer than the ready-made variety. In Italy, pork is often cooked with rosemary; it is good also with juniper berries and with thyme, and, of course, a loin of pork is wonderful with truffles.

As for vegetable side dishes, all the members of the brassica family, led by sweet-and-sour red cabbage, are naturals for pork. The more delicate roasts, such as leg or loin, look most appetizing with something fresh such as little carrots or turnips, leeks, bright green cabbage or spinach. Young peas and artichoke hearts in butter make one of the best combinations. A plain lettuce salad, eaten from the same plate after a broiled or fried chop, and bathed in the meat juices, is extremely delicious.

**Broiling and frying** A medium chop

should take about 20 minutes at medium heat. Turn it from time to time as it cooks, and test it by piercing—when the juices run clear, it is ready to serve.

**Roasting** must be thorough. Allow a full 30 minutes per 1 lb/450 g for smaller, thinner cuts, plus 20 minutes over, at about 350°F/180°C and 35 minutes per 1 lb/450 g and 25 minutes over, for thicker pieces like leg or a shoulder cut. If you buy pork with the skin, ask the butcher to score it closely and deeply with his special knife, right through the rind to the fat, to help the heat penetrate to the center. In many countries, the skin is peeled off the meat before it is sold and supplied separately, to be cooked alongside the meat, enriching the gravy. It turns into the hardest leather by this process. (The Normans found this *cuir bouilli* an effective protection against their enemies' arrows.) So if you like crisp crackling—and many people think this is possibly the best part of a piece of roast pork—do not allow the meat to sit in the fat in the pan or you render part of the skin inedible. Instead, roast the cut on a rack, having rubbed the skin with oil or salt (but not both together) for extra crispness. Increase the oven temperature a little before the end of cooking and do not baste the crackling during cooking—it just makes it tough.

**Braising and pot roasting** On top of the stove, simmer pork over a medium

heat, or set the oven at 325°F/170°C.
**Boiling** It is not very usual to boil fresh pork, except, of course, for the feet, but any of the pickled cuts make perfect candidates for boiling, or rather simmering. These may need soaking beforehand: ask the butcher for how long, as he alone knows for how long the meat has been salted.

## The cuts

There is no single cut of pork that cannot satisfactorily be roasted—the pig is too lethargic a beast to develop much by way of tough muscle and connective tissue. The coarser cuts with little visible fat may be better casseroled or slowly stewed. A coarse, fat cut will still make a lovely braise or stew, provided it is trimmed of most of the fat, which would make the sauce too rich and indigestible.

### The leg
A whole leg makes a really imposing dish. But even a small one—and one from a pig should weigh no more than 6–7 lb/2.5–3 kg —can be rather daunting, so it is usually divided into the shank or leg end and the fillet end, which the French confusingly call jambon frais and which in America is referred to as the fresh ham rump.
**The shank end** is easier to cook evenly when it is boned and rolled, but it then looks less handsome on the platter. When cooking it on the bone, it is a good idea to protect the thinner bony bit by wrapping it in foil halfway through the cooking time, leaving the meatier end exposed to the full heat.
**The rump end** of the leg is cooked as a roast, or may be cut by the butcher into lean slices about $\frac{1}{2}$–1 in/1–2.5 cm thick. Such a slice makes a huge meal—cook it as you would a steak. The rump end of leg may be cut into cubes to be cooked as kebabs.

A leg is sometimes, especially in Italy, first simmered in milk and then cooked on in the oven, surrounded by quantities of garlic (the milk ends up as a light, golden gravy), while some countries pickle the leg, to be boiled and eaten with the mash of green split peas that is known and loved as pease pudding in the north of England.

### The loin end
This fleshy part of the loin is usually cut into delicious large chops—the butterfly chops of America—but this is another cut that may be roasted on the bone or off, seasoned with sage, rosemary or thyme.

### The loin
Delicate and very tender, the loin itself makes a wonderful meal if boned, filled with chopped garlic and a couple of mushrooms or even truffles, and rolled and roasted. On the bone, a loin cut is sometimes served sitting on a bed of unsweetened apples and sweet chestnuts.

It is the loin that provides most of the pork chops: to be fried plain or broiled after being lightly brushed with oil, or pounded, egg-and-crumbed and fried *alla milanese*, or braised, moistened with beer or cider.

Chops taken from the sirloin end of the loin may bring with them a slice of kidney and a portion of the fillet or tenderloin.

### The tenderloin
In young pigs the fillet or tenderloin is usually much too small to be separated out, but many butchers remove it in its entirety from larger carcasses, where it may weigh about 1 lb/450 g. Trimmed of its fat, it is good roasted—perhaps scored down the middle and stuffed, or wrapped in bacon and roasted whole like a miniature roast. It may also be cut into medallions or scallops, but their taste, like those of veal, from which they are almost indistinguishable, is delicate, so some interesting flavoring is needed to give them character: in France apples or prunes are used as garnish for fillet cuts, which are lovely cooked with crushed juniper berries, and in Germany they are cooked with caraway seeds or a rich sauce made of sour cream and the delicious pan juices.

### Blade or shoulder
This rather rich cut can be roasted, or ground up or chopped for pork pies or meatballs and for the famous scrapple of Philadelphia—a cooked mixture of pork and cornmeal, sliced and fried in bacon drippings.

Meat from the shoulder can be sliced into steaks that are particularly good when cooked over charcoal.

### Picnic shoulder and hock
An awkwardly shaped piece which is often divided into a variety of cuts for stewing, but whole it makes a good, large, economical roast, although the meat is marginally coarser than that of the leg. This cut is a particularly difficult one to carve unless you know exactly how the bones run, but the butcher will advise you if you ask him, or will even bone and roll it for you.

### Spareribs
These come from the upper part of the rib cage and are either sold in sheets or separated into meaty single or double bones, each with its cartilage. The sheets of ribs are sometimes cooked sandwiched together with a stuffing in between: the Pennsylvania Dutch like to spread this sandwich with apples, the Germans with cabbage and caraway. The separated ribs are barbecued and often eaten with a sweet-sour sauce, said to have been introduced to America by Chinese railway workers, who used to cook this meat as they worked on the line.
**Chinese spareribs,** as we know them, are not the meaty slices from the upper parts of the rib cage, but the lower ends of the rib bones. These have very little meat on them, but are extremely good barbecued and served with chili sauce. Eat them with the fingers, allowing about 3 lb/1.5 kg for 2 people because these spareribs are so bony.

### Pork belly
The abdominal wall provides rather fatty meat; it is usually cured for bacon and is good for enriching dishes of beans, lentils and cabbage and is useful in pâtés. If you can't find fresh pork belly use salt pork—preferably a piece with a good streak of lean—that has been soaked to freshen.

### Suckling pig
These young pigs, which have been slaughtered between the ages of three and eight weeks, contain proportionally little meat, however what there is, is perhaps the sweetest and richest of all pork.

In northern Spain, suckling pigs are a specialty. These Spanish suckling pigs start their short lives on a diet of mothers' milk and wild herbs. They are traditionally roasted in a slow-burning wood oven and served with potatoes and applesauce.
**Choosing suckling pig** You will need to order one specially from your butcher. They range in size from 6–20 lb/2.5–9 kg, and a medium-size one will be a good buy as it will have developed enough meaty parts without sacrificing any of the tender succulence of the smaller pigs. As a rough guide, a 12 lb/5.5 kg pig should feed about 10 people.
**Roasting a suckling pig** Suckling pig, which should have been cleaned for you by the butcher, can be stuffed with any stuffing suitable for pork (a combination of bread crumbs, parsley, onions, sausage, chestnuts and brandy is good), or simply brushed with oil or rubbed with coarse salt and lemon juice and sprinkled with herbs. Place the suckling pig on a rack and prick the skin before and during roasting to allow the fat to ooze out into the roasting pan. It won't need basting and the skin will turn a shiny crisp brown. A medium-size stuffed pig will take about $2\frac{1}{2}$–3 hours to cook, an unstuffed one will be ready in 2 hours. Allow 20 minutes per 1 lb/450 g at 350°F/180°C.

Suckling pigs are usually reserved for festive occasions, such as the colorful Hawaiian luaus, or beach barbecues, where the central feature is a spit-roasted suckling pig, liberally basted with barbecue sauce and presented on a tray with a red apple in its mouth.

Some of the best dishes in the world are made with humble pieces of meat that are collectively known as variety meats. They are treated with special respect in France and the Mediterranean countries, where their distinctive flavors and textures are preserved by careful cooking.

Luckily, many of these meats are among the most economical buys. While some of them, particularly those from veal, may command a high price, only small amounts need to be purchased because of their rich flavor and lack of bones, while meats from less expensive animals are full of wholesome flavor. Whichever type you buy, make sure it is fresh and cook it as soon as possible.

## Sweetbreads

A fine delicacy, sweetbreads are sold in pairs, being two parts of the thymus gland found in the throat and chest of young animals. The rounder, fatter one is the better of the two. (The sweetbreads that come from the pancreas gland and are sometimes referred to as stomach sweetbreads, or beef breads, are coarser than true sweetbreads.) Veal sweetbreads are the best, especially the very large ones from milk-fed veal. They are whiter and larger than lamb's sweetbreads, less fussy to prepare and have a finer flavor. Pork sweetbreads are small and not particularly good.

No matter how they are to be cooked, all sweetbreads need to be cooked first to make them white and firm. One of the best ways of cooking them after the initial preparation is to egg-and-crumb them and fry them gently in butter until brown.

## Brains

Calf's brains are decidedly the best, although lamb's brains are also quite good. Neither pork nor beef brains are eaten with any enthusiasm. Like sweetbreads, brains need preparation before they are used. They can then be gently fried or poached. *Beurre noir*, with a few capers added, is the classic sauce. Brains are also good *à la meunière*—fried and served with brown butter (*beurre noisette*), lemon and parsley.

## Liver

Fresh liver is the most nutritious of all variety meats. It is sold either whole or in slices and is often already trimmed, but if it still has a thin covering of membrane, this needs to be removed or the liver will curl up in the pan. Less delicate livers such as pork or beef liver will become more tender if they are soaked in milk before cooking.

**Calf's liver** Pale and plump, liver from milk-fed veal is the most delicious but it is expensive. Liver from grass-fed veal will be thinner, darker and not as mild. Fried liver is delicious if it is cooked very lightly and rapidly and is still rosy inside—overcooking makes liver tough, dry and leathery. In the famous *fegato alla Veneziana*, calf's liver is cut into the thinnest slices, fried for mere seconds and served on a bed of golden fried onions. Liver is also good with bacon and watercress.

**Lamb's liver** is a deeper color than calf's liver and has a less good flavor but is as tender. It is served in the same ways as calf's liver.

**Pork liver** is not ideal for frying, as its texture is granular and its taste rather powerful. It is best used in pâtés, or braised in one large piece with wine and vegetables.

**Beef liver** is the coarsest and strongest flavored of livers and is eaten braised with onions. Simmer it for 1–2 hours until tender and serve with mashed potatoes.

## Kidneys

All kidneys, whether they come encased in their fresh white surrounding fat or not, should be firm and smell sweet. Once they have been skinned, halved, and their gristly core has been removed, they can be broiled or sautéed briefly or simmered slowly and for a long time—anything in between and they will be tough and rubbery.

**Veal kidneys** These multilobed kidneys will be very large and pale when they come from milk-fed veal, and darker and much smaller from grass-fed veal. They are best when grilled over charcoal and served with bacon, or briskly browned in butter to seal in their juices. The piquancy of a mustard and cream sauce is the perfect complement. They can also be roasted, encased in their own fat. This takes about an hour and the resulting kidneys will be pink and succulent.

**Lamb's kidneys** These have a mild but delicious flavor and are excellent fried in butter. With the two halves not quite severed they form an essential part of a mixed grill.

**Pork kidneys** are larger than lamb's kidneys and thought by some people to be strong flavored, but they are tender enough to be broiled or fried and are a favorite dish on the menu in French brasseries. They are also good cooked slowly in wine and served with boiled potatoes to offset their richness.

**Beef kidneys** are dark, strong flavored and really only suitable for braising. They also provide just the right flavor and plenty of rich gravy in steak and kidney pies.

## Tongue

While tongue can be purchased fresh, it is more usual to find it salted and possibly smoked. It is a very smooth meat: beef tongue is best; veal tongue, although good, has less flavor and lamb's tongue is inclined to be rather dull.

Whether fresh or salted, choose a tongue that feels soft to the touch. Soak salted tongue overnight if necessary to remove the salt, and then simmer it with vegetables and herbs until tender. Skin it carefully and serve it hot with salsa verde, walnut or raisin sauce, and mashed or boiled new potatoes. Cold, it is usually eaten with pickles, horseradish or mustard, and green salad.

Pressed tongue can be made by placing a weighted plate over a warm, cooked tongue, curled up in a round cake pan with a spoonful or two of its own cooking liquid.

## Tripe

Usually from beef or calf, tripe is the lining of the first and second stomachs. It comes in a variety of textures, some honeycombed, which are considered the best, some just slightly rough and some smooth. In France it is cooked with wine and vegetables; in Italy with wine and Parmesan. An authentic *tripe à la mode de Caen*, the Normandy dish flavored with vegetables and Calvados, needs about 12 hours of simmering before it is at its gelatinous best.

Always buy tripe that looks white and fresh. Pickled tripe will need to be freshened before it is cooked.

## Hearts

A heart is a hard-working muscle and is never especially tender. Beef heart is particularly tough and is best sliced and braised with plenty of onions to give it a good flavor. Lamb's, veal and pork hearts, being more tender, can be blanched, stuffed, wrapped in bacon and roasted. Italian cooks like to fry sliced veal hearts very fast with chili peppers and serve them with lemon.

## Heads, tails and feet

Although not always available, heads, tails and feet are often well worth the trouble and the long, slow cooking needed to make them tender and to bring out their velvety gelatinous qualities.

## Heads

Daunting to look at, the head of a calf, pig or sheep can be a lengthy business to prepare, but an obliging butcher will do this for you and split it into manageable pieces.

**Pig's head** makes brawn or head cheese, the chopped meat suspended in a translucent aspic flavored with herbs, spices and vinegar (heads are very gelatinous) and eaten cold with mustard and green salad.

**Calf's head**, cooked, boned and chopped and covered with a vinaigrette containing capers and onions, makes the *tête de veau vinaigrette* sold readymade in charcuteries. **Sheep's head** makes a broth much liked in Scotland but thought depressing elsewhere. **Calf's and pig's ears** are cartilaginous and considered a delicacy by the Chinese. Braised pig's ears sometimes appear in *choucroute garnie*—garnished sauerkraut—beloved in Alsace, and they can be coated with egg and bread crumbs and fried.

## Oxtail

Oxtail stew, in winter, is one of the very best and most warming dishes. Choose an oxtail with a high proportion of lean, and with fresh, creamy fat. Allow a whole oxtail for two to three people. It needs long, slow cooking to develop its excellent gelatinous texture. The large amounts of fat that rise to the surface will be easier to remove if the stew is made the day before serving and allowed to get completely cold. Oxtail stew reheats particularly well.

## Feet

Calf's foot and pig's feet both yield plenty of gelatine—the type with which to fill a homemade meat pie.

**Pig's feet** These are sold fresh or pickled. They are usually split in half and can be quite plump and meaty. Often they are just simmered and served hot with sauerkraut or cold in their own gelatine, and they are very good cooked and then bread crumbed and broiled, served with mustard, or fried and served with tomato sauce. Pig's feet go into some stews, and they strengthen the jellying powers of stocks and consommés. **Calf's foot** can be stewed and goes into the making of jellied stocks and glazes.

## Gelatine

Extracted from calf's feet, pig's knuckles and the like, gelatine is sold either in powdered form in individual packets, or in shiny sheets. A good gelatine will have virtually no taste and will dissolve into a clear liquid—so necessary when making galantines, when the meat and vegetables shine through the aspic. Sheet or leaf gelatine is less likely than powdered to go lumpy. Do not boil gelatine but dissolve it with a little liquid in a cup standing in a shallow pan of hot water. Gelatine does not take kindly to freezing. An alternative to animal gelatine is agar-agar, the jellying agent extracted from seaweed.

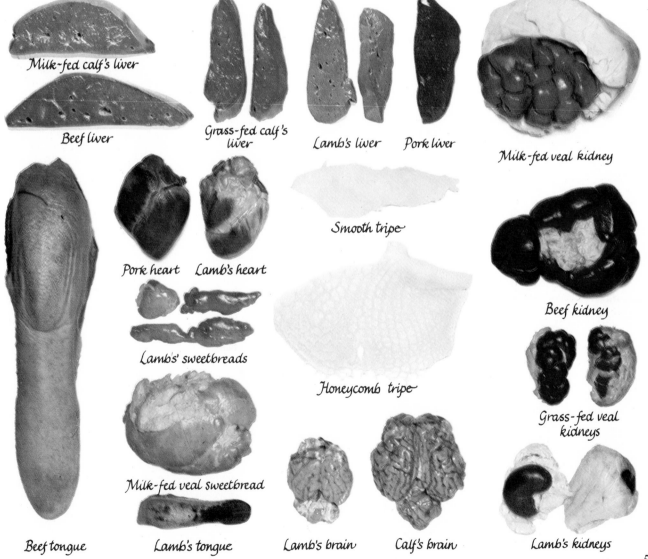

Milk-fed calf's liver

Beef liver

Grass-fed calf's liver

Lamb's liver

Pork liver

Milk-fed veal kidney

Pork heart

Lamb's heart

Smooth tripe

Beef kidney

Lamb's sweetbreads

Honeycomb tripe

Grass-fed veal kidneys

Milk-fed veal sweetbread

Beef tongue

Lamb's tongue

Lamb's brain

Calf's brain

Lamb's kidneys

**Preparing a tenderloin of beef**

**1.** *With the rounded, neater side of the meat uppermost, start cutting and pulling away the fat from the wide end.*

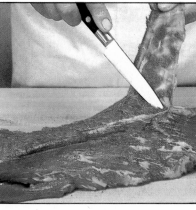

**5.** *Return the meat to its original position and with the aid of a sharp knife pull off the covering layer of sinew. This should leave the meat completely free of fat, sinew and gristle.*

**2.** *Cut away all the fat and gristle that lie along one side of the tenderloin.*

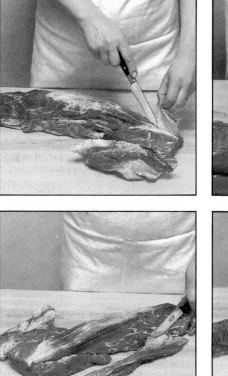

**6.** *Prepare the meat for roasting whole by securing any loose ends neatly with trussing string.*

**3.** *Sever the large lump of fat that is attached to the wide end.*

**7.** *Alternatively, trim the tenderloin to neaten it, and cut small filets mignons from the thin end, medium-size tournedos from the center. The wide end can be used as a Chateaubriand: wrap it in a clean cloth, turn it on its side and flatten it to half its original height.*

**4.** *Turn the tenderloin over and pull and cut away the strip of gristle and fat.*

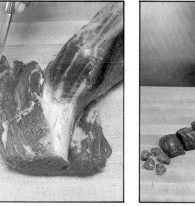

**8.** *In this way the tenderloin has been divided into a Chateaubriand (bottom), three tournedos (top) and three filets mignons. Use the trimmings for beef Stroganoff or steak tartare.*

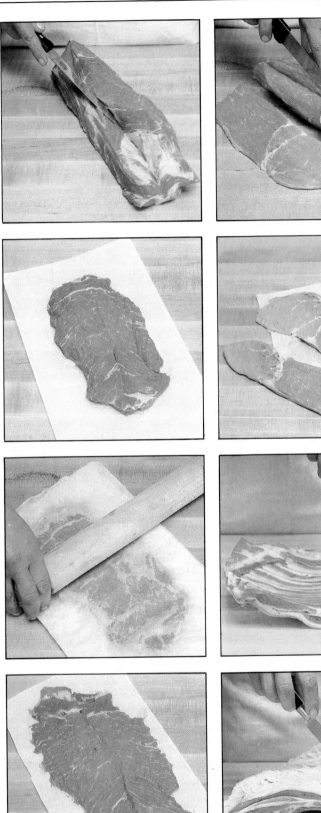

**Preparing pork scallops**

1. *Take a tenderloin of pork and slit it down the middle, being careful not to cut right through it.*

2. *Open the meat out 'like a book and place it on a dampened piece of wax paper.*

3. *Cover the meat with a second piece of damp wax paper and flatten it gently but firmly with a rolling pin.*

4. *Here, the scallop is ready for use. Alternatively, cut the scallop into smaller pieces and use as scallopini —small scallops.*

**Preparing veal scallops**

1. *Cut even slices from a leg cut of veal, using a very sharp knife.*

2. *Flatten each slice between two pieces of dampened wax paper in the same way as for pork scallops. Here, a scallop is compared with a freshly cut slice.*

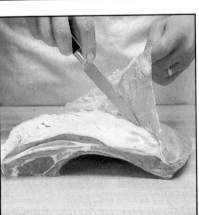

**Preparing rack of lamb, Guard of Honor and Crown Roast**

1. *Take two racks of lamb from the rib section and, if the butcher has not already done so, cut away the bony part, or chine, from the meaty end of each rack, using a strong, sharp knife or a cleaver.*

2. *Peel the fatty skin from each rack, exposing the layer of fat beneath.*

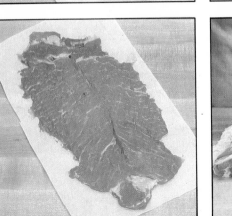

Pork tenderloin **49**

Veal scallops **44, 45**
Lamb rib **47**

# Meat /*Preparing roasts*

**3.** *Strip off the first 2 in/5 cm of flesh from the tapered ends of the ribs.*

**7.** *Bend each of the racks backwards, with the skin side innermost, to make a semicircle. Truss the racks together to make a complete circle or "crown."*

**4.** *Rack of lamb trimmed to this stage can be roasted without further preparation.*

**Preparing saddle of lamb**
**1.** *Lay the saddle skin side down and cut away the kidneys and their surrounding fat.*

**5.** *To make a Guard of Honor, fit the two racks together, interlocking the rib ends, and secure them in place with trussing string. You can now, if you like, push stuffing between the two racks.*

**2.** *Trim the fatty ends of the skirt on either side of the saddle.*

**6.** *To prepare a Crown Roast, make a short incision between each rib on the inside of the thicker, meaty end of each rack. This makes the racks more flexible.*

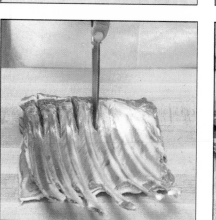

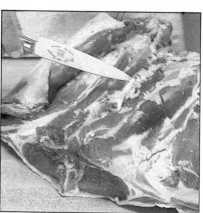

**3.** *Cut away the fat and sinews that lie along and to either side of the saddle's central bone.*

**4.** *Turn the saddle over and slice away the fat, leaving only a thin protective layer on top of the meat.*

**2.** *Stuff the pig with herb stuffing and sausage meat.*

**5.** *Tuck the flaps under the saddle to make a neat roll and tie securely with trussing string. Prick the large sinew all the way down the spine to prevent contraction during cooking. The kidneys can be skewered to the saddle for flavor and decoration.*

**3.** *Sew up the belly, using a trussing needle and string.*

### Scoring pork for crackling
*Before roasting pork, score parallel lines across the skin at ½ in/1 cm intervals and rub salt into the cuts. This will turn the skin and fat crisp and appetizing during cooking.*

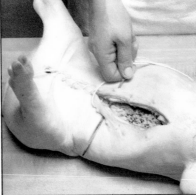

**4.** *Wrap the feet, ears and nose in foil to prevent them burning.*

### Preparing suckling pig
**1.** *Dry the inside of the pig with a paper towel. Suckling pig will have been gutted for you by the butcher.*

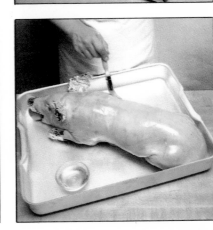

**5.** *Arrange the pig in a roasting pan, tucking the feet well under the body. Put an apple or a block of wood in the mouth. Brush the skin liberally with oil. It is now ready for the oven.*

Roasting pork **48**
Suckling pig **49**

Sausage meat **68**
Trussing needle **382, *382***

# Meat / *Trimming and boning*

## Preparing lamb chops

**1.** *Take a chined rack of lamb and cut cleanly between each rib with a sharp knife.*

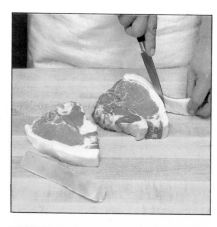

## Stuffing pork chops

**1.** *Trim the skin from the chop if the butcher has not already done so.*

**2.** *Trim the fat from the outside edge of each chop.*

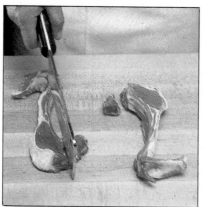

**2.** *If it is a thick chop, slit a pocket in the meat, cutting into the fatty edge. An alternative method is to slit open the eye of the chop to create a neat hollow.*

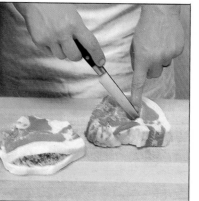

**3.** *Cut away the awkward corner bone, using a cleaver.*

**3.** *Push the stuffing into the slit or hollow, using a teaspoon, and pack it in well.*

**4.** *Trim the rib bone ends to neaten the shape of the chops.*

**4.** *Cut several nicks in the fat to prevent the chop curling during cooking.*

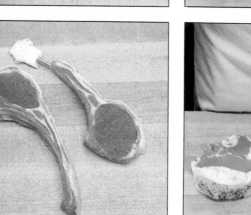

**Trimming oxtail**
1. *Oxtail is usually sold jointed and needs only to be trimmed of any large lumps of fat. Generally only the meatier upper joints need trimming.*

3. *Divide the roll into noisettes by cutting between the pieces of string with a sharp, long-bladed knife.*

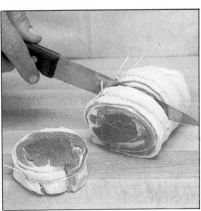

2. *Here the oxtail is fully prepared. The discarded fat is on the left-hand plate.*

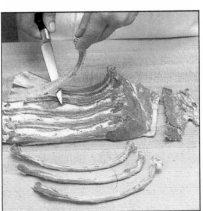

**Boning a leg of lamb**
1. *Take hold of the broad, curved hip bone, which protrudes at the wider end of the leg, and carefully run a sharp knife around it. Pull the bone out of the meat.*

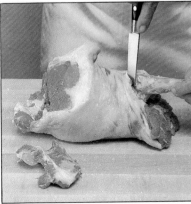

**Preparing lamb noisettes**
1. *Take a trimmed and chined rack of lamb and carefully cut the rib bones away from the flesh with a sharp, short-bladed knife. On the right of the picture lies the chine bone, which has been cut away from the rack.*

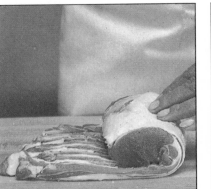

2. *Approach the leg from the narrow end, grasp the shank bone, cut it away from the flesh and lift it out.*

2. *When all the ribs have been removed, roll up the boned meat, starting from the meaty end. Trim any excess fat from the scraggy end and tie the roll at 1 in/2.5 cm intervals with trussing string.*

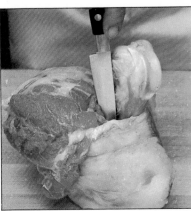

3. *Sit the meat up with the wide end uppermost and tunnel into the cavity left by the hip bone, cutting closely around the middle bone.*

**4.** *When all the flesh has been cut back from the middle bone, pull the bone out of the hip cavity. Trim any excess fat from the meat.*

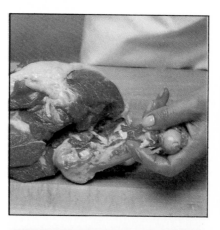

**2.** *Cut into the joint between the foreleg and the middle bone and then bend the foreleg back until the joint breaks. Remove the foreleg.*

**5.** *Arranged counter-clockwise around the meat lie a lump of excess fat, the hip bone, the middle bone and the shank bone. Above the shank bone lies the continuation of the shank, which may well have been severed by the butcher.*

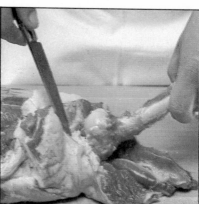

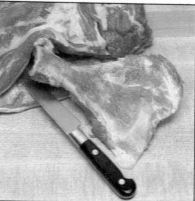

**3.** *Grasp the exposed end of the middle bone and cut back the meat in the same way as with the foreleg, keeping as close to the bone as possible. Avoid piercing the surface of the skin. Pull the middle bone apart from the shoulder blade to which it is attached and prise it from the center.*

**6.** *Tuck the shank end of the meat into the cavity left by the bones and truss the meat as shown.*

**4.** *Turn the meat around so that the triangular shoulder blade is nearest you. Insert the knife into the side of the meat where you can feel the shoulder blade and cut the meat away from either side of the flat bone. Pull this last bone out and trim any excess fat from the meat.*

## Boning a shoulder of lamb

**1.** *Lay the shoulder skin side down and take hold of the exposed end of the foreleg. Cut around the bone with a sharp knife, pushing the meat back as you progress towards the joint.*

**5.** *Roll up the boned meat with the skin outermost and secure it with trussing string. The three bones that have been removed are, from left to right, the shoulder blade, the middle bone and the foreleg.*

## Boning and stuffing a veal breast

**1.** *Starting from one corner of the breast, peel off the thick skin, easing it away with a knife wherever necessary.*

**2.** *Cut back the natural flap of meat until three or four white bones are visible.*

**3.** *Lift out the first few bones, cutting them away from the flesh with the point of a knife.*

**4.** *Continue along the breast, cutting away the long, slender ribs.*

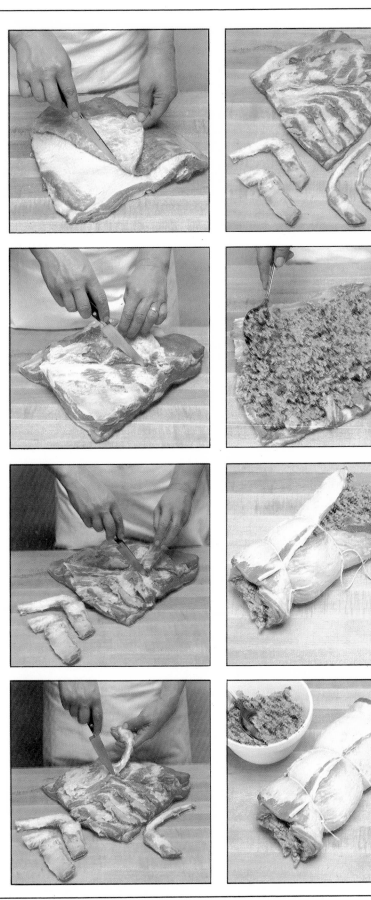

**5.** *Make sure that every bone is removed. Feel the breast carefully for any lingering flexible ribs or bits of bone.*

**6.** *Spread an herb stuffing over the boned breast.*

**7.** *Carefully roll up the veal, tucking one edge neatly under the other.*

**8.** *Tie the breast securely with trussing string. It is now ready to go into the oven.*

# Variety Meats / *Cleaning and trimming*

**Preparing liver**

**1.** *Pull the thin veil of membrane away from the liver. The liver used here is a calf's liver.*

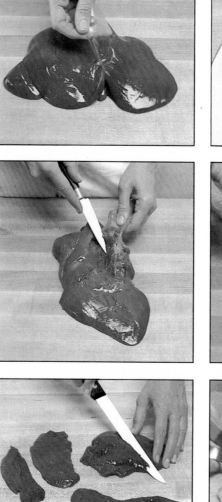

**2.** *Slice each kidney open and snip out the pale inner core with a pair of kitchen scissors.*

**2.** *Cut away any fat and gristle that might be adhering to the liver.*

**3.** *Veal kidneys are prepared in a similar way. Peel off the surrounding fat with a very sharp knife or pair of scissors, remove the thin inner membrane, then cut out the gristly core that runs through the center of the kidney.*

**3.** *Cut the liver into slices about ¼ in/5 mm thick.*

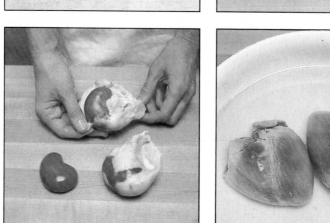

**Preparing heart**

**1.** *Snip out the pipes and tendons from the core of the heart with a sharp pair of scissors. The heart being prepared here is a pork heart.*

**Preparing kidneys**

**1.** *Peel away the casings of fat and the thin inner membrane. These are lambs' kidneys.*

**2.** *Hearts need to be soaked in cold water for an hour before they are cooked to draw out the blood.*

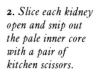

**Preparing brains**

1. *Soak the brains in tepid water for 1–2 hours to whiten them.*

**Preparing sweetbreads**

1. *Soak the sweetbreads in salted water for 2 hours, changing the water from time to time, until they lose all trace of pinkness and turn white.*

2. *Carefully remove as much as possible of the skin and membrane with a sharp pair of scissors.*

2. *Put them in a pan of cold salted water, bring to the boil, simmer for 2 minutes and then rinse them under cold running water. This process stiffens the sweetbreads and makes them easier to handle.*

3. *Pick out as many of the red veins as possible with thumb and forefinger.*

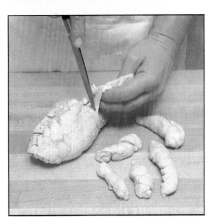

3. *Peel away the skin, connective tissues and gristle— some sweetbreads will fall naturally into smaller portions. These are veal sweetbreads; lambs' sweetbreads are prepared in the same way.*

4. *Simmer the brains for 15 minutes in salted water acidulated with lemon juice. If they are still too delicate to handle, chill them in the refrigerator or freezer until firm. Finish by removing any remaining veins, after which the brains will be ready to use. These are calves' brains.*

4. *The sweetbreads are now ready to be flattened between two plates for an hour before being poached or fried.*

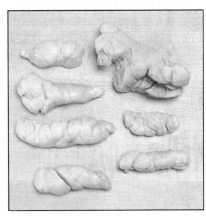

# Ham, Bacon and Salted Pork

Theoretically, and indeed in practice, every kind of meat can be cured, but pork has long been the prime candidate—not only because of pork's doubtful keeping qualities in the days before refrigeration, but also because this fine-grained and well-lubricated meat emerges from the cure in a succulent and delicious state, and remains so juicy and tender when it is boiled, fried or roasted.

Dry air, salt and smoke are the age-old curing agents. Saltpeter, added in minute quantities to reinforce the preservative powers of salt, is a comparative newcomer, and it is this ingredient that causes the pinkness in cured pork products.

## Ham

Pigs used for ham tend to be longer and leaner, as well as older and heavier, than those that yield fresh pork for our tables. Before the cure, their meat is deep pink or clear red, and the fat is firm and white rather than ivory colored. After the cure, the outside skin may be from creamy-grey to mahogany, depending on whether it has been smoked or not.

Not all hams are smoked: some of the finest are simply salted, either in a bath of brine, often with brine first injected into the flesh to speed up the process before it goes into the bath, or by the dry-salt method, which involves repeated massaging, rinsing and drying. This is a slow process, but ensures that the minimum of salt necessary for preservation penetrates the meat; the brine treatment is faster but tends to introduce more salt into the flesh. In both cases, certain flavoring agents—herbs, spices and

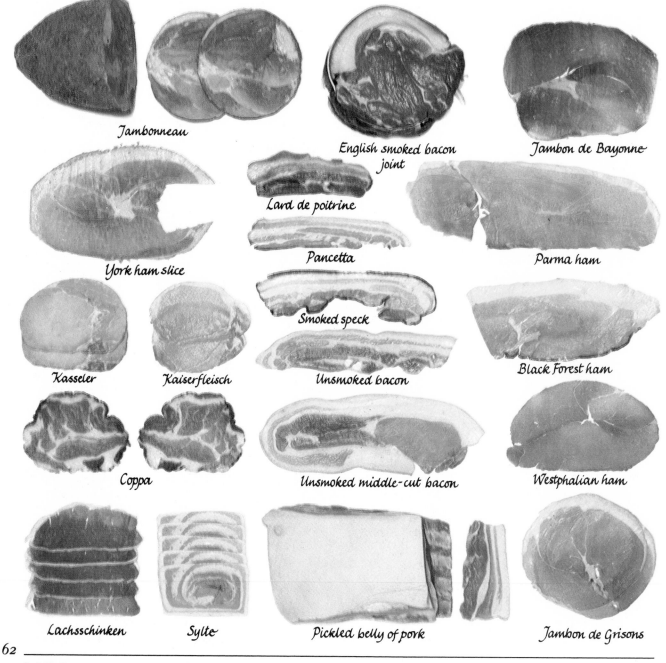

Jambonneau

English smoked bacon joint

Jambon de Bayonne

York ham slice

Lard de poitrine

Pancetta

Parma ham

Kasseler

Kaiserfleisch

Smoked speck

Unsmoked bacon

Black Forest ham

Coppa

Unsmoked middle-cut bacon

Westphalian ham

Lachsschinken

Sylte

Pickled belly of pork

Jambon de Grisons

sweeteners—may be added. When sugar is added the ham may be labelled "sweet cure."

Once salted, all hams are matured. The time and methods for this process vary from place to place (some are buried in wood ash, some hung up in an airy place for months on end) and it is to these differences, as well as to the type and diet of the pigs before slaughter, that we owe our immense variety of hams. There are also differences in the cuts themselves. Strictly speaking, hams are the hind legs of pigs, cut high and at an angle, but there are other parts of the pig's anatomy, such as the loin, the fore-hock and the shoulder, which are cured in similar ways.

### Boiled and boiling hams

Whole boiling hams may be bought cooked or uncooked. If you mean to have a stately boiled ham for Christmas, make your enquiries in good time, since you (or your supplier, who may boil to order) will need time to soak the ham for several days, to simmer it for about 45 minutes per 1 lb/450 g, to cool it in its own liquid, and then to skin it and perhaps to glaze and bake it, or simply to egg-and-crumb it.

Boiled ham is a most versatile meat: it can be served whole as a hot main course with parsley or Cumberland sauce and young vegetables, or plain with velvety spinach. It may also be eaten with stout vegetables, such as roots or any type of cabbage, or dried peas and beans, which may themselves be cooked together with a ham bone, or a piece of bacon. Sliced reasonably thickly, it often comes in a mustard, cream, tomato or Madeira sauce, although gourmets insist that a spoonful of champagne is all the moistening a first-class boiled ham really needs. Cold, in thinner slices, boiled ham can make a first course, or, with a salad, a nice lunch. Chopped, it adds flavor and character to a vast number of dishes.

When buying a whole ham to cook at home, do not be put off by a little bloom or mold on its rind, since this indicates that the ham is cured to perfection. It must, however, be scraped off before the ham is immersed in the cooking liquid.

**York ham** Firm and tender, this is the best known of the British boiling hams. It is delicately pink, with fat that is white and translucent. It is cured by the dry-salt method and smoked over oak sawdust until it develops its fine, mild flavor.

**Suffolk ham** Traditionally cured in brine with spices and honey, this ham is then smoked and hung to mature. During this process it develops its characteristic blue mold and a full, delicate flavor.

**Bradenham ham** With its coal-black skin and deep red flesh, this is another famous English ham. It is cured with molasses and so has a sweet but robust flavor. If bought uncooked, it should be soaked for at least a week before cooking, otherwise it will tend to taste very salty.

**Gammon or Wiltshire ham** Unlike true hams, which are first cut and then cured, English gammon is cured as part of the whole bacon pig, which is then divided into various cuts. It is extremely mild and does not keep so well as most other hams. Like bacon, it is sold smoked or unsmoked and comes in a variety of cuts such as steaks, the little wedges called slippers, the lean fine-grained corner and the succulent middle gammon, as well as the bony hocks. It is best boiled and served with root vegetables or dried peas or beans.

**Virginia ham** This is among the so-called "country-cured" hams of America. Pigs destined to become Virginia hams are fattened on peanuts and acorns, and the meat is usually smoked over some scented hickory and applewood.

**Smithfield ham** This ham is cured and smoked in Smithfield, Virginia. It comes from pigs that feed on peanuts, and is spiced with pepper and heavily smoked.

**Kentucky ham** This is another American country ham and is perhaps a little drier than the Virginia hams. It owes its flavor to a large proportion of clover in the young pigs' food and a diet of grain towards the end of their lives.

**Prague ham** is perhaps the most admired of the central European hams. It is traditionally salted and then mildly brined before being lightly smoked over beechwood embers, from which it emerges as perhaps the sweetest of all smoked boiling hams.

**Jambon de Paris** In France, ham for boiling is sold as jambon de Paris, and boiled ham as jambon glacé.

**Jambonneau**, a small ham from the shank part of the leg, is sold covered in bread crumbs and ready to eat.

**Other boiled hams** Whole hams are a substantial investment usually reserved for festive occasions, and so ham is usually sold in portions. Like the small jambonneau, "half-hams" come from the meaty, more expensive rump end of the leg, or from the bonier but cheaper shank portion. Hams are also sold boned and these are usually bought by the slice. Some are just boiled, while others may have been baked or topped with bread crumbs. Boneless hams can be bought with the fat and rind, or skinless with the fat trimmed. Skinless hams, although popular, tend to lack the flavor of hams with their skin and fat still intact.

Hams may also be bought canned, the best known being the Dutch, Danish and Polish. Lean and full flavored, they are boneless and ready to eat, but taste better baked with cider, brown sugar, mustard and cloves.

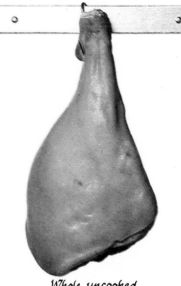

*Whole uncooked York ham*

### Kaiserfleisch and Kasseler

Other cured pork products include the delicate smoked Austrian Kaiserfleisch, and the Kasseler so popular in Germany, Denmark and Poland. Taken from the loin of the pig, these cuts look like a row of pork chops, but they may also be bought by the cutlet, boned or unboned, or sliced. In Germany, Kasseler is so popular that pigs have been bred with an extra set of ribs to yield more of this cut. Austrians eat Kaiserfleisch with bread-based dumplings and red cabbage; German Kasseler is sold uncooked in its native country, but is most often encountered elsewhere cooked and sold by the slice.

### Raw hams

Local differences in the traditional cures show most clearly in the hams that are not meant to be cooked but eaten raw.

**Parma ham** When you go into a shop in Italy to buy prosciutto, you will be asked if you want it *cotto* (cooked) or *crudo* (raw), but outside Italy, prosciutto means raw ham, and the best comes from Parma.

Parma ham is lightly salted and air-cured for many months. A crown stamped upon its golden hide tells you that it is the genuine article produced from local pigs. The thousands of hams sent to Parma for the cure from all over Italy are less delicate and do not bear this hallmark.

Eat Parma ham in transparently thin slices with melon, fresh figs, or simply butter.

**Culatello** Looking like a half-size Parma, culatello comes from the choice rump end of the leg. It is less fatty and more spicy than a whole Parma.

**Coppa** When Italian recipes specify raw

# Ham, Bacon and Salted Pork

ham, most Italian housewives tend to use coppa. This is the cured, unboiled shoulder and neck portion of a pig, and is fattier and less expensive than prosciutto. It can also be thinly sliced and served as an antipasto.

**Bayonne** This most celebrated of hams comes from the Basses-Pyrenees. Wine plays an important part in the curing process, and accounts for its special taste. Locally, Bayonne ham is eaten with eggs or added at the last moment to stews, but it is most delicious eaten raw like Parma ham, but sliced more thickly.

**Westphalian ham** is the best known of the German hams and the star of a German schinkenplatte, a plate of assorted cold hams. Traditionally, it is smoked over ash or beech with a bit of juniper until it is a deep golden pink. Juniper berries used in the cure give it its special flavor. Eat it thinly sliced on dark bread such as pumpernickel.

**Black Forest ham,** strongly brined and strongly smoked, has well-flavored flesh and milk-white fat. Its robust taste goes well with sourdough bread.

**Jambons de campagne, country hams** The Dordogne area of France is well known for its splendid farm-cured hams, often rather salty and hard as the cure is very heavy, but delicious sliced thickly and served with unsalted butter and French bread. Spanish and Italian country hams are also excellent.

**Jambon de Grisons** This Swiss delicacy comes from a region with a climate that is ideal for the curing of meats. It is first lightly salted and then dried in the cold, clear air of the Alps.

**Lachsschinken** is the smoked foreloin of the pig, wrapped in snow-white pork fat and bound with string, and it should be pink and moist inside. It can be bought sliced or in its expensive entirety, but should be eaten thinly sliced or minutely diced, with crusty buttered rolls.

**Jamon serrano** This highly esteemed delicacy is eaten raw and comes from the province of Huelva, in Spain. Cured in the Sierra Morena mountains, it is delicious on rough peasant bread. It is reputed to be the sweetest ham in the world, and although it is produced in other parts of Spain, the variety from Huelva is thought to be best.

## Bacon

Bacon may be bought smoked or—if you can find it—unsmoked, or "green." You can tell the difference if the rind is still on. Smoking makes the rind look golden and the flesh a nice deep pink. Unsmoked flesh is pale pink, and the rind looks anything from off-white to dark cream. As far as the taste is concerned, smoking adds great depth and interest to the flavor.

## Bacon roasts

In those countries, especially England, where entire carcasses of pigs are cured in brine, a number of ham-like cuts appear on the market. The leaner cuts are good hot or cold, boiled with onions and root vegetables, or first boiled and then liberally basted with fruit juice or cider and roasted. Broil or fry bacon chops and steaks and serve them with applesauce.

## Fat bacon

It is the fat of a bacon piece that imparts the most flavor, since it melts slowly, amalgamating with whatever other ingredients are in the pot. Cured flank or belly are therefore the most useful parts to use in cooked dishes. Whether you buy pancetta, lard de poitrine, poitrine fumé, speck, paprika-schinken, or tocino, what you carry home is cured pork belly—either sliced or in a slab that can be cut into chunks for use in stews and soups.

**Pancetta** is pink and white in even proportions and may be smoked or green. It goes into such Italian dishes as *spaghetti alla carbonara*, other pasta sauces, risotto and bean casseroles.

**Lard de poitrine** France's version of streaky bacon can be extremely fatty and generally has less lean meat than the pickled petit salé. Lard de poitrine is given a proper bacon cure and comes smoked, when it is called poitrine fumé, or green. It is used to enrich stews and farces, and is an essential part of coq au vin and many beef stews.

**Poitrine fumé** is splendid sliced and fried like bacon, or added to omelets.

**Speck, spek,** is basically fat with a thin layer of lean. When it is more striped with lean it becomes schinkenspeck. In Germany, Holland, Scandinavia and other northern countries, speck, which can be smoked or unsmoked, appears as a garnish on dishes that need the taste of bacon fat. Speck yields such a quantity of drippings that part of it is often poured off and eaten on bread. The rendered fat is also used as a frying medium for potatoes or mushrooms, and for browning pieces of beef or veal before roasting.

**Paprika speck,** translucent white and rindless, powdered on the outside with bright red paprika, is not used so much in cookery, but may turn up on a platter of cold cuts.

**Tocino,** the Spanish version of speck, is strong flavored and stored in salt crystals. It goes into *fabadas*—bean stews slowly simmered with vegetables and sausages.

## Breakfast bacon

When streaky bacon appears in fried slices for American breakfasts, it tends to curl up: the pigs' diet causes their fat to be on the soft side, so that it melts easily, causing the bacon to become crisp and crumbly. In other parts of the world, crisping is only possible if streaky bacon is sliced extra thin.

Lean bacon cuts are also made from the back of the pig, and those cut from the meaty leg area are considered to be very good. In England, top back slices are lean; middle-cut bacon slices have long tails of streaky attached and a good eye of solid pink meat at the top end. The oyster-cut from the hind end of the back comes sometimes in the piece and sometimes sliced, and is beautifully succulent. Shortback, with a nice edge of fat and plenty of lean meat, may come in thin slices or in thicker ones, which are meant for broiling. Long back slices are the leanest and most expensive of all.

When Americans buy their breakfast bacon under the name of Irish bacon, or country style, top back is what is usually offered, while Canadian bacon from the loin is quite lean and smoked and needs a little fat in the pan before frying.

## Salted pork

The petit salé of France, the pickled pork belly of Great Britain, and the salt pork of the United States fall into a category all of their own, being not fully cured but lightly salted in brine.

**Petit salé,** lightly brined, can be either flank end of belly, or the fatty parts of collar and neck. It is eaten in the traditional French potée, a rich cabbage soup containing other cured meats and vegetables. It may also sit in pink and white slices on top of puréed peas and beans, or on a dish of cabbage, when it is called *petit salé aux choux.*

**Pickled pork** tends to be slightly more heavily cured in brine, with sugar added. It usually consists of belly, although shanks are sometimes also prepared in the same way. This meat may need soaking before it is simmered with carrots, turnips, rutabagas or other root vegetables. Pease pudding is its traditional British accompaniment.

**Salt pork** Not to be confused with fatback, salt pork comes from the belly and may be well streaked or virtually all fat. The streaked salt pork from the leaner end is what goes into Boston baked beans. Salt pork is also known as sowbelly and is chiefly used as a flavoring agent. As such, it has become an essential ingredient of a New England clam chowder.

**Sylte** is pickled pork belly, rolled around crushed peppercorns and mustard seed. It is delicious thinly sliced and often appears at Scandinavian cold tables.

**Smoked jowls** England offers breadcrumbed bath chaps, which come from pig's cheeks. They are cured like hams, and are good if they are not too fatty. In America, where they are known as jowls, they are served with black-eyed peas.

# Cured Meat and Poultry

By far the greatest number of preserved meats, whether brined, air-dried, smoked, potted or canned, contain pork and pork mixtures. But other meats, game and poultry also lend themselves to the curing process, producing interesting and luxurious alternatives to ham.

## Salted beef

There are many ways to treat a salted cut of beef, most of them a welcome legacy from kosher Jewish cuisine.

**Salt beef** is simply beef soaked in brine—the addition of saltpeter makes it red, as in its natural state it is greyish-brown. Some types of salt beef are so heavily brined that some soaking will be necessary before the meat goes into the pot, while others may be ready for cooking just as they are, so check with your butcher. Salt beef—bottom round is the traditional cut—is often boiled with plenty of carrots and served with potatoes.

**Corned beef** Corning is the old term for salting, and corned beef is the term used in America to describe the salted and well-spiced briskets that go whole into a New England boiled dinner and chopped into corned-beef hash. To most Europeans, however, corned beef means canned, pressed, salted beef, pink in color and usually caked with fat, that is eaten without further cooking.

**Pastrami** In the Balkans, the word pastrami is used to describe any kind of preserved meat from beef, pork and lamb to goose. Elsewhere, it has come to mean salt beef that has been smoked and seasoned, usually with black peppercorns. Since the people of Romania, above all other Balkan countries, excel in making pastrami, their method is the model for the rest of the world, and the words "Romanian style" often feature on the packaging. Sold cooked in slabs or slices, it is good with rye bread.

## Dried beef

This is beef spiced and salted and then air-dried to the very essence of beefiness.

**Bündnerfleisch** Grisons in Switzerland is the home of this mountain air-cured beef. As it tends to be dry, scraped slivers of it are eaten with an oil and vinegar dressing.

**Bresaola,** the Italian counterpart, is a specialty of Lombardy and is similarly served, although the usual dressing is made with oil, chopped parsley and lemon.

**Chipped beef** is a rather poor American relation sold ready-sliced. It is sometimes served in a cream sauce on toast, or is mixed with scrambled eggs.

## Smoked mutton

"No sort of meat," say the Scots, "is more improved by smoking with aromatic woods than mutton." The people of Norway are in perfect agreement. Norwegian *fenalar* is smoked and air-dried until it develops a highly concentrated flavor, to be enjoyed with crisp Norwegian flatbrød and butter. The Scottish mutton ham has a rich, interesting flavor and is good sliced and eaten raw, or braised with vegetables.

## Smoked poultry and game

Unlike hams, poultry and game are always hot-smoked, or first cooked and then smoked. They can be bought whole or sliced and resemble ham in flavor, but are as perishable as fresh-roasted birds. Smoked guinea fowl, smoked chicken and smoked turkey breasts offer plenty of delicate flesh; smoked duck is excellent and smoked quail extravagant, but the most prized of all is smoked goose breast from the Baltic coast of Germany, where the geese tend to be the most bosomy. Also excellent is smoked reindeer meat from Scandinavia, particularly from Lapland.

## Confit d'oie, confit de canard

An everyday food in southwestern France, where vast numbers of geese and ducks are fattened for foie gras, confits are simply salted pieces of goose or duck preserved in fat. Confit can be bought in jars and will keep for several months, but all that is needed to make it in one's kitchen is the bird, its rendered fat and coarse salt. The salted meat simmers in the fat until it is well permeated, then it is drained, scored and covered with the strained fat.

A portion of confit is an essential ingredient in a cassoulet, but confit can also be eaten on its own, gently sautéed in a little of its preserving fat.

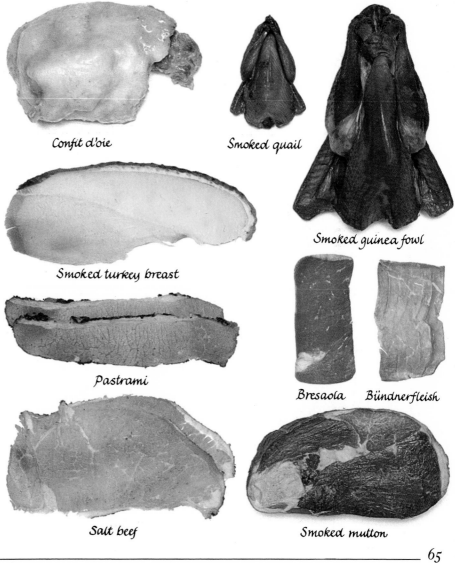

*Confit d'oie*

*Smoked quail*

*Smoked turkey breast*

*Smoked guinea fowl*

*Pastrami*

*Bresaola*     *Bündnerfleisch*

*Salt beef*

*Smoked mutton*

# Sausages and Salamis

When country people killed their own animals, particularly pigs, to provide themselves with meat, there was always a tremendous amount of work to be done to make sure that every part of the animal could be either eaten at once or, for the most part, stored for later use.

The liver, heart, kidneys and so forth were eaten at once, while legs, bellies, shoulders, feet and heads were salted for the winter, and all the scraps were gathered together and turned into sausages, with the animals' own guts serving as casings. These sausages were either spiced, to help prolong their life by a few days, and eaten fresh, or dried and preserved by various means for eating later.

The type of meat, the proportion of fat to lean, the endless variations of seasonings and cures, account for the myriad different sausages we enjoy today. What makes the ideal sausage is largely a matter of regional taste. Some like sausages so coarse that the meat seems to be chopped, not ground; others prefer the stuffing ground to a paste; but all agree that the meatiest sausages are the best. The seasonings also vary tremendously from country to country and from region to region.

Most interested sausage eaters prefer their sausages in natural casings, true gut being marginally more digestible than the artificial kind, less liable to burst during cooking, and producing a more attractive, rustic, natural-looking result. Natural casing can be recognized by the fine, slim knots between the links; artificial casings tend to untwist, leaving air spaces between the individual sausages.

## Fresh sausages

While fresh homemade sausages are fairly simple to make and easily rival the best store-bought ones, country markets and butchers' shops still offer some very good fresh sausages. These should be treated like fresh meat and eaten within a few days of purchase, or they develop a strange flavor. They need really slow cooking—too much heat and they burst their skins, as the contents swell at a faster rate than the casings. Prick them in one or two places before frying in some pork drippings or oil, and make sure they are cooked right through. In England, fresh sausages and sausage meat go into sausage rolls, pies and toad-in-the-hole. In Italy and France sausages are poached and boiled and used in soups, and in France they are sometimes wrapped in brioche dough and then baked.

## English and American sausages

Usually bought by weight, these can be made from fresh pork, or, less good, from fresh beef, or a combination of the two. Sage is their usual seasoning and the best are made of pure, coarsely chopped pork. Accompanied by mashed potatoes, they are called bangers and mash in England and are often eaten with mustard. Broiled and served with fried eggs, fat sausages make a filling and delicious breakfast. (Slender, half-size sausages, filled with pork or beef, are called chipolatas in England.)

Unless they are labelled 100 percent meat, sausages are likely to contain a cereal binder: being descendants of the old *boudins*, or puddings, this cereal was once fresh bread crumbs, but rusk is now generally used. They also contain a good deal of moisture, since crushed ice is introduced into the sausage machine to prevent overheating the meat as it is ground up.

## Cumberland sausage

This meatiest of all British pork sausages is made in a continuous spiral, rather than being twisted into links. The filling should be coarsely cut and spiced with black peppercorns. It is sold by length and is usually fried.

## Weisswurst and bratwurst

These fine-grained, pale, almost white sausages—the best known are those from Bavaria and Switzerland—are usually made of veal. Called "frying sausages," they may indeed be fried, or they may be first poached and then briefly broiled so that they are branded with golden stripes on the upper side. They are of a fine consistency and have a delicate taste.

## Saucisses

Small fresh sausages in France generally go under the name of saucisses, while larger ones are saucissons. Regional recipes make for differences of texture and taste, but whether coarse or fine, highly seasoned or not, all are made of pure meat, which is so important when making saucisses *en brioche* and other sausage pastries if the result is to be light and delicate. Throughout France there are any number of excellent locally made country sausages—saucisses de campagne—which go into cabbage soups and stuffings as well as being broiled. A wide variety of seasonings is used, ranging from pistachio nuts, chard, truffles or champagne to sage, peppers or parsley.

**Saucisses de Toulouse** These delicately seasoned sausages are made from coarsely chopped pork and are an essential ingredient of cassoulets, but are also fried or broiled and served with plenty of fried apples and mashed potatoes.

**Saucisses d'Auvergne** These are saucisses fumées, or smoked sausages. They are eaten broiled or fried, and combine their rich flavor beautifully with a hot potato salad.

## Kielbasa

In Poland any number of fresh sausages, called kielbasa, are added to hearty *bigos*—cabbage and meat stews—but elsewhere kielbasa refers to a particular garlicky and spicy sausage sold either fresh or fully cooked. It is good broiled and served with sauerkraut and a mild mustard.

## Luganeghe

This sausage from northern Italy, made of pure pork shoulder seasoned with Parmesan cheese, is made in enormous lengths; it is slim, unlinked and cut to the customer's order. Italian housewives fry it in oil, adding tomatoes or sage, and serve it with polenta, or they may simply scrape all the meat out of the skins and use it as a basis for a thick pasta sauce.

## Salsicces or Italian sausages

Seen hanging in Italian shops, salsicces have a rustic flavor and may be highly spiced with chili peppers, or very mild, especially if they are made simply with ground pork and pancetta. In America salsicces are seasoned with fennel seeds and are usually referred to as Italian sausages.

## Other cooking sausages

Apart from fresh raw sausages, there are those that have been treated in some way to preserve them. Some, such as the frankfurter, have been fully cooked, but are reheated and served hot. Others have been salted and smoked and then left to mature but still require further cooking.

## Frankfurters

It is the light smoking that gives the skins of frankfurters their familiar color. Unless marked kosher, in which case they are made of pure beef, frankfurters contain a mixture of finely ground beef and pork, and are usually quite highly spiced and salted. Genuine frankfurters are always sold in pairs—the best are fresh, while those that are heat-sealed in a vacuum pack come next. Canned varieties are overcooked and lack texture, flavor and robustness. The classic accompaniments to frankfurters are hot or cold potato salad, or sauerkraut and mustard; they are sometimes added to potato or split-pea soup.

In Austria a piece of lean roast beef becomes a wurstelbraten when small frankfurter-type sausages called wurstel are inserted into the meat before braising. When frankfurters appear in long rolls as hot dogs or dogs (or, today, foot-longs), they owe their name to America, where they were once known as dachshund sausages because of their shape. They are eaten with mustard.

When heating frankfurters it is best to put them into a saucepan filled with water that is just off the boil; too much heat and their thin skins will split.

## Knackwurst

This short, stumpy sausage is made of finely ground pork, beef and fresh pork fat, flavored with salt, cumin and garlic. Saltpeter is added to give the meat a good color. Knackwurst are usually sold in pairs or in long links.

## Bockwurst

These sausages are prepared in the same way as frankfurters. In Germany they are traditionally made in the spring, when the winter-made bock beer is ready to drink. The Berliner bockwurst is a smoky red sausage, while a Düsseldorf favorite is bockwurst wrapped in bacon with mustard.

## Saucisson-cervelas

This is similar to the small French saucisse except that it has matured longer and is therefore drier. It is best poached and served with *choucroute* or a hot potato salad. The English version, the saveloy, is a poor and stodgy shadow of its French relation.

## Cotechino

From northern Italy, this sausage is made of pork moistened with white wine and subtly seasoned with spices. It comes in various sizes and is usually salted for a few days—it is eaten after being simmered with white beans, lentils or other peas or beans, or is sometimes served simply with rather thin mashed potatoes. It is one of the essential ingredients of *bollito misto*—an Italian dish of mixed boiled meats.

## Zampone and stuffed goose neck

Besides guts, stomachs and bladders, which medieval jesters used indecently to flaunt—accounting for the German Punch-figure's name of Hanswurst and indeed for Mr Punch's own traditional accessory of strung sausages—other parts of animals can be turned into interesting sausages.

**Zampone**, a specialty of Modena, Italy, is one such example and is really a cotechino stuffed into a boned pig's foot. Fresh, it needs soaking and then simmering for an hour, but those that are packaged are precooked and only need heating through.

**Stuffed goose neck** The fat skin of a goose is used in a similar way. The filling consists of innards—liver, stomach, heart—perhaps

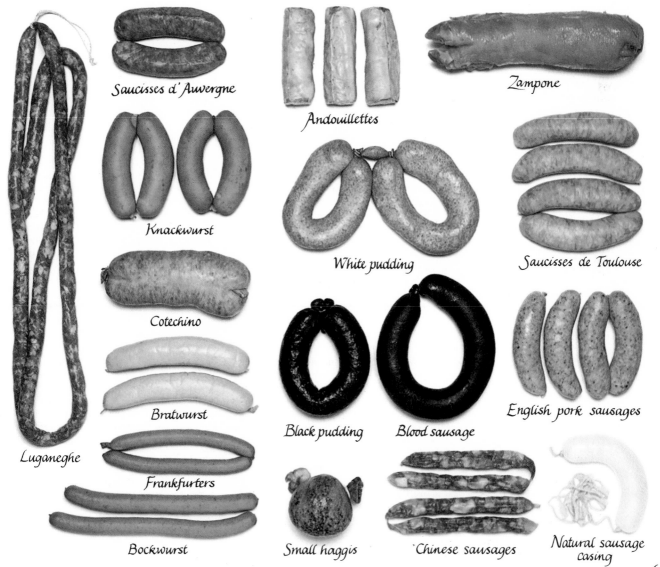

Saucisses d'Auvergne

Andouillettes

Zampone

Knackwurst

White pudding

Saucisses de Toulouse

Cotechino

Bratwurst

Black pudding    Blood sausage

English pork sausages

Luganeghe

Frankfurters

Bockwurst

Small haggis

Chinese sausages

Natural sausage casing

# Sausages and Salamis

morel mushrooms, air-cured bacon, bread crumbs, and an egg for binding it all together. It is sewn up or tied at both ends and may then be fried to a golden brown, poached and pressed between boards and eaten in slices, or simply poached in stock fortified with a little white wine.

## Loukanika

Sliced and served as a Greek *meze*—hors d'oeuvre—a loukanika usually means coarsely ground pork seasoned with coriander, marinated in red wine, stuffed and left to dry. A loukanika in America, however, is a combination of ground lamb and pork seasoned with orange rind, and is usually grilled and served at barbecues or broiled for breakfast.

## Chinese sausages

These sausages are cured and air-dried. Salami-like, dark red with white bits of fat, they need no further cooking. They flavor a number of Chinese chicken and vegetable dishes, and are sometimes mixed with rice.

## Andouillettes and andouilles

Andouillettes contain tripe and chitterlings, which are pork guts boiled to a gelatinous tenderness. They often come covered in lard, and are broiled and eaten with mashed potatoes or fried apples. The larger andouilles, which may be black skinned, are hung to dry and are sliced and eaten cold.

---

## Pudding sausages

These are the ancestors of all the fresh sausages and contain cereal as well as meat.

## Black puddings

These get their color from pigs' blood, their richness from cubes of pork fat and their body from oatmeal—at least it is this cereal that is always used in Scotland and northern England. Elsewhere, other cereals, even bread crumbs, may be used. In Ireland, lambs' blood goes into the local version, which is called drisheen. The French *boudins noirs* may, variously, also contain onions, apples, chestnuts, eggs, garlic and the leaves of chard. They are simmered by their makers, but may afterwards be boiled, baked or fried. In France, they are sometimes served on onions fried with bits of liver, but are at their best when broiled and served with fried apples.

## White puddings

Made of white meat such as chicken, veal, rabbit or pale pork, with bread crumbs or ground rice, cream and perhaps eggs, these are first simmered, and may be gently fried or broiled or wrapped in buttered parchment paper and baked.

## Blood sausages

These are also known as black sausages, but differ from black puddings in that they have fewer cereal additives and less seasoning. They always contain pigs' blood and come in a great variety.

**Blutwurst** There are many varieties of German blood sausages, but perhaps the blutwurst is the best known. It is made of diced bacon, veal or pork lungs and is seasoned with cloves, mace and marjoram. It is often served with boiled potatoes and cooked apples. Other German blood sausages include rotwurst, which is usually sliced and eaten on bread, and schwarzwurst, which is smoked and air-dried, and seasoned with garlic, cloves and a sprinkling of pepper and salt.

**Morcilla** Made and smoked in Asturias, Spain, this blood sausage is made of pigs' blood, fat, spices and onions, and is an essential ingredient of *fabada asturiana*, or bean stew. There are two varieties—ordinary morcilla, which is the most popular and has a strong smoky flavor, and morcilla dulce, which has a sweet, spicy flavor that is slightly reminiscent of a rich Christmas pudding.

## Haggis

Although called a glorified sausage, a haggis is really in a class of its own. In Scotland it is created with reverence and solemnly piped in (announced by a bagpiper) on special occasions such as Burns' Night on 25 January. It is made of roughly chopped, freshly cooked sheep's pluck (liver, lungs and heart), toasted oatmeal, onions, suet and herbs, all loosely packed into a sheep's stomach, which is then sewn up. The filling swells as the haggis is boiled and makes it look like a greyish rugby ball. A haggis merely needs to be steamed to heat it through, but it must be piping hot to be good.

## Faggots

These little round parcels are made like crépinettes but contain pigs' fry—liver and lungs—cereal and fat salt pork or bacon. They are wrapped in caul fat—the fatty membrane from around the stomach and guts of a pig, previously soaked and softened in warm water—and are cooked slowly in the oven. Also known as poor man's goose or savory duck, they are best when homemade from good ground meats, with plenty of onion, nutmeg and other spices. If caul fat is a problem to obtain, they may be put unwrapped into the oven, sitting closely together in the pan.

## Cayettes, caillettes

These delicious flat sausages from the Ardèche, in France, contain chopped chard leaves, and for the rest they are a mixture of ground pork, liver, garlic, herbs and seasonings, wrapped in caul fat. They are cooked in the oven, like faggots.

---

## Homemade sausages

Once you have made fresh sausages you will realize how simple the procedure is. While it may be a fussy job to stuff the sausage meat into its casings, nothing can be more rewarding than to see links of fresh homemade sausages emerging in your own kitchen. Using a basic chopped or ground pork mixture, any number of delicious varieties of sausages can be made by simply adding various herbs and spices, and if you have your own smoking equipment in which to smoke the sausages the possibilities become even greater. Seasonings can range from sage, oregano, marjoram, onions or garlic to sliced truffles or pistachio nuts. Chopped pancetta or bits of ham or smoked tongue can also be added and the whole mixture can be enriched with eggs.

## Sausage meat

A basic sausage meat consists of about one-half lean to one-half fat. For pure pork sausages, use lean meat from the shoulder, neck or loin, and add fatback in an equal quantity. For other sausages, veal and game such as hare and venison can be used, and smoked fish is good. Fatback is the best fat to use for any type of sausage, but any scraps of fat from the belly or even the fat trimmed from pork chops or spareribs can be used. Trim the fat of any rind or gristle, cut it into cubes with the meat and put them through a grinder, or chop briefly in a food processor, which works particularly well, especially for the coarser-textured sausages. Take care to remove gristle and strings from the chopped meat. The ground ingredients should be mixed well before the seasonings are added. The best way to determine how the sausages will finally taste is to fry a little of the mixture and, after tasting it, to adjust the seasonings accordingly.

## Casings

Some sausages such as crépinettes—the flat little sausages made in vast varieties in France—cayettes and faggots are merely encased in caul fat. Others can be skinless, in which case they are bound with eggs or dipped in beaten egg and bread crumbs or simply floured. Sausage meat can also be poached in a muslin bag, but natural casings are best for neatly bound sausages.

Casings can be bought in small sets from butchers' suppliers or through mail order. The small $1\frac{1}{4}$ in/3 cm hog casings usually come in approximately 20 ft/6 m lengths and can be cut as required. Store them, in salt, in a screwtop jar in the refrigerator.

## Stuffing sausages

It is not difficult to force the freshly ground, seasoned meat into the casings, and although there is a certain amount of domestic machinery available to help you turn out professional-looking specimens, you really only need a funnel and a pastry bag, some string, a prodder, such as the handle of a wooden spoon, and a faucet.

After disentangling and soaking the casing, slip it over the faucet and run cold water through it, cutting out any bits with holes. Then cut lengths for convenient handling and wrinkle each one up over the funnel, leaving a good bit dangling at the end. Tie it up and start feeding in your mixture; force out any air bubbles, and tie or twist the casing at intervals. Dry your handiwork for about 24 hours—in an airy place if the weather is cool, on a rack in the refrigerator if not—and then cook in the usual way.

## Slicing sausages

These are always cooked or smoked. They are eaten cold, often in sandwiches or as part of a simple lunch, accompanied by bread, olives and red wine. They are best bought uncut or freshly sliced, although it is important to remember that once they are sliced they don't last very well. The varieties that are sold presliced in vacuum-packed bags are frequently mass produced and of inferior quality.

## Mortadella

Made of finely ground pure pork, this is the best and most famous of all slicing sausages, patterned perhaps with green flecks of pistachio nuts and white cubes of fat. The best mortadellas, which are made in enormous sizes, come from Bologna, where only the best ingredients are used, and where the flavorings include wine and coriander.

There are, however, other varieties: some good, some very pasty. Although these have never been seen anywhere near Bologna, they are still called Bologna sausages or, rather contemptuously, baloney. Americans are very fond of this sausage, and it comes in a variety of shapes: variously sized balloons, rings and sticks, and even a square one to fit bread baked in pans. They vary in texture and flavor depending on whether they are made of pork, beef or veal, or mixtures of these meats, and their taste varies according to the spices used.

Eat mortadella as cold cuts with mixed salamis, or in sandwiches, or use it as part of a meaty stuffing for ravioli.

## Jagdwurst

This sausage owes its character to quite sizeable pieces of pork fat and rosy pork meat embedded in its pale pink paste, which is slightly porous due to the fact that it has been made by a process which involves the use of moist heat.

## Bierwurst

Although much larger in circumference than jagdwurst, this sausage has a similar paste. Ham bierwurst, or bierschinken, shows bits of ham in each of its large slices. It is also known as ham bologna in America because of its kinship with Bologna sausage, and is often flavored with garlic.

## Mettwurst

The word mett is the medieval name for lean pounded pork. There is grosse mettwurst, which is coarse in texture and red, and feine mettwurst, which is smooth and pink.

## Zungenwurst

When a blutwurst is interlarded with bits of tongue, it becomes a zungenwurst. Bits of pork fat and a lot of pigs' blood, heated carefully to setting point without curdling, make this black sausage, which does not usually contain any cereal additives.

## Hungarian brawn sausage

Reminiscent of a head cheese, Hungarian brawn sausage, also known as presswurst, consists of meat from the pig's head, neck and feet, blood and seasonings. Cased or uncased, it is cooked, lightly pressed and cooled until the mixture jellifies. Sage is the most usual flavoring.

## Sulzwurst

Similar to brawn, this sausage is made of large pork pieces. It can be eaten spread on bread, or with sliced onions and an oil and vinegar dressing.

## Cervelat sausages

Almost always smoked, cervelats are far less stiff than salamis because their maturing time is half as long. There is, however, a slight resemblance between the two. They are always moist, and being made of finely pounded meat and fat, they have, when cut, a velvety surface and a color of mottled pink. Fat or thin, cervelats are always pliable and look rather like large frankfurters.

## German cervelats

Made of finely ground beef and pork, these are very popular in Germany and are exported in various diameters. They are mild, delicate and easy to slice.

## Holsteinerwurst

Elastic enough to be sold in rings as well as straight, the Holsteinerwurst originated in Holstein on the German–Danish border. Although counted among the cervelat-type sausages, the Holstein is so heavily smoked that it could also be counted among the German country sausages—the sort that used to hang above heather, beech or peat smoke in northern chimneys.

## Plockwurst

With its smoke-darkened skin and dark meat, which contains a high proportion of beef, this sausage often comes studded with whole peppercorns.

## Katenrauchwurst

This cottage-smoked sausage is produced in some quantity. It is made of coarse pieces of pork, is dark and firm and should be cut diagonally in thick oval slices.

## Danish cervelat

Air-dried and hot-smoked, this is rather a bouncy cervelat. Its skin is usually varnished and looks a glossy red.

## Thuringer

Among the American cervelats—also sometimes called summer sausages because their surfaces do not sweat so badly in the hot months—is the coriander-spiced variety called Thuringer. It is named after a sausage-producing area in central Germany.

## Salamis

Among the thousands of traditional sausages, it is the salami, or *salame*, which is perhaps the most celebrated. The Italian salamis—and there are almost as many regional variations as there are villages in Italy—may be considered by purists to be the only authentic salamis, but it is worth noting that most of central Europe has made this type of tightly stuffed sausage for a number of centuries, so that Danish, German and Hungarian salamis, for example, are not pale imitations of the Italian original but indigenous sausages: only the Italian name is borrowed.

Most salamis, wherever they are made, consist of a mixture of lean pork and pork fat and sometimes beef. Occasionally veal takes the place of beef, and sometimes wild boar is used. They can be flavored with red or white wine, with rum, with peppercorns, fennel or garlic, paprika and perhaps a few teaspoons of sugar.

Only a few types of salami are smoked, but all are matured for periods varying from a few weeks to a few months. During this time they lose a good deal of weight in the form of moisture, while the flavor of the meats and the seasonings—wine, spices, garlic—becomes more concentrated.

Buy salami that is a fine fresh red or pink, not brown or greasy, on its outside surface. If you squeeze it and it gives a little, you can

# Sausages and Salamis

be sure that it will be fresh and fragrant. The harder the salami sausage, the more thinly it should be sliced. Cut it at an angle, whether you serve it as an hors d'oeuvre, as in Italy (where the Genoese eat their local salami with raw young green beans), or whether you mean to serve it as a meal in its own right with bread and butter.

### Genoa salami
This is one of the salamis that traditionally contains a high proportion of veal. To make up for the possible dryness of this meat, a little more pork fat than usual goes into the mixture, so that the result is quite fatty.

### Salami di Felino
Made near Parma, this pure pork sausage is among the best of all the Italian salamis. Since it is made by hand, it is less geometrical than most of the others. It contains white wine, garlic and whole peppercorns, and is subtle in flavor and succulent in texture. It does not keep well, but when sent abroad is encased in wax for a longer life.

### Salami Napolitano
Seasoned with chili pepper, this salami is made with pork and beef. It is usually garlicky and extremely peppery and hot.

### Salami Finocchiona
This pure pork salami has the unusual but very good flavor of fennel seeds. A similar salami, known as *frizzes*, is flavored with aniseed and comes in both mild-sweet and spicy varieties.

### German salami
Because this is not usually cured for long, it is fairly moist. It is mild with a whiff of garlic and usually has a medium texture.

### Danish salami
This is bright pink or red because it usually contains coloring. Made since the fifteenth century, this is one of the types that is salted and then sometimes hung over smoke, which is just cool enough to make the flavor more interesting and to brown the casing but not warm enough to cook the meat. Danish salami tends to be fine textured, rather fatty and to have a bland, rather predictable flavor.

### Hungarian salami
One of the densest of salamis, this is not necessarily made in Hungary. Other countries, especially Italy, also produce this type, which contains paprika as well as other peppers. It is surprisingly mild and is often

smoked. Since it is matured for about six months, it is one of the really hard salamis and ideal for slicing.

### Saucisson de Lyon
In France, salami is known as saucisson sec. Perhaps the most famous of the French salami-type sausages is the saucisson de Lyon, which, with its criss-cross cording, is made of pure pork. Cording is used to keep the salami straight while it dries. It is coarsely cut and a good rose-pink color, and has an excellent flavor.

### Garlic sausage
Many of the sausages of France, no less than those of Italy, are flavored with garlic. However, the one known as garlic sausage is different insofar as it is only lightly spiced, so that the strong distinct taste of garlic predominates.

### Chorizos
These are popular throughout Spain and are coarsely textured and quite spicy. In Spain they are widely used in cooking, and elsewhere they are usually sold air-dried and are suitable for slicing or cutting into chunks. Chorizo de Lomo is one of the finest chorizos for slicing and eating.

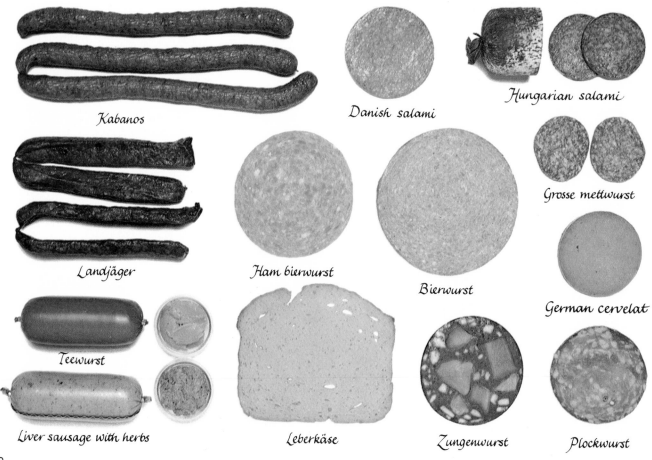

Kabanos

Danish salami

Hungarian salami

Landjäger

Grosse mettwurst

Ham bierwurst

Bierwurst

German cervelat

Teewurst

Liver sausage with herbs

Leberkäse

Zungenwurst

Plockwurst

Herbs and spices **166–175**

Meat slicers **358**, *358*
Knife for cold meat **355**

## Salsicha

This Spanish sausage is similar to a salami and is usually served as a snack. It is made of finely chopped pork, pork fat and whole white peppercorns.

## Small salamis

These are usually bought whole rather than by the slice and can be short or long.

## Rosette

Perhaps the finest of the Lyonnaise sausages is the rosette, which is slowly matured and, due to its extra fat and thick casing, is more moist than other salamis.

## Kabanos

These slim, garlic-flavored sausages of Polish origin are smoked until they show wrinkles. Too thin to slice, they are bought whole and eaten in chunks.

## Landjäger, gendarmes, cacciatore

Landjäger and gendarmes presumably owe their names to uniformed officials who used to patrol and administrate the German and French Alpine regions, carrying a good supply of these hard, salami-type sausages in the pockets of their tunics. The sausages are usually smoked in little frames, which accounts for their strap-like shape. They are usually eaten in chunks.

The Italian version, called cacciatore, or hunter's sausage, is somewhat thicker than the others. It is not usually smoked but briefly cured and matured and is just about large enough to slice. Chunks of these sausages are sometimes added to Italian stews, which they enrich and flavor.

## Pepperoni

This Sardinian salami can be mild or spicy. It is usually eaten hot, or sliced into a pepperoni salad or onto pizza.

## Pâté-type sausages

Some sausages such as liver sausages, leberkäse and teewurst can be soft in consistency and are meant for spreading, while others are firm enough to be sliced.

## Liver sausages

These may be large or small, curved or straight, finely milled or coarse, and their paste may also contain chunks of fat, bits of liver (which is especially good in the case of goose-liver sausage), truffles and any number of finely chopped herbs. Some liver sausages are soft and pasty and meant for spreading, while others, such as the Strasbourg liver sausage, which also includes pork meat and is smoked, are meant to be thickly sliced.

All liver sausages can be eaten as they are, but occasionally form an essential ingredient of cooked dishes: the Swedish black soup, for example, needs the Swedish gåsleverkorv. Flavorings, besides herbs and truffles, may include nutmeg, cinnamon, browned onions or anchovies; where anchovies predominate, the liver sausage is known as a sardellenwurst.

Most liver sausages are made of pork liver mixed with pork or veal—some may contain other innards as well as liver—but there are also pure liver sausages. Calves' liver sausages are particularly good, and there are also sausages made of poultry livers.

**German liver sausages** Authentic German liver sausage is almost invariably smoked. It is prepared by a scalding process, which tends to lead to a harmless whitish film forming on natural casings.

**French liver sausages** These have more in common with black puddings than with the creamy Germanic liver sausages. They are eaten hot, often with apple rings.

**Danish liver sausages** These are made of pork or calves' livers to which anchovy is often added. They are excellent spread on dark Danish rye bread, garnished with slices of cucumber.

## Leberkäse

A mixture of pork and liver baked in an oblong pan, this sausage has no skin. Sliced, it can be eaten as it is, or it can be fried.

## Teewurst

This is the name given to small sausages of the spreadable variety. They are usually made of a spiced, finely pounded mixture of pork and beef.

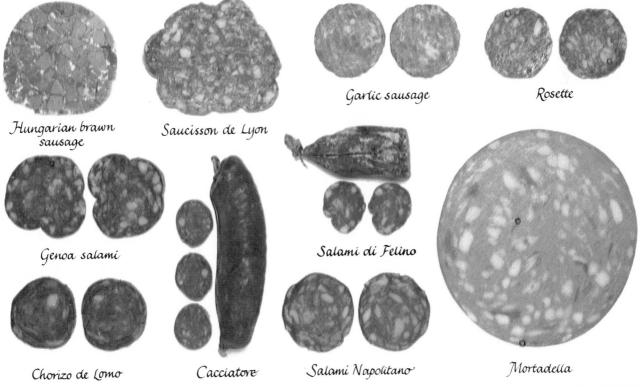

*Hungarian brawn sausage*

*Saucisson de Lyon*

*Garlic sausage*

*Rosette*

*Genoa salami*

*Salami di Felino*

*Chorizo de Lomo*

*Cacciatore*

*Salami Napolitano*

*Mortadella*

# Game/Furred

In town most game is a luxury and only the best restaurants feature it on their menus. It is usually served with a great deal of ceremony from trolleys shining with silver and with a flourish of traditional accompaniments.

The situation is different in the English countryside where, even if there is no local dealer selling game fairly cheaply during the open season, you are likely to be given some as a present. The only drawback is that it probably arrives in the kitchen with its fur and guts intact, but once you have mastered the art of preparing it for cooking, this meat above any other is worth your time, skill and attention. Apart from the subtlety of flavor and texture, it is also considered to be one of the healthiest of meats.

To tenderize the more athletic and older creatures, a marinade is useful. This, as a rule, contains vinegar to break down tough fibers, oil to add succulence, and wine, herbs and spices to permeate the meat with flavor. There are cooked and uncooked marinades, the cooked ones being more powerful. The marinade should completely cover the meat, which should be turned periodically during the time it is steeped. This period may vary from a mere 12 hours or so for a hare to at least two weeks for a haunch of wild boar.

All game is protected by laws, which vary from country to country. These are laid down to prevent the shooting of creatures that are too young, to allow mating and the rearing of young to take place and also because the game population of any given area varies from year to year. As a further safeguard, the numbers of any species allowed to be shot by each sportsman are also limited in many parts of the world. Some species of game have been hunted almost to extinction; the American buffalo is an example, but fortunately it has been reintroduced and may now only be hunted on game farms, under strict control.

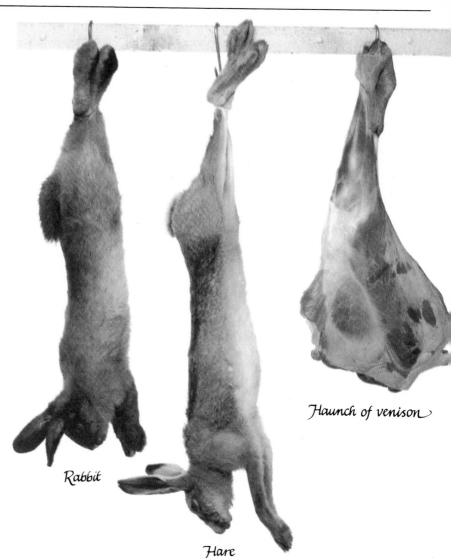

Rabbit

Hare

Haunch of venison

## Venison

Once bagged, deer becomes venison. It does not matter whether it started life in the wild as red deer, roe deer, fallow deer, white-tailed Virginia deer or the black-tailed variety called mule deer, or even as reindeer, caribou, elk or moose. Nor does it matter if these animals have been bred especially for the table, lived in the wild or, as in the case of roe and fallow deer, in parks; wild or semi-tame, they all become venison.

Venison is not always easy to obtain, since the hand-reared variety is mostly sold to hotels and restaurants, while the wild deer

shot by the sportsman is usually sold privately. When venison does appear it is usually in the most expensive stores. It is, however, sometimes to be found in country shops or market stalls, costing rather less than beef, only to be ignored. Contrary to custom, unfamiliarity seems to have bred contempt, but venison prepared with real devotion makes a memorable meal.

The buck is supposed to be better than the doe, but neither should be eaten too young since the flesh, although tender, will not have had time to develop its characteristic flavor. The tendency these days is towards fresh venison, but if a gamy taste is preferred the animal should hang, head down, in a cool, airy place free of flies for 12 to 21 days, depending on the weather—the cooler the weather the longer it can hang.

The saddle, the loin and the haunch, which is the whole leg, make the best roasting cuts. The loin can also be eaten as chops, while the rest of the animal is usually used

for ragouts, game pies and pâtés. The head is rarely used in the kitchen, although smoked reindeer tongue is a delicacy in Scandinavia, as is smoked and salted reindeer meat, and moose in all forms.

When buying venison, make sure that the flesh is dark and close grained and that the fat is clear and bright, but trim off the fat before cooking because it is not good to eat. Venison is by nature a dry meat and the fat should be replaced by pork or bacon fat before cooking, the venison having been placed first in a marinade of oil, vinegar, spices and plenty of red wine to which juniper berries have been added. In Italy, venison is sometimes soaked in olive oil with excellent results.

When it is time to cook the meat, lift it out of the marinade and wipe it dry. Then wrap it in a jacket of good white pork fat or, even better, lard it with thick strips of pork fatback, and cover it all over with oiled parchment paper, tying it on with string.

Alternatively, instead of parchment use a jacket of aluminum foil, which does the job just as well. When cooking venison, it is usual to allow 25 minutes per 1 lb/450 g for the buck and 20 minutes for the doe, in a fairly hot oven. It is cooked when, on piercing the skin, the juices run clear. Any sign of blood indicates that the meat needs more time.

Venison has a strong but muted flavor, sometimes described as old lamb that tastes of beef. It needs the encouragement of some sharp, sweet, spicy or piquant accompaniment to taste at its best, so serve it with red currant or rowan jelly, cranberry sauce, spiced cherries or Cumberland sauce. Other flavors that marry well with venison include those of juniper berries, rosemary, Seville orange or lemon juice and spices such as cloves, cinnamon, mace, allspice, nutmeg.

Among the many dishes that have an affinity with venison are wild rice, which is traditional—but expensive—with all game in America; and the noodles or dumplings, made of pasta dough, eaten in southern Germany, Switzerland and Austria, where venison is also sometimes served with a sauce made of sour cream blended with the pan juices. This sauce also accompanies it in northern Germany and in Scandinavia, where it is mopped up with mashed potatoes or potato dumplings. Spiced red cabbage often appears with venison in these countries, and chestnut purée is invariably served with it in France, while celery or celeriac complement its taste and suede-like texture beautifully.

## Hare

The flesh of the hare is a dark mahogany brown regardless of the color of its coat, which varies from species to species. In the Champagne district of France, the much-prized hares are golden, while northern France offers a mottled variety. German hares are almost russet colored, English hares are fawn to grey and the Scotch blue hare of the Highlands is the color of Scotch mist.

The blue Scotch hare is a first cousin of the arctic hare of America, called the snowshoe rabbit; this name is an example of the linguistic confusion that has overtaken the hare, which is not helped by the fact that the highly palatable, domestically bred Belgian hare is, in fact, a rabbit. Jack rabbits are actually American hares, which becomes clear when it comes to eating them as there can be no confusion between the strong, gamy flavor of hare and the mild, more delicate taste of rabbit.

The hare, a common but usually distant sight in open farmland in autumn, is surprisingly large when seen close to. Its hind legs are heavily built for speed and it is these and the fleshy saddle that are particularly esteemed in *haute cuisine*. A cut consisting of the back or saddle goes under the culinary name of *râble*, and when the hind legs are included it is called *train de lièvre* or *baron de lièvre*. These are the classic cuts, but a tender, less muscular foreleg can be more succulent than either.

Hare is best eaten when young and luckily its age is easy to determine. A leveret, as a hare under one year of age is called, has a white belly and pliable ears, easily split skin and a barely noticeable harelip. Its claws are almost hidden under the fur of its paws and it is also easily recognizable by its fur, which should be soft and smooth—the fur only becomes matted with advancing age. Long sharp claws and yellow teeth are a definite sign of adulthood.

Leverets are always tender and although the doe remains so during its second year the buck begins to become tough. A hare is usually hung for a few days by the feet. It is then paunched, or gutted, and skinned, after which the inner bluish iridescent layer of muscle that covers the saddle must be removed. If the hare is bought from a game dealer, he will perform this service and probably also joint or truss the animal. Hares are sold minus their heads and innards, but ask for the liver, taking care to remove the gall, which lies between its lobes. You can use the liver to make a forcemeat stuffing, which can be pushed into the diaphragm cavity to make the traditional British "hare with a pudding in its belly."

Hare should be well marinated and then larded or wrapped in pork fat to counteract its tendency to be dry. It can then be roasted slowly and served quite rosy if young and tender. The larger the hare, the longer it should be cooked—give it 20–25 minutes per 1 lb/450 g in a medium oven.

Allow about 6 oz/170 g of hare per person if you plan to jug it. The original method was to place it in a jug with herbs, vegetables, spices and port and then to put the jug in a pot of boiling water. Nowadays, however, jugged hare is often stewed or braised in the normal way, and it is a good idea to keep the saddle separate and roast it for another meal. Recipes for jugged hare often tell you to collect some of the hare's blood in a paper cup attached to its nose as it hangs head down, gutted, but still in its fur.

A few drops of red wine vinegar in the cup will prevent the blood coagulating. If the blood has not been kept or the smell of it is too overpowering, a fine jugged hare can still be made without it.

The flavor of hare, which should never be high, is improved by the addition of cloves in moderation and red wine in abundance, and also by port, red currant jelly, fat bacon, mushrooms, shallots, juniper berries and cream, particularly sour cream. In France noodles, in Italy polenta and in Switzerland celeriac purée are served with roast or braised hare.

## Rabbit

The rabbit is both the ancient enemy and old friend of the countryman; ancient enemy because it eats crops and old friend because it can, in turn, be eaten.

Wild rabbits, still rampant—although reduced in number wherever that unfortunate disease myxomatosis has struck—are stronger tasting and, with age, ranker than tame ones. They are also less plump and tender. Perhaps the best is a fat white rabbit that is not too young, when it is tasteless; not too old, when it becomes dry and tough; and certainly not stale, when it becomes yellow and discolored and loses its resilience and glossiness.

Rabbits are paunched, or drawn, as soon as they have been killed and can be eaten immediately. They do not have to be marinated or hung, although a large, elderly, wild rabbit will develop a good aroma if it is marinated. When choosing rabbit in its fur, pick one that is plump and compact rather than heavy, long and rangy. If buying it skinned, look for pink meat and do not be put off by a bluish sheen. Frozen rabbit pieces have a mild but good flavor and are best in ragouts and mustard sauce. Allow half a rabbit per person.

Although it has a definite flavor of its own, rabbit also makes a good vehicle for other flavors. This works to the cook's advantage in the case of cooking the wild rabbits of Provence, which feed on the tender shoots of wild rosemary and thyme and come with an added herby flavor. Backyard bunnies, however, brought up on lettuce leaves and dandelions, are unlikely to offer unexpected flavors, so it is worth adding a variety of herbs and spices to make them more interesting.

Apart from the famous French rabbit dishes such as *lapin aux trois herbes* or *lapin au moutarde*, there are some splendid traditional English recipes such as rabbit pie, flavored with salt pork or bacon, grated lemon rind and nutmeg, or rabbit stew with bay leaves, carrots and onions. In some parts of England the stew is moistened with cider, which gives a delicious flavor.

In Spain, rabbit is practically a staple food. When it is not roasted, covered in olive oil and sprinkled with sprigs of rosemary or chopped garlic and parsley, it is stewed in wine or served in a light case of potato pastry. In Italy it is cooked with Marsala, tomatoes, eggplant, ham or bacon, and

Sicilians, true to their early Moslem heritage, eat it with pine nuts and an *agrodolce* sauce made with raisins, herbs, stock and vinegar.

Scandinavians roast rabbit like hare and serve it with red cabbage; and when rabbits used to be regarded as "frontier food" in America, pioneers used to enjoy them in a delicate fricassée.

## Wild boar

Any wild pig, male or female, once killed becomes wild boar. Pig sticking, that dangerous sport, is almost a thing of the past, and although wild pigs still roam the woods of the world, especially in the Causse district of southern France, most of the wild boar —or *sanglier*, as wild boar is also known— found in a butcher's or in a game and poultry store have been reared in boar pens, an environment as close as possible to the wild woods, but where the animals can be fed and can raise their young successfully.

A young wild boar is called a *marcassin* up to the age of six months, after which time it becomes a *bête rousse*. After it is one year old it does not make such good eating, and in old age (wild boars can live up to the age of 30) only the head is still considered to be edible.

Wild boar meat should be dark, almost black, with little fat. It tastes of pork with strong gamy overtones and, like pork, has a certain natural succulence. While *marcassin* may need only hanging, a *bête rousse* is usually tougher and requires marinating as well as hanging before being cooked. The top part of the leg and the saddle make noble roasts; the smaller cuts such as steaks and chops are often broiled or braised. But no matter how you cook wild boar it is a lengthy operation and, again like pork, it must be cooked right through with no trace of pinkness.

In elegant French country restaurants the mounted mask of a ferocious boar with its tusks at a war-like angle may look down on you as you are served, in the autumn, with *marcassin* accompanied by chestnut purée and a poivrade sauce, which owes its flavor to wine, spices and cognac. In German country inns wild boar is served with a sour-cream sauce, plain boiled potatoes and a side dish of golden chanterelles. As with venison, a spicy accompaniment is required such as cranberry sauce, spiced cherries, or bottled sour cherries poached in red wine flavored with cinnamon.

Since boar is eaten wherever it is found, and the method of its preparation follows national traditions, it is no surprise that it is made into curry in India. In America, where boar was introduced from Germany in the early twentieth century, its steaks are broiled and eaten with a sweet pepper and mushroom sauce, flavored with plenty of garlic and onion. It is also often marinated in cider and served with applesauce.

## Other game

**Bear** is now so rare that few housewives will be faced with the problem of having to prepare it for the pot. Those who are should know that the paw is reckoned to be the best bit and that every part of the animal needs to be thoroughly cooked, for bear, like pork, can be dangerous if it is eaten underdone.

**Squirrel and opossum** The squirrel was once highly sought after. A sixteenth-century cook's manual ends its recipe for rabbit pie with the words: "If you cook for a lord, use squirrel instead of coney—it is the fitter meat for the table." The squirrel, however, is no longer regarded as a delicacy in Europe; indeed it is not eaten at all and as a result has become a destructive pest.

Squirrel is skinned like rabbit, while the opossum, which is considered a delicacy in some rural parts of America, is scalded and then its hair is scraped off. If young, both animals can be roasted or fried; if old, they benefit from longer cooking and are better made into a stew.

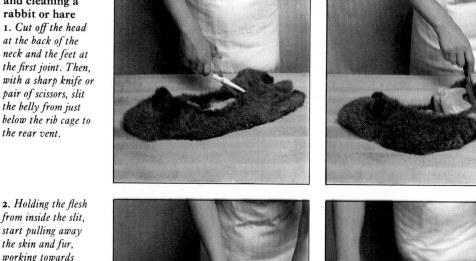

**Skinning and cleaning a rabbit or hare**
**1.** *Cut off the head at the back of the neck and the feet at the first joint. Then, with a sharp knife or pair of scissors, slit the belly from just below the rib cage to the rear vent.*

**2.** *Holding the flesh from inside the slit, start pulling away the skin and fur, working towards the tail end.*

**3.** *When you have pulled the hind legs out of the skin, sever the tail from the rest of the body.*

**4.** *Grip the animal by its hind legs and pull it up and away from the skin, working towards the shoulder.*

**5.** *Ease the front legs free and then pull the animal right out of its skin.*

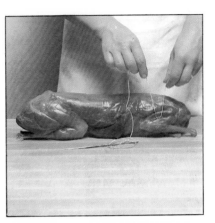

**3.** *Bend back the forelegs to sit neatly under the body and truss them in place by drawing a threaded trussing needle through both the legs and the body.*

**6.** *Remove all the entrails, reserving the heart, liver and the kidneys.*

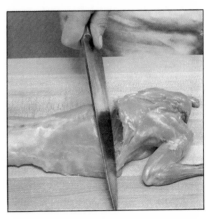

### Jointing a rabbit or hare

**1.** *Take a skinned and gutted rabbit or hare and cut off the hind legs by inserting a strong, pointed knife into the ball and socket joint, just above each thigh.*

### Preparing a rabbit or hare for roasting whole

**1.** *Take a skinned and gutted rabbit or hare—in this case a hare is being used— and sever the sinews behind the knee of each hind leg. This is to prevent the legs contracting and distorting during cooking.*

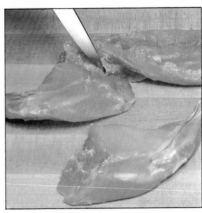

**2.** *Cut the forequarters off in one piece, slicing cleanly through the rib cage.*

**2.** *Tuck the hind legs under the body and tie them in place with trussing string.*

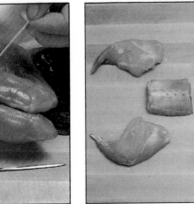

**3.** *Split the forequarters down the middle and, if you do not want to keep the saddle whole for roasting, cut the remaining body or saddle into serving-size pieces. The forequarters, saddle and hind quarters of this rabbit have divided into six pieces.*

One of the great pleasures of autumn is the arrival of game on our tables. In Great Britain shooting begins in August with the open season on grouse—the "Glorious Twelfth"—a red-letter day for those who make an annual expedition to the Scottish moors, and by the 13th grouse features on the menu of every stylish restaurant.

However, do not be in too much of a hurry for your first taste. Most game needs time to hang to develop its flavor and tenderness, especially if you like the *haut-goût*—although the day is passing when pheasants were judged fit to eat only when head and tail feathers fell out of their own accord, and when maggots showered down from them like so much rice. Today the ripeness of game birds is judged by smell and by the condition of the bird around the vent. This becomes moist and fragile when the bird is well hung—don't worry about a blue or greenish tint to the skin. A high bird smells powerfully gamy while a bird that is rotten smells bad, like any other bad meat.

Hang pheasant, partridge and grouse heads up; hang wildfowl, including geese, by the feet. Apart from helping the meat to mature slowly and magnificently (especially in cold weather, best for the slow mellowing of game), this helps to retain moisture—and if game has a fault, it is that it tends to be dry. If very smelly once plucked, it is helpful to wipe the meat with a cheesecloth dampened with diluted vinegar.

### Wild geese

These migratory birds fly vast distances and as a result are normally less well covered and more muscular than the fat domestic goose. Choose a young bird with bright-colored legs and a pliable underbill. Like the duck, the wild goose—whichever the species, such as Barnacle, Brent or Chinese—should be eaten within a day or two of being shot. It is best well larded and roasted with a moist stuffing of apples or prunes. An older bird is best stuffed and braised in red wine or cider. Serve wild goose with red cabbage, sour-cream sauce, or any of the tart orange- and endive-based salads that go so well with waterfowl.

### Wildfowl

**The mallard** is the most common variety of wild duck and also the largest—a fat mallard will feed from two to three people. **The widgeon** is considered superior to the mallard in flavor. One bird will feed one hungry person, or two at a pinch.

**The teal** is an ornamental duck, tender, and almost too pretty to eat. It will feed one.

Other varieties include the excellent pintail, and the American canvasback, which obligingly feeds on wild celery and tape grass which make its flavor interesting and delicate, lacking any fishy overtones.

Most species of wild duck, however, enjoy a diet of plants growing below the water and so the flavor is, according to their particular biochemical processes, more or less strong, distinctly aquatic and, not to put too fine a point on it, fishy. This can be countered by placing a raw onion inside the bird for an hour or two (remove it before cooking) or by rubbing the bird inside and out with half a lemon dipped in salt; or you may find that it is enough just to spike the gravy with lemon juice and cayenne or Tabasco.

No matter what the species, the duck is preferable to the drake, which tends to be tougher and may therefore need to be marinated. Wild duck should be cooked within 24 hours of killing, unless it is bled so that bacteria do not have the chance to develop. The two small nodules by the tail, which exude a fluid that helps to waterproof the bird, should be removed as they can give the flesh a musky taste.

Leaner and dryer than domestic ducks, all species of wild duck should be well larded and roasted fairly fast on a rack, alternately basted with fresh butter and whisky, red wine or port. They must be served juicy and slightly pink—the longer they cook the tougher they get. The juices that run out when the bird is cut make the best gravy, mixed with orange or lemon juice, red wine, port and Tabasco. Skim the drippings in the roasting pan and taste—if the juices are not bitter, they too can be added to the gravy. Both duck and gravy must be very hot. Serve with homemade potato chips, fried bread crumbs and a sharp salad of orange, celery and watercress. Braised wild duck is good with red cabbage.

### Quail

In Egypt and around the Mediterranean, particularly in southern Italy and Sicily, these migrating birds, exhausted by their journey to or from North Africa, are easily caught in their millions. There is some evidence that even quail in fine fettle will stand around just waiting to be killed. It is this that has earned one American breed the name fool-quail. Nowadays, since wild quail are scarce and are even protected all the year round in many parts of the world, most of the birds that find their way into kitchens come from quail farms.

Once their feathers have been removed, quail are so small that they are scarcely worth eating. Only if there are at least two apiece, supported by small pieces of fried bread or toast, do they give the impression of being enough. They are best roasted in butter, first on one side, then the other and finally breasts upwards. This keeps the meat moist, what there is of it. Make the gravy with the pan juices and a little Madeira, and if you like add a few tablespoons of cream and some soaked raisins. Or they can be wrapped in vine leaves and roasted, or cooked in a casserole with chopped shallots and garlic, softened in butter. In America, quail is the largest of several small game birds that can be prepared in the same ways.

### Ortolan, woodcock and snipe

Woodcock and snipe are sometimes cooked with their trail—meaning innards—intact. Due to their habit of excreting during flight they are white and clean inside.

**Ortolans** are the tiniest of the trio. They are almost too small for the piece of toast on which they are served, plainly broiled or, for preference, threaded like pearls on a necklace and cooked on a spit. They can also be wrapped in vine leaves and cooked, tightly packed, in the oven.

**Woodcock**, gently dappled and speckled with a brown-leaf light-and-shade pattern, has a long, distinctive beak. It eats greedily of almost anything it comes across, and as a result of its omnivorous diet of heather, insects, worms and moss it should be a fat little bird with a fair amount of meat for its size. One bird is just the right amount for one person. It is plainly roasted with its head on, complete with beak, and the head is split after cooking to expose the brains, which are considered a delicacy. It is eaten on toast on which the cooked mashed entrails have been spread.

**The snipe** is a smaller bird than the woodcock, with a similar beak, and it is often trussed with its beak through its body. It is cooked like woodcock, but its lesser size has also given it a cooking method of its own: beak threaded through one wing or through the body, it is encased in a hollowed baking potato that has been cut in two and is then carefully tied together again. When the potato is done, so is the bird. Like woodcock, it is served with its head split open so that the brains can be eaten.

### Pigeons and squab

All varieties of pigeon—wood pigeon, mourning pigeon, ring doves, turtle doves, stock doves and rock doves—and squab (specially reared young pigeons) have an agreeably beefy flavor and produce a most appetizing brown gravy. If pigeons have

*Teal*

*Widgeon*

*Mallard*

*Wild goose*

sugar and the same quantity of salt. A liquid will soon form: turn it in this for two or three days. Alternatively, the birds can be steeped in a red wine marinade. Squab, on the other hand, are plump, tender young birds. Not as gamy as pigeons, they can be roasted or braised, and make a useful addition to a game pie.

If you shoot your own pigeons, hang them by the feet to bleed and pluck them while still warm, when the job is much easier. A Malayan recipe recommends that the pigeons be given a final swig of alcohol before their intoxicated and unsuspected despatch. This is thought to be both kinder and taste improving. They are then rubbed with aniseed inside and honey outside and

fallen from favor, it is because they can be so tough that the work of plucking and drawing them hardly seems worth the pain. The difficulty lies in choosing a young bird. Look at the feet, which should be without scales, soft and supple, and if in any doubt perhaps make a stew or casserole instead of braised or roast pigeon. There is, however, an infallible method of softening up a tough old bird: rub it with a tablespoon of

Squab pie **259**
Game pie **230**

fried in sesame-seed oil. In the Western world, it is usual to serve pigeons with petits pois, braised onions and mushrooms, cabbage and bacon or, for a more gamy dish, with braised red cabbage or lentils.

## Partridges

In Britain, these are the round little birds that explode from the stubble during autumnal country walks. They are always pretty, but are more delicate to eat if they are of the greyish-brown, grey-legged variety. The red-legged partridge is definitely duller. Partridges make the best eating when they are young—about three months old, weighing about 1 lb/450 g, most of which is supplied by the plump breast. Allow one bird per person.

Roast partridge is a great delicacy, while *partridge en Chartreuse*—a pie of partridge, cabbage, sausage, carrots, onions and cloves covered with pastry—is a tremendous dish for a cold winter's day, as is a deep-dish pie made with partridge, mushrooms and a suet crust. Use old birds for pies. (Experts can distinguish the old from the young: the older birds have blunt tips to their flight feathers.)

Young partridges require only a little hanging, as their delicate taste should not be overpowered by highness. Clear gravy, homemade potato chips and watercress are all that are needed with roast partridge.

## The grouse family

The flavor of grouse is one of the greatest treats of late summer and early autumn. In the controversy about what makes better eating, partridge or grouse, it is the northern British red grouse, *Lagopus scoticus*, that is being held up for comparison. Its numerous cousins all have merit, but none can match the red grouse, which tastes of game at its gamiest. In America, the ruffed grouse is considered quite choice.

Since young grouse look surprisingly like old ones (except that, as with partridges, there is a difference in the tip to their flight feathers), and you can't get to know very much about grouse just by eating it a few times in a decade, it is best to go to a really expert purveyor of game for these expensive little birds.

For all their gamy taste, grouse are very clean-feeding birds whose diet is heather, berries and small insects, and they are quite easy to cook to perfection. Young birds, born in the year they are eaten, need to be wrapped in bacon and roasted in a quick oven for 15–20 minutes, until they are pink and slightly underdone. The nicest way to serve them is to sit them on a piece of toast or fried bread with a few straw potatoes

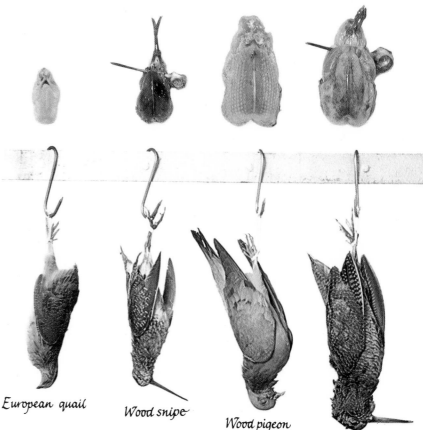

European quail

Wood snipe

Wood pigeon

Woodcock

and a little watercress. Older birds, while very delicious, take more time to prepare. They are good in game pies and in pâtés and terrines, or braised in red wine and stock with celery, onions and carrots, and button onions added just before the end of their cooking.

**The capercaillie** is the largest of the European grouse tribe. It is almost 3 ft/ 90 cm long, weighs between 7 and 10 lb/ 3–4.5 kg and has spectacular plumage of green, black, red and white. It is a northern bird, and owing to its habit of feeding off the tops of young pine trees it tastes distinctly of turpentine, which is not agreeable. Old English recipes variously suggest that to remove the pungent tang the bird should be soaked in milk or vinegar or buried in the ground for 24 hours. A good method of improving a cock bird is to stuff it with raw potatoes, which are discarded after cooking.

In Scandinavia cream plays a great part in the cooking process. In Denmark this might take place in a lidded oven dish, the breastbone of the bird having been broken down to make the lid fit. Towards the end of the lengthy cooking time the bird is allowed to brown and it is served in its sauce with a

sharp cranberry jelly, little gherkins and potatoes. In Norway a creamy, cheesy sauce is poured over the carved bird, which has been roasted in the ordinary way.

**The blackcock and the greyhen** The cock will feed three or four people, but the greyhen two at most, for the cock, with his glossy plumage with white bars and his tail feathers curved like a lyre, is twice as large as his wife. Roasted, both need a good lump of butter in the belly, but blackcock is also casseroled, and made into pies and salmis; in fact, it is treated much like red grouse, although its taste is less delicate.

**The ptarmigan,** which is also called the rock partridge, is getting scarcer. Its size is similar to that of the red grouse, as is its taste, which makes it excellent eating. It is cooked in much the same way as grouse, but in northern Europe, where it is extremely popular, slices of bacon are sometimes inserted under the skin as well as tied over the top. Sour cream goes into the sauce, or there might be a cold sauce of apples cooked in wine, blended with mayonnaise.

Partridge

Grouse

Hen pheasant

Cock pheasant

## Pheasant

The pheasant stands out like a target among the quietly feathered birds of the autumn landscape, and a target is just what he is, hand reared with loving care to offer sport for countrymen. And who can complain when pheasants make such delicious eating. The cock pheasant is the more handsome, but the hen, although slighter and less gloriously plumaged, is often the plumper, juicier bird. A hen makes a superlative meal for two; a large cock can just feed four.

To choose a pheasant in its plumage, feel the width of the breast to see if it is plump, and see that the legs are smooth and the feet soft. It is easy to tell a young cock by its spurs: rounded and without points in the first year, pointed but still short in the second year.

Make sure the bird is hung to your liking before you cook it, as this improves its succulence and flavor. Without hanging—the

time depends on your taste and on the weather—pheasant can taste rather like a dry version of the chicken (to which it is closely related). Since pheasant tends towards dryness in any case, it needs to be wrapped in bacon. It also needs basting with butter, partly to keep it moist, partly to make the skin crisp. Traditionally a young pheasant is served roasted, together with brussels sprouts, braised celeriac, creamed celery or braised endive, and with watercress, clear gravy, fried bread crumbs and faintly clove-scented bread sauce.

A plump pheasant boiled, its skin unbroken, on a bed of celery and served with a

celery sauce with the merest dash of lemon juice, has been described as a dish for the gods. Roast pheasant with bitter orange is also good: the juice of a Seville orange is used to baste the bird towards the end of the cooking. Spiced cabbage, even mild sauerkraut, accompanies pheasant in parts of Europe. But it is generally accepted that the natural foods of bird or beast provide the best and most appropriate dressing with which to send it to the table. So cranberries, juniper berries, rowanberries and sweet chestnuts, as well as watercress and celery, play their part in game and fowl recipes.

Pheasant with celery **252**
Normandy pheasant **254**
Bread sauce **206**

Pheasant with chestnuts **253**
Pheasant with raisin sauce **253**
Pheasant pâté **233**
Pheasant eggs **89,** *89*

# Birds/*Plucking, cleaning and boning*

**Plucking and cleaning a pheasant**

**1.** Hold the legs firmly with one hand and start plucking from the breast area. Pull the feathers down in the direction of growth. Pluck firmly but gently and try to avoid tearing the skin.

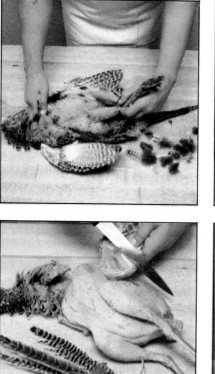

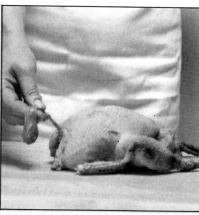

**5.** Withdraw the crop from just inside the neck cavity and discard it.

**2.** When the body is completely plucked, cut the tough flight feathers from the end of each wing.

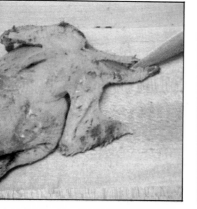

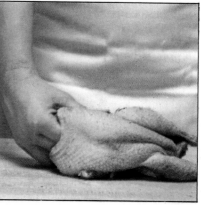

**6.** Feel inside the neck cavity and detach the entrails from the body. This makes it easier to draw them out from the opposite end.

**3.** Turn the bird breast down, cut off the head and slit open the skin encasing the neck.

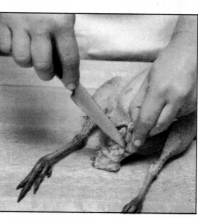

**7.** Cut around the rear vent without piercing the intestine, which is attached to the vent and lies just inside.

**4.** Open out the neck skin and sever the neck. Reserve this for making gravy.

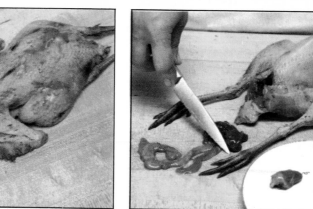

**8.** Pull out the entrails, reserving the liver and heart for making gravy.

**9.** *Run a knife around each leg just below the joint, snap the bone and twist off the foot, pulling with it the stringy tendons.*

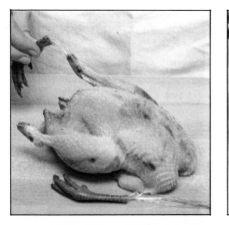

**3.** *Place the knife between the ball and socket of the thigh joint and twist the knife to sever the thigh bone. Do the same on the other side.*

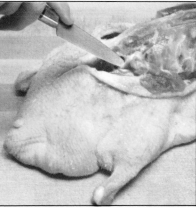

**10.** *This pheasant is cleaned and trussed ready for roasting, with the liver, heart and neck set aside for making gravy. All poultry and game birds can be plucked and cleaned in the same way. Turkeys should be plucked while still warm, starting with the tough wing feathers.*

**4.** *Slide the knife in the other direction towards the neck until the shoulder bone is well exposed. Free the other shoulder bone in the same way.*

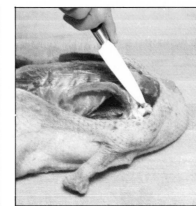

**Boning and stuffing a duck**

**1.** *Lay the duck breast down and with a strong, sharp, short-bladed knife split the skin along the center of the back from neck to parson's nose.*

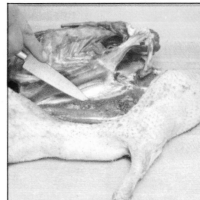

**5.** *Cut through the wing joints and continue to cut, keeping the bones as free of flesh as possible, until you reach the breastbone.*

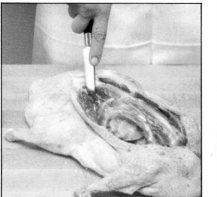

**2.** *Cut down each side of the backbone, starting a little below the neck cavity, and peel back the skin and flesh until you encounter the joint of the thigh bone.*

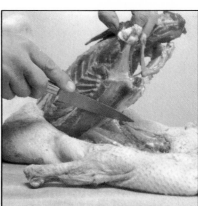

**6.** *Lift up the bones, cutting away the remnants of flesh. Take care not to puncture the breast.*

**7.** *Finally, sever the bony framework at the parson's nose, separating it completely from the flesh.*

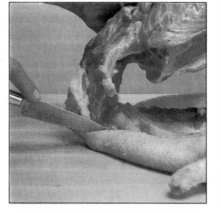

**8.** *Remove the leg bones from the body, working down each with the knife edge. Start from the inside of the duck and push down on the flesh, keeping the skin as intact as possible.*

**9.** *Slip out each wing bone in exactly the same way as the leg bones.*

**10.** *Fill the bird with stuffing of your choice, but do not pack it too tightly or the duck will burst during cooking. Sew up the slit with trussing string.*

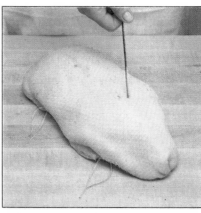

**11.** *Push the duck into a long, oval shape, truss and then prick the bird all over to allow the fat to run out freely while roasting.*

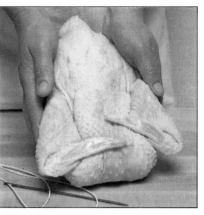

**Trussing a chicken**
**1.** *Take a cleaned chicken, stretch the neck flap firmly under the bird and fold back the wing tips to secure the flap in place.*

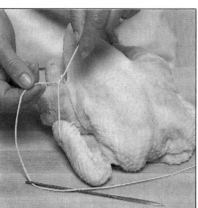

**2.** *Push a threaded trussing needle right through the body just above the wings. Return it through the body, but this time pierce the wings. Tie and trim the two loose ends of string. Re-thread the trussing needle.*

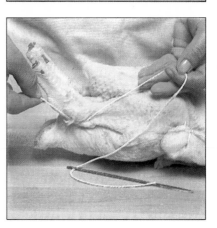

**3.** *Push the needle through the skin just under the drumstick joint, then through the gristle on either side of the parson's nose and emerge through the skin under the far drumstick. Return the needle through the bird, just to one side of the original path. Tie securely and trim the ends.*

**Jointing chicken**
1. *With a short, sharp knife cut off each of the chicken's legs at the point where they join the carcass. Do this by forcing the knife blade between the ball and socket joint and slicing down to either side of the parson's nose.*

5. *Discard the breastbone and cut each side of the chicken in half.*

2. *Slide a large, heavy knife inside the bird and make two cuts, one on either side of the backbone.*

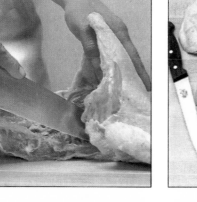

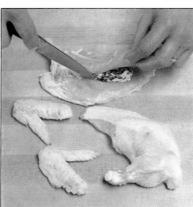

6. *The resulting portions are two legs, two wings and two breasts.*

3. *The backbone, which should be as bare of flesh as possible, can now be withdrawn from the body and reserved for making soup or stock.*

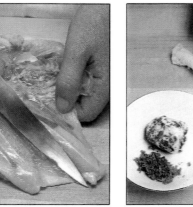

**Stuffing chicken breasts**
1. *Take a breast of chicken, with wing bone attached, and cut off the wing tip at the second joint. Lay the breast skin side down and push a roll of chilled garlic and herb butter under the natural flap of flesh.*

4. *Turn the bird over and cut along either side of the breastbone.*

2. *Seal the flap closed by pressing the outer edges together, and then roll the breast up from the tip towards the wing bone. Tie with cotton or trussing string to make a neat parcel.*

Garlic and herb butter **206**

# Poultry

Squab chicken

Broiler

Boiling fowl

Capon

Turkey

When Henri IV of Navarre summed up his plans for making his people happy, he wished that all his subjects should be prosperous enough to enjoy a succulent *poule au pot* every Sunday. But in spite of his best intentions, it is only fairly recently that poultry has moved out of the luxury class.

## Chicken

In the days before intensive farming, when chicken was a rare Sunday treat, young farmyard fowls had to be specially fattened for the table. In France a young fowl would be roasted, an older bird, nicely stuffed and boiled with plenty of vegetables, would become *poule au pot*, and a large, heavy cockerel would go into a *coq au vin* with its heady smell of wine, onions, mushrooms and herbs. The backhähndl of Austria (a young roasted rooster) was accompanied by a paprika-sprinkled salad of cucumber cut transparently thin, while in England chicken was always stuffed and served roasted, surrounded by sausages, rolls of bacon, roast

potatoes and brussels sprouts or fresh garden peas, and with its crisp skin and juicy flesh it is still always a success. And then, of course, there is the Jewish mother's panacea for any kind of debilitation from flu to stress—chicken soup made from a fully matured hen, which is by far the best provider of sustaining broth.

Today we eat chicken often and in a thousand and one ways. Unlike its ancestors, the battery-bred chicken is fattened so fast and killed so young that it does not have time to develop its full flavor. Sad though this is, a modern chicken responds to being enhanced and improved, and makes a good vehicle for a number of different flavors. Even so, it pays to begin with the best chicken you can find. Free-range birds undoubtedly have the best flavor because of the variety of their diet as they scratch happily for their living, and the fact that they have

been able to run about in the sunshine gives them altogether more character. But even among the battery-reared supermarket poultry there are varying degrees of taste.

There is the fresh-chilled chicken, which may or may not be plastic wrapped and has been gutted and stored at just above freezing point. The giblets (not necessarily its own) are found neatly wrapped inside it. You can cook it at once—which one can never do in the case of a frozen chicken

84

Poultry recipes **259–267**
Pies, pâtés, galantines **228–235**
Poultry preparation **80–83**
Carving poultry **386–387**

Coq au vin **261**

Stocks **194–196**

*Guinea fowl*

*Duck*

*Goose*

—and fresh-chilled chicken has a good texture and plenty of meat on it.

Birds sold by poultry dealers will not be free-range unless specifically advertised as such, and they are sadly hard to come by, especially in cities. The majority will be un-frozen battery birds, complete with innards. Ungutted birds should not be kept for more than seven days, including the time in the store. The poultry dealer will oblige by drawing and trussing the bird for you, and handing you the giblets, which should never be turned down, since they greatly improve the flavor of homemade chicken stock, and can be used in other ways as well.

The plastic-wrapped chicken that has been blast-frozen at a temperature of o°F/−18°C or less is usually the cheapest variety that is available. From the seller's point of view, it has the edge over fresh poultry because no skilled labor is needed for the drawing and trussing. Also, provided the bird is stored at the correct temperature it will not deteriorate, and the wrapping film not only helps to preserve its bright appearance but substantially retards weight loss through evaporation.

All this is good news for the trade and is also welcomed by economists and nutrition-ists, because these birds are a cheap source of energy-giving protein. It is not such good news for the cook because frozen chicken can be rather characterless, needing quite a lot of flavoring and enhancement to make it taste of anything.

When buying frozen chicken, avoid any with freezer burn (they will be dry and taste-less) and also those with noticeable chunks of ice between them and the bottom of their wrappings—these have at some time been partially thawed and refrozen, which is not good for the quality of the flesh. All chick-ens, fresh-chilled or frozen, are drawn through a bath of water as soon as they have

# Poultry

been plucked and drawn. In the case of the fresh-chilled bird, the water has dried off before it reaches your kitchen. In the case of the deep-frozen bird, however, the water drains off only when the chicken is defrosted at home, and the bird ends up in a pool of pink liquid which you have paid for at chicken prices.

Thaw your deep-frozen bird most thoroughly. Not to do so is dangerous, since bacteria develop as the bird is exposed to the heat of the oven and must be killed by thorough cooking. This is impossible if the chicken goes into the pan with a frozen spine (especially if you mean to stuff it), so check not only the meat but also the interior of the chicken before you cook it. Any sign of ice crystals on the inside, or indeed of undue coldness, and the bird is not ready to go into the oven.

Thawing is best done slowly in the refrigerator. The second-best method is to thaw the bird at room temperature in the kitchen. Third comes plunging the bird into cold water. Never give a stiffly frozen chicken a bath of warm water: rapid defrosting spoils the texture of the meat beyond redemption and, whichever recipe you follow, it will come out as dry, stringy chicken in some sort of disguise, the meat having lost all resilience and juiciness.

As soon as you can while it is thawing, remove the wrapped giblets from the chicken so that air can get to the cavity, and never forget to remove the giblet package from any bird before it goes into the oven. This may sound a little basic, but there have been too many surprise stuffings for the advice not to bear repetition.

## Squab chickens and Rock Cornish hens
Squab chickens are small, immature birds and are, generally speaking, rather dull, but they can be good split and grilled over charcoal or under fierce heat. Rock Cornish hens are tastier and can be cooked in the same ways, but are best when roasted, perhaps with a wild rice stuffing. Allow one squab chicken or Cornish hen per person.

## Poulardes
These are fat, neutered young hens, firm and tender and as prized as capons. The most famous come from Bresse, in France, a district so jealous of its superiority that a true *poularde de Bresse* proclaims its provenance by a metal disc clipped to its wing and is displayed with great pride at the poulterer's or the restaurant.

## Capons
These are young neutered roosters fattened on corn, sometimes to an immense girth. Often considered the best chicken available, they are extra succulent because their flesh is marbled with fat, which melts during the cooking process.

A word of warning—the birds may be neutered by hormone pellets implanted in their necks (although in France this method is illegal and caponizing is done by performing a small operation on each bird). The implant method means that by using the neck in cooking you can pass the hormones on to your family, so throw the neck away if you eat capons at all frequently.

## Boiling fowl
Once abundant, these are now hard to find, but any of the old recipes that specify boiling fowl can be made at a pinch with a young roasting bird. The boiler is an older bird and therefore a good deal tougher as well as cheaper. But treated to long, gentle simmering it can be made tender and has both light and dark meat like a turkey, each with a pronounced flavor of its own. Useful in pies and salads, it also provides a quantity of very good broth.

## Broilers and chicken pieces
Young broilers are the most popular sort available and can be used for most chicken recipes. Allow a $3\frac{1}{2}$–4 lb/1.75–2 kg broiler to feed 4–6 people.

Of course you can also buy chicken portions in the shape of the legs, or breast and wing, or a mixture of both. Comparatively, these are a little more expensive than a whole chicken but very convenient if you are short of time. Deep fried with lovely crisp golden batter, chicken pieces eaten with corn bread and fried bananas become chicken Maryland. Chicken breasts wrapped around a piece of chilled garlic butter, egg-and-crumbed and deep fried make the delicious chicken Kiev that spurts hot garlic butter into the eater's eye.

## Cooking with chickens
Since chicken is such a good vehicle for flavors, there are as many ways of preparing it as there are regional tastes. In Morocco, it is rubbed with honey and stuffed with ground almonds and sweet basil or with dried apricots and raisins. It is served with peanuts in the West Indies and with almonds in China, and in West Africa it is cooked inside a scooped out melon. It is poached with truffle slivers under its skin *en demi-deuil* (in half-mourning) in the higher reaches of French gastronomy and, as one might expect, it comes with tomatoes and garlic in Italy, where, plain roasted, it is also eaten with a *salsa de fegatini*—a sauce made of chicken livers, diced ham, mushrooms, chicken stock and Marsala.

If chicken can be said to have a special affinity with any herb, it is with tarragon. Marjoram or oregano, thyme and of course parsley are good too. The best additions and flavorings for cooking a chicken are bacon, garlic, cream, yogurt, white wine, sherry, saffron, curry powder, ginger, nutmeg, cumin or paprika; the best accompaniments: shallots, mushrooms, tomatoes, rice. The best fruits and nuts are raisins, walnuts, lemons, apricots, pine nuts and almonds.

## Turkey
An English Christmas and an American Thanksgiving would be incomplete without a fine, plump, roasted turkey, served with all the ceremonial trappings. Calculate 1 lb/450 g of dressed weight per person—thus a 20 lb/9 kg bird will provide 20 helpings as well as seemingly endless supplies of stock and soup.

The bird to look for is a broad, compact one, hen rather than cock, with a fresh looking but not moist skin and a pearly white tint to the flesh rather than purple or blue. It should have been hung for at least three days, otherwise it will have very little flavor. This makes a fresh turkey your best buy, because although frozen birds can, of course, be quite good, they are sometimes frozen as soon as they have been killed, which means that although they may be juicy the taste may be rather dull.

A frozen turkey takes about 48 hours to thaw. Simply put it in the refrigerator two days before you want it (three days if it is extra large) and let it thaw gradually. Then let it spend a few hours at room temperature just to make certain that it has properly thawed. It won't be cooked in the middle if it hasn't, and domestic birds not cooked through are as dangerous as undercooked pork and much nastier. Once it has thawed, it should be cooked soon. Resist the temptation to prestuff the turkey in order to save time on the day of the dinner, even though there will be so many other traditional bits and pieces to see to. Get the stuffing ready on the eve of the day by all means, but put it inside the bird just before it goes into the oven, as the stuffing may spoil if it sits around inside the bird, even if the stuffed bird is kept in the refrigerator.

## Cooking with turkey
Everybody has a favorite stuffing for turkey—perhaps one for the neck cavity to make a nicely plumped out shape under the skin and a different one to go inside the bird. The purpose of the stuffing in the main cavity is, of course, to help keep the bird moist: sausage meat is the usual basis, or a forcemeat of pork belly, and many people like chestnuts in the mixture. A seasoned and buttered bread stuffing, or an oyster one, are both popular. A marjoram and onion stuffing flavored with lemon peel is

good, but might be rather dry unless it has a large lump of butter worked into it.

Some people like to cook a turkey simply in butter, starting it off, like a chicken, breast downwards. This is an excellent way of keeping what is by nature rather a dry-fleshed bird succulent. Others like to bard it with bacon, others still to roast it wrapped in foil, which must, however, be folded back towards the end of the cooking time to give the breast a chance to become brown and crisp. In very slow cooking, which gives good results, a glass or two of white wine can be added to the juices in the roasting pan halfway through the cooking.

André Simon, the great wine and food expert, compares big birds like the turkey to cygnets and peacocks which once upon a time counted among the greatest delicacies. "One should be content to meet them occasionally at some friend's dinner table," he says, "without troubling to order them when one is the host." Unless one is very lucky with one's turkey, it is easy to agree with him, except on traditional occasions.

For Thanksgiving, turkey is traditionally served with sweet potatoes, creamed onions or creamed celery, succotash (which is a mixture of green lima beans and corn off the cob), creamy giblet gravy and cranberry sauce. For English Christmas dinner, the turkey comes with roast potatoes, brussels sprouts and chestnuts, clear gravy, bread sauce and perhaps, if there is no sausage stuffing, a chain of crisp little sausages draped about its bosom, like the Lord Mayor's chains of office. On national holidays in Mexico—the home of the ancestral turkey, from which the domestic variety descends—the bird is eaten with a dark, non-sweet, velvety chocolate sauce, spiced with aniseed, and the Spanish, in a festive mood, will stuff their turkey with sweetbreads and truffles.

All these rich meals are best enjoyed once a year and then forgotten until next time. However, we meet turkey with increasing frequency on non-feast days. Supermarkets now sell turkey throughout the year in the form of rolled turkey breasts to be roasted, turkey drumsticks, breasts and other portions, and young birds, suitably split, are sold as broilers for summer barbecues.

The turkey is, of course, very nourishing, and all-year-round sales are a good thing for the trade even though they endanger the turkey's aura of the special occasion.

## Goose

Martinmas, on 11 November, is the traditional day for eating goose in northern Europe. It is, presumably, an extended annual punishment meted out to these birds, whose cackling once gave away the farmyard hiding place of the modest St. Martin as he was attempting to evade admiring followers who wanted him to be Pope. (The raucous cry of geese saved the ancient Romans from barbarian invasion—but that has not stopped the Italians from eating goose, richly stuffed with sausage meat, olives and truffles.)

In England goose used to be eaten on Michaelmas. This was not so much because this saint and all his angels had a grudge against geese, but because his day, 29 September, was, like St. Martin's, a fast day —one of so many that people were getting heartily sick of being forced to eat fish. Waterfowl—including geese—didn't count as meat and so could be eaten without offense to God or man. Moreover, both saints' days fell in the season when the geese were getting fat, having gleaned the stubble fields since the harvest had been brought in. So Michaelmas geese were the stubble geese, slightly more mature than the green geese of the summer which had fed mainly on grass, but less magnificent than the Martinmas geese, which had an extra six weeks to fatten on grain.

When buying a goose for the table, choose a young bird with downy feathers around the legs and a pliable lower beak and breastbone. A well-filled plump breast denotes succulence and value for money. Look for creamy skin with a warm tinge to it, almost pale apricot, without a trace of blue or brown.

A gosling, or green goose, of no more than three months old weighs up to about 5 lb/ 2 kg and can hardly help being tender and delicate. At 8–9 months old it becomes a goose (in culinary terms it is never a gander). At 8–9 months the goose, weighing 6–12 lb/ 2.5–5.5 kg, is in its prime; with advancing age it becomes both fatter and tougher, needing longer and longer periods of braising or stewing—very delicious, but perhaps not quite the rare treat that goose is usually expected to be.

You will need to trust in the expertise of your supplier in keeping fresh, chilled or frozen birds in the right condition—the goose should be hung for a few days before it is gutted and plucked. If by any chance you have to pluck the goose at home, put it into a large bowl and pour boiling water over it to loosen the feathers, or the job is likely to take you all day.

### Cooking with goose

Geese are eaten on high days and holidays, especially in northern Europe where goose is the traditional Christmas bird and comes to the feast magnificently brown, with crackling skin, copious gravy and a stuffing of sharp apples, which may be layered with boiled chestnuts or raisins, or, in Scandinavia, with prunes. (Sausage meat, it is rightly agreed, makes this bird too rich.) In Ireland geese are stuffed with boiled potatoes which sop up the fat, and this method is also known in America, where bread or rice stuffings are used to the same effect.

The skin of a roasting goose needs to be well pricked, like that of a duck, and it should be roasted on a high rack so that it stands clear of the fat that pours out. (Although it is a hot and messy job, it is a good idea to pour off some of the fat halfway through the cooking.) Shortly before the end, some people like to dredge the top of the bird with a little flour, which forms dark crusty speckles where it lands. But the best finishing touch is to increase the heat for a few minutes just before the goose comes out of the oven and to splash the bird with drops of cold water, which hiss and evaporate as they would on a hot iron, leaving the skin delicately crisp.

Rendered goose fat spread on bread is delicious to eat and it makes a wonderful cooking medium, particularly good for frying potatoes. It is more highly flavored than duck fat, and each bird yields so much that in days gone by it was used to good purpose not only in the kitchen but also on the farm: cows' udders were rubbed with it to prevent chapping, as were the hands of the dairymaids; harness and leatherwork were kept supple by its liberal application, and cold plasters made of brown paper coated with goose grease were a common household remedy for colds.

## Duck

A duck is nobody's best buy: it is a bony creature covered in fat, with a shallow breast. When you come to carve it—and here you may come to blows with the bird before you have finished—you will find that there is not enough breast to go around; but hot or cold, duck has such an excellent flavor, richness and succulence that it is well worth the occasional extravagance.

The very best French ducks are the small Nantais, and the larger Rouen, which is suffocated to retain the blood so that its flesh stays dark, giving it a strong flavor which is something of an acquired taste. The Rouen duck should be cooked within 24 hours of its demise. Roasted very rare and divested of breast, drumsticks and wings, it is this duck which is pressed, together with its lightly cooked giblets, in the great silvery duck presses which are still a feature of elegant French restaurants, to make the juice for the gravy.

The most famous English duck is the Aylesbury and the most popular American variety is the Long Island duckling. This, like the Nantais, the Rouen and the Aylesbury, is a descendant of the Imperial Peking duck, a Chinese snow-white breed of special excellence, which was once reserved for the Emperor alone.

"Duckling" was once, strictly, the term for birds under two months old, but it is now used until the birds are six months or so. Duckling sounds more tender than duck, but it is a mistake to invest in too young a bird as it does not have enough meat on its bones to be worth eating. However, the best eating age and weight varies with the breed. Make sure that the duck's underbill is soft enough to be bent back easily, that the webbing of its feet is pliable and that its breast, when pinched, feels meaty.

As for how many persons a duck will feed, it is hard to say. A wit once observed that the duck was a difficult bird—too much for one, too little for two. However, two people can dine more than well even on a Nantais; and three, or even four if helpings are modest, on an Aylesbury or a Long Island duckling.

Ducks take quite kindly to freezing—their greater fat content, compared with that of the chicken, assures that when defrosted they retain their moistness, and the stronger flavor is not so easily frozen out. Like the chicken, the duck comes both fresh-chilled and deep frozen, and the same rules regarding defrosting apply. Fresh is still better than frozen, and free-range better than battery. But unlike the battery chickens, who may never have set foot to ground throughout their lives, battery ducklings may have been allowed to waddle about the yard in their youth, before the fattening up process put an end to exercise.

### Cooking with duck

Before roasting a duck, it is best to prick its skin in all the fatty places so that some of the subcutaneous fat which insulates it against cold water (even though it may never have had a swim in its life) can run out during cooking. This makes a wonderful fat to eat with salt on bread or to use for frying potatoes. To crisp the skin, the bird should be roasted on a rack.

Like chicken, duck is cooked and eaten in countless ways. The Chinese, especially, who have domesticated ducks for more than 2,000 years, have thousands of delicious dishes composed of crisp duck morsels with a variety of stir-fried vegetables. They also have deep-fried ducks which are first steamed to remove the fat; sometimes called lacquered ducks, these are a glistening reddish-mahogany color and so soft that the flesh comes away at a touch. The Chinese even like to chew the brittle bones, saying that the crunchiness is the chief attraction of these vividly glazed ducks, which are often seen hanging in the windows of Chinese restaurants. The Danes and the Swedes boil their ducks with herbs. The Danes serve theirs with mustard and dark rye bread; the Swedes dish up boiled duck with a creamy horseradish sauce.

The classic flavors with duck include oranges, both bitter and sweet, turnips and onions—all designed to offset the somewhat richly flavored meat. Other classic accompaniments are young peas, morello cherries, green olives, red wine and vermouth. Newer inventions include duck with limes and duck with apples, walnuts and prunes.

### Guinea fowl

This elegantly spotted fowl, of West African ancestry, is an endearing but stupid bird. Looking somewhat like a walking cushion, its feathers are a marvel of pattern, white-spotted on black like old ladies' dresses, or sometimes a delicate lavender. The semi-domesticated breeds are delicious to eat, plumper than their wild counterparts, but both have a tendency to be dry and thus require regular basting during cooking with seasoned butter, or barding and larding with bacon fat. It is nice to put a sprig of marjoram under the waistcoat of fat if you do not plan to stuff the bird.

Guinea fowl are often seen in European shops wearing their wing feathers—perhaps to distinguish them from young chickens, which they resemble in size. They taste like a slightly gamy chicken and recipes for pheasant, partridge or young roasting chicken will do justice to their delicate flavor.

To be enjoyed at their best, guinea fowl should hang, unbled, in a cool place for one or two days to tenderize the meat. Ask the poultry supplier to pluck it, gut it and truss it for you. The demand for guinea fowl is not enormous so they are not always available, but they are on the market all year round. In America they are either home-raised or available only in specialty stores.

### Cooking with guinea fowl

The prime concern is to keep the flesh moist, so recipes which call for a stuffing of vegetables and butter or *fromage blanc* under the skin will certainly enhance the texture. In Poland guinea fowl is rubbed inside and out with ground ginger an hour before roasting and is served with chestnut purée. The traditional English way is to stuff it, roast it and serve it with giblet gravy and bread sauce, just like turkey. In the west of England it is braised in cider.

Older birds are good casseroled with stock and cream. Breasts of guinea fowl can be sautéed in butter and served with a sauce of sherry, cream, paprika and Worcestershire sauce; and a spit-roasted bird, stuffed with buttered fresh bread crumbs, shallots and marjoram, well larded with bacon, flambéed in cognac and served with a well-seasoned "jus" will satisfy any gourmet.

### Giblets

The giblets—the neck, heart, gizzard and liver—of most poultry are usually packed inside the body cavity or handed over by the poulterer. Giblets make a wonderful stock for gravy and can be eaten in stews or pies. To prepare them for cooking, remove the yellowish gall bladder sac from the liver and trim away all yellowish patches, which will give a bitter taste. Trim the fat, blood vessels and membrane from the heart and discard the outer skin and inner sac containing stones and grit from the gizzard. When making a giblet stock, it seems wasteful to boil up the liver, which can be enjoyed in many different ways.

### Poultry livers

Chopped, these are a well-known feature of Jewish cooking and an essential ingredient in many pâtés, terrines and stuffings for poultry. Whole, they are delicious wrapped in bacon and skewered and broiled, or lightly seasoned and sautéed in butter with a dash of dry vermouth.

Chicken livers, especially, appear in almost every national cuisine: in sauces for spaghetti, in risottos and pilafs, in grand mousses and simple spreads. They can be bought fresh or frozen. The fine-grained pale livers are considered to be the best.

### Foie gras and goose liver

The wit of the English Regency, the Reverend Sydney Smith, defined his idea of heaven as "eating foie gras to the sound of trumpets." Indeed, there can be nothing to compare with the exquisite, pale, fattened liver of the goose, for which the bird is expressly bred, particularly in areas of south-western France.

To make foie gras the geese are force-fed until their livers weigh around 4 lb/2 kg apiece. The best comes from a breed already known to the ancient Romans. These geese, unlike table geese, have an extra pleat of skin under the breast, which neatly accommodates the enlarged liver. Ducks are also increasingly being bred for foie gras, with the result that fresh foie gras is becoming much more widely available than ever before.

The liver of a goose on a normal diet weighs about 4 oz/115 g. Soaked in milk it will swell a little and become even more tender. It is good sliced and fried and eaten with rice or with scrambled eggs. Pounded, together with white bread crumbs, marjoram, chopped mushrooms and diced bacon and bound with egg, it is used to stuff the fat skin of the neck, which is then tied at both ends and poached in giblet broth and white wine, or fried in goose drippings. In France, no part of a goose is wasted, and in some country areas even the blood is eaten in the form of little cakes flavored with garlic.

# Eggs

For primitive man, with a mind far less tortuous than ours, there was no such thing as a chicken-and-egg dilemma: he recognized the egg as the beginning of life and celebrated it as such. It was in this context that people began to decorate eggs, as a symbol of springtime and fertility.

In the kitchen the hen's egg is celebrated still. Indispensable to the cook and rich in vitamins and minerals, it is one of the most versatile and valuable of foods.

There is a popular misconception in Europe that brown eggs are somehow better than white, whereas in the United States, white are usually preferred. But shell color reflects neither flavor nor nutritional content, merely the breed of the laying bird. The best egg, brown or white, large or small, is one that has been freshly laid by a free-range hen—properties difficult to ascertain in the store or supermarket, where boxes enticingly labelled "farm fresh" may contain factory eggs up to four or five weeks old.

From the time an egg is laid, the membranes weaken and the flavor changes. The white of a fresh egg is thick (making wonderful fried and poached eggs), getting runnier and thinner as time goes by. It is easy enough to tell if an egg is fresh or stale once you get it home. At the rounded end of the egg, between the shell and the membrane, there is a small air chamber, all but invisible when the egg is fresh, increasingly large as the egg gets older and loses moisture through its pores. So one way of assessing freshness is to hold the egg upright against a strong light and examine the size of the air space. Another is to weigh it in your hand: the heavier for its size the better; yet another is to immerse it horizontally in cold water. A perfectly fresh egg will stay put; older eggs will tilt; if more than three weeks old they will float. If the egg rises to a vertical position it is really getting old.

Large eggs are good for breakfast, but when cookbooks specify eggs they generally mean medium-size ones. Eighteenth- and nineteenth-century recipes instructing the cook to "take three dozen eggs" should cause less amusement than they do, since the average egg used to be a great deal smaller than it is today and was probably laid by bantam hens. There are still dozens of different bantam species, all as pretty as chrysanthemums, and they still make the best "sitters"—on farms they are sometimes used for hatching eggs of larger hens bred for laying rather than motherhood. But no bantam, however devoted, can be as efficient as a mechanized battery. "Factory" eggs are no less nutritious, their flavor is standard and good, if rather slight, but they fail to give as much pleasure as eggs from contented hens scratching about for their food in the farmyard. These "free-range" eggs arrive in the stores ready boxed, often with a token bit of down attached, and it is probably a sign of the times that in parts of California the token feather is of hygienic plastic. Eat genuine farm-fresh eggs as soon as possible, especially if they have been cleaned, as washing removes the natural protective film from the shell.

Because eggshells are porous they are highly susceptible to neighboring smells, which is fine if they are intended for truffle omelets and stored in an egg basket with a truffle, as they are in parts of Périgord, but not such a good thing if their near neighbors are unwrapped, strong-smelling foods such as onions and particularly ripe cheese. Eggs should be kept in a cool place—not necessarily a refrigerator—standing with the rounded end up to allow the air space to breathe." For cooking, they should be at room temperature—eggs straight from the refrigerator will crack if plunged into boiling water, a cold yolk will not emulsify reliably and cold whites will not whisk well.

## Cooking with eggs

A beaten egg will thicken soups, stews and sauces because heat causes the egg to coagulate, thus holding the liquid in suspension. The raw yolk will hold oil or butter in suspension and to this happy fact we owe such good things as mayonnaise and hollandaise sauce. An egg is sticky and so will bind mixtures for croquettes and stuffings or hamburgers. As for food that is to be deep fried, a dip into a beaten egg will not only keep the bread crumbs in place but the film of egg will protect the food from becoming sodden with fat. A beaten egg gives a handsome sheen to pastry, and a whole whisked egg with its millions of tiny trapped air bubbles gives a rise to cakes and batters.

The volume of beaten egg white—so essential for light soufflés and mousses—depends on the eggs being at room temperature before you start and the way you whisk them —electric food processors are too fast and produce a dense texture. Big "balloon" wire whisks, while taking a little more time and energy, do produce the desired airy froth.

Apart from omelets and batters, which are cooked briefly over a high heat, eggs respond best to gentle warmth—too high a heat and too long a cooking time makes them leathery.

## Other eggs

No other bird has proved anywhere near so obliging as the domestic hen, which lays up to 250 eggs a year, but hens' eggs are by no means the whole story.

**Ostrich eggs** (one ostrich egg is equal to two dozen hen's eggs) are rarely sold these days—but Queen Victoria once tasted one made into a giant omelet and declared it to be very good.

**Duck eggs** are extremely rich with somewhat gelatinous whites, so although they taste quite good alone they are best in custards, mousses and other puddings.

**Goose eggs** are also rich and make very good omelets, custards and mousses.

**Quail eggs** come both fresh and preserved. Fresh, they make a good first course served hard boiled with celery salt.

Gulls' eggs, plovers' eggs and pheasants' eggs are sometimes to be found, but in many countries they are, quite rightly, protected from the unheeding gourmet.

White hen egg · Brown hen egg · Duck egg · Goose egg · Quail egg · Pheasant egg · Gull egg

# Milk, Cream and Butter

The cow is a good friend to mankind, providing us with one of our most complete foods. Milk contains most of the nutrients required by the human body— proteins, vitamins and minerals, especially calcium — and since cows are so generous with their supply, milk and its products are still good value for money.

## Milk

Most children and quite a number of adults enjoy drinking milk and it is also used in a variety of ways, including for cooking. In Italy and Germany it is even used for roasting pork, the meat bubbling away under a golden skin that eventually caramelizes with the pan juice into a delicious gravy, and in Saudi Arabia lamb cooked with rice in milk is the descendant of an ancient dish. There are also many other sauces and dishes cooked all over the world that are based on using up milk that would not have kept for long in the days before refrigeration.

It is said that milk is not so much a drink as a liquid food. It contains proteins, vitamins and minerals, and has most of the nutrients needed by the human body. There is even an official scale of desirable milk consumption: 2½ cups/6 dl a day for children and young people between the ages of two and 21; 5 cups/1 liter a day for expectant mothers; 1¼ cups/3 dl for other adults.

The majority of milk on the market today is pasteurized. Pasteurization was one of the successes of Louis Pasteur, whose work in the field of microbiology led to the eradication of many animal-borne diseases. It involves heating the milk to a point where any potentially dangerous bacilli are killed but the flavor of the milk is not impaired.

Milk that has not been pasteurized is sold as raw or unheated milk. It must always be certified or attested—that is, stringently tested at the farm to make sure that no harmful bacteria are present.

Milk should always be heated slowly and cooked at low temperatures. A skin that is either liked or detested forms on the top when it reaches high temperatures, helping it to boil over the sides of the pan—with the resulting characteristic smell that gives the impression things are getting out of hand in the kitchen. This skin is solidified proteins and milk fat—to avoid it do not boil but scald the milk: that is, remove it from the heat just as it shows a wreath of tiny bubbles around the edge. To guard against the milk scorching on the bottom of the saucepan, rinse the pan with cold water before putting in the milk.

If the recipe calls for the addition of flour or sugar, these, too, help prevent a skin forming. To prevent the skin that appears on the top of a milk-based sauce, rub a small piece of butter over the surface on the point of a knife. This makes a protective film and can be stirred in at the last minute.

### Fresh milks

There are three main types of fresh milk, which need to be kept as cool as possible.

**Whole milk** This is milk with its natural cream intact and has one of the best flavors of all milk sold. In summer the cream rises to the top of the milk in a thick golden layer, while in winter, due to the lack of rich grass for the cows, the cream tends to be paler and thinner.

The creamiest milk usually comes from Jersey and Guernsey cows, but today many farmers are producing good quality milk from Friesians and Holsteins. Their milk used to be thin, watery and blue, but now they have been bred and rebred to produce better milk. The cream can be shaken back into the milk, or it can be carefully poured off and used in coffee or on breakfast cereals or fresh berries.

**Homogenized milk** The cream is still present in homogenized milk, but as the name suggests it has been evenly suspended throughout instead of being allowed to float to the top as in whole milk. Homogenized milk is good for making ice cream as it freezes well.

**Skimmed and low-fat milk** Skimmed milk is milk that has been divested of its rich, delicious cream. Our ancestors went to great pains to avoid their milk being skimmed, even to the extent of making the urban dairyman bring his cow to the city streets to be milked on the spot so that the customers could see for themselves the cream going into the jug.

The cream is removed by centrifugal force and the resulting almost fat-free milk is good in low-fat diets, since it contains only 0.1 percent fat. Low-fat milk, which is slightly less watery, contains 2 percent fat. These milks are sometimes given extra milk solids and vitamins to restore something of the nutrients they have lost in skimming.

### Long-life milks

These milks will keep, unopened, for much longer than ordinary pasteurized milks and are therefore extremely useful for people who are frequently away from home or without refrigerators. Once opened, however, or reconstituted, they will keep only as long as fresh milk.

**Sterilized milk** This is pasteurized, homogenized and then held at a high temperature until all the bacteria have been destroyed. It will keep unopened for about seven days but has a slightly peculiar taste due to the caramelization of the sugar present in milk, known as lactose.

**UHT (Ultra Heat Treated) milk** First pasteurized, this milk is then treated at a temperature of 270°F/132°C for a single second, which means that the lactose does not caramelize to such an extent that the flavor is impaired. It will keep unopened for several months and is an invaluable standby in case one runs out of fresh milk.

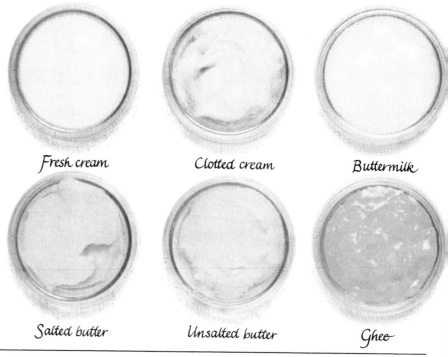

Fresh cream     Clotted cream     Buttermilk

Salted butter     Unsalted butter     Ghee

**Evaporated and condensed milk** Evaporated milk is the less sweet and sticky of the two, but the extra sugar in condensed milk helps it to keep better once the can has been opened. Condensed milk tends, however, to taste more like toffee than milk. Both can be used in cooking and can even be whipped. If doing the latter, chill the milk first in the freezing tray of the refrigerator until soft crystals have formed around the edge.

The quality of these milks in cooking is open to controversy; some hold that they enrich foods while others feel that they impart a strange, oversweet taste.

**Dehydrated milk** This has a flat but unobjectionable flavor that bears little resemblance to real milk. It can be used in cooking either in reconstituted or dried form and can also be used to make yogurt: a few tablespoons of dried milk powder stirred into the measured quantity of milk before incubating gives a thicker and slightly richer yogurt.

### Milk substitutes

These are whiteners that are used in tea or coffee by those who are allergic to real milk. They are usually made with vegetable or coconut oil or soybeans. Other additives such as artificial color, emulsifiers and sugar are also often present.

### Other milks

Although Western society drinks mainly cows' milk, there are many other kinds such as sheep's, goats' and water buffaloes' milk. The latter huge, black, curly horned beasts stand up to hot weather better than cows and are found in India and the hottest parts of southern Italy. Desert dwellers drink camels' milk, Tibetans drink yaks' and asses' milk, while the Kurds like mares' milk, riding along on their milk supply.

Both ewes and goats give milk for delicious cheeses such as pecorino, Roquefort and Spanish manchego, while buffaloes' milk is a fine basis for mozzarella.

Goats' milk has the special quality of being highly digestible and is excellent for babies and for people with poor digestions and for those who are allergic to cows' milk. It should, however, be avoided by those who are unable to cope with a full cream content since the cream does not separate as easily from goats' milk as it does from cows' milk.

### Soured milk products

Milk that has been soured is often looked upon as a food. It also makes a drink that is enjoyed in various parts of the world under different names and soured by various methods. Kefir is from the Caucasus and is slightly fermented. The Russian koumiss is made from mares' milk that turns sour as it hangs in leather bags on the mares' own warm sides. Viili is a Finnish sour milk

drink, and yogurt has long been a daily food in the Balkans, parts of India, the USSR, Turkey, Greece and the Middle East.

It is the presence of living lactic acid bacteria in milk that makes it go sour. This used to be a real problem before pasteurization, and it was the need to use milk before it became too sour that led to making yogurt and cheese. Pasteurization, however, kills the lactic acid bacteria and now milk, if left, does not go sour but merely bad, so a souring culture must be introduced in order to achieve soured milk products.

**Acidophilus milk** The bacteria *lactibacillus acidophilus*, killed during pasteurization, is reintroduced in a dormant state to pasteurized milk to produce acidophilus milk. This milk has been found to be easily digestible even by those who cannot manage ordinary milk and is called "the milk of the future" by some nutritionists. It looks and tastes like fresh pasteurized milk and the bacteria is said to be extremely beneficial, since it helps to achieve a better bacterial balance in the digestive tract.

**Buttermilk** This used to be a favorite drink of farmers' children. It had a fresh, slightly acid flavor and was made from the liquid left over when butter was made on the farm. It was also used in cooking to activate the bicarbonate of soda that was used as a leavening agent in baking to give a soft, tender quality to cakes and scones. The buttermilk sold today is still delicious but it is thicker than the old farm variety and is made with a culture.

**Yogurt** Credited with powers of increasing health and prolonging life, yogurt is made daily in those countries where it has a long history. It is eaten as a dessert and is used extensively as a marinade for meat, in soups and salads, and even in cooked dishes. For the latter it must first be treated to prevent it separating.

Good yogurt is easily made at home with the simplest of all equipment, an earthenware bowl, or in a small yogurt maker.

Commercially made yogurts are made by injecting a low-fat or skimmed milk with a culture of *lactobacillus bulgaricus, lactobacillus acidophilus* or *streptococcus thermophilus*. A combination of these strains produces the most acidic yogurts, often considered to have the best flavor. Some, especially the varieties with fruit in them, have had milk solids, cream or edible gum and gelatine added, but none of these contributes to the acid flavor of yogurt, which is particularly desirable in cooking, nor do they taste particularly like yogurt. And they are not suitable, as plain yogurt is, for those who are on a low-fat diet.

Although only some yogurts are labelled "live," the only ones that are in fact not live are those that have been sterilized.

### Cream

*The friendly cow all red and white*
*I love with all my heart.*
*She gives me cream with all her might*
*To eat with apple tart.*

Robert Louis Stevenson

Creams vary in thickness and richness according to the amount of butterfat present —the thicker the cream the more butterfat it contains and the richer it will be.

The thickest cream is for spooning over strawberries, for syllabubs and for filling cakes, éclairs and so on, and is whipped for decorating cakes and puddings. Thin, light creams are ideal for soups and sauces, for pouring over puddings and desserts and for putting into coffee.

Whipping creams are usually used in soufflés, ice creams and mousses. A thin cream will not whip no matter how long you work at it, as there is not enough butterfat to trap the air bubbles, so buy heavy cream.

Whipped cream should be light, airy and about doubled in volume—a balloon or spiral whisk will achieve the best result. A blender is too fast and even a rotary whisk is too fierce. To achieve the right texture the cream, bowl and whisk should all be cold. A spoonful of cold milk or a crushed ice cube added to each $\frac{2}{3}$ cup/1.5 dl of cream as it thickens gives a lighter result, and if you add a little sugar to the cream the whipped result will not separate so easily but will not be so pure in flavor.

As well as varying in texture cream can be fresh, which is the best for all purposes, sterilized, when it acquires an odd, flat, sweetish flavor, or treated to a version of UHT, when it has a long life but is not the best choice when flavor is important. Fresh cream is obviously the first choice and this will keep, refrigerated, for up to four days in summer and seven days in winter. In America some heavy creams will keep for several weeks. Some farms still deliver untreated cream to local stores and this is the cream with the best flavor of all.

**Clotted cream** This is a specialty of the west of England, where great pans filled with milk are heated, cooled and then skimmed of their thick, wrinkled, creamy crust. This cream is usually eaten in Devon and Cornwall piled onto scones with strawberry jam. A commercial variety can be bought but is not nearly so good.

**Crème fraîche or crème double** This French cream is treated with a special culture that helps it to stay fresh longer and gives it a lively though not exactly sour taste. It is this cream that is required when French recipes call for cream. A tablespoonful of buttermilk added to $2\frac{1}{2}$ cups/6 dl of cream—heavy whipping cream is best—and

# Milk, Cream and Butter

put in a warm place, between 75–85°F/24–29°C, for a few hours will produce the authentic taste.

**Soured cream** Light or heavy cream treated with a souring culture is known as soured cream. It is sometimes sold by its Russian name smetana, and in that country it is served on borsch, salads and is used in marinades. Germany, Austria and Scandinavia include it in sauces, which it makes glossy and slightly acid. A plain broiled pork chop eaten from the same plate as a cucumber salad dressed with sour cream produces the most delicious mixture as the meat juices mingle with the dressing. To make your own sour cream, simply add a few drops of lemon juice to fresh heavy cream.

## Butter

Experts can tell where butter comes from by the color, texture, smell and taste. Normandy butter, ivory colored and rich, is the most admired, especially the Norman butter of Issigny. Melted, it resembles cream. Spread on bread, its taste is sweet and nutty and its texture firm and smooth. There are no visible beads of water—if butter has a water content of more than 12 percent it will not cream well. When pressed it does not crumble and its aroma is delicate and mild. It is all that a butter could hope to be and is worth buying for a special treat, expensive though it is, if you know of a specialty store that stocks it.

But for normal everyday use we tend to buy butter by brand name or by price, cheaper butters being the blended ones. Both for eating and cooking it is always better to buy a good-quality butter, since a low-grade butter can have such an overpowering flavor that it quite spoils such things as fresh vegetables and delicate sauces such as hollandaise. Buy only a week's supply at a time and take it out of the refrigerator about 15 minutes before using so that it loses its hardness. Rewrap what has not been used before replacing it and keep it well away from strong-smelling foods, particularly anything flavored with garlic, and soft fruits such as strawberries, since butter absorbs these flavors and once tainted no amount of airing will make it recover.

Butter can either be salted or unsalted. Salting used to make all the difference between butter that kept fresh and butter that went rancid fast. It still improves the keeping qualities of butter.

Unsalted butter has a much sweeter taste than salted butter. It makes an excellent table butter and is preferred in cooking. Its delicate flavor lends itself particularly well to cakes, and it is better than salted butter for frying—salted butter contains deposits that burn at a fairly low temperature, making it

an unsuitable medium for cooking. Unsalted butter has fewer of these deposits and can therefore withstand higher temperatures.

Butter can be blended with a number of ingredients to make delicious garnishes and fillings for sandwiches. Mix it with garlic to make the classic accompaniment for snails, or with herbs, especially parsley, to serve with fish or meat. With Roquefort cheese it is delicious with steak, and with pounded anchovies, lobster coral or mustard it makes an excellent garnish for fish.

There are also many types of butter sauces, including beurre blanc—velvety butter flavored with a touch of vinegar and shallot; sauce meunière, a combination of foaming butter and lemon juice; and beurre noir, which should on no account be black, but dark golden brown.

The addition of a little oil will prevent butter burning when cooking but will also impair the buttery flavor, so the best butter for frying very delicate foods is clarified butter, from which all the milk solid deposits have been removed. This is the ghee used in India, but only for special occasions—less expensive vegetable ghee is used for everyday cooking. Clarified butter, however, no longer has the fresh taste that makes it so nice on vegetables and new or baked potatoes. For these purposes there is nothing so good as fresh butter.

**Fresh cream butter** This can be salted or unsalted and is also known as sweet cream butter, made from unripened cream. The cream is pasteurized, deodorized and cooled before being placed in ageing tanks for at least 12 hours. Salt, which acts as a preservative, can be added during this time. American, British and New Zealand butters tend to be of this type.

**Ripened butter** This is also known as lactic butter and like fresh cream butter can be either salted or unsalted. A pure culture of lactic bacteria is introduced to the cream, which is then allowed to ripen to develop a delicious, slightly acid flavor before the butter is made. This butter has a slightly more pronounced taste than fresh cream butter and is also softer.

## Making your own dairy foods

Many milk-based products can be made quite easily at home. Starter packets for cultured products such as buttermilk and yogurt can be bought from health food stores, or a little unflavored ready-made product can be used. All you need then are very clean, well-covered bowls or jars (not metal), an undisturbed environment and a constant temperature to allow the culture to grow. Keep in the refrigerator and always set a little aside to start your next batch.

**Sour milk** This must be made with raw or

unpasteurized milk—pasteurized milk will not go sour but merely bad. The milk can be put in a bowl and left to stand in a warm place for several days until it thickens and sets (this is old-fashioned sour milk), but sour milk tastes better if it is soured quickly —in about eight hours—by adding a starter. Enjoy it very fresh with a sprinkling of sugar or with a slice of black bread and butter, or strain it to make a fresh-tasting curd cheese.

**Buttermilk** Add approximately two tablespoons of cultured buttermilk to every 2½ cups/6 dl of pasteurized, skimmed milk, cover and leave to stand in a warm place for about 12 hours. Buttermilk can be served as a drink or used to make scones and soda bread.

**Clotted cream** This can only be made with fresh, unpasteurized cream, which should be left to stand for six hours in summer, 12 in winter, in a heatproof dish. The cream is then scalded, but never boiled, over a low heat until small bubbles appear on the surface. Remove it from the heat immediately and store in a cold place for 12 hours. The thick, clotted cream can then be skimmed off the top.

**Yogurt** Any kind of milk except condensed milk can be used to make yogurt. The milk should be brought almost to the boil and maintained at 170–180°F/75–80°C for a few minutes, then cooled to about 110°F/43°C. This temperature needs to be maintained throughout the rest of the process so that the bacteria can grow. Stir one teaspoon of live yogurt or a packet of culture into each 5 cups/1 liter of milk and leave to stand overnight—a thermos bottle is excellent, or wrap the covered jars or bowls in a blanket so that the temperature is maintained. When the yogurt has reached the consistency of a thick custard, fruit, nuts and so forth can be added if you like. The yogurt should then go straight in the refrigerator.

When cooking with homemade yogurt it needs to be stabilized first to prevent it curdling. Make a little paste with cornstarch or potato flour and water. Heat the yogurt, stir in the paste and simmer for about 10 minutes until it thickens, then proceed with the recipe.

A delicious fresh cheese similar to *fromage blanc* can be made by putting yogurt in a cheesecloth bag and suspending it (attaching it to the taps over the sink is a good method) overnight to drip.

## To clarify butter

Melt the butter in a small saucepan and cook it for a few moments over a gentle heat, without browning. When it separates, remove from the heat, allow to settle for 10 minutes and then strain into a bowl through a paper towel moistened with hot water and placed over a sieve. Store in the refrigerator.

There are no rules about serving cheese at home, but if you want to enjoy this most splendid and noble of foods in all its variations, the first thing to do is to find a good cheese store run by someone who really cares, where the cheeses are kept in good condition and allowed to ripen to perfection quite naturally. (If cheeses are stored in a refrigerated storeroom or cabinet they will not mature properly.)

Having found your dealer, buy only one or two types of cheese at a time, taking one generous cheese or piece of cheese in perfect condition, rather than all sorts of bits and pieces. Keep it, if possible, in a cool place such as a cellar, between 50° and 60°F/10° and 15°C, rather than in a refrigerator, with the cut surfaces covered and the crust free to breathe, but protected from flies. If no cool place is available, keep it loosely wrapped (in transparent wrap that allows the passage of air) in a large airtight container in the bottom of the refrigerator. Take the cheese out a good hour before you serve it, to give it time to recover, and do not leave it too long before you eat it.

The serving of cheese varies from country to country. In France it is generally served after the salad, which has then done its job of refreshing the palate, with crusty French bread and good unsalted butter, which sets off the subtlest cheese flavor and will not spoil the most delicate. (Some of the richer Normandy cheeses obviously don't need any butter at all.) The Burgundy or Bordeaux served with the main course is finished off and appreciated with the cheese.

In Britain cheese is either eaten plain and hearty as a whole meal, with a nice hunk of fresh bread, or if it is a serious dinner it is brought to the table at the end of the meal, after the pudding, and is traditionally accompanied by good port. There are usually homemade breads and water biscuits or some other neutral crackers on the table for those who want them, and, again, unsalted butter. A strong cheese may be served with walnuts or celery or perhaps with crisp apples.

When cooking with cheese, it is unwise to use up any old scraps or ends of moldy cheese. The best results are obtained by using the best cheese. A piece of good, mature farmhouse Cheddar will be worth any amount of cheap factory-made block cheese—and, whatever the manufacturers may say, it is possible to tell the difference. Another thing to notice is the difference between cheeses made from pasteurized and unpasteurized milk. The unpasteurized cheese will go on developing and maturing because the milk that the cheese was made from was "alive," while pasteurized milk does not have the ability to develop the same subtle flavors and textures.

### Fresh cheeses

These are the simplest of all cheeses. They are made from the curds of soured milk or from milk that has been coagulated with the help of rennet—a curdling substance obtained from the stomachs of unweaned calves. They can also be made from whey, the thin liquid left over from cheese making. The milk used for making fresh cheese has often been skimmed of its fat content, but some fresh "cream" cheeses have a high fat content and make some of the world's most fattening desserts—cheesecake for one.

These cheeses used to be made on country or mountain farms from surplus milk or milk and cream, but are now usually mass produced in factories from pasteurized milk, and sadly in the process have become rather bland. Some fresh cheeses, however, are left to ripen and ferment for weeks or months, during which time they develop a characteristic bloom and an agreeable sharpness.

**Curd or cottage cheese** Made from the curds of skimmed milk and therefore having a low fat content, this cheese is popular with people trying to lose weight. The curds are broken into different sizes and cream is sometimes added, in which case it becomes creamed cottage cheese. Its slightly acid taste makes it a refreshing accompaniment to a summer fruit salad. In Germany, where a version known as quark is popular, it is often mixed with fruit purées, while in

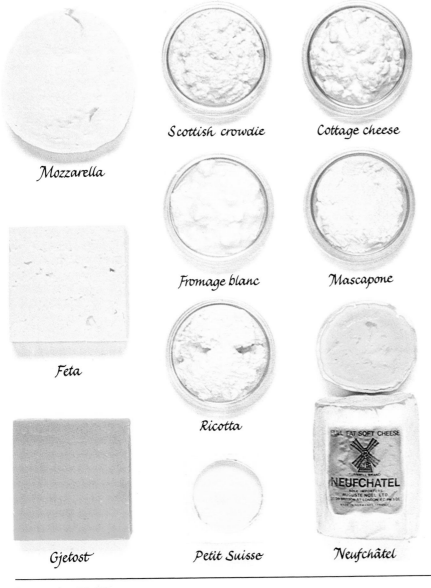

*Mozzarella*

*Scottish crowdie*

*Cottage cheese*

*Feta*

*Fromage blanc*

*Mascapone*

*Ricotta*

*Gjetost*

*Petit Suisse*

*Neufchâtel*

Provence a similar homemade white cheese is traditionally eaten with tiny new potatoes cooked in their skins. American pot cheese is a cottage cheese made from a large curd with no salt, while Scottish crowdie, also a cottage cheese, is made from fresh sweet milk and butter.

**Liptauer or Liptoi** Originally from Hungary, this ripened curd cheese is usually made from goats' or ewes' milk. It has a piquant taste and is delicious when blended with butter, seasoned with salt, paprika and caraway seeds and spread on rye bread.

**Mysost and Gjetost** In Norway any cheese which has been made from thickening the whey after it has been separated from the prepared curd is known as Mysost. There are several varieties, but the most popular is Gjetost. It is cooked until it looks like fudge and has a sweet flavor.

**Gomost** This Norwegian fresh cheese is made from soured, unsalted milk, and in France is known as Caillebotte. White and creamy, it is sometimes eaten with sugar or mixed with stewed or fresh ripe fruit.

**Pultost** This is also a Norwegian curd cheese but is stiffer and harsher than Gomost. It is made from whey or buttermilk and caraway seeds are often added.

**Ricotta** Traditionally made from the whey left over from making the Italian ewes'-milk pecorino cheese, this can also be made from the whey of other cheeses. Its dry, bland texture makes it ideal for mixing with fruit and raisins, or it can be eaten—as it is in Rome—with salt, or with cinnamon and sugar. It is especially good used with Parmesan, spinach and chard to stuff ravioli.

**Fromage blanc** One of the main ingredients of the delicate sauces of *Cuisine Minceur*, this popular French cheese is made from skimmed milk soured with a culture. An acceptable substitute can be made by combining equal parts of cottage cheese and yogurt with a squeeze of lemon juice and then whipping them in a food processor to a fine consistency. It is excellent with fresh raspberries or other berries.

**Cream cheese** Rich and creamy, soft and mild, this cheese can be made from whole milk or a combination of whole milk and cream. It is delicious when mixed with chopped raw vegetables or nuts and raisins and is also an essential ingredient of American cheesecakes. In France a vast number of fresh cream cheeses are sold, with varying fat contents: *double crème, triple crème* and, when put into heart-shaped molds and drained, *coeur à la crème*, eaten with wild strawberries and powdered sugar.

**Fontainebleau** Rarely available outside its native France, this cream cheese is made from a mixture of curd and whipped cream and is usually eaten with sugar. It can be made at home by blending demi-sel or Petit Suisse with whipped cream, but one is unlikely to produce the super-aerated result achieved by commercial manufacturers.

**Petit Suisse** French in origin, but called Swiss because a French-employed Swiss dairyman is credited with its invention, this mild, light little cream cheese is delicious with fruit and excellent in any recipe where cream cheese is required.

**Demi-sel** Small and square, soft and white,

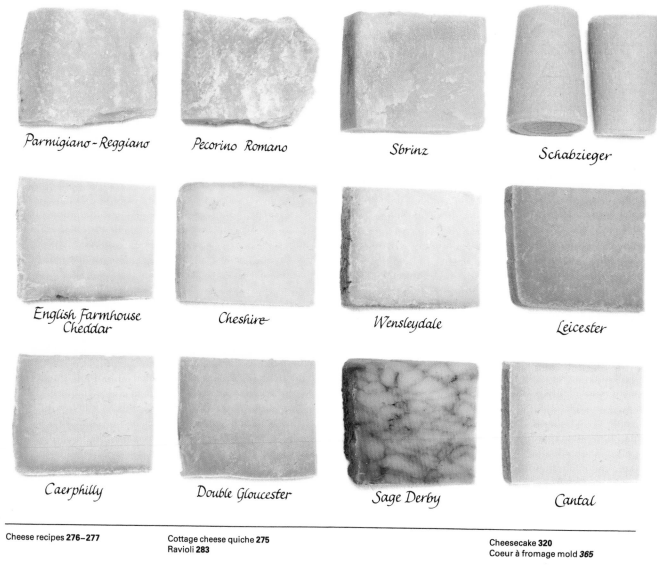

Parmigiano-Reggiano

Pecorino Romano

Sbrinz

Schabzieger

English Farmhouse Cheddar

Cheshire

Wensleydale

Leicester

Caerphilly

Double Gloucester

Sage Derby

Cantal

Cheese recipes **276–277**

Cottage cheese quiche **275**
Ravioli **283**

Cheesecake **320**
Coeur à fromage mold ***365***

this wrapped cheese is sold under a number of brand names but is especially good when it has been made in Normandy, where it originated. It has a high fat content and, as its name implies, is slightly salted.

**Neufchâtel** This whole cows'-milk cheese comes from Normandy. It is either eaten fresh, when it has the first growth of a soft white down and a delicate taste, or allowed to ripen until it is firm and pungent with a warm-colored, bloomy rind. It comes in a variety of shapes.

**Mascapone** Made in Lombardy and Tuscany, this cheese is enjoyed all over Italy, where it is sold in muslin bags and eaten with fruit or sugar and cinnamon.

**Mozzarella** This rubbery white cheese was originally made from water buffaloes' milk, but now cows' milk is often used; it is sold swimming in its own milk and is springy when fresh. It is served as an hors d'oeuvre in southern Italy, with olive oil and freshly ground pepper, and is ideal for cooking, being a traditional ingredient of pizza. Keep mozzarella fresh for days in a bowl of milky water in the lower part of the refrigerator.

**Feta** Crumbly and salty, this is the best known of the white cheeses ripened in brine or salt and known as "pickled" cheeses. It was originally made from ewes' milk by shepherds in the mountain regions near Athens and is popular in Greek cooking, especially crumbled into salads with tomatoes, cucumbers, black olives and olive oil. It can be made less salty by soaking it in milky water.

## Hard cheeses

The word "hard," when applied to cheeses, means that they have been subjected to pressure to make them dense. They will be softer or firmer according to their age.

Hard cheeses develop their various characteristics according to the milk used and the methods by which they are made. The speed of coagulation, the way the curd is cut, and whether the curd is then left or cut again, all affect the taste and texture, as does the treatment the cheese receives during the ripening process.

Some of these cheeses are derivations of more famous originals, but while some remain copies, others have developed a character of their own and deserve to be thought of as cheeses in their own right.

### Grana cheeses

The hard, grainy cheeses known collectively as grana are the well-known Italian grating cheeses, familiar to anyone who has ever eaten a plate of pasta or a bowl of minestrone soup. Their slow ageing process and low moisture content give them their long-keeping qualities and their crumbly texture.

The younger grana cheeses are more delicate and are delicious when broken in chunks and eaten accompanied by white wine.

**Parmesan**, or, more correctly, Parmigiano-Reggiano, the most famous and expensive of all the granas, is sweet and fragrant. It keeps for years, growing harder and fuller as it ages. When young, it can be eaten at the end of meals; it is an essential ingredient of many of the best and most characteristic northern Italian dishes, and is grated and then scattered on top of soups and pasta.

When buying Parmesan, the name Parmigiano-Reggiano burned in dots on the rind is proof of authenticity. The cheese should be straw colored and brittle, with pinpoint holes that are scarcely visible but give it a rocky surface. It should never be grey, sweaty or waxy, and should always smell fresh. It is possible to buy ground Parmesan, but it will be a poor substitute for fresh.

**Pecorino** is the name given to grana cheeses made from ewes' milk, which are used in much the same way as Parmesan. A pecorino is round, hard and white, with a yellow crust when mature (except for that made in Siena, which is red). The taste is strong, pungent and salty, and there are many varieties which often go by the names of the districts in which they are made. Pecorino Romano is the original variety and is still considered to be the best.

**Grana Padano** This is made in the Po valley and since it is cheaper than true Parmesan is often used in cooking.

**Sbrinz** This ancient and splendid Swiss cheese is equal in virtue (although distinct from) Parmesan. Its texture is granular and brittle and it has an uneven surface with pinprick holes. In central Switzerland it is often shaved in thin slivers and served with a glass of wine. It is also ideal for cooking.

**Schabzieger** Also known as green cheese, or in America as sapsago, this is a hard, truncated little green cone. Made from skimmed cows' milk, it ferments naturally and is mixed with pulverized blue melilot, or sweet clover, which gives it its green color and characteristic pungent flavor. It smells of coriander or cumin, and is used as a condiment for a variety of dishes.

### Cheddar-type cheeses

These are the real grass-root cheeses, made and eaten all over the world and used indiscriminately in recipes that call for cheese.

**English Cheddar** No hard cheese has been more widely imitated than English Cheddar, which originated in the small town of Cheddar, in Somerset, and was well established by the sixteenth century. It is a splendid all-purpose cheese, good to eat and to cook with. It has a sweet, full flavor when young and mild, and a sharp nutty flavor (often referred to as "tasty") when mature.

Mature English farmhouse Cheddars, still made on some farms and ripened for months or years, are among the world's greatest cheeses. They compress more than ten times their weight of creamy milk when pressed into a cylindrical form and wrapped in a cloth, which may then be waxed. A traditional Cheddar weighs about 50–60 lb/22.5–27 kg, while small, whole Cheddars, known as truckles, usually weigh about 14 lb/6 kg. English Cheddar is also made in large blocks, but these do not develop and mature like the traditional aged cheeses.

Smaller Cheddars of various shapes are made outside England, but may vary widely from the true Cheddar flavor. In New York state, the home of the first Cheddar-cheese factory in America, a number of Cheddars are still made in varying sizes. Wisconsin, Oregon and Vermont are also known for the quality of their Cheddars, but these, and most other Cheddars, like the Australian and New Zealand varieties, are made from pasteurized milk and lack the authentic taste of the English farmhouse variety. Canadian Cheddar, however, which is still sometimes made of unpasteurized milk, may have the characteristic tangy, nutty flavor. Look for Belleville-Brockville Cheddar (in a plain waxed cloth), or Black Diamond (with a black waxed surface).

**Cantal** Sometimes called the French Cheddar, Cantal has a smooth texture and, if the truth be told, a duller flavor than Cheddar. It is large, hard and yellow and is made in cylindrical forms, to which it may owe its old name, "fourme de Cantal." Cantal can be good if allowed to mature—it takes as long to ripen as Cheddar.

**Cheshire** Usually known as "Chester" abroad, and well liked under this name in France and Italy, this is the oldest of the British cheeses. It is crumbly, nutty and salty and can be red, white or blue. The red, which is dyed with anatto and is a marigold-orange, makes excellent eating as well as first-class soufflés. It is fat and rich, with a special piquancy that is also to be found in the white and blue varieties. The white variety, which is in fact a pale cream, is sharper than the red. It ripens faster but does not keep so well. The blue Cheshire is farmhouse made, and there is also an accidental blue Cheshire, which can start either white or red and is called, rather confusingly, Green Fade.

**Gloucester** This hard, robust English cheese originated in Gloucestershire and is now made in Somerset. It used to be made in two sizes—the well-matured double and the thinner and milder single—but only the large Double Gloucester survives. In taste it lies between Cheddar and Cheshire, although there is none of Cheshire's crumble about it. Farmhouse Gloucester, with its natural hard crust, should not be darker than straw colored. It is a good cooking cheese and makes delicious cheese straws.

**Caerphilly** One of the mildest, softest, crumbliest and fastest-ripening of the British hard cheeses, this was once known as the Welsh miners' cheese because it was the favorite ingredient of their packed lunch. But the best Caerphilly today is made on Somerset farms. Made of skimmed milk, it is slightly sour and is eaten rather immature. Its melting quality makes it suitable for dishes calling for a mild cheese flavor.

**Wensleydale** This is similar to Stilton in shape but smaller. White, moist and flaky, it has a delicately sour buttermilk flavor.

**Leicester** The largest English cheese in circumference, Leicester is a rich orange color and shaped like a millstone. It is mild and nutty, moist and flaky, and very different from Cheddar in texture and flavor, since the curd is shredded rather than milled into knobs. It is ideal for cheese sauce.

**Sage Derby** Once made for eating at harvest suppers, this farmhouse cheese is a sage-flavored version of plain Derby, which is similar to Cheddar but closer textured and more distinct in flavor. It should be aged for at least nine months and be mottled with natural-looking sage-green streaks, but at its worst it is heavily marbled with a vivid green, is artificial in taste and too waxy in texture to even recall the real thing.

Vermont sage cheese is a similar cheese, spicy and succulent.

## Gouda-type cheeses

Firm and fat, these familiar round cheeses become drier and sharper with age. Flavored with cumin or caraway seeds, they are good with rye bread and wine.

**Gouda** Made in the town of Gouda, outside Amsterdam, this is the archetypal Dutch cheese. It is creamy, golden and flattish, with a yellow paraffin-waxed protective skin. A mature Gouda will be more pungent than a youthful one. A black skin indicates that it is seven or more years old, when it becomes known as an Alt Gouda. Gouda étuve has been subjected to a prolonged maturing period or to artificially accelerated ripening. It is a simple eating cheese, which in its native Holland appears for breakfast, and in the kitchen it is fried with potatoes, grated into sauces and melted to make a type of fondue.

**Edam** Made from partially skimmed milk, Edam, encased in bright red or yellow livery for the export market, has a lower fat content than Gouda and is less smooth and round flavored. When young it tends to be boring, but once aged and ripened it acquires a rather pleasant mellowness.

**Mimolette** This is similar to Edam but bright orange inside, turning a rich red with age. The best Mimolettes are aged for up to two years, look like cannon balls dug up from an Armada wreck and when chipped away at have a glorious rich flavor, but most are young and flabby.

**Leyden** Resembling Gouda, this cheese has a sharp, tangy flavor. It is usually flavored with caraway seeds, but varieties with cloves and cumin are also available. It is branded with the crossed keys of the arms of the Dutch city of Leyden.

## Gruyère-type cheeses

Reminiscent of alpine meadows, these cheeses range from mild flavored to a rich, full nuttiness. Straw yellow in color, characterized by holes caused by gas forming during ripening, they are the cheeses most popular with French cooks who appreciate their melting qualities, so well suited to the making of gratins and sauces.

**Gruyère** This Swiss cheese is made of cows' milk and has a fairly smooth rind. Ivory-yellow with tiny pinprick holes spaced far apart, it should have a waxy rather than

*Alt Gouda*        *Leyden*        *Baby Edam*        *Edam*

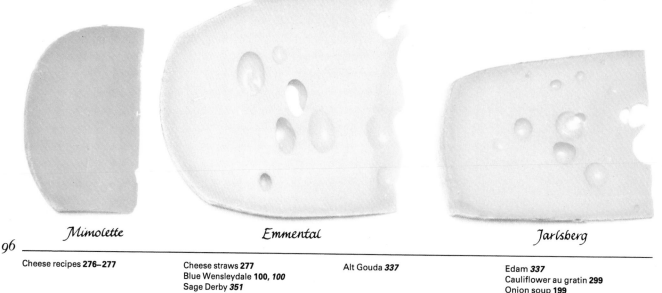

*Mimolette*        *Emmental*        *Jarlsberg*

a velvety surface. It is a main ingredient of the classic cheese fondue because of its fine melting qualities, and is also often served after a meal with grapes, figs or pears.

**Comté** Made in the Franche-Comté, this is a first cousin to Gruyère. The best "fruitiest" cheeses are made in village one-man dairies, or fruitières, to which the village farmers bring their milk, and can be identified by a green oval plaque on the outside of the whole cheese. These cheeses often have almost no holes at all, and are matured in the Franche-Comté itself.

**Emmental** This is the famous cheese with the large holes. It comes in huge, shiny golden wheels and its ivory-colored paste is riddled with bubbles, which form during its fermentation and cooling period. It has a sweet flavor that grows fuller with age and is excellent for eating and cooking.

**Fontina** Made in the Piedmont area of Italy and also in Switzerland, this is a fat, rich, softish cheese. Experts recommend the Swiss version as a table cheese and the Italian one for cooking. It melts beautifully and is used for Piedmontese fonduta, a fondue served with sliced white truffles.

**Appenzell** A Swiss relation of Emmental, washed in a mixture of white wine and brine, this makes a tasty element in a fondue when young. Mature, it is firm but buttery with a rich, sweet flavor.

**Jarlsberg** This popular Norwegian cheese is similar to Emmental but milder and more rubbery. Its taste is slightly nutty.

## Semi-hard cheeses

These cheeses, some of which resemble Cheddar, are characterized by their firm but elastic feel. They are sometimes soft and tender, but, unlike truly soft cheeses, do not become runny as they mature.

**Cacciocavallo** Made from cows' milk, this is often smoked. An ivory-white cheese with a golden-yellow to grey rind, it is sold in pairs joined by a string and is usually eaten at the end of a meal. It is one of the pasta filata, or drawn curd cheeses, so named because they are stretched into strands in hot water during their making.

**Provolone** There are two main types of Provolone: a pasta filata, or drawn curd cows'-milk cheese *dolce*, which is young and usually dull, and *piccante*, sometimes available from good Italian delicatessens, which is sharp, strong and often very salty, but a good cheese. It is sometimes smoked, and is molded by hand into various shapes.

**Monterey Jack** This pale California cheese, with small interior holes, comes in various shapes and degrees of softness. When it has a high moisture content and is quite soft, it is often called Jack, while the harder grating varieties are called Monterey.

**Colby** This cheese of Wisconsin origin is similar to Cheddar but has a more open texture. It is a soft, mild, bland cheese and does not keep so well as Cheddar.

**Tilsit** German in origin, this yellow cheese is pungent with a slight smear to its surface. It is sometimes made with caraway seeds.

**Danbo and Samsoe** These firm, nutty cheeses are the national standbys of Denmark, just as Cheddar is the standby of Britain (Samsoe is named after the island where it is made).

**Manchego** Made in Spain, this cheese has a high fat content, can be made from cows' or ewes' milk and is matured for up to three years, sometimes spending a year ripening in olive oil. It may be white or yellow, with or without eyes, and varies widely in taste.

## Soft cheeses

The characteristic flavor of the creamy white soft cheeses comes from bacterial growths, which begin at the outer edges of the cheese and move into the center. A ripe cheese will be soft at the center and can be tested by pressing lightly around the middle with the fingers. The bloomy white rinds are also a result of bacterial growth, natural in farm or artisan production, where the mold is established in the ripening premises, or induced in many factory-made cheeses by penicillin sprayed onto the crust. (In cheeses with a russet mold, which have a washed crust, the same applies.)

These cheeses are considered ready for eating when they are soft, with a bulge in the middle of the cut surface but no trace of runniness. Any smell of ammonia indicates that the cheese is past its best. Soft cheeses are delicious on French bread. The most famous varieties come from Normandy,

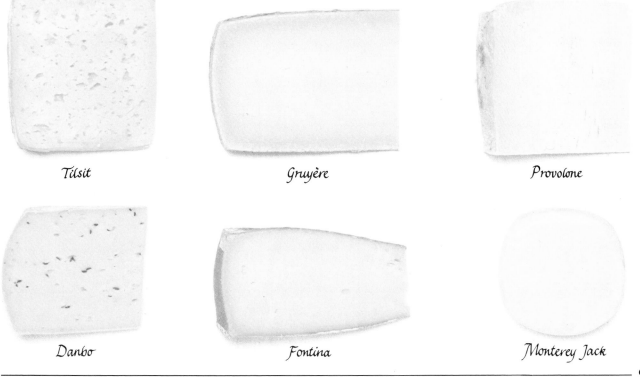

Tilsit

Gruyère

Provolone

Danbo

Fontina

Monterey Jack

which has some of the best pastures producing the richest, creamiest milk in the world (although Normandy farmers say artificial fertilizers are changing the quality of this wonderful milk).

**Camembert** A farmhouse Camembert is made from raw milk, while the more common factory-produced Camembert is always made from pasteurized milk. The best Camemberts are from Normandy, and are made in rounds weighing 8–9 oz/225–255 g. Camembert is also available in half moons and in portions, but unfortunately is only reliable if ripened as a whole cheese: proportion and thickness of crust and consistency of the interior are all affected by alteration of size or shape before ripening. A really fine Camembert is never chalky.

**Brie** A whole round, flat Brie usually measures 14 in/35.5 cm across and is sold in wedges. The unliquefied part in the center of a ripe Brie is important and is called "the soul of the Brie." Farmhouse Brie, known as Brie de Meaux fermier, is the creamiest variety and has a bouquet that is full and mild. (Nowadays Bries are mainly produced in factories and there are many imitations, but obtain unpasteurized farmhouse Brie from Normandy should you ever get the chance.) The Brie de Melun affiné, a smaller cheese, is one of the finest of all.

**Pont-l'Evêque** This cheese is square, soft and fat, with a shiny golden or reddish salty rind and warm farmyard taste. It should always have Pays d'Auge and *lait cru* or *non-pasteurisé* stamped somewhere on the wrapping paper or box, proving that it comes from unpasteurized milk.

**Livarot** This cheese, still made at its place of origin and elsewhere in the Pays d'Auge, is round, weighs about 1 lb/450 g and is about twice the depth of a Pont l'Evêque. It has a thicker crust and, although it is obviously of the same family, quite a distinct flavor. Traditionally it is bound with five strips of raffia-like leaf or paper.

**Vacherin** Usually banded with spruce bark, which not only saves it from collapse but also gives it a faint aroma of resin, Vacherin is a seasonal cheese, made in winter by the Comté-producing farms when there isn't enough milk, or transport is too difficult to produce the Comté they make in summer. Slice it like a Brie with a very sharp knife to cut the bark, as the outside crust is delicious and should not be wasted.

**Maroilles** Square and strong smelling, this comes from Flanders and is ripened for up to four months, with much crust-washing. It is delicious with a full-bodied wine and is used to make *goyère* and *flamiche*, the cheese pies peculiar to Flanders.

**Reblochon** This fine cheese from Savoy is smooth and creamy with a pinkish-gold crust and a strong farmyard flavor.

**Port-Salut** Also called Port au Salut—haven of rest—after the Trappist abbey where it was first made, this is a velvety smooth whole-milk cheese, semi-soft or semi-hard, and mildly pungent. One variety is still made by the monks under the name of Fermiers-Réunis at their Champagne dairy from the unpasteurized milk of their cows. Commercial Port-Salut, made by a farmers' cooperative at Entrammes, is a more rubbery and less tasty affair, as is the Bricquebec—a similar cheese made in the monastic dairy.

**Taleggio** Made from whole cows' milk, this comes from Lombardy in Italy. It has a smooth pink skin with a straw-colored interior, and is fruity in flavor.

**Munster** Originating in the Vosges, this is the national cheese of Alsace. Its paste is firm and its rind red and smooth. It has a pungent smell and flavor, and is traditionally eaten with rye bread, caraway seeds and chopped onions.

**Limburger** This cheese may take the form of a log, a corrugated roll or a little disc or blob and has a moist, pale rind and an overpowering smell. It is an acquired taste and should be eaten with robust country bread.

**Liederkranz** Rather like a non-odorous Limburger, this gold crusted, tawny cheese is America's best soft cheese.

**Bel Paese** is the trade name for a soft, cream-colored cheese of which there are many local and factory-made variations throughout Italy. It is tender and mild.

**Tommes** This is the family name of a large number of rustic cheeses, made of ewes', goats' or cows' milk in almost any shape. The Tommes are from Savoy, all along the southern mountain ranges of France and in the east of Switzerland. Tomme au Marc is coated in fermented grape "marc"—made from the pressed skins and seeds of grapes left over from wine-making, which gives it its characteristic taste, while Tomme de Savoie has a nutty flavor.

**Saint Nectaire** A mountain cheese from the Auvergne, this is a round, flat cheese with a dark rind and a soft, supple but not creamy, straw-colored inside. It has a nice light flavor.

**Epoisses** A very smelly cows'-milk cheese from Burgundy, this is cylindrical and reddish on the outside, and soft, oozy and rich inside with a strong earthy taste. It is traditionally aged in brine and marc.

**Soumaintrain** Like Epoisses, this flat, round cheese comes from Burgundy. It is semi-soft with a sticky red-brown crust, a strong smell and an earthy taste.

**Chaource** is one of those small, deep, white, downy, luxurious-looking cheeses that give a fresh note to an otherwise heavy meal. It has a faintly acid, fruity flavor and a velvety rather than creamy texture.

## Goats' cheeses

There are infinite varieties of goats' cheeses, of which the vast majority are simply described as "chèvres" and have no distinguishing names. They are made on small farms and dairies all over France and throughout the Mediterranean, and are usually known as "frais" or "mi-frais," which means fresh; "affiné," which has been matured and should be velvety, occasionally creamy and fairly soft; and "vieux," which is well aged and varies from soft and creamy to rock hard. They should not be chalky or soapy—this may be a sign that they have been refrigerated.

The flavors of goats' cheeses vary according to the ripening period, the locality and altitude, which have a bearing on the taste and quality of the milk, and the different mold cultures, which affect flavor and texture. But in general goats' cheeses, whether strong or mild, should taste nutty and sweet with a goaty piquancy. Some are flavored with chives or garlic and other fresh herbs, while others are rolled in mountain ash. Some goat cheeses are sold sitting on the straw mat on which they have been drained. These are delicious tasting and have a distinct country flavor.

## Blue cheeses

Blue cheeses originally started to turn blue by a happy accident. Roquefort, the ancestral blue cheese, was, at first, just a humble curd cheese made of ewes' milk, and had it not been for a lovelorn shepherd who, as legend has it, set off in pursuit of a country girl, leaving his luncheon cheese in a limestone cave, the blue mold might never have happened. However, returning after a week or so of dalliance, the shepherd found that his lunch had changed in texture, color and taste and become "blue." Since that time, the penicillin molds that turn cheese blue have been isolated and identified, and blue cheeses have multiplied. The cheese's paste itself may be firm or creamy, buttery or brittle, and any color from chalk white to deep golden-yellow. The only thing that the paste of a blue cheese should never be is brown and dingy.

**Roquefort** The veining of Roquefort, a ewes'-milk cheese, is due to *Penicillium glaucum*—now better known as *Penicillium roquefortii*—which thrives in the caves high upon the Cambalou plateau. These ancient caves, cool and damp owing to underground springs, are still used for maturing Roquefort. The blue veining is now accelerated by layering the curd with crumbled bread molds, but even so, the ripening process still takes about three months, and the cheese will not be at its best until it is at least six months old.

A Roquefort in its prime is creamy, with green-blue veins. Persillé—parsleyed—is the French term. It is smooth, firm and buttery when cut, but crumbly owing to the mold, which should be evenly distributed. It is strong, with the fine grain and the extra pungency that ewes' milk produces. It should not, however, be salty —although those for export tend to be over-salted as a precaution against spoiling.

**Bleu de Corse** is a cheese made by Corsican shepherds and sent to the Roquefort caves to become blue and to mature. It is similar to Roquefort in taste.

**Gorgonzola** Once exclusive to the Italian village of that name, this cheese is now produced all over the lush plain of Lombardy. The squat, cylindrical cheeses, made of cows' milk, are no longer matured in the local caves but in the great maturing houses in the district. *Penicillium mycelium* accounts for the streaking. Although Gorgonzola is often described as an early copy of Roquefort, it is softer, milder, creamier and less salty. It should have very little rind, being wrapped in foil, and should be rather smooth and blue-grey. The cheese should be springy to the touch. It may smell a little musty, but should never be overpowering. Other Italian blues include the creamy factory-made

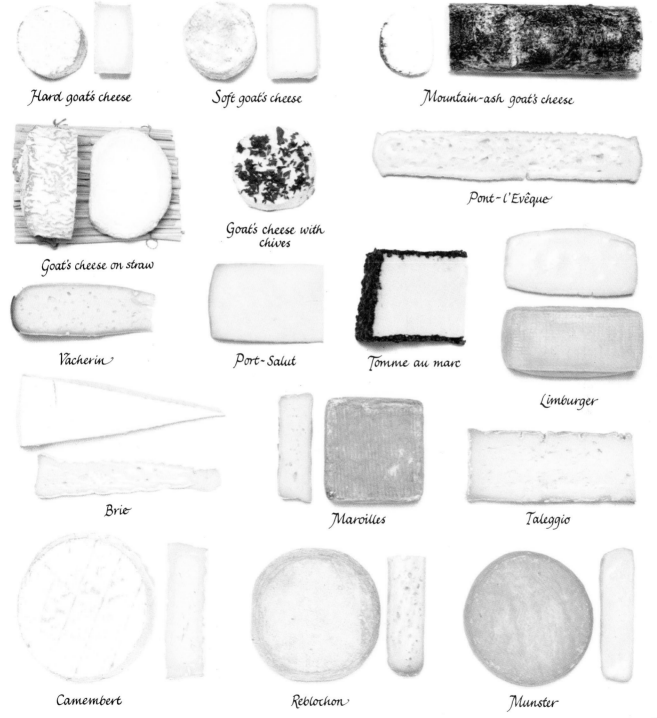

Hard goat's cheese

Soft goat's cheese

Mountain-ash goat's cheese

Goat's cheese on straw

Goat's cheese with chives

Pont-l'Evêque

Vacherin

Port-Salut

Tomme au marc

Limburger

Brie

Maroilles

Taleggio

Camembert

Reblochon

Munster

Dolcelatte and Mountain Gorgonzola, which is smaller than a true Gorgonzola.

**Pipo Crème**, a cylindrical cheese, was first produced as a counter-attraction to Gorgonzola but has a quite distinct character.

**Danish Blue** is similar to Roquefort but is made with cows' milk. It can be cylindrical, rectangular or square, and is white with blue veins. It has a high fat content and the saltiness inevitable in this type of cheese.

**Bresse Bleu** A French cheese similar to Gorgonzola, this soft blue cheese comes from the Bresse region, which also produces a more stodgy blue called, confusingly, Bleu de Bresse, another stodgy one called France Bresse, and most recently Belle Bressane, with a hole in the middle.

**Torta di Gordenza**, also marketed as Gorgonzola con Mascapone, is a cheese made from layers of piquant Gorgonzola and fresh Mascapone—a delicious combination, like fresh clotted cream.

**Bleu de Causses** This is a cheese of high quality, somewhat similar to Roquefort, coming from the same region and having the same mold, but made with cows' milk.

**Fourme d'Ambert** A naturally blued cows'-milk cheese, this is from the Auvergne. It is exceptional in being almost the only non-English blue cheese to have a hard crust, which is grey flecked with yellow and red. It comes in cylinders weighing about 3 lb/1.5 kg and is sharp and strong.

**Stilton** One of the very few English foods to be admired by the French, this is a highly protected cheese made only in Derbyshire, Leicestershire and parts of Nottinghamshire. Although a noble cheese, Stilton is a comparative latecomer and in fact was never made at Stilton, but it was there, at the Bell Inn in the eighteenth century, that it was first served. It should be a creamy ivory color with greenish-blue veining throughout. The paste should be open textured, velvety and never dry, hard or salty.

Stilton is served with a white napkin wrapped around it, and should be stored wrapped in cloth. Should the cheese become dry in spite of this, it helps to moisten the cloth and to leave it until the dampness restores the cheese's proper consistency.

**Blue Wensleydale** Among the other English blue cheeses is Blue Wensleydale (now made in Derbyshire). Claimed by its admirers to be even better than Stilton, it should be creamier, sweeter and nuttier, but is nowadays not as soft as it should be.

**Dorset Blue** is a hard white cheese with bright blue veining. It is made of skimmed milk, which makes it agreeably sharp.

**Other blues** There are a number of little-known blue cheeses made in France and elsewhere, and a mysterious blue Brie, apparently made in Germany, has appeared, and is actually rather good. Also worth trying if you see them are the strong and fruity Bleu de Quercy and Bleu de Sassenage, the delicate Saingorlou and the very pungent Bleu de Tignes and Bleu de Sainte-Foy. There are also the cheeses called "Persillé" —Persillé des Aravis, du Grand Bornand and de Thônes are goats'-milk blues.

Gorgonzola

Blue Wensleydale

Torta of Mascapone and Gorgonzola

Stilton

Roquefort

Dolcelatte

Danish Blue

Bresse Bleu

# Cooking Fats and Oils

Every cook in the world uses fat or oil of some kind as a cooking medium. In cool northern regions the fats from grass- and grain-fed animals are traditionally used, while in the hot Mediterranean countries, where the blessed olive tree grows, olive oil is the essential ingredient. Other regions may use goose fat or mustard seed oil, grapeseed oil or sesame oil, each giving its distinctive flavor to the local dishes.

Today, the limitations of climate count for far less than they used to and we can obtain and cook with almost any medium we choose. But the flavor of food depends very much on what fat or oil is used, and a good cook will always try to use the right medium for the right dish in order to keep the flavor as authentic as possible.

Unfortunately, the amount of fat, whether animal or vegetable, in our Western diets has come under major criticism from doctors and nutritionists. Not only do we get our chief source of energy from fats that are an "invisible" part of most foods, but we are all too likely to load up on rich fats in the form of butter, lard and oils. While vegetable fats, unlike the traditionally suspect animal fats, contain no cholesterol, the cook should use either type only as part of a well-balanced diet that includes plenty of fibrous, non-fatty foods such as vegetables and fruit.

## Fats

To the cook, fats are for the most part of animal origin and are either purchased, or collected at home from a roasting joint and then left to solidify. It is this quality of solidifying naturally that distinguishes fats from oils. However, vegetable oils can now be solidified by various chemical processes, so we have solid blocks of vegetable fats at our disposal as well as animal fats, and very often margarines and shortenings are a blend of the two.

### Margarines

All margarines are based on fats and oils, and most contain skimmed milk or whey. Many contain animal fats together with fish and vegetable oils, unless the label specifically reads "edible vegetable oils" as opposed to simply "edible oils."

The taste and texture of margarine differ slightly according to brand but, with the exception of the all-important flavor, its characteristics in the kitchen are somewhat similar to those of butter, except that it is not particularly suitable for frying since it splutters and burns easily. Soft margarines are too soft to be rubbed into flour, so when making pastry with this type of fat mix the margarine, water and only a third of the flour at the start. Gradually add the rest of the flour until you have a smooth ball of dough which can then be kneaded and rolled out as usual.

Low-fat spreads, which usually appear on supermarket shelves alongside margarines, are designed simply for spreading and cannot be satisfactorily used for cooking.

### Suet

The word suet comes from the Latin for tallow, and suet was once used instead of wax to make candles. Like wax, suet is stiff and melts slowly. It is the firm, white fat surrounding beef or lambs' kidneys, but beef suet is the one you are more likely to find. If you are shredding suet, a little flour sprinkled over the suet will keep it from getting too sticky. Beef suet has a wide range of uses. It goes into sweet puddings such as Christmas pudding and jam roly-poly, and into savory ones like steak-and-kidney and steak-and-mushroom puddings. A good suet crust, made with self-rising flour and mixed with a light hand, is one of the most satisfying of winter foods.

### Lard

Before technology took a hand lard had to be used fresh, had a strong taste and no creaming properties. Now it is usually light and clean tasting and is used mainly for frying—it is the traditional medium for deep frying doughnuts and fish and chips—and for baking, where its creaming properties are appreciated. Lard is the essential ingredient in making a good raised crust for pork pies (when making pastry, a mixture of butter and lard produces a crisp, light, crumbly texture). It also adds lightness to scones.

The best lards are those rendered from the stomach fat—the flare or leaf fat—of the bacon pig, and from the fat that lies directly under the skin of the back. Lard made from other pig fat has a stronger taste and is the lard most widely sold; add a sprig or two of rosemary to the melted fat to overcome any porky taste when frying potatoes and other delicate foods.

**Caul fat** After the fat has been removed to make fine quality leaf lard, a very thin membrane of fat that surrounds the stomach is separated to become the delicious and delicate caul fat, or lace fat. This fat with its lace-like appearance is sold in large white sheets in French, German and Chinese shops. It needs to be soaked in warm water until it softens and becomes pliable for wrapping around sausages and chopped meats as in French charcuterie, while the English use it to enclose fresh faggots. In Chinese cooking, caul fat is used to envelop poultry before it is deep fried or baked. The fat provides a basting layer, melts into nothing and leaves behind a delicate, delicious golden brown crust.

**Fatback** This is the fat from the loin of the pig. When cut thinly and beaten into long pieces it is used primarily for larding dry meats—veal and game birds, particularly pheasant and partridge. The pieces are tied over the birds like a waistcoat and baste the flesh during cooking. Cut into strips called lardons, they can be inserted with a special needle into the flesh of dry meat to keep it succulent while it cooks.

It is also used for lining terrines for pâtés and for rendering lard at home. This is done by cutting the fatback into very small cubes and then gently melting the cubes with a little water in a very low oven. When the water has evaporated, the clear liquid fat is poured off into a jar until all that is left in the pan are the crisp brown scratchings, or grattons. These are sometimes mixed into the lard to give extra flavor and texture.

### Drippings

A good old-fashioned way of acquiring a delicious fat is to strain and reserve the fat that has dripped off roasting meat. Once these drippings have solidified, the jelly or juice underneath is removed (it is excellent in gravy or stock) and any sediment from the bottom of the cake of drippings is scraped away and disposed of.

Drippings from different kinds of meat should not be mixed. Beef drippings can be used to fry the meat for beef stews; pork drippings can be used for any savory dish. Chicken fat, when rendered, is fine and delicate and is much used in Jewish cooking, where it replaces lard. Use the fat from geese or ducks for poultry dishes and fried potatoes, or eat it on hot toast. Lamb drippings smell and taste rather unpleasant and are not used very much, except in the Middle East where lambs' tail fat is widely used.

### Shortenings

All hard fats are shortenings, meaning that they are capable of producing a crumbly "short" crust (the greater the amount of fat in the mixture, the greater the shortening effect). However it is the white cooking fats that are neither pure lard nor drippings that have claimed the name.

White cooking fats may be made of blended vegetable oils or a mixture of vegetable and animal fats or fish oils, depending on what is cheapest on the world market at any particular time. In taste they are bland, in texture light and fluffy. When using white fat for frying, break it into small pieces so that it all heats up at the same rate. If you use

# Cooking Fats and Oils

shortening for making pastry, look for a variety that has been aerated or whipped. This will certainly make creaming and rubbing in easier, but remember that it is totally flavorless and will not contribute one iota towards the flavor of a pie or tart.

## Oils

Unlike fats, oils are liquid at room temperature. They perform the same function as fat in shallow and deep frying, but oils have the advantage of being reusable, as long as they are not overheated and are carefully strained after each use. (But beware of the taint of overused or overheated oil, which spoils the flavor of so many fried foods eaten in restaurants.)

When frying, oils should be heated slowly to the correct temperature. Underheating causes too much oil to be absorbed by the food and overheating is dangerous. An overheated oil decomposes and will start to smoke and eventually, if heated further, develops toxins and will finally burst into flames. Any oil if overheated by accident should be thrown away. A simple rule is to wait for a blue haze to rise from the oil but never allow it to smoke. Test the temperature of the oil with a thermometer: it should be around 320°F/160°C for meat and up to 360°F/180°C for French fries and other vegetables. Poultry and fish come in between. If you lack a thermometer, fry a small cube of day-old bread in the heated oil: if the bread turns golden and crisp in one minute, the temperature is roughly right.

The object of deep frying is to seal the surface of the food; the pieces to be fried should be as nearly as possible of uniform size so that they cook evenly. The crisp outside crust encloses a food whose inside is cooked in the heat of its own steam. If you dip the food in batter, the excess should be drained off before you put it into the oil, and if you bread crumb it, press the crumbs in well so that the oil remains as free as possible of small, dark brown and finally burned crumbs, which give the oil a bitter flavor.

A good oil should last for up to five fryings. Strain it well after each use. When reused it should neither foam nor smoke excessively: the smoke point gradually decreases with age. It should not smell or look dark or thick. These are definite signs that the oil has reached the end of its useful life.

There are a great many oils in the world. Even without going into such exotics as brazil-nut oil, used as a hair dressing by the inhabitants of the Amazon rain forests, or juniper oil for gin or even clove oil for toothache, the subject of oils is a complex one. To start with—and this goes a long way to help one make a sensible choice—there is the distinction between oils that are unrefined and refined.

**Unrefined oils** are those that have simply been cold pressed and then left to mellow for a few months before being bottled. They tend to be cloudy but come to the customer in full possession of their natural flavor and color. Often called cold-pressed oils, they are—not surprisingly—more expensive than their refined counterparts.

**Refined oils** have been extracted by pressure under heat. They are then degummed, neutralized, heated and blanched, "winterized" to keep them from going cloudy, deodorized by an injection of steam and finally given artificial preservatives to make up for those that they have lost in the processing.

## Olive oil

Indispensable for pasta, salads and many Mediterranean recipes, olive oil, the finest of all oils, varies in character from country to country. Choice is often a matter of personal preference. Generally speaking, Spanish olive oil has a strong flavor, Greek a heavy texture, Provençal a fruity and Italian a nutty taste.

The very best and most expensive olive oil, from whatever country it originates, is virgin oil from the first cold pressing of the olives. The best virgin oils come from green Provençal or Tuscan olives (the town of Lucca is reputed to produce the best Tuscan olive oil).

Virgin oil is usually a greenish color—often helped by putting a few leaves into the press—but may also be golden yellow. It is best for salads and for mayonnaise, where its beautiful, fruity flavor can be most appreciated.

Subsequent pressings produce olive oil with a blander and less characterful taste and a paler color. These cheaper grades are sometimes blended with one another and might then be mixed with a proportion of virgin oil to improve the taste. Use the less expensive grades for cooking. When used for shallow-frying vegetables, olive oil imparts a glorious mellow flavor particularly complementary to Mediterranean cooking, and it is essential for making ratatouille and cold vegetable dishes. Olive oil is unsuitable for deep frying as it cannot tolerate high frying temperatures.

## Peanut oil

Known also as groundnut oil, arachide oil, *huile d'arachides* and arachis oil, this is the favorite cooking oil of those French chefs who do not cling to olive oil. It is often considered a good replacement for olive oil, particularly when used for frying, as it has very little smell and no flavor.

Peanut oil is used for salads and mayonnaise when a delicate flavor is wanted,

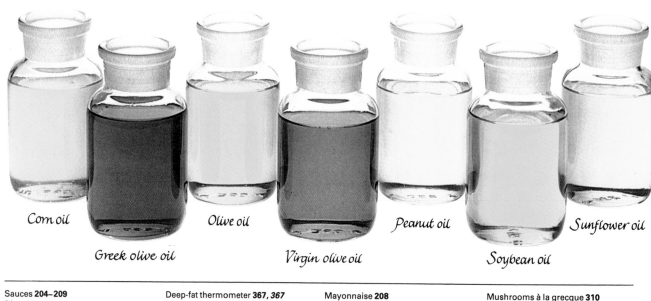

Corn oil    Greek olive oil    Olive oil    Virgin olive oil    Peanut oil    Soybean oil    Sunflower oil

although extra seasoning, lemon juice or vinegar may be required.

Less refined oil can impart a slight peanut flavor to food such as fried chicken. The Chinese, who use this bland oil a great deal in their cooking, like to flavor it by frying a few slices of fresh ginger, garlic or a scallion in it before use.

## Corn oil

This is one of the most economical oils for shallow and deep frying, having one of the highest smoke points. Corn oil can also be used for salad dressings. Its admirers say it is rich and bland; its detractors find it lifeless, weak and flabby. Unrefined, it has a strong taste of maize about it. Refined, it is practically tasteless when cold, but surprisingly produces a strong and not very agreeable smell during frying.

## Sesame oil

There are various types of sesame oil. The thicker and browner the oil, the more aromatic it is—the Chinese use this dark oil, made from toasted sesame seeds, more for seasoning than for frying, as it burns easily.

The pale yellowish oil that appears in many Indian and Middle Eastern dishes is quite different from the brown; it is odorless and light textured.

Ali Baba's efficacious formula "Open Sesame" was based on the fact that sesame pods burst open with a sharp sound to release their seeds. The jars in which the thieves hid were no doubt waiting for that year's sesame oil.

## Sunflower oil

In the USSR, the main producer of this oil, people crack sunflower seeds between their teeth as a health-giving snack. Sunflower oil is light, mild and thinly textured.

Excellent for cooking with and good for using with more expensive oils when making delicate salad dressings, it is the best oil for all recipes where a fairly neutral oil is required.

## Safflower oil

This oil, so often confused with sunflower oil, is made from the safflower, a pretty thistle-like plant with orange, red or yellow flowers. Usually a deep golden color, safflower oil is found refined in supermarkets and unrefined in health food stores. It is very light and used in the same way as sunflower oil. It is also the oil most recommended for use in the low-cholesterol diets of heart patients.

## Mustard seed oil

Although mustard seed oil has a distinctive smell and taste when cold, most of this is driven off when the oil is heated. This oil is used in parts of India as an alternative to ghee. It is also used in Kashmiri curries and as a preservative in pickles, including Italy's colorful *mostarda di frutta*.

## Rapeseed oil

This oil, also known as colza, is widely used in Mediterranean countries and the East for frying and salads.

Rapeseed oil is also often blended with other oils by the makers of margarines.

## Soybean oil

More oil is produced from soybean than from any other plant and most of it goes into the blending of oils, cooking fats and margarines. A good brand, marked 100 percent soybean oil, is quite pleasant in salads, although it tends to have a heavy texture. When heated, it smells rather of the seaside, and has a strong flavor.

## Grapeseed oil

This light, aromatic oil is a by-product of the wine industry and is popular in France and Italy. The seeds yield a golden oil.

Used in salads and for gentle frying, this oil comes into its own as the best cooking medium for fondue bourguignonne.

## Walnut oil

Cold pressed from dried walnuts, strong, with a deliciously nutty flavor, this is an unusual salad oil. It is especially good on a spinach salad, with a few walnuts added.

Walnut oil does not keep well and should be bought in small quantities. It is also very expensive, and is seldom used for frying or baking.

## Almond oil

When almond kernels are simply pressed they produce a clear, pale yellow oil. Oil obtained from the bitter almond is used to make sweet almond oil, a fatty oil that can be used at home for confectionery making. When further processed this oil becomes oil of bitter almonds, an essential flavoring, now often produced synthetically.

## Wheat germ oil

Extracted by cold pressing, this pleasant, nutty-tasting oil is mainly taken by the spoonful as a vitamin E supplement. It is also used in salad dressings, either by itself or, since it is expensive, blended with other oils. It can be used to flavor yogurt.

## Vegetable oils

The most economical oils on the market are the highly refined pale golden oils that are a blend of various vegetable products—soybean oil, cottonseed oil, rapeseed oil, palm oil and coconut oil. They have a high smoke point, little taste and are good for frying.

*Grapeseed oil*     *Sesame oil*     *Chinese sesame oil*     *Walnut oil*     *Almond oil*     *Wheat germ oil*     *Safflower oil*

# Grains, Breads and Thickening Agents

Besides yielding flour for our daily bread, grains are the staple foods of a great many countries. The porridge of Scotland, the polenta of Italy, the couscous of North Africa, the kasha of Russia and countless other grain dishes are all basically the same thing: the local grain, in one form or another, cooked in boiling water until swollen and tender and then eaten plain or with whatever else makes up the national diet.

## Wheat

One of the first cereals ever to be cultivated, wheat has become the most valuable of all food grains, widely used in all its stages from whole and unadulterated to finely milled and sifted. When "flour" is called for in modern recipes it is invariably wheaten flour that is meant. Broadly speaking, the wheat flours can be divided into those made from the high-gluten, hard or strong wheats grown in hot, dry areas and used for bread and pasta, and the soft-grained or weak varieties grown in temperate places, suitable for cakes, cookies and general use.

**Whole wheat grain** is available in health food stores. To eat it as a grain, soak it overnight before cooking and then boil it in plenty of water for about two hours. Eat it in the same way as rice with meat, fish or vegetables, or mixed into a salad. In earlier times it was cooked overnight at a low temperature, ready to eat as a sort of porridge called "frumenty," delicious with honey.

**Cracked or kibbled wheat** is simply the whole wheat grain cracked between rollers. It is eaten in the same way as whole wheat but takes only about 20 minutes to cook. It is also good cooked like porridge as a hot breakfast cereal.

**Burghul or bulgur** is cracked wheat that has been hulled and parboiled, a process which makes the grain easier to cook and gives it a less pronounced flavor and a lighter texture. Eat it in place of rice, or in the Lebanese salad called *tabbouleh*, for which burghul is mixed with chopped onions, parsley and mint.

**Bran** consists of the thin, papery outer covering of the wheat grain. It is a by-product of the refining processes of the whole wheat grain and can be bought in health food stores and some supermarkets. For extra roughage, sprinkle it on breakfast cereals, eat plain with milk and sugar, or add it to bread, cake and cookie mixtures.

**Wheat germ**, the heart of the wheat grain, is often extracted or destroyed during wheat refining processes. It can be bought toasted from supermarkets and raw from health food stores. The raw variety should be kept in the refrigerator, since the oil in the germ quickly goes rancid (it is often extracted from flour to improve the flour's keeping qualities). Sprinkle it on breakfast cereals or mix it with yogurt. When baking bread, sprinkle wheat germ on the sides of the bread pan for a nice finish to the loaf.

**Semolina** is wheat in its intermediate stage between grain and flour. When wheat grain is first milled it is separated into bran, wheat germ and endosperm. The first millings of the floury yellow endosperm are known as semolina and can be found in Italian specialty stores.

When medium-ground, semolina is quite widely used in making desserts ranging from milk and fruit puddings to the powerfully sweet, round Indian cakes, for which the semolina is first fried and then mixed with raisins, nuts and honey. The finest ground semolina is used to make one kind of Italian gnocchi. Semolina made from hard durum wheat is used commercially to make pasta, but it is unsuitable for home pasta making. (To make your own pasta use a good, un-bleached, plain flour.) Flour-coated semolina grains make couscous, part of the excellent North African dish of the same name. Couscous semolina can be purchased precooked.

**Farina** Similar to semolina, this well-known breakfast cereal can be used as a substitute in recipes calling for semolina but because it has been processed it will not produce the full-flavored results of semolina.

**Whole grain or graham flour** This consists of the whole of the wheat grain. Stone-ground flour has a better flavor than roller milled since the slow grinding of the stones doesn't overheat and destroy the vitamins in the wheat germ, but it does not keep as well so do not buy more than a month's supply at a time and keep it in a cool place. It makes a dense loaf with the warm earthy taste of the wheat. For a less heavy loaf, a good compromise is to mix whole grain flour half and half with white flour. For a nutty wheat pastry, sieve the flour first and use the fine part to make the dough. Then when the dough is kneaded and ready for shaping, roll it in the remaining coarse particles of bran.

**Whole wheat flours** are actually flours from which some of the bran and germ have been removed, leaving behind between 80 and 90 percent of the grain. The resulting flour is lighter in texture than whole grain flour and so produces a less dense dough. Loaves made from whole wheat flour rise well, have a smooth crust and still retain some of the sweet nutty taste of the wheat. The name whole wheat is often applied to whole grain flour.

**All-purpose flour** In the United States, this accommodating, general-purpose flour is milled and refined from a blend of hard and soft wheats. It contains virtually none of the grain's bran and germ but is required by law to be "enriched," which means that some of the lost nutrients are restored during processing. As its name suggests, it is suitable for all types of cooking from bread to sponge cakes, for coating and thickening and for all pastry making. The unbleached variety, which has been allowed to whiten and mature naturally, has a creamy color and a better flavor than the bleached variety, which will have been whitened or "bleached" artificially.

**Cake flour** is the refined and bleached product of soft wheat. Soft wheat flours produce only a small amount of gluten and so give a light, short texture in baking. Its fine silky consistency is particularly good for producing even-textured cakes but it is not recommended for general use.

**Self-rising flour** is plain, soft flour mixed with baking powder and salt. These chemicals, however, gradually lose their potency, so it is best to use a bag of self-rising flour within two or three months. Use it for making cakes and in any recipe that calls for the addition of baking powder.

**Strong plain white flour**, familiar in Britain, is usually a blend of soft and hard wheats. This type of flour is suitable for all yeast baking and produces excellent loaves, buns and pizza dough. It is also good for puff and flaky pastry.

## Corn

Second in importance only to wheat, there are countless varieties of corn—some hard, some soft, some creamy, some golden, some red, some purple.

**Hominy** is an old American Indian name for hulled and dried white corn. It can be bought either dry or ready-cooked in cans. The dried grains must be soaked overnight before use. Hominy is also available ground and is then known as hominy grits. The whole grains are cooked and eaten as a side dish and as an addition to stews. Coarse-ground hominy grits cooked in milk and served with butter and syrup or with gravy is a traditional breakfast dish in the southern states of America. Finer ground grits are used in cakes and puddings and to give body to casseroles and stews.

**Cornmeal, maize meal, polenta**, ground from white or yellow corn, is available in coarse and medium grinds. The best cornmeal is ground by the old millstone method, but it does not keep as well as cornmeal ground by more modern processes so should be bought in smaller quantities and kept in a cool place or in the refrigerator.

In the United States there are a number of simple cornmeal dishes such as griddled jonnycakes, deep-fried hushpuppies and spoonbreads lightened with egg whites. In the southern states corn bread, leavened with baking powder, is served hot with fried chicken or ham or as a dessert with syrup.

In the south of France, cornmeal is mixed with wheat flour to make various rough, flattish loaves, while the traditional northern Italian dish of polenta is made by boiling coarse-ground, yellow cornmeal until it becomes a stiff porridge. This is then poured onto a board in a large flat moon shape and allowed to set, and is then sliced and eaten steamed, broiled or fried. The tortillas of Central America are made from *masa harina*—a fine cornmeal ground from white corn which is soaked in limewater. *Masa harina* can be bought as a wet dough, or dehydrated.

**Cornstarch, cornflour** is the white heart of the corn kernel, ground to a silken powder. Used primarily as a thickening agent, it can also be added to cakes, shortbread and cookies to give a fine-textured result. A little cornstarch added to an egg custard will stop it from curdling.

## Oats

These are among the most nutritious of all cereals. Being rich in oils they soon become rancid, so do not buy more oat products than you can use in about three weeks and keep them in a cool place.

**Oatmeal** comes in three grades, pinhead or coarse, medium and fine. The coarser the meal, the longer it will take to cook. Medium oatmeal is traditionally used to make porridge. It is also used to give bulk to sausages and haggis, and can be added to wheat flour when making bread. Pinhead oatmeal is good in thick soups and stews. Fine oatmeal

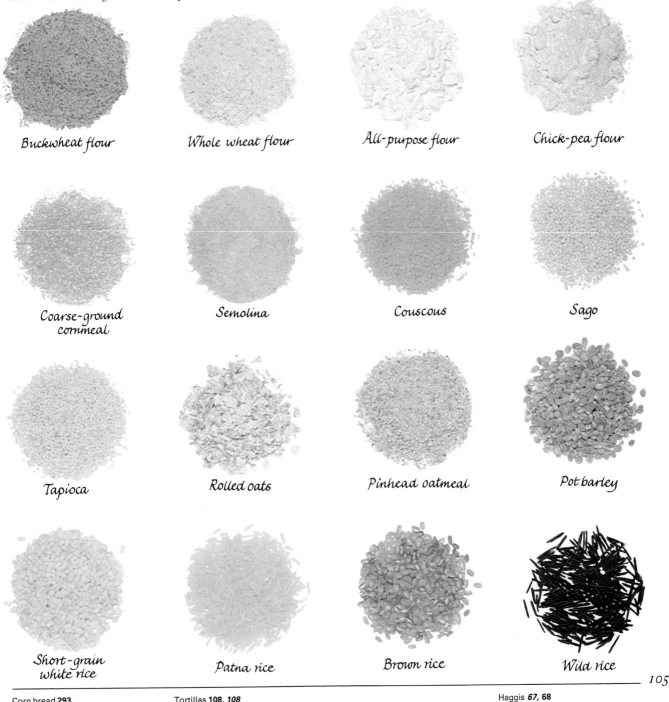

Buckwheat flour

Whole wheat flour

All-purpose flour

Chick-pea flour

Coarse-ground cornmeal

Semolina

Couscous

Sago

Tapioca

Rolled oats

Pinhead oatmeal

Pot barley

Short-grain white rice

Patna rice

Brown rice

Wild rice

# Grains, Breads and Thickening Agents

is used in baking oatcakes, scones and cookies. Fine-grade meal is also used for oatmeal pancakes and is good for flouring Scottish herrings before they go into the frying pan.

**Rolled oats, oat flakes, porridge oats** are oats which have been steamed and flattened between rollers, a process which makes them quicker to cook. Porridge takes only ten minutes to make when using rolled oats. They are also used to make English flapjacks —sticky, chewy, teatime cookies. Uncooked rolled or toasted oats are the main ingredient of the Swiss breakfast cereal muesli.

## Rye

This strong-flavored, hardy grain is particularly popular in Scandinavia, Russia and Germany. It has a tough kernel which, if bought whole, needs to be cracked with a rolling pin and then soaked before being cooked.

**Whole rye kernels**, boiled until tender, can be added to stews or mixed with rice.

**Rye flour**, which makes a rather heavy, distinctive loaf, is widely used in bread making in many parts of Europe. Coarsely ground whole rye flour goes into pumpernickel, a bread which is more steamed than baked. Finer ground flour is used for black bread; light-colored rye breads are made with rye flour and wheat flour mixed. European rye breads are traditionally made with a starter of fermented sour dough. Rye flour is also used to make crisp breads.

## Barley

Although more widely used for brewing than eating, barley has a pleasant nutty taste and can be cooked in a variety of ways.

**Pot or Scotch barley** is the whole grain with only the outer husk removed. It requires overnight steeping and several hours' cooking. Eat it like rice or add it to stews.

**Pearl barley**, the polished grain, is more widely available than pot barley and will cook to tenderness in about $1\frac{1}{2}$ hours. It is traditionally used in Scotch broth, to which it adds body and a smooth taste. In Ireland it is cooked in buttermilk and eaten as a dessert with syrup.

**Barley meal and barley flour** The first is ground pot barley, the second is ground pearl barley. Both can be added to wheat flour when making bread.

## Rice

At least a third of mankind eats rice as its staple food. There is an enormous number of varieties, each with its own special properties, and it is important to choose the right variety of rice for the right dish.

**Brown rice** is any rice that has been hulled but has not lost its bran. To the regret of dieticians, polished white rice is usually preferred to brown rice which contains more nutrients, particularly vitamin B, a deficiency of which causes beriberi. It takes rather longer to cook than the white variety and is much improved by being soaked first. Boil for 40–45 minutes in plenty of salted water. Brown rice is available in short, medium and long grains. Long and medium grains are best eaten as a vegetable, or as a basis for a pilaf. Short grains are delicious in puddings. You may need to cook less brown rice as it is rather more filling than its polished, white counterparts.

**Patna rice** has a long, milk-white grain. It can either be cooked in plenty of salted boiling water for up to 15 minutes or until just tender, or as for basmati rice. The center of each grain, when cooked, should have a slight resistance but no hint of chalkiness. Patna, cooked to perfection, produces a beautiful mound of separate grains, good for pilafs, salads, stuffings and all dishes where the rice is served dry.

**Converted rice** For those who cannot wait the 15 minutes or so that long-grain white rice takes to cook, there is a more expensive fast-cooking variety. This is steam treated and more nutritious than one might think because it is processed before it is hulled, and so has the chance to absorb the bran's nutrients before this is discarded.

**Basmati rice**, available in Asian food stores, is a superior long-grain rice. It is slightly more expensive than patna but its better flavor and consistency is well worth the extra cost. Before cooking, it sometimes needs to be carefully picked over for any bits of grit and husk and should then be washed thoroughly under running water to remove excess starch.

Basmati consistently produces good results if cooked in the following way: add one part rice to three parts cold salted water, bring to boiling point, stir, cover the pan and turn down the heat until the water is barely simmering. After 12–15 minutes the rice will have absorbed all the water and, when forked up, the grains will be beautifully dry and separate. It is ideal for pilaus and as a filling and soothing foil for highly spiced Indian dishes.

**Carolina rice and Java rice**—not to be confused with the American brand name Carolina rice, the "extra long-grain rice"— are in fact, shortish versions of long-grain species. When cooked, the grains swell enormously without disintegrating. They are very suitable for milk puddings, whether baked in the oven until caramel colored within and brown on top as in England, or cooked plain on top of the stove and served with sugar and cinnamon as in Germany,

or blended with whipped cream and layered with black cherries as is traditional in Switzerland. These types of rice are also suitable for making molds and stuffings.

**Italian Piedmontese rice, Arborio rice** These are Italian risotto rices and have short, round grains that are either white or pale yellow. Their special asset is that their grains can absorb a great deal of liquid over a long period without becoming soft. This, and their distinctive flavor, makes them ideal for risottos and any dish such as paella or jambalaya that needs long, gentle cooking. Italian rice is an excellent vehicle for strong-flavored foods such as squid, white truffles and wild mushrooms.

**Wild rice** is the seed of an aquatic grass related to the rice family, which grows in the United States. It is hard to find and prohibitively expensive but has a rare, distinctive, nutty flavor not to be missed if you are really interested in food. To cook wild rice bring it to the boil in salted water, drain and then cook in a minimum of fresh water for about half an hour or until the grains are just beginning to open. Serve plain or mix into stuffings for poultry and game birds.

**Ground rice**, ground from polished grains, can be purchased loose or, more usually, packaged. Cook with milk for a fine-textured dessert or add it to a shortcake mixture for extra crunchiness.

**Rice flour** is polished rice very finely ground to a silky consistency. Health food stores also sell a more coarse, off-white rice flour ground from brown rice. A little rice flour can go into a walnut or hazelnut cake of the type that uses no flour, only grated nuts, and is a useful thickener for dishes that are to be deep frozen as it will prevent the mixture separating when heated.

## Buckwheat

Also known as saracen corn or beechwheat, buckwheat grows in great quantities in northeast Europe—the whole grains when roasted are sometimes labelled kasha, after the Russian dish of that name. Buckwheat is the correct flour to use for Russian blini— small, speckled, yeast-risen pancakes that are eaten with caviar. It is also used to make crêpes and can be added to other, lighter flours when making bread.

## Millet and sorghum

These are closely related and are invariably sold shelled as the husk is extremely hard. Their greatest characteristic is that they swell enormously—at least five parts water are needed to one part millet or sorghum. Both have a blandish, slightly nutty taste. They are best cooked and eaten like rice, but bear in mind that a small handful produces a large helping. To reduce cooking time, toast the grains a little in a dry, heavy pan on top of the stove before putting them in the pot to boil. Millet and sorghum flours produce flattish breads.

## Sago and tapioca

The starch obtained from the stem of the southeast Asian sago palm, sago is usually exported in pearled form. It comes in varying sizes and consists purely of starch. It is most commonly made into sweet milk puddings, which are thought to be easily digestible and so are fed to children and the elderly. In Norway it is made into a soup with sugar, egg and sherry.

Tapioca, prepared from the tuberous roots of the tropical cassava or manioc shrub, is as tasteless and starchy as sago and comes both pearled and powdered. Pearled, it is made into creamy milk puddings.

## Thickeners

All starchy meals and flours will, in the presence of heat and moisture, act as thickeners. They cannot be used indiscriminately, but the cook can experiment with the two broad categories. Finer flours, before being added to the pan, must first be blended to a lump-free paste with a little of the cooking liquid or with some butter, to make a roux or beurre manié.

As an alternative to plain all-purpose flour for thickening soups, stews, gravies and other such dishes, try using something a little more robust such as fine-ground cornmeal or whole wheat, sorghum, barley or chick-pea flour. These will add flavor and color as well as body. If you have none of these at hand, a crustless slice of bread or a boiled potato, blended with a little of the liquid, will work too. Chick-pea flour, also known as gram flour or besan, also makes a very good batter and is used to make *pakoras*, spicy little Indian fritters.

*Fécule* is the general French name for starchy powders used in cooking. It is usually associated with potato flour, which is the thickening agent used by continental cooks when making soups and gravies. The other very fine, quick-thickening flours such as cornstarch, arrowroot, tapioca flour and rice flour are all virtually tasteless. They have double the thickening power of flour, turn translucent when cooked and are suitable for thickening delicate chicken or game dishes and sauces to accompany sweetbreads. Arrowroot and potato flour are particularly suitable for thickening fruit sauces because they turn completely clear when cooked, and arrowroot has the added feature of being ideal for cooking at low temperatures—an advantage when making such things as egg sauces. Take care not to overcook these fine flours as they have a tendency to turn thin again.

## Yeast and baking powders

When buying flour for baking you will probably also need a leavening agent such as yeast for bread, pizza dough and buns, and baking powder for scones and cakes.

**Compressed or fresh yeast** is a pale beige, pasty substance which should be solid but able to crumble easily and should have a clean, sweet, fruity smell. It will keep for a couple of weeks in the refrigerator and for several months if stored in the freezer, in which case it will need to be thawed thoroughly and brought back to room temperature before it is used. Look for it in health food stores, the refrigerated section of supermarkets and at small bakeries.

**Dried granular or active dry yeast** has virtually replaced fresh yeast; it has been freeze dried and so will keep for several months if stored in a cool, dry place, but it needs a warmer liquid than fresh yeast in which to dissolve. Never use more of this yeast than the recipe states or you will find that you have a coarse, sour loaf that will quickly go stale.

**Brewer's yeast** Old cook books called for brewer's yeast, or ale barm, which was bought at breweries or skimmed off the top of homemade beer and was very temperamental. The brewer's yeast sold these days for home brewing is too bitter, however, for baking purposes.

**Debittered brewer's yeast,** found in health food stores, has no leavening properties but is high in vitamin B. It should be treated as a nutritional additive to mix into drinks and sprinkle over foods.

**Baking powder** combines acid and alkaline substances that act together when in contact with moisture to create air bubbles, which expand during baking to give a fine, delicate-textured result. It is usually sold in airtight containers and great care should be taken to keep it dry, as any hint of moisture will set the chemicals working. When adding the milk or water to a baking powder and flour mixture, work quickly so that the resulting carbon dioxide does not have a chance of escaping. Double acting or SAS baking powder, widely available in America, is easier to use because the chemicals spring into full action only when they are exposed to the heat of the oven.

**Bicarbonate of soda and cream of tartar** You can make your own baking powder by mixing these in the proportion of one teaspoon of soda to two of cream of tartar for every cup of flour. Bicarbonate of soda, the alkalin, will work alone if used in a recipe in which there is an acid ingredient such as the sour milk in soda bread and the molasses in gingerbread. A little cream of tartar—a fine white powder crystallized from grape acid and an ingredient of commercial baking powders—helps increase the volume and stability of whisked egg whites. **Salt of hartshorn,** chemically imitated these days with ammonium carbonate, is used in Scandinavian countries as a baking powder to produce light, crisp cookies.

## Breads

The qualities of the plain white loaf are, of course, proper for such things as croûtons, melba toast and English bread sauce, but there is a host of other breads, of completely different tastes and textures.

**French bread,** which is most often seen in long sticks or *baguettes*, has a hard, crisp crust and a wide-holed crumb. When made in the authentic French manner it will only keep a few hours, but it is bread at its very best. A thick slice, plain or toasted, is often floated in soups and consommés.

**Malt loaf,** a dark, moist, sweet bread enriched with syrup and malt extract, often comes wrapped and may contain raisins. It is a splendid tea bread eaten with butter and jam or jelly, and keeps well for days.

**Light rye bread,** with a satisfying sour flavor, is popular for sandwiches, particularly in the United States where it is filled with roast beef, corned beef, pastrami or ham and cheese.

**Dark rye bread, pumpernickel and vollkornbrot** A dark rye loaf with its hard, thick crust keeps fresh for a week or more, while pumpernickel and vollkornbrot (a slightly lighter variety) lose their moisture quickly and keep best wrapped in foil and stored in a cool place. They should all be sliced very thinly and are good served as open sandwiches.

**Bagels,** ring-shaped rolls that are boiled before baking, are a Jewish specialty, very good with cream cheese, smoked salmon or jam. There are endless varieties of these shiny, chewy rolls, including an English version with a savory topping.

**Croissants,** the soft doughy crescents that are such an essential part of the French breakfast, are made of a rich dough of milk and flour liberally interleaved with butter. Eat hot with butter and jam, or plain with a cup of good coffee.

**Brioches,** rich, featherlight little loaves with a crisp golden crust, made from a dough of milk, water, eggs and butter, also come as large loaves. Eat warm with butter and jam, sliced and toasted, or hollowed out and stuffed with perhaps mushrooms or pâté de foie gras.

**English muffins,** popular in the United

# Grains, Breads and Thickening Agents

States for breakfast or brunch, are pulled or "forked" apart and toasted. Top with anything, sweet or non-sweet.

**Crumpets** should be first toasted on the underside and then on the holey top. Eat piping hot and dripping with butter.

**Baps**, soft, floury breakfast rolls from Scotland, are eaten straight from the oven, split and spread with butter.

**Pita bread**, originally from the Middle East, is only slightly leavened and forms flat, hollow rounds that look like oriental leather slippers. Eaten hot, they are sometimes cut in half and filled with broiled lamb and salad. They are always eaten plain with Greek meals, at which it is customary to tear off a bit at a time to use as a scoop for hummus and taramasalata.

**Pizza**, a flattish but yeast-leavened Italian bread, is available from some bakeries, baked plain without its usual topping. It is best eaten hot and cut in triangles to accompany a main course.

**Tortilla** This Mexican unleavened bread is made with *masa harina* or with whole wheat flour. Corn tortillas are fried and filled to make *tacos*, or simply fried until crisp to make *tostadas*. Whole wheat tortillas are for eating hot accompanying a main course, tearing off a piece at a time with which to scoop up chili con carne, or they are filled and rolled to make *enchiladas*.

**Chapati** Indian unleavened bread made from *atta*—fine-ground whole wheat flour—chapatis are eaten hot with curries and other Indian dishes, being used to pick up the food.

**Puri** This is a deep-fried, air-filled chapati. Buy and eat as for chapati.

**Paratha** is a shallow-fried, butter-enriched variety of chapati.

**Naan** Tear-drop shaped, this rich, leavened variation on the chapati is traditionally slapped on the side of a charcoal tandoori oven to cook.

## Crisp breads

There is a huge array of crisp breads on the market, ranging from rusks to water biscuits. There are a few varieties, however, which deserve special mention.

**Scandinavian crisp breads** are generally made from whole rye and are popular as a slimming aid, as rye is the most filling cereal and so gives one a feeling of satisfaction with fewer calories. They can be eaten spread with anything, sweet or salty, and are available in light and dark varieties, sometimes sprinkled with sesame seeds.

**Matzo** This Jewish wheaten crisp bread, similar to water biscuits, is traditionally eaten during Passover. Eat as bread, especially with cheese and spreads. It is completely unsalted.

**Poppadoms** These wafer-thin Indian chips are available plain or spiced and need only to be broiled or deep fried for a few seconds. Eat immediately, broken up over curries or with drinks.

**Pretzels**, often studded with salt crystals, are available twisted into many shapes and sizes. They are usually crisp but some varieties are soft in the middle. Best served with drinks or cheese; the soft ones are good with spicy mustard.

**Bread sticks**, known also by the Italian name, *grissini*, are long, thin sticks of bread with a fine texture, baked and dried until crisp. Eat with drinks, or accompanying an Italian meal instead of rolls.

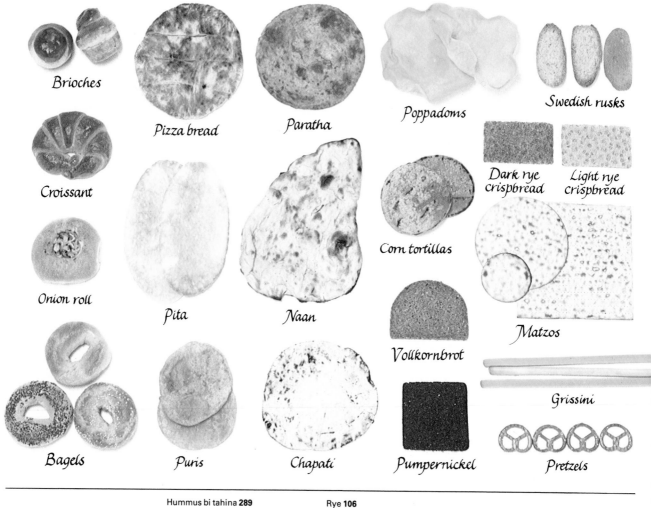

Brioches

Pizza bread

Paratha

Poppadoms

Swedish rusks

Croissant

Dark rye crispbread

Light rye crispbread

Onion roll

Pita

Naan

Corn tortillas

Matzos

Bagels

Puris

Chapati

Vollkornbrot

Pumpernickel

Grissini

Pretzels

# Pasta and Noodles

Six hundred or so pasta shapes are made in Italy—most Italians rely on a daily supply of pasta in one form or another to keep up their spirits—and many more come from China and Japan, where noodles and stuffed pasta dumplings are an important and ancient part of the classic cuisine.

## Pasta

Records show that the Chinese were eating pasta as long ago as the Shang dynasty, some 3,500 years ago, and it was long believed, rather romantically, that Marco Polo brought pasta to Italy from the court of Kubla Khan. But Etruscan murals in Tuscany show all the kitchen equipment needed for pasta making, from the kind of wooden table still used to roll it on (so far laminated plastics have not replaced it) to the fluted wheel with which to cut pappardelle, lasagne and ravioli. Even without the murals the story had been put in doubt by the estate of a military man who died in the thirteenth century, leaving among his effects a precious chest of *maccheroni*.

Whatever its origins, the Neapolitans have always been Italy's most serious pasta eaters and Naples and the surrounding area have long been regarded as the center of the dried pasta industry. Certainly the best flour for pasta making, made from the extra hard wheat *Amber durum*, comes from the hot, dry south. This absorbs the minimum of water as it cooks. The warm, dry, windy climate means, too, that spaghetti can be dried in the open air, swathed like curtains over long canes that are supported on tall stands—although with industrialization, modern factories have taken the place of the old traditional family enterprises.

When buying dried pasta look for that made in southern Italy, especially the Abruzzi, and make sure it is a clear yellow color without any chalky greyish tinge. Thinner pastas should be translucent when held up to the light, with the exception of dried egg pastas, which should be a sunny bright yellow.

Most pastas can generally be described as long or short; round, tubular or flat; smooth or ridged; solid or hollow. An attempt to classify their shapes by name, however, is a problem, since one shape can have several different names and sizes. The north of Italy insists on one appellation, the south another, and even different regions quite close together cannot reach agreement. Miniature pastas, or *pastina*, which come in every shape you can think of from stars to motorcars to apple seeds, are in a category of their own. They can be made from fresh or dried egg pasta or plain dried pasta (without eggs) and are generally cooked and served *in brodo* —in chicken or beef broth.

The long, round, solid pastas that are coiled around the fork, such as vermicelli, spaghetti and spaghettini, are generally eaten dry (*asciutta*) with oil or butter, a tomato-based sauce or a seafood sauce. Meat sauces, with the exception of *ragú bolognese*, are not generally eaten with these as they do not cling to the pasta well. Short, hollow pastas such as conchigliette, elbow macaroni or penne are the ones to serve with meat as the pieces catch easily in the hollows and curves of the pasta.

The larger short, hollow pastas such as cannelloni and manicotti are usually boiled and then stuffed with cheese or meat before baking. Macaroni and rigatoni are sometimes boiled and then baked in a sauce in the oven, perhaps as part of a molded shape called *timballi* which is among the oldest of all pasta dishes. Two egg pastas, lasagne and tagliatelle, can also be baked in this way, as can farfalle, conchiglie, ruote and lumachine.

Serve cream sauces with short, ridged, hollow pastas, since these catch the cream and do not slip off the fork. Tagliatelle and other flat fresh pastas are generally eaten with rich meat or vegetable sauces, and the same fresh pasta dough is used to make stuffed pastas such as ravioli, anolini, tortelloni, tortellini, conchiglie and lumachine.

Having said all this, of course, one can eat any pasta with any sauce and have a perfectly good meal.

## Spaghetti

This is the best known of all pastas and always comes in long, straight bundles. It is marketed in a number of widths that go under such names as cappellini, spaghettini, vermicelli, vermicelloni and thin or thick spaghetti. The thicker ones are better with rich sauces while the thinner ones are better with plainer sauces.

Spaghetti has long been the traditional pasta of Naples and the traditional way of eating it is still *alla napoletana*—first turned in oil and then topped with a ladleful of tomato sauce. Naples also eats its spaghetti *all'aglio e olio*—pasta bathed in olive oil and mixed with sautéed garlic. Grated grana cheese such as Parmesan or pecorino is served with all spaghetti except those with seafood additions such as spaghetti alla vongole. This is made with tiny clams and is another Neapolitan specialty, although it is, of course, much enjoyed all over Italy.

## Macaroni

It is not known how the idea of making the tubular pasta called macaroni or *maccheroni* started. But the most likely theory is that someone wrapped a piece of rolled-out pasta around a filling, leaving the ends open.

Macaroni comes in an even greater range of sizes than spaghetti. Apart from the long variety, with bore holes that can be measured in millimeters, there are also those that can be measured in centimeters, culminating in cannelloni, but these are despised by purists as too modern an invention, designed solely to make filling our pasta easier. However, we ought to be grateful that we are not obliged, as was the composer Rossini, to fill our macaroni with the aid of a silver syringe. He is said to have used this for filling tubes of pasta with foie gras, for which he had a well-known passion.

Apart from cannelloni there are ribbed rigatoni, mafalde, zite, penne—cut like quills—and elbow macaroni—the curved, short lengths of macaroni used in baked pasta dishes and, of course, for the ubiquitous macaroni and cheese.

Macaroni used to be virtually the only pasta known and loved by English-speaking countries. Called macrow, it had been eaten at the court of Richard II of England. It fell into decline, but was rediscovered by eighteenth-century Englishmen in the Italian part of their grand tours and taken back to Britain. Soon macaroni and cheese became an important high-tea dish, and it is still eaten at home by many British as well as American families.

## Egg pasta

In northern Italy housewives traditionally made egg pasta or *pasta all'uovo* daily at home with eggs and flour. Emilia-Romagna, the area with the richest farming land in Italy, was renowned for its beautiful handmade pasta, and young women from that region were keenly courted by young men and their mothers for their pasta-making skills. Egg pastas are richer and lighter than ordinary pastas.

Pasta making is a craft and to see an expert rolling out a golden circle of dough, as thin as fine suede, to the size of a small tablecloth is a wonderful experience. In Bologna, the gastronomic center of Emilia-Romagna, you can watch it being made in a shop window. It is then turned into tortellini— little stuffed, folded-over pasta triangles—at lightning speed in front of your eyes.

Fresh pasta can be made at home, when it becomes known as *pasta casalinga*, either by hand or with a pasta machine, but perfectionists say that the former is better since the machine squeezes the pasta and tends to give it a slippery surface that does not hold the sauce so well.

In fact a great deal of the *pasta all'uovo* now eaten in Italy and elsewhere is made in factories, where by law it must contain five eggs to each kilo of flour. It is sold in nests or in

# Pasta and Noodles

Cannelloni

Ruote

Ravioli

Ditalini

Tagliarini verdi

Lasagne

Whole wheat lasagne

Farfalle

Tortellini

Conchigliette

Farfalline

Anellini

Whole wheat elbow
macaroni

Conchiglie

plain  buckwheat
Spaghetti

Lumachine

Tortiglioni

Tagliatelle verdi

Tagliatelle

Lasagne verdi

Stelline

Zite

Mafaldine

Pasta recipes **278–284**

skeins that loosen when boiled. Buy it wrapped in cellophane or loose, if you can; boxed pasta is more expensive, the size of the box often bears little relation to the contents, and it is impossible to see if the brittle pasta inside is whole or broken.

The best-known egg pasta is tagliatelle, or —as it is called in Rome—fettucine: those golden strands that were supposed to have been inspired by the long blonde hair of Lucretia Borgia. In Bologna and Parma and all the other places of gastronomic pilgrimage with which northern Italy abounds, the tagliarini (thin tagliatelle) is still normally freshly rolled out every day.

Tagliatelle is, of course, not only eaten *alla bolognese*, even in Bologna, but also *in bianco*, mixed with plenty of melted butter, freshly grated Parmesan and cream, or *al burro*, with the cream left out. Bologna also eats its tagliatelle mixed with strips of delicious sautéed pancetta and grated Parmesan.

### Green pasta

Lasagne verdi and tagliatelle verdi prove that spinach has a special affinity with pasta. Both are colored by a small amount of spinach purée that is worked into the dough. **Lasagne** can be bought in long, wide, flat strips or in curly pieces which do not stick together as easily as flat pieces when boiling. It can also be bought as squares which are easier to fit into a baking dish. In Bologna strips of green lasagne or the narrower lasagnette are alternately layered with uncolored strips and with Bolognese sauce and rich creamy béchamel sauce. This dish is baked in the oven and emerges, glazed here and there with deep golden flecks, as *lasagne al forno*.

**Tagliatelle** Tuscany and Umbria make a pretty mixture of yellow and green tagliatelle or tagliolini, which is called *paglia e fieno*, meaning straw and hay. It is eaten with melted butter and cream and sprinkled as usual with Parmesan.

### Whole wheat and buckwheat pasta

Although Venice has always had its thick whole wheat spaghetti called *bigoli*, it is not common throughout Italy. There are, however, some relative newcomers in the health food stores, such as the buckwheat and whole wheat pastas.

Whole wheat lasagne and macaroni and buckwheat spaghetti are some examples. These have a nutty flavor and are richer in vitamins and minerals than the traditional pale pastas. They take longer to cook as they contain five times as much fiber as pale pasta. The Italian whole wheat pastas are, on the whole, lighter than those made elsewhere.

Whole wheat and buckwheat noodles also feature in Japanese cooking and are often eaten cold as a late afternoon snack.

### Stuffed pasta

Pasta stuffed with a large variety of finely ground fillings is eaten throughout Italy. Parmesan cheese and mortadella sausage with pork and veal, diced or pounded and mixed with minced turkey breasts, provide the traditional stuffing for tortellini and tortelloni. These are the coiled half-moons which are the famous Bolognese version of ravioli and are by custom eaten on Christmas Eve and for big celebrations. Perugia, in Tuscany, on these occasions eats cappelletti, or little hats, whose stuffing includes finely ground veal and sweetbreads or brains. The hollowed shells called conchiglie or the larger conchiglioni and even lumache can also be stuffed.

Throughout the length and breadth of Italy ravioli with delicious spinach, beet leaf or chard fillings are to be found. The chopped leaves are mixed with soft white cheese such as ricotta and with Parmesan or pecorino, bound with egg and flavored with a touch of nutmeg or garlic depending on the local taste.

### Soup pasta

If the dough and the basic shape of pasta *asciutta* are fairly consistent—allowing for a thousand and one small regional variations —the same cannot be said of soup pastas. The range is vast and includes anellini and stelline, which are used for serving *in brodo*, while the larger varieties such as farfalline, conchigliette and ditaline are used for making hearty soups such as minestrone or *pasta e fagioli*.

Italy garnishes its soups with tiny car radiators, cogs and wheels, with flying saucers, hats, boots, letters and numerals, all made of pasta. The more traditional shapes include grains of rice and melon seeds, twisted bow ties, butterflies, stars, crescent moons, seashells of every description, rings, hoops, elbow macaroni and noodles which are as thin as matchsticks.

These garnishes are sometimes cooked separately and added to the soup just before serving, as they tend to shed a bit of starch, which can make a clear broth cloudy.

### Pasta sauces

Pasta of one kind or another is the main part of most Italians' daily diet, and there are almost as many pasta sauces to be found as there are types of pasta.

All the classic pasta sauces have their origins in regional cookery. They are made from what is readily to hand. Piedmont, with its famous white truffles, makes a delicious sauce of truffled chicken livers. Tuscany makes a richly flavored sauce with hare. Pounded anchovy, truffles, garlic, tomatoes and onions go into the sauce that in Spoleto makes pasta *alla spoletina*. In Sorrento there

is a sauce made of zucchini. Pesto, a mixture of fresh basil, pine nuts, garlic and Parmesan or pecorino, is served with pasta in Genoa, and when Tuscany offers a cream sauce with its tagliarini it saves the sauce from blandness by adding meat glaze.

*Spaghetti alla carbonara*, despite its reputation of having been created during World War II to please the Allied armies with their vast appetites for eggs and bacon, is a specialty of Rome. The sauce consists of pancetta mixed into a hot cooked spaghetti with a raw beaten egg that partly sets in the steam, combined with Parmesan. The secret is not to drain the spaghetti too enthusiastically or the result will be dry.

In the Abruzzi and Molise, a favorite sauce is made with lamb and sweet green peppers, another of smoked pork with tomatoes. The pasta eaten here is *maccheroni alla chitarra*—long strands cut on a frame strung with wires like a guitar. In the Marches, black olives preserved in a special brine are incorporated in the sauces, not only for pasta made with the conventional dough but also for a local variation that is made with a yeast-like bread dough. Chickpeas also appear in a dish called thunder and lightning (*tuono e lampo*), which is a mixture of chick-peas and pasta.

Towards the south, sauces include sweet red peppers, green peppers and a fiery dash of chili pepper. Since the sea is not far from any spot in Italy, there are often marine accompaniments such as cockles and clams.

### Nudels, nouilles and dumplings

In the German-speaking countries, which are supposed to have introduced nudels into Italy in the Middle Ages, flat nudels have been consistently eaten for centuries. They are often baked with raisins and sweetened lemon-flavored curd cheese and served as a pudding. In Alsace they are known as nouilles and are prepared in countless savory and delicious ways. *Coq au vin*, for example, is often accompanied by nouilles, which are always better when fresh.

In Alsace we also find the ancestral dumpling known as noque, while farther south it appears under the name of nockerln. By whatever name, it is a pasta dumpling and can be eaten with a variety of sauces.

### Gnocchi

In Italy, gnocchi are eaten in the same way as pasta and at the same point in the meal, but they are not strictly speaking pasta. There are several local variations and they can be made from ricotta cheese and spinach, or semolina, or mashed potato or potato flour. They are usually poached in boiling salted water until cooked, when they rise to

# Pasta and Noodles

the surface. They are then served with a variety of sauces. Gnocchi are generally made fresh, the semolina variety being extremely easy to make.

## Chinese noodles

Wheat flour, rice flour, arrowroot or pea starch are the main ingredients of Chinese noodles. They come in a variety of thicknesses and shapes, can be used interchangeably and are often tied in bundles or coiled into square packages. The majority, however, are long, as this is thought to symbolize and encourage long life.

Although most Chinese buy their noodles, some do make their own. Fresh noodles are obtainable from Chinese supermarkets and taste best when they are first parboiled and then steamed in a colander over boiling water. Once boiled or steamed, Chinese noodles become part of more elaborate preparations that often involve several cooking methods for one dish.

## Soup noodles

These are traditionally served in broth with a topping of finely cut meat or seafood and bright, fresh-looking vegetables. The cooked noodles are put into the bottom of the bowl, the hot broth is poured over them, then come the vegetables, previously stir-fried with the meat or seafood, as the garnish.

In the north of China, where wheat is the primary grain, wheat noodles, with or without egg, are used. Egg noodles are often sold in little nests while pure wheat noodles may be packaged like Italian spaghetti as well as in square-shaped nests. In the southern districts of China, where paddy fields abound, rice noodles are used. These range from square packets of coiled rice sticks to the thin thread-like rice vermicelli that comes tied in bundles. White arrowroot vermicelli is also available.

## Fried noodles

Crispy fried noodles, known as chow mein, are a Cantonese specialty, and since most Chinese restaurants in the West are Cantonese these are perhaps the best known of all noodle dishes. They can either be flattened in a frying pan with plenty of seasoned oil and then turned like a pancake, or they can be fried gently with leftover vegetables and meat from a noodle and soup dish.

Pea starch noodles can also be used if a crisp garnish is all that is required.

## Sauced noodles

In the West, where Chinese thickeners such as lotus root flour are not readily available, sauced noodles or lu mein are usually served in sauces thickened with cornstarch. Since texture is just as important to the Chinese as taste, a crunchy element is often introduced to these sauces with matchstick slivers of bamboo shoots or crisp stalks of scallions and leeks. Protein is provided by adding meat such as chicken, shelled shrimps or oysters. Lu mein dishes are usually served at birthday celebrations.

Pea starch noodles, also known as transparent or cellophane noodles, are never served in their own right but are generally used in lu mein dishes. Since they absorb liquid at the rate of four times their weight they are ideal. They are usually cooked as part of the savory dish and then the entire dish is served with rice.

## Dumplings

Chinese dumplings or wontons are similar to the Italian ravioli. The delicate ingredients, finely ground and variously flavored, are wrapped in squares of fine noodle dough. They may be purchased in Chinese supermarkets, but can be made at home in the same way as fresh pasta. Boiled or steamed they are often served floating in a clear broth.

One of the prettiest dishes available in a Chinese restaurant arrives at the table as a towering pagoda of baskets. Each one fits into the other and contains bite-size packages of dumplings called dim sum. These contain pork, shrimp or other meat or fish fillings and are ideal for a light lunch.

## Japanese noodles

There are four main types of Japanese noodle, all of which play an important part in the national cuisine. Soba are thin, brownish noodles made from buckwheat flour. They are used in soups and sometimes served cold with a garnish. Harusame are equivalent to the Chinese pea starch noodles and can be deep fried, or soaked and then cooked in various dishes. Somen are very fine white noodles—you can substitute vermicelli if somen are not available. Udon are made from white flour and are more substantial.

Wonton wrappers

Fresh rice noodles

Soup vermicelli

Chow mein noodles

Wheat noodles

Arrowroot vermicelli

Rice vermicelli

Wheat noodles

Cellophane noodles

Fresh egg noodles

Fresh wheat noodles

Rice sticks

Egg noodles

# Dried Peas and Beans

The dried seeds of podded plants were first popular many thousands of years ago. In Egypt, the pyramids have been found to contain little mounds of dried beans—not only to sustain departed pharaohs on their journey to the next world but also because Egyptians believed beans to be particularly helpful in conveying the soul to heaven.

Unfortunately, apart from being an excellent and sustaining food, very suitable for those about to embark on long journeys, beans have the annoying property of engendering flatulence. Perhaps this characteristic helped lead to their gradual banishment, after medieval times, from Europe's more elegant tables. Another probable reason for their steady decline in appeal was the greater availability of fresh vegetables at that time.

It was not until this century, when the Western world found a new taste for simple, sturdy, regional foods, that dried beans and peas were seriously rediscovered. A growing interest in Indian and Middle Eastern cooking brought Eastern species to Western shelves, and with them the Indian word gram, which is one of the collective names for dried beans and peas, particularly the chick-pea. In England the collective name is pulse, originating from the ancient Roman word puls, meaning pottage.

Although thousands of species of beans and peas, botanically known as Leguminosae, now exist, they have many common characteristics. Flavor and mealiness may vary, but all have a straightforward earthy taste and satisfying sturdy quality. All are a rich source of protein and, being a healthy and body-building form of food, make a very sound substitute for meat, especially when combined with cereals. Hence their label "poor man's meat."

A popular misconception is that dried peas and beans have an indefinite shelf life. In fact, they should not be stored longer than a year for they harden with age and become difficult to cook. There are two methods of preparing them, both of which help to clean and tenderize them. The most common method is soaking, to which all dried peas and beans respond, preferably in soft water. The dried peas and beans that are prepared for supermarkets are sure to be clean and may not need to be soaked: the label should tell you. The alternative to soaking, useful when you are short of time, is to put them into a pan of cold, unsalted water, bring them to the boil, then simmer them for five minutes. Cover the pan, remove it from the heat and allow the peas or beans to cool. Then cook them in whatever way the recipe calls for.

All these vegetables should be cooked in soft water—a pinch of bicarbonate of soda will soften hard water—and simmered rather than rapidly boiled. Unless very fresh, they require lengthy cooking. They should be salted towards the end of cooking—if salted at the outset, the skins will split and the insides will harden. A little fat in with the cooking water—salt pork, bacon or oil—improves the texture of all dried peas and beans. When bought canned rather than loose or packaged, they are already cooked and only need heating.

## Haricot beans

The word haricot covers the botanical species of beans Phaseolus. It derives from medieval times when dried beans were used chiefly to go into a pot containing a haricot or halicot of meat—haricot meaning simply that the meat was cut in chunks for stewing. When English and French cook books specify haricots, what is meant are white beans, smooth and oval rather than kidney shaped. In the United States they are known, sensibly enough, as white beans.

Soissons are generally considered the finest haricot beans. They originated in northern France, but are used to greatest effect in the famous regional dish cassoulet, from Toulouse, cooked with preserved goose, mutton and sausage.

Flageolets, in a semi-dried state, are an important ingredient in another classic French dish, gigot d'agneau. Usually, however, they are found only dried, either green or white. The green are the more interesting, having a delicate flavor and a lovely color.

Cannellini are Italian haricots, slightly fatter than the English or French ones and popular in Tuscany in soups and in dishes such as tonno e fagioli—served cold with tuna fish in a garlicky vinaigrette.

Navy beans or Yankee beans are very popular in the United States, particularly for making Boston baked beans. At one time, these small round beans were served by the US Navy, hence their name.

Pea beans are sought out by discerning New Englanders for authentic Boston baked beans, but they are used interchangeably with navy beans in canning.

Brown Dutch beans are also used to make Boston baked beans and are available in England as well as the United States.

## Lima beans

Also known as butter beans, these can be large or small. Although, when fresh, they are highly prized, especially in America, the large dried bean easily becomes mushy when cooked and so is best when used in soups and purées. When recipes for other dishes call for either haricot or butter beans, it is the smaller bean that should be used.

## Red kidney beans

Best known outside Mexico for their part in chili con carne—which is not, as it happens, a true Mexican dish—red kidney beans are a staple in Central America and are the beans that, with black beans, were cooked by the Central American Indians in their earthenware pots (still much the best receptacle for baked beans, which should never be decanted before serving). After the introduction of lard from Spain, beans were often mashed, formed into a stiff paste and then fried to become frijoles refritos—still one of the most popular ways of eating beans in Mexico. In this form they may be used as an accompaniment to a main dish, or as a filling for tacos, tostadas and tamales, those crisply fried corncakes which are popular far beyond the borders of Mexico itself. Red kidney beans also appear in many dishes in New Orleans.

## Black beans

As well as being used interchangeably with red kidney and pinto beans to make frijoles refritos, black beans, with their glistening black skins and creamy flesh, are the staple of many soups and stews in South and Central America. There they are often baked with ham or other cured pork and flavored with garlic, cumin and much chili pepper. In the southern states of the United States, black bean soup is a great favorite. The beans are cooked with a ham bone or hock, blended to the consistency of a heavy sauce and served with slices of hard-boiled egg and lemon floating on top.

## Borlotti beans and pinto beans

Both these beans are often mottled in color. The pink-splotched pinto bean grows freely all over Latin America and, like the borlotti bean from Italy, is an ingredient in many regional stews and is often mixed with rice. The borlotti bean is also mixed with pasta to make the soup pasta e fagioli.

## Black-eyed peas

These white peas with their characteristic black splotch came to Europe and America from Africa, brought over in the seventeenth century by the slave traders. The bean thrives in warm climates and has become a favorite food crop in the southern United States, where it is eaten fresh as well as dried. It is often served with pork and corn

# Dried Peas and Beans

*Ful medames*

*Green split peas*

*Large lima beans*

*Black beans*

*Brown lentils*

*Borlotti beans*

*Tur dhal*

*Chick-peas*

*Black-eyed peas*

*Yellow split peas*

*Adzuki beans*

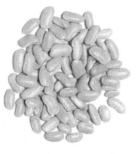

*Flageolets*

*Kidney beans*

*Fava beans*

*Small lima beans*

*Green lentils*

*Soybeans*

*Mung beans*

*Split red lentils*

*Small haricot beans*

Dried peas and
beans recipes **288–290**
Fresh peas and beans **126–127**

bread, and is the essential ingredient in a traditional southern dish called Hoppin' John—a mixture of peas, brown rice, bacon and plenty of oil.

## Fava beans

Sometimes known as broad beans, these are the strongly flavored beans that form the basis of the Egyptian *ta'amia* or falafel: deep-fried little patties made with soaked and pounded raw beans and flavored with garlic, onions, cumin, coriander and parsley. Most often used in their fresh green state, as in the rib-sticking *fabada* from northern Spain—a mixture of beans, cured meats, sausage and plenty of garlic—they become brown when dried.

## Ful medames or Egyptian brown beans

Also known as the field bean in England, these small, brown, nobbly beans are grown in southeast Asia and Egypt, where they are a staple food. There the beans are usually sprinkled with garlic and parsley, with oil and seasonings passed around separately. They also make a filling for an Arabian bread to become a sort of meatless hamburger, eaten with tomato and onion salad. They are also good when served in a tomato sauce, but they do require lengthy soaking and cooking.

## Chick-peas

The botanical name for this pea (which is, strictly speaking, not a pea at all) is *Cicer arietinum* because of its alleged resemblance to the skull of a ram, although to those of us with a less discerning eye it looks more like the kernel of a small hazelnut.

The flavor of chick-peas vaguely recalls that of roasted nuts and they are eaten with drinks in Greece. Large ones are a better buy than small ones as they do not need such long soaking. However, they will still sometimes need as much as 10 hours' soaking and 5–6 hours of gentle simmering to become completely tender.

Once cooked, *ceci*, as they are called in Italy, are very good dressed simply with oil and eaten as a salad. The Italians also make chick-pea soup and mix them with pasta—a dish known as thunder and lightning. In France, where chick-peas are called *pois chiches*, they are stewed in good stock with herbs to make *pois chiches en estouffade*, and also used in soups and as a garnish. In Spain, *garbanzos* form the basis of *olla podrida* (which means rotten pot) and in Portugal they are combined with spinach and eaten with bacalhau—dried salted cod—and other dishes. In the Middle East chick-peas are combined with tahina paste, lemon and garlic to make the delicious spread, hummus, and Israel uses them for its version of falafel, which is so widely eaten that it has almost become the national dish. They are a common ingredient of couscous and are also mixed with beef and vegetables to make a rich and filling Israeli dish called Dfeene or Daphna. They are an important crop in India, where they are often cooked with garlic and chili peppers and turned in aromatics before being fried with herbs and spices in clarified butter.

## Split peas

Although there are still some dingy grey dried peas to be had, most are now sold skinned, split and bright green or golden yellow. Thick yellow pea soup—*ärter med flask*—is the traditional Thursday evening dish in Sweden, keeping alive the memory of the unpopular King Eric XIV whose last supper on earth, on a Thursday, consisted of this very dish. His brother had contrived to slip a dash of arsenic into this humble food, which would hardly have crossed royal lips had Eric not been imprisoned at the time by his eventual successor.

Green split peas form the basis of a traditional English dish, pease pudding, which is usually eaten in slices with gammon. Although an egg is sometimes beaten into the mushy pea mixture to make it creamier still, it is one of the characteristics of split peas, yellow or green, that they turn into a purée by themselves and do not have to be mashed.

## Lentils

Red, brown and green lentils have all the virtues of dried peas and beans, and the additional one of needing less cooking time, particularly split lentils. The small red split lentil, originally a native of India, needs no soaking and becomes tender within about 20 minutes' cooking, quickly turning into a mush if overcooked. The brown lentil, also known as the German lentil, and the green lentil of France, *lentille de Puy*, take a little longer to cook.

Lentils make excellent purées and soups. In Germany they sometimes accompany roast duck, while in France lentils cooked with garlic and flavored with a squeeze of lemon juice are eaten with a *petit salé*—hot salt pork.

## Dhals

These are not a particular type of bean but the Hindi word for dried beans and peas, and most packages labelled dhal in the West will contain split varieties such as chick-peas, lentils and the pigeon-pea, which is known as the tur dhal. They are not soaked but are cooked for 40–45 minutes and served spiced as a thick purée, or are mashed to make thick soups. Another of the dhals, the urd dhal, is often ground and becomes the basis of the poppadom, without which no curry would be complete.

## Mung beans

These beans, called green gram or golden gram, can of course be cooked in the usual way, but they tend to become rather sticky. They are now chiefly used, like alfalfa seeds and soybeans, for sprouting.

## Soybeans

The soybean is the most nutritious of all beans and the most easily digested. Better known for its products than for the bean itself, it is one of the few known sources of complete protein. It has been periodically rediscovered by the West, but was first brought to Europe in the eighteenth century, when it confounded scientists with its amazing qualities and is still the subject of considerable research.

But while the West has only recently started knitting soybeans into steaks and processing it into cheese, the Chinese have for thousands of years called them "the meat of the earth," and have used soybean curds —a bland substance known as *tofu*, which soaks up other flavors—as a substitute for meat, fish and chicken. The extracted "milk" is used in cooking many vegetable dishes, soy sauce is used for flavoring and a dark paste made from the bean is sweetened and used in desserts in the manner of jam.

Of the thousand or so known varieties, two soybeans are chiefly cultivated—one sort for commercial purposes, the other to be eaten both fresh (when young) and dried, in which case they are prepared and cooked just like other dried beans.

## Adzuki beans

The adzuki bean, also known as the asuki bean and the aduki bean, is one of the most delicious and also one of the more expensive of the dried beans.

A native of Japan, it is small and red with a curious keel-shaped ridge. It is a fairly recent arrival in the West and is found mainly in health food stores. It is cooked in exactly the same ways as other dried beans, both in Japan and abroad, but since it is very much sweeter than most other beans its flour is also much used for cakes and pastries in Japan, and the crushed bean is made into puddings and ice cream by the Chinese. It is one of the most easily digestible of all the dried beans.

It was that scholarly seventeenth-century figure, John Evelyn, who said of a salad that it should be composed like a piece of music, with each ingredient playing its due part without being overpowered by anything of strong taste. Since his time, a salad has come to be widely regarded as an attractive and nutritious proposition, so much so that in many countries it is served as a second vegetable dish.

Exactly at what point of the meal to serve a green salad is a matter of taste. Ancient Romans, who regarded the lettuce as a panacea for all ills, believed that its milky juices "lined the stomach," enabling people to drink more with their food. Accordingly, lettuce was served as a first course, as it is still sometimes eaten, although hardly for the same reason, in the United States. It is more usual to eat it with or after the main course: immediately following, as in France and England; or at the same time, on a side plate or, not so agreeably, on the same plate —although this has something to recommend it in the case of such dishes as chops, steaks or roast chicken: the meat juices mingle so delectably with the dressing.

Green salads should not meet their dressings until they are on the point of being served, since once dressed they rapidly become limp. A good compromise is to prepare the dressing in the bowl, and to place the leaves lightly on top without mixing them. Some people prefer to mix the dressing at the table, while Italians simply pour olive oil and then vinegar onto the salad—they say you need a generous person for the oil, a miser for the vinegar, a judge for the salt and a madman to mix it.

To make sure that your "sallet herbs," as John Evelyn called them, are fresh and good, see that the leaves look vigorous and show no sign of brown. Inspect the cut parts: they should be sound, neither blackened nor soggy. The heavier the lettuce the more tightly packed it will be, giving you more leaves for your money.

A salad plant in good condition will stay fresh in the refrigerator if it is wrapped in a plastic bag to retard the evaporation of its moisture. Should it have wilted, it can be refreshed by being plunged into water, shaken dry and put into a large covered pan, or in the refrigerator in a plastic bag or wrapped in a damp dish towel.

Salad leaves should be washed and dried —either by absorbing the moisture with a clean dish towel or by getting rid of it in a salad shaker. The leaves should be torn rather than cut, to avoid bruising. For such dishes as seafood cocktail, which require shredded lettuce, a knife has to be used, but only just before the greenery is needed since it wilts so quickly after being cut.

Apart from being used in salads, lettuces and other leafy plants can be cooked. The less substantial the leaf, the faster it collapses, and while heavier leaves may retain a bit of body, lighter ones do not. For braising, choose small plump lettuces and cut them in half or braise them whole.

## Round or cabbage lettuces

These vary greatly in size and crispness but have in common their general round shape. Although there are many varieties of cabbage lettuce, ranging from soft to very crisp, there are three main types.

**Butterheads** are floppy, loosely packed and delicate. A particularly melting one, Bibb, is prized in the United States. Another, Continuity, is grown in England and sports leaves with a reddish tinge to them. It is often sold by name as a special delicacy. Butterheads tend to be floppy, a characteristic which is by no means a defect as long as the loose leaves are fresh.

**Icebergs** Whereas there is not much joy in eating a tired and wilting butterhead, these hearty lettuces, when fading on the outside, may still be full of vitality in the middle. Icebergs, such as Webb's Wonderful, are by far the crispest lettuces—they are also called Crispheads and are often sold without their aureole of outer leaves, looking like tightly wrapped heads of cabbage.

**Looseheads** are cabbage lettuces which have no heart at all. Instead of the leaves, which are often crinkled, becoming more tightly packed towards the center, they all splay outwards from the middle.

## Romaine or cos lettuce

Far more elongated in shape than round cabbage lettuces is the romaine or cos lettuce. Tall and large with a nutty flavor to its vigorous leaves, it has a beautifully crisp and tender heart. Its two names—cos in England and romaine in France and the United States—testify to its origins: the Romans found it on the Greek island of Cos and brought it back to Rome, whence it was introduced to the rest of Europe.

## Chinese cabbage or Chinese leaves

A wide variety of these are grown in China, and they frequently end up in large wooden barrels, coarsely chopped and pickled in brine. They are often used for dishes that need a piquancy or bite to them.

The Chinese cabbage with which we are becoming increasingly familiar is a variety called, in Chinese, *pe-tsai*. It resembles a large, pale romaine lettuce and is crisp and delicate with a faint cabbage flavor. Its crinkly inner leaves are best in salads, while the outer leaves, once divested of their tough ribs, can be braised, stir-fried, simmered, or treated like ordinary cabbages.

Less familiar is the Chinese *bok-choy*. It looks more like spinach, and indeed is also known as Chinese mustard spinach. The large coarse leaves radiate loosely from the stalk. This variety is often used for pickling by the Chinese since the leaves taste somewhat harsh.

## Celtuce

This tall Far-Eastern specimen is among the less well-known salad plants. So called because it tastes slightly of celery and looks rather like a head of lettuce, with long pale stalks and a head of leaves, it used also to be called asparagus lettuce. However, it tastes neither like asparagus nor much like celery or even lettuce. The similarity to celery lies mostly in the crunch of the stalks, which, like celery, can be eaten raw, making a good salad when peeled and chopped. The similarity to lettuce is confined to the tender central leaves. The stalks can also be cooked like Swiss chard, and make a similar vegetable dish to be eaten with butter or a creamy sauce, while the tough outer leaves can be cooked like spinach.

## Corn salad or lamb's lettuce

This is what you are served when you order a dish of *mâche* in France. The spoon-shaped leaves grow in dark green rosettes, which are difficult to wash since they harbor sand. It is more substantial than lettuce and has a nutty taste which blends particularly well with the sweetness of beets for an excellent winter salad.

## Chicory, endive and escarole

**Wild chicory** with its pretty blue flowers is the ancestor of varieties that are now grown primarily for their roots, which are roasted and ground to make a coffee substitute. Its leaves have a bitter taste and are sometimes mixed with other salad leaves.

**Belgian endive or witloof** First bred in Belgium, which explains its Flemish name, this is the best known of the cultivated chicories. It is blanched by being grown in the dark or under peat, and with its tightly furled leaves it resembles a fat white cigar. A yellowish frill bands the juicy white parts, which are in fact the broad, succulent center ribs of an underdeveloped leaf. Sliced across or with the leaves separated, it makes a fresh and interesting salad. It can also be mixed with sliced orange or a little watercress and some oil and lemon juice.

What little bitterness there is in Belgian endive tends to come to the fore when it is cooked, so it is usually blanched in a little stock and a few drops of lemon juice before being braised. In this way it is particularly good with ham, veal, chicken and pigeon.

**Radiccio or ciccorio** There are several types of this chicory introduced from Italy. Looking like miniature colored lettuces, the plants can be either deep ruby-red, cream splashed with a fine wine-red, or marbled pink when they have been grown in the dark. When they have not been carefully shaded they look green or dark copper colored and less pretty. It is its beauty that recommends radiccio: it tastes

much like a lettuce, but with more bitterness and has somewhat tougher ribs. It makes a very beautiful salad mixed with green lettuce and pale yellow escarole.

**Curly or frizzy endive and escarole** The curly-leaved endive and the broad-leaved escarole are more robust than the lettuce tribe. Although by nature they are bitter, they become less so when the jagged rosettes are shielded from the light and

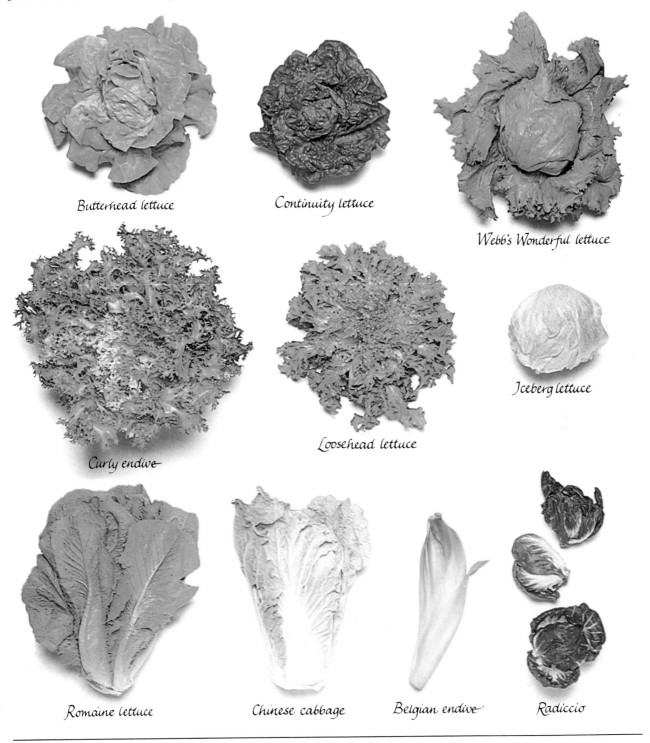

*Butterhead lettuce*

*Continuity lettuce*

*Webb's Wonderful lettuce*

*Curly endive*

*Loosehead lettuce*

*Iceberg lettuce*

*Romaine lettuce*

*Chinese cabbage*

*Belgian endive*

*Radiccio*

blanched to a succulent pale golden-green. Look for these in winter—they have much more character than most hothouse-reared winter lettuces. Curly endive looks like a pale greenish-white mop, and escarole has broad crinkled strap-shaped leaves with a rather leathery texture. Prepare curly endive and escarole as you would a lettuce, but with a more highly flavored dressing; use them to give texture to a salad made of more delicate leaves or on their own. A few walnuts with perhaps some strips of bacon make a good addition, and this is the salad to eat with Roquefort dressing.

Escarole is often called by its variety name, Batavia, while the different names used for curly endive must stem from its Latin name, *Chicorium endiva*—in France it is known as *chicorée frisée*, and in the United States it is called chicory as frequently as it is known as curly endive.

## Cresses

**Watercress** Dark green, bunched sprigs of watercress make a beautiful garnish for broiled kidneys, chops and game, and little sprigs enhance both the taste and look of a green or an orange salad. A watercress sauce is an excellent and pretty complement for fish. When buying watercress, the rule is the darker and the larger the leaves, the better. Use it soon after purchase, keeping it meanwhile in the refrigerator in a plastic bag or, better still, in a cool place in water, like a bouquet in a jam jar or, even better, completely submerged in a bowl.

**Mustard and cress** The tiny embryonic leaves of mustard and salad or garden cress are usually found in the thinnest and most delicate sandwiches—especially those containing egg or chicken, to which they bring a warm, sharp flavor—and as a garnish sprinkled over salads. If you don't grow mustard and cress yourself, what you are most likely to buy growing in little boxes is simply cress, the smaller of the two.

## Radishes

As a family, these roots belong to the mustard tribe, which, considering their hot pungency, is not surprising. In shape and color they range from little scarlet or white globes to long red and white types such as the Icicle radish. There is even a black radish, which has ice-white flesh.

Pungency varies not only according to type but also according to the soil in which the plants are grown. The red and white type tends to be the mildest and goes by the name of French Breakfast radish, although one has yet to meet a Frenchman who actually eats them first thing in the morning. The most pungent of the pure white radishes is the type offered in Bavarian beer halls to encourage thirst.

Except in the East, where radishes are eaten as a fully fledged vegetable, they mostly provide an appetizer. "As they carry their pepper within," they are simply dipped in salt and eaten with crusty French bread and butter, or themselves buttered. In Italy thin white slices of radish with their pretty red edges are scattered over green salads, perhaps with some equally thin slices of carrot.

**Winter radishes** This term is applied to those large varieties with flesh that is compact and firm. They are cooked or grated into salads, and can also be curried.

**The daikon, or mouli,** is the winter radish from the Far East, the birthplace of radishes. Long, white, cylindrical and enormous, it can be pickled, or grated and mixed with grated ginger roots to make a sauce for fried vegetables, and features in tempura dishes.

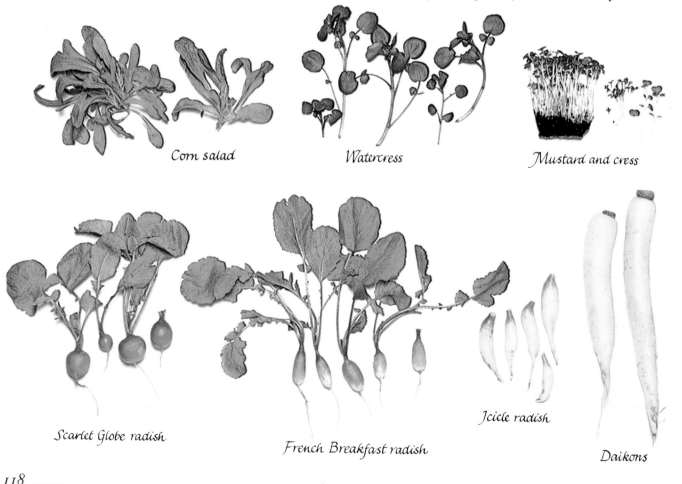

Corn salad

Watercress

Mustard and cress

Scarlet Globe radish

French Breakfast radish

Icicle radish

Daikons

Vegetable recipes **296–311**
Bowls **364**

Salade frisée au lard **297**
Light watercress soup **198**
Watercress quiche **275**

Mustard seeds **178**, *178*

Radis au beurre **297**

This group of green-leaved vegetables includes several that are now considered to be weeds. Once they were as well known as spinach, which since its wide cultivation has displaced them. But while spinach is the most widely grown and popular of all our leaf vegetables, there should still be a place in the kitchen for its old-fashioned relations.

## Spinach

The long cultivation of spinach, since its first appearance in Persia many thousands of years ago, has resulted in succulent leaves of a beautiful green, which may be small and rounded—the best for salads—or larger and more pointed.

Since spinach greatly reduces in volume when cooked, you need to allow $\frac{1}{2}$ lb/225 g for each person. It is customary to remove the stalks and, if they are coarse, the midribs from each leaf, which is done by folding the leaf inwards and pulling the stalk towards the tip. The spinach should then be well washed in several changes of water to remove the grit which it often contains. It should be cooked on a low flame, pan uncovered, with only the water that clings to the leaves. As the lower layer softens, stir the spinach and continue in this way until all the leaves have wilted down. It must be very well drained as it tends to exude water after it is cooked.

Spinach can be used in a multitude of ways. As an accompanying vegetable it can be served simply with masses of butter, or in a mornay sauce, or as a purée with cream. In *Cuisine Minceur* spinach is mixed with pears for a beautiful light green purée. Sweet spinach purée, although it sounds unfamiliar, is an ancient dish: Elizabeth I sat down to a pipkin of boiled spinach mixed with rosewater, raisins, vinegar, butter and sugar. And a pastry shell filled with spinach, candied orange and lemon peel and bathed in a rich creamy custard is a Christmas dish of southern France.

In Italy there are dozens of lovely spinach recipes: spinach is eaten in soufflés, frittatas and dumplings; mixed with ricotta, Parmesan and nutmeg to make a filling for stuffed pasta; and used to make fresh green pasta, which looks so pretty with a cream or tomato sauce. No wonder that spinach garnish goes under the Italian name of *alla fiorentina*. Eggs Florentine are eggs arranged on a bed of cooked spinach under a covering of cream or mornay sauce; fish and sweetbreads *à la florentine* have spinach in the filling. So it is not surprising that the thin, sweet florentines, all almonds, nuts and candied fruit held together, it seems, by chocolate alone, once contained spinach too.

Spinach can also be eaten raw: delicious salads can be made with small, fresh spinach leaves garnished with pieces of crisply fried bacon and hard-boiled eggs, tossed in a garlic-laden vinaigrette.

There are also some wild plants that are reminiscent of spinach in flavor, two of them so close to spinach in taste that they are sometimes cultivated.

**New Zealand spinach** is a fleshy leaved plant discovered by Sir Joseph Banks, botanist on Captain Cook's *Endeavour*, who brought it back to Europe. It is still grown outside its native land, flourishing where excessive heat and lack of water would prevent true spinach growing well. Somewhat tougher than true spinach, it is often sold in local French markets, where it is called *tetragon*.

**Malabar spinach** This thrives in tropical Asia and in tropical parts of America. The large, bright, shiny leaves have a distinctive but good taste, and are treated in the same way as spinach. In China it is cultivated for its fleshy berries, which yield a dye that has been used by women as a rouge and by high-ranking officials for sealing documents.

## Cabbage greens

Any member of the cabbage family which does not form a proper head becomes simply "greens," also known as spring or winter greens in England and collards in the United States. All greens should be very fresh and need to be bought in generous quantities, since they reduce in volume when cooked. They should be cheap enough to allow any woody stems, coarse midribs or damaged leaves to be ruthlessly discarded. See that the midribs are crisp and snappy.

**Collards, or spring and winter greens,** are the Cinderellas of the vegetable world, but, like Cinderella, they are good and can be quite splendid when properly dressed. The leaves are particularly tender and delicate when cooked, and are excellent for sustaining dishes such as New England's "mess o' greens," which usually contains salt pork and is much like the southern United States' dish called "pot likker," always eaten with corn bread to sop up the broth.

**Kale and curly kale** Of the two, curly kale is the better known and certainly the better tasting. Kale, with its smooth, greyish-green leaves, is less succulent than other greens but is good when stir-fried.

Curly kale has crimped leaves, like giant parsley. It was known by the early Greeks and Romans, whose climate was too warm to grow cabbage. There are many varieties; some are grown as ornamental plants, and there is even one type whose stems become so hard and woody that when dried they are made into walking sticks. The edible ones taste rather like collards but stronger and can be used for all cabbage recipes.

## Beet greens or spinach beet

Beets are not only cultivated for their excellent red roots but also specially for their leaves. The first-century Roman gourmet Apicius included in his book recipes for beet greens with mustard, oil and vinegar, and for barley soup with beet greens. In fact, in his day only the leaves were considered worth eating.

Beet greens are grown extensively in eastern districts of France where, together with Swiss chard, they are known as *blettes* and are used interchangeably with both Swiss chard and seakale beet. They are often mixed with sorrel to counteract the latter's acidity, being themselves extremely mild. When cooked, they are used like spinach, and in Italy are very popular as a stuffing for ravioli or agnolotti, together with ricotta and Parmesan cheese.

## Sorrel, dandelions and purslane

**Sorrel** Of all the different types of sorrel, it is the cultivated French variety that is best for eating, adding an acid, lemony note to salads, soups, purées, sauces and omelets. The classic potage Germiny consists of sorrel cut into delicate ribbons—called a chiffonade—cooked in butter and then moistened with chicken stock and thickened with egg yolk. Because sorrel, even more than spinach, is rich in oxalic acid, it should be eaten in moderation, but a purée of sorrel is the traditional accompaniment to broiled shad and is also an exceedingly good foil for salmon.

**Dandelions** In some countries gardeners wage constant, if ineffectual, war against this golden flower, as a noisome weed. In others they buy packets of seed and take great trouble earthing up the plants to keep them tender and white for the salad. In France, housewives buy them on market stalls. Those addicted to dandelions should be warned that in France they are called *pissenlits*, and one of their many local English names is piss-a-bed, illustrating their diuretic properties.

Weed though they may be, they are certainly useful. The roots can be used as a caffeine-free coffee substitute and the leaves make excellent salads. Perhaps the best is *pissenlits au lard*, a bowl of small, fat, juicy, whole dandelion plants in vinaigrette, over which is thrown a panful of sizzling pieces of salt pork or bacon and bacon fat.

You can remove most of the bitterness from wild dandelions by placing a plate or tile over a patch of young plants, but the juiciest, least bitter dandelions are those grown from a packet of seed. Blanch them before they start to produce flower buds and pick them young.

**Purslane** A native of India, where it has grown wild for thousands of years, fleshy leaved purslane spread to England in the Middle Ages and was popular as a pickle and salad. It was introduced to America by the early colonists, but today most people discard it as a weed. In England, too, it was once cultivated in gardens, but it is now uncommon. The French are more astute and still consider purslane—known as *pourpier* in France—to be a salad plant worth cultivating. The succulent leaves can also be boiled, and are good when briskly fried in butter and then cooked in an omelet. In the Middle East, where it is also cultivated, it is an important ingredient in *fattoush*— a salad mixture including tomatoes and cucumber eaten with pita bread.

## Wild greens

There are still many edible green-leaved plants growing wild and free which, if nothing else, can be regarded as survival food. However, much enjoyment can be had gathering these plants on country walks and experimenting with cooking and eating them at home. Make sure, though, that you know exactly what you are gathering. If you are uncertain of what the plants look like, take sketches with you of the plants you want to find so that you can identify them.

**Nettles** Northern countries used to prize the nettle, but it is now something most people avoid because of its sting (which completely disappears when the nettle is cooked). In Scandinavia the leaves were boiled like spinach, and the coarse fibers of the stalks used for cloth, in the manner of flax. (This explains, without making it any less sad, the task of the fairy-tale maiden set to stitching nettle garments for her seven brothers, to lift the spell that had transformed them into swans.) Ireland combined nettles and oats in a broth, but her nettle haggis—a purée of nettles, leeks, cabbage, bacon and oatmeal boiled in a bag —would not, one imagines, pass muster with a Scot. Italians still eat nettle purée or soup in the spring as it is supposed to be excellent for cleansing the blood.

Nettles should be picked when they are only about a finger-length high; later on they become bitter and tough. Remember to wear gloves and use scissors to snip off the leaves.

**Goosefoots** The two best-known members of this family are the delightfully named Good King Henry and Fat Hen, both of which were staples in antiquity but have now been superseded by spinach. Fat Hen is a tall, stiff-stemmed plant, which grows prodigiously wherever there are people—or weeds. It tastes much like spinach but is considerably milder. The leaves of Good King Henry are also treated like spinach, and some suggest that the shoots can be prepared and eaten like asparagus.

**Amaranthes** The green leaves of this species, known as pigweed, also have a taste similar to spinach, although more tender and sweet. The celery-like stalks taste somewhat of artichokes.

**Chickweed**, so called because poultry have a particular yen for it, grows in all temperate climates of the world. Probably the most common of all edible weeds, it is a tender vegetable which, cooked in butter with chopped onion, goes well with rich meats.

**Brooklime** This makes a perfectly acceptable, though slightly bitter, substitute for watercress. Brooklime is found by streams and in marshy places in North America and in northern Europe.

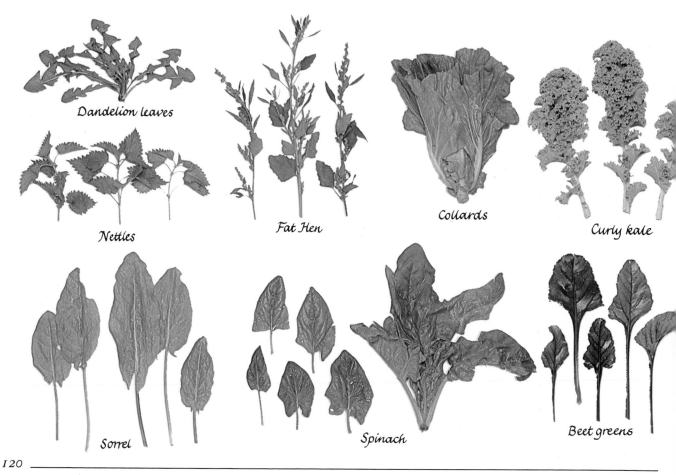

Dandelion leaves

Nettles

Fat Hen

Collards

Curly kale

Sorrel

Spinach

Beet greens

Cabbages which form into a head are members of the vast brassica family, which also includes cauliflowers, broccoli and brussels sprouts (as well as turnips and kohlrabi, which are eaten, respectively, for their roots and their swollen stems).

All brassicas are descendants of the wild cabbage which still grows in coastal regions of Italy and France—a tough, tall plant, almost all trunk. They are rich in vitamin C and minerals, but half the vitamin content is lost when they are cooked, and they all contain sulfur compounds which give them their characteristic "cabbagey" smell when they are overcooked.

## Cabbages

There are three main types of cabbage which form into a head, distinguished mainly by color: green, white and red.

**Green cabbages** Early green cabbages are a deeper green and more loosely packed than the later ones, often with pointed heads. Buy them in the spring, checking that the leaves—frequently curly at the edges—are fresh and crisp, and do not worry about the lack of heart—they simply have not had time to develop the firmness associated with the later kind, but even the outer leaves should be tender.

The later green cabbages are altogether tougher, but have solid hearts. They include the crimped variety, called the Savoy cabbage, which is particularly tender and mild flavored and needs less cooking than other varieties. The Savoy's head is firm, for all its crinkliness, and is a beautiful green with a touch of blue; it stands up well to frosty weather and is therefore readily available throughout late winter.

**White cabbages** are in fact the very palest of green, almost white, and are sometimes called Dutch cabbages. Like red cabbages, they have smooth leaves, and should be quite hard and firm.

**Red cabbages** Although these have magenta or dark purple skins, the color fades during cooking unless a little vinegar is added. The flavor is improved by the added sharpness, too. Some raw beet grated into the cooking liquid towards the end of cooking also gives a brilliant red color. They are best stewed with plenty of spices and flavorings and are also good when they are pickled.

### Buying and storing cabbages

When buying cabbages, no matter what kind, look not only at the leaves, which should be sound and unblemished, but also at the cut trunk. This should be neither dry and split nor woody and slimy. Those with wilted outer leaves or a puffy appearance should be avoided.

The firmer the cabbage, the longer it will keep—Savoys can be kept in a cool place for several days; white and red cabbages will keep for at least a week.

### Cooking cabbages

Red cabbage is cooked very differently from green and white varieties, with such ingredients as wine vinegar, red wine, apples, currants, onions, brown sugar and spices going into the pot after the cabbage has been gently sautéed in lard, oil, butter or goose fat. A sweet and sour red cabbage dish is also much improved by the addition of some dried prunes during the cooking. Red cabbage is traditionally served with the Christmas goose in many northern countries and is also excellent with pork or game. Pickled red cabbage is one of the best of all pickles to eat with cold meats.

The simplest way of cooking a green or white cabbage is to boil it, after removing the core and thickest stalks, and washing it in a bowl of cold water with a tablespoon of salt to deal with the creatures that might lurk between the leaves. Cut into quarters or shreds, it needs no more than 8–10 minutes to cook—the moment it starts to sink it is ready—and it should be cooked uncovered.

The sodden leaves which mark overcooked cabbage have to take much of the blame for the ruin of Britain's culinary reputation. Yet cabbage that has been carefully cooked and gently but thoroughly drained, and then

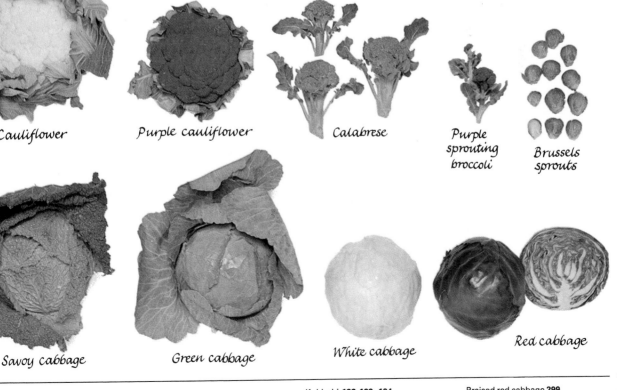

*Cauliflower*

*Purple cauliflower*

*Calabrese*

*Purple sprouting broccoli*

*Brussels sprouts*

*Savoy cabbage*

*Green cabbage*

*White cabbage*

*Red cabbage*

gently heated with a generous quantity of butter, makes a delicate, light vegetable dish. Long, slow cooking gives an excellent texture quite different from cabbage cooked fast and served green.

There are several good slowly cooked dishes in which the cabbage is started off with lard and onions and then cooked on with meat: partridges, no longer young, for *perdrix au chou*; lamb, beef or spiced salt beef for Irish-American "boiled dinners." Then there are the filling, stock-based cabbage soups, poured over slices of bread for extra body, which make complete meals by themselves.

In northern Germany there is the famous hunter's cabbage, made with golden cubes of fat bacon bathed in a piquant sauce, which accompanies the equally famous brat-wurst. In Bavaria cabbage is braised with chopped bacon, caraway seeds and white wine, while the nineteenth-century King of the dream castles, the eccentric Ludwig, liked to eat his cabbage casseroled with pike and served with a crayfish sauce.

Stuffed cabbages are a subject on their own: stuffings of all descriptions are layered between the blanched and semi-unfurled leaves. Ingredients may include different kinds of meat, bacon, chicken livers, herbs, rice, onions and chestnuts, all bound with eggs and possibly rice or bread crumbs. Cabbages can also be stuffed after being hollowed out, with their tops cut off but replaced before going into the oven, or the individual leaves can be stuffed and tied into little parcels.

Sweet-sour cabbage dishes are popular with Jewish Americans and in Russia, where cabbage baked with apples is eaten with smoked meats. From sweet-sour it is only a small step to sour; cabbage ferments and becomes sauerkraut when packed in a barrel with salt. Fresh sauerkraut for immediate use is preferable to the bottled versions. Raw white cabbage makes a good salad either as coleslaw, with its thick creamy dressing, or simply shredded into a bowl and dressed with oil and vinegar.

## Cauliflowers

Since early cauliflowers used to be no larger than tennis balls, one can justify the complaint made by six seventeenth-century travellers to Italy who rose from the table in a marble palazzo as hungry as they arrived, having shared between them one cauliflower, a dish of anchovies and three hard-boiled eggs. Modern cauliflowers can be enormous, although ironically a strain no larger than golf balls is being grown for the freezer; people are not happy, it appears, with the more usual stalky frozen flowerets. A type of cauliflower grown in Sardinia and

southern Italy is purple, but turns green when cooked unless it is carefully steamed.

A fresh head of cauliflower will have a compact cluster of creamy white flowerets, or curds—so called because they resemble soured-milk curds—and feel heavy for its size. Loose or spreading flowerets mean the cauliflower is overmature.

When cooking cauliflower, start testing for tenderness after five minutes or so by carefully sticking a skewer into a side stalk, and continue testing until there is little, but still some, resistance. A whole head in boiling water cooks in about 25 minutes; flowerets take about eight minutes and will cook more evenly. Overcooking turns the flowerets into a flavorless mush.

Boiled cauliflower needs sauce: a tomato sauce, or light creamy sauce flavored with cheese or mustard, or perhaps an Italian sauce incorporating chopped onion, capers, olives and anchovies, or fried bread crumbs and chopped hard-boiled eggs. Cauliflower and cheese have a special affinity: cauliflower au gratin is a classic, and the English nursery dish, cauliflower cheese, can be delicious if cooked well. Flowerets of raw cauliflower, arranged around a bowl of mustardy mayonnaise, make a good cocktail party offering, and cold cooked flowerets in a mustardy vinaigrette dressing make a delicious salad.

## Broccoli

Like the cauliflower, broccoli started life in the Mediterranean region where the warm, dry climate encouraged wild cabbages to shoot into buds rather than concentrate on making leaves. The earliest broccoli was the purple sprouting type with green stalks and loose green rudimentary flowers. The best and most luxurious of the broccolis is Calabrese. It is a delicate vegetable and combines the subtle, fresh texture of cauliflower with the succulence of asparagus.

**Purple sprouting broccoli** This was the type the Romans ate cooked in wine, or dressed in oil and sharp *garum*—a sauce of fermented fish—and as a garnish in a soup of chick-peas and lentils, peas and barley. In Sicily broccoli is still cooked in the oven with anchovies and onions. In the rest of Italy it is often parboiled and finished off with oil and garlic in the frying pan, and perhaps eaten with pasta.

Although less succulent than Calabrese, purple sprouting broccoli is a very fine vegetable. Its stalks are usually cooked whole with the small loose flowerbuds and served drenched in butter. There are also white and green sprouting broccoli and these are treated in the same way. The flavor of all is excellent but they must be picked young or they become stringy and

tough. Purple sprouting broccoli turns green on being cooked; the others keep their original color.

**Calabrese broccoli** Named after the Italian province of Calabria, where it was first grown, this beautiful bluish-green broccoli keeps its color when it is cooked. The large flowerheads sit on succulent spikes, and one of the tests for freshness is to see that the spike snaps cleanly: however, one's eye can also tell one whether they are juicy and stiff. Avoid flowerets that show the least sign of turning yellow.

Broccoli of whatever kind is best boiled briefly so that it still preserves some crispness, and it can be used for all cauliflower recipes. In fact, a white head of cauliflower looks particularly appetizing when surrounded by green broccoli flowerets. Broccoli alone is often eaten with a hollandaise or béarnaise sauce, or simply with butter and a squeeze of lemon juice.

## Brussels sprouts

At their best, brussels sprouts look like tiny green buds, at their worst, like miniature full-blown cabbages. Developed in Flanders, the vegetable garden of Europe, some time in the Middle Ages, brussels sprouts grow at the intersection of leaf and stalk on a tall plant that much resembles the old wild cabbage. They have a delicate nutty taste, especially when they are small. Cooked until just tender but not too soft, they are an excellent vegetable.

The ideal size for brussels sprouts is just a little larger than hazelnuts. These, however, are usually sold at some expense in baskets, while the ordinary medium-size ones are sold loose or in nets. Do not waste much time before using them—they soon turn yellow. Look for compact green heads and uniform size so that they will cook evenly. Some people cut a cross in the stem, but this is really only necessary in large specimens with coarse, wide stalks; fresh small ones do not need such incisions. They need to be washed, trimmed of any yellowing leaves, and to be cooked in fast-boiling well-salted water without a lid so that they preserve their good green color.

Brussels sprouts very often accompany the turkey, with separately cooked chestnuts, for a traditional Christmas dinner. On less festive occasions they appear simply tossed in butter, or with brown butter and bread crumbs. They are also good "au jus," with the addition of some good clear gravy. If used to garnish a meat dish or game birds in France, the dish is called *à la bruxelloise*. Some people like them with a béchamel or mornay sauce, or with slices of crisply fried bacon. They are also good braised in butter and lemon juice.

# Vegetables/*Stalks and Shoots*

Although shoots and buds often look appetizing, there are in fact only a handful that make serious eating: the buds of the palm tree are familiar as hearts of palm, and asparagus and bamboo shoots are two of the best vegetables there are—particularly asparagus, one of nature's kindest gifts to man. Stalks are mainly enjoyed in the form of celery and sweet fennel, chard and cardoons, while the globe artichoke, a companion delicacy, is a flower head.

### Florence fennel

Looking like a short, bulbous celery plant, Florence fennel, also called sweet fennel or finocchio, is a close relation of the herb, and the same feathery leaves can be seen emerging from its fat overlapping stalks. Like the herb, it tastes of anise and its leaves can be used to flavor court bouillons for fish

dishes. Southern Italians eat it raw, dressed in oil or with an aïoli sauce, and it makes a very good addition to a green salad.

When braising fennel, allow one head per person, trim away the stalks and string it as you would celery, and halve or quarter it. Choose fat round bulbs in preference to long flat ones. Buy fennel as fresh as possible; it should be white with a greenish cast—any yellowness is a sign of age. It will keep crisp in a plastic bag in the refrigerator.

### Asparagus

Although there are many species of asparagus, from the thorny ones of Spain to the shiny ones of the Far East, asparagus is always something of a luxury because its season is so short. There are also many differences in the way it is raised: French asparagus is cut near the crown when the top part has emerged above the soil; English and American asparagus is allowed to grow above the ground, which gives it its green color all the way down the stalk; Dutch and German ivory-tipped asparagus is

always grown under mounds of soil, which helps to blanch it, and it is cut as soon as the tips begin to show.

Whatever the color, the thick varieties of asparagus are the ones which are most prized. Those of Argenteuil, with their white stalks showing a purple tinge towards the top and their pointed green and purple heads, are considered to be the very best, certainly in France, but this does not stop England and America from believing their asparagus to have a superior flavor. In fact each of the great asparagus-growing areas—Argenteuil, Candes, Fribourg, Schwetzingen, Bassano and Norfolk and many parts of the United States—tends to prefer its own asparagus, because although asparagus travels well it starts to lose flavor from the moment it is cut; it is a revelation to eat asparagus fresh from the garden, cut and cooked within the hour or even sooner.

Thick or thin, the tips are the best part and this is the part to inspect when buying asparagus. The tips should be tightly furled with the scales close together, and none of them discolored or moist. Loose asparagus,

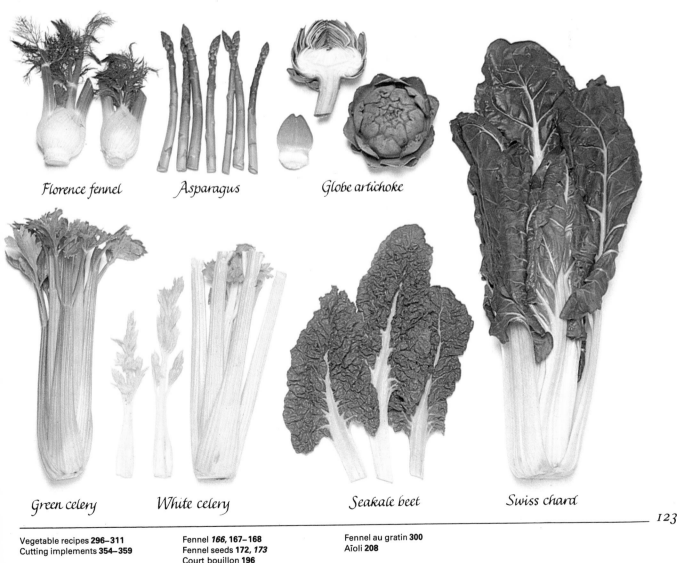

*Florence fennel*     *Asparagus*     *Globe artichoke*

*Green celery*     *White celery*     *Seakale beet*     *Swiss chard*

which is sometimes thin and often short, and may be sold as "grass" or "sprue" asparagus, is usually well worth having.

The difficulty encountered in cooking asparagus arises from the fact that the tips, being much more tender than the stalks, cook more quickly and may break off when you transfer the asparagus to the serving dish. The answer is to cook asparagus in an asparagus kettle, a special pan with a rack, but failing this, cook them tied together in bundles in a wide pan, in which case it is extremely important not to overcook them or boil them too fast, otherwise the tips will become damaged.

To prepare the asparagus, wash it well, cut off the hard ends and pare the lower part of the stalks with a knife or potato peeler, then tie the asparagus into two or three bundles. Bring a deep saucepan of well-salted water to the boil, lower the bundles into it so that the stalks are in water and the tips in the steam, and return to the boil as rapidly as possible. Cover with a loose dome of foil to help retain the steam and boil for 15–18 minutes, until the lower parts of the stalks are easily pierced with the tip of a knife. Don't overcook them—they should be just tender when pierced and will go rather slimy if boiled for too long.

Save the asparagus water and a few token asparagus for making soup. Serve the rest, carefully drained, and slightly less than hot. In Britain, thick asparagus is always served as a separate course, usually at the beginning of the meal, occasionally at the end, and it is always best eaten with the fingers, the delicate tips first.

Served warm, thick asparagus is good with melted or whipped butter or hollandaise, or with mousseline sauce, or *à la flamande* with halved hard-boiled eggs and noisette butter served separately. Served *à la polonaise*, the noisette butter—butter heated in a pan until it is a pale hazelnut color—is poured over the tips that have been sprinkled with finely chopped hard-boiled eggs.

In Italy, asparagus is eaten with Parmesan and butter over the tips, melted for a moment under a broiler. If served cold, mayonnaise or vinaigrette are the usual accompaniments. As asparagus contains a certain amount of sulfur it spoils the taste of wine, so save this for other courses.

Thin asparagus makes a good vegetable dish and goes well with delicate, light kinds of meat: veal, brains, sweetbreads, chicken breasts, slices of turkey or rosy boiled ham, thinly sliced. Broken asparagus can also go into quiches or omelets. In restaurant dishes, the presence of asparagus tips is indicated by the words *à la princesse*, but in all but the very best establishments these tips will most likely be the limp canned variety as opposed to fresh specimens.

## Celery

This can be white, which means that it has been blanched during cultivation or is the self-blanching kind that is naturally golden-white, or it can be green. The white varieties are usually more tender and less bitter than those that are green.

Celery is usually sold neatly packaged in transparent wrap and already washed, ready for use. The stalks should be thick and crisp, the leaves green and full of vitality and the base sound. When the leaves and the outer stalks are missing (which you can see when examining the base), the celery is not likely to be very fresh, but limp celery can be revived by wrapping it in moist paper and standing it in a jar of water. Raw celery sticks are often served with cheese in a tall pitcher with their decorative leaves intact, but the coarse outer strings should be removed first by cutting partway through the stalk bases and pulling off the attached strings down the length of the stalks.

Raw celery is excellent with cheese and, chopped, it is good mixed with cream cheese and in sandwich fillings. Celery also goes into poultry stuffings and sauces, and can be stewed with butter and lemon juice as an accompaniment to game. It is delicious parboiled, stuffed and served *au gratin*, and is equally good when braised plain, or *à la grecque*, when it is eaten cold.

## Sea kale

Highly popular in earlier times, although less often seen now, this frail, pale vegetable grows wild in English coastal districts, forcing its stalks up through piled up sand so that they emerge perfectly white. Cultivated sea kale is cut when its leaves are no more than a yellow frill edged with purple, and is boiled in seawater, or in salted water by those who are distant from the shore. The juicy but delicate stems are sometimes found in the stores wrapped in dark blue tissue paper, for once they are exposed to the light they very soon lose both their pallor and their flavor.

Sea kale should be boiled for about 18–20 minutes to become tender, or it can be parboiled and then braised. Plain boiled in little bunches, it makes, like asparagus, a course of its own, and is served with the same sauces as asparagus. It is also good raw, like celery, with cheese.

## Swiss chard and seakale beet

No relation to the seakale of coastal areas, these varieties of beets are grown primarily for their pale, wide midribs. Their green leaves can also be prepared like spinach or beet greens (whose stalks are not big enough to be cooked separately).

The large, silvery Swiss chard, also known as silver seakale beet, has a delicate flavor and, like the smaller seakale beet, is extremely succulent when boiled or steamed. Both can be served *au gratin* or simply dressed with melted butter. In France chard, or *blettes*, are served with béchamel sauce and sausages.

## Cardoons

A relation of the globe artichoke, the cardoon is cultivated for its leaf stalks and has a flavor that faintly resembles the artichoke. Left to itself, it produces a smaller, spikier head than the artichoke, which can be picked and eaten in exactly the same way, but what comes into the stores are the bottom ends of the plant, looking like overgrown grey-green celery. Like celery, cardoons are earthed up to blanch the stalks, which gives them their delicate texture and delicious flavor.

The finest cardoons are those grown in the region of Tours, but since Italians enjoy their *cardoni* even more than do the French, you are most likely to come across cardoons in Italian shops.

To prepare them, trim off the skin, which is fibrous and prickly at the ridges, blanch them in boiling water and then cook them for about 30 minutes in acidulated water—like artichokes, cardoons discolor easily when cooked. Serve them with a béchamel or cheese sauce, or *alla piedmontese*—dipped in a sauce of anchovies, oil and garlic—or simply eat them with melted butter.

## Bamboo shoots and palm hearts

Edible young bamboo shoots—and not all bamboos are edible—are bought fresh in the Far East and, stripped of their tough brown outer skins, the insides are eaten. Their texture is similar to celery and their taste to a globe artichoke.

The canned variety is the most readily available kind outside the Far East and needs no peeling, but it should be rinsed before use because it is preserved in brine. Chopped bamboo shoots can be used in a number of stir-fried vegetable and meat dishes, and as a garnish for clear chicken broth. They can also be served with any of the sauces that are suitable for asparagus.

Fresh palm hearts, which are the buds of cabbage palm trees, need to be blanched before being cooked to get rid of their bitter flavor. They can then be simmered in wine, perhaps, or braised. When hot, they are eaten with any of the sauces suitable for asparagus; cold, they need a vinaigrette dressing. They are also good in mixed salads. Hot or cold, they are usually served cut in half lengthwise.

## Hop shoots

While the dried flowers of hops are used for brewing, the young blanched shoots, cooked and eaten with melted butter, make a useful substitute for asparagus—in France, where they are known as *jets de houblon*, they are considered a delicacy. Like asparagus, they should simply be rinsed well to clean them of any soil and sand, then tied in bundles and boiled. Their delicate flavor goes well with creamy sauces, and in Belgium young hop shoots are served with eggs.

## Globe artichokes

Although not strictly a stalk, shoot or bud, the globe artichoke is usually considered in the same group as delicacies such as asparagus. While some of its flavor lies in the fat base of each of its leaves, the best part—the heart, or *fond*—lies deep within its center.

When you buy artichokes—they can be green or purplish—make sure they still have a good bloom on their leaves and that the centers have not unduly darkened, ready to burst into great purple thistle-like flower heads. They don't keep well and should be used at once, but if you must keep them, place their stalks—they are usually sold with about 4 in/10 cm of stalk—into water.

To prepare them for cooking, twist off the stalks, which will also remove some of the tougher fibers from the base. Then, with a stainless-steel knife, cut the globe flush so that it won't wobble on the plate when it is served and rub the cut surface with lemon to prevent it turning black. If the leaves are very spiky, cut them into a pretty V shape. Wash the artichoke and then boil it in acidulated water in a non-oxidizing pan, perhaps with a piece of lemon tied to its base. Test for readiness by tugging at a leaf: when it comes away and is tender, the artichoke is done and ready to be drained upside down on a rack.

One of the best ways of eating globe artichokes is simply to take each leaf in the fingers and dip the fleshy part in turn into melted butter or into vinaigrette or hollandaise. Then draw it through the teeth, eating the fleshy part and putting the remains of the leaf onto your plate. When you come towards the end of the vegetable, and the tiny pale leaves seem to be arranged in the form of a little pointed hat, grasp it tightly at its top and pull off the whole rosette. Pull away and discard the prickly straw-like choke, which may come away with one tug or need a bit of scraping, and eat the heart, which is slightly pitted, with a knife and fork.

It is possible to remove the choke before cooking, to form little cups. This is usually done in good restaurants, where instead of a simple butter or vinaigrette dressing you may be offered various sauces such as puréed shallots reduced in wine. The hearts can also be stuffed, perhaps with a béchamel enriched with egg yolks and Parmesan, or a mixture of bread crumbs and chopped ham or bacon, or bread crumbs, eggs and cheese. They are usually parboiled before they are stuffed, and then go into the oven, surrounded by vegetables and anointed with oil or butter, until the stuffing is cooked. For delicate dishes or when artichoke hearts are required as a garnish, remove the green leaves, keeping the firm white-green part.

Among the many ways of preparing artichokes, the Italians have produced the most inventive. They simmer large globes in broth or wine, or in wine with oil, tomatoes and garlic, and fry small, tender ones in oil; sometimes they blanch them and then dip them in batter before deep frying them. As elsewhere, they are also eaten cold.

Chopped cooked artichoke hearts may be mixed with peas and ham or scrambled eggs for an interesting first course, and if you are given a soup called Chatelaine you will find that it is made of puréed hearts. In the south of France and some parts of Italy, tiny young artichokes no larger than walnuts are eaten raw, either whole with aïoli or *bagna cauda*—a hot anchovy and garlic flavored dip—or thinly sliced with Parmesan in olive oil.

### Preparing globe artichoke hearts

**1.** *Snap off the stalk, drawing with it the fibers from the heart.*

**2.** *Trim the stem end with a stainless-steel knife, just exposing the white base, and trim away all the tough outer leaves. Have a lemon handy to rub on the exposed parts to prevent them discoloring.*

**3.** *Slice off the top of the artichoke so that the pink tips of the choke are just visible.*

**4.** *Scoop out the prickly choke with a sharp-sided stainless-steel teaspoon until you are left with a pale empty cup-like heart. Put this immediately into a bowl of water, acidulated with lemon juice.*

From the moment they are picked, peas, beans and sweet corn start converting their sugar into starch. Because this process subtly alters both their taste and texture, it is freshness just as much as youth that matters and they should be chosen carefully and eaten the very day they are bought. Freezing, however, arrests these changes, which is why frozen peas, beans and sweet corn retain their sweetness and melting consistency so well.

## Peas

Once inordinately expensive and considered a great luxury, peas have become one of the best loved of all vegetables and endless varieties have been developed, especially in England where the climate suits them to perfection.

**Snow peas and asparagus peas** Snow peas, also known as mangetout and sugar peas, are, as their French name suggests, eaten pods and all. There are many varieties, all bred with the minimum of thin, tough membrane that lines the pod of the common green pea, so both the large, flat snow pea pod with immature seeds and the smaller, darker kind make tender eating, provided they are very young. If they have threads at the sides, these should be removed in the kitchen during topping and tailing.

Snow peas taste best when they are briefly boiled, in plenty of well-salted water; the salt helps them retain their color. When cooked, they should still have a little bite to them, and they are best served perfectly plain with enough butter to coat each pod. Very young snow peas are good in salads, and all snow peas are excellent when they are stir-fried.

Asparagus peas, not a relation of the asparagus but of the cow pea, and in fact not a true pea at all, are rarely seen these days. They have winged pods which, like the snow pea, are eaten as well as the seed, but they are only good when they are very young and 2 in/5 cm long or less.

**Garden peas and petits pois** Contrary to popular belief, petits pois are not small because they are immature but are a dwarf variety. These are the peas canned in vast quantities by the French and Belgians, and they are excellent: tiny, dull green and very sweet, quite unlike most other canned peas, especially the fat, ugly canned peas sold in Britain, swimming in green dye. These are best avoided altogether.

Gardeners make a distinction between two types of garden pea: the larger marrowfat, which is wrinkled when dried, and the varieties that remain smooth when dried. The former is much sweeter and is the one most often frozen.

The reason for the disappearance of many varieties of green pea is, of course, the ubiquitous frozen pea; more expensive to be sure, but a great timesaver. And by the time peas bought in their pods have been shelled, the actual price difference does become blurred.

Shelled peas respond to all sorts of treatment: in England they are liked best plain, boiled and bathed in butter, but some cooks like to add a small sprig of fresh mint. In Italy peas are often mixed with fine shreds of raw ham, or with rice, in which case the dish becomes *risi e bisi*. In the countries where vegetables are habitually served in a light coating of béchamel sauce peas, too, are given this treatment. They are often mixed with carrots, *à la flamande*.

*Petits pois à la française* are peas cooked in a lettuce-lined saucepan with a little sugar, some tiny silver onions, a lump of butter and only as much water as clings to the lettuce leaves after washing. Cooked in this way, the peas turn a delicate yellowish color and have a most delicious flavor; even peas on the mealy side become melting and young tasting. Really solid older peas are best for fresh green-pea soup or purées.

## Pole beans

This is a group of beans, eaten for their pods, which came to market in colors ranging from deep green and purple to pale yellow. The two main types are the French or green beans, and the runner or pole beans.

Of the French beans there are dozens of varieties. Snap or string beans, a fairly fat, fleshy variety, should snap in half juicily if they are fresh. The highly prized haricot vert is slim and delicate and should be eaten very young and when no larger than the prong of a carving fork. The yellow wax-bean is also a French bean and is somewhat mild in taste.

Runner beans have long, rough and usually stringy pods, although stringless varieties are available. As their name suggests they are a type of climbing bean, as are the delicious purple-podded beans, which have stringless purple pods, but turn the normal green when they are cooked.

Whatever the type, podded beans should be crisp and bright—avoid buying wilted ones or overly mature beans with tough-looking pods. They all need topping and tailing, and some types still need de-stringing. Test for stringiness by keeping the top or tail end just attached to the pod and drawing it downwards: if a portion of stout thread comes away, careful de-stringing is indicated.

All podded beans are cooked in the same way. Too often they are overcooked, but they should be plunged into well-salted, rapidly boiling water and cooked until just *al dente*. Once drained, they can be tossed in butter until they glisten, or French beans can be served in a sauce containing shallots, or cream and butter with chives, or bathed in a tomato paste with a touch of onion.

## Fava beans and lima beans

In their first youth, neither fava beans nor lima beans strictly require shelling, but the pods are nearly always discarded to reveal large, flattish seeds.

Fava beans—also known as broad beans or Windsor beans—are the original Old World bean, much appreciated in Italy and Spain. These large, lumpy beans with their furry lined pods should be shelled immediately before going into the pot, unless they are very young, in which case they need only to be topped and tailed and can then be cut up, cooked and eaten pods and all.

Lima beans, named after the capital of Peru, are most familiar in America in their shelled and frozen state, but are at their best when they can be bought fresh and in their shells. They appear in the American Indian dish succotash, which also includes sweet corn, and are known in the southern American states as butter beans. There are two types of lima bean—the baby Sievas, pale in color, and the larger Fordhooks.

For a plain dish of fava beans or lima beans, plunge them into rapidly boiling water and cook until just tender, but not a moment longer. They are also delicious with cooked ham or bacon. Elderly beans need skinning after they are cooked.

## Okra

These curved and pointed seed pods came originally from Africa, but travelled to America and feature a great deal in Creole cooking. The flavor resembles that of eggplant but the texture is mucilaginous, and this is what gives the body to the Creole stews and gumbos to which okra is added.

Crossbreeding has produced a range of colors and surfaces, but the slim green octagonal okra is the one usually sold in the West. Look for crisp pods and avoid any that are shrivelled or bruised. To cook okra whole, trim off the tip and the cap, but be sure not to expose the seeds and sticky juices inside or the okra will split and lose shape during cooking. Cooked in boiling salted water until just tender, they can be served with a tomato sauce or simply tossed in butter.

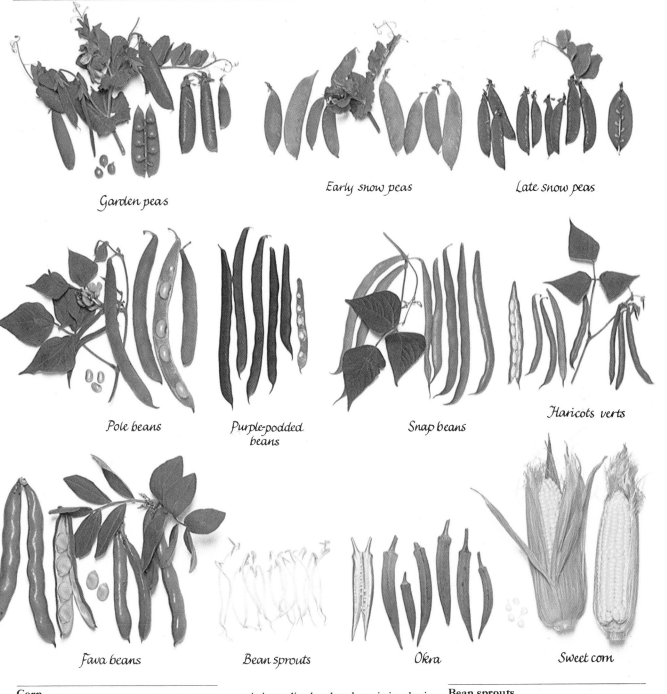

Garden peas

Early snow peas

Late snow peas

Pole beans

Purple-podded beans

Snap beans

Haricots verts

Fava beans

Bean sprouts

Okra

Sweet corn

## Corn

One of the delights of late summer is the appearance on the market of fresh, tender young sweet corn. The husks should be clean and green, the silk tassels bright and golden brown with no sign of dampness or matting, the kernels plump, well filled and milky, with no space between the rows. Avoid cobs with immature white kernels or older large ones that look tough and dry.

With fresh sweet corn, time is of the essence—the briefer the span between picking and eating, the sweeter and more tender the corn will be. But if you can't

use it immediately, then keep it in plastic bags in the refrigerator for two or three days. Allow corn plenty of space—if the cobs are piled on top of each other, this tends to generate warmth and "cook" the corn.

To cook corn on the cob, strip away the green packaging and silk tassel and plunge into briskly boiling water or milk and water. A little sugar can be added for extra sweetness—especially for the corn sold in Europe, which is never quite as sweet and tender as American corn.

Serve with plenty of butter, salt and freshly ground pepper, and large napkins.

## Bean sprouts

The sprouts that can be bought in plastic bags and are the main ingredient of chop suey have usually been sprouted from mung beans or soybeans. Look for crisp, pale sprouts; even a hint of exuding brown juice means that they are past their prime. Mild flavored, they add a crunchy texture to salads, or they can be stir-fried briefly over high heat and seasoned with soy sauce and scallions. Serve them immediately or they will lose their crunch. Keep sprouts in a plastic bag or box in the refrigerator while they are waiting to be used.

Corn on the cob **302**, *347*          Mung beans *114*, **115**

The onion family, including garlic and leeks, has a great many members, both cultivated and wild. It is because the onion is such an ancient vegetable that it has been bred in so many forms, and while many of these can be used interchangeably, each type has a particular use.

## Onions

Being both flavoring agent and vegetable in its own right, the onion is something that no kitchen can ever be without. There are few non-sweet dishes that don't start with a sliced or chopped onion, and few that would be good without it. Then there are onions in onion soup, creamy or clear; sauce soubise or onion sauce to go with lamb; flans like zwiebelkuchen from Austria or the French *tarte à l'oignon*; as well as all the garnishes that this versatile vegetable provides. Among these are the glazed, bronzed button onions, good with any plainly roasted meat, particularly veal; fried onion rings that go with steak and liver; little pickled onions, and the smaller, fresh green-tailed onions that are eaten with cheese.

### Green or fresh onions
These are eaten fresh in salads, but can also be cooked. There are two types of green onions, so called because of the green leaves that form above the white part. They are scallions or spring onions, and Welsh onions or Japanese bunching onions.
**Scallions or spring onions** may be slim and tiny, like miniature leeks, except that their leaves are tubular, or they may have been lifted from the soil after small silvery bulbs have formed just above the roots. They taste mild and quite delicate, and both the white bottoms and the green tops are used as lively additions to salads. When cooked they are added to some dishes in which other onions would be too strong, and they are also good chopped finely and mixed with mashed potato, and in omelets.
**Welsh onions or Japanese bunching onions** If you find scallions mentioned in Chinese or Japanese recipes, these are the onions you should use, if you can get them —they are not widely known in the West and certainly not in Wales, despite their Welsh name. The other name for the species, Japanese bunching onion, is more precise, since they are very popular in the Far East. The difference between scallions and Welsh onions is that the bulbs, or enlargements, of the Welsh onions are covered with dry outer coats. They grow in a cluster and can be used early in the year as scallions, then as fresh bulb onions.

### Globe or dry-skinned onions
It is a good idea to try to buy globe onions in assorted sizes, or to choose smaller rather than larger specimens as, once cut, they do not keep well. To keep back the tears when peeling an onion, try skinning it under running water. Holding a piece of bread between your teeth is said to be helpful too.

Chopping an onion into dice can be quite a fast business if efficiently tackled. Peel the onion but do not cut off the root end. Halve the onion through the root and lay the half onion cut side down. Slice down into narrow strips from tip end to root end, but do not let the strips fall apart. Now, holding the half onion together, cut strips lengthwise, at right angles to the first cuts, remove the root end and the onion will fall into dice.

Once chopped, the onion is often sweated in hot fat—which means allowing it to become transparent without coloring—or fried to a more or less deep gold to develop its characteristic flavor. It is then incorporated into the dish in the making.

Globe onions come in all sizes from pearly button onions to coppery spheres as large as a grapefruit, and in a variety of shapes: oval, round, slender and flat. All come to a peak at the top, like the domes of the Kremlin, which owe their shape to the fact that the many-layered onion—"a sky within a sky" —was regarded as a symbol of eternity in its native Asia and beyond.
**Yellow onions**, so called although their outer skin is golden brown rather than yellow, are considered to be the most pungent of all the globe onions. Look for sound specimens, dry, with no trace of moisture at the base or the neck and with no growth of light greenery at the top—a sign that they have begun to sprout again at the expense of the soundness of their core. Yellow onions are the basic all-purpose onion. The smallest are often offered as pickling onions, but do as well for the pot.
**Spanish onions** These large, flattened, brown or pale copper-colored onions are generally inclined to be milder and sweeter than the yellow variety. Their size makes them particularly suitable for stuffing and baking, and their comparative gentleness makes them ideal as fried onions, in salads and for use in dishes that need their substance, such as creamy soups and sauces.
**Italian onions** These are large, relatively mild and distinguished by their deep red skin and the red-tinged layers below the skin. They can be used for the same purposes as Spanish onions and are good to eat raw in antipasti and in salads.
**Bermuda onions** As large as the Italian onions but rather more squat, these can be used in the same ways as Italian onions and are ideal with hamburgers.
**White or silver onions** These relatively mild little onions have shimmery silver skins. They are about the size of a walnut and are best either added to stews or served in a cream sauce. Very tiny white onions are called pearl or cocktail onions. Sold in jars, these are used as a garnish in various cocktails such as the Gibson—which is what a martini becomes when an onion replaces the usual olive. Slightly larger white onions are used for pickling, and in many French dishes such as *coq au vin*.
**Tree onions** A curiosity for the gardener, the tree or Egyptian onion produces its cluster of little copper-colored bulbs at the top, where one normally expects to see only flowers. Although fiddly to use they are quite an acceptable substitute for other onions, particularly for pickling.

## Shallots

These slender, pear-shaped bulbs with long necks and skins that range from grey to copper are intense in taste without being unduly pungent. They grow singly or in clusters and are more seasonal than onions, since they do not keep as well. The crisp layers of their flesh are finely textured, and since shallots taste sweet and delicate they are mostly used for flavoring. No other onion produces such an exquisite flavor in a sauce such as *beurre blanc*, a butter sauce which features shallots cooked in wine or in wine vinegar.

When recipes specify shallots, they should be used. On the other hand, it is sometimes perfectly in order, although extravagant, to use shallots instead of onion. The exception comes when browning is involved—this makes shallots taste a little bitter.

Shallots are an important ingredient in the cooking of northern France, featuring in *marchand de vin* sauces, made by reducing shallots to a purée with wine, to go with steak, and in fish dishes.

## Garlic

By far the most pungent of the onion family, garlic grows in a cluster of pointed bulbs, called cloves, from a single base. Many people are prejudiced against garlic because it lingers on the breath, but by way of compensation when garlic is eaten in company the nose develops a tolerance of the garlic-laden breath of others. And it is said that vast quantities of garlic eaten at a single sitting will not have much effect on the breath. It is certainly true that a slowly cooked dish using a great deal of garlic— say a chicken cooked on a bed of whole cloves of garlic—or even whole heads of garlic, which can be roasted unpeeled and eaten by picking up the cloves at the end and squeezing the content into the mouth, taste much sweeter and far less garlicky than something like a salad with raw peeled and bruised garlic in the dressing.

Garlic grown in a hot climate is considered to be the most pungent. As a flavoring agent it is therefore most economical in use. But wherever it comes from, and whether it is sold tied in strings or bunches, in little nets or loose, and whether it is snow-white, grey, purple or pinkish, look for fat, round, hard bulbs.

Fresh new-season's garlic, available in the summer, has a specially subtle flavor and, with its suede-like inner skin, is liked by connoisseurs for their salads. However, most garlic is allowed to dry off: it keeps well in a dry airy place. Too much moisture in the air, and it will start sprouting in due course; too much warmth, and the interior cloves turn to black dust—but this takes a matter of months rather than weeks.

To prepare garlic, carefully skin as many cloves as you plan to use. Whether you chop them in the ordinary way, mash them with salt under the point of a knife, or crush them in a garlic press is a matter of taste: the finer the result, the more of the pungent oils are released and it is probably true that the garlic press produces the least subtle taste.

There are many dishes to which garlic gives its essential flavor. It blends well with meat, particularly lamb, with fish and many vegetables, especially the Mediterranean ones such as tomatoes and eggplant, and with mushrooms, whose flavor it enhances. Without it there would be no aïoli, the garlic-laden mayonnaise served with fish soups, boiled chicken and every sort of fresh vegetable, and it is an essential ingredient in the cooking of southern Europe.

## Leeks

The leeks that good Welshmen used to wear in their hats on St. David's Day were in fact their native non-bulb forming onions, and leeks were once used interchangeably with onions. But they are, with their flat leaves arranged in chevron formation, more delicate in taste than onions. A leek is certainly a more subtle flavoring for broth, earning it the title of "king of the soup onions." Scotland's cock-a-leekie is a justifiably renowned soup composed of chicken and leeks, and the leek's talents were taken to their logical end when the *chef des chefs* of New York's Ritz-Carlton hotel invented his *crème vichyssoise*.

Sadly, many cooks quite ignore the leek's virtues as a plain accompanying vegetable; it is excellent simmered in butter, stewed in red wine, or lightly browned and then cooked in a tomato sauce.

If they have a drawback, it is that they can be rather a bore to clean. There is no problem when recipes call for chopped leeks, when it is a case of chopping first—after pulling off the outer membrane and trimming the wilted part of the greenery—and cleaning later. This is best done by placing the chopped leeks in a colander set in a bowl and running cold water over them until all the grit has settled at the bottom of the bowl. But when recipes call for sliced leeks, it is necessary to loosen the leaves gently so that the water can run right into the furled vegetable. Most leeks on sale look quite clean, but it is only the outside dirt that has been removed by the growers; in the kitchen it is usually a question of making little slits with the point of a knife in appropriate places and of rinsing until all the grit has gone, or cutting them almost in half down the middle if they are very gritty.

When you buy leeks, examine them at both ends. The white part should be firm and unblemished; the green part fresh and lively, since it is useful for soups or stock even if your main dish only calls for the white part. When leeks are sold trimmed, without much greenery, you may suspect that they are not only elderly, but so mature as already to have formed a solid tubular flower stalk in the middle, which you will have to discard, being left with a disappointingly hollow stem as a result.

Spanish onions

Garlic

Yellow globe onions

Leeks

Pickling onions

Shallots

Scallions

# Vegetables/*Roots and Tubers*

The root vegetables and tubers —carrots, parsnips and potatoes, turnips and rutabagas—certainly make rather a humble-sounding list when they are all lumped together. It is true they are of the earth, rustic, robust and ordinary, but it is because of this that they have always been so useful.

In hard times, when people couldn't afford to obtain bread, or were forced to make it out of fern roots, it was herbs and root vegetables, particularly turnips, that kept them alive, since herbs can be gathered wild and roots, surviving the worst rains or droughts, can be stored through the winter. In better times, roots were the vegetables that were liked best in most households, alongside a piece of boiled or roasted meat —hence boiled beef and carrots, roast duck with turnips, haggis with mashed rutabagas and everything with potatoes.

## Potatoes

Potatoes, whose mysterious underground swellings make better use of their patch of ground than any cereal, are one of the world's most important food crops. They are a most obliging and good-natured vegetable. Easy to grow, cheap to buy, simple to cook and tremendously filling, they also seem to be the one vegetable, apart perhaps from tomatoes, that nobody ever seems to get tired of.

There are endless varieties of potatoes to suit all sorts of uses. Popular varieties change rapidly, coming into favor with the growers because they keep well or are resistant to disease, and then being ousted by newer, even hardier kinds with higher yields or fewer eyes. This makes it extremely difficult to make a catalogue of varieties.

However, different types of potatoes, round, oval or kidney shaped, pink, red or white, do have very different qualities, and a well-informed supplier will be able to tell you which variety is which. There are floury or mealy potatoes, ideal for mashing and baking, but annoying if you want to boil them whole as they tend to fall apart in the water. They are also useless for making French fries. Waxy potatoes are very firm fleshed and not at all good for mashing, as they become glutinous, but they make excellent potato salads, lovely boiled potatoes, and excellent pommes dauphinoise, when the potatoes are cooked in slices that are supposed to remain whole.

There are also all-purpose potatoes, whose texture is described as firm. These can be used for almost anything, except perhaps potato salads. They don't disintegrate, can be made into French fries and are good for baking. But they don't always have the best flavor, so it is a good idea to try different varieties as you come across them, and then keep to the ones you like best.

As well as different varieties there are, of course, new and old potatoes. Potatoes which are called new or early are simply those dug early in the season while they are still small and sweet. Old potatoes, or maincrop, are lifted when they are mature and fully grown, and have converted their sugar into starch. These can be stored through the winter and until the beginning of the next season when the new potatoes— tremendously welcome—reappear.

### Buying and storing potatoes

New potatoes should be small and faintly translucent under a coating of slightly damp loam; if the skin is a little ragged and so tender that you can pull it off in strips, so much the better—this shows that the

*New, or early, potatoes for boiling*

*Old, or maincrop, all-purpose yellows*

*Old, or maincrop, all-purpose whites*

*Waxy maincrop for boiling*

*Waxy salad potatoes*

*Yam*

*Sweet potatoes*

Roots and tubers recipes 303–306
Knives 354–356
Cutting implements 357–359

Pommes dauphinoise 304

potatoes are fresh and will be easy to scrape. New potatoes do not keep particularly well, becoming more difficult to scrape (in which case scrub them and cook them in their skins). They also lose their flavor after a few days, so buy them in small quantities and keep them in a cool, dark place.

Old potatoes are more amenable and can be stored in a cool, dark, dry place for months on end. Choose dry potatoes with some earth on them, free of sprouts and without the green patches that appear when potatoes are exposed to light—these contain poisonous alkaloids. If they do have green parts, cut them off. Avoid potatoes that have scaly or rotting patches and, if buying washed potatoes in bags, avoid those that look damp or show signs of condensation as you may find that they have an unpleasant, moldy flavor.

### Potatoes for boiling

The very best dish in the world is probably new potatoes boiled and served with a good deal of melted butter and a sprinkling of coarse salt. For perfection, choose walnut-sized potatoes, scrape or scrub them and drop them into already boiling salted water. Bring them back to the boil, and after about 10 minutes of gentle boiling start testing frequently with a kitchen needle or skewer. Drain as soon as they are tender. A small sprig of fresh mint added to the water heightens the flavor.

For a delicate, somewhat earthy flavor, old potatoes can be scrubbed and boiled in their skins—this conserves the vitamins, too—and then peeled while they are still hot, unless you want to be rustic and serve them with skins on. But skinning hot potatoes can be painful and tedious, so don't attempt it when you are preparing potatoes for more than two or three people.

Otherwise, old potatoes should be peeled as thinly as possible, as many of the vitamins are concentrated just under the skin. If they are not to be cooked immediately they must be put straight into a bowl of water or they will dry out, and some varieties will discolor on contact with air, but don't soak them too long as this can also lead to a loss of vitamins.

When ready to cook them, put them in a pan of salted cold water, bring them to the boil and then cook them fairly gently—fast boiling causes them to bump against each other, which breaks them up. When they are just tender, drain them thoroughly and return them to the pan. Let them steam for a minute, then drop in a few nuts of butter and turn the potatoes over gently until they are well coated. Some people like to leave potatoes after they are cooked and drained in a warm place with a folded napkin placed over the pan to absorb the steam.

Boiled potatoes are very absorbent and good for all dishes with a lot of gravy to mop up. In some countries raw potatoes are dropped into the top of stews about 25 minutes before the stews are ready to serve. They absorb any fat that has risen to the top of the casserole and also help to stretch the dish a bit further.

### Potatoes for sautéing

The dry, firm texture of yellow-fleshed maincrop potatoes makes them ideal for sautéing. Cut them up and drop them into boiling, well-salted water for about five minutes before frying them, or fry them raw, drying them in a cloth before putting them into the hot fat.

Potatoes can also be grated before they are sautéed. Rösti, the Swiss national dish, is usually made with potatoes that have been boiled the previous day and kept overnight, traditionally in the snow but the refrigerator will do, to dry them out a little. They are then grated and fried gently in butter, formed into a pancake and inverted on to a plate with the golden crust uppermost. Pommes lyonnaise are potatoes sautéed with fried onions.

### Potatoes for frying

Whether you call deep-fried potato sticks French fries or chips, choose firm, dry potatoes. The yellow-fleshed varieties are best, although whites are also good. These are also the potatoes to use for croquettes, game chips, gaufrettes—waffle-cut game chips—matchsticks, ribbons, potato puffs and all the many other varieties of fried potatoes.

When frying raw sliced or chipped potatoes, they should be soaked in cold water for at least half an hour to rid them of their surface starch, otherwise the pieces will stick together when fried. Dry them well, since hot fat foams up over wet potatoes and could easily bubble over. Fried potatoes should be salted after cooking, and like other fried foods they will turn soft if covered after cooking.

### Potatoes for roasting

Most maincrop varieties are fine for roasting, but small potatoes should be avoided because roasting tends to dry them out, and new potatoes do not roast well (make them into pommes rissolées). Potatoes roast better if they are first boiled in well-salted water for about five minutes, drained and then returned to the pan to dry off over a low heat, uncovered, for a minute or two.

### Potatoes for mashing

Dry, floury, "old" potatoes are ideal for mashing. Peel and boil them until they are very tender, drain them well and then mash them thoroughly before adding any liquid, which should be hot for best results. Add butter at the end, beat thoroughly and taste for seasoning—they always need more salt. In France, meat juices are sometimes added to mashed potatoes instead of milk.

The habit of piping mashed potatoes around the edge of certain dishes such as coquilles St. Jacques is a very poor one. By the time the potato, stiffened with egg, has been piped, rebaked to set it and served, it has lost all its fresh flavor and it looks pretentious too.

### Potatoes for baking

Dry, floury potatoes such as the long, white-skinned varieties are ideal for baking. They have a white, creamy flesh and are usually large or medium size, which is what is needed for baking. So-called russet potatoes are also good. Baked potatoes are extremely health giving since there is no loss of goodness or flavor into water that is then thrown away. They are also a wonderful vehicle for toppings such as cheese, sour cream, bacon bits and chives.

### Potatoes for salads

The classic potato salad is plainly boiled and sliced waxy potatoes mixed with a simple vinaigrette while they are still hot. A little more dressing is added just before serving. Another version is mixed first with a little dressing while still warm, and then with some good, creamy homemade mayonnaise when cool. Celery, freshly cooked French beans or dill are good additions to fresh potato salad. Serve it with frankfurters or salt herrings—its bland flavor is an excellent foil.

### Sweet potatoes

The tuberous roots of a tropical vine, sweet potatoes have a taste of faintly scented artichoke. The small or medium-size ones are best; they should be firm and well shaped. Avoid cracks and damp patches.

Sweet potatoes are an important ingredient in Creole cookery and are eaten fried, whipped up into purées or soufflés and as an accompaniment to sugar-cured Virginia ham. In the southern United States they are often boiled and mashed with nutmeg, or made into a sweet-potato pie. Candied, they are a traditional accompaniment for a Thanksgiving turkey, and in Australia they are parboiled and roasted with pork.

### Yams, taro and cassava

Yams belong to a family of climbing plants that flourish in South and Central America and the West Indies. They come in a large number of shapes and sizes and the flesh is white or yellow, with a texture similar to potatoes. In North America, where true yams are not cultivated, orange-fleshed sweet potatoes with brownish skins are known as yams. The true yam, however, is much sweeter and moister than the sweet potato, although both are usually prepared in much the same ways, boiled and served with butter, nutmeg and other spices as well as apples, oranges and nuts. Like sweet potatoes, they are delicious when fried.

Looking much like yams (and found in the same markets) are taro root, or dasheen, and cassava roots—the source of tapioca. They taste similar to potatoes and can be prepared in the same ways, but the taro root will turn a greyish-green color when boiled.

## Carrots

These range from slim little slips, pale apricot in color and no longer than a little finger, to long, stout cylinders, light orange to the deep color of nectarines.

Young carrots, tender and melting, have a most delicate flavor. Washed and simply thrown into boiling water for no more than seven minutes, then tossed in butter and sprinkled with parsley, they are one of the celebratory dishes of early summer. Parboiled and glazed in a stout pan with butter and possibly a little sugar to emphasize their natural sweetness, they become one of the garnishes of haute cuisine.

When young carrots are boiled in their skins, then drained and rubbed in a towel, the skin will slip off quite easily and in this way the smooth, transparent inner skin, beneath which the vitamins lie, is retained.

Mature carrots are the great standby for hearty winter dishes. They accompany boiled beef and dumplings and it is to them, together with onions, celery and leeks, that good warming broths owe their flavor—but don't put in too many or the broth will become so sweet that people will think there is sugar in it. They are also used to make the excellent carrot soup, potage de Crécy.

The stubby, bright, almost translucent carrots of uniform size usually found in supermarkets are bred more for the convenience of the seller than the buyer, because they travel well. Although their flavor is a little elusive they are delicious eaten raw and make a good dish on their own, either as carrots Vichy—sliced and cooked in Vichy water and sprinkled with parsley—or simply served with butter and parsley. Their main advantage is that they stay crisp for longer during cooking.

### Buying and storing carrots
Avoid specimens that are rubbery, blemished or cracked with age. The green discoloration sometimes seen at the top of certain carrots denotes immaturity but does not diminish their flavor. If storing carrots in the vegetable compartment of the refrigerator, take them out of their plastic wrapping. Outside the refrigerator, they should be kept in a cool, airy place to preserve their crispness.

## Parsnips

Related to the carrot, parsnips are almost as sweet but blander. They are delicious in soups and stews, and there are many old country recipes for parsnip flans and puddings which make good use of their sweetness. This is often emphasized by the addition of ginger, spices and honey. Sweet parsnip dishes are part of the English country tradition, as is parsnip wine, a clear, pale gold drink that is delicious in the year it is made, but even better 12 months on. Boiled parsnips mixed with mayonnaise were once served as mock lobster, but they are probably nicer without the pretentious title.

Available from early autumn until spring, parsnips are at their best in midwinter, especially when their ivory skin has been touched by frost. They can be bought washed, or with traces of soil still clinging to them, in which case they keep better. Those with brown patches or those that look wizened or dry should be avoided, but parsnips with "fangs" and blemishes can be cheap buys and as good and as nutritious as perfect specimens.

Store parsnips in a cool place—the Dutch seventeenth-century paintings that show root vegetables spread around the housewife's feet do not signify untidiness but the fact that the tiled floor of the kitchen was the coolest place. An airy larder or the crisper compartment of the refrigerator is more convenient nowadays.

## Salsify

Black-skinned salsify, which has snowy white flesh, is known as scorzonera; white salsify is also called the oyster plant because its taste is supposedly reminiscent of oysters. In fact, the flavor of both has a nodding acquaintance with that of asparagus; it is just as delicate and therefore at its best when simply boiled or poached and served with a good knob of butter, or perhaps a creamy white sauce made of a roux moistened with the cooking liquid and a dash of cream.

Salsify is neither easy to peel nor to clean, so is best boiled in its skin and peeled afterwards, or skinned thinly with a swivelling potato peeler and plunged immediately into a saucepan containing a "blanc"— water to which a tablespoon of flour has been added (vegetables cooked in a blanc will keep their color). The white stalks should then be cooled and gently reheated with a little butter. As they are water retaining, they will neither fry nor burn providing the pan has a well-fitting lid.

When buying salsify, choose those with a topknot of fresh-looking leaves, avoiding any that look sad or shrivelled, or buy canned salsify, since this is one of the few vegetables that lends itself really well to the canning process.

## Celeriac

The edible root of a certain kind of celery, celeriac is not a neat-looking vegetable and needs to be peeled with a sharp knife. Under its brown exterior the flesh is pale, but discolors when exposed to the air so should be plunged immediately into a bowl of acidulated water. Cooked, its texture is similar to that of a potato, but less smooth and with more bite to it. Celeriac is a great standby, not only because soups and broths are often improved by a slight celery flavor and it is in season when celery perhaps is not, but also because céleri rémoulade—one of the delights of French cuisine—cannot of course be made without it. Boiled and diced, celeriac is delicious in potato salads, and in Germany it is served with diced apples, potatoes and beets in a herring salad. Puréed, it is excellent with game.

## Beets

Globe shaped or long and pointed, beets come in bunches with edible greenery at the top when young, loose and trimmed of leaves when mature. When buying raw beets make sure that their whiskers are intact and that they have at least 2 in/5 cm of stalk at the top—if they are too closely trimmed they will bleed, meaning that they will give up their color to the cooking water and be no more than pale shadows of themselves when they are cooked. For the same reason, beets are never peeled before they are cooked.

When making borsch, the ruby-colored Russian soup that is as good iced as it is hot, make use of the beets' tendency to bleed and don't worry about keeping the skin intact. It is a good idea, though, to cook one or two specimens whole to add at the end, cut into julienne strips, to bring their fine dark red color to the soup.

To prepare sliced beets as a vegetable dish, sauté them gently, moistening them with wine vinegar to set the brilliant color and give them a perfect flavor. The greenery attached to young beets can be cooked and tastes like spinach.

Beets are not always red but also golden and white; they may taste the same and are sometimes served with hare and venison, but they are rather disappointing to look at after the glorious red ones.

If buying beets already cooked, make sure the skins are still moist. It is best to buy them on the day they have been boiled, while they are still warm and steaming. (Avoid like the plague those that have already been steeped in vinegar—they are violent and indigestible.) In France beets are cooked in the oven or in the ashes of a wood fire, which gives them a charred skin and a smoky flavor.

## Rutabagas and turnips

Both these roots are, in fact, members of the cabbage family and so closely related that it is not surprising to find their names sometimes used interchangeably. To add to the confusion, rutabagas are also called swedes, while in Scotland they are known as neeps and are considered to be turnips, and they are also sometimes called Swedish turnips. Rutabagas, however, with their pale, dense flesh, grow to immense sizes without impairment to taste or texture, while white-fleshed turnips coarsen if they are allowed to become larger than tennis balls. They should be heavy with no spongy patches, worm holes or large blemishes. Specimens that have grown side roots should be avoided.

**Rutabagas** make a delicious winter dish when mashed alone and are the essential ingredient for "mashed neeps," a Scottish dish served with haggis, in which the rutabagas are mashed with potatoes and butter.

**Baby turnips**, globe shaped, conical or flattened, are as different from maincrop turnips as new potatoes are from old. They should not be peeled before cooking, but rubbed afterwards: the skin comes off easily and beneath it lies their flavor and goodness. Although it seems a pity to do more to any young vegetable than to boil it for a few minutes, glazed baby turnips are delicious and the classic accompaniment to roast duck. Their fresh greenery can be cooked in the same way as collards.

**Mature turnips** may have a purplish tinge on their nether regions and are peeled before roasting or boiling.

## Kohlrabi

White, pale green or purple, kohlrabi is a member of the brassica family but is bred for its bulbous stem; it looks like a horizontally ridged turnip and is at its best when young and small, since it becomes coarse and fibrous as it grows larger. The leaves, which grow in stalks from the spaced-out ridges, can be used in the same way as

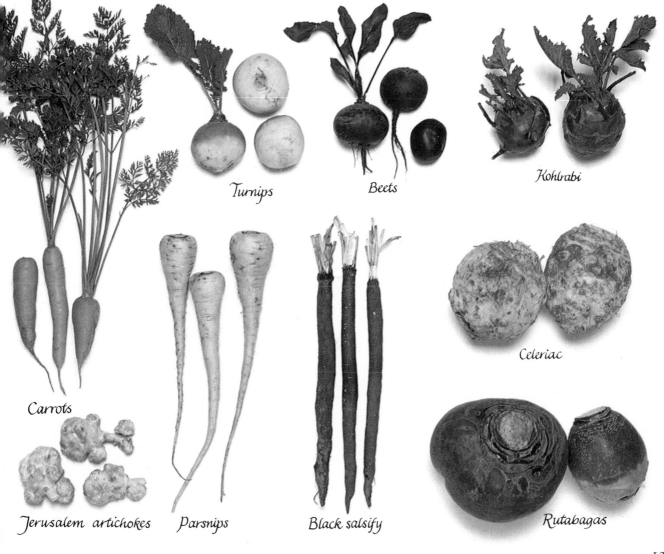

Turnips

Beets

Kohlrabi

Carrots

Jerusalem artichokes

Parsnips

Black salsify

Celeriac

Rutabagas

young turnip tops, but are usually removed before they are marketed. The skin can be peeled easily with a kitchen knife to expose the pale green flesh below. Tiny kohlrabi can be cooked whole, but the larger ones need to be sliced. They can then be eaten with fresh butter or a creamy sauce and served with any meat that responds to a delicate cabbagey taste.

### Jerusalem artichokes

These knobbly tubers are neither artichokes nor do they come from the Holy City, but from the New World. Like the sunflowers to which they are related, they were christened girasole—from whence "Jerusalem"—because their yellow flowers tend to turn towards the sun.

Jerusalem artichokes are at their best in late autumn and winter. When buying them, look for neat specimens with the minimum of knobs. Their skin is brownish, like that of potatoes but more delicate, and the white flesh must not be exposed to the air as it quickly turns a grey-purple color. When boiling artichokes, add a squeeze of lemon juice to the water—this will prevent them turning color, especially if you plan to make the delicious white soup, sometimes called Palestine soup, which owes its pearly color as much to the artichokes as it does to the milk or cream that goes into its making.

**Crosnes**, also known as Chinese artichokes, knotroot or chrogi, taste similar to Jerusalem artichokes but are nuttier and more delicate. They dry out too quickly after being lifted to be widely available; dried-out tubers are sometimes treacherously revived in water and sold as fresh, but the deception can usually be spotted by a brown discoloration. The yellowish patches that tend to develop on fresh white crosnes in no way impair the flavor. They should be scrubbed—a fiddly job as they are so tiny—and cooked very briefly in boiling salted water, then tossed in plenty of butter.

**Preparing celeriac**

*1. Peel off the rough skin and root parts with a sharp knife or potato peeler.*

**Preparing kohlrabi**

*1. Trim away any leaves. The young sprouting leaves can be cooked in the same way as spinach. The kohlrabi shown here is a green one; there is also a purple variety.*

*2. Slice thinly and then cut into delicate julienne strips.*

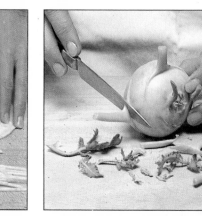

*2. Cut off all the stalks, and the fibrous part where the stem has been cut.*

*3. Alternatively, celeriac can be grated. If it begins to turn brown, put it into a bowl of acidulated water.*

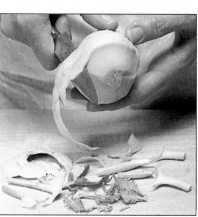

*3. Peel the kohlrabi thickly or, if you prefer, leave the peeling until the vegetable is cooked.*

# Vegetable-Fruits

Glossy black olives, rich purple eggplant, bright scarlet peppers and tomatoes, and green and yellow cucumbers need hot sun to ripen, and these vegetables bring Mediterranean color and warmth into the kitchen, while avocados, tender squashes and huge pumpkins provide exotic shapes, textures and tastes.

## Tomatoes

Ripened to a marvellous blazing red in the sun, tomatoes are one of the cook's most essential provisions. Ideally, one should have tomatoes in the larder at all times, both fresh and in cans (fortunately, tomatoes are one of the very few vegetables that take happily to being canned).

Belonging to the nightshade family, tomatoes used to be considered unhealthy and were not eaten fresh for many centuries after they had arrived from their native Central America. Spain was the first country to use them in cooked dishes, and the rest of Europe followed suit, but it was not until the middle of the nineteenth century that tomatoes *en salade* began to appear, and even then they do not seem to have been highly thought of.

Today, however, there is no better salad than a tomato salad, preferably scattered with fresh basil leaves, which have a great affinity with tomatoes. The Italians often add slices of mozzarella, a bland cheese that goes well with tomatoes. To dress it, a good sun-ripened tomato only needs olive oil, since it provides its own astringency, but a duller one needs vinaigrette. Tomatoes should never be allowed to sit about in their dressing, which will turn them soggy.

### Buying and storing tomatoes

The best tomatoes are those that have been allowed to ripen slowly on the vine, developing their flavor in the warm sun.

Buy bright red tomatoes for immediate use; for use in the near future, choose a paler pink color—after a day or two in a cool spot they will be a vivid red. If tomatoes have been picked when green but after reaching maturity, they are called "mature green" and will redden well if kept in a drawer or in a brown paper bag (they will ripen faster with a red tomato keeping them company, exuding its ethylene gas, which is responsible for the color change). Tomatoes picked when green and unripe will never turn red and are best used for making pickles and chutneys.

The large, ridged tomatoes, deep red or orange and green and often quite misshapen, tend to be the best, with rather fewer seeds than the smaller, more ordinary globe tomatoes, grown to uniform size and often with very little flavor. The cherry tomatoes, or Tom Thumbs, can be used whole in salads, while the richly flavored Italian plum tomatoes, with relatively small seed clusters and pulp that is inclined to be dry, are best for sauces and purées. Fleshy tomatoes are best for sandwiches because there is less liquid to turn the bread soggy. Slice them across rather than downward.

Golden-yellow tomatoes are like red tomatoes in every aspect except color, and make a pretty salad when mixed with the reds or on their own. There is also a tomato bred especially for stuffing, with an interior that is practically hollow, and even a cubic tomato, bred for sandwich making, which can only be considered as a victory of commercial interests over taste.

### Cooking with tomatoes

The traditional tomato dishes include tomato soup, which may be delicate and translucent or creamy and strong, perhaps flavored with basil or chives; tomatoes with stuffings of cooked seasoned rice mixed with lamb, currants, onion and garlic, or with bread crumb-bound fillings of rice and olives, herbs or mushrooms; and fragrant tomatoes *provençale*, which are simply broiled with a sprinkling of herbs, garlic and olive oil. *A la provençale* invariably means the presence of tomatoes in a dish, and just as Provençal cookery relies on tomatoes, so does Italian cookery, using them liberally with pastas and pizzas, in soups and vegetable stews.

Many recipes require tomatoes that have been *concasséed*—skinned, seeded and roughly chopped. In the case of Italian plum tomatoes the skin usually comes off perfectly easily, but globe tomatoes need a quick dip in boiling water first. To seed tomatoes, cut them in half crosswise and squeeze them in the palm of your hand over a bowl, giving a little shake as you do so. You can sieve the contents of the bowl and use the seedless liquid as stock—it will be too watery to serve as tomato juice.

## Peppers (Capsicums)

Peppers may be mild, sweet, hot or unbearably fiery, but they are all members of the Capsicum family. The large Capsicums are known as sweet peppers, bell or bullnose peppers because of their shape, and may be red, yellow or green. There are fiery types, but generally only the mild varieties are sold.

Chili peppers are the hot peppers that add heat rather than flavor to a dish, although some of them are quite mild. They can be green, red, yellow or black, and in general the smaller the pepper the hotter it is. When testing them for heat, simply touch a piece of the broken flesh to your tongue.

Most peppers are green to begin with, ripening to red and finally becoming red-brown when dried, although some peppers turn a pale yellow when ripe or a deep mahogany color. Peppers that are sold half ripe—part red and part green—will never ripen to full red but will simply shrivel.

### Sweet peppers

Bought fresh, large sweet peppers (which are rich in vitamin C) are quite light in weight. Red peppers are sweeter than the green ones, and the yellow ones are closer in flavor to red peppers than green.

Capsicum means box, and the fleshy walls of sweet peppers contain no more than a few ribs and a cluster of seeds. These should all be discarded to the last flat seed, which even in the mildest pepper can occasionally be bitingly hot. The empty boxes can then be filled with any number of stuffings—cooked rice mixed with ground meat and perhaps yogurt, or a mixture of anchovies, tomatoes, onions and garlic, or olives and capers. They are then put side by side in a baking pan and slowly cooked in oil. Some people like to blanch the peppers in boiling water for a minute or two before stuffing them.

As well as being stuffed, sweet peppers can be cut into strips and used in a variety of dishes. Sicilians make lovely salads with broiled red or yellow peppers, mixing them with anchovy fillets, capers, garlic and olive oil. Yugoslavians have a similar salad, using peppers roasted until they have blistered and then skinning them, and in the south of France there is the beautiful pipérade, a mixture of sweet peppers, tomatoes, onions, garlic and sometimes bacon, to which beaten eggs are added at the last moment. Sweet peppers are also sometimes combined with chili peppers, as in rouille—the bright orange, fiery sauce that floats in the center of a bowl of bouillabaisse, and is served with a number of other fish dishes that have their origins in the south of France.

### Chili peppers

These should look fresh and bright—dullness is a sure sign of overmaturity—with no brown patches or black spots.

With chili peppers, not only the seeds but the box itself is pungent, and except in Central America, notably Mexico, where they are second only to corn in their importance in cooking, people wisely use them sparingly. Even Mexican restaurants will cook two versions of the same dish: one hot and traditionally Mexican, the other much cooler for the tourists who have not yet developed a tolerance for the volatile oil called capsicin that accounts for the heat.

Capsicin irritates the skin and especially

# Vegetable-Fruits

Red sweet peppers

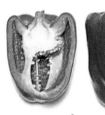

Green sweet peppers

Yellow sweet peppers

Cayenne chili peppers

Serrano chili peppers

Mild chili peppers

Hot black chili peppers

Ancho chili peppers

Summer avocado

Winter avocados

Green olives

Black olives

Eggplant

Cherry tomatoes  Yellow tomatoes

Globe tomatoes

Large ridged tomatoes

Plum tomatoes

the eyes, so keep your hands—even after washing—away from your eyes for an hour after you have prepared chili peppers, and rinse the peppers in cold water, not hot, or the irritating fumes may rise into your face. To prepare the peppers, pull off their stems and break each one in half, all under cold running water. Chili peppers soaked for a while in cold salted water will be less hot, and they can also be blistered under the broiler to give them a lovely smoky flavor.

Canned chili peppers should be washed to remove the brine in which they have been preserved. They may be already sliced or diced, or they may need seeding like fresh ones. Dried peppers, torn into small pieces, can be used as they are to season simple Mediterranean dishes, or they can be steeped in water first. For a much milder flavor, put them into a pan of cold water, bring slowly to the boil and then drain. You can now use your peppers, more or less discreetly, for any fiery dish such as chili con carne, for curries or any number of Creole dishes, especially those that include shrimps or pork. Chili experts, of course, can distinguish between the flavors of the various peppers, but non-experts tend to differentiate only between the hot and the unbearable. The cayenne chili peppers are not one particular type but a group of peppers, always hot and used for making chili pastes and sauces. Serrano chili peppers are extremely hot, while ancho peppers, looking like small sweet peppers, are quite sweet and only faintly hot.

## Eggplant

These can be long and slim or as fat as zeppelins, with glossy purple or almost black skins, or plump ivory-white ovals (to which version they owe their American name, eggplant, instead of the French aubergine), but they all have the same slightly acrid taste. The difference lies in their consistency: the plump ones, marginally juicier, are the ones to use for such dishes as moussaka, with its golden layers, or the Balkan okrochka, similarly layered but without the béchamel or eggs. The long, slim ones, being rather dryer, are best for frying.

When buying eggplant, those that feel heavy for their size are likely to have the smallest seed channels because their flesh will have filled out. They should have smooth, unblemished skins with no rough, spongy patches or brown spots.

It is a good idea to salt eggplant before cooking to sweat out some of the moisture and possible bitterness, although the slim ones do not really need this treatment. To salt them, cut them into thin slices, sprinkle with fine salt and allow them to drain in a colander for about half an hour, then rinse them and pat them dry.

It is not usual to peel eggplant because the skin contributes to their flavor and color, and in dishes such as stuffed eggplant it prevents them disintegrating. But in dishes that involve mashed eggplant, such as "poor man's caviar," the traditional way of peeling them is to roast them in their skins over a fire or under a broiler until they blister, and then to scoop out the flesh, which will have acquired a delicious smoky taste. (Poor man's caviar, a mixture of mashed eggplant, onions, oil and lemon, got its name in the region around the Caspian Sea, where it is eaten by the fishermen who have spent the day dealing with caviar, catching sturgeon for city dwellers.)

Although ratatouille—the delicious Provençal stew of eggplant, tomatoes, zucchini, onions and sweet peppers—is one of the great Mediterranean dishes, the best eggplant recipes come from southern Italy and the Middle East. In the Middle East eggplant purées are flavored with tahina and garlic and served as a salad, or with milk, butter, lemon juice and cheese and served with poultry and meat.

The most famous of the eggplant dishes is the Turkish *Imam Bayildi*, or "the Imam has fainted," for this is apparently what an *imam*, or Turkish priest, did when presented with an incredibly rich dish of fried eggplant mixed with onions, tomatoes, spices and sultanas, all swimming in oil.

Eggplant may be halved and stuffed, or filled from the stem end after the seeds and a portion of the flesh have been removed to make room for the stuffing. They look very beautiful if they are first peeled in strips so that white flesh and purple skin make handsome stripes around the outside. Fill them with ground lamb or beef, rice, tomatoes, garlic and plenty of onions and spices, and their own chopped and cooked pulp.

Whether eaten hot or cold, *à la grecque* or in batter, eggplant are always first fried in hot olive oil; if you fry them fast they do not become so oil laden, while still giving you a combination of delicious flavors.

## Avocados

The avocado was once called the butter pear because of its consistency, and the alligator pear because its original Spanish name, based on the Aztec, was too difficult to pronounce. It is, strictly speaking, a fruit, but is used mainly as a vegetable because its flavor is bland, mild and nutty.

Particularly rich in oils, proteins and vitamins, it was used by the ancient Mayans, Incas and Aztecs both as a food and for skin care, but avocados were a luxury in northern countries until Californians began to cultivate them in the nineteenth century. Some people consider these comparatively northerly avocados to be only pale replicas of those grown in the tropics, but they are still very good, as are the Israeli avocados which supply many European markets in their season.

There are two main types of avocado: those that appear in the summer and those that appear in the winter. The summer variety, with a rough, pebbly skin that is green when unripe and purple-black when ripe, has golden-yellow flesh. The winter ones are more pear shaped, with smooth green skin and pale green to yellow flesh. With the winter avocados, skin color is no indication of ripeness, and the test for this is to apply gentle pressure at the thin end: if there is some give, the avocado is ready.

Avocados appear in some unlikely dishes. In Mexico, where they are abundant, they are eaten in soups, salads and stews. They are also the essential ingredient in guacamole—an avocado purée with green chili pepper, chopped onions and lemon juice, and perhaps a dash of fiery Tabasco, which may be eaten alone, with corn chips, or with tortillas. It is best to purée avocado shortly before it is to be eaten because it turns a dirty brown color when exposed to the air. So does the flesh of a cut avocado, so either halve it just before serving or rub the cut surfaces with lemon.

In the Caribbean avocados baked in their shells are sometimes served with turkey and chicken. But there is no better way to serve them than halved, with a good vinaigrette, or even more simply with a sprinkling of fresh lime juice and salt.

## Olives

Groves of gnarled olive trees flourish in the Mediterranean countries and in California, producing a great variety of olives, large and small. Greek and Italian olives are reckoned to be the finest—in ancient Rome olives were eaten both at the beginning and at the end of meals from sheer greed.

Whether olives are green or black (which may in fact be brown or purple) is not a matter of type but of timing: olives picked young are still hard and pale green; black olives have had time to ripen and darken on the tree and have developed more of their oil. They are soaked in an alkaline solution —once rainwater and wood ash (lye), now more likely to be caustic soda—and exposed to the air to develop their characteristic black color.

Green olives are treated rather differently, first steeped in an alkaline solution and then put into tightly sealed barrels of brine and left for up to 12 months to develop their olive green, smooth succulence. Olives destined for the oil presses are allowed to ripen fully; some of these, looking a little shrivelled and quite small, are also cured in salt and eaten, and can be the best of all.

Among the many olives on the market, the most common are the big, green, solid, Spanish ones, called Queens, which are slightly acid and which connoisseurs like to dip in olive oil before eating, and the small, succulent Manzanillas. These are often stuffed with strips of red pimento, or less frequently with almonds, anchovies, lemon or orange peel or pieces of black olive—they are meant for cocktail-party offerings, and are not the favorites of olive aficionados.

Olives are preserved in a number of ways. The black ones range from those preserved in oil with herbs to those in brine. There are also cracked olives—green olives pickled with garlic, spices or herbs—and the pitted, pressed green olives packed with chili peppers, which are very fine.

Black olives feature in a good many dishes: chopped or whole they go into Mediterranean stuffings with bread crumbs, mushrooms, anchovies and herbs; moistened with more oil, they make an olive pâté that is popular in the Balkans; unchopped, they make beautiful glossy black additions to some rice and pasta dishes and to a great variety of salads.

The Italian olives, such as the large green Cerignola, or the black olives from Castellamare, or the tiny black wrinkled ones from around Rome, go on top of pizzas. Salty olives, such as those from Greece, go into a salad with tomatoes and onion rings, and the black olives of Provence into rich estouffades and daubes.

Besides the best-known green and black olives, there are also the pale or dark brown ones found in Italy and Cyprus, and the straw-colored California olives which some people prefer above all others.

If you buy too many olives and do not use them all at once, store them in the refrigerator, or better still in the larder, in a jar of olive oil or in a mixture of water, oil and vinegar. It is a good idea to roll olives in fresh olive oil, perhaps with a few crushed coriander seeds, to liven them up before you eat them. If you want black olives without pits for cooking, use an olive pitter, or *chasse noyau*, or simply split the flesh and remove the pit. The firmer green olives can be cut in a spiral from the pointed top to the stalk end with a small vegetable knife. The fat ribbon that results, carefully detached from the pit, can then be reshaped.

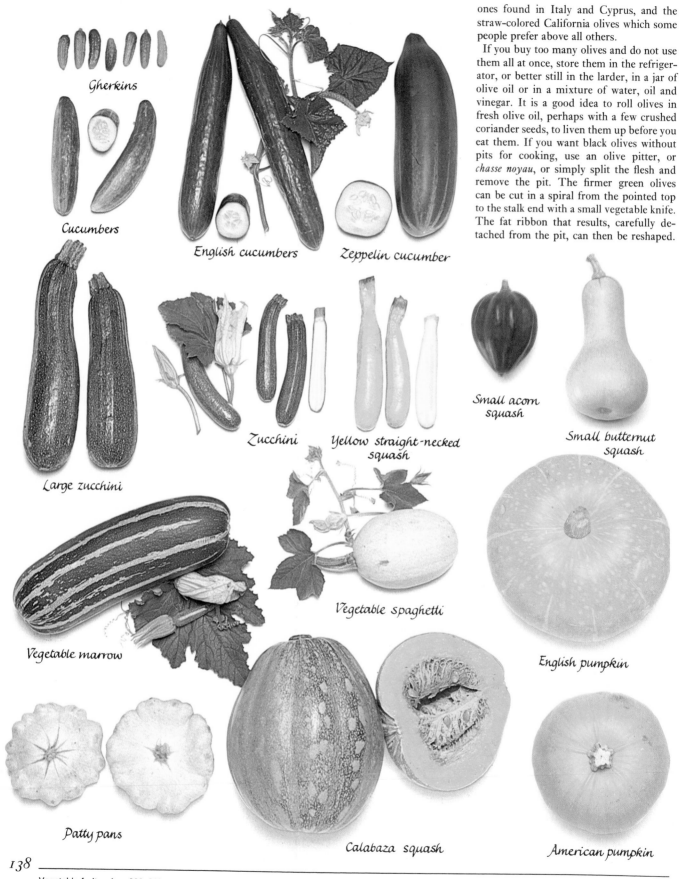

Gherkins

Cucumbers

English cucumbers

Zeppelin cucumber

Large zucchini

Zucchini

Yellow straight-necked squash

Small acorn squash

Small butternut squash

Vegetable marrow

Vegetable spaghetti

English pumpkin

Patty pans

Calabaza squash

American pumpkin

## Cucumbers and gherkins

Before cucumbers had the bitterness bred out of them they were invariably peeled and salted and drained. This is no longer necessary, unless you want to make a delicate Austrian or French cucumber salad, for which salting and draining are essential. Otherwise, cucumber salads are likely to consist of slices cut transparently thin on a mandoline and dressed with sour cream or vinaigrette, or, in the Hungarian version, of little dice dressed with yogurt and chives and sprinkled with paprika. Cucumbers are also interesting cooked and served hot.

Small ridge cucumbers have plentiful seeds and smooth, dark green skins (their name comes from the way they are grown on ridges). If ridge cucumbers have been waxed, as they often are in the United States, they need to be peeled before they are used. Unwaxed and unpeeled, they are the cucumbers that are brined, or pickled with a head of dill.

The long, clear green cucumber (known in America as the English cucumber) has fewer seeds and an exceedingly thin skin and is often sold in a tight plastic jacket to keep it fresh. Largest is the Zeppelin, firm and juicy, that turns a pale yellow when fully ripe. The apple or lemon cucumber, almost round and with crisp, juicy flesh and tough yellowish skin, should always be peeled.

Cucumbers are best when they are young and tender and look as if they are bursting with juice. They can be stored in the refrigerator for about a week at most, but do not like very low temperatures.

Gherkins, covered in warts, are usually found pickled in unsweetened vinegar and are eaten with cold meats, with hot *boeuf bouilli*, or chopped and incorporated in sauces such as tartare sauce.

## Squashes and pumpkins

These belong to the climbing family known as Cucurbitas, together with melons and cucumbers and the decorative autumn gourds. Some are soft skinned and for eating when young and tender, which is why they are often known as summer squashes; others are best when they have been allowed to mature slowly to develop hard, sweet flesh.

### Soft-skinned or summer squashes

These should be cooked as soon as possible after they have been picked.

**Zucchini** are infinitely superior to the larger squashes, with a much more interesting and delicate taste. There is hardly any work involved in their preparation: just give them a little wash, and then leave tiny ones whole and cut larger ones into circles or slice them lengthwise into halves or quarters. Give them a very few minutes' boiling, steaming or frying, add some herbs such as basil or parsley, with perhaps a dash of cream, or a quantity of butter or olive oil, and an extremely good vegetable dish is ready to eat. But don't keep it waiting, because the vegetable continues to soften even after it has been taken off the heat.

Zucchini are excellent fried in oil, either plain or in batter, and their big golden flowers are also sometimes stuffed and deep fried in a crisp batter. They form part of an Italian *fritto misto* in which there may also be apples, artichoke hearts, eggplant, brains, or veal cut into little strips as beef is for *boeuf stroganoff.*

**Straightnecks, crooknecks and cocozelles** Much like small zucchini in flavor and texture, these can be used in the same ways. The crookneck has bumpy yellow skin and curves at the neck; the cocozelle looks like a large zucchini, but its pale skin is striped with green.

**Vegetable marrows** Grown to enormous size, these peculiarly English squashes are not very delicate as a vegetable and, to some tastes at least, are even less acceptable transformed into jam. Boiled into a watery mush, medium-size specimens can be equally disappointing, but started off with a little butter and chopped onion and steamed in their own juice, and sprinkled with a generous handful of chopped parsley, they can be fresh looking and delicious, especially when tomatoes are added.

A barboiled or blanched marrow or large zucchini, halved and hollowed out, makes a good vehicle for a ground beef and onion stuffing bound with an egg, or a rice and meat stuffing, but both need lively flavoring because the flesh itself is bland.

**Vegetable spaghettis** These stubby yellow squashes are grown with particular attention to the squash's tendency to produce stringy flesh and are eaten, with sauce, just like spaghetti, and wrapped around a fork. They are always boiled, the end pierced so that the heat reaches the interior, and are served cut in half lengthwise. Pass a tomato sauce separately. They are also good eaten simply with butter and grated cheese.

**Patty pans** Usually creamy in color, although they also come in shades of yellow and green, these taste rather like zucchini. They are best up to 4 in/10 cm across, when the skin is soft and the interior tender, and their scalloped shape need not be spoiled by slicing. Boil them and then cut off the tops, scoop out the seeds and fill the hollow with melted butter, and eat them with a spoon.

**Chayotes** Small and pear shaped, these squashes have a large single seed, which in very young chayotes is edible. They feature in Central and South American cooking, where besides being used as a vegetable they are candied, filled with nuts and raisins and eaten as a dessert.

**Chinese hairy melon, or wax gourd** Looking like a large torpedo, this can be bought in Chinese supermarkets. When young it is covered with a silky fuzz, which is easily washed off by running the hand over the skin under cold running water. In maturity it is usually coated with wax, which also washes off. It has a slight bitterness but is excellent stir-fried.

## Pumpkins and winter squashes

With bright autumn-colored or green skins, these have flesh that is firm and floury.

**Winter squashes** A favorite winter vegetable in America, these include the Acorn squash, which can be green or orange or a combination of the two; the Butternut, looking like a huge, pale orange peanut, and the smooth-skinned Buttercup, which swells to a turban shape towards the blossom end; the bumpy skinned Turban squashes and the large, warty Hubbards, often sold in wedges. Look for firm, unbruised specimens, or wedges that show no signs of softening around the edges.

Peeled, cut into pieces and boiled for about 20 minutes, squash can be served mashed with butter, salt and pepper or a little orange juice. The smaller squashes can be left unpeeled, halved and baked in the oven for about 30 minutes with butter and brown sugar or maple syrup.

**Calabaza squash** Often sold in wedges to display its golden-orange flesh, this West Indian variety features in Caribbean soups; otherwise it can be used for any hard-skinned squash or pumpkin recipe.

**Pumpkins** Best known and best liked are the handsome golden field pumpkins that go into American pumpkin pie, pumpkin soup and pumpkin bread, and are carved into smiling, gap-toothed faces for Hallowe'en.

The earliest pumpkin pies were not the familiar spiced golden ones now eaten at Thanksgiving. For the Pilgrim Fathers, pumpkin pie was simply a pumpkin with its head sawn off and its seeds removed, with the cavity filled with milk, spices and honey and baked until tender. Nowadays, because of the business of baking, straining, seeding, scraping and puréeing the pumpkin, many people use canned purée—one of the few foods that can be better canned than fresh. For pumpkin soup, which looks so pretty served in a hollowed-out shell, canned purée can also be used, but for baked and fried pumpkin you need fresh ones.

English pumpkins are much softer fleshed, and because they cook so readily into a mush they are best used for pumpkin soup, or they can be combined with potatoes or root vegetables to give them a little extra body when used in vegetable dishes.

# Mushrooms and other Fungi

In many countries the mushroom forage is an autumn treat, with whole families combing the ground for the 80 or so edible species of fungi which are either sold in the local markets, dried, or enjoyed fresh as a luxurious addition to the normal diet.

It is important to remember however that for the amateur picker going out in the morning dew, the business of mushrooming is fraught with risk. Some mushrooms are indigestible; a few are lethal. In France and Germany, where mushroom gathering is particularly popular, pharmacists will check the morning's pick.

Meanwhile, plenty of wild mushrooms do find their way to the world's vegetable markets, harvested by people with a long tradition of mushroom gathering. As a change from the ubiquitous cultivated mushroom, it is one of the pleasures of autumn to see a selection of wild forms, including the fat brown cep and the golden-pleated chanterelle, both worldwide in distribution and probably far and away the best of the woodland mushrooms. These two, along with the morel, which is a spring-time delicacy, are the truly great mushrooms of fine cookery, but for those who can find an expert to tell them which varieties to choose, there are many other pleasant treats.

## Wild mushrooms

**Cep** (*Boletus edulis*) A strong, meaty, bun-shaped fungus known to the French as *cèpe*, to the Germans as *steinpilze* and to the Italians as *porcini*, this is the archetypal mushroom, smooth and shiny and with the texture of fine kid gloves. Unlike many other wild mushrooms, it does not collapse in cooking but keeps its texture. Except when using ceps in soup, however, it is advisable to draw off some of their ample water content by stewing them gently for a few minutes in oil or butter. After draining, the liquor is saved for future use and the ceps can be cooked in fresh oil or butter.

The French usually sauté their ceps, with garlic and parsley, for use in omelets or with fish, game, poultry or practically any meat. The Germans turn them into a popular vegetable dish and use them for a hearty soup. In Italy they are often broiled, with olive oil in the caps and a sprinkling of chopped garlic, or sliced, dipped in batter and fried until golden, or stuffed with a mixture of bread crumbs, ham, parsley and grated cheese and cooked in the oven.

Dried ceps need soaking in warm water for about half an hour, and the liquid as well as the ceps is used to flavor the dish. When dried they are used almost like stock cubes.

**Chanterelle** (*Cantharellus cibarius*) The frilly, trumpet-shaped chanterelle, common in woodlands in summer and autumn, is quite unlike any other edible mushroom and there are many varieties. Most are bright yellow and have an odor reminiscent of apricots and a delicate flavor. Like most mushrooms they do not improve with immersion in water, but whereas many can simply be wiped with a damp cloth, the chanterelle is harder to clean because of the grit or sand trapped in the pleated gills. The best method is to run cold water over them, and then shake them dry.

Somewhat rubbery in texture, chanterelles take a long time to cook. They should be started off gently, like ceps, and left to exude their liquid, which is better replaced with butter rather than oil. They can be served with scrambled eggs on toast, with chicken, veal, or any other pale dish where the color can be seen to effect. Treat dried chanterelles to a soaking in lukewarm water for 20 to 30 minutes before cooking.

**Morel** (*Morchella esculenta*) The handsome morel is the first mushroom of the year, appearing with the cowslips in spring. It is as delicate as a natural sponge and varies in color from pale beige to dark brownish-black and has a meaty flavor.

Cut in half and carefully washed and dried, morels can be put into a casserole dish with a little butter. Sauté for a few minutes and then add a squeeze of lemon juice. Stir around a few times, add salt and pepper, cover the pan and simmer for up to an hour, adding a little stock from time to time. When the mushrooms are tender, thicken the juice with egg yolk, season and serve hot with toast. Also, once cooked, morels make a memorable addition to an omelet or to braised chicken, pheasant or veal.

Retaining a good flavor, dried morels are best soaked for ten minutes and then pressed dry before they are added to soups or stews; or they can be softened in butter, sprinkled with flour and then enriched with cream, and seasoned with salt and pepper.

**Blewit** (*Lepista* species) Still to be found in rural vegetable markets in northerly climates, blewits look somewhat like common mushrooms but have whitish gills and plain, lilac-tinged stems. An autumn mushroom, blewits are delicious cooked like field or cultivated mushrooms.

**Horn of plenty** (*Craterellus cornucopoides*) is a very good mushroom although it has a rather unprepossessing appearance, being trumpet shaped, somewhat ragged and almost black. Sometimes called the trumpet mushroom, it is eaten sautéed in butter, with or without chopped shallots or garlic, and goes into stews and soups.

**Oyster mushroom** (*Pleurotus ostreatus*) These ear-like grey or greyish-brown "bracket" mushrooms grow in clumps on deciduous trees. They need careful cooking as they may be tough, but have an excellent flavor. Cook them in butter with parsley and garlic or coat with egg and crumbs and deep fry until golden.

**Shaggy cap, shaggy ink cap** (*Coprinus comatus*) These singular and graceful mushrooms grow in groups in rich pastures. They push up like white folded umbrellas and this is the time to eat them, when they are as delicate and tender as fillets of sole. As they age they blacken, become bell shaped and finally dissolve into a pool of black ink. Cook young shaggy caps as soon as possible after picking, either baking them in cream or sautéing them gently in butter.

Their close relative *Coprinus atramentarius*, which is similar but grey and without scales, is also edible (although known by some country people as toad's meat), but do not drink alcohol if eating it, as the combination could make you sick.

## Cultivated mushrooms

Although lacking the pleasing diversity of wild mushrooms gathered by season, cultivated forms have the merit of year-round availability. Moreover they are consistent—there is no waste on cultivated mushrooms bought and used fresh—and utterly safe. Most common, of course, is the silky champignon, cultivated relative of the field and horse mushrooms, which is sold in three grades: button, cup, and open or flat.

**Button mushrooms**, small and succulent, are slightly weaker in flavor than the more mature grades. Remaining pale (although an aluminum saucepan may darken them slightly), they are useful for white, creamy sauces and also for salads.

**Cup mushrooms**, the kind where the membrane is just breaking to expose the gills, can be kept pale if rubbed with a cut lemon, or if a few drops of lemon juice or white wine are added to the cooking liquor.

Left unpeeled—cultivated mushrooms never need peeling—cup champignons are ideal for stews and casseroles. The larger ones can be stuffed or the cups filled with cream, and, with the stalks trimmed off level with the cap, cooked in the oven.

**Open or flat mushrooms** most resemble their wild cousins and are almost as penetrating in taste. Fully mature, these are the kind to eat broiled with bacon, or on toast, briskly sautéed with garlic and plenty of black pepper and chopped parsley. They can be used in dark soups or casseroles, but are troublesome cooked with chicken, for example, as they turn it an unattractive grey.

It is best to buy mushrooms a few at a

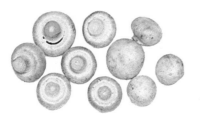

*Button mushrooms*

*Cup mushrooms*

*Field mushrooms*

*Fresh white truffles*

*Bottled black truffles*

*Dried morels*

*Fresh morel*

*Fresh ceps*

*Dried ceps*

*Dried Chinese cloud ears*

*Horn of plenty*

*Chanterelles*

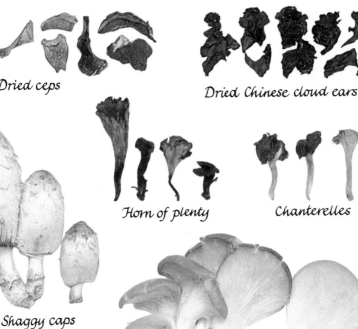

*Shaggy caps*

*Oyster mushrooms*

time and often. Button mushrooms become cups even in the refrigerator, and their flesh soon starts to shrivel. To limit evaporation they can be wrapped in plastic or foil. All but the densely fleshed button mushrooms act like sponges when they are cooking, absorbing more than their own weight in liquid, so add them to stews or casseroles towards the end of the cooking time.

## Japanese tree mushrooms

Long before mushrooms were first cultivated in Europe, the Japanese were harvesting *take* specially grown in the water-softened bark of various tree trunks. Best known today are the *shiitake*, which grow on hardwood (*shii*), principally oak, and the meaty tasting *matsutake*, grown on pine logs. Another favorite, the *enok*, is also cultivated in California. With a slightly acid taste, it can be used in salads or cooked, but only briefly or it becomes bitter and tough.

## Chinese dried mushrooms

Dark-colored Chinese mushrooms (the kind served in Chinese restaurants) must be soaked for at least half an hour to revive the meaty texture; the tough stems are discarded. Also available in Chinese supermarkets is the stemless type known as cloud ears, used for texture rather than flavor.

## Truffles

One of the rarest and certainly the most expensive of all fungi, the black Périgord truffle (*Tuber melanosporum*) grows on the roots of certain oak trees in the Périgueux region of southwest France. This is the most sought-after of the truffle species, detected beneath the soil by pigs or specially trained truffle hounds.

With its rich, mold-like flavor, a little of the black truffle goes a long way—one of the good reasons it is used sparingly in such things as omelets, scrambled eggs or stuffing for roast chicken. The classic dish *truffe sous cendre*—truffle wrapped in bacon fat or pastry, baked and served with a bottle of St. Emilion—is rated by gourmets as the experience of a lifetime. Unfortunately, truffles found in pâtés often have no flavor at all and are probably canned.

Used more liberally and with less reverence, the white truffle of Piedmont is larger, stronger in flavor and almost as expensive as its Périgord cousin. While the latter is invariably eaten cooked, the Italians use their white truffle raw, grating it in showers over risottos and salads. One of the great Florentine specialties is a delicate little bridge roll which contains a paste of raw white truffle, Parmesan and butter.

Leeks with truffles **303**
Scrambled eggs **271**

Apples and pears, although frequently bracketed as if they were almost one and the same fruit, could scarcely be more different.

Apples are the most common, the most easy-going and the most useful of all fruits, both to eat casually at any time of the day and to cook with—there are more apple puddings than any other sort. Pears on the other hand are a fragile luxury—large, aesthetically pleasing and opulent, they make a grand ending to a grand meal, and speak to the diner of sunny orchards and of careful harvesting and marketing.

## Apples

Today, unfortunately, the choice and variety of apples is getting smaller and smaller; although there are several thousand different apples cultivated in gardens and nurseries, very few find their way into commercial orchards, where the fruit grown must keep well and be tough, disease resistant and good at travelling. Of the 7,000 varieties known in the United States only 50 are seriously marketed, while the British are limited almost entirely to Cox's, Granny Smiths and Golden Delicious, with Red Delicious and Bramleys as runners-up.

It is sad that this is the case, since there are so many aromatic old-fashioned apples that are worth growing. So hunt through the countryside in the autumn and you may find interesting varieties for sale that are worth trying. Apples sold as windfalls are also good buys and are perfect for cooking, since unripe apples have plenty of acid, essential to the flavor of apple pies, tarts and crumbles. The best eating apples are those that retain some of their acidity even in their final sweetness, and have a mellow flavor and a firm, juicy texture. The eating apples known as reinettes, with their red-flushed golden skins, are especially good.

### Buying and storing apples

While obviously one should avoid apples with bruises and soft spots, do not be put off by dull, rough, brown patches on sound apples. This is called russeting and in the case of apples that go by the name of russets will extend over the whole surface. Russets are splendid with cheese, and cook well.

Those buying for the trade test for ripeness by grasping apples around the middle and applying gentle pressure: if the skin wrinkles slightly the apples are at the peak of perfection. But it takes a bold shopper to emulate this practice in a store or market. Fragrance is important when testing for ripeness and the fruit should be firm.

Apples continue to ripen after they have been picked. If they are to be stored they should be spread out so that they are not touching each other. If you want to buy apples in quantity, at one of the pick-your-own orchards for example, keep them on racks or in special fiber apple trays in a cool, dry, dark place. A cool loft is the ideal place to store apples.

### Cooking with apples

Selecting the right apples for cooking is important if you do not want your pies to end up watery or your baked apples to collapse in a frothy mess all over the oven. Some apples, such as America's favorite eating apple, the Red Delicious, are too tender for cooking and lack the acidity that gives apple dishes their delicious flavor. The hard, crisp apples such as the popular Granny Smith or some of the russets will require longer cooking than the softer-fleshed ones.

**Apple purées** When making these, choose crisp, juicy apples with plenty of acid—adding sugar towards the end of cooking time—as these will quickly turn to a froth. Tart apples give a sweet-acid taste that is delicious with pork, pheasant or goose.

**Cooking apple slices** Many of the dishes involving apples, such as tarts, turnovers and fritters, depend on apples retaining their shape. Sugar and/or butter added at the beginning of the cooking helps to prevent them from disintegrating. Europe's favorite reinettes and russets, noted for their unique subtle flavor, are excellent for cooking. These are the apples that French cooks use when making *tartes aux pommes*—with their neat rings of apple slices nicely browned on the upper edges. The Golden Delicious, one of the most popular and common of today's apples, retains its shape well, but lacks the flavor of the reinettes and russets, so cook it with cinnamon and plenty of butter and sugar.

**Stewing apples** When stewing apples use the same varieties as you would use for pies and tarts. To vary the flavor you can add cloves, cinnamon, or perhaps coriander seeds and grated lemon rind. Rum or Calvados and butter are also good with stewed apples. Some savory stews such as Persia's *khoresh* involve apples with cinnamon and onions. In West Germany apples are stewed, sprinkled with bread crumbs and gently fried, and then served with ham.

**Baking apples** These are cored with an apple corer and the cavity filled with sugar, butter and perhaps almonds, blackberries or raisins. They are then baked, possibly basted or flamed with Calvados or brandy, and served with thick cream. The best apples for baking are the large ones. Run your knife around the circumference of the apple (to prevent the skin from splitting)

| NAME | APPEARANCE | FLESH | TYPE |
|---|---|---|---|
| Cox's Orange Pippin | small, round, greenish-yellow tinged with red russeting | crisp, juicy, firm, sweet, some acidity | reinette |
| Orleans Reinette | small, flat, golden tinged with crimson russeting | crisp, juicy, firm, some acidity | reinette |
| Egremont Russet | medium, round with brown-orange russeting | soft, very sweet, some acidity | russet |
| Laxton's Superb | medium, round, greenish-yellow flushed with red | juicy, firm, sweet, some acidity | russet |
| Golden Delicious | large, conical, green, ripening to yellow | tender, very sweet, no acidity when ripe | all purpose |
| Rome Beauty | large, elongated, thick skinned, shiny red | crisp, firm, juicy, slightly tart | eating only |
| Granny Smith | medium to large, conical, green with small, whitish flecks | crisp, juicy, mild but acid | green crisp |
| Crispin | medium to large, yellow-green | crisp, juicy, mild but acid | green crisp |
| Bramley's Seedling | extra large, irregular, green flushed with red | crisp, juicy acid | tart green |
| Red Delicious | large, elongated, thick skinned, shiny red | juicy, very tender, no acidity | eating only |
| Worcester Pearmain | medium, conical, firm, two-tone red and green | crisp, juicy, sweet, slightly tart | all purpose |
| McIntosh | small to medium, round, firm, two-tone red and green | crisp, juicy, slightly tart | all purpose |

before you stuff them and put them in the baking pan. Thick-skinned varieties such as Rome Beauty are ideal, since their skins are less likely to burst. The harder the apple, the longer it will take to bake: it is done when the top is frothy and seeping with juice.
**Fried apples** A classic accompaniment to fried or broiled *boudin noir* is peeled, sliced apples fried golden in butter. They are also very good with pheasant.

## Raw apple slices

These when added to salads give a crisp, crunchy texture—the famous Waldorf salad of celery, apples and walnuts tossed in mayonnaise is especially good. A squeeze of lemon juice will prevent the slices from turning brown. Any crisp, sharp eating apple will make a good salad.

## Crabapples, quinces and medlars

These three fruits, like the apple, are related to the rose family and used to be called the fruits of Merrie England.
**Crabapples** Roasted and still hot, the crabapples that "hissed in the bowl" in the hot spiced ale punches of Shakespeare's day were most likely the small, sour apples that still grow wild or in gardens and are the ancestors of all our modern apple varieties. These beautiful tiny fruits, which can be yellow, red or green, are no longer eaten (except by birds) because they are generally not worth the bother, being mostly core and often very sour. They do, however, make a

lovely clear, golden-pink jelly, which is excellent on bread and butter and with Petit Suisse. The larger crabapples are slightly sweeter and grow from the seeds of cultivated apples that have become wild. They have a crisp, tart flavor.
**Quinces** came originally from Portugal, where they are called marmelos, and until they were supplanted by oranges they were the fruit from which marmalade was made. Yellow-gold and aromatic, they are a pleasing sight on the kitchen table in autumn and are usually used to make jellies, jams and cheeses, but a slice or two added to an apple pie or tart gives these dishes a delicious scent and flavor. Quinces can also be boiled down with sugar to a thick paste, which is then dried and eaten as a dessert.
**Medlars** are never found in stores, but are sometimes seen growing wild on roadsides. They look like open cups of a warm golden brown and resemble a large rose hip insofar as each is crowned with a five-tailed calyx. Since they do not ripen on the tree they need to be well on the way to being rotten, or "bletted," before they are edible. In the past this was done by laying the fruit in straw or packing it in bran, except in the warm south where medlars ripen in the normal way. The ripe state is easily recognizable, as the unripe fruit is rock hard. Once bletted, medlars are usually baked, or made into a slightly bitter jam or jelly, or the flesh is scraped out of the cup and eaten with sugar and cream. The taste and texture are slightly reminiscent of marzipan.

## Pears

This fruit, which can be so delicious, is more temperamental than the apple. It has an unpleasant habit of becoming mealy from the core outwards, a state described by fruiterers as "sleepiness," and it does not keep so well as the apple.

Pears come in almost as great a variety as apples. Europe has about 5,000 named varieties and America about 1,000, but as with apples only a small proportion reach the market. Three shapes predominate: the ordinary pear shape, the long-necked shape called calabash, and the oval, almost round shape. Colors, too, vary a great deal, from a soft blurred brown to bright green with dark brown, grey-black or green flecks, to golden with a handsome red-gold flush.
**The Comice pear**, Doyenné de Comice, is considered to be one of the best pears. It has a perfect balance of sweetness and acidity, a certain spiciness, and its juicy, sweet flesh is buttery—meaning that it is melting and not grainy. Large and greenish-yellow, it has a red blush where it has been exposed to the sun. Its thick, shiny skin is stippled with tiny grey spots and fawn patches.
**Williams' Bon Chrétien** This pear is usually known as the Williams or Bartlett pear, due to the fact that it was propagated by an English grower called Williams and introduced to America by an American called Bartlett. It has a sweet, musky flavor and a smooth skin that turns from dark green to yellow as it ripens: eat it when its speckles are still surrounded by a tiny halo

Golden Delicious    Laxton's Superb    Worcester Pearmain    Crispin

Granny Smith    Orleans Reinette    Cox's Orange Pippin    Egremont Russet

Red Delicious    Mc Intosh    Rome Beauty    Bramley's Seedling

Large crabapples          Crabapples          Medlars

Quinces     Comice pears     Bartlett pears     Conference pears

of green on an otherwise golden skin. These superb pears are unfortunately bad travellers and extremely perishable.

**Packham's Triumph** This descendant of the Bartlett or Williams pear looks somewhat like its distinguished ancestor but is not nearly so delicate. It keeps well and is therefore exported in great numbers from Australia, where it is grown in profusion.

**The Conference pear** A favorite English pear, this was so called when it won the top prize at a fruit growers' conference for its fine, tender, melting flesh and delicious flavor. It is slim, calabash shaped, stippled with fawn and grey russeting and turns pale yellow when ripe. Kept in controlled cold storage by the trade, it is ripened and released as the market demands, so although it is an early pear it may be found later on in the season.

**Beurré Hardy, Beurré Bosc** A number of pear varieties with the French word for butter in their names are characterized by their creamy, melting quality. The Beurré Bosc, so named in honor of a former director of the Jardin des Plantes in Paris, who propagated it, is also known as the Emperor Alexander as a compliment to the nineteenth-century Czar. It has a calabash shape and a fine brown russeting.

Juicier than the Beurré Bosc, the Beurré Hardy takes its name from a nineteenth-century Belgian and is a plumper pear. Both pears in their youth have enough juice for delicious eating and are also excellent when stewed.

**Bonne Louise** de Longueval and d'Avranches, named after its grower and the place of its birth in Normandy, is now also known as Louise Bonne de Jersey and in German-speaking countries as gute Louise von Avranches. Good it certainly is, and well known not only in its native country but wherever French pears are exported. Smooth skinned, with the merest speckle of russeting, Louise tends to be greenish on the shaded side and yellow washed with pink on the side ripened in the sun. It can be stored without loss of flavor and is an excellent dessert pear.

**Seckel**, or seckle, was discovered growing wild in America by an eighteenth-century trapper. It is small, long necked and very popular since it is so sweet, juicy and spicy.

**Clapp's** Large, yellow with some russeting and occasionally faintly red cheeks, this is a popular American variety.

**Passe crassane** This fat, juicy, rounded Italian pear has a lovely flavor and makes an excellent dessert pear. It keeps well and is known as the queen of winter pears.

### Buying pears

Pears for eating or cooking should always be sound. Test for ripeness near the stem end, where there should be more than a little give, and at the blossom end, where there should be no oozing softness, since this usually indicates trouble within. Pears are at their best for a very short time, and although they can be left to mature for a little while they must be inspected frequently.

### Cooking with pears

Most pears are eating pears, although some are juicier than others. All pears, however, can also be poached in wine or light syrup, and well-flavored eaters such as Bartlett are in fact best for such dishes as pear sherbet and Poires Belle Hélène, the dish in which pears are served on a bed of vanilla ice cream and covered with a hot chocolate sauce.

Cooking pears, which may be sold as such, are harder and less perfumed than the eaters. Poached in vanilla-flavored syrup, they make good compotes and can also be cooked in spiced red wine, in the process of which they become dyed, as the Tudors said, to "a fine oriental red." In Italy they are baked in Marsala, the cavity of each half-pear stuffed with a mixture of ground almonds and crystallized fruit. They can also be made into a relish with lemon juice and ginger or with horseradish, mustard seeds and black pepper, or they can be preserved or pickled with sugar, cinnamon and white wine vinegar. Cooked "brown" with butter and sugar, they used to be served hot with game in Germany. They are still served cold there, poached in lemon juice with cranberries.

Around the North Sea pears also go into main dishes: Frieslanders boil them with green beans, potatoes and beef, while in Hamburg they are cooked with beans and bacon or with salt meat. Boiled potatoes mixed with pears and a dash of vinegar are also sometimes served in northern Europe, while in the *nouvelle cuisine* a purée of pears and spinach can accompany roast duck.

# Fruit/*Citrus*

The beautiful citrus fruits all have one thing in common: they ripen while they are still on the tree. Once they have been picked they stop developing and will not get sweeter or improve their flavor. But most of them travel well and remain in good condition for many weeks in the right environment, and only gradually lose weight and pliancy as their juices and oils lose freshness.

Natural untreated citrus fruits are also subject to regreening. This does not necessarily mean that they are unripe but is simply a matter of temperature; the chlorophyll in ripe fruit fades as the thermometer drops and revives as it rises again. Inside the skin the fruit remains unaffected, but since green patches are unattractive on citrus fruit that should by rights be orange or lemon-yellow, they are often treated with ethylene gas, which fades the chlorophyll,

making them more acceptable to the consumer. When buying citrus fruits, choose those that feel heavy for their size as this means plenty of juice. The fruit should be sound with no sign of bruising, damp patches or soft spots.

## Citrons

These fruits are the elders of the citrus tribe. They are large with a thick corrugated skin and resemble large avocados. Since their pulp is too bitter to eat, they are now mostly grown to make the most translucently green, beautiful candied peel, which is used in fruit cakes.

## Oranges

There are three main varieties of oranges: the smooth, thin-skinned sweet oranges such as the Valencias and blood oranges, that range from bright gold to blood red and are full of juice; the larger, rougher, thick-skinned seedless navel oranges that have the best flavor and are easy to peel;

and the bitter oranges, also known as Seville or Bigarade oranges, that are used for making the best marmalade.

Invented in Scotland, orange marmalade owes it origins to a boatload of Portuguese oranges which arrived in Dundee in the eighteenth century and unexpectedly turned out to be extremely bitter. Bitter oranges still come onto the market in their short New Year season and marmalade making is about the only occasion on which we boil oranges to good purpose.

For the most part, however, we like our oranges fresh. In Trinidad they are sold in the street, halved and sprinkled with salt. Orange juice, freshly squeezed and served with ice, used to be standard refreshment in many countries. In Sicily, a paradise for oranges, the juice is drunk not so much as an appetizer but as a final bonne-bouche after a meal, especially the glorious tomato-red juice of blood oranges, which is particularly sweet and full of flavor.

When making orange juice, thin-skinned oranges such as the virtually seedless Valencias are the best buy. This is not

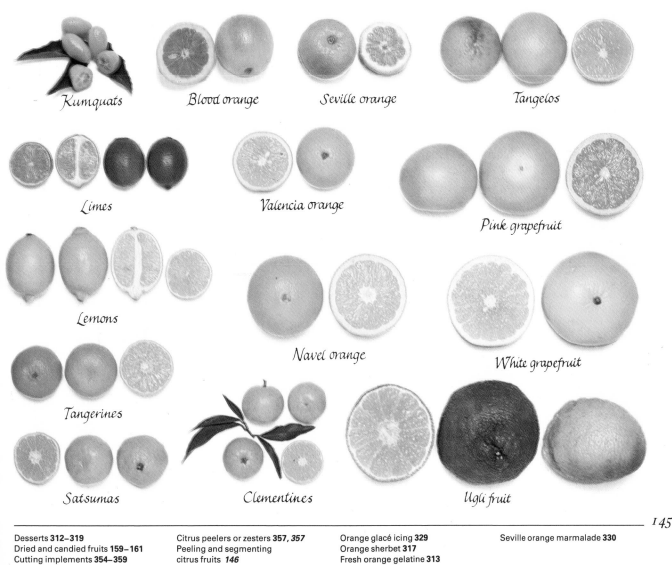

Kumquats · Blood orange · Seville orange · Tangelos

Limes · Valencia orange · Pink grapefruit

Lemons · Navel orange · White grapefruit

Tangerines · Satsumas · Clementines · Ugli fruit

so much because navel oranges lack juice but because their imposing size makes them more expensive, and since their skins have a thick padding of pith a lot of what we pay for is thrown away. The navel orange, which can be peeled neatly and is also virtually seedless, is the best to eat as a dessert.

## Mandarins and tangerines

These and their many cultivars such as clementines and satsumas are the smaller members of the citrus family and their names are sometimes used interchangeably. All are distinguished by having skin that does not cling to the fruit and flesh that separates easily into segments. They are known as various mandarin cultivars to the botanist but to the shopper as different types of tangerines. Those of North African descent, grown in Tangiers with loose-fitting skins and perfumed juice, are responsible for the name tangerine. Canned segments, however, are sold as mandarins.
**Clementines** are thought by some to be mandarins crossed with the Algerian wild orange, but are generally recognized as a variety of tangerine. They are usually tiny with a very good flavor—children are particularly fond of them.
**Satsumas** are the tangerines grown and exported from Japan and Cyprus. They can be quite sour and are very refreshing.
**Ortaniques, kings, tangors and murcotts,** along with many other small hybrids, are related to both tangerines and oranges and are often found growing on the same tree, which shows how easily they cross with each other. They are sweet, spicy dessert fruits and are easy to peel.

## Kumquats

These originated in Japan and have recently been cast from the citrus family by botanists although they continue to look and taste like tiny oranges. They are usually eaten with their skin and are often sold in glass jars, unpeeled and preserved in heavy syrup.

## Grapefruit

These large familiar globes that are either yellow, when they are called white, or rosy, when they are called pink, are descendants of the pomelo, a citrus plant carried from Polynesia to the West Indies in the seventeenth century by an English sea captain. A modern variety of this fruit, pink fleshed and with the merest trace of bitterness, is still marketed under its original name.

The grapefruit is more popular in America than anywhere else. It is primarily a breakfast fruit but often starts meals in the shape of cocktails, or in the half shell with the segments precut. It ends meals in mousses and sherbets and in between turns up in salads mixed with avocado, or with oranges and mint and served on beds of lettuce.

## Tangelos and uglis

Tangelos are a cross between tangerines and grapefruits. They are loose skinned and often stamped "color added" when marketed, since their skin does not color well naturally. The minneola variety is particularly juicy and easy to peel.

The same fruit is also marketed under the name of ugli fruit or, as it is called in Jamaica, hoogli fruit. No cosmetic treatment is applied to it in this guise and its extraordinary bumpy, mottled skin remains greenish-yellow. The light orange flesh is sweet and juicy and delicately flavored with a flower-like perfume.

## Lemons

Rich in vitamin C, these most indispensable of fruits can be large or small, with a smooth, thin skin or a thick knobbly one. For culinary purposes such as puddings and sherbets, lemon butters, lemon soups, frothy sauces and for the wedges served with fish and shellfish, and with iced tea, it is better to use smooth-skinned lemons, which have more juice.

Choose specimens that are truly lemon-yellow. Butter-yellow lemons may have lost some of their acidity in ripening, and lemons that look dull and do not have a moist-looking sheen may be dry and "ricy," meaning that the almost invisible little sacs containing the juice have turned grainy through evaporation.

Lemons owe much of their flavor and aroma to the oil in the outer part of their skin, which is known as the zest. When serving lemon quarters they should be cut lengthwise so that when squeezed the juice will be directed downwards onto the food. Lemon juice should be added whenever possible to dishes after they are cooked, to avoid loss of vitamin C, which disappears when it is heated.

Apart from flavoring, lemon juice has certain other qualities. A teaspoonful of lemon juice added to every cup of water will help prevent fruit breaking up or losing its shape while it is stewing. A few squeezes of juice will help poached eggs and boiled rice to keep their color, and a few drops will acidulate water sufficiently to prevent the discoloration of vegetables such as sweet potatoes and Jerusalem artichokes. It can be used instead of vinegar in salad dressings, and since it helps to counteract the richness of foods it can aid digestion when used with fried foods.

## Limes

These can be pale or dark green and have a tart greenish pulp; if their skins are yellowish this usually means that their tang has gone. The West Indian or Mexican lime, which features so much in Creole cooking, is sharp and aromatic, as are the larger Tahitian limes of which the Persian and the Bearss are two types. The Key limes of Florida have a delicious sharpness and are used to make Key lime pie.

Limes are the most perishable of all the citrus fruits. They can be used for the same purposes as lemons and their juice, pale when fresh but often with added green color when commercially extracted, goes into daiquiris and margheritas.

**Peeling and segmenting citrus fruit**
*1. Using a serrated knife, cut a slice from the top of the fruit to expose the flesh. Peel the fruit in the same way as you would an apple, cutting just beneath the pith.*

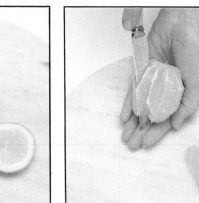

*2. Hold the fruit in one hand and cut out each segment, freeing it from its protective membrane as you cut. The resulting segments should be completely free of membrane and pith. This method is suitable for all citrus fruits.*

Although hothouse peaches can be found almost all the year round, there is still something wonderfully seasonal about stone fruits. Their year begins with the first cherries and ends with the last of the plums, with outdoor peaches, greengage and damson plums, nectarines and apricots in between. All are closely related members of the Prunus family and when talked about collectively are known as drupes.

## Cherries

Firmly fleshed or melting, deepest lip-staining black or the palest cream tinged with a rosy blush, cherries come in hundreds of varieties and are generally classified by their growers as sweet or sour. There is also a third type, which is a mixture of sweet and sour, known as Dukes or Royales. Usually black or transparent red, these are all-purpose cherries and can be both eaten and cooked in a variety of ways.

The wild sweet cherry known as the mazzard is the ancestor of all our varieties.

### Sweet cherries

Sweet cherries used to be neatly divided into the hard, crisp bigarreaus and the soft, sweet cherries known as guignes in France, or geans in England. Now, however, with the appearance of many hybrids, the distinction has become blurred.

Among the most delicious of the bigarreaus are the Napoleons, or Naps—big, crisp and golden with a red cheek. They are also known as Royal Annes, and in nineteenth-century England were for a time called Wellingtons. This politically inspired name, however, did not catch on, and to restore the balance England named a dark red cherry the Waterloo. A favorite American cherry, the Bing, is also a bigarreau—large, heart shaped, deep red to almost black, with firm, sweet flesh.

Another red-black cherry that is tender and has an excellent flavor is the Black Tartarian, a type of guigne. It is said to have made its way to Europe from the Caucasus, the seed probably carried by birds. Early Rivers, another of the guigne type of cherry, is a prolific variety with red to deep red flesh.

Sweet, juicy black guignes are used to make the delicious dessert clafoutis, which comes from the Dordogne region of France, while in Kent, England's cherry-orchard county, a similar dish goes by the name of battered cherries. The same juicy type of cherries also go into the exquisite Swiss black cherry jam, slippery and shiny and full of whole cherries. The cheaper versions with chopped-up cherry pulp trying to pass off as the real thing are best avoided.

### Sour cherries

If the word sweet is sometimes used too optimistically as far as cherries are concerned, sour is almost an understatement. The dark, short-stemmed, juicy morellos, or griottes as they are known in France, are so acid that they are almost impossible to eat. They are small and round and deep red to almost black. The famous Black Forest cherry cake called schwarzwälder kirschtorte is authentically made with morellos grown in the Black Forest region, and with kirschwasser, the Black Forest version of cherry brandy. Amarelle cherries such as the Montmorency, brighter in color and with pale, clear juice, are so sour that they are not usually eaten uncooked.

Sour cherries go into translucent jams, into pickles to eat with game, pork and poultry, and into liqueurs and cherry brandies. Duck Montmorency, now something of a cliché, requires cherries for its fruity, winy sauce, although they do not necessarily have to be the sour Montmorency cherries of France; any acid red cherries will do. And cherries set alight in a brandy sauce and poured over vanilla ice cream make Cherries Jubilee. Morello cherries are often preserved in jars and make excellent tarts and pies.

### Maraschino cherries

The sweet, sticky liqueur maraschino is made from a small, wild Dalmatian cherry called damasca, or marasca, but maraschino cherries, which were originally preserved by being steeped in the liqueur, are now more likely to be cherries that have been bleached and then steeped in syrup flavored with oil of bitter almonds.

### Buying and storing cherries

Look for brightly colored fruit; whether heart shaped or spherical, the plump ones are always best. The fruit should be clean and glossy, with unbroken skins and stalks that are fresh and green. Ripe cherries are perishable, but will keep for a few days in the refrigerator; wash them just before they are to be eaten.

### Cooking with cherries

Prepare cherries for cooking by pushing out the stones with a cherry pitter or hooking them out with the U-bend of a bobby pin or paper clips. If you try to squeeze the pits out, too much juice is lost.

Canned cherries lack firmness and flavor and are best used in sweet dishes, although they still won't be very good. It is best to avoid them if possible.

## Plums

No other fruit, said Pliny, has been so cleverly crossed, and since he wrote this some 2,000 years ago, the growers have not been idle. Some plums are grown primarily to be eaten fresh, although many, like the greengages, are equally delicious cooked.

### Dessert plums

These are usually larger and juicier than cooking plums, with a higher sugar content. **Gages** Of all the plums, none is more sweetly perfumed than the greengage, known in France as the reine-claude after Francis I's queen. Round and firm fleshed, the old greengage with its rose-flushed cheek is still grown, although there are now other varieties such as the Black Diamond and the juicy Jefferson. There are also many golden descendants of the old French "transparent gage," large and translucent, with the delicious honeyed flesh that is characteristic of all the gages.

**The Santa Rosa and Burbank** These are pleasantly tart plums grown largely in California, where the climate suits their warm temperament. Derivatives of the wild Asiatic plum, they are often referred to as Japanese plums, although in fact they were grown originally in China.

**The Gaviota** This is one of the newer varieties, grown to giant proportions; it is sweet and juicy and ruby-colored right through to the pit.

**The Victoria** Golden red and pink bloomed, the Victoria is one of the most prolific of plums. Oval shaped with golden flesh, it is a favorite in the kitchen as well as being an excellent dessert plum.

### Cooking plums

These are usually the smaller, drier, sharp-flavored plums that retain enough acidity to make them delicious when cooked. **Sloes and bullaces** Dark and mouth drying, the sloe is the wild European plum that grows on spiky hedges and is used for making sloe gin. The bullace, larger than the sloe, is less acid and can be stewed, jellied or preserved.

**Damsons** These have a lovely acidity even when ripe and are used for jams, pies and desserts, and in England for damson cheese, an old country confection made of sieved fruit and plenty of sugar, which is potted and aged before it is ready to eat. It also used to be dried in slabs, decorated with almonds and served with a dousing of port as a dessert. Damson cheese is a close relation to the more pliable "mus," the cheese made from Zwetschen, which used to be frequently eaten, especially in Germany.

**Zwetschen**, Quetschen or, in the Slavonic languages, slivy, are small, dark blue plums with a heavy bloom. They thrive in central

Europe, where slivovitz is made, and in Germany and in Alsace, where they are used to make quetsch—a fruit brandy that is clear and potent.

**Cherry plums**, also called myrobalans, are very small, with red or yellow skins and yellow flesh. They are soft and juicy and are excellent stewed or made into jams.

**Beach plums** These grow wild in the United States, especially around Cape Cod, where the dark purple fruits grow in large clusters and are keenly gathered and made into beach-plum jelly.

### Buying and storing plums

When buying plums make sure that they are firm and free from damage. They should be stored in a cool place, but not for too long; ripened plums do not keep for more than two or three days. If you buy them already ripe, they need to be eaten as soon as possible as they will quickly go bad.

### Cooking with plums

All dark plums and some of the lighter varieties such as the small golden-yellow Mirabelle, have bitter skins which make a delicious contrast to the sweetness of their flesh when cooked. They can be used to make jams and jellies which are transparently luminous when freshly cooked, but darken with overcooking and ageing. These are the plums, too, that are used to make a delicious sweet-sour sauce that can be served with meat and with the crêpes that sometimes accompany Peking duck.

In Austria plums, fresh or dried, go into the middle of lovely deep-fried little dumplings that are rolled in sugar mixed with grated chocolate, and also go into strudels. Throughout Germany the plum season means Pflaumenkuchen—plums riding on a yeast-based dough that absorbs the juice of the fruit. In Britain, however, many recipes such as plum duff or plum pudding do not require plums at all, the word being used to mean raisins.

### Peaches

The flesh of peaches ranges from almost silvery white to deep gold—the white-fleshed peaches being tender and juicy, the yellow ones slightly coarser but often very

Apricots

Gaviota plums

Santa Rosa plums

Burbank plums

Cherry plums

Peaches

Royal Anne cherries

Early Rivers cherries

Nectarines

Black Tartarian cherries

Bottled morello cherries

good. With some peaches the flesh clings to the stone, hence clingstone peaches, while with freestone varieties the flesh comes away easily and cleanly. In Europe this distinction seems not to weigh so heavily on the shopper, although it is always a shame when too much of the flesh—rightly described as voluptuous—refuses to part in any way from the stone.

Known as *Prunus persica*, the peach reached Greece from its native China via Persia, and Rome and the rest of Europe via Greece. It arrived in America by way of stones carried by Columbus, and the American soil and climate suited the peach tree so well that it spread faster than the settlers. But it is Georgia, especially, which is often known as the peach state. The freestone Belle of Georgia, crimson cheeked, its creamy flesh delicately marbled and its stone sitting in a carmine-tinted pit, comes from seed sent directly from China at the end of the nineteenth century. Elberta, another favorite Georgian, has juicy yellow flesh, firm but

*Victoria plums*

*Greengage plums*

*Damson plums*

tender. It is equally popular fresh or canned, but while canned peaches in heavy syrup are nice enough, they differ almost more than any other fruit from their fresh counterparts: perhaps it is because canned peaches are cooked in a heavily sweetened syrup, for even the sweetest fresh peach never has a cloying quality.

### Buying and storing peaches

Large peaches command the highest price but are not always the most delicately flavored. (The native peach of China, venerated ancestor of all the peach trees in the world, bears fruit that is relatively small with a large stone, yet its flavor is said to be unsurpassed by any of our hybrids.)

Peaches are a fragile fruit and should be handled very gently. They should feel firm with a little give; greenish fruit should be avoided as it will never ripen at home. Store ripe peaches in the refrigerator, but those that are still a little too firm are best kept at room temperature.

### Cooking with peaches

Spiced or pickled peaches are excellent with ham, and some people eat them in salads, but it is as puddings or desserts that they come into real use. Peach sherbets and ice creams are both delicate and subtle, and there are scores of coupes and sundaes made with peaches, the most famous of which must undoubtedly be Peach Melba. Invented by Escoffier for a late diner, Dame Nellie Melba, the opera singer, this involves a ripe fresh peach gently poached in syrup, with vanilla ice cream and whipped fresh cream, and crushed fresh raspberries for the sauce. In France, peaches and raspberries make an exquisite fruit dessert.

*Sloes*

*Bullaces*

### Nectarines

One of the most beautiful of all fruits, with rosy cheeks like blushing girls, nectarines are smooth skinned like plums and are very like ripe plums in texture, but taste of peach, although they are a little sharper and more scented. They can be used in all the same ways as peaches, but are usually devoured, messily, as a dessert fruit—much juicier than peaches, they are rarely skinned as their skin is much thinner. Called brugnons in France, they are eaten there in vast quantities in July and August. They are grown in California and are widely marketed throughout America.

### Apricots

Even in the days when fresh fruit was regarded with suspicion, apricots were generally accepted as wholesome food. Known as *Prunus armeniaca* because the Romans obtained them from the Far East via Armenia, they span the spectrum of gentle orangey tones from the very pale to the very rich. Depth of color, however, is not necessarily an indication of flavor; it merely means that some varieties have more carotene than others and are richer in vitamin A. The dark apricot called Moorpark is always sweet and delicious.

The flesh of apricots, unlike that of peaches and nectarines, is dry and mealy, which makes them ideal for cooking as well as for eating fresh because they will not turn into a mush, thereby ruining your pastry or whatever else.

### Buying and storing apricots

An apricot picked before its time does not sweeten, it only matures a little, so test for ripeness by pressing the fruit between two fingers; it should feel soft. Ripe fruit will keep in the refrigerator for a few days. Unripe, they will keep for longer, and if they are too hard and sour to be eaten fresh, they can be cooked and made into tarts, or pickled in vinegar with cloves for an excellent relish which is delicious when eaten with cold pork or ham.

### Cooking with apricots

In France large, fresh apricots make the most mouthwatering flans and tarts, arranged on light flaky pastry, and a compote of apricots, sometimes flavored with Madeira, is served hot on crisp, golden croûtons. Austria's knoedels, or apricot dumplings, are made from fresh skinned apricots individually wrapped in thin pastry, and then poached and eaten with hot melted butter, sugar and cinnamon. And brandied apricots are delicious, the fruit poached with sugar and put up with brandy in equal quantity to the syrup.

# Fruit/*Berries and Rhubarb*

The arrival of berries heralds the coming of summer, but they will not be so fully flavored and sweet as later on in the season and they are also likely to be expensive. In the case of most berries, however, it is a pleasure to buy at least a few early ones for decorating creamy desserts, to which they give an allure that is quite disproportionate to their numbers.

The real feasting begins in the high season and it is then that most berries taste best, simply dredged with sugar and eaten with creamy milk, cream or possibly sprinkled with wine. Later on, when the first flush of excitement has worn off somewhat, they can be combined with other fruit or made into ice creams and sherbets.

There are usually at least two weeks each summer when a great number of berries are available simultaneously. This is the time to make summer desserts or to offer great bowls of mixed berries, sugared well beforehand so that they yield some of their juice. Later in the season, when the smaller berries (which are delicious but cheaper) arrive, it is time to think about making jams, jellies and syrups.

When buying berries it is important to look not only at the top of the little box in which they are likely to be packed but also at the underside. Bad staining or wetness underneath suggests squashed, sad fruit below, which will soon go moldy. Some packers still call to mind the Elizabethan "strawberry wives" who, according to their monarch, were given to "laying two or three great ones at the mouth of their pot, and all the rest were little ones."

If you buy berries loose, ask for them to be weighed in small quantities since this prevents them being crushed by their own weight on the way home. If you go fruit picking at a farm—every year more of them open their gates to the public—take plenty of small shallow containers so that your harvest remains in good condition.

Berries, whether bought or picked, are fragile and perishable, so the sooner you eat them the better. If they must be stored, put them in a darkish, airy place, spreading them out well so that furry casualties do not infect their neighbors. No berries, except perhaps the harder ones that come in the autumn, thrive in the refrigerator, for although it is cold and dark, it is too humid, and also the highly scented berries such as raspberries and strawberries tend to permeate other foods, particularly butter, with their smell.

## Strawberries

"Doubtless God could have made a better fruit than the strawberry, but doubtless, God never did." Best loved among the soft fruits, strawberries conjure up all the well-being of summer. In England they are built into the summer way of life—tea at Wimbledon and Henley and garden parties at Buckingham Palace traditionally include what a sixteenth-century writer described as "strawberries swimming in the cream."

Somewhat surprisingly, perhaps, the ancestor of the cultivated strawberries we delight in these days was American, introduced to Europe from Virginia by early colonists. It was smaller than today's prize specimen, but a positive giant compared with the indigenous fragrant wood strawberries (*fraises des bois*) that had long been transplanted into gardens and regarded as a cure for all ills. Alpine strawberries (*fraises des alpes*) have slightly larger fruits and some are completely white in color. Both these wild varieties have not changed in their intense fragrance and size and still remain the best of all strawberries.

The advent of the Virginian strawberry led to unceasing attempts to grow even larger strawberries. Sadly, it was found that what the fruit gained in size it lost in flavor, and it was not until a particularly fragrant strawberry arrived from Chile, and crossbred with the Virginian, that the balance between size and taste was finally adjusted. This hybrid is the ancestral strawberry of all modern varieties cultivated on both sides of the Atlantic.

Nowadays new varieties of strawberries are regularly introduced and old ones discarded as being too fragile or not sufficiently resistant to disease, or possibly too small: size rather than flavor is the important factor in marketing and the big strawberries command the highest prices. They may look particularly luscious but from the eater's point of view bigger is not necessarily better; nor do the deep scarlet varieties necessarily taste best.

Do not be put off by the lighter berries or those that have paler tips, but make sure that the strawberries are plump and glossy. They should be bought with their green frills intact, and if washing them, do it immediately before hulling. Hulled strawberries yield their juice when sugared. Only in jam making should strawberries be cooked at all. Even when making strawberry sauce to go with ice creams or sherbets, simply liquidize the fresh fruit with sugar and perhaps a little lemon juice.

The way in which strawberries are served is a matter of taste. Some people like them hulled and sugared, simply hulled or, which is especially pretty, arranged in a pyramid with strawberry leaves tucked in here and there, while others prefer them with a dusting of pepper or a sprinkling of orange or lemon juice to bring out the flavor. There is also a school of thought that considers a sprinkling or even a dousing of beaujolais, claret or champagne, perfection.

## Raspberries

These beautiful, velvety berries from which the liqueur crème de framboises is made are at their best when a deep garnet red. Black raspberries taste much like the red ones, as do the white ones, which do not often find their way onto the market. Raspberries are always sold hulled, which makes them fragile and particularly vulnerable to crushing. When picking them, gently slide the beaded lantern shape off its conical center, as this turns brown and mushy and quickly spoils the flavor of the fruit.

The flavor of raspberries is intense and their presence will be apparent even if only a handful is mixed with some other fruit, or the juice of a few is mixed with the juice of, say, red currants, for the Scandinavian dessert called rødgrød.

Raspberry juice is much loved in Germany and Scandinavia as a refreshing drink. It also often appears at table to be poured over rice puddings, blancmanges and flummeries. And in Berlin when you order a *weisse mit Schuss* in a beerhall, you will be served a goblet containing a fizzy drink made from pale ale, raspberry syrup and soda. Finally among the raspberry-flavored liquids is raspberry vinegar, which is made by steeping crushed berries in wine vinegar. It makes a delicious addition to fruit salads and when mixed with sugar and water and poured over ice it makes a wonderfully cool, quenching drink.

A few non-sweet dishes are improved by the addition of raspberries. The Scots stuff grouse and blackcock with the wild raspberries that grow in abundance in the hedges. It is in desserts, however, that raspberries come into their own, either served quite plain with a dollop of whipped cream, crushed in fresh sherbets or puréed with a little sugar and served as a sauce.

## Blackberries and dewberries

From the shopper's point of view, the distinction between these two berries is purely academic. From the picker's point of view, these relations of the raspberry are distinguished by their growing habits: upright plants are thought of as blackberry bushes, trailing ones as dewberries.

Although blackberries are generally larger than dewberries, and shiny while dewberries are dull, sometimes with a white bloom, their names are used interchangeably

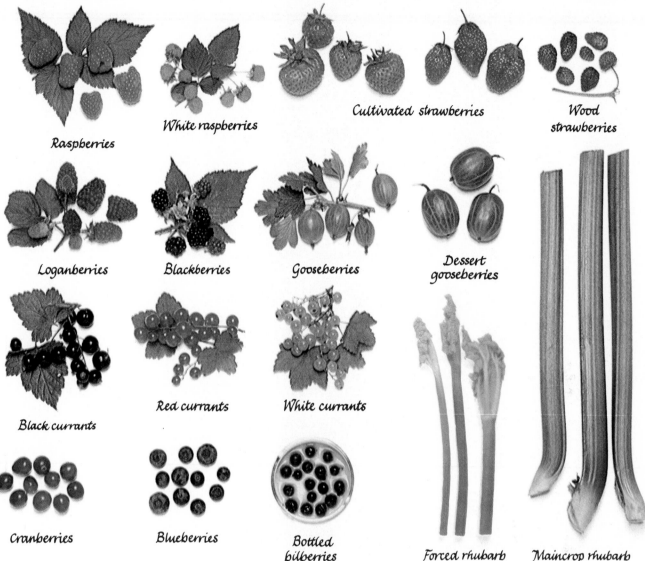

Raspberries

White raspberries

Cultivated strawberries

Wood strawberries

Loganberries

Blackberries

Gooseberries

Dessert gooseberries

Black currants

Red currants

White currants

Cranberries

Blueberries

Bottled bilberries

Forced rhubarb

Maincrop rhubarb

in many places. Neither their taste nor their properties differ and both are exceptionally rich in vitamin C. Both remain sour for a long time after turning black and are only fully ripe when they are soft to the touch.

The plant grows freely and English hedges tend to be black with berries from September to November. During these weeks pickers are out in full force and kitchens are filled with the aroma of the berries, which, besides preserves, are also made into wine, syrup and any number of desserts. Like raspberries, blackberries can also be eaten with sugar and cream, but this is a success only when they are ripe and fresh since, once off the brambles, wild blackberries lose their flavor fast.

Cultivated blackberries are more stable and keep their taste longer. They are always sold with their core but without their green stalks. They, too, make lovely pies, tarts, fools and crumbles. Blackberries

are particularly good when cooked with apples, not only because apples give an agreeable texture to the dish but also because their mellowness accentuates the blackberry's delicious acid flavor.

## Loganberries, youngberries and boysenberries

Whether in an attempt to improve the humble blackberry or to make the raspberry more robust, Messrs. Logan, Young and Boysen in turn did us a great service in crossbreeding. America's youngberries and boysenberries are used for the same purpose as loganberries, which are more familiar in Europe. All can be made into cooked and uncooked desserts and preserves using any recipe in which raspberries are called for.

**The loganberry**, basically a cross between a blackberry and a raspberry, is more acid than the blackberry but less intensely

flavored than the raspberry. It is purple with a delicate bloom, almost conical in shape and has no troublesome seeds. It needs plenty of sugar if it is to be eaten raw.

**The youngberry**, the result of crossing a dewberry with a raspberry, looks like an elongated blackberry and tastes rather like a loganberry.

**The boysenberry** is a cross between a youngberry and a raspberry and has a similar taste to the latter. The size of this fruit causes amazement to those unfamiliar with this fairly recent breed, as it is twice or even three times the size of its ancestors.

## Cloudberries and mulberries

**The cloudberry** is the raspberry's slow-ripening, cold-weather cousin. It has been found as far north as the Arctic Circle and grows in Siberia, Canada, cold districts of northern America and in Scandinavia, where it forms the basis of many fruit desserts and soups. Fully ripe, it is orange, tinged with red where it catches the sun, and resembles a golden mulberry. Its taste is reminiscent of apples with honey and in Canada it is called the baked-apple berry.

**The mulberry,** although it is not botanically related to the raspberry members of the Rubus tribe, is used in much the same way. The leaves of the mulberry tree form the silkworm's diet and many trees of great antiquity are to be found in old gardens, dropping their purple fruit to the ground below. Ripe, sweet scented and deeply staining, mulberries are good to eat fresh, although sometimes a little musty and watery. They also make delicious ice creams, sherbets and summer desserts.

### Gooseberries

These can be golden, green or red globes, translucent or opaque, covered in whiskers or smooth, and there is one variety that is milky white. They are the only berries among the soft fruits that make the most delicious dishes when they are unripe. No matter what their final color, immature gooseberries are pea-green.

Cook them, topped and tailed, into a purée with a little water over the lowest heat, using sugar to taste. They are always sour and require some sweetening even when making the classic sauce for mackerel, to which a little fennel is sometimes added. For pies and crumbles, gooseberries are also best when they are slightly immature. A cream-colored sprig of elderflowers laid on top of the fruit is a traditional British addition; it scents the gooseberries and makes them taste a little like muscat grapes.

When fully ripe, the big dessert varieties, full globes of yellow or red, make glorious eating. The common or garden green gooseberries are also good to eat, but are really better for jam making.

### Currants

Red currants, white currants and black currants are, like gooseberries, of the Rubus tribe, but here the similarity ends. They hang like tiny translucent grapes in little bunches on the bush, and the longer they hang, the sweeter they become. They are, however, never really sweet and even the ripest retain a good percentage of pectin.

**Red currants** There are those who love eating fresh red currants, raked off their stalks with a fork and covered with sugar and milk. Others prefer them in a berry mixture, or bathed in a real vanilla custard to mitigate the acid. They are delicious with melon and an essential ingredient of summer pudding.

Best loved of all red currant preparations, however, is red currant jelly. Eat it with mutton and lamb, or like jam with croissants and butter. Add a spoonful when cooking red cabbage or when jugging hare. Transform it, with the addition of port, orange juice and peel, into sweet-sharp Cumberland sauce to serve with ham and game.

**White currants** are less acid than their red counterparts and can be eaten just as they are, their thin, almost transparent skins liberally dusted with sugar.

**Black currants** These, too, make lovely jams and jellies but are rarely eaten fresh, except by those who like acid-tasting berries. The Russians, who often add spoonfuls of jam to lemon tea, add black currant jam to the actual brew in cases of colds and coughs. Black currants are rich in vitamin C and a tisane made of their leaves is often taken as a health-giving drink. A few black currant leaves are also sometimes included when making a purée for desserts, and there is a nice sherbet made with lemons and black currant leaves.

### Blueberries and bilberries

These berries, borne by shrubs found on acid soils and in peaty districts wherever heather grows, come from different species of the same genus and are used for similar purposes. Both have a silvery bloom that intensifies their blueness. They can be small or large depending on the soil, although blueberries are usually larger than bilberries, especially the blue cultivars that are widely grown in America.

Both were once so widespread that there was little to be commercially gained by putting them under cultivation. But their numbers declined as our appetite increased for berry crêpes, cheesecake and pie, cobblers and grunts—delicious concoctions of cooked fruit and dumplings—and now it is possible to buy cultivated berries that are the size of marbles and twice the size of the wild ones. Flavor has suffered considerably with cultivation, but becomes stronger when the berries are cooked and turn to a deep, teeth-staining purple.

### Cranberries

In northern Europe where these berries are plentiful they traditionally go into the sharp fruit relish that accompanies venison and roast game birds. They used to be as popular in Britain as elsewhere, but with the advent of red currants fell out of favor. America, however, reintroduced the larger, redder cranberry, much eaten as a sauce with turkey at Thanksgiving, and they are still traditional in Britain at Christmas.

When buying cranberries, make sure that

they are bright, dry, plump and unshrivelled. They will keep unwashed in the refrigerator for up to two weeks and also freeze well. When preparing them for fritters, jellies, compotes, sauces, relishes, muffins or pies, cook them slowly with plenty of sugar and a little water until they pop their skins and turn into a ruby-colored purée.

### Elderberries, rowanberries, rose hips

These berries are not usually found in the stores but each is well worth picking.

**Elderberries,** growing black and shiny in flat clusters, are a good addition to blackberry puddings and ripen at about the same time. On their own they may be a little sickly, but the syrup, made of the berries, can add a delicious flavor to apple pies all winter long. Sprigs of the cream-colored flower heads can be dipped in batter and eaten as fritters; they are surprisingly good, light and delicate.

**Rowanberries** are the fruit of the mountain ash, which in autumn is a mass of decorative orange-scarlet berries. They are delicious when made into a bittersweet jelly and served with venison or lamb.

**Rose hips,** either the scarlet ovals that appear in the hedges when the wild roses have blown, or the flat squat fruits of the Rugosa roses, are the essential ingredients of rose hip syrup, the well-known repository of vitamin C. They also make a delicate, health-giving jelly.

Care must always be taken to strain out the sharp, prickly hairs that surround the abundant seeds in each hip, so after steeping the ground hips in boiling water, pass the liquid at least twice through double cheesecloth or jelly bags.

### Rhubarb

Odd man out in the world of fruit, rhubarb is used for the same type of dishes that also call for gooseberries, apples and plums. It is probably best known in pies and crumbles —in fact, it used to be known as the pie plant—and its tart taste combines well with blander, sweeter fruits. When buying rhubarb, look for stalks that are crisp and firm. Use them as soon as possible as they are very perishable, or keep them in the refrigerator until ready to cook them.

Forced rhubarb stalks with their delicate texture need only the briefest of cooking as they soften so quickly. Tougher maincrop rhubarb takes longer and both need quantities of sugar. If very acid, a teaspoon of red currant jelly added to the cooking water often helps. Rhubarb is usually sold with its leaves as these prevent it wilting, but they must be discarded before cooking as they contain toxic amounts of oxalic acid.

# Fruits of the Vine/*Grapes*

Grapes can be pale, straw-colored and amber, shades of green, rose and scarlet, and deepest blue-black with a rich silvery bloom. They can be tear shaped, oval or round, large or small, in tight or straggly bunches, and all of today's grapes are descended from the wild grape vine.

The main role of grapes, of course, is to provide us with "God's choicest gift to man"—wine. The grape contains all that is necessary for making wine: it has yeast in its bloom, natural sugar to feed the yeast, tannin in the skin and seeds, and natural acids to help provide the right environment for the yeast to make alcohol.

But grapes have been long, and rightly, celebrated for more than the wine they yield. Fresh grape juice featured largely in medieval kitchens. The acid juice that characterizes grapes when they are unripe and sour was pressed out for *verjuice*—a piquant green liquid used in the place of vinegar for flavoring sharp sauces—and the sweet juice of mature grapes, when not concentrated by sun-drying which transformed the grapes into currants, raisins and sultanas, was boiled down into a syrup which was used as an alternative to honey.

Grape "cures," too, were once very popular. Edwardian society, after a season's over-eating, would spend a week or so eating nothing but grapes, in an attempt to restore the figure and cleanse the system. These grapes would have been huge, perfectly flavored hothouse muscats—still the most elegant of all the dessert grapes—which became the pride of gentlemen all over northern Europe as soon as greenhouses appeared in the seventeenth century.

## Muscats

These are to be seen in the stores almost all the year round sometimes swaddled in tissue paper to protect their yeasty bloom, or hanging in full glory in store windows. They may be translucent green with a golden tinge, in which case they are known as white muscats, or a deep blue (known as black muscats), or from scarlet to purple (the red muscats). They are all large, with the richly perfumed flesh that makes muscat wines so distinctive, and they all have seeds.

**White muscats** include the amber, oval-shaped Muscat of Alexandria, with a bloom that rubs off all too easily unless carefully handled; the prized Golden Chasselas, green with an amber tinge which means that it has developed its full flavor; and the fleshy green Almeria, of Spanish stock.

**Black muscats** Among these are the delicately flavored Gros Colmar; the large, round Royal with its heavy bloom, very juicy and sweet; Ribier, oval shaped and sweetly perfumed, with a vine-like flavor; and Black Alicante, oval, firm, not as sweet as the Royal but very juicy.

**Red muscats** range from the Cardinal, scarlet and crisp and delightfully aromatic, to the Flame Tokay, a lovely deep red, and Emperor, red or purple, firm and bland.

## Sweetwaters

Sweet and juicy, as their name implies, and with thin skins, the sweetwaters include the sturdy Black Hamburgh; a cutting of this type, planted at Hampton Court in 1769, flourishes there still.

## Seedless grapes

These have much less tannin than the varieties with seeds, and make the best canned grapes, since tannin tends to alter the flavor of the grapes in the canning process. Sweet, juicy and green, with smallish fruit, varieties such as Thompson Seedless and the smaller Sultana are among the most abundant grape varieties in the world, enjoyed both fresh and dried.

## Labruscas and Muscadines

The *labrusca*—not to be confused with Lambrusco, the sparkling red wine of Lombardy—is the native American vine that thrives in the colder climate of the eastern United States, where more tender varieties of grape refuse to grow. With tough skins that slip easily off the flesh, labruscas such as the round, blue-black Concord are rich in pectin and ideal for making grape juice and grape jelly. Delaware, small and a lovely pale rose-red, has a juicy, sweet flesh, and Catawba is red-purple and sweet.

Muscadines such as the large, bronze, sweet-fleshed Scuppernong are grown mainly in the southern states of America and have a rich, spicy flavor.

## Buying grapes

Although some grapes have ceased to be seasonal, and are either issued from storage as the market demands or from the greenhouses where they are nurtured all the year round, the end of summer is the traditional grape season. A few stores have taken to naming the grapes on sale, but most sell them unlabelled and few stores offer such a profusion of varieties as to put the shopper in a quandary.

When buying grapes, make sure that the red or black kinds have lost any tinge of green, and that white ones have a tone of amber about them. The stems of both kinds should be fresh looking but show at least a few brown patches, with the exception of Emperor grapes whose stems should be woody-brown all over.

From the trade's point of view the perfect bunch consists of grapes that are uniform in size, with no lurking tiny ones, and all of them firmly attached to their stalks. From the consumer's viewpoint, bunches with a tendency to shedding are often the sweetest, as anyone can testify who has bought local grapes from a huge mound in an open market, through a haze of wasps, and come away with straggly bunches and loose grapes, and found them perfectly delicious and more aromatic than the cosseted sort. But if perfect fruit is desired, it should be plump with no sign of wrinkling in the skin and no brown patches. Avoid bunches with little or no bloom, which shows they have been handled too much, or with any small, shrivelled grapes; these are sour.

## Storing grapes

Grapes will keep in good condition for about three weeks in the refrigerator, wrapped in perforated plastic wrap, or for two weeks in a cool larder—a long way on from the barrels in which the ancient Romans sealed their oil-dipped grapes, hoping to keep them fresh and luscious. But since part of the pleasure of grapes is their appearance, it seems a pity to banish them from sight. A fine bunch in a glass bowl or a basket makes a perfect centerpiece for the dining table; silver epergnes loaded with hothouse grapes were a frequent table decoration at grand Victorian dinners, and talented Victorians would set a bunch of grapes complete with a few leaves and tendrils in a mold of white wine gelatine as an edible showpiece.

## Serving grapes

Grapes are usually served at the end of a meal, either alone or with one of the soft cheeses from Normandy or perhaps the hard cheeses from Switzerland, where grapes are a frequent accompaniment to cheese. In Italy you may be offered your grapes in a huge bowl of ice water, with a few floating ice cubes—chilling makes grapes extra refreshing, but room temperature brings out their flavor better.

In the kitchen, grapes are used to make sherbets, jam, jelly and juice, and can also be frosted with egg white and sugar. A Calabrian specialty is a small pastry turnover filled with rum-flavored grape jam, together with walnuts and grated chocolate. In France, grape juice is sometimes boiled until it is syrupy, and then boiled again with

# Fruits of the Vine/*Grapes*

sliced apples, quinces, pears or lemons until it is sticky: such fruit is called *raisiné*.

Sole becomes sole Véronique when the rolled, poached fillets in a light white wine sauce are garnished with white muscat grapes. Muscat grapes are good, too, with duck foie gras, sometimes served hot, and pheasant and guinea fowl are sometimes stuffed with peeled, seeded grapes.

Some types of grape slip easily out of their skins, but others may need to be dipped in scalding water for a minute or so. Seeding, too, is simplicity itself if the grapes are first halved. If you want to keep them intact, use the U-bend of a new hairpin or paperclip to extract the seeds.

If you like salads with fresh fruit, try grapes in a mixture of apple and watercress, dressed with oil and lemon. Grapes and cottage cheese also combine well. Make fruit salads prettier with the addition of black grapes, seeded but not peeled, even though the skins of black grapes may be tougher than those of the white varieties. To preserve black or muscat grapes in brandy, prick each grape to make sure that it does not shrivel and then seal the grapes in equal parts of alcohol and sugar. Turn the jar once or twice during the week of maceration. After that, the fruit is ready to eat, poured over ice cream, or the strained brandy can be used in puddings or served in little glasses to accompany the grapes.

Emperor grapes

Gros Colmar grapes

Muscat of Alexandria grapes

Sultana grapes

Sugar Baby watermelon

Ogen melon

Charentais melon

Tiger watermelon

Honeydew melon

Muskmelon

Desserts 312–319

Impromptu fruit salad 312

A melon is a luxurious thing. Beautiful and intricately patterned on the outside, a ripe melon no larger than an orange can fill a large room with its fragrance. Inside, cool and full of juice, it offers to quench your thirst and provide you with a delicate sensation rather like eating snow. "There is," say the Arabs, "a blessing in melons. He who fills his belly with melons fills it with light."

Sweet melons, ribbed and encrusted with lacy patterns, were brought to Spain by the Moors, who had in turn received them from Persia or from the depths of Africa—both the Middle East and Africa claim to be the home of this honey-sweet fruit, described as "the masterpiece of Apollo" and celebrated for being as beneficial as the sun itself. Melons appeared in France towards the end of the fifteenth century, to extravagant praise, and were eaten in astonishing quantities by royalty. Served in pyramids and mountains, "as if it were necessary to eat to the point of suffocation, and as if everyone in the company ought to eat a dozen," they were washed down with draughts of muscat wine.

At that time, of course, sweet melons were no larger than oranges, but over the centuries they have been cultivated and improved in both their size and variety.

## Muskmelons

It is most likely that the muskmelon, or "nutmeg" melon as it is sometimes known, was the kind eaten by the Ancients, who served it with a sprinkling of powdered musk to accentuate the flavor.

Muskmelons are recognized by their distinctive raised netting, which may be coarse like crochet work or fine like lace. This is why they are also called "embroidered" melons in France and "netted" melons in Britain and America. They may be sharply segmented or grooved, with a green or yellow-orange skin, and the flesh ranges from green to salmon-pink.

Americans know their most famous melon of this type as cantaloupe, which is a misnomer. The true cantaloupe melon is not grown commercially in the United States.

## Cantaloupes

These are among the most aromatic types of melon. The rind is ribbed and warty and the flesh is usually a pale orange, rich and juicy. The French prefer to grow this type, especially the Charentais with its deep orange, faintly scented flesh, although new, similar hybrids are always being introduced. The delicate, pale yellow-fleshed Ogen melon from Israel is a small smooth-skinned cantaloupe hybrid.

## Winter melons

These are smooth or shallowly ribbed and less aromatic than the muskmelons. The principal varieties include the onion-shaped Casaba with its thick golden-yellow skin and creamy-white to golden flesh; the Cranshaw with green-gold skin and aromatic golden-salmon flesh; and the ubiquitous pale green or yellow honeydew melon with delicate green flesh.

## Buying sweet melons

Whatever type of melon you buy, there are a few sound rules to follow. Choose firm, plump melons with clean scars at the stem ends (a roughness here indicates they were picked before they were fully ripe). Netted melons should have no bald patches—this is a sign that the melon suffered a check during its development. Reject any fruits that are soft, scarred or show moist bruises on the skin. It is a bad sign, too, if the stem has started to rot, but light cracking at the stem end is a sign of ripeness. If you press them gently at the blossom end, the cantaloupes and the honeydew winter melons should feel slightly elastic to the touch.

If you are able to shake the melon before buying it and you hear a sloshing sound, the fruit is too ripe and may have started to deteriorate. All melons should feel heavy for their size and—most important—ripe melons should have a pleasant, sweet melon scent about them.

## Storing melons

A cool, airy place is best for storing all types of melons—warmer if you suspect that your melon is not quite ripe. When you think that it is ready to eat, and if you do not want it to scent everything in your refrigerator, put your melon to chill in a tightly closed plastic bag before cutting it.

## Serving melons

Although the most scented varieties are nicest plain for dessert, melon can be served in salads with leaves of fresh mint and an oil and lemon dressing; with oranges and watercress; or with finely chopped celery, onions, olives and mayonnaise. This mixture may sound strange, but it rests on an old tradition: a seventeenth-century list of "sallet" herbs includes the melon, and ideas for eating it with salt and pepper.

Ground ginger sometimes mixed with sugar has taken the place of pepper—which had ousted powdered musk—as the melon's usual condiment. Plain sugar is often served for the sweet-toothed because even the sweetest melon will be enhanced by a fine dusting of sugar, but the British way of pouring port or other fortified wines into the cavity of a melon is a mistake since it ruins both. Melon slices, resting on the rind from which they have been separated with a sharp knife, beside thin, translucent slices of raw ham—prosciutto—is as delicious a meal-starter as one could hope for. The French used to offer melons only as an hors d'oeuvre; usually chilled, halved cantaloupes sitting in a bowl of crushed ice, but sometimes, in the case of larger light-fleshed varieties, in wedges, the flesh already cut and resting on the rind in a sawtooth arrangement.

These days, melons have rightly taken a place in the dessert course and are to be met in fruit salads, filled with an assortment of fresh fruit, diced and mixed with grapes or red currants, or as melon sherbet or melon ice cream, made with orange and lemon juice and served, if possible, with wild strawberries. The best melons, of course, really need no dressing up, but a cool and refreshing sweet melon salad can be made with an assortment of melon balls or cubes—orange, white, green and scarlet—sugared and chilled: a feast for the eye and an opportunity for the palate to distinguish between the slightly different flavors of the fruits.

## Watermelons

The watermelon—which Mark Twain called "the food that angels eat"—is a different proposition. Much larger than the sweet melons, and oblong or round in shape, it is an entirely different species and originated in tropical Africa.

Small round watermelons from 6–10 lb/ 2.5–4.5 kg, with sweet red flesh and pitch-black seeds, may have deep green rinds with a bloom, such as the Sugar Baby, or they may be striped on a light green background, such as the appropriately named Tiger. But the favorites at family picnics are the large spherical or oblong watermelons, often sold in wedges. These usually have a much paler flesh than the smaller varieties because of their higher water content.

When buying a watermelon, it should have a bloom on its skin and the spot where it rested on the ground should be amber colored, not white or green. It should sound hollow when tapped. If you buy your melon by the piece avoid pieces with visible fibers: the flesh should not have any hard white streaks in it.

Watermelon is usually eaten in slices or as part of a fruit dessert.

# Fruit/*Tropical and Mediterranean*

Before steamships began to cross the seas regularly in the nineteenth century, trading in perishable tropical fruits such as bananas and pineapples was an impossibility. Now, unfamiliar fruits appear by boat or plane and make strange, exotic-looking piles among the more familiar fruits appearing, conveniently, just at the time of year when most fresh fruit is usually rather scarce in the market.

## Bananas

There are many varieties of this perfectly packaged fruit. Cooking bananas, called plantains, tend to be starchier and less sweet than the eating variety and are often used before they ripen. One variety is grown only for making beer, and there are red bananas, purple bananas and pink bananas, slim bananas and fat ones like little pigs. Bananas for the table are picked while they are still hard and green and may not be quite ripe when they reach the market. They will, however, ripen quickly at room temperature, turning first yellow, then spotted when they are ready for eating, and finally black when they can still be used to make banana bread. Buy them in the bunch rather than loose since the skin of loose bananas may well be ripped at the top, thus exposing the flesh.

The first bananas to be exported came from the Caribbean, and early northern desserts using bananas have a distinctly Creole flavor: demerara sugar and rum, coffee flavoring and rice, or coffee ice cream feature widely. Bananas are also eaten baked with slices of lemon, or plain out of their jackets. Chicken Maryland is often accompanied by peeled bananas fried in butter, and in Central America and the Caribbean ripe plantains are found boiled, fried or baked in many dishes.

Bananas, however, are most enjoyed in their fresh state. Sliced, they form part of many savory dishes, including curries and Creole rice. In fruit mixtures their slightly scented taste and smooth texture complement juicy or crisp fruits such as oranges and apples. Raw or fried, they also make a perfect dessert.

## Pineapples

A whole pineapple on the table is a truly luxurious sight. Fresh pineapples form part of many main courses in their native tropical habitat, where they are plentiful and cheap, and it is in the tropics that the idea of serving them hot as an accompaniment to poultry, pork chops and ham originated.

It is when fresh and simply served with sugar and perhaps kirsch that the pineapple is really at its best, although now that they are imported in quantity they are sometimes fried, baked in the shell, flambéed with cinnamon and rum, sprinkled with lime juice and used to make a variety of fillings for sweet omelets.

When buying a pineapple it should be fully ripe and fragrant. If the stalk end is moldy or discolored, the fruit bruised or the leaves wilting, the pineapple is not at its best. A pineapple will continue to ripen after it is picked and one that is almost ripe will ripen completely at home, but an unripe pineapple that has no scent and is not uniformly colored will never develop its flavor to the full. Small pineapples often have a more delicate flavor than large ones.

## Mangoes

These beautiful fruits, shaped like large eggs, may be as big as melons or as small as apples. They may be green, gold, rosy or a mixture of all three. The vivid pinky-golden flesh of ripe mangoes is smooth and fiberless with a taste that has been compared to that of peaches, apricots, melons and pineapples.

When buying mangoes make sure that they are just soft and have a good perfume. If they are completely green they will not ripen properly, and those with large black areas tend to be overripe.

Mangoes are embarrassingly difficult to eat. They are usually either scored from top to bottom in several places, peeled and eaten with a spoon, or cut in half and eaten with a spoon or just sucked up.

Chilled mangoes are sometimes served halved in their shells, sprinkled with lemon

Prickly pears

Lychees

Pomegranate

Papaya

Plantains

Guavas

Cape gooseberries

juice, sugar, rum or ginger. Pared and cut they are delicious in fruit desserts and they make excellent sherbets.

It was in India that Britain found its original taste for mango chutney. Green unripe mangoes are used for this, as they are for poached and baked mango dishes.

## Papayas and pawpaws

Columbus anticipated Mark Twain—in a different context—by declaring that these fruits that he called tree melons tasted, when ripe, like the "food of the angels." The unripe papaya, also called *lechosa*, is used like a vegetable and tastes like a squash.

The papaya's skin is green to golden, its flesh orangey and its seeds black and shiny. It usually comes onto the market when it is ripening and is sweet and subtly flavored. When buying papayas make sure that they are firm, unblemished except for their speckles and just turning yellow, then allow them to ripen at home.

Like a squash, the unripe papaya may be served stuffed or baked with butter, or it may be added to salads or simply pickled. South American Indians wrap its leaves, freshly plucked, around tough meat to act as a tenderizer, as the plant contains a powerful enzyme that breaks down protein. The food industry also taps it for a substance called papain to make a tenderizing powder for meat. The ripe papaya is distinctive in fruit salads, pies and sherbets and can also be served simply sprinkled with lemon or lime juice, or sugar or ginger.

The papaya is sometimes called pawpaw, as is another fruit which is similar to look at but is in fact related to the custard-apple.

The true pawpaw is usually green with a bloom to its skin and an unpleasant scent and flavor, although there is one variety that becomes almost black-skinned in maturity and is sweet and good to eat.

## Guavas

Pink fleshed and sweet, these can be as small as a walnut or as large as an apple. They can be served puréed or baked, or eaten fresh with sugar and cream, and they also go well with other fruit such as pineapples or bananas. They are best known, however, for their jelly, which is served with meat or game as an alternative to

Mangoes

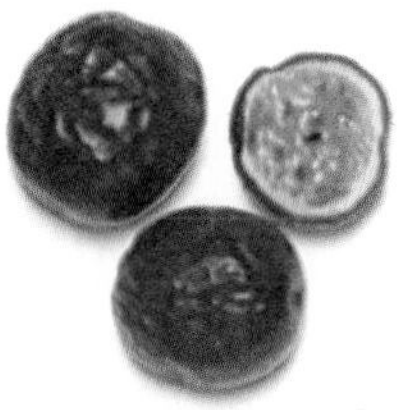

Passion fruit

Bananas

Pineapple

Persimmon

Kiwi fruit

Fresh figs

Fresh dates

the usual red currant jelly. If you make it at home, a few drops of Worcestershire sauce in the juice will give a more interesting flavor. Guava jelly is also delicious spread on hot toast.

## Pomegranates

The lark, which Shakespeare's Juliet insisted was a nightingale, "sang on yon pomegranate tree"—a shrub-like plant introduced to the West from Persia via Africa. Its beautifully shaped fruit, golden outside and filled with crimson beads, each with its central seed, is an intricate construction.

To admire its crimson glory at its best, cut the fruit in half or in segments, slicing through the leather-like, pink-flushed skin. Although the juicy pulp surrounding each of the seeds is beautifully refreshing and aromatic it is rather tiresome to eat. You can take a few grains, suck the flesh off the seeds, discard the seeds and continue to eat and discard until the shell is empty. A much easier way, however, is to crunch and swallow the seeds, which have a nice texture.

## Persimmons

These, when they are ripe and good, are often compared in taste to rather cloying guavas, apricots, tomatoes and mangoes, but their astringency when less than perfect "draws the mouth awry with much torment." Wrinkled fruit should therefore never be shunned, since by the time it has reached this stage the acidity and tannin are sure to have disappeared.

The handsome, orange-red persimmons, however, do stay glossy and plump when they have been plucked early and artificially matured. Provided they are ripe and soft, with cap and stem intact, their tough skin can be cut downwards and peeled back and the jelly can then be eaten like pulp.

## Kiwi fruit

The brown furry skin covering this egg-shaped fruit hides glistening translucent green flesh with decorative edible black seeds. Once known as the carambola, Chinese and Coromandel gooseberry, it is now best known by the name of New Zealand's national bird, the kiwi. The fruit is used to best effect when it is peeled and thinly sliced, since the pattern of the black seeds in the green flesh is so pleasing.

## Passion fruit

This fruit is so called because the flower of the plant is thought to evoke the Passion of Christ. The fruit of some species of the passion-flower is also called granadilla and calabesh in the West Indies. It is the size and shape of an egg with a purple-brown hard skin that becomes crinkly as the fruit gradually ripens.

The aromatic flesh is inseparable from the many small black seeds, which are edible. The fruit is usually halved and perhaps sprinkled with sherry or cream, or the flesh is scooped out and mixed in fruit salads.

## Custard apples

These are the fleshy, round or elongated, thick-skinned fruit of the large family of *Anona* trees of the American tropics. There is the apple-shaped cherimoya, and the llama, whose taste has been compared to that of a banana and pineapple. The soncoya is similar but larger, and the sweet-sop is green with flesh that is soft, sweet, aromatic and custard flavored. The sour-sop is green, heart shaped and more acid, with a taste similar to that of a black currant. All are eaten fresh, often chilled for breakfast, the flesh being spooned from the shell.

## Loquats

Also known as Japanese medlars, loquats are the size of crabapples but more conical. Although thirst-quenching, they do not have much flavor when raw and are principally used to make jams, jellies and sauces. A few of the seeds are usually included as these give a delicious bitter-almond flavor to any preserve or sauce to which they are added.

## Cape gooseberries

Native to tropical America, these acid-sweet, pleasant, small fruits of the shrub *Physalis peruviana* are encased in papery balloons shaped like Chinese lanterns. In South Africa they are grown on such a large scale that they have come to be known as Cape gooseberries. Golden when ripe, the berries can be eaten in the fingers or coated with fondant and served with *petits fours*, but are chiefly used to make the most delicious jellies and jams.

## Lychees and rambutans

Lychees or litchis are perhaps best known when served in syrup after a Chinese meal. They appear as translucent half-moons without their knobbly shells and bright red or brown glossy stones. In China, the lychee has been cultivated for thousands of years and has been used for its sweet-acid flavor to complement pork and duck dishes in much the same way as apples and oranges are used in the West.

A rambutan has a hairier shell than a lychee but is used for similar purposes in southeast Asia. Both fruits can be bought in the West, but should be avoided if they look shrivelled, since this means that their pulp is turning black and their delicate flavor will be lost.

## Prickly pears

These are the fruit of a cactus called the tuna and are sometimes known as cactus pears or Indian figs. They are pear shaped, vary in color from green to rosy and are covered with sharp prickles.

When buying prickly pears make sure that they are reasonably bright in color and firm, but not too hard. They are mild flavored and sweet and are usually eaten raw. The fruit should be slit lengthwise and the prickly skin will come off easily. The flesh can then be eaten with sugar and cream or sprinkled with lemon juice.

## Mangosteens

These delicate purple fruits with their shiny skin and white, soft, acid-sweet flesh segmented like that of an orange are very popular in southeast Asia. Their taste is refreshing and similar to that of a pineapple.

## Figs

These are perhaps the most sensual of all fruits with their bloomy, bursting skins and luscious flesh. Ancient Greeks thought figs so health giving that they formed part of the athletes' diet for the original Olympic games, and so delicious that poets and philosophers sang their praises. White, green, brown or purple, they are always beautiful and when cut open reveal their pulpy flesh, deep purple, red or pink, embedded with tiny seeds.

The entire fruit is edible and in Italy, where the Sicilian figs are most prized, they are served with prosciutto or as a dessert. In France the purple, white-fleshed Barbillone and many other varieties are also served as a dessert. All are good, especially when eaten fresh and ripe. Being perishable, they will not keep for longer than three days in the refrigerator, but should not be served chilled since the cold tends to numb their delicate flavor.

## Dates

In their fresh state, dates have a shiny brown skin that sadly promises more juice than the flesh actually delivers. Even the plumpest date has a warm, fudge-like consistency. When buying fresh dates make sure that you pick out fat, smooth-skinned and non-sticky specimens.

Making jam **330**                    Impromptu fruit salad **312,** *350, 351*                    Prosciutto **63**
Dried figs *159,* **160**
Dried dates *159,* **160**

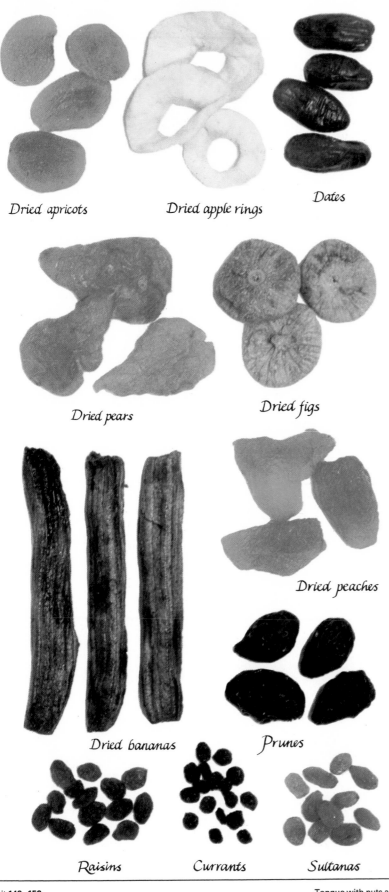

Dried apricots

Dried apple rings

Dates

Dried pears

Dried figs

Dried bananas

Prunes

Dried peaches

Raisins

Currants

Sultanas

Dried fruit does not so much prolong the taste of summer as provide us with sweetness of a different kind. Drying concentrates the sugar content of the fresh fruit, and although vitamin C is usually lost, vitamin A and the minerals remain.

Dried fruits such as "datyes, figges and great raysings" have been valued in Europe since they were imported in the thirteenth century from the Levant, to sit in the larder alongside domestic "prunellas, apricocks and pippins." There were also dried pears (a special delicacy) and the dried cherries and berries that the medieval housewife would put by in due season. This dried fruit went into a number of what now seem curious dishes. The taste was for the sweet-savory—the sort of dish still found in countries that were once part of the great Ottoman Empire. In Turkey, Iran, Arabia and North Africa, traditional cookery still allies lamb with prunes, apricots and almonds, honey and spices. Chicken is still simmered with prunes, or with quinces, dates or raisins.

Medieval Europe ate veal tartlets with prunes and dates, pickled fish was enhanced with raisins and figs, and mallards were smothered with fruit. The Great Pyes, without which no great dinner was complete, contained a mixture of beef, chicken, marrow, eggs, dates, prunes and raisins, all highly spiced and saffroned before being entombed in the "coffyn," as the crust was called. The taste for such things lives on. The seventeenth-century recipe for raisin sauce to eat with ham differs very little from that found in modern American cook books, or the raisin sauce eaten with boiled tongue in northern Europe. And the eighteenth-century ham stuffed with "apricocks" is not far from Virginia ham with peaches.

Indeed, that most British of institutions the plum pudding is a descendant of the sweet-savory puddings of the Middle Ages —until the eighteenth century, one of its main ingredients was a leg or shank of beef. Now there is only the suet to remind us of the old days. Look further back and you find that the Christmas pudding is not English at all, but of ancient Greek origin— a less astonishing fact when you think that the very word currant is derived from Corinth, its place of origin.

### Raisins

The large, sweet raisins made from muscat grapes and called muscatels used to be the kings of the tribe. Now, similar giants are produced in other places in the world, especially California. It is these that are eaten as a dessert fruit; they used to appear in the stores at Christmastime, but are now available, seedless or complete with seeds, all the year round and are useful in cooking when making pilaus, sauces for quail and hare and in stuffings. Smaller raisins are sold loose and in packs for cake making. Raisins also come packed together with peanuts, shelled hazelnuts and almonds. This once inexpensive mixture is known as Studenten Futter in Germany, because the sugar content of the raisins and the protein content of the nuts quickly revives the energy of poor scholars while they pore over their books.

## Currants and sultanas

The currant comes from the small black seedless grape that is a native of the slopes around Corinth in Greece, while sultanas, also known as golden raisins, are made from the seedless white grapes once grown only in the neighborhood of biblical Smyrna. Although both varieties have long been produced elsewhere, the old names have stuck.

In some parts of the world, currants and sultanas are still sun-dried, without the help of chemical treatments. In other centers, science gives nature a helping hand and the fruit is artificially dried. But welcome the fact that your currants and sultanas, which you can buy separately or mixed and with the addition of finely chopped peel, are likely to have been already washed and tumble-dried. This means that you can forget about picking them over for bits of stalk and grit, and doing your own washing and drying. However, if you mean to use the fruit with yeast for baking, it is a good idea to place it in a sieve over a pot of boiling water for a few minutes. This warms and moistens the fruit just enough to prevent it retarding fermentation of the temperamental yeast.

The too-liberal use of liquid paraffin to keep dried fruit from becoming too dry is a deplorable innovation. The flavor can and occasionally does permeate the fruit and cannot be removed by soaking.

## Candied peel

The delicate green variety is the candied, aromatic skin of the citron—a large, scented, extremely thick-skinned cousin of the lemon. It is citron peel that decorates the top of a traditional Madeira cake.

Orange peel—sometimes sold mixed with citron—and lemon peel can both be bought in large pieces. If you buy peel in a large slice, you will find that it has more flavor than the "cut" peel, not only because there

has been less chance for its essential oils to evaporate but also because only the fattest, juiciest peels are sent to market in their entirety. Peel is perfectly easy to cut into neat dice yourself. If the pieces are very sticky, separate them with a dusting of flour and use that much less flour in your recipe. Store peel in airtight jars or it becomes tough and difficult to cut.

Mixed peel is sold for use in cakes, puddings and tea breads, but it is always better to chop your own whenever possible.

## Dried figs

The yellow figs of Smyrna were traditionally the most highly prized, and these are now extensively grown elsewhere, together with many other varieties. Although figs pack and travel well, blocks of squashed figs can have a depressing look; so if you mean to enjoy figs with dessert wine after a winter dinner, look for those whose plump, cushion shapes are still discernible. In Provence, a dessert offered at New Year and known as *mendiants*, or "the four mendicants," is a mixture of figs, raisins, hazelnuts and almonds, their colors recalling the habits worn by the four Roman Catholic mendicant Orders.

For compotes or puddings, dried figs need soaking for a few hours before use: try wine instead of water for a good flavor.

## Dried bananas

Often called "banana figs," dried bananas are quite unconnected with figs and don't have the fig's laxative properties. They are, however, used in the same way as dried figs. Look for them in health food stores.

## Dates

Only the stickiest, juiciest dates—"candy that grows on trees"—are sent into the world from their native Arabia, Iran and North Africa, and of them all the Tunisian date, the Deglet Noor, "date of the light," is considered the finest.

These are the dates that have been left on their palm trees to sweeten and mature in the sun, and are then packed in boxes with desert scenes on the lid. You used to find them packed "on the stem," but now the stem is often made of plastic, although the top layer of dates is still "arranged." The bottom layer, however, looks more higgledy-piggledy, so if you buy your dates for both eating and for adding to dishes, dig down to the bottom ones to use in cookery. If you plan to stuff dates with nuts or marzipan, making *petits fours* sitting in frilled paper cases to be offered after dinner, you would, of course, use the handsomest dates you can

find. Inexpensive pressed blocks of dates are perfectly adequate to use in breads, puddings and cakes.

## Prunes

Until the nineteenth century, prunes were far more popular than plums. Traditionally eaten with game, goose and pork, prunes can also be cooked with red cabbage and are used in the United States to make delicate whips, soufflés, molds and ice creams. The drying process makes prunes good keepers, and nothing is easier than to reconstitute their plumpness by soaking them overnight.

The finest prunes are from the red and purple plums of Agen and from those of Tours, the orchard of France. It is these varieties that are grown in California and have made the Santa Clara Valley the center of the excellent American prune industry. Some of the French maintain that the flesh of a California plum is less delicate than that of their native produce, but then in France, plum drying has developed into a fine art. The Perdrigon plum, for instance, is not simply dried. It may be either skinned, pitted, exposed to the sun and flattened to become a *pistole*, or it may be scalded in its entirety and slowly dried in the shade to become a *brignole* or *pruneau fleuri*. This is plumper and less wrinkled than the humble grocery prune and somewhat resembles the Karlsbad plum, a glamorous prune with a blue sheen, tasting strongly of fruit, that is on sale around Christmastime packed in handsome wooden boxes.

## Dried peaches, pears and apricots

Dried peaches and pears are most delicious eaten raw: their taste is delicate and does not always survive cooking.

On the tart side even when ripe, dried apricots keep a good deal of their original flavor. Of all the dried fruits, they are the least sickly-sweet. Soaked and cooked, they can be used to make a sharp, fragrant purée, good for puddings, sauces and jam making. Roughly chopped, they can go into pilafs; soaked, they make a good stuffing for lamb and poultry.

Apricots from health food stores are most likely to be sun-dried. Supermarket packaged apricots may have been assisted in drying by sulfur dioxide—the label will reveal the process. Some delicatessens stock commercially "sugar-cured" apricots—tender, chewy fruit which tastes strongly of itself and doesn't need soaking. Apricot paste, a sweetmeat much appreciated in Arabian countries, where it is called *kem-reddine*, "moon of religion," can be found in the more exotic stores.

## Dried apples

These can be reminiscent of faintly scented rings of chamois leather; only by shopping around, particularly at health food stores, can you find dried apples actually tasting of fruit.

Apple rings have only come into fashion during the last century or so. Before that, and before apple-drying became a commercial operation, there were several methods for drying apples whole—all of them considerably more trouble than to simply core, peel and slice apples, soak them for a few minutes in salted water to prevent discoloration, and thread them onto string looped around the ceiling, where air can circulate around them, until the rings are thoroughly dried.

In whatever way apples have been dried, they have many uses. Applesauce for pork can be made from dried apples that have been soaked and then cooked in plenty of water in a closed pot in the oven. Chopped and mixed with currants and sultanas they usefully stretch a cake mixture. If you use dried apples as a compote, stew them slowly with cinnamon or cloves and add a dash of lemon juice for tartness. If you make your own muesli, you can add chopped dried apple together with the raisins. Indeed, dried apples with any other dried fruit and every type of nut make nourishing winter fruit salads—much nicer if you add fresh oranges and bananas to the mixture.

## Cherries

Cherries for cakes are candied and glazed with a heavy syrup to aid their preservation. This accounts for their extreme stickiness, and makes it advisable to wash and dry them, or steam them for 5–10 minutes in a sieve placed over a pan of boiling water and then dry them, before adding them to a cake mixture. Without this precaution, they are too heavy to float and may sink to the bottom of the cake. A dusting of flour helps to keep them separate and suspended. No need, of course, to wash those cherries you use for decoration—for this, their charm depends on their glistening lusciousness. Beware of "cherries" that are not cherries at all but a cheap and nasty jelly-like substitute, flavored and colored to look like cherries.

## Crystallized fruit and flowers

Strictly speaking, crystallized fruit is candied fruit with a coating of granulated sugar. Glacé refers to the glossy coating of sugar syrup found, for instance, on cherries, pineapple rings and whole candied fruit such as oranges, clementines and figs. The terms, however, have become almost interchangeable.

Angelica, used for decorating cakes, is quite easy to candy yourself. If you have the plant growing in your garden, gather the stalks in midsummer. Blanch them and peel off the outer skin, and boil the inner stems, with a few vine leaves to keep them a bright green, in a syrup made of $\frac{2}{3}$ cup/1.5 dl water and 1 cup/225 g sugar. When the stems are soft and transparent, let them cool and then soak in the syrup for two weeks. Dry the sticks in a cool oven. The same system works for all sorts of small fruit, or chunks or segments of larger fruit.

To crystallize violets, cowslips, primroses or rose petals, you need a light hand. Make a syrup of confectioners' sugar and water, letting it boil until it crisps when dropped into cold water. Draw it off the heat, drop petals or flower heads into it for a minute (in the case of violets, you can dip a little posy at a time) and dry them in a sieve, sprinkling them with more sugar. Sift off the surplus sugar and scatter the flowers over creamy white puddings, or use them to decorate chocolate mousse and trifle.

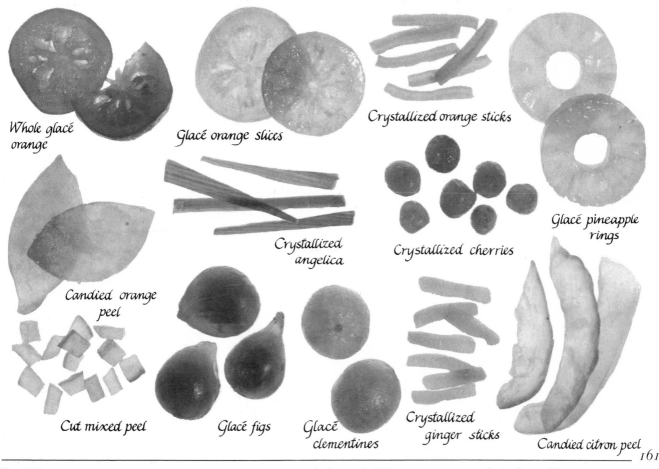

Whole glacé orange

Glacé orange slices

Crystallized orange sticks

Crystallized angelica

Crystallized cherries

Glacé pineapple rings

Candied orange peel

Cut mixed peel

Glacé figs

Glacé clementines

Crystallized ginger sticks

Candied citron peel

# Nuts

The cracking of nuts has always been a pleasant accompaniment to conversation: "after-dinner talk across the walnuts and the wine" is Tennyson's description of the Northern nut ritual, while in the Middle East pistachio nuts and almonds are eaten before a meal as part of the varied *mezze*, the morsels that precede a meal, and are "savored accompanied by feelings of peace and serenity."

As well as spreading serenity and tranquil enjoyment, nuts have also been used since earliest times in a huge variety of cooked dishes. Egyptians and Persians, many of whose favorite recipes have changed very little for almost twelve centuries, use almonds and pine nuts to thicken their sauces, in stuffings for lamb, chicken and vegetables and in all kinds of pastries and sweets—dates stuffed with walnuts and almonds was one of the earliest sweets invented. In India, pilaus and rich rice dishes are decorated with almonds or cashew nuts, and coconut is an important flavoring of curries in many areas, particularly in Kerala in the southwest, while peanuts are used throughout Africa in all sorts of stews.

In Europe, chestnuts are much liked with turkey and with game of all sorts; the British love black pickled walnuts and the Italians use fresh pine nuts to make pesto—their superb green basil sauce for fresh pasta. The French serve wonderful green salads sprinkled with fresh walnuts, and enjoy almonds with trout, while Eastern Europe specializes in rich nut cakes with ground almonds or hazelnuts taking the place of flour. Pecan pie is one of the traditional great American dishes, and of course nut-flavored ice creams abound.

Since nuts are so rich in protein, vitamins, calcium, iron and oils (nut cooking oils are used everywhere) and are so extremely versatile, no good cook should be without them. Buy them in small quantities and often, preferably in their shells, and store them in a cool environment, since their high oil content makes them subject to dire alterations of flavor if they get hot or are kept too long. Make a particular point of enjoying fresh nuts in the autumn and early winter when they are sweet and milky.

## Cashews (*Anacardium occidentale*)

Kidney-shaped cashew nuts come from a tropical tree, which found its way from South America to the rest of the world by way of the early Portuguese explorers. Cashews are widely eaten throughout South America, India and Asia and often appear—plain, roasted or salted—with drinks or as dessert nuts in the colder continents (they are easy to toast and salt yourself at home). In Brazil, they are also used for making wine and for the production of the famous anacard or cashew nut vinegar. In Chinese cooking, of course, they often appear as an ingredient, especially in chicken dishes. Use plain cashews for cooking, there is no need to go to the expense of buying toasted and salted "cocktail" nuts to put into the pot.

## Pine nuts (*Pinus pinea*)

These nuts actually do come from the beautiful glossy cones of pine trees. They are contained inside hard little torpedo-shaped shells which are covered with a sooty dust. In the Mediterranean they can be found lying all over the sand or rocks in September, wherever the handsome umbrella-shaped Stone Pines grow, and more can be shaken out of the open cones if the weather is dry.

These are the classic pine kernels used in Mediterranean cooking. They are delicious in stuffed vegetables—eggplant, zucchini or vine leaves—and form part of the liaison in pesto sauce—the smooth green paste of basil that is so irresistible with fresh tagliatelle or linguine. They combine with rice and raisins in a rich stuffing for chicken,

Peanuts    Cashews    Pistachios    Macadamias    Pine nuts

Pecans    Chestnuts    Brazil nuts and whole husk

Nutcrackers **382**, *382*
Pilau rice **286**

Lamb korma **242**
Pesto alla genovese **280**

duck or turkey, and are mixed with prunes, dried apricots, pomegranate seeds and almonds in *khoshaf*—exotic dried-fruit salad, flavored with rosewater.

Pine nuts can generally be found in Italian delicatessens, but don't store them for too long because their resinous oil spoils easily and they start to taste musty.

## Macadamias (*Macadamia ternifolia*)

Sweet and buttery, these are of the predinner drinks and dessert-nut variety. Native to Australia, where they are also known as "Queensland" nuts, they are also grown in Hawaii, California and Florida; their hard shiny shells are cracked open and the kernels roasted in coconut oil before being marketed.

## Almonds (*Prunus dulcis*)

No other nut features as widely in old recipe books as almonds. Milk of almonds—the juice extracted from ground almonds steeped in water—used to take the place of milk on fast days or in hot weather (it is almost as rich in calcium). This technique of dealing with ground almonds is still used in such dishes as almond soup. Slivered almonds, fried golden, were much used for seasoning: they are still often scattered on fried river fish, particularly trout.

Ground almonds do more than provide their liquor. They can be used in the place of flour for rich, moist cakes and for crisp cookies. Sweet almonds are the chief ingredient of marzipan for coating cakes, and smooth sugared almonds, ovoids in silver, white, pink and pale blue, in silver baskets, traditionally grace French wedding feasts (and confectionery stores). "Burnt almonds," cooked in sugar, nobbly and the color of burnt sienna—the classic praline—are superb in ice cream. In delicate Mogul cooking they are combined with chicken in a variety of ways, while fresh almonds in their delicate green velvet coats form part of the early autumn *corbeille des fruits* in France and Italy.

Almonds can be bought in their shells or out of them, and also come ready blanched, flaked, shredded, diced and pounded. Good stores stock not only sweet but also bitter almonds (*Prunus amara*), which some recipes for cookies and candies may specify. The pungent taste of bitter almonds—like that of the crushed peach kernels you would add to jam—is due to the same enzyme reaction by which prussic acid is produced. Although they are inedible raw, bitter almonds, like peach kernels, are quite safe to use in cooking, because the poison is highly volatile and evaporates when heated. Once heated, they retain the flavor of ratafia (indeed, ratafia essence and the liqueur by that name

rely on the essential oils of both sweet and bitter almonds). One bitter almond can bring out the flavor of a dish using sweet almonds, but store them in a jar apart, well marked to avoid confusion.

## Peanuts (*Arachis hypogaea*)

Whether you know them as peanuts, ground nuts or monkey nuts, these are the success story of our age. Dry-roasted, salted, shelled or unshelled, they come to more cocktail parties than any other nut. In North African countries you will find whole peanuts scattered over couscous; in Indonesia ground peanuts go into savory sauces; and all over the world pressed peanuts give peanut or arachide oil—a light, delicate oil for use in cooking and as a salad oil.

Raw peanuts have a faint taste of green beans—which is not surprising, as the peanut is a member of the legume family. These are the peanuts that can be so useful in cooking. You can roast raw peanuts by first tossing them in a little heated oil and a little salt, then toasting them to a light golden color in a moderate oven. To devil them, toss them in oil with a little chili powder instead of salt, or season the oil with ground coriander, cumin and red pepper.

When you buy peanut butter you may find the highly nutritious oil sitting on top—stir it in before you start spreading. You can

*Filberts*

*Fresh giant filberts*

*Walnuts:
green, pickled and mature*

*Coconut*

*Almonds*

*Betel
nuts*

# Nuts

make your own by grinding whole shelled peanuts, with their skins removed, together with a little peanut oil in a blender. Add a little salt and do not make too much at a time, as fresh peanut butter is inclined to go rancid. However, it will soon be used up if you make peanut butter cookies or use it as a foundation for peanut fudge, in which to encase chopped, blanched nuts.

## Pistachio nuts (*Pistacia vera*)

These exquisite pale green nuts, with usefully half-open shells and papery skins marked with a rosy fingerprint, are the greatest luxury. They come from the Middle East and are usually roasted and salted—sometimes also flavored with rosewater—to eat between meals, or with drinks. They are also found, blanched and skinned, studding the galantines and terrines in good restaurants (you can use hazelnuts instead in duck pâté). The best Turkish delight and nougat contain pistachio nuts, and the nuts were originally used in ice cream making, although pistachio ice cream nowadays, unless made at home, probably owes more to almond essence and green coloring than to the nuts themselves.

## Betel nuts (*Areca catechu*)

These are the tough little nuts much beloved in India. Chopped and mixed with spices, pink-dyed coconut shreds, other nuts, or tiny candy balls, they are wrapped in betel leaves to make the small triangular packages called *paans* which Indian hostesses (and restaurants) may offer to guests after a meal. Chewing these little parcels is said to aid the digestion and sweeten the breath. It can also turn the mouth an alarming red. Betel nuts can be bought whole (in which case you need a special cutter called a *sarota*) or ready shredded at supermarkets.

## Pecans (*Carya illinoensis*)

These are not so easy to find outside the United States, their natural home. Their very name is American Indian, and the nut was widely used in tribal cookery. Pecans, heavier in fats than walnuts, which belong to the same family and which pecans somewhat resemble in taste and in the appearance of their kernels, were particularly cherished for their oil. Their flesh, ground to a fine meal, was used to thicken soups and stews.

Nowadays, pecans are used to enrich cakes, confectionery and ice cream, but their proudest moment comes at Thanksgiving, in dark toffee-colored pecan pie—a rich sweet mixture of syrup, brown sugar, eggs, vanilla and nuts which traditionally follows the turkey. Pecans can be tracked down in the more elegant stores outside the United States, but if they prove to be elusive, walnuts can usually be substituted in recipes that specify pecans.

## Hazels, cobs and filberts (genus *Corylus*)

These are the joy of the autumn countryside. If you don't have the chance to go gathering your own nuts—in England the terms hazel and cob are used for the same nut, known to Americans as filbert, and the nut known in Europe as the filbert is called in America the giant filbert—you can buy them, fresh, moist and juicy, in good stores. By Christmas, the pretty leafy husk will have shrivelled, the shells hardened, and darkened to the familiar hazel color. The kernels themselves will be less milky, but, in their own way, as good to eat and to use in the kitchen.

The ubiquitous peanut butter has rather overshadowed hazelnut butter, which is a very pleasant compound; and although almonds are the more usual garnish for fish, trout with hazelnuts is both good and interesting. But where hazelnuts come into their own is in the preparation of desserts, cakes and ice cream. To make cakes and cookies you need neither flour nor fat: hazelnuts have enough oil, balanced with mealiness, to provide it all. Just combine them, ground, with eggs and sugar and/or cream, as the case may be, and you have a whole repertoire of rich dishes and sweets. In grocery stores and supermarkets you can buy shelled hazelnuts whole, ground or chopped. In some shops they'll be sold complete with shells—the heavier the nut, the fuller the kernel and the better the buy.

## Chestnuts (*Castanea sativa*)

Edible chestnuts, also called Spanish chestnuts, are first cousins to horse chestnuts. They are a prettier shape, but have none of their cousin's flamboyant mahogany sheen. Their pointed shell encloses a truly delicious nut—good to eat with moist leafy vegetables such as brussels sprouts; wonderful for stuffings; warming—and a joy—roasted over the fire on a winter's day.

*Marrons glacés* are easy to make, and a great treat, although they do not often look as stunning as those bought, at some expense, sitting in individual frilled paper cups. Puréed sweet chestnuts make the basis for the creamy and delicious *marrons mont blanc* and for iced Nesselrode pudding (invented for the nobleman of that name by his gifted cook). In Italy, chestnuts are stewed in wine, and in France, these useful nuts, braised or puréed, provide garnishes for chickens, pigeons and young turkeys.

When shopping for fresh chestnuts, look for smooth, shiny shells and buy nuts that feel heavy for their size. Preserved chestnuts come canned in water, in syrup, or, of course, in the form of purée (which can also be bought in tubes). Chestnuts are also sold dried, ready to be soaked and then cooked to make chestnut purée, which makes a traditional accompaniment for roast game.

## Brazils (*Bertholletia excelsa*)

These are the seeds of a mighty tree that towers above the Brazilian jungle. The trees have never been cultivated: their seeds are gathered and buried by the cotia, the Amazonian hare, and those that the hare forgets to retrieve take root. The fruit the tree produces is as large as a coconut and a considerable weight; it falls to the ground when ripe, and inside the hard, woody shell are the twelve to twenty triangular seeds, packed tightly together like segments of an orange. These are the brazils that we buy in the stores, either in their shells (don't buy those that rattle or feel light) or shelled in packets. Rich and creamy fleshed, brazils are available all year, but are best in winter.

## Walnuts (*Juglans regia*)

Fresh walnuts have flesh that is pearly white, soft, easily peeled inner skins, and shells that still have a trace of moisture about them. These are called green walnuts, perhaps because their husks—called "chucks"—are green at the time of harvesting. Green walnuts are a great delicacy, eaten raw and as soon as possible after you've acquired them so that their moisture has had no chance to evaporate. At an even younger age, when the shells are still not hardened, green walnuts are suitable for pickling in vinegar, which turns them black. They also make walnut ketchup.

After the first flush of youth, walnuts become both drier and more oily in consistency. It is in this state that their kernels, halved or chopped, are used in cooking. Chopped walnuts are good in stuffings, pressed into cream cheese, in buns, breads and cakes, and are an essential ingredient of a winter fruit salad of prunes, pears and dried apricots, cooked in spiced red wine. Walnut toffee (or taffy) and walnut fudge are delicious, and so are halved nuts, candied and threaded on a stick, and toasted around a bonfire, while nothing goes better with after-dinner port than a dish of fat walnuts (and a pair of nutcrackers).

Black walnuts (*Juglans nigra*) and butternuts, or white walnuts (*Juglans cinerea*), are the North American branch of the family. Black walnuts are inclined to be larger than the average European walnut and their shells are so hard that special nutcrackers need to be used. The kernels give a stronger taste to confectionery, ice cream and cakes than other walnuts. Butternuts are not as difficult to crack and have a rich flavor.

## Coconuts (*Cocos nucifera*)

Coconuts, known to us as hard, brown, hairy objects, are harvested when their outer husks are green, their shells pliable and their flesh soft and moist. They grow in great clusters on giant palm trees, once found only in Malaysia, but now cultivated on tropical coasts all over the world. This is because, apart from providing useful ingredients for cookery, the coconut palm also supplies a huge range of products, from coir for matting to palm wine. And in our kitchens, the coconut proves its versatility in any number of ways.

By the time it arrives in the Western World, its shell is dark, its flesh thick, a great deal of the coconut juice—the thin white liquid present in the center of the unripe nut—will have been absorbed. When you buy a coconut, weight is the factor to watch—the heavier the nut, the juicier it will be. When you have opened it and extracted the juice, which makes a sweet, refreshing drink, you only have to pare away the brown skin with a sharp knife and grate your coconut meat to use in curry, pies, cakes, puddings and sweets. You can also mix fresh grated coconut with boiling water and then squeeze the liquid from the shreds to get coconut milk, the *sine qua non* of the true Indian curry. To make coconut cream, simply use less water, or you can skim the cream from coconut milk that has been allowed to stand for a while.

Coconut is also useful in its shredded form. This is made from copra—dried coconut meat from which most of the oil has been extracted for other purposes—and has less flavor than the fresh grated flesh, but it can be infused for a short time in hot water and then squeezed to produce a quite reasonable coconut milk or cream.

**Blanching almonds**
*Plunge shelled almonds into boiling water for a few seconds until the skins expand and loosen. Drain, and then pinch the kernels free.*

**Skinning hazelnuts**
*Toast shelled nuts under broiler until the skins begin to color and loosen, then put them all in a paper bag and rub them against one another to free the skins from the kernels.*

**Peeling chestnuts**
*With a sharp, pointed knife score a cross on the side of each nut. Boil the scored chestnuts for a few minutes, drain them and then while still warm peel away the hard outer shell and the furry inner skin.*

**Splitting a coconut**
*1. Pierce two of the eyes with a strong, sharp instrument such as a robust kitchen skewer or, as shown here, a workshop bradawl.*

*2. Shake out the milk; bake the empty nut in a hot oven for 15 minutes.*

*3. Lay the hot nut down and give the center of the shell a sharp blow with a hammer; it should break cleanly in two.*

# Herbs

Each herb used in the kitchen has a special and well-known affinity with certain kinds of food—fresh basil with tomatoes, mint with new potatoes, rosemary with lamb, sage with pork—but there are no rules laid down about these harmonies, and one of the pleasures of preparing food is to find one's own combinations.

This is especially enjoyable for those who can stroll out into the herb garden for inspiration and cast their eye over the fresh greenery growing so pleasantly there. The judicious use of dried herbs, too, can lead to some memorable discoveries, so always keep a wide variety at hand—not simply a pot of mixed herbs to fling into everything.

Herbs from the garden can be dried at home, but they must be picked at the right moment, just before they flower, or they lose their strength. Gather them on a dry but grey day and wash them quickly.

Divide small-leafed herbs such as thyme, tarragon and savory into bunches and tie them loosely with string. Either hang them up in muslin bags or spread them on a cloth or on newspaper laid over a rack and leave them to dry in a warm place.

Large-leafed herbs such as bay, sage and mint can be tied loosely and dried in the same way, or dipped into boiling water for a minute, shaken dry and dried to a crisp in a very slow oven. Parsley is more difficult, as it is a very moist herb. Dry it on a rack in a hot oven (400°F/200°C) for one minute, then turn the heat right down and leave the parsley until it is quite crisp.

If you want to crush dried herbs for storage in glass jars, use a rolling pin or whizz them in a little grinder, which will turn them a nice green color again. Fill the jars loosely to the top and make sure the tops fit properly to preserve the aroma.

Most of the more tender herbs—mint, tarragon, parsley, chives, dill, basil, chervil and so forth—can be frozen. They will darken in color when they thaw, but the flavor is well preserved. Since herbs are extremely strongly scented, store them in airtight boxes or they will flavor everything in the freezer.

## Bouquet garni

Traditionally this is a few sprigs of parsley, some thyme and a bay leaf; tied with thread it goes into the soup, stew or whatever dish calls for it and is discarded when the dish is cooked. It can also be a mixture of dried herbs tied up in a little square or bag of cheesecloth, and a bouquet of fresh herbs to flavor a stock can simply be tied inside a stick of celery. To the basic bouquet can be added a piece of orange peel, a clove of garlic, a few celery leaves, a couple of twigs of fennel or whatever herbs you choose to go with the dish you are making, but too many herbs together cancel each other out.

## Fines herbes

This is a delicate mixture of the more tender herbs—parsley, chervil, chives and sometimes tarragon—all chopped very fine. The alchemy of this mixture has a hundred and one uses, from flavoring all kinds of subtly cooked eggs to poached sole or any delicate fish with a cream and white wine sauce. *Fines herbes* are delicious, too, in melted butter with a squeeze of lemon, poured over roasted, broiled or fried chicken, or veal scallops. They go into tartare and bearnaise sauce, and can be mixed into mayonnaise to make an excellent sauce to accompany shrimps and, of course, hard-boiled eggs—the mayonnaise should be green with herbs.

## Parsley (*Petroselinum crispum*)

The most serviceable of herbs and one that you can always buy fresh, parsley seems to have just as much affinity with garlic and hard-flavored Sicilian dishes, salty with olives, anchovies, goats' cheese and capers, as it does with the potato soups and fresh cod of the north, and many a dreary looking dish has been saved with a sprinkling of this chopped greenery. Flat-leafed parsley is tastier than the curled, and parsley roots—the roots of Hamburg parsley—are good for flavoring stews. Use parsley in court bouillons, soups and of course parsley sauce, *Jambon persillé*—a dish of chunks of ham set in an aspic quite solid with green chopped parsley—is a Burgundian dish well worth trying. To make parsley sandwiches, wash and chop very finely some freshly gathered parsley, mix it with a little butter and spread thickly between two thin slices of dark bread and butter.

## Chervil (*Anthriscus cerefolium*)

One of the classic *fines herbes*, chervil has a delicate, aniseedy flavor, so subtle that it needs to be used lavishly. It is good in green salads, with eggs and as an herb butter for steak of sole. In Korea it is used as a salad instead of lettuce, served by itself or with a dish of broiled or curried shrimps. It makes a very good light soup, and chervil and sorrel, both shredded fairly finely, are a traditional garnish for chicken soup. Chervil can be bought canned, and fresh chervil can be frozen, but it doesn't dry very well.

Parsley

Chives

Fennel

*Hamburg parsley*

*Chervil*

*French tarragon*

*Dill*

*Coriander*

*Sweet cicely*

## Chives (*Allium schoenoprasum*)

With a flavor faintly redolent of onions but far finer and more delicate, chives are best with eggs, especially omelets, with potatoes—particularly baked potatoes split open and piled with sour cream mixed with chopped chives—and with raw or cooked tomatoes. As they are such a clean, fresh green they look pretty, cut up small with scissors to prevent them bruising, sprinkled over puréed soups—tomato, vichyssoise, avocado, potato or artichoke—in a lettuce salad and as a garnish for potato salad and glazed carrots. Chives freeze well but do not dry.

## Tarragon (*Artemisia dracunculus*)

Like basil and dill, tarragon has an addictive flavor—that is to say, those who have eaten it fresh can't very well get through the summer without it, since it is so delicious. French tarragon tastes sweetly of vanilla and aniseed and harmonizes completely with all kinds of egg dishes, with cream and with chicken or ham. It is good in green salads, potato salad and with cold salmon or trout, and tarragon vinegar makes an excellent mayonnaise for potato salad or chicken. Dried tarragon takes on an uncharacteristic, hay-like flavor, but frozen tarragon is very good.

Russian tarragon (*Artemisia dracunculoides*), unlike the true French herb, has a dull and disappointing flavor.

## Dill (*Anethum graveolens*)

Scandinavians are as fond of dill as they are of summer, the height of which is the first day of the kräfta season, when thousands of crayfish are cooked with quantities of dill, served in their scarlet shells on a bed of green dill and accompanied by numerous glasses of akvavit, interspersed with beer. Dill is the flavor that makes Scandinavian pickled salmon (gravlax) so delicious, and is used as a matter of course with boiled and mashed potatoes. With white fish, serve dill either in melted butter or made into a sauce rather like parsley sauce. To preserve dill, freeze it in plastic bags, or use dill seeds or dried dill weed when fresh dill is out of season.

## Fennel (*Foeniculum vulgare*)

The sweet herb fennel—not to be confused with Florence fennel—is used both as an herb and for its seeds. A few small twigs are invaluable for bouillabaisse, bourride and with sardines, and if you catch your own crayfish and cook them in boiling water with a jungle of fennel, it gives them a most delicate flavor and is a good alternative to dill. Burn a few dried twigs when you are

167

# Herbs

grilling fish or lamb outdoors, and put twigs inside a fish and under it when you bake it in the oven. The anise-flavored oils permeate the food with a wonderfully sympathetic flavor. In Sardinia, wild fennel is often used to flavor a bean and pork stew, and occasionally lamb.

## Coriander (*Coriandrum sativum*)

The soft, floppy green leaves of coriander look like rather lacy, flat parsley. They don't smell particularly strong unless you bruise them, and their taste, on its own, is harsh with a green note and not very attractive (in fact, said to be reminiscent of bed bugs), quite unlike the warm flavor of the seeds. But chopped and used sparingly in meatballs and lamb stews, or with lamb or pork kebabs, coriander has a superb flavor. It is also an essential flavor in many types of curry, particularly shrimp and lamb, and a very good addition to meat or chicken curry is a paste made from fresh ginger, garlic, green chili pepper and fresh coriander all pounded together. It does not dry well, but can be frozen or preserved with salt in oil.

## Sweet cicely (*Myrrhis odorata*)

A pretty, old-fashioned herb, also known as anise chervil, sweet cicely can be used like parsley in salads or as part of a bouquet garni. Both the leaves and the green seeds can be used—they taste fragrant and sugary, somewhere between anise and licorice. The ripe seeds were once used in the making of furniture polish to clean and perfume oak floors and furniture.

## Basil (*Ocimum basilicum*)

Sweet basil, so necessary to the well-being of anyone who loves the Mediterranean, has large, tender leaves that bruise easily and smell sweetly of cloves. It should be picked young and eaten raw, or almost so, since the aroma and flavor are fugitive. Use it lavishly on tomato salad—it has a great affinity with tomatoes—and with eggplant, zucchini and other squashes. In the south of France, a few chopped leaves are sometimes thrust into a dish of ratatouille at the last moment. The famous pesto alla Genovese—basil and pine nut paste—is one of the greatest spaghetti sauces, and *soupe au pistou* would be no more than an ordinary vegetable soup if it were not for the "pommade" made with oil, garlic and basil pounded together and added to the bowl at the last moment. Fresh basil is also delicious with mozzarella cheese, potato salad or on a salad of dried haricot beans, and with rabbit and chicken.

To preserve basil, push the leaves into a jar, sprinkling a little salt between the layers, and fill the jar with olive oil. Both leaves (which become black) and oil are good, and carry the flavor into whatever they are added to. Basil can also be preserved by deep-freezing, after a brief blanching. Commercially dried basil is useful for making a winter version of pesto sauce, but the flavor of dried basil can never compare with that of the freshly pickled herb.

## Marjoram (*Origanum majorana*)

Sweet or knotted marjoram smells very sweet, both when it is fresh and the bees are enjoying it and when it is cut, just after flowering, and dried in bunches like thyme and sage. Use fresh leaves in a salad or on lamb kebabs, roast lamb or in stuffing for chicken or guinea fowl, rabbit or hare, and put dried marjoram in spaghetti and tomato sauces and any tomato-based soup or stew.

Pot marjoram (*Origanum onites*) is slightly less warm flavored than sweet marjoram but can be used in the same ways.

*Rigani* is the wild marjoram of Greece—use the dried flowers rather than the leaves to give the authentic Greek flavor to lamb kebabs and the Greek salad of feta cheese, tomatoes, olives and onions.

## Oregano (*Origanum vulgare*)

This wild Mediterranean marjoram has a wonderfully warm, heady scent and flavor. In Italy it is used for the same dishes as marjoram. The dried leaves give a strong, spicy flavor to an oil and lemon sauce for fish and roast meat, to pizza and spaghetti sauce, chicken broth, beef stews and broiled fish, especially red snapper. Oregano is one of the flavors in the best chili con carne and is delicious with mozzarella and tomatoes.

## Rosemary (*Rosmarinus officinalis*)

One of the prettiest of shrubs, rosemary loves the baking heat and dryness of the Mediterranean, but will grow to quite a good size in northern climates if given a warm, dry, sheltered place. It particularly likes the seaside—its name comes from the Latin for "dew of the sea." It has a great affinity with veal, lamb and pork and also with rabbit—put a sprig under a rack or leg of veal or lamb before roasting or into the butter in which you are sautéing onions for a veal or rabbit stew, and drop a sprig into the fat or oil in which you are frying potatoes. Rosemary is better fresh than dried and fresh rosemary has the added advantage of staying in one piece in the cooking—which is lucky as it is very disagreeable to eat a mouthful of the dried, needle-like leaves.

## Bay (*Laurus nobilis*)

Everybody who is familiar with cooking is familiar with the sweet, resinous smell of bay. The leaves and twigs go into court bouillons for fish, into stocks, broths and marinades, pickles and stews, daubes and spaghetti sauces—into anything, in fact, that demands a bouquet garni. The best decoration for a terrine is a fresh bay leaf, and in the past bay leaves were used to flavor milk puddings—bay infused in boiled milk gives a very agreeable flavor, much nicer than synthetic vanilla. To dry bay leaves, spread them on newspaper and leave them to dry in the dark to preserve their color. Avoid buying old bay leaves; if they are more than a year old they will have lost their flavor as well as their color. In France, bay leaves are called laurier, dangerously translated as laurel leaves in many French cook books.

## Sage (*Salvia officinalis*)

Sage was once believed to give wisdom and prolong life. It is certainly a powerful herb, harsh and dry but fragrant. The leaves go into stuffings for roast pork and goose, and sage is an important ingredient—usefully lessening the impact of the fat—in pork pies and sausages. Partridge is sometimes cooked with sage, and eel and bacon wrapped in sage and broiled makes an extremely good dish. In Italy, fresh sage is fried in the oil in which veal or calf's liver is to be cooked to give an interesting flavor.

## Thyme (*Thymus vulgaris*)

Sun loving, tiny leafed but tough, thyme tastes and smells warm, earthy and flowery. Use it in every kind of long-simmered and red-wine dish, with rabbit, veal and chicken in all their tomatoey forms, in a bouquet garni and marinades and—instead of rosemary—with lamb. In Marseilles, thyme is sprinkled into everything including vinaigrette dressing, and over fish to be grilled on a wood fire. It gives pungency to pâtés, terrines and meatballs, and has an affinity with Mediterranean vegetables such as eggplant, zucchini and sweet peppers. Lemon thyme (*Thymus citriodorus*) is superb in stuffings for pork and veal. Home-dried or frozen thyme is incomparably better than commercially dried or powdered thyme—to dry it, hang bunches in a warm place, then rub the leaves off and store in a jar.

## Summer savory (*Satureja hortensis*)

Aromatic and pleasantly bitter with a scent a little like thyme, summer savory was used by the Romans to flavor vinegar in much the same way as the English use mint in mint

Basil

Sweet marjoram

Pot marjoram

Oregano

Rosemary

Bay

Sage

Thyme

Summer savory

# Herbs

sauce. In France, where it is called sarriette, it is used with thyme to flavor rabbit, and fresh sprigs are cooked with fava beans and peas. It dries well and is used with other herbs in stuffings for turkey and veal.

## Mint (*Mentha*)

One of the oldest and most familiar of herbs, mint has almost as many varieties as it has uses. Spearmint (*Mentha spicata*), with its pointed leaves and fresh taste, is the most commonly used, but apple mint (*Mentha rotundifolia*), which is much prettier and has woolly, rounded leaves, has a superior flavor—its woolliness disappears when it is chopped.

In America, mint is best known as an accompaniment to roast lamb in mint jelly, but it is also used a good deal in the Middle East: finely chopped and stirred into yogurt it makes a dressing for cucumber salad.

Mint is often boiled with new potatoes, when it is delicious, and with garden peas, when it is a mistake. It is also used in the making of desserts that contain fresh oranges (with which it has an affinity) and with shellfish, particularly broiled shrimp. Sprigs of mint go into fruit drinks, wine cups and juleps, and in northern India chopped mint is used in fresh chutney—mixed with fresh green chili pepper and yogurt, it is good with Tandoori chicken.

## Burnet (*Poterium sanguisorba*)

Salad burnet, with its grey-green leaves and cool cucumber flavor, was eaten a great deal by our ancestors. The young leaves are very tender and can be sprinkled into the salad bowl with the lettuce. Used a great deal in France and Italy, burnet can also be used, like borage, in cooling drinks, and is an excellent flavoring for vinegar.

## Rocket (*Eruca sativa*)

This neglected salad herb with its pale yellow flowers looks like mustard and has a peppery flavor. The young leaves give a dry, aromatic taste to plain green salads, and in southern Italy wild rocket is used as an extra flavor in the mixed salads eaten with pasta or veal. But be careful which herb you use—the name rocket applies to a number of other plants some of them far too bitter to be eaten.

## Balm or lemon balm (*Melissa officinalis*)

Beloved of bees—and of beekeepers, who use it to increase the honey harvest—balm was the vital ingredient of Paracelsus' *elixir vital*, designed to make man immortal. It now gives its essence to Chartreuse, that

Mint

Salad burnet

Balm

Borage

Lovage

Angelica

*Rocket*

*Sweet woodruff*

*Horseradish*

green and potent liqueur made by monks, who keep most of the other ingredients a secret. The fresh, lemon-scented leaves and small white flowers are delicious in white wine cups, and in a German claret cup made with cucumber, orange and soda water. A few freshly picked leaves can also go into a green salad.

### Borage (*Borago officinalis*)

A hairy, bristly plant which stings the fingers, borage makes up for the discomfort it inflicts by its flowers, which are a heart-breaking blue and which, together with the cucumber-flavored leaves, complete that fruit salad of an English summer drink called Pimms. The flowers also make a pretty decoration for crab salad.

### Sweet woodruff (*Asperula odorata*)

A small woodland herb, sweet woodruff has a ravishing hay-like perfume and is used in May, before it flowers, to flavor a delicate wine cup. Steep the well-washed plants in a pitcher of white wine overnight in the re-frigerator, add brandy and sugar or Bene-dictine and serve with a garnish of leaves.

### Lovage (*Ligusticum officinalis*)

This old-fashioned herb looks rather like immensely tall celery that has got out of hand. It has a very strange, pleasant but heavy smell and is called the Maggi plant in Holland because the flavor is reminiscent of stock cubes, with monosodium glutamate lurking somewhere in its nuances. It is a strong-flavored herb and should be used sparingly to season stocks or soups when a meaty flavor is wanted.

### Angelica (*Angelica archangelica*)

Nobody knows why angelica is associated with angels, although it has been helpful in its time for curing coughs, colds and colic. It is best known today as a candied stem used for decorating desserts and cakes, and freshly shredded leaves are a good flavoring for rhubarb and can be used in making jam, particularly rhubarb jam.

### Horseradish (*Armoracia rusticana*)

A fresh, stinging horseradish sauce with roast beef is one of life's pleasures and is very good, too, with hot boiled tongue. In Germany, horseradish is grated and mixed with vinegar as a sauce for fish, and it can be mixed with mayonnaise as a dressing for hard-boiled eggs. Commercially dried Swedish or American horseradish flakes are a reasonable substitute for the fresh root.

## Garden leaves and flowers

**Peach** (*Prunus persica*) Fresh peach leaves make a delicate flavoring for custard, more interesting than the usual vanilla and tasting faintly of almonds. Pick five or six fresh leaves and infuse them in the milk for 5–10 minutes, then proceed with the custard in the usual way.

**Vine leaves** (*Vitis*) Every vine that pro-duces edible grapes produces leaves that are edible when young. As dolmades and as a wrapping, with bacon, for little birds such as quail, partridge and snipe, they impart a delicious faint lemon flavor. Choose large, tender young leaves and blanch them in boiling salted water to soften them before they are used.

**Geranium** (*Pelargonium graveolens*) The curling, slightly furry leaves of the rose-scented geranium add a delicate rose fra-grance to a clear amber-pink crabapple jelly or to lemon water ice. Pick the larger leaves, just as they begin to turn yellow.

**Marigold** (*Calendula officinalis*) This pretty golden flower used to be used a great deal to decorate salads—especially shrimp, crab or lobster—and to color and flavor fish soups and meat broth. It still sometimes colors butter and cheese, and can be used as a substitute for saffron if you don't like the strong flavor of the spice. The petals can be fresh or dried, but don't use the flower centers.

**Nasturtium** (*Trapaeolum majus*) Almost every part of this tender plant has a place in the kitchen. The flowers and young leaves can be used in salads—the leaves taste like watercress, but don't use too many because they are very hot. The buds and seeds can be pickled to make false capers. Gather the seeds as soon as the blossoms have fallen, before they get hard, wash them in cold water and soak overnight in cold salted water. Drain and cover with cold spiced vinegar, seal and keep for twelve months before using.

**Roses** (fam. Rosaceae) Much of life must have been far from rosy in medieval days, but it must have been a great pleasure, on a fine day, gathering dark red rose petals to make into rose syrup, rose candy and rose vinegar. In the Middle East roses are still definitely the domain of the cook, who will sprinkle rosewater into fruit salads made with pomegranates and make clear, rose petal jelly with nuts suspended in it. The Victorians made rose petal sandwiches—lay deep red petals on and under a large, flat piece of butter in the refrigerator, and the next day spread the butter onto thin slices of crustless white bread. Lay a few fresh petals on top and allow them to show around the edges of the sandwich. Cream cheese and cinnamon can also be added. Rose petals are also good in cherry pie.

# Spices

The spices once used so effectively in Elizabethan dishes rather fell into disrepute as "good plain cooking" followed in the wake of the Puritans. Now the heady, aromatic smells of the bazaars are back, with the wave of new ethnic food shops, and with them a revived interest in the cooking of India and the Middle East.

Kitchen cupboards are loaded with little pots of cumin, coriander and cardamom, which are becoming as familiar as the ginger, cloves and curry powders many cooks have relied on in the past. Buy in small quantities and use whole spices whenever possible, pounding or grinding them freshly for each dish that calls for ground spice.

## Mixtures

**Pickling spice** Ready mixed, this will probably contain a great deal of mustard seed, some small dried chili peppers, white peppercorns, allspice, cloves, mace, a few coriander seeds and perhaps some ginger. But it is better to use weighed amounts of the separate spices in pickling, as quantities and ingredients vary from vegetable to vegetable and recipe to recipe.

**Mixed spices** (*quatre épices*) Made up to a personal recipe by every spice merchant, this powdered mixture is used in the making of pâtés, pies, sausages and brawns. It is likely to be a compound of white pepper or allspice, cloves, nutmeg, cinnamon or ginger. Buy or make only a small quantity at a time.

**Five spices** This is a Chinese mixture of powdered anise, fennel, cloves, cinnamon and anise pepper. Its subtle aniseed flavor is particularly good with roast pork.

## Anise (*Pimpinella anisum*)

Also known as sweet cumin, anise flavors Pernod, ouzo and other addictive drinks of the same genre. From a delicate bush of the hemlock family, the seeds give a sweet, aniseed flavor to fish and particularly to mussels, to sweets and creams and, in some parts of Europe, to cakes and bread. In the Middle East, anise flavors green figs and jam, and it is a flavoring in some Indian vegetable and fish curries. Buy anise in small quantities as it quickly loses its strength.

## Star anise (*Illicium verum*)

The fruit of a small evergreen tree that belongs to the magnolia family, star anise has the same essential oil that gives anise its characteristic flavor but is much stronger and more licorice like. It is used in Chinese cooking, particularly with pork and duck, and is an ingredient—together with anise pepper, cinnamon, cloves and fennel seeds —in Chinese five spice powder.

## Anise pepper (*Xanthoxylum piperitum*)

The dried red berries of a small shrub, this spice—also known as Szechwan pepper—comes from the Szechwan region in China. It has a peculiar delayed reaction: nothing happens when you bite it, then it floods your mouth with a strong, hot flavor.

## Dill seeds (*Anethum graveolens*)

Firmly associated with pickled cucumbers, sprigs of dill complete with half-ripe seeds are a familiar sight in jars of gherkins and dill vinegar. Dill seeds are also excellent in a court bouillon and as a flavoring in fish soups and stews. They can be used, too, to flavor cakes, much like caraway seeds, although dill is considerably more delicate.

## Fennel seeds (*Foeniculum vulgare*)

These have a sweet, aniseed flavor, and a few seeds chewed after meals will help the digestion and sweeten the breath. They are used in the manufacture of a marvellous salami called finocchiona, and—again in Italy—are found in a kind of nougat called mandorlotto. Try using them to flavor the milk in which fish is cooked for fish soup or pie, or scatter them onto mashed potatoes.

## Juniper berries (*Juniperus communis*)

The flavor of the juniper berry, familiar to gin drinkers and especially to those who drink Dutch gin, is strangely harsh and turpentiny on its own. The hard, blue-purple berries, borne on a pretty but prickly evergreen bush, take two years to ripen, so that green and ripe berries appear together. Gathering them is a painful business but is worth the trouble, for when combined with game, red cabbage, fried pork fillets, stewed rabbit or beef they give a delicious, rather somber, spicy background flavor. They are good in pork-based pâté, in marinades for game and in stuffings for small game birds.

## Celery seed (*Apium graveolens*)

Although inclined to be bitter, celery seeds give a lift to soups and stews when fresh celery isn't available. They can also go into dishes that combine rice with tomatoes, and into savory bread, but are much more familiar in celery salt—usually reserved for eating with quails' and gulls' eggs but good, too, with ordinary hard-boiled eggs.

## Sesame seeds (*Sesamum indicum*)

The nutty taste of toasted sesame seeds is probably most familiar topping bread and cakes, but sesame comes in many guises. Tahina, the oily paste made from finely ground seeds, is used with chick-peas to make hummus, a delicious smooth cream into which hot bread is dipped—an hors d'oeuvre well known to everyone who has eaten a Greek meal. Halva, a sweet, compressed, oily bar of crushed sesame seeds, has a delicate scrunch and is good as an unusual dessert. *Gomasio*—a seasoning popular in macrobiotic cooking—is a mixture of lightly toasted sesame seeds and sea salt. A delicious Chinese dish is a layer of sesame seeds, shrimps and bread deep fried to make an oriental sandwich.

## Poppy seeds (*Papaver somniferum*)

Although they come from a variety of the opium poppy, there is nothing narcotic about poppy seeds. The blue-grey seeds, scattered over loaves and rolls, add a pretty decoration and have a bread crumb flavor themselves, warm and dusty. The creamy-yellow seeds used in India are ground to make a floury curry spice that adds texture rather than flavor. They are also sprinkled into the whole wheat flour from which puris and chapatis (rounds of unleavened bread) are made. Poppy seed chutney, made from the Indian seeds, is delicious freshly made and eaten with all kinds of curry. To make this "chutney," Mrs. Grace Johnson, who wrote for Anglo-Indian Service wives in the 1890s, instructed that one tablespoon of poppy seeds fried in ghee (use clarified butter), two red chili peppers, a little tamarind, two beads (cloves) of garlic and salt to taste should be pounded well until like a paste. A little lime juice or fresh lemon juice can be used instead of tamarind.

## Caraway seeds (*Carum carvi*)

It could be the fact that they aid digestion that makes these an ingredient of so much heavy, delicious rye bread. They are also used when making seed cake, with its dry, sandy inside, and treacle sponge—the seeds taste very pleasant with the syrupy part. In Germany, caraway is called kümmel and gives the typical flavor to the liqueur of the same name—a warm and comforting drink. With anise, star anise, fennel and coriander it also flavors akvavit, the superb but lethal white spirit tossed down by the Scandinavians with herrings, crayfish and smoked eel, and there are at least a dozen good cheeses flecked with caraway seeds. However, if you find caraway in a recipe for curry it is probably a mistranslation for cumin, and the confusion is not helped by

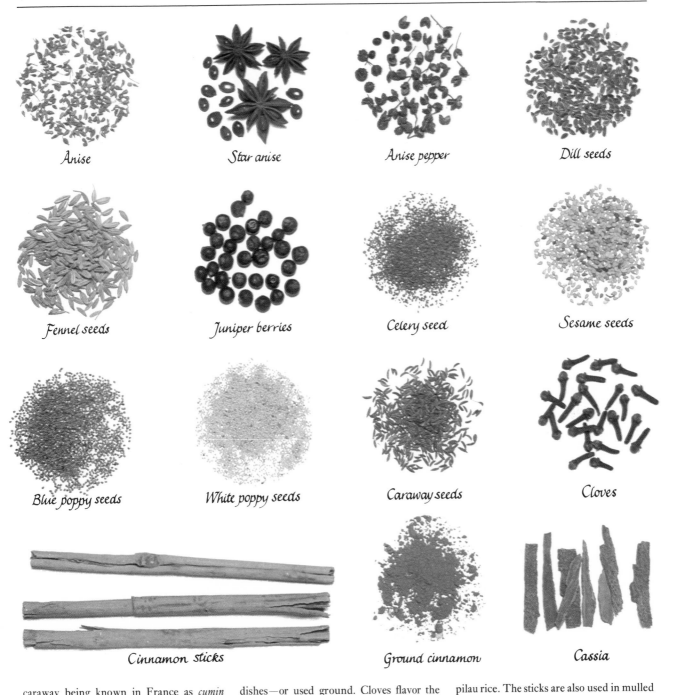

Anise

Star anise

Anise pepper

Dill seeds

Fennel seeds

Juniper berries

Celery seed

Sesame seeds

Blue poppy seeds

White poppy seeds

Caraway seeds

Cloves

Cinnamon sticks

Ground cinnamon

Cassia

caraway being known in France as *cumin des prés*—wild cumin—as well as by its correct French name *carvi*.

## Cloves (*Eugenia caryophyllus*)

Cloves have the scent of the Spice Islands, sweet and warm, with a rather numbing quality that has also made them since the earliest days of medicine a sovereign remedy for toothache. They are not, however, particularly pleasant to bite on when found floating in the dinner, so are usually fixed firmly in an onion—for oxtail stew, jugged hare and other gamy, long-cooked meat dishes—or used ground. Cloves flavor the best bread sauce, spiced beef, hams, pilau rice and curry, and are traditional with cooked apples and pears, in mead, sweet spiced pickles, hot toddies and claret cups. The best cloves are large, dark and plump, and not easily broken.

## Cinnamon (*Cinnamomum zeylanicum*)

Cinnamon sticks are curled, paper-thin pieces of the bark of the cinnamon tree, packed one inside the other. Use them for flavoring the milk for rice puddings and crème caramel, and put a few pieces in a pilau rice. The sticks are also used in mulled wine, hot punches and in sweet pickles.

Ground cinnamon is used in baking—in cinnamon rolls and hot-cross buns—in rum butter and cinnamon toast, and in spiced dishes all over the Middle East and India. In Italy it appears on doughnuts and in sweet fritters of ricotta cheese, and it has a marvellous affinity with chocolate.

## Cassia (*Cinnamomum cassia*)

In thicker rolls than true cinnamon, less delicate, more pungent and less expensive, cassia is better suited to stronger dishes such

Bread sauce **206**
Pilau rice **286**
Pears in red wine **313**
Wyvern's chicken curry **264**

Crème caramel **316**

Cinnamon sugar **183**
Glögg **334**

# Spices

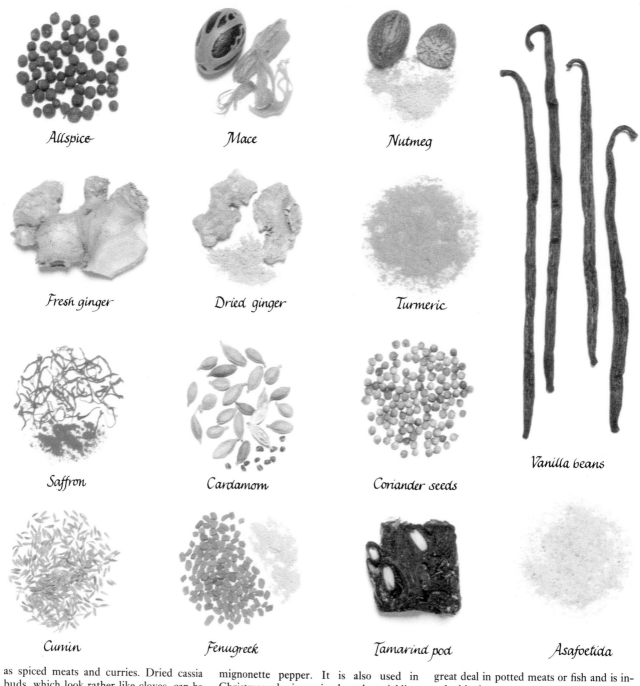

Allspice

Mace

Nutmeg

Fresh ginger

Dried ginger

Turmeric

Saffron

Cardamom

Coriander seeds

Vanilla beans

Cumin

Fenugreek

Tamarind pod

Asafoetida

as spiced meats and curries. Dried cassia buds, which look rather like cloves, can be used in much the same ways as the rolls.

## Allspice (*Pimenta dioica*)

Allspice, or Jamaica pepper, is a hard brown berry, larger and smoother than a peppercorn. It tastes faintly of cinnamon, strongly of cloves and has a touch of nutmeg about it, which is why it is sometimes mistakenly thought to be a mixture of spices when it is bought ready ground. Pounded, it can go into pâtés, sausages and pork pies, along with coarsely pounded mignonette pepper. It is also used in Christmas cake, in marinades, when pickling pork, with soused herrings and salt beef, and seems to impart something of a peppery as well as a spicy flavor. In autumn when country people make elderberries into a port-like, sweet, dark purple wine, allspice is one of the flavorings used, together with cloves and ginger.

## Mace (*Myristica fragrans*)

This is the frond-like outer coat, or aril, of the nutmeg, dried to an orange-brown. More delicate than nutmeg, it is used a great deal in potted meats or fish and is invaluable in sausages, pâtés, terrines and pork pies, and in marinades and pickles. Its warm, sweet, spicy flavor is delicious in cakes and puddings, and in Italy it flavors the milk for béchamel and cheese sauces.

## Nutmeg (*Myristica fragrans*)

Beautifully aromatic with a warm, slightly bitter flavor, nutmeg is equally at home in sweet and non-sweet dishes. While its pretty outer coating is dried to make mace, the nutmeg or seed is dried slowly in the sun or over charcoal and will keep, whole, for several months and sometimes for years. Buy a good-quality, large nutmeg rather than ground nutmeg, and grate it as you need it. Use it in sausages, terrines, pâtés and potted meat, in egg dishes, with mashed potatoes, spinach, and in sweet dishes—custards, rice puddings, apple pies and spiced fruits.

Northern Italians use nutmeg in many of their stuffed pastas and in India it is a frequent ingredient of garam masala—that fragrant fresh mixture of spices used to flavor so many meats and vegetables. Nutmeg is also essential in mulled wines, ale and brandy—an excellent sleeping potion, since nutmeg is mildly narcotic.

### Vanilla (*Vanilla planifolia*)

Vanilla is associated with the exotic because of the drowsy, lotus-eating quality of its perfume. In fact it does have an exotic quality, for it comes from a climbing orchid found in tropical rain forests. It was used to flavor chocolate by the Aztecs, the original chocolate addicts, and produces yellow beans that are picked unripe and allowed to cure to a dark brown. When you buy them the beans should be somewhat soft, ribbed, pointed at one end and have a frosting of crystals—the vanillin essence. A favorite way of using vanilla beans is to keep them in a jar of sugar, keeping the jar replenished as you use the sugar in rice puddings, crème caramel, and so forth. Another method, useful when making ice cream and crème brûlée, is to infuse the bruised bean in the milk or cream. The bean can then be gently washed and dried and stored for another time. It imparts a flowery and spicy aroma.

### Ginger (*Zingiber officinale*)

This romantic spice is associated with the East. The fresh root is used a great deal in Chinese cooking with pork, fish and chicken, duck, shrimps, crab and beef. It has a delicious rosemary scent and a crisp texture, and if you can't buy fresh ginger root the best substitute in Chinese cooking, rather than dried ginger, is scallions. In India fresh ginger is a favorite curry ingredient. Dried root ginger needs to be bruised before it is used to break open its fibers and release the hot flavor. Powdered ginger—Jamaican is best—goes into ginger cookies, brandy snaps and gingerbread, and is mixed with sugar to sprinkle on chilled melon, the pleasant contrast of hot and fiery with icy and juicy being interesting if slightly detrimental to the flavor of the melon. Stem ginger preserved in syrup and packed in Chinese jars goes, with its syrup, into puddings, with rhubarb dishes and over—and sometimes into—ice cream.

### Turmeric (*Curcuma longa*)

Turmeric has a harsh taste, bitter and somehow reminiscent of freshly scrubbed wood, but its color is indisputably useful—not as pretty and golden as saffron, but a deep yellow ochre that turns curries with dark spices to a warm mahogany color, and others made with yogurt and pale spices a sharp appetizing yellow. Use it in moderation and do not try to use it in place of true saffron—the flavor is quite different.

### Saffron (*Crocus sativus*)

True saffron is fabulously expensive—each red-gold shred is a crocus stigma, and each saffron crocus has only three stigmas to be hand-gathered and dried.

It is in Spain that one becomes truly addicted to the flavor of saffron, although it is used a great deal in the south of France for soups, particularly fish soups, and is essential in Milanese risotto. But the Spanish must have it. They like their rice bright yellow, and they have saffron in their fish stews, in vegetable soups, with mussels and shrimps. Very little is needed: a pinch soaked in a little warm water or white wine will diffuse the liquid with its powerful flavor—which is somewhere in the realms of warm sap, varnish and flowers—and characteristic color. Saffron is almost always added with the liquid in which the dish is cooked, but sometimes it is kept until the end of the cooking and then stirred in for a dish of many shades of yellow.

Saffron powder, also expensive and liable to be adulterated, is a poor substitute for saffron strands, and there is a strong Spanish powder, *colorante alimentario*, which adds color without flavor, for a little economy and not much point.

Saffron and turmeric are sometimes substituted for each other, but this is a mistake. Saffron is perfect with garlic, fennel, white wine, mussels and fish, while turmeric belongs with vegetables and meat.

### Cardamom (*Elettaria cardamomum*)

Genuine cardomom is costly and has a great many inferior relatives, so it pays to look carefully at what you are buying. The best cardamom pods are the size of peas, pale brown or greenish, and the tiny seeds, when you split a pod open, should be dark, shiny and richly aromatic. Larger hairy black pods are best avoided. The flavor of cardamom is essential in curry—it has a warm, oily but sharp taste, and an anesthetic effect on the tongue. Sometimes the whole pod is used, but usually the seeds are taken out and freshly ground with other spices. You can buy powdered cardamom, but it has a much more floury flavor than

the seeds. In Arabian countries cardamom is put into the coffee, which is sweet like Turkish coffee, and in Scandinavian countries it flavors cakes and pastries.

### Coriander seeds (*Coriandrum sativum*)

These round, brittle, easily crushed seeds are the basis of all that is delicious in homemade curries and vegetables *à la grecque*. They have a warm, faintly orangey fragrance that is much enhanced if they are parched by gentle heating in an iron frying pan just before use. Coriander seeds, together with lemon peel, make a delicate substitute for vanilla in custards and ice creams, and an excellent flavoring for cooked apples—puréed, in apple tart or in a pie—and their flavor harmonizes well with lentils.

### Cumin (*Cuminum cyminum*)

Cumin is essential in curry. Its scent is hard to define; powerful, warm, sweet and slightly oily, but quite unmistakable—which is fortunate, because it looks rather like caraway and the two are often confused. In Spain, cumin is the traditional seasoning for chick-peas, in Mexican cooking it is part of the background in chili con carne and in the Canary Islands it flavors fish soup. In North Africa and the Levant it is used in couscous, on kebabs, with stewed lamb, and to spice rice and vegetable dishes.

### Fenugreek (*Trigonella foenum-graecum*)

Floury, somewhat bitter and smelling of maple or fresh hay, the ground seeds of fenugreek are used as a curry spice and are a common ingredient of made-up curry powders. The hard seeds need to be lightly roasted before they are ground, but don't overroast them or they become bitter.

### Tamarind (*Tamarindus indica*)

Sharply sour, the sticky, dried pods of the tamarind tree—also known as Indian dates—are used instead of limes or lemons to add an acid note to curries, and go into delicious fresh chutneys to eat with curry. To obtain tamarind juice, steep the pulp in a bowl of hot water until the sour brown juice can easily be squeezed out.

### Asafoetida (*Ferula asafoetida*)

An ingredient in some curries and Indian vegetable dishes and pickles, asafoetida is an evil-smelling resin from equally evil-smelling plants of the giant fennel family. It should be used in exceedingly small quantities, or it can be omitted altogether from recipes that call for it.

# Salt and Pepper

It has long been considered a measure of a cook's talent as to whether food can be sent perfectly seasoned to the table, and of all the condiments salt and pepper are the cook's greatest allies. But there are two aspects to the proper seasoning of food. One is what goes into the food in the kitchen, the other is what goes onto it at the table.

## Salt

One of the properties of salt—which is an invaluable preservative as well as a seasoning—is to draw the moisture out of foods. This is an advantage with vegetables such as eggplant that have bitter juices; they can be sliced and salted before cooking so that the bitterness is drawn out. Fresh meat, however, should not be salted before frying or roasting, as the moisture raised on its surface will prevent it sealing and browning.

Salt also toughens food, which can be an advantage when pickling with vinegar—food salted before being pickled will not go soft and soggy in the jar. But again this is a disadvantage when cooking meat, and with legumes such as dried beans, so start these in fresh unsalted water and do not add salt until at least 15 minutes after they have reached simmering point.

**Sea salt** This is the best of all salts for both kitchen and table. It is made by evaporating sea water, either naturally by sun and wind or by artificial heat. (Technically, sea salt gained by natural evaporation is called bay salt, but the two terms have become interchangeable.) The result is large crystals of pure salt which retain their natural iodine and have no bitter aftertaste. They can be sprinkled directly onto food, like Maldon salt, or ground in a salt mill or wooden mortar. This is also the salt to sprinkle over certain breads, rolls and pretzels before they go into the oven—the crystals dissolve so slowly that they will still be a sparkling presence after baking. Fine sea salt is the best to use in cooking.

**Sel gris** is a coarse, greyish, unrefined sea salt that contains traces of other minerals. It is for kitchen use rather than at table.

**Common salt** Ordinary domestic salt is made by dissolving the salt found in underground deposits (formed by the drying up of ancient seas) and then drying it in a vacuum. It can be coarse-grained for kitchen use or refined into table salt, in which case it has to be coated with magnesium carbonate or some other additive to prevent it absorbing moisture from the air. This type of salt, although useful because it can be sprinkled finely, has a decidedly bitter aftertaste, but it is better than any other salt for baking.

**Iodized salt** This is domestic salt to which iodine has been added. It is useful in areas where the water and soils are lacking in this essential trace element.

**Rock salt,** known in France as *sel-gemme*, is a hard, coarse, crystalline salt that needs a salt mill or mortar to make it manageable. At its best, it can be the finest flavored of all the salts, but it must not be confused with non-edible freezing salt, also called rock salt, which is often used in the United States when making homemade ice creams.

**Block salt,** also known as canning salt, is pure, refined rock salt. It is good for all cooking and is the salt to use for pickling, because it has no additives that might spoil the clarity of the pickling liquid. Other names for it are pickling and dairy salt.

**Seasoned salts** Salts such as garlic salt and celery salt contain extracts of the vegetable—and, in the case of celery salt, the seeds—that give the salt its name, but they give an instantly recognizable "package" flavor so often found in convenience foods. *Gomasio*, sprinkled on southeast Asian dishes, contains one part salt to nine parts lightly toasted crushed sesame seeds. The various "chef's salts" usually contain flavoring agents plus monosodium glutamate.

**Monosodium glutamate** The sodium salt of glutamic acid, MSG is a chemical that "wakes up the palate." It accentuates other flavors already present in the food and is used extensively in Chinese cooking, but it is a lazy way of giving flavor to food and is not a good thing to have in the kitchen and is frowned upon by nutritionists.

**Saltpeter** Potassium nitrate is a preservative, and has been used in the making of brines and dry salt mixtures for hundreds of years. It has the culinary quality of turning meat a beautiful pink—in France, many restaurateurs put a pinch of saltpeter in their pâté to keep it a wholesome rosy color—and is present in bacon, ham, sausages, salt beef, salami and so on. It has been found to be harmful when eaten in large quantities, so it is probably wise to think twice before flinging an unmeasured amount into every pâté you make.

## Pepper

The vine that gives us peppercorns and chili peppers and sweet pepper plants that give us chili powders, cayenne and paprika are not related, although all these seasonings add a pungent savor to food.

Ready-ground pepper soon tastes dull and dusty, and inferior brands are sometimes adulterated with such things as powdered date stones, so buy whole peppercorns—they should be evenly colored, aromatic, free from dust and too hard to be crushed between the fingers. Nothing could be easier than keeping a pepper mill in the kitchen and on the table, and the aroma and flavor of freshly ground pepper, black or white, is quite different from the dry smell and taste of the powdered product.

Different peppers vary in pungency and size of corn. Usually they are called after their place of origin—Malabar black, for instance, is one of the best of the black peppercorns.

**Black peppercorns** are the dried, shrivelled berries of the pepper vine, *Piper nigrum*. They are picked before they are quite ripe and dried in the sun, where they blacken within a day or two.

**White peppercorns** are the ripened berries, soaked, rubbed to remove their husks and then dried. White pepper is slightly less warm and spicy than black pepper, and it has a drier smell; it is useful when making pale soups or sauces when black specks would spoil their appearance.

**Mignonette pepper,** also called shot pepper, consists of coarsely crushed black and white peppercorns. It is used in pâtés and terrines, to which it gives an aromatic flavor without bringing tears to the eyes, as happens when peppercorns are thrown in whole. It is also the pepper for *steak au poivre*.

**Green peppercorns** are fresh, unripe pepper berries, milder than dried peppercorns and with a nice crisp texture. Picked when green, they become black within a day or two and so are only found fresh in the very best and most expensive stores such as Fauchon in Paris. Freeze-dried and canned green peppercorns, however, are a good substitute. Use them in a sauce for lamb, steak or duck, in pâtés, fish terrines, and with shellfish and smoked fish.

**Pink peppercorns** More subtle than green peppercorns and with little of the hotness associated with pepper, these are much used in the south of France in fish dishes, particularly with red mullet. Preserved in vinegar and sold in jars, they are quite soft and lend themselves to being mashed.

**Chili powders** are dried and ground chili peppers, either red or black, and they vary enormously. They can be pungent, mild, tasty or absolutely red-hot, and only by experience can you know what you are getting. Once you have found a good source of chili, or made your own powder at home by grinding a blend of dried chili peppers, and have the measure of it—knowing how much or how little to add—it is a good idea to stick to that or you may give yourself and other people some unpleasant surprises. Use chili powder in curry, chili con carne, with beans and chick-peas and in couscous—although authentically for couscous you should use harissa, a very hot Tunisian mixture of crushed dried chili peppers, ground cumin and salt. You can also buy chili powders mixed with spices such as cumin and oregano, made specifically for chili con carne.

**Cayenne pepper** is made from ground dried chili peppers, originally from Cayenne in French Guiana, that give an orange powder, very hot and rather delicious. (It is the long red cayenne, which is easily dried, that is used in Tabasco sauce.) It is used in potted shrimps and in dishes such as devilled turkey and with devilled almonds, and in the gravy served with roasted wild-fowl, particularly mallard. Cayenne also makes a pretty finish for egg mayonnaise.

**Paprika** Although it may be faintly hot, paprika by nature has a sweet flavor and is made from sweet red peppers. In Spain and Portugal it is used in fish stews, potato and vegetable soups and with salt cod, as well as in most of the *chorizos* and *salsichas* (salamis and sausages). But it is in Hungary that paprika really comes into its own, so the best to buy is the original mild Hungarian paprika, described as "noble and sweet." The combination of paprika and sour cream has the most appetizing delicacy, and although chicken paprika and goulash may be somewhat overworked dishes, both are wonderful food. Hungarians sometimes use paprika and cayenne in the same dish—in cabbage soup, for example.

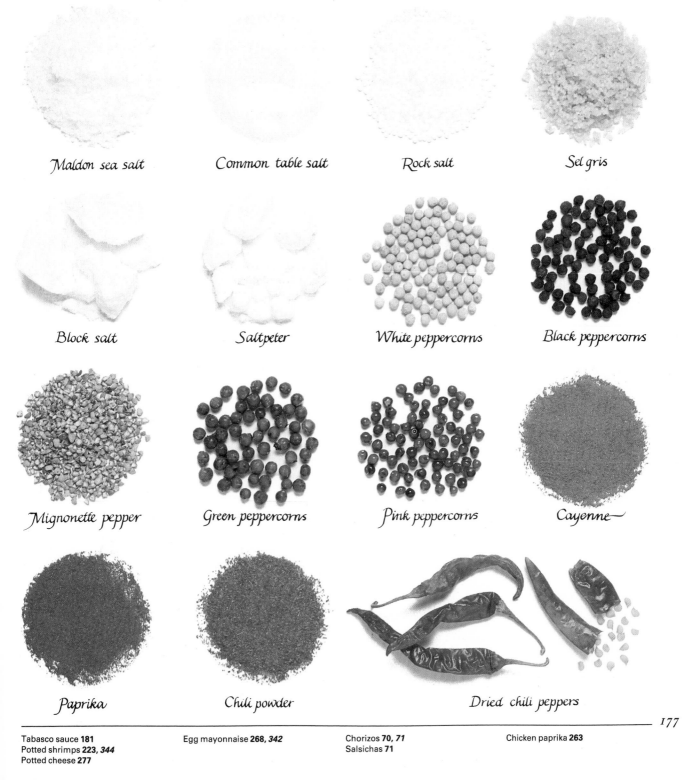

Maldon sea salt

Common table salt

Rock salt

Sel gris

Block salt

Saltpeter

White peppercorns

Black peppercorns

Mignonette pepper

Green peppercorns

Pink peppercorns

Cayenne

Paprika

Chili powder

Dried chili peppers

# Mustard

Mustard has been adding its hot spiciness to food for thousands of years—the ancient Egyptians, Greeks and early Romans used to crunch the seeds between their teeth during meals, and the Romans used mustard to preserve vegetables—their pickled turnips in mustard were the forerunners of our fierce piccalilli.

In the course of time, it was discovered that mustard helps the digestion, and it came to be eaten particularly with pork dishes and with cheese, which was thought to "sit heavy on the stomach." It had a place in home medicine, too: hot mustard poultices were applied to relieve aching joints, and sportsmen, when they came home cold and wet from the hunt, used to thrust their feet into a comforting mustard bath to ward off chills.

Mustard as we know it is basically a paste made from the ground seeds of black mustard (*nigra*) and white mustard (*alba*), which is also called yellow mustard. *Nigra* is hot. *Alba* is cooler. It is *alba* which will obligingly grow on moist cotton to provide young mustard for mustard and cress sandwiches, and *alba*, mature, which yields the seeds that are used whole in pickling. There is a third, brown, variety in the mustard family called *juncea*, or Indian mustard. Less harsh than *nigra*, this is the whole mustard seed that is usually called for in recipes for curry.

## French mustards

The most famous of these are the mustards of Dijon, Bordeaux and Meaux.

In Dijon, mustard center of the world, the mustard is blended with salt, spices and white wine or verjuice—an acid juice made from unripe green grapes. Some Dijon mustards rival English mustard in strength, but can be distinguished from it by their creamy grey-lemon color and by a more subtle flavor. Other Dijon mustards are milky pale and delicate rather than sharp. The famous house of Poupon—one of the sights of Dijon—sells dozens of different blends and exports them all over the world.

Most cooks use Dijon mustard in preference to any other: for vinaigrettes, for mayonnaise (which mustard helps to emulsify), for the more delicate creamy sauces

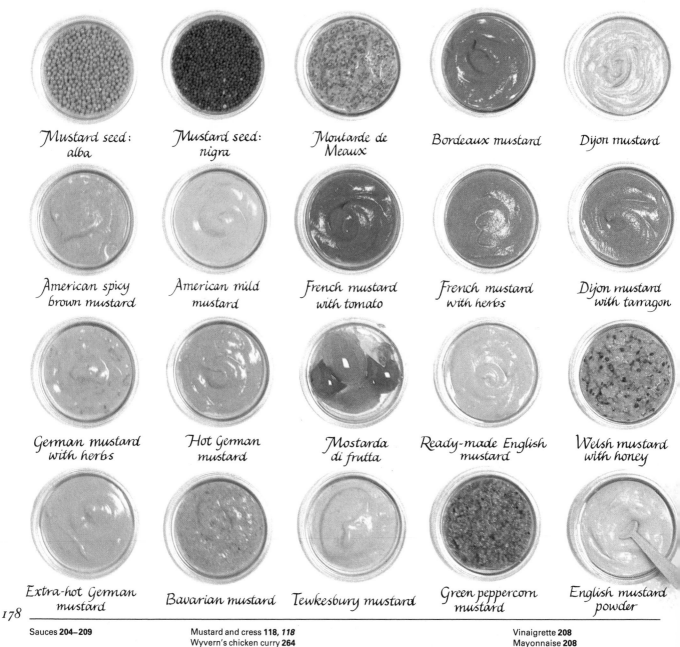

Mustard seed: alba

Mustard seed: nigra

Moutarde de Meaux

Bordeaux mustard

Dijon mustard

American spicy brown mustard

American mild mustard

French mustard with tomato

French mustard with herbs

Dijon mustard with tarragon

German mustard with herbs

Hot German mustard

Mostarda di frutta

Ready-made English mustard

Welsh mustard with honey

Extra-hot German mustard

Bavarian mustard

Tewkesbury mustard

Green peppercorn mustard

English mustard powder

to go with kidneys, egg dishes and chicken or fish. As a general rule, when mustard is called for in a recipe it is safe to use a strong Dijon, such as Grey-Poupon.

Blended with unfermented Bordeaux wine, Bordeaux mustard is strong, dark brown and both more acid and more aromatic than that of Dijon. It is unsurpassed for eating with steak, complementing rather than overpowering the flavor of the meat. When you are offered a choice of French or English mustard in a restaurant, the French variety is almost certainly Bordeaux, the darkest of them all and the one that differs most, in looks and taste, from the hot, bright yellow English type.

*Moutarde de Meaux* is an interesting mixture of ground and half-ground seeds, with a grainy texture and an attractive musty taste. It is pleasantly hot, and was described by Brillat-Savarin—the eighteenth-century French *bon viveur*—as "the gourmet's mustard." It comes in wide-mouthed stoneware jars, their corks secured by sealing wax, and is made to a formula that has been a closely guarded secret since 1760, when it was handed by the abbots of Meaux to the Pommery family, of Champagne fame. The most superior of the coarse-grained mustards, with a taste all its own, it is best appreciated when eaten with humble food—sausages, ham, cold meats and pork pies—and it makes an interesting addition to a French dressing.

There are, of course, other French mustards: sometimes tarragon is added, or a mixture of fresh herbs (which produce a pleasant tasting but rather alarming looking result). There is a mustard containing tomato purée, making a red-brown mustard that is designed to go with hamburgers; and a mustard that is basically mild, but with the bite of crushed green peppercorns, called *moutarde au poivre vert*.

### English mustard

Its color is a hot yellow, it is made of blended seeds, finely ground, and its taste is straightforward and hot, good with plain English food. For its texture we owe a debt to an eighteenth-century housewife from Durham, England, who decided to grind and sift her mustard seeds rather than simply pound them. She took her new mustard flour to London, it was taken up by George I and commercial production soon followed. Mr. Colman began milling his mustard powder in 1814.

Today you can buy Colman's mustard in powder form or—convenient but not as good—ready-mixed. A straightforward blend of ground and sifted seeds, flour and spices, it contains no wine or vinegar to lessen the natural impact of the seeds.

To mix "common" English mustard, simply add cold water to the powder—the water must never be hot or it will release bitter oils that spoil the taste. To be at its best, the mustard should be freshly made up in a small quantity—a quarter of a teaspoonful of mixed mustard per person is usually sufficient. Allow it to stand, well covered, for about half an hour before use, to develop its full flavor and heat.

To make mild mustard, use milk, a teaspoon or two of cream and a few grains of sugar. To make a thick Tewkesbury-type mustard, which has a delicate flavor and a biting aftertaste, moisten the powder with wine vinegar, grape or apple juice, or with red wine or ale.

Common English mustard is perfect with roast beef, its classic partner, with other plain roast meat, gammon and ham, pork pie and beef or pork sausages. It goes well with Cheddar cheese, especially with welsh rarebit, and it is the proper mustard to use when making strong mustard sauce to go with richly flavored oily fish such as herring or mackerel. But simmered for any length of time in dishes that call for mustard, even English mustard loses some of its taste and piquancy, and mustard sauces benefit from being given a boost of a little more mustard shortly before the end of cooking.

There are other ready-made mustards, many of them resembling the coarse-grained mustards of France. One contains honey (good with pork), and commercially made Tewkesbury mustard is blended with fresh horseradish root.

### German mustards

Made from a blend of strong mustard flour and vinegar, German mustard—*Senf*—generally combines pungency with aroma, and comes halfway between hot, sharp English mustard and the earthy, aromatic flavor of that of Bordeaux. In northern Germany it is ladled out by the spoonful. Stronger palates go for mustard that is *scharf* or *extra scharf*—hot or extra hot.

A lot of mustard is consumed in Germany: it is specifically designed to be eaten with the profusion of sausages of the frankfurter type—knackwurst, bockwurst and dampfwurst, and of course with frankfurters themselves. So it is not surprising that the Bavarians and other South Germans, whose pale local sausage is made of veal and called weisswurst, have a mild, pale mustard to go with it: coarse-grained and sweet, it is just right for this bland sausage, which is eaten fried to a golden color.

The Rhineland favors an herb mustard, thought to be excellent with lamb by those who have not learned in the nursery that "mustard with mutton is the sign of a glutton," and so fond is Germany of the condiment as a whole that there is even a mustard called Diätsenf—dietary mustard—which is green and devoid of salt, made for people on the saltless regime.

### American mustards

Owing to the wide range of national tastes, every kind of mustard, plain and spiced, can be found in American supermarkets. What is thought of as the true American mustard, however, is yellow, mild and sweet, and has a consistency rather more like a thick sauce than a mustard. It is made from *alba* mustard seeds, flavored with sugar, vinegar or white wine, which accounts for its cool character and for the fact that it can be applied in such quantities to hot dogs that it oozes over the sides of the buns, and is even lavished on that other American specialty, the hamburger.

This is also the mustard that is frequently used when making mayonnaise, not only to speed up the emulsion of the egg yolks and the oil but also to give the mayonnaise a distinct mustard flavor, which improves any salad that contains hard-boiled eggs—potato salad and tuna fish salad being the main candidates.

### Italian mostarda di frutta

This is a confection of fruits—figs and cherries, chunks of pears, lemons and peaches—preserved in a syrup containing mustard oil. Enjoyed from about the sixteenth century on, it is still eaten, like jam, by the spoonful on bread. Its delicate, strange, sweet-sharp flavor makes it an interesting relish for cold meats, particularly boiled beef.

### Making your own mustard

Experimenting with your own blends can be interesting. To grind the seeds, use a small coffee grinder (clean it very well after use) or, for a coarser mixture, simply pound them in a mortar.

The first time you make your own mustard, use equal amounts of black and white seeds and, if necessary, gradually alter the balance according to taste. Moisten the ground mustard with water until just saturated, then add white wine vinegar, salt and the flavorings of your choice—tarragon, green peppercorns, horseradish, honey, etc—and leave to ferment for several days. A little olive oil takes the edge off a hot mixture. Store in a cork-topped jar in a cool larder or in the refrigerator.

To enjoy all mustards at their best, they should be used fairly rapidly and certainly not kept longer than six months.

# Vinegar

*Vinaigre*, the French word for vinegar, means sour wine, and this is what wine vinegar is, being produced by an acid fermentation of fresh wine. By the same process, malt vinegar is made from malt liquor, cider vinegar from cider, and Chinese and Japanese sweet-sour vinegars from fermented *sake*—rice wine.

"The grateful acid," as vinegar was called by a seventeenth-century writer, has had its abuses. In Elizabethan days salads were served swimming in malt vinegar—a condiment much loved by the British—without benefit of either salt or oil. But things have improved since then. Although vinegary pickles still go well with rich foods such as cold pork, the biting character of vinegar has been tempered—first by the increased use of wine vinegar, which is an altogether milder affair than malt vinegar, partly by reducing the quantity of vinegar used in such things as salad dressings and increasing the proportion of oil, and partly—which is rather a pity—by the increased use of sugar. (If you want to avoid using sugar as a seasoning for salad dressing, use sherry vinegar as a base for the dressing or mix red or white wine vinegar half and half with wine of the same color.)

Apart from its role in salad dressings vinegar can be used instead of lemon juice in mayonnaise, hollandaise and bearnaise, and is essential in mint and horseradish sauces. It is used in marinades for meat and game, and a little vinegar can improve the flavor of stews and welsh rarebit—a dash of vinegar certainly works wonders with a dull sauce or gravy. A little vinegar in the water when steaming food stops the pan from discoloring, but vinegar is corrosive, so when cooking food that includes vinegar use pots of stainless steel, glass or earthenware, or enamelled ones.

Good vinegars are always worth their price. Cheap vinegars are usually inferior, frequently synthetic and nearly always nasty.

**Wine vinegar** The best wine vinegar is made by a slow, gentle process that allows it to mature naturally. Look for the French wine vinegars from Orléans, still probably the best and purest. Wine vinegar can be red or white and is sometimes very powerful, but it has a delicious flavor. If it is stronger than you like, dilute it, for salad dressing, with wine of the same color.

If you are offered a "vinegar mother," accept her with alacrity. She is a fungus that lives in wine and will turn all your leftover wine into excellent vinegar. Keep her in a warm place in an earthenware jar with a loose-fitting lid, so that air can get in, and give her wine as often as you have it to spare. If she is not very active, feed her a large dose of cheap wine and a pinch of sugar.

When the wine vinegar smells strongly acetic, decant it carefully into a bottle and let it stand for a month to mature and mellow before using it. Red wine seems to produce the best-flavored vinegar, but white is more useful in mayonnaise and even in most vinaigrettes, as the red turns them a curious pink color.

**Cider vinegar** If we are to believe all we read about it, cider vinegar is a cure for all ills. As a seasoning, it has a strong, distinctive taste of cider and in sharpness is midway between wine vinegar and malt vinegar. Use it when making pickles and fruit chutneys, especially those with apples in them, and for a refreshing vinaigrette to use with fresh tomatoes.

**Malt vinegar** Brewed from malted barley, malt vinegar is colored with caramel to varying shades of brown. The color is no longer an indication of the strength of the vinegar, although originally a deeper color probably did mean a well-matured vinegar, since it was kept in oak barrels, which colored the clear vinegar as it aged.

The best malt vinegar, with an acetic acid content of at least five percent, is excellent for pickling, which needs a strong vinegar.

**Distilled vinegar** Being colorless, this is often labelled white vinegar and is the vinegar to use for pickling silver onions and for any pickling when color is important.

**Spirit vinegar** This is strong and slightly alcoholic—flavored with lemon, it makes a good addition to a vinaigrette.

**Sherry vinegar** A delicious vinegar made from sweet sherry, sherry vinegar used half and half with lemon juice in a vinaigrette tastes very nutty, almost like walnut oil. French chefs sometimes use sherry vinegar in *poulet au vinaigre*.

**Rice vinegar** features in Japanese cooking, where its sweet, delicate flavor is used in *sushi*—vinegared rice—dishes.

**Flavored vinegars** Wine vinegar can be flavored by putting fresh herbs—tarragon, basil, mint, thyme, burnet—into a jar, covering the herb with vinegar and keeping it in a warmish place—a warm kitchen, for example—for a week, giving the jar an occasional shake. Then decant the vinegar, keeping a token sprig of herb to show what's what. Three tablespoons of fresh herb to 5 cups/1 liter of wine vinegar is ample.

To make garlic vinegar, crush the garlic and leave it in the vinegar for 24 hours. For a really good chili vinegar, the chili peppers need steeping for ten days and should be given a daily shake.

Tarragon makes the best home-flavored vinegar, excellent for hollandaise sauce and on salads. Use chili vinegar with shellfish, especially lobster salad, burnet vinegar for mayonnaise to eat with fish, garlic vinegar for salad dressings when sharp flavors such as anchovies and capers are being used.

*White wine vinegar*    *Distilled vinegar*    *Cider vinegar*    *Spirit vinegar with lemon*

*Malt vinegar*    *Thyme vinegar*    *Tarragon vinegar*    *Red wine vinegar*    *Mint vinegar*

# Sauces, Flavorings and Colorings

There is no dispute that sauces, relishes and essences are best made at home, but in a busy world it is not always possible to brew great batches of ketchups, to crack the secret formula of Worcestershire sauce, or to find the time to extract the essence from an anchovy.

## Sauces, ketchups and pastes

Some store-bought sauces have withstood the tests of time and changing tastes, and are to be found in almost every kitchen.

**Tomato ketchup** must head the list. Properly made, it is thick and clotted in appearance. It should be bright red and contain no artificial coloring. Homemade ketchup is delicious, of course, but only viable if you grow your own tomatoes; failing this, Heinz make irreproachable ketchup from pure ingredients.

**Tomato paste** is used in cooking rather than at table and is highly concentrated—a tablespoonful will improve a stew, a teaspoonful will brighten a sad-looking sauce.

**Walnut and mushroom ketchups** were once highly popular condiments. Walnut ketchup used to flavor stews and cheese dishes, while mushroom ketchup came into its own when the menu included a robust sort of meat or a none-too-delicate fish. They are both good used with restraint in dark, non-sweet sauces, in hearty dishes such as steak and kidney pies and in onion sauce for broiled beef steak.

**Worcestershire sauce** There is only one true variety, which is of Indian origin, although there are many types of this concoction, including the "steak" sauces. The real thing is hot, spicy and vinegary and contains tamarinds, molasses, sugar, anchovies, garlic, salt and other natural flavors. Worcestershire sauce, besides adding its own ineffable taste, heightens the flavor of whatever is being cooked. It is wonderful in devil sauces and in sauces for reheating cold meat, and in tomato juice.

**Harvey sauce** is more of a relish than a sauce. It includes anchovies, garlic, soy, cayenne and vinegar and is used in the same way as Worcestershire sauce.

**Chili sauce** is a thick, hot, oriental sauce. Use it sparingly in stews and discreetly as a dip for morsels of Chinese food or spareribs.

**Tabasco** is an exceedingly hot, peppery liquid made from vinegar, red chili peppers and salt. The label suggests a multitude of uses: soup, gravy, breakfast eggs, even milk, and insists "no seafood to be eaten without it." It also adds its heat to Creole cookery.

**Anchovy essence** or extract is a thick, pinkish sauce once widely used to flavor any kind of non-sweet dish; now its salty taste is usefully employed in cheering up fish pies and sauces. Use it sparingly: a few drops suffice. Mixed with soy sauce it can be used as a substitute for the powerful fish sauces called for in oriental cooking.

**Anchovy paste** (one brand is Patum Peperium or Gentlemen's Relish) is for spreading very thinly on hot buttered toast.

**Shrimp paste** or sauce is a common general flavoring in Far Eastern cooking. It is thick, dark and pungent.

**Oyster sauce**, a flavoring used a great deal by the Chinese, is a thick, brown sauce made with oysters cooked in soy sauce and brine. One of its classic uses is in Cantonese pork-filled dumplings.

## Angostura bitters

Originally made up as a remedy for fever, Angostura is clove-scented, spiced and pink in color. Found more often in the bar than in the kitchen, this bitter liquid can do a great deal more than flavor champagne cocktails and tinge gin pink. In cooking, it makes a good contribution to several sauces, particularly mustard sauce and tarragon sauce, and a few drops will improve such nourishing mainstays as shepherd's pie, beef stew, or a dish of baked beans.

## Soy sauces

True soy sauce is a strange oriental concoction of fermented dough made from soybeans and wheat or barley flour. Most commercially prepared brands are chemically fermented from defatted bean pulp and lack both flavor and natural vegetable protein.

**Tamari and Shoyu** are pure, naturally fermented soy sauces complete with nutritious oils and free from artificial coloring and flavorings. When buying soy sauce, shake the bottle vigorously until bubbles form at the top. Naturally fermented soy will form a thick, foamy head that takes quite a while to disperse.

Good soy sauce has a rich aroma and a flavor both salty and pungent. It heightens the flavor of whatever is being eaten with it. In China and Japan it is a staple condiment, used extensively in cooking and at the table in place of salt. In Western cooking it has become a common ingredient in marinades and barbecue sauces.

**Miso** tastes much like soy sauce but is a thickened paste, used in oriental cooking to make soups and to enrich sauces.

## Capers

These little green flower buds, tasting of goats and the sea, are both a seasoning and a condiment. They are an essential part of Italian and Provençal cooking. Use capers in any sharp sauce to be eaten with fish or tongue, or with black butter and lemon juice as a sauce for skate or for calves' brains. Steak tartare would be almost unthinkable without its seasoning of capers.

## Stock cubes and extracts

While they are sometimes extremely useful, stock cubes are thin and do not add anything in the way of texture to soups and sauces and they have the added disadvantage of being utterly consistent. The more often you use them, the more bored you become with the unmistakable flavors—monosodium glutamate and sometimes yeast.

**Meat and yeast extracts** are best made into hot drinks, or spread on toast. In cooking they tend to make everything taste rather similar.

**Chicken stock cubes,** in a very diluted form, are marginally less intrusive than beef. Fish stock cubes, curry stock cubes and vegetable stock cubes are all available, all sharing the same disadvantages—a very diluted chicken cube is generally preferable.

## Flavoring extracts

These volatile substances are the essential oils extracted from flowers, nuts, fruits and herbs. There are, of course, endless synthetic flavorings which are cheaper than the true essences and are not so hard to find, but if one has ever tasted the real thing one will know and appreciate the difference.

## Colorings

In countries where the sun shines brightest —Sicily, for example, and southern Italy, India and South America—food tends to be extravagantly brightly colored. Shocking pink and silver, bright orange and magenta and glaring yellow and green make the dinner table look like a carnival and the food rather daunting to those of us who live in the more misty and soft-hued north. But even here processed food is often artificially colored with chemicals that are potentially harmful.

Cooks at home can avoid artificial colorings: throw away the garish chemicals and gravy brownings and use the gentler natural colorings. Use saffron or anatto for a beautiful golden yellow; turmeric for a brighter, harsher yellow; onion skins for golden broths; a tiny pinch of red-colored rang powder to make Tandoori chicken orangey-red; spinach juice or chopped herbs for green sauces and mayonnaise; beet juice for a ruby-colored soup and tomato paste for healthy reddish-brown stews, or delicately pink sauces for shellfish.

# Honey, Syrups and Sugars

Man was probably born with a sweet tooth. Wild fruits and honey taken from wild bees provided the first sweet foods, and since then our craving for sweet things has gone on unabated.

Obviously, any sensible household is now aware that it is unwise to eat too many sweet things, but sweeteners do have an important part to play in the kitchen. As seasonings and preservatives, they have always been as important as salt to the cook. There are many foods too bitter, like Seville oranges and cocoa; too sour, like plums and lemons; too acid, like damsons, rhubarb and gooseberries, or too bland, like apple pie, to be enjoyable without the addition of sweeteners. Without sugar we couldn't preserve strawberries and raspberries in the form of jam, and there would be no breakfast marmalade.

By using honey, syrups and sugars in their original roles, and cutting down on our intake of highly sweetened manufactured foods and drinks, we can enjoy sweet things and not do ourselves any harm.

## Honey

Like all natural things, honey can vary enormously. It can be runny, or gritty, or so stiff that you can hardly dig it out of the pot. It can vary in color from darkest amber to almost white. Connoisseurs look for a honey with a clean, straightforward flavor, uncomplicated by undertones of bitterness.

For a single pot of honey, bees have to visit more than two million flowers, and the honey's taste, color and viscosity depend on the sort of flowers they choose. Normally, the bees' main diet will be written on the label—clover, lavender, heather, and so on.

Generally, the paler honeys, gathered from meadow flowers such as clover, have a mild, clean, delicate flavor. Heather honey is light golden with an aromatic tang to it. Exotic honeys such as California orange blossom, lavender from Provence, or the dark Greek Hymettus honeys have heavily scented flavors. Blended honeys, labelled as coming from various countries, although not the finest, are reliable and consistent.

Clover honey is best for all-round cooking and eating, lovely in honey cakes or rich fruit cakes. If you bake honey buns, note that the presence of honey slightly delays the yeasting, and if you substitute honey for sugar in any recipe, remember that honey is much sweeter than sugar so you need less of it. Yogurt and ice cream sweetened with honey are very good, but ice creams that are made with honey will usually result in a softer consistency than those sweetened with sugar because the freezing point of honey is lower.

Honeycombs give us the honey sealed in the cells with a capping of wax (cut or scoop horizontally so that the honey does not run out); chunk honey includes pieces of the comb bottled in liquid honey. Clear, runny honeys have usually been heat treated to prevent them crystallizing—which most honeys will do naturally within a few weeks of being taken out of the comb. If your honey does begin to crystallize, set the jar in hot water (but not hotter than 160°F/70°C) until it reliquefies. Granulated or creamed honeys should be smooth and fine grained, with no coarse or gritty crystals.

## Syrups

Some syrups are made by God, others are made by man.

**Maple syrup,** among the former, is the best known and most delicious: the grades generally considered to be among the best are light in color, crystal clear and come from the maples of Vermont. Tapped from the trunks as a clear, thin sap, it is boiled for hours to reduce it to the syrup that goes onto hot buttered waffles, pancakes and over ice creams. There are also various maple-flavored syrups on the market, less pure, less fragrant and less expensive.

**Palm syrup,** another natural syrup, is the sap of date palms (which also gives us palm sugar). Very dark and extremely sticky, it can be bought in oriental grocery stores, usually under the Indian name of *jaggery*, and often features in Indian recipes.

**Golden Syrup,** a light golden treacle, is a by-product of sugar refining that has been through its own refining process. Used in cakes and desserts, it is less sweet than sugar so when it is used in baking, sugar is usually added. It can be useful when making such things as brandy snaps, since it is not as granular as sugar when heated.

**Corn syrup,** made from certain varieties of corn, can be light or dark (the dark syrup tastes stronger), and is used in the same way as Golden Syrup in cakes and puddings, icings and candies.

**Carob syrup,** extracted from the pods of the carob tree, is mild, sweetly flavored and is dark brown in color. Rich in vitamins and minerals, it can be used as a sweetener in place of honey or sugar.

## Molasses and black treacle

These dark, heavy syrups are good friends to the cook. Far less sweet than honey, they go into the making of gingerbreads and hefty fruit cakes—unless brown sugars are used instead—and into such traditional American dishes as Boston baked beans and Indian pudding. Black treacle, a molasses-like sugar syrup, is sweeter than molasses, which is the natural syrup drained from sugarcane, but the difference is slight enough for them to be interchangeable in most recipes that call for one or the other.

Molasses

Granulated clover honey

Hymettus honey

Honeycomb

Orange blossom honey with comb

Maple syrup

Golden Syrup

Clear clover honey

Scottish heather honey

## Sugars

Sugar first started to replace honey as a sweetener in European kitchens in medieval times, although it was being used in China and India more than 2,000 years ago. It was introduced into the Americas by Columbus, and it was the first sugar plantations that formed the basis for the slave trade.

While the natural brown sugars still bring us some of the flavor and goodness of the sugarcane from which they come, the white sugars contain no proteins, no minerals and no vitamins—simply instant energy. For the cook, however, sugar, used discriminately, is an indispensable ally.

### Brown sugars

The natural brown sugars come from raw sugarcane, and if you like the warm taste of molasses that still clings to them you can use them all the time. Being moist they have a tendency to go hard in the bag or jar, but if covered with a damp cloth for a few hours they soften up again.

**Molasses sugar** is also known as black Barbados and demerara molasses. Soft, fine grained and very moist, it is good in dark, rich fruit cakes and dried fruit puddings, gingerbread and homemade toffee.

**Muscovado** Dark muscovado, sometimes called Barbados sugar, can be used in the same ways as molasses sugar. Pale muscovado is excellent for making crunchy toppings, and in pickles and chutneys.

**Demerara**, gritty with large golden crystals, can be used in the same ways as pale muscovado. Although, like honey, demerara slightly retards yeasting in the early stages, it is particularly good in spiced breads and yeast baking, giving a nice creamy color and good flavor.

**Turbinado**, one stage beyond demerara and lighter in color, can be used in recipes that call for demerara.

Many of the other brown sugars, usually labelled light brown or soft dark brown, are simply fully refined white sugars that have been tossed in syrup or molasses. They are usually drier than the natural browns and don't have as much flavor. Coffee crystals, which dissolve slowly in hot liquid, are sugar crystals to which sugar syrup and colorings have been added. The simple way to tell whether brown sugar is natural or manufactured is to read the label: if it lists ingredients and no country of origin, the sugar will be the manufactured sort.

### White sugars

All white sugars are equally sweet, but the finer the sugar, the faster it dissolves and the sweeter it seems. There is one thing that white sugars have in common: they taste sweeter hot than cool. This is why ice cream mixtures, before freezing, need to taste almost too sweet, and why recipes for hot desserts specify, as a rule, less sugar than for cold ones.

**Granulated sugar** is a highly refined white crystal sugar usually used in tea, with cooked fruit and for making desserts, sauces, fudges, toffees and fondants. If there is such a thing as an all-purpose sugar, this is it.

**Lump sugar** is granulated sugar pressed into little cubes to use with tea or coffee.

**Superfine sugar** is a smaller grained crystal. It is very fine and dissolves easily; use it for soft fruit, meringues and in cake making, in custards, mousses and crumbles, and whenever it is desirable for the sugar to dissolve before the mixture starts cooking. Use it, too, to make your own vanilla sugar by sticking a bean or two into a large storage jar of sugar and leaving it for at least two weeks. Make cinnamon sugar—good on pancakes, *pain perdu* and cream cheese—in the same way, substituting two cinnamon sticks for the vanilla beans. (For a faster result, mix some ground cinnamon with a little bowlful of the sugar to make the beige, stronger mixture you need for cinnamon toast.) Or try rosemary sugar: clean and dry sprigs of rosemary, put them in the sugar, shake well, and after 24 hours shake again and leave for a week. This unusual sugar is good with any milk pudding.

**Confectioners' sugar** tastes the sweetest of all and dissolves the fastest. Apart from its obvious use making frosting for cakes, it is sprinkled (through a sieve to keep it powdery) over pies and sponge cakes; because it dissolves so quickly it is the sugar to use in sherbets made with uncooked fruit purées.

**Preserving sugar** is a sugar made for jam-making: the large crystals retain enough air between them to prevent the sugar sinking in a solid mass to the bottom of the pan, so they dissolve evenly and quickly without burning or forming too much scum. Jams, jellies and marmalades will need less skimming, and will be crystal clear.

Light brown sugar    Superfine sugar    Dark brown sugar    Rainbow coffee crystals    Lump sugar    Molasses sugar

Dark muscovado sugar    Preserving sugar    Brown lump sugar    Demerara sugar    Confectioners' sugar    Coffee crystals    Granulated sugar

# Cooking with Alcohol

In a good restaurant kitchen there will be, within easy reach of the bubbling and simmering pans, a lineup of interesting bottles of wines, fortified wines and eaux-de-vie. This alcohol supply is not for fortifying the cooks but to be used judiciously as an ingredient in cooking—an ingredient as vital as butter, flour, salt, pepper or eggs.

There is no reason why the home cook should not emulate the professional here. Buy miniatures of the more exotic spirits as and when you need them, use leftover wine for cooking and raid the bar cupboard for sherry, port, rum, vermouth, brandy and so on. Do not make false economies—"cooking" sherry, cheap brandy and wine-flavored concentrates will defeat the object, which is not to swamp food in alcohol (which evaporates in cooking anyway) but to add flavor. If a wine or spirit is too awful to drink, then it is too awful to cook with.

Wine is an important ingredient in marinades. It impregnates food with its flavor and will soften the fibers of meat and draw out the juices from fruit. Wines for cooking should, in general, be young and dry. It is easy enough to find a reasonably priced red, but cheap white wines do tend to sourness—a light French vermouth such as Chambery or Noilly Prat is an excellent substitute. Use a wooden spoon when cooking with alcohol—the tang of metal is all too easily transferred.

Beers have their place in the kitchen, too—beer makes an interesting addition to a soup or a stew, ale is a good addition to beef casseroles and even hard cider complements hare and pork. Cooking with champagne may seem deplorably extravagant, but often a glass or two is all that is required to make a superlative sauce for sole or scallops or an unforgettable sherbet.

Eaux-de-vie will turn a simple dish of fruit into a deliciously alcoholic dessert worthy of any occasion. Spirits of all kinds from brandies to schnapps are often abused for pretentious displays of pyrotechnics in the dining room. Apart from flaming Christmas puddings and crêpes suzette, *flambéing* should be practiced in the privacy of the kitchen. The purpose of pouring alcohol over food and igniting it is not to impress the guests but to burn off fat—to degrease the dish, in other words—and of course to flavor it.

These charts are not intended to be exhaustive lists—merely a guide to inspire you to tip the right bottle into dishes that will benefit from the added flavor.

Liqueurs and eaux-de-vie distilled from fruit or flavored with it have an obvious affinity with the fruit from which they were made—hence oranges in Grand Marnier—and they share with the parent fruit affinities with certain foods—hence pork cooked with Calvados. The same logic applies to liqueurs flavored with essences and herbs.

| Liqueur | Made from | Uses |
|---|---|---|
| Advocaat | Eggs and brandy | Whip into cream for trifles |
| Apricot brandy, Abricotine | Apricots | Flame over roast chicken, soak dried apricots |
| Cointreau, Curaçao, Grand Marnier | The rind of bitter oranges, Oranges | Chicken, duck, lemon soufflé, chocolate mousse, sweet omelets, crêpes, fruit salads, apples, pears, figs, strawberries, oranges |
| Cassis | Black currants | Pour over ice creams, in sherbets |
| Amaretto, Crème d'amandes | Almonds and apricot kernels | Cookies, frostings, cakes |
| Crème de cacao | Chocolate flavored with vanilla | Ice cream, mousses, cakes |
| Calvados | Apples | Pheasant, partridge, pork and veal dishes, cooked apple desserts |
| Maraschino, Kirsch | Cherries | Black Forest cake, compotes, cheese fondue, fruit salad, strawberries, pineapple, cherries, clafoutis, figs, peaches, apples |
| Izarra | Herbs and mimosa honey | Jellies and sweet fruity desserts |
| Kahlua, Tia Maria | Coffee | Cakes, gâteaux, puddings and ice cream |
| Kümmel | Caraway, cumin, fennel and orris | Cabbage, sauerkraut |
| Crème de menthe | Peppermint | Pour over ice cream, in milk shakes |
| Pernod, Anis, Pastis | Anise | Trout, sea bass, striped mullet, Florence fennel |
| Mirabelle, Prunelle, Slivovitz | Yellow plums, Sloes, Plums | Plum desserts, compotes |
| Southern Comfort | Bourbon flavored with peaches | Peach desserts |
| Williamine | Pears | Pear desserts |
| Fraise, Framboise | Strawberries, Raspberries | Strawberries, raspberries, melon, sherbets |

| Wines and Spirits | Soup | Fish and Shellfish | | Poultry | Game | Meat | Vegetables | Sauces | Fruit and Desserts | Cheese and Eggs |
|---|---|---|---|---|---|---|---|---|---|---|
| **Red Wine** | Cherry | Mackerel Salmon Sole | | Chicken Duck Goose Guinea fowl | Hare Mallard Partridge Pheasant Pigeon Quail Teal Venison | Beef casseroles, steaks and braises Kidneys Lamb Liver Oxtail Pork Veal | Broccoli Leeks Red cabbage | Pan gravy (meat) | Cherries Peaches Pears Prunes Raspberries Strawberries | Poached eggs |
| **White Wine** (substitute dry vermouth or dry sherry) | Crab and Lobster bisque Strawberry | Haddock Herring Mackerel Red mullet Salmon Sole Trout Turbot | Clams Lobster Mussels Scallops Shrimps | Pâtés Chicken Duck Guinea fowl | Pâtés Hare Pigeon Rabbit Teal | Pâtés Beef casseroles Ham Lamb Liver Pork Sausages Sweetbreads Veal | Artichoke hearts Carrots Cauliflower Green beans Leeks Sauerkraut | Court bouillon Sauces for: Fish Poultry Vegetables | Peaches Raspberries Sherbet Syllabub | Creamed Brie Fondue |
| **Rosé Wine** | Shrimp | Salmon | | Chicken | | | | | | |
| **Champagne** | | Salmon Sole Turbot | | Chicken | | Ham Sweetbreads | Potato salad | Sauce for turkey | Peaches Raspberries Sherbet Strawberries | |
| **Sherry** | Asparagus Chicken Consommé Peanut Pheasant Tomato Turtle | Salmon White fish | Lobster | Pâtés Chicken Chicken livers Duck | Pâtés Pheasant | Pâtés Beef Veal | | Applesauce Pan gravy (meat) Sauce for poultry Seafood sauce | Apricots Avocados Fruit cake Oranges Syllabub Trifle Zabaglione | Potted cheese Welsh rarebit |
| **Port** | Duck Hare | | | Duck | Hare Teal | | Mushrooms | Applesauce | Cherries Melon Peaches Plums Prunes Strawberries Trifle | |
| **Madeira** | Consommé Kidney Turtle | | Crab Lobster | Pâtés Chicken Duck | Pâtés Quail | Pâtés Kidneys | | | Cakes Tea breads Trifle | |
| **Marsala** | | | | Chicken livers | | Veal scallops | | | Pears Zabaglione | |
| **Vermouth** | | Sole | | | | Pork | | Sauce for fish | | |
| **Brandy** | All bisques | Sole | All shellfish, especially lobster | Pâtés Chicken Chicken livers Duck | Pâtés Grouse Partridge Quail Rabbit Venison Woodcock | Pâtés Beef casseroles and steaks Kidneys Lamb | Mushrooms | Brandy butter Brandy cream Lobster sauce | Apricots Cherries Christmas pudding Mince pies Oranges Peaches | Egg custard |
| **Rum** | | | Oysters | | | | | Rum butter | Apple puddings Baked apples Baked bananas Compotes Ice cream Mixed berries Oranges Rum baba Trifle | Omelets Soufflés |
| **Whisky and Whiskey** | | | Lobster | | | | | | Mincemeat Trifle | |
| **Gin** | | | | | Quail | Kidneys | | | | |

# Coffee

In the Arab world, where coffee is drunk throughout the day in countless ceremonial cups, the old rule for a good brew is that it should be "as black as hell and as sweet as sin."

Good coffee, to suit the Western palate, is made from freshly roasted beans of the kind you like best, ground just before brewing. There must be a generous quantity of beans to the cup, the grind must be suitable for your method of making coffee and the water freshly drawn. Our breakfast coffee loses nothing by the addition of milk, or our after-dinner coffee by a layer of cream.

Sadly, however, the promise in the delicious smell of real coffee is not always fulfilled. This is one of the reasons why coffee-making has become surrounded by mystique—quite unnecessarily—for it is really only a matter of knowing a little bit about the properties of coffee, the way it has been roasted, the grind and the method of infusion. But the beginning of a good cup of coffee lies in the beans themselves.

## The beans

These are, in fact, not beans at all but the twin seeds of the cherry-red fruit produced by the tropical coffee plant. The seeds lie, flat sides facing, in a parchment-like caul. If, as occasionally happens, one occurs on its own, it is called a peaberry because of its rounded shape. (This singleton is noted for its even roasting qualities and is therefore especially good for home roasting.)

Picked and partially depulped, the fruit is usually, but not always, fermented in water for varying periods. The seeds are then extracted from their natural wrappings, dried, washed and dried again and then graded according to size.

Before roasting, coffee beans are quite pale. The *Mochas* are yellowish, and are small, uneven beans, the Bourbon *Santos* are the same color but oblong and a little larger, and the *Martiniques* are greenish, rounder and larger still.

True *Mocha* from the Yemen is now a rarity. There had been hardly enough to go around when only the Arab and Levantine world drank what was described by an astonished British traveller as "that black liquid called kahveh." But when Europe took to coffee in the seventeenth century, enterprising colonists were quick to spread the tree now known as *Coffea arabica* to new parts of the world. The Dutch were soon providing coffee from plantations in their East Indian possessions, while in France the ever-growing demand for coffee led to its cultivation in Martinique: a young

French naval officer introduced a single seedling, which became the ancestral plant of most Central and South American coffee. France was also to grow coffee on its Indian Ocean island of Bourbon—now called Réunion; it is from here that the Brazilians imported the seed for the famous *Bourbon Santos* coffee.

These *arabica* coffees all do best at high altitudes; they are often labelled "mountain grown" and are a good deal more temperamental than the group of coffees called *robusta*. The *robustas* can be grown in lower regions and are, as the name implies, hardier, easier to grow and therefore cheaper. Mostly grown in Africa (which also grows *arabicas*), the *robustas* are less delicately flavored but they are steadily being improved.

However, the *arabicas*, which the trade now also divides into the Brazilians and the Milds (which does not mean that they are not strong), make up most of the quality coffees you are likely to encounter at a specialist coffee merchant's.

**Brazil**, the world's largest coffee grower, produces all grades from exquisite to indifferent. *Santos* is the word to look out for: the *Brazilian Santos*, especially *Bourbon Santos*, give a good, full-bodied cup of coffee. "Prime Brazilian" on a coffee label is meaningless as far as flavor goes.

**Colombia** Second only to Brazil as a coffee exporter, Colombia produces some coffees that are quite excellent and which brew so well that you need fewer beans than of other coffee to any given quantity of water. Among the best Colombians are *Medellin*, mildly acid, which means that it has a much-valued

sharpness, just short of being sour, *Manizales*, a little sharper, and *Excelsio*, which is slightly bitter.

**Jamaica** If you find *Jamaican Blue Ridge Mountain* coffee, which is rarely available, you can be sure that it is mellow and "sweet" —it is rich in natural sugars, which caramelize during roasting. It is also agreeably acid and hailed by many as the best coffee in the world. The *Jamaican High Mountain Supremes* are a little less full-bodied.

**Venezuela** Coffee from Venezuela, if it has grown in the mountain districts, can be rich, winy and light in body.

**Guatemala** Mountain-grown coffees from Guatemala are noted for their acidity and fullness. *Antiguas* and *Cobans* are the best. Other regions of Guatemala produce beans renowned for their zest but not for body.

**Costa Rica** Coffee grown in the high areas of Costa Rica is renowned for its acidity—it has the reputation of being able to curdle the milk in the cup—but other Costa Rican *arabicas* are famed for their fragrance, mild flavor and full body.

**Mexico** Coffee grown in Mexico is light, mellow and on the bitter side.

**Hawaii** This is where *Kona* coffee comes from. It is rich, mellow, full-bodied and full of flavor, with a good straightforward taste.

**Sumatra and Java** Sumatra *arabica* coffee is wonderful: sweet, mellow and full-bodied. It is Sumatra coffee that is still most sought-after by the Dutch, who take great pride in perfect coffee-making. However, both Sumatra and Java now also grow *robustas*, so ask specifically for a *Sumatran arabica*. Take the same precaution when you buy Java coffee. *Old Java* (old means that it

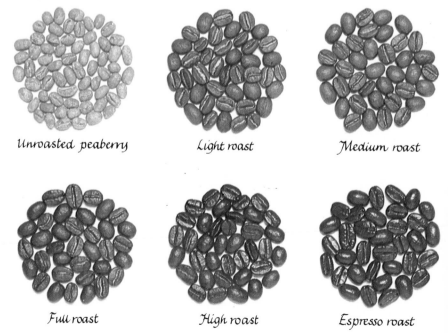

Unroasted peaberry     Light roast     Medium roast

Full roast     High roast     Espresso roast

has been stored in tropical conditions for a decade or so) is always of the *arabica* variety; the *robustas* are not worth storing for so long and would not in a hundred years develop the fine special flavor that is associated with *Old Java*.

**Mysore** This Indian coffee is velvety, acidy and aromatic. It is delicious, especially when, as is so often the case, it is blended with *Mocha*.

**Ethiopia** This coffee is acid and is also described as "gamy," which means that its aroma is slightly spicy. A type known as *Longberry Harrar* is now replacing the traditional descendants of *Yemen Mocha*, and in this there is a kind of poetic justice: the Yemen's first coffee came from Ethiopia, shortly after a legendary Abyssinian goatherd observed his goats skipping and dancing after feeding off the hitherto ignored coffee plant growing in the wild.

**Kenya** The *arabicas* of Kenya are among the quality coffees: one, the *Kenya peaberry*, a variant producing a single round bean, is much admired for its flavor and is one of the coffees drunk straight and unmixed with any other.

Although there are these, and many more, distinctive varieties of coffee beans, most coffees are blended, producing a pleasant balance of body, flavor, sweetness and acidity. This is where the skill and knowledge of the specialist coffee merchant is an invaluable help. The names of house blends —Director's Choice, Connoisseur and such like—signify nothing, so it pays to cultivate a discerning coffee merchant who can be relied upon to offer freshly roasted beans, and will explain which combinations of beans constitute his particular blends.

## The roast

Roasting brings out the flavor inherent in the bean and determines the mellowness, richness, nuttiness, smoothness or otherwise of the final brew. The roast does not determine the strength of the coffee—this depends directly on the ratio of coffee to water when brewing.

**Light roast,** also called a light city roast, gives a cinnamon-colored bean and a brew that is called delicate by those who like it and thin by those who don't. This roast is used for mild-flavored beans.

**Medium roast, brown roast or city roast** will give beans a stronger character and more flavor.

**Full roast or full city roast** produces dark brown beans and a flavor that is deeper still.

**High roast, double roast or continental roast** practically burns the beans black, for after-dinner coffee with a strong kick.

**French roast** produces shiny beans, burnt amber in color, for coffee that is still smooth, but only just.

**Italian or espresso roast** is dark to the point of carbonization.

**Spanish roast, or French/Italian roast,** makes espresso without quite the same kick.

The higher the roast, the lower the acidity of the bean and the less subtle the aroma, so the most precious beans are not used for very high roasts. However, the high-roasted coffees are distinctly preferred by many coffee connoisseurs who dislike the acid flavors of lightly roasted beans.

Only countries that take their coffee-drinking very seriously indeed go in for large-scale home-roasting, with appropriate machinery. Formerly, drums agitated by a turning handle and heated with spirit lamps set underneath were used; now, electric roasters have taken their place. If you want to try roasting your own "green" beans (which can be obtained from specialist coffee stores) but lack the apparatus, use a frying pan, shaking it continuously over the heat until the beans are the right color all over (the spherical peaberries are the easiest beans to handle). However, for the very best coffee it is easier to buy your beans freshly roasted and in small quantities. Store them in an airtight jar to preserve their aroma. In this state they will keep in good condition for up to three weeks.

If you buy your coffee ready-ground in vacuum packs, you will not be told on the pack the types of beans that have been used to make the blend, but you should be informed of the degree of roast and grind. Many of these coffees are excellent, blended for constancy of flavor year in and year out, although coffees, like wines, do vary according to weather conditions during the growing season. Once the pack has been opened, store the ground coffee in an airtight jar and use it up within a week if possible.

## The grind

Choosing the right grind is essential. The finer the grind, the greater the surface area of coffee that is exposed to the water and the longer the water takes to run through it. A coarser grind has less surface area and the water passes through more rapidly. The various machines for making coffee are designed so that with the right grind the coffee is exposed to the water for just the right length of time. If the grind is not right, it will result in under-extraction, which is wasteful and gives a weak-bodied brew, or over-extraction, which makes coffee bitter. If you don't grind your coffee yourself, tell the shop where you buy the beans by what method you make your coffee and have it ground accordingly.

**Turkish grind** Powder-fine, this is the grind that is used to make intensely strong, sweet Greek, Arabian and Turkish coffee.

**Very fine grind** is the grind to use for the paper-filter method. It is too fine to use in an infusion—the fine grounds would turn into an unsievable mud.

**Drip or fine grind** This is the sort to use in an espresso machine and in the drip pot, which Brillat-Savarin, the French gastronome, writing on coffee in the early eighteenth century, preferred to all others and which the French still call for when they order *un filtre*.

**Regular or medium grind** is the one to use in an automatic coffee maker, percolator or jug, since it requires an extraction time of 6–8 minutes.

## The brew

When making coffee, it is important to use coffee and water in the right proportions. Nineteenth-century visitors to England—notorious for its awful coffee—were urged by experienced travellers to specify the precise number of beans to the cup, otherwise they would be served with a prodigious quantity of pale brown liquid. "Waiter, is this tea? Bring me a cup of coffee. Or is this coffee? In that case bring me a cup of tea"—ran a famous joke in *Punch*. Sixty-five beans to the cup was Brillat-Savarin's recipe, but he and his contemporaries liked their coffee extra strong. ("I know it is a poison," said Voltaire, whose clarity of thought Brillat-Savarin ascribed to copious coffee consumption, "but it is a slow one." He was over 80 at the time.)

Today, the recommended amount of ground coffee is two level tablespoons per large coffee cup. For Turkish coffee, drunk in the very smallest cup, a heaping teaspoon is sufficient.

There is much controversy among coffee aficionados over which method produces the best brew. Internationally recognized styles of serving coffee include:

**Café au lait or café con leche,** the breakfast drink served in France—traditionally in a bowl—and in Spain, made with equal amounts of hot, strong French- or Spanish-roasted coffee and hot milk.

**Demitasse,** an after-dinner coffee that is a regular brown-roasted coffee served double strength.

**Espresso,** the Italian favorite, a rich, strong, foaming cup, is the product of a machine which forces steam and boiling water through finely ground Italian-roast coffee. Use a high-roast after-dinner coffee at double strength to make espresso at home. It should be drunk as soon as it is made, otherwise, the Italians say, it dies in the cup.

**Cappuccino** is espresso served with steaming, frothy milk from the espresso machine

*187*

Coffee grinders 360, *360, 361*
Coffee mill 379, *381*
Sugar for coffee 183, *183*

# Coffee

(the same effect can be produced with hot milk in the blender at home) and can be dusted with cinnamon or powdered cocoa.

**Viennese coffee** is made with beans that are roasted darker (but not as dark as the French) and the brew is topped with sweetened, whipped cream, often spiced with cinnamon and nutmeg. The term Viennese coffee is also used for a brew to which dried figs are added.

**Irish or Gaelic coffee** is a strong brew laced with Irish whiskey and topped with floating cream.

**Turkish or Greek coffee**, usually drunk very sweet and after dinner, is traditionally made in an *ibrik*, a long-handled copper jug. However, an ordinary saucepan will do. The powdered beans, sugar—plenty of it—and water are brought to the boil and simmered to a froth. This rich, thick coffee is served in a tiny cup and should not be drunk until the grounds have settled to a sludge at the bottom.

By long tradition the enjoyment of really good coffee is something of an event. There are still individual flourishes to be seen in Africa and the Middle East. The Moroccans, for instance, add whole peppercorns to the brew for extra kick. The Ethiopians take it with a pinch of salt, and in some Arab countries freshly pounded saffron and cardamom pods are added to a foam called the "face of the coffee." Most evocative of all, perhaps, when the Turks gather around the polished *ibrik*, is the practice of taking coffee with extra sugar for happy occasions such as a wedding, but with no sugar at all at somber gatherings such as funerals.

## Additives and extractions

Unless you are positively fond of the taste, avoid coffees that are "stretched" with additives, or coffee substitutes. The reason for using them is, of course, economy, but chicory "coffee" and other mixtures that appear in abundance whenever the Brazilian crops are decimated by frost are, even so, quite popular in their own right. In various parts of the world, such things as dandelion roots, toasted and ground, sometimes feature in mass-produced coffee; so do toasted figs and toasted barley, which makes malt-coffee. If you buy packaged coffee, the label will tell you what it contains.

**Decaffeinated coffee** is pure coffee from which the stimulating properties have been extracted. With them, alas, goes a proportion of the aromatics: to get a product that is 97 percent caffeine free, the beans have to swirl in a solvent and then be dried off 24 times over. Decaffeinated coffee beans, which are available ready ground or whole, need a higher, darker roast than unprocessed ones to develop their flavor.

## Instant coffees

Purists may despise them, but these are nevertheless pure coffee, if not of the most delicately flavored sort; few (but discriminating) are the people who insist on making the real thing for every cup they drink. Instant coffee is also an asset in the kitchen when you want a coffee flavor but not an extra quantity of liquid.

What is true is that instant coffees vary. Their taste is not only affected by the blends of coffee going into their making (they are made entirely from *robustas*) but by the way they are produced. The freeze-dried varieties are most like the real thing. For these, brewed coffee is frozen and the resulting ice is ground and vacuum-dried. The strongest and most flavorsome are the individual sachets of Italian espresso coffee. Other, cheaper, varieties are spray-dried at high temperatures, which drive away the aromatics; these are sometimes reintroduced by means of a spray of coffee oil, which evaporates as soon as the jar is opened —the result is a poor apology for the real thing. Some of the instantly soluble coffees are composed of partly freeze-dried and partly spray-dried types.

Of course, with instant coffee one gains in convenience but loses in excellence of flavor and the delicious aroma that heralds a pot of fresh coffee in the making.

| APPARATUS/METHOD | | | |
| --- | --- | --- | --- |
| Turkish | Ibrik | | |
| Very fine | Filter paper drip | | |
| Drip/fine | Espresso | Drip pot | Napoletana |
| Regular/medium | Cona | Cafetière | Jug |

# Cocoa, Chocolate and Carob

Bitter chocolate

Cocoa powder

Carob powder

Carob pod

A century before coffee arrived in the West, the Spanish conquistadores had brought chocolate home with them from the New World. They had seen the Aztecs whisk up a hot, frothy drink called *cacahuatl*, "bitter water," and at the court of Montezuma, the Mexican emperor, they had savored a thicker, richer brew the Mexicans called *chocolatl*.

Cocoa beans, each the size of an almond, grow 30 or 40 at a time, like the seeds of a melon, in large pods. Their characteristics vary enormously depending on the region in which they are grown and one of the closely guarded secrets of the chocolate industry is the formula for handling and blending the different varieties.

When cocoa beans are fermented, roasted, hulled and ground, a rich reddish-brown liquid is extracted which contains about 50 percent of a fat called cocoa butter. It is at this stage that cocoa and chocolate undergo their separate processes.

## Cocoa

In order to make cocoa, a proportion of the cocoa butter—it varies from one manufacturer to the next—is removed from the liquid. The remaining liquid sets rock hard and is then pulverized. This pure, naturally acid cocoa has a good, bitter flavor but needs to be sweetened before it becomes palatable. "Dutch" cocoa undergoes a further process known as "Dutching" to neutralize the acids, making it mellower in flavor and darker in color.

Cocoa has starch in it, so when making it into a hot drink it should, like flour, be mixed to a paste with a little milk or water before being added to the hot milk, otherwise it will become lumpy. To improve the flavor and digestibility of drinking cocoa, let it boil for two minutes and then whisk it vigorously to a velvety froth before serving. Instant cocoa, also known as drinking chocolate, is precooked cocoa to which sugar and flavorings have been added. It

blends easily into hot or cold milk without forming lumps and should not be boiled.

Cocoa and drinking chocolate are very popular in Europe, particularly during the long winters; in France, cream is often added, and in Spain they make a rich drink thick enough to eat with a spoon. In the United States, steaming cups of cocoa are traditionally drunk with whipped cream or a melting marshmallow floating on the top. In Russia and Brazil, coffee is added (when coffee is added to cocoa or chocolate, the resulting flavor is called mocha).

Cocoa powder can also be used as a flavoring for cakes, cookies and desserts. When unsweetened cooking chocolate is called for in a recipe, you can use three level tablespoons of cocoa plus 1 tablespoon/15 g of vegetable shortening or unsalted butter for each 1 oz/30 g of chocolate. If bitter chocolate is required, do the same, adding also an extra three tablespoons of sugar.

## Chocolate

Unlike cocoa, chocolate retains all the natural cocoa butter found in the liquid extracted from the beans and so is a richer product than cocoa. In fact, in some instances extra cocoa butter is added to the liquid to make the chocolate richer still. The melted liquid is poured into molds and allowed to set; in its unsweetened state it is sold as bakers' chocolate, often in premarked 1 oz/30 g squares, eight to a bar. Chocolate to which sugar and extra cocoa butter has been added ranges from the dark, bitter cooking slabs to mild milk chocolate bars.

When cooking with chocolate, it is generally best to use the least sweet variety that you can find (the less sugar that is added to chocolate, the stronger and more chocolatey will be the flavor). To ensure the best flavor, buy from top-class confectioners; if they do not stock cooking chocolate, buy their finest bitter chocolate. For icings, however, semi-sweet chocolate is always better: it has a higher fat content than the unsweetened chocolate so is easier to melt, and the sugar in it produces a good sheen when dry. Beware of cheap cooking chocolates, which have often been blended from rather inferior beans.

Great care is needed when melting any sort of chocolate: it should be done either in a very low oven or over boiling water in a double boiler—if it is overheated it scorches. It is also important to avoid any steam or the smallest drop of water coming into contact with the melting chocolate, as this, too, will ruin it.

Chocolate is, of course, essential to the making of some of the world's most delicious cakes and candies, truffles, éclairs and desserts. It has a special affinity with rum and brandy, particularly in mousses and ice creams. Chocolate cakes, cookies and candies should be cooked at a slightly lower temperature than other cakes and so forth as they scorch more easily. To make a particularly rich and glorious drink, melt grated chocolate slowly with sugar and then whisk in hot milk.

Unsweetened chocolate is also used as a flavoring in some extraordinary dishes such as the Mexican national holiday dish, *mole poblano de guajolote*—turkey in Pueblan sauce—while in Spain two casseroles, one of veal tongue *a la aragonesa* and one of braised pigeon, *pichones estofados*, are served in sauce containing chocolate.

## Carob

Naturally sweet and nutritious, carob provides a satisfying alternative to chocolate. In their natural state carob beans are the long, elegant pods of a Mediterranean tree belonging to the legume family (it is the carob, or locust bean, on which St. John reputedly lived in the wilderness).

Carob contains fewer calories than chocolate and none of the substance theobromine, found in chocolate, that can be a cause of migraine. Carob powder, or flour, is ground from the whole pod, which is also very palatable in its natural state. As a flour, carob can be used in the same way as cocoa in cakes, cookies and homemade candies, but carob is sweeter than cocoa so use less sweetener with it. Its mild, milk chocolate taste is good in honey and nut pudding, date loaves, cake icings and ice creams, but it is not recommended for use in recipes that require a really strong chocolate flavor such as mousses and rich chocolate cakes.

Chocolate molds **365**

Brownies **326**, *347*
Devil's food cake **328**, *347*
Chocolate cream filling **330**

Chocolate mousses **316–317**
Cream puffs **325**
Chocolate ice cream **318**
Carob syrup **182**

# Teas and Tisanes

When, in the early seventeenth century, the Dutch first brought tea to the West—it had been cultivated in China for centuries—it was the rich who savored its various aromas, not the poor. For another century or more ordinary people continued drinking their habitual cheap ale, wine and sack, while the gentry sipped the costly new brew from the East.

It was not until the middle of the eighteenth century that tea became a popular drink as a result of the British East India Company cutting prices and opening up the trade. Today, still single-minded about their tea, the British lead the field in consumption, drinking three times as much as the Japanese (to whom tea is as much a ceremony as a refreshment) and ten times as much as the Americans. In Russia tea is served very strong, sometimes with lemon but never with milk, while the Moroccans like their tea very sweet, adding great quantities of sugar and honey.

What is a curious anomaly, now that tea is such a universal beverage, is that the terminology under which it is graded and sold remains utterly cryptic to the bulk of the tea-buying public. True, most people readily distinguish black tea, the kind most commonly drunk in the West, from green, which is the favorite in the East. But other terms are for the most part incomprehensible outside the trade. The term Orange Pekoe, for instance, on the label of many black teas, simply indicates the size of the leaf and has nothing to do with the taste of the tea.

Although all tea comes from variants of the same evergreen plant, *Camellia sinensis*, it varies noticeably according to the region in which it is grown and after which it tends to be named. The factors mainly associated with superior teas are good soil and water conditions, high elevation, attentive plucking and a favorable plucking season.

Generally the finest flavors are to be found among what are known as high-grown teas—varieties cultivated on terraced hillsides at high altitude. Scarcer and more difficult to harvest, these hill varieties invariably cost more than the lowland teas.

Following the harvest, what happens to the leaf during processing has considerable bearing on the quality of tea in the cup. Tea processing not only changes the leaf to bring out its inherent qualities but also ensures that the finished leaf will not spoil, and confirms it in one of the three classifications into which all teas are grouped: black tea, fermented and with the highest concentration of essential oil; green tea, which is unfermented and retains the closest resemblance to the natural leaf; and oolong, semi-fermented tea.

## Black tea

Rich, aromatic and full-flavored, black teas account for by far the largest proportion of international tea sales. The oxidation that takes place during fermentation largely accounts for their flavor, strength, body and color—all characteristics which hinge on chemical changes in the tea tannin and the development of the essential oil. The longer tannin ferments, the more color it has and the less pungent it is to the taste, so that a very black tea might, in fact, have little pungency—in tea terms, astringency without bitterness.

Black teas are graded by the size of the leaf into leaf teas—those with large leaves, which develop flavor and color more slowly to give a lighter, more fragrant brew—and broken-leaf teas, covering the smaller, broken leaves which yield a stronger, darker, quicker brew.

Among the leaf teas, the term Orange Pekoe means that the leaves are long and well defined, perhaps mixed with a few yellow tips or leaf buds. (A thousand years ago, the term pekoe—white haired—was applied by the Chinese to teas which showed a touch of white on the leaves and to which they sometimes added orange blossoms for extra fragrance, but the name no longer denotes this agreeable custom.) Pekoe, smaller and more tightly rolled, produces a brew darker but not necessarily stronger than Orange Pekoe. Souchong, the largest, coarsest leaf picked, makes a tea that is pale and quite pungent.

Of the broken-leaf teas, Broken Orange Pekoe, which gives good strength and color in the cup, is the one most often used as the mainstay of a blend. Fannings, much smaller, give a strong, quick brew, as does Dust, the smallest grade produced.

Outstanding among the black teas are Keemun, a full-bodied, aromatic tea from North

Black: Darjeeling

Blend: Ceylon spiced with lemon

Japanese three-year tea

Green: Taiwan Special Chun Mee

Oolong: Pouchong with jasmine

Blend: English Breakfast

Oolong: Formosa

Blend: Earl Grey

Iced tea 334

China, which, with its penetrating bouquet, makes a good alternative to after-dinner coffee; and the rich, smoky flavored Lapsang Souchong from South China and Taiwan, which is best with lemon.

The classic Indian teas include high-grown Darjeeling, one of the world's most prized teas, with a rich, golden-red liquor and exquisite, penetrating aroma; and the full, strong, malty-tasting Assam. Ceylon teas are generally softer in character than other blacks and the high-grown varieties are known for their strength, delicacy of flavor and scented aroma. Dimbula, a rich, mellow Ceylon, makes a good nightcap. Indonesian black teas are taken mainly by Dutch blenders and packers.

## Green tea

Primarily from China, Japan and Taiwan, green tea is cool, clean and refreshing. Said to aid digestion, it is often served with highly flavored or fried foods. It has a mellow, subtle flavor and brews to a pale golden green, but where green tea is concerned pallor does not signify lack of strength: the lighter the liquor, the younger the leaf and the better the brew.

Green tea is steamed and heat dried but not fermented, and is graded by the age as well as the size of the leaf. The top grades are Gunpowder, young leaves rolled into tiny balls, and Young Hyson, long, thinly rolled leaves. Other grades are Imperial, loosely balled leaves, and Hyson, a mixture of Young Hyson and Imperial.

Among the Chinese green teas, look for the type known as moyunes, made from soft, tender leaves that give a tea celebrated for its richness and clarity, and Dragon Well, a variety that takes its name from a spring outside Hangchow and is considered to be the best green in China.

Japan, which meets a good deal of the United States' demand for green tea, grows its finest varieties in the district of Yamashiro, near Kyoto. Sadly, the most prized, Gyokuro or "Pearl Dew," is not normally exported, nor is the leaf from which Mattcha, the ceremonial tea of Japan, is made. Most of Japan's tea is Sencha, or "ordinary" tea, which finds its way abroad as pan-fired —delicate, light colored and similar to the Young Hyson of China—and the long-leaf, basket-fired teas, which have been cured to a dark olive green.

The green teas of Taiwan are graded into Special Chun Mee, Chun Mee, Sow Mee and Gunpowder.

## Oolong tea

Named from the Chinese words *wu* (black) and *lung* (dragon), the oolongs combine the qualities of black and green teas. Best known —and the best of all teas, some experts believe—are those from Taiwan, known as Formosa oolongs, with their deep amber color and magnificent fruity taste. Also very distinctive is Pouchong—oolong mixed with highly scented flowers such as jasmine and gardenia.

Much better than other countries (China included) at cultivating oolongs, Taiwan is the one exception to the high-altitude rule: here on this subtropical island the best teas are grown on the yellow clay soils of the *teela*, or broken lands, many of which are at sea level. It is the summer pluckings which yield the highest grade, rich golden oolongs.

## Blended teas

Perhaps not surprisingly, the hub of the tea trade is London. Here firms base their bidding on the verdicts of tea tasters, who are much preoccupied with appearance, aroma and taste. For although there are only three basic types of tea, there are something like 3,000 commercial blends.

Given the fluctuations in price and availability from year to year, the major tea packers mostly market products that are blends using perhaps 15 or 20 varieties. The most distinguished of these blends include English Breakfast, traditionally a straight Keemun but now more likely to be a strong blend of India and Ceylon teas; Irish Breakfast, high-grown Ceylon with hearty Assam; Russian Style (also known as Russian Caravan or Russian Blossom), a blend of Keemun, Assam and China green well suited to the samovar; and Uva, a blended Ceylon, golden when brewed and with a distinctive flowery bouquet.

Another well-known blend is Earl Grey— so called because its secret was said to have been passed by a Chinese mandarin in 1830 to the Earl Grey, who had it made up for himself by a London tea merchant. Earl Grey is a blend of Indian and oriental teas scented with bergamot. Ideal for late-afternoon tea, it yields a pale, clear liquor with a

Black: Keemun

Green: China Young Hyson

Black: Assam

Green: Japanese Sencha pan-fired

Black: Ceylon

Blend: Uva

Blend: Irish Breakfast

Green: China Gunpowder

# Teas and Tisanes

slight citrus flavor—a reminder of how well a hint of citrus combines with tea.

Spiced blends on the market, such as the orange-flavored Constant Comment, popular in the United States, usually feature a smooth-drinking Ceylon tea with added clove, dried orange peel or lemon. Various teas can also be deliciously spiced with cinnamon, anise or cardamom.

Japanese three-year tea, also known as twig tea or kukicha, is a natural tea with no caffeine, made from the roasted three-year-old twigs and leaves of the tea bush. It is best sipped slowly after meals.

## Tisanes

Long eclipsed by ordinary tea, tisanes are making a comeback as more and more people realize that, as well as being refreshing in summer and a fragrant reminder in winter of sunny gardens, tisanes can also be soothing and beneficial.

Modern-day tisanes and herbal blends are sold either in packages, complete with instructions, in the ubiquitous tea bag, or loose, by retailers who should be able to advise on their use. The ingredients can also be gathered from the garden, as long as one keeps to the absolutely safe, well-known plants. The flowers, leaves, seeds or roots can then be used fresh or dried gently, out of the sun, to use later.

Most dried herb, flower and leaf tisanes are infused—made like tea—in a stainless steel or ceramic container (never aluminum or iron). Measure about a teaspoonful of the tisane per cup of water, add boiling water as if making ordinary tea, cover and allow to stand no more than five minutes—long enough to bring out the fragrance, but not too long or the tisane will become bitter. Strain and, if you like, flavor with lemon or honey. Teas made from seeds, roots or bark are prepared by decoction. Allow two tablespoons of seeds for every 2½ cups/6 dl of water, bring to the boil, cover and allow to simmer gently for about 15 minutes. Strain into a teapot, cover and leave the tisane to steep for a few minutes.

**Ginseng** (*Panax quinquefolium*) **and mu tea** An ancient Chinese cure-all and aphrodisiac, said to be good for the mind, ginseng gives tisanes a licorice-like taste. Ginseng root, with 15 other herbs, features in the powerful, spicy, Japanese **mu** tea.

**Lime or linden** (*Tilia vulgaris, Tilia americana*) Beautifully scented lime flowers are dried to yield relaxing lime-blossom tea, which can be drunk hot, or cold and mixed with lemonade. A pale, amber liquid, this is known as basswood tea in the United States. The leaves also make a good tea.

**Raspberry/black currant** The leaves from both bushes make lightly flavored tisanes faintly evocative of the fruits. Black currant leaves, a source of vitamin C, contain tannin.

**Rose hips** (fam. Rosaceae) Wild rose hips yield a sweet, astringent tea popular for its high vitamin C content; a fragrant tea is also made from rose petals.

**Bergamot** (*Monarda didyma, citriodora, fistulosa*) Tea made from the leaves and flowers has a slightly bitter taste. Refreshing and relaxing, it is also known as Oswego tea.

**Mint** (fam. Labiatae) A great Arabian beverage, mint tea is served hot, in glasses, with a sprig of fresh mint. This refreshing tea is stimulating and a good aid to digestion. The many mints include peppermint, with menthol coolness, giving a pungent tea, and sharp, aromatic spearmint.

**Lemon balm** (*Melissa officinalis*) Believed by the Ancient Greeks to promote long life, balm makes a delicious lemon-flavored tea, calming and relaxing.

**Camomile** (*Anthemis nobilis*) The dried flowers of camomile make a rather bitter but soothing tisane, excellent for settling the stomach.

**Elder** (*Sambucus nigra*, Europe; *Sambucus canadensis*, North America) Elder flowers, fresh or dried, feature in many old-fashioned tisanes. The tea is honey-like, slightly bitter.

**Maté** (*Ilex paraguensis*) Tea made from the dried and crumbled leaves of this small tropical tree is a favorite South American drink. Also known as yerba maté or Paraguay tea, it can be drunk hot or cold.

**Yarrow or milfoil** (*Achillea millefolium*) Feathery green leaves and white flowers give a tea that is astringent and bitter, and believed by the French to have stimulating properties.

**Lemon verbena** (*Lippia citriodora*) The lemon-scented leaves make a delicious tea, strongly reminiscent of lemon and excellent for the digestion.

**Marigold** (*Calendula officinalis*) The warm orange flowers of pot marigold make a very pretty but somewhat bitter tisane; make it weak and sweeten it, or mix a few marigold flowers with verbena tea.

Yarrow     Peppermint     Bergamot     Rose hip

Ginseng     Japanese mu     Lime     Raspberry leaf

# PART TWO

## Recipes

*Good food, simply cooked*

# Stocks

The ingredients for stock should never be expensive. You can use bones and pieces of meat the butcher has no use for, or the chicken giblets that many customers don't want, or the remains of the Sunday roast. If you haven't any vegetables, you can do without; if you have only vegetables, you can still make a reasonable stock, although it is probably better to resort to a stock cube on these occasions, adding half a cube to the water with the vegetables.

## Jellied stock

This adds a velvety texture to sauces, gravies and soups. If you make a well-flavored light chicken or beef stock but include a high proportion of veal bones, or a calf's foot chopped in pieces, or two pig's feet and other gelatinous things such as skin or heads, you will have a stock that jellies firmly when it is cold.

## Meat glazes

If you reduce your rich jellied stock, after straining, to one-quarter of its original volume, you will have a syrupy jelly called a glaze. It is an important ingredient of French restaurant cooking and the basis of many classic sauces, but most domestic cooking can be absolutely delicious without the bother of making a glaze; just use a good concentrated stock.

## Everyday chicken stock

This is the easiest and quickest stock to make and also one of the best bases for homemade soup. It is made from the bones and carcass of a roast chicken. Use it for most vegetable soups, chicken and rabbit stews, for braising white meat such as sweetbreads, poaching brains and so forth, and whenever a light-colored stock with a good flavor is needed. Chicken feet, if you can get them, previously boiled for 5 minutes in salt water and then skinned, or chopped veal bones, can be added to make a stock that will set more firmly.

SUGGESTED INGREDIENTS:

*1 chicken (or duck) carcass and giblets, chicken feet or chopped veal bones (optional), 2 onions or shallots, 2 carrots, 2 leeks, 2 sticks celery (or a selection as available), bunch of thyme, parsley and bay leaf, 6 black peppercorns, 3 quarts/2.75 liters water, glass of white wine (optional), salt*

Put all the bones and, if you have not already used them for gravy, the giblets in a large pan, together with the prepared chicken feet or veal bones, if you are using them. Cover with cold water, bring slowly to the boil, skim off all the scum and froth that rise and then add the onions or shallots, the carrots, leeks, celery, whatever you happen to have—a combination of onions and celery is particularly good in chicken stock—the tied bunch of herbs, the peppercorns and perhaps a glass of white wine. If you want a very pale stock, peel the onions, otherwise they can be left in their skins, which will give the liquid a clear golden tint. Don't put in cabbage or any of the brassicas, they go sour rather quickly, and add salt only lightly or at the end—as the stock becomes concentrated, so does the taste of the salt.

When your stock has been simmering for 2–3 hours (boiling makes it cloudy) and is well reduced, take it off the heat, strain it into a bowl, pressing the vegetables lightly to extract all the liquid, and as soon as it is cold put it, covered with a plate, into a cool place or the refrigerator. The fat can then be taken off with a teaspoon.

## Light veal or beef stock

Somewhat stronger, but not such a well-flavored stock as the pale chicken stock, this is used when making gravy, veal or beef stews, braised veal dishes and daubes, or as a substitute for chicken stock.

The bones from young animals contain the most gelatine, so use some veal bones for a rich, unctuous texture. Beef shank and knuckle bones are the best choice for flavor, neck bones second best. Ideally, use a combination of the two. Long, slow cooking extracts the gelatine, salts and flavor. Bone marrow contains a good deal of flavor, as does any meat that is left on the bones, but the stock will have a more interesting flavor if you add some extra meat —beef shank, a duck or chicken carcass or giblets,

*194*

Meat **39–49**
Variety meats **50–51**
Poultry **84–88**
Skimmers **362–363**

Stock cubes **181**

Brassicas **121–122**
Bone marrow **43**

and if possible a piece of beef liver for flavor and to keep the broth relatively clear.

SUGGESTED INGREDIENTS:

*3 lb/1.5 kg veal and beef bones, chopped up by the butcher, ¾ lb/340 g beef shank, 3 quarts/2.75 liters water, 2 onions, 3 leeks, 2 carrots, 2 sticks celery, bunch of thyme, parsley and bay leaf, 6 black peppercorns, glass of white wine (optional), pinch of salt*

Cover the bones and meat with cold water and bring slowly to the boil. Skim off the froth and scum that rise and cook very gently for 4–5 hours on top of the stove or 45 minutes in a pressure cooker. Add the vegetables, chopped, the herbs, peppercorns and glass of wine (if using) halfway through the cooking time, but not more than a pinch of salt until later. If you hate the smell of stock cooking, bring it to the boil on top of the stove and then transfer it, covered, to a very slow oven.

# Brown beef or veal stock

Brown stock is used for strong beefy soups such as borsch, onion soup, oxtail soup, goulash soup, when making stews such as oxtail, beef stew and hot pot, and in ground-meat dishes, Bolognese sauce, etc. The bones left over from an underdone roast of beef will make a good brown beef stock.

SUGGESTED INGREDIENTS:

*3 lb/1.5 kg beef or veal knuckle bones, ¾ lb/340 g or more beef shank, 2 tablespoons/30 g beef drippings or lard, 3 quarts/2.75 liters water, 2 sticks celery, 2–3 carrots, 2 onions, 2 leeks, 2 tomatoes, 2 cloves, thyme and a bay leaf, glass of red wine (optional), salt*

Brown the knuckle bones and shank in the stockpot in a little of the fat until they are nicely colored, or you can brown them in a hot oven, 425°F/220°C, in an uncovered roasting pan. Pour off the fat, add cold water and bring slowly to the boil. Skim and simmer, and keep skimming whenever you pass by. After 2–3 hours chop the celery, carrots, onions (some in their skins) and leeks and fry these until brown in the rest of the fat in a separate pan. Drain off the fat and add these vegetables, the tomatoes, cloves, thyme and bay leaf, and the glass of red wine (if using) to the bones and cook for a further 2 hours. If you add the vegetables at the start of the cooking

time for the bones, they can become so overcooked that they make the liquid bitter. Add onion skins— those from the onions you are using plus an extra one or two—to give the stock a good color. Strain the stock and when it is quite cold the fat can easily be removed from the top, where it sets in a solid layer. This stock can be reduced to make a glaze.

# Ham stock

If you can charm your butcher into selling you a ham bone—it should cost very little—you have the basis of a really good stock for all the soups made with dried beans, dried split peas, lentils or other legumes, or *pasta e fagioli.*

If, in addition to this, you can add a small piece of salt pork, you will have an even better flavored stock. Soak salt pork overnight before use as a precaution against too much salt.

SUGGESTED INGREDIENTS:

*a medium ham bone or hock, ½ lb/225 g piece of salt pork (optional), 1 large onion stuck with a clove, 2 sticks celery, 2 carrots, bay leaf*

It is easiest to put the ham bone and, if you are using it, the salt pork to cook with the peas, beans or lentils, and make soup and stock together in the same pot. But if you want to keep the stock for a day or two, simply cover the ham bone and salt pork with cold water, bring to the boil, add the onion and clove, celery, carrots and bay leaf and simmer for 3 hours. Strain and cool the stock rapidly and keep it in the refrigerator.

# Chicken broth

The only chicken broth worth eating is the transparently clear amber-tinted liquid obtained from boiling a chicken. It must be good enough to eat without adornment.

Chicken broth is understood best by the Italians; they use it as a base for countless delicate soups— stracciatella, zuppa pavese, with eggs stirred or dropped into it—with pasta or peas or tomatoes, or with cubes of custard or a scattering of Parmesan cheese and semolina. In Greece it is used to make avgolemono soup and sauce, and in England it makes sturdy chicken soup with rice.

SUGGESTED INGREDIENTS:

*a 3½–4 lb/1.75–2 kg boiling or roasting chicken, together with its giblets, 2¼ quarts/2.25 liters pale jellied chicken stock or water, glass of white wine, 6 black peppercorns, large bunch of parsley, 2 shallots, 2 onions with their skins on, celery, carrots, leeks, salt*

Put the chicken, breast downwards, in a large pan with all the other ingredients and bring slowly to the boil. Skim and simmer gently until the chicken is tender. A roasting chicken will be done quite quickly—in about an hour—but will not give such a rich flavor as a good old boiling fowl, which will need at least 2–2½ hours of slow, steady simmering. Enjoy the broth, carefully strained and with the fat spooned off (chicken fat is excellent for frying), at the same time as the chicken or at another meal.

# Consommé

This is a rich, clarified stock, so concentrated that it sets to a firm jelly. It should be so delicious that it can be eaten cold, although it is often served hot, and should have the transparency and tint of sherry, with which it is often lightly flavored.

In classic French cuisine there are literally hundreds of ways of garnishing consommé, from consommé Argenteuil, which is chicken consommé garnished with asparagus tips and flavored with the liquor of asparagus, to consommé Valetta, garnished with fine strips of tangerine peel and with skinned quarters of tangerine served separately.

Consommé can be made with any good stock, but the most usual are chicken and beef.

**Chicken consommé**: rich chicken broth with the addition of a calf's foot or two pig's feet cut in pieces, cooked for 3 hours and then carefully clarified, makes very delicious consommé with a small glass of sherry dashed into it.

**Beef consommé**: make brown beef stock with the addition of a chopped calf's foot or two chopped pig's feet. Reduce, clarify, season and add sherry.

**To clarify consommé**: bring the strained broth to the boil, whisk in two stiffly beaten egg whites and let them rise up the pan, carrying all the bits and pieces with them. Remove the pan from the heat

before it boils over and don't whisk the stock after the egg whites have clotted. Return the pan to a low heat and let the stock simmer under its raft of egg white for a good 20 minutes before straining it into a bowl through a layer of damp paper towel or, better still, a fine cloth in a wire sieve.

If you add about 2 tablespoons of ground beef with the egg whites this helps to improve the flavor, somewhat exhausted by the process of clarification. Allow it to simmer for 1 hour before straining.

Any well-flavored jellied stock can be clarified like this, and the jelly used as a soup or as a glaze.

# Court bouillon

This is the stock in which to poach many types of fish and it is also the basis of many fish soups.

SUGGESTED INGREDIENTS:

*2–3 small onions, 3 carrots, 2 bay leaves, small bunch of parsley, 2 slices lemon, 1 tablespoon/15 g butter, 1 tablespoon salt, 5–6 black peppercorns, 5 cups/1 liter water, 2½ cups/6 dl white wine or 1¼ cups/3 dl wine vinegar*

Skin and slice the onions and carrots. Put all the ingredients in a large pan, bring to the boil, cover and simmer for 20 minutes. Always allow court bouillon to cool to lukewarm before you put in the fish.

# Fish fumet

Strain and reduce this fish stock to become the basis of a sauce, or it can be turned into an aspic with which to glaze fish that are to be served cold. If you cannot obtain sole trimmings, use the better-flavored fish such as cod or salmon.

SUGGESTED INGREDIENTS:

*The bones and trimmings of 2–3 sole, 2–3 outside sticks of celery, 2 onions, 1 carrot, 1 bay leaf, a little salt, 2½ quarts/2.25 liters water*

Skin and slice the vegetables. Put everything in a large pan—not too much salt because the liquid reduces during the cooking—bring to the boil and simmer, uncovered, for 30–45 minutes. This makes about 2 quarts/1.75 liters. If you like, substitute 1–2 glasses of dry white wine for some of the water.

## Delicate carrot soup

| |
|---|
| 6 carrots, peeled |
| 2–3 potatoes, peeled |
| 2 onions, peeled |
| 2 tablespoons/30 g butter |
| 1 quart/9 dl chicken stock |
| 3 tablespoons heavy cream |
| 1 egg yolk |
| salt and freshly ground pepper |
| 2 teaspoons finely chopped chervil or parsley |

SERVES 4–6

Coarsely grate all the vegetables, put them in a large heavy pan with the butter and stir them around over a medium heat until the butter melts. Cover the pan and leave it over a low heat for 10 minutes, removing the lid from time to time to give the vegetables a stir. Add the stock, bring the soup to the boil and simmer for 20 minutes until the vegetables are tender.

Purée the soup using a food processor or the fine blade of a food mill. Pour back into the pan and bring to the boil. Whisk the cream and egg yolk in a bowl for 2–3 minutes. Remove the soup from the heat and pour it slowly onto the cream and egg mixture, whisking all the time. Return the soup to the pan once more, heat very gently, stirring continuously. Do not allow it to boil. Taste for seasoning, stir in the chervil or parsley and serve at once.

## Mushroom soup

| |
|---|
| $\frac{1}{2}$ lb/225 g mushrooms |
| 8 small onions or shallots |
| 1–2 cloves garlic |
| $\frac{1}{2}$ stick/55 g butter |
| 2–3 tablespoons dry white vermouth |
| 5 cups/1 liter mild chicken stock |
| 3 large or 4 small egg yolks |
| 1$\frac{1}{4}$ cups/3 dl heavy cream |
| 1–2 teaspoons chopped parsley |
| salt and freshly ground white pepper |

SERVES 6

Peel and chop the onions and garlic finely and melt the butter in a large pan. Sweat the onions and garlic in the butter while you chop the mushrooms finely. Add the mushrooms to the onions and stir them around for a few minutes, and then add the vermouth. In another pan, bring the stock to the boil and then pour it onto the vegetables. Simmer for 15 minutes or until the taste of the mushrooms has really permeated the broth.

Beat the egg yolks with the cream, add a few ladles of the soup, then pour the mixture into the pan. Add the parsley and seasoning and heat very slowly, stirring all the time. Do not allow the soup to boil or it will curdle. When the mushrooms are suspended in the soup, serve immediately.

## Tomato soup

| |
|---|
| 1 lb/450 g tomatoes |
| 2 leeks |
| 2 small potatoes |
| 5 cups/1 liter chicken stock |
| salt and freshly ground white pepper |
| 3–4 tablespoons heavy cream |

SERVES 4–6

Cut the tomatoes into quarters—there is no need to skin them. Clean the leeks and chop them coarsely. Peel and cube the potatoes. Put the vegetables in a large pan and cover them with the stock. Bring to the boil and simmer for 25–30 minutes, but no longer than is necessary to make all the vegetables tender. Purée, using a food processor or the finest blade of a food mill, and then strain the soup through a wire sieve. Taste for seasoning, add salt and white pepper and stir in half the cream. Serve with a teaspoonful of cream poured into each bowl at the last moment.

## Cold cucumber soup

| |
|---|
| 4 cucumbers or 1$\frac{1}{2}$ English cucumbers |
| 1$\frac{1}{4}$ cups/3 dl each of sour cream and natural yogurt |
| 2 cups/4.5 dl chicken stock |
| salt and a good pinch of paprika or cayenne |
| handful of chopped mint |
| few spoonfuls of whipped cream |

SERVES 6–8

In a blender purée the chopped, unpeeled cucumber, sour cream and yogurt. Add the stock, salt and mint and stir. Chill, and serve with a dollop of cream and a sprinkling of paprika or cayenne.

## *Gazpacho*

| |
|---|
| *1 lb/450 g tomatoes, skinned* |
| *3–6 cloves garlic* |
| *½ teaspoon salt* |
| *⅔ cup/1.5 dl olive oil* |
| *2½ cups–1 quart/6–9 dl water* |
| *¼ Spanish onion* |
| *1 tablespoon wine vinegar* |
| *1 green sweet pepper* |
| *1 cucumber* |
| *2 slices white bread, crusts removed* |

SERVES 4–6

Peel the garlic and pound it together with the salt to make a purée. Reserve one of the tomatoes, chop the rest and sieve them into the garlic. Add the olive oil to this mixture drop by drop, stirring all the time to emulsify it. Then add the water, stirring well. Peel the onion, chop it finely and soak it in the wine vinegar. Seed and chop the sweet pepper, the cucumber and the remaining tomato into small cubes and add them to the soup. Stir in the onion and vinegar, and put the soup to chill.

Cut the bread into cubes and dry them in a very low oven while the soup chills. Add them just as you serve the soup.

ALTERNATIVES: *you can serve gazpacho with bread cubes only, or with just a few cubes of cucumber. In Spain this soup is made in hundreds of different ways; sometimes it has bread crumbs in the mixture, sometimes it is a biting pearly emulsion made only with the vegetables, oil, garlic and water.*

---

## *Light watercress soup*

| |
|---|
| *2 bunches watercress* |
| *2 large potatoes, just under 1 lb/450 g* |
| *1 onion* |
| *2 small leeks* |
| *2 tablespoons/30 g butter* |
| *5 cups/1 liter good chicken stock* |
| *salt and freshly ground pepper* |
| *⅔ cup/1.5 dl milk* |
| *a little butter or ⅔ cup/1.5 dl heavy cream* |

SERVES 6

Peel and cut up the potatoes, skin and chop the onion, wash and slice the leeks. Melt the butter in a fairly large pan and put in the chopped vegetables.

Let them sweat and soften over a low heat for 10 minutes, stirring from time to time to prevent them browning. Cover with the stock, add a little salt and bring to the boil. Simmer for 10 minutes, then add, apart from a sprig or two, the coarsely chopped, well-washed watercress, stalks and all. Taste the broth, add a little more salt if necessary and simmer until all the vegetables are tender but the cress is still a good green. It will take about 15 minutes after the watercress goes in.

Purée coarsely for a green-flecked soup or finely for a soup of a more uniform green, using either a food mill or a food processor and add some of the milk if the mixture is too thick. Return the soup to the pan, add the rest of the milk, taste for seasoning and reheat.

For a plain family soup, serve as it is with a small lump of butter in each bowl. For a more extravagant version, whip some cream to a soft, light snow, until it sticks to the whisk, and then, at the last moment, whisk it briefly into the pan of very hot soup. You can float a leaf or two of raw watercress on the top of each bowl when you serve the soup.

---

## *Sorrel soup*

| |
|---|
| *¾ lb/340 g sorrel* |
| *1 onion* |
| *3 tablespoons/45 g butter* |
| *1 small head of lettuce* |
| *several sprigs of chervil* |
| *1 quart/9 dl boiling chicken stock* |
| *salt and freshly ground pepper* |
| *2 large or 3 small egg yolks* |
| *a little butter or 4–6 tablespoons heavy cream* |
| *2–3 tablespoons tiny freshly made croûtons* |

SERVES 4–6

Chop the onion and sweat it in the butter in a large pan for 5–10 minutes while you wash the sorrel, lettuce and chervil and chop them coarsely. Put the greenery in with the onion and allow to wilt; the sorrel melts and changes color immediately from bright green to pond green, the lettuce takes a little longer. Pour on the boiling stock, season and simmer, uncovered, until the vegetables are cooked through, about 10–15 minutes. Press through a wire sieve, or purée them, using the medium blade of a food mill or a food processor. A blender cannot cope with the hair-like fibers in the sorrel, so if you use one, strain the soup through a wire sieve after blending.

Return the soup to the pan and heat it through without boiling. Beat the egg yolks in a bowl and stir in a few tablespoons of the soup. Pour the egg mixture into the pan and stir continually over a very low heat, without boiling, until slightly thickened.

Sorrel, when cooked, has a beautiful velvety consistency; the egg yolks make it smoother still. Serve with a knob of butter or a spoonful of cream in each bowl and a spoonful of very hot croûtons. This is a refreshing, acid soup, very useful for lifting jaded appetites.

ALTERNATIVE: **Spinach soup**. *Substitute spinach for the sorrel and lettuce.*

# Beet soup

| |
|---|
| 2 raw beets and 1 cooked beet |
| ½ white cabbage |
| 2 leeks |
| 2–3 sticks celery |
| 2 onions |
| 2 tablespoons/30 g butter |
| 2½ quarts/2.25 liters best strong beef stock |
| 1 teaspoon caraway seeds |
| small bouquet garni of 1 sprig thyme, 1 bay leaf and 1 sprig parsley |
| salt and freshly ground pepper |
| pinch of grated nutmeg |
| 2 tablespoons red wine vinegar |
| 2 teaspoons sugar |
| 1 glass red wine |
| ⅔ cup/1.5 dl sour cream |

SERVES 4–6

Clean and chop all the vegetables fairly finely except for the cooked beet. Melt the butter in a large frying pan and sweat the chopped vegetables in it for 10 minutes. Add the skimmed beef stock, caraway seeds and bouquet garni and season sparingly with salt, pepper and nutmeg. Simmer gently for 1 hour. Add the vinegar, sugar and red wine and simmer for a further 20 minutes. At the last minute grate the cooked beet, or cut it into fine strips, and add it to the soup. Season to taste. Remove the bouquet garni, heat the soup through and serve, adding a tablespoon of sour cream to each bowl.

# Jerusalem artichoke soup

| |
|---|
| 1 lb/450 g Jerusalem artichokes |
| 2 potatoes |
| 2 onions |
| 1 stick celery |
| ¾ stick/85 g butter |
| small bouquet garni of 1 sprig parsley, a few celery leaves and 1 sprig thyme |
| 1 quart/9 dl chicken stock |
| 2 cups/4.5 dl milk |
| salt and freshly ground pepper |
| ⅔ cup/1.5 dl heavy cream (optional) |

SERVES 6

Peel and quarter the artichokes and potatoes and skin and slice the onions. Chop the celery into small pieces. Melt half the butter in a large pan and add the onions and celery, and stir from time to time until soft. Add the artichokes, potatoes, herbs and stock. Bring to the boil and simmer until the artichokes are cooked through. Remove the bouquet garni and purée the soup, using either a food processor or the fine blade of a food mill. If using a blender, strain the purée through a wire sieve.

Pour back into the pan with enough milk to make a thickish soup, add plenty of seasoning and some cream if you have it. Heat through and serve with a nut of butter stirred into each bowl.

This soup is sometimes called Palestine soup, presumably because it is made with Jerusalem artichokes. It is creamy and delicious but has a somewhat flatulent effect.

# Onion soup

| |
|---|
| 1 lb/450 g Spanish onions |
| ½ stick/55 g butter |
| 5 cups/1 liter rich beef stock |
| 2 sticks and leaves of fennel |
| 1 clove |
| salt and freshly ground pepper |
| 1 teaspoon sugar |
| 1 French loaf |
| dash of brandy |
| 4–6 oz/115–170 g Gruyère, freshly grated |

SERVES 4 AS A MAIN DISH OR 6 AS A FIRST COURSE

Peel and slice the onions. Melt the butter in a large pan. Sweat the onions gently in the butter until they are transparent and golden. Bring the stock to the boil in another pan and pour it onto the onions. Add the fennel, clove, salt and pepper. In a soup spoon, carefully hold the sugar under the broiler or over a gas flame until it caramelizes and turns deep brown. Stir this into the soup and it will give it a deep, mellow color. Simmer for 30 minutes.

Heat the broiler. Cut the French bread into thick slices, slightly diagonally rather than straight across the loaf, and toast them. Add the brandy to the soup and ladle it into bowls. Thickly cover each piece of toast with the Gruyère. Float a slice or two of toast in each bowl and then put the bowls under a very high heat for 1–2 minutes, until the cheese is bubbling. Serve this extremely filling soup as piping hot as possible.

## Vichyssoise

| |
|---|
| 1½ lb/700 g leeks |
| 2 shallots or 1 small onion |
| 2 small potatoes |
| ½ stick/55 g butter |
| 2 cups/4.5 dl chicken stock |
| ⅔ cup/1.5 dl dry white wine |
| salt and freshly ground pepper |
| grating of nutmeg |
| 1 quart/9 dl milk |
| ⅔ cup/1.5 dl heavy cream |
| 3 tablespoons chopped chives |

SERVES 6

Trim the leeks and peel and chop the onion and potatoes. Put the vegetables in a large heavy pan with the butter and let them sweat and soften without burning for about 10 minutes. Add the stock and wine. Bring to the boil, season and simmer for 20–25 minutes until the vegetables are tender. Purée the soup using the fine blade of a food mill or alternatively use a food processor. Mix in the milk. If you prefer to use half chicken stock and half milk this is all right, but the stock should not be at all greasy.

Cool and chill the soup and serve topped with the cream and chives.

This is a particularly fresh and delicate version of vichyssoise, which for a summer soup is often far too rich and heavy.

ALTERNATIVES: **Cauliflower soup.** *Substitute a cauliflower for the leeks, omit the chives and serve with croûtons.*

**Green pea soup.** *Instead of leeks and potatoes, use shelled peas straight from the pod and a few outer lettuce leaves. Serve with triangles of fried bread.*

## Pumpkin soup

| |
|---|
| 1 pumpkin or slice of pumpkin, weighing about 1 lb/450 g |
| 2 large leeks |
| 1¼–2 cups/3–4.5 dl milk |
| 5 cups/1 liter chicken stock |
| 2 sprigs fresh basil or ½ teaspoon dried basil |
| pinch of grated nutmeg |
| salt and freshly ground pepper |
| 2 tablespoons/30 g butter |
| 2–3 tablespoons heavy cream |

SERVES 4

Trim and wash the leeks, reserving the green tops, and finely slice the white part. Remove the seeds and pith from the pumpkin, cut the flesh away from the skin and chop it into cubes. Put the sliced white leek and the cubed pumpkin into a saucepan with a few tablespoons of water, just enough to cover the bottom of the pan. Put it over a gentle heat and allow the vegetables to soften and melt to a mush. Stir from time to time to make sure they do not stick to the pan. When they are tender, purée them either in a food mill, using the medium blade, or in a food processor.

Return the mixture to the cleaned pan and add the milk, stock, basil, nutmeg and salt and pepper. Finely slice about half a teacupful of the green leek tops, cutting them into rings. Melt the butter in a small saucepan, add the green rings of leek tops and sweat until just tender.

Stir the leek tops and the cream into the soup just before serving.

If you are making this to serve in a pumpkin shell, double the quantities.

## Avgolemono soup

| |
|---|
| ¼–⅓ cup/55–85 g short-grain Italian rice |
| 5 cups–2 quarts/1–1.75 liters good chicken broth |
| salt |

*2 egg yolks*

*juice of 1 lemon*

*large pinch of cinnamon*

SERVES 4

Wash the rice in several changes of water. Bring the stock to the boil in a large pan, add the rice and bring back to the boil. Skim and simmer until the rice is just cooked. Season with salt—it needs quite a lot. Beat the egg yolks and lemon juice together in a large bowl. Whisk the soup into the egg and lemon mixture—it must be this way round so that the egg will not curdle—then return it all to the pan. Heat through gently until slightly thickened, but on no account let it boil.

Serve the soup sprinkled with cinnamon. It is very fresh and light and makes the perfect start to a summer lunch or supper.

---

# Yellow pea soup

*½ lb/225 g dried yellow peas, soaked overnight*

*1 carrot*

*2 potatoes*

*1 ham bone or piece of bacon soaked overnight*

*or ½ lb/225 g salt pork*

*2½ quarts/2.25 liters water or ham stock*

*bouquet garni of 1 sprig parsley, 1 sprig thyme and 1 bay leaf*

*salt and freshly ground pepper*

*½ lb/225 g smoked boiling sausage, sliced*

*⅔ cup/1.5 dl heavy cream or ½ stick/55 g butter*

SERVES 4–6

Peel and coarsely chop the carrot and potatoes and put them in a large pan with the drained peas and ham bone, bacon or salt pork. Cover with the cold water or stock, add the bouquet garni, pepper and a very little salt and bring to the boil. Skim and allow to simmer for about 1¼–1½ hours until everything is tender. Remove the ham bone or bacon and the herbs. Purée the soup using the fine blade of a food mill or liquidize it in a food processor.

Return to the pan and taste for seasoning. Add the sliced boiling sausage, simmer for 15 minutes and serve very hot. This soup is very delicious with cream stirred into it, but is more traditionally served with a knob of butter added to each bowl and plenty of freshly ground black pepper.

ALTERNATIVE: **Lentil soup.** *Substitute brown or green lentils for yellow peas, add 4 sticks of celery to the carrot and potatoes, and add a teaspoon of olive oil to each bowl in place of cream or butter.*

---

# Minestrone

*6 oz/170 g dried borlotti beans, soaked overnight*

*2½ quarts/2.25 liters boiling water*

*2 large cloves garlic*

*¼ lb/115 g salt pork or pancetta*

*2 tablespoons chopped parsley*

*1 tablespoon olive oil*

*2 onions*

*2 carrots*

*1 stick celery*

*1 potato*

*2 zucchini*

*6–7 leaves Swiss chard or ½ lb/225 g spinach*

*3 tomatoes, skinned, or 4 canned tomatoes*

*1 teaspoon tomato paste*

*salt and freshly ground pepper*

*¼ lb/115 g penne or elbow macaroni*

*2 tablespoons chopped basil*

*freshly grated Parmesan*

SERVES 10

Cook the beans for about 1¾ hours in half the water until almost tender. Peel and crush the garlic and chop the salt pork or pancetta into small pieces. Fry the garlic, pork and parsley gently in the olive oil in a large pan until the fat runs from the pork. Peel and chop the onions and scrub and chop the carrots and celery. Add the onions to the pan, allow them to sweat and soften, then add the beans in their liquid and the carrots and celery. Pour in the rest of the water and simmer until the vegetables are almost cooked.

Peel and dice the potato, cut the zucchini in half lengthwise, slice, wash and coarsely chop the greens and chop the tomatoes. Add these to the rest of the vegetables, return the soup to the boil, add the tomato paste, season and boil for 10 minutes.

Scoop out a large ladleful of the soup and throw the pasta into the pan. Let it cook while you sieve the ladleful of soup to a purée. When the pasta is done, return the puréed beans and vegetables to the soup in the pan. Add the basil, more salt and pepper if it is needed and heat through. Serve the soup with a generous bowlful of freshly grated Parmesan. It is impractical to make minestrone soup for fewer people than 10, but it does reheat particularly well if you don't eat it all at once. It can also be eaten cool —not cold—in the summer as a very filling sort of bean stew.

ALTERNATIVE: **Pasta e fagioli.** *Use fresh maltagliate or dried ruotini and double the quantity of beans. Omit the meat, zucchini, potato and greens and add a little extra garlic. Purée two-thirds of the cooked beans before adding them to the pasta. Pasta e fagioli is a very thick soup.*

## Soupe au pistou

| |
|---|
| *1 lb/450 g tomatoes, skinned, or a 1 lb/450 g can tomatoes* |
| *1 large onion* |
| *2–3 tablespoons olive oil* |
| *1 lb/450 g green beans* |
| *1 large zucchini* |
| *2 potatoes* |
| *5 cups/1 liter water* |
| *salt and freshly ground pepper* |
| *¼ lb/115 g dried white beans, soaked and cooked, or a 1 lb/450 g can of white beans* |
| *3 tablespoons vermicelli* |

**for the pistou:**

| |
|---|
| *3 cloves garlic* |
| *handful of large basil sprigs* |
| *3 tablespoons olive oil* |
| *salt and freshly ground pepper* |
| *3–4 oz/85–115 g Emmental, freshly grated* |

SERVES 4–6

Chop the tomatoes. Peel and chop the onion fairly finely and sweat it in the oil in a large pan. Add the tomatoes and cook for 10–15 minutes while you prepare the other vegetables. Top and tail the green beans and cut them into short lengths. Cut the zucchini in half lengthwise and then into smallish chunks. Peel and cube the potatoes.

Pour the water into the tomato mixture, season, bring to the boil and throw in the green beans, zucchini and potatoes. Boil for 10 minutes, then add the white beans and the vermicelli and boil until everything is tender. Taste for seasoning.

To make the pistou, peel and chop the garlic and put it with the basil into a food processor or blender, or use a pestle and mortar, and purée coarsely, adding the oil in a thin stream so that you have an oily green paste. Season to taste. Stir this into the soup just before serving and put a bowl of grated Emmental on the table for each person to sprinkle some onto the soup.

This soup reheats well, but do not add the pistou until the last moment.

## Almond soup

| |
|---|
| *¼ lb/115 g ground almonds* |
| *6 cups/1.5 liters best chicken stock, very hot* |
| *salt and freshly ground white pepper* |
| *⅔ cup/1.5 dl cream, light or heavy according to taste* |
| *2 egg yolks* |
| *handful of finely chopped chives (optional)* |

SERVES 6

Put the ground almonds in a bowl and gradually add 1¼ cups/3 dl of the stock, working it with a spoon or pestle to keep the mixture smooth. Put this with the rest of the stock in a large pan. Heat, stirring, add a little salt if it is needed and some pepper and simmer for about 30 minutes.

Just before serving, whisk the cream with the egg yolks in a bowl, then whisk in 2 or 3 tablespoons of the soup. Away from the heat, pour this mixture into the soup in the pan, then heat through gently until slightly thickened but do not boil. The soup should be pearly white and creamy. It looks beautiful without any decoration, but if you want to make it look less plain sprinkle some chives over the top of each bowl.

This attractive and rich soup comes from a cook book written in the seventeenth century, a time when almonds were a popular cooking ingredient, and, although comparatively cheap and simple to make, it is very luxurious.

## Fish chowder

| |
|---|
| *1½ lb/700 g cod or haddock on the bone* |
| *1 quart/9 dl water* |
| *1 large onion* |
| *¼ lb/115 g salt pork* |
| *3 potatoes* |
| *salt and freshly ground pepper* |
| *2 cups/4.5 dl milk* |

*⅔ cup/1.5 dl heavy cream*

*2–4 tablespoons/30–55 g butter*

SERVES 6

Remove the bones and skin from the fish and put them, broken up, into a pan containing half the water. Bring to the boil and simmer for 15 minutes. Peel and thinly slice the onion and chop the salt pork into small cubes. Sauté the pork gently until the fat starts to run, then add the onion, stir around, cover and cook over a gentle heat for 15 minutes.

Peel and slice the potatoes. Put them in a large pan with the remaining water and a pinch of salt, cover and cook for 15 minutes. Cut the fish into large pieces, 1 in/2.5 cm or more across, and add to the potatoes together with the milk, strained stock, salt pork and onion. Simmer for a further 10 minutes. Heat the cream in a small saucepan and pour it into the chowder. Add the butter and season to taste. Heat through gently and thoroughly but do not boil. This chowder should be a mild but delicious, steaming, cream-colored stew, slightly thickened by potatoes and cream, on which float beads of yellow melted butter. It is both pretty and cheap as well as being very soothing and appetizing.

ALTERNATIVES: *shelled chopped clams or, if you feel really extravagant, oysters, together with their juices, can be added at the end and just heated through.*

# Shrimp bisque

*1 lb/450 g cooked shrimps in their shells*

*5 cups/1 liter fish fumet*

*1 head Florence fennel, sliced, or a few fresh green fennel twigs*

*1 sprig parsley*

*2 bay leaves*

*2 onions, peeled and sliced*

*⅔ cup/1.5 dl dry white wine*

*½ stick/55 g butter*

*1 sprig thyme*

*½ cup/55 g flour*

*1¼ cups/3 dl milk*

*4 tablespoons heavy cream*

*1 tablespoon brandy*

SERVES 6

Shell the shrimps, put the shells in a pan with the fish fumet and add the green top of the Florence fennel or the fresh fennel twigs, the parsley, 1 bay leaf, half the sliced onion and the wine. Bring to the boil, simmer for 25 minutes and strain.

Roughly chop the shrimps. Heat all but a little of the butter in another large pan and stir in the remaining onion, bay leaf and the thyme. When the onion is almost tender, add the shrimps and sauté for 2 minutes, then stir in the flour. Gradually add the liquid from the shells until you have a pan of pinkish sauce. Simmer for 20 minutes, purée in a blender or food processor and add the milk.

If using Florence fennel, put the rest of it, with the remaining butter, in a saucepan; when soft, add to the soup. Add the cream and brandy and serve.

# Bouillabaisse

*3 lb/1.5 kg assorted fish, preferably on the bone; those closest to the Mediterranean varieties include eel, red snapper, sea bass, haddock and flounder*

*2–3 large tomatoes*

*3–4 cloves garlic*

*2 onions*

*large bouquet garni of several fennel twigs, few sprigs thyme, a bay leaf and a piece of orange peel*

*¼ cup olive oil*

*salt and freshly ground pepper*

*large pinch of saffron strands*

*4–6 rounds of French bread, dried in the oven*

*few spoonfuls of rouille*

*2 tablespoons chopped parsley*

SERVES 4–6

Clean and scale the fish and cut them in thick slices or chunks. Skin and chop the tomatoes and peel and chop the garlic. Peel and chop the onions and put them in a large pan together with the tomatoes, garlic, herbs and olive oil. Season with salt, pepper and saffron and boil rapidly for 5 minutes to soften the onion. Throw in all the fish except the flounder, pour in just enough water to cover the fish and bring to a rapid boil. Allow to boil furiously for 5 minutes—this amalgamates the oil and water, which is essential when making proper bouillabaisse. Add the flounder and boil rapidly for a further 2–3 minutes.

Remove the herbs and serve the broth in bowls with the rounds of French bread, spread with rouille, floating on top. Serve the fish separately, sprinkled with parsley and accompanied by more rouille.

# Sauces

## Béchamel sauce

3 tablespoons/45 g butter

4 tablespoons/30 g flour

2 cups/4.5 dl milk

salt and freshly ground white pepper

Melt two-thirds of the butter in a small saucepan, stir in the flour and let it cook gently for 1–2 minutes without browning. Add the milk, little by little, each time stirring with a wooden spoon until the milk has been absorbed. When all the milk has been incorporated and the sauce is smooth and creamy, season with salt and pepper. Half cover the pan with a tilted lid and simmer for 15 minutes, stirring from time to time to prevent the sauce catching on the bottom. Beat in the remaining butter in small pieces to give the sauce a velvety texture.

ALTERNATIVES: *this sauce can also be made with hot milk instead of cold. Allow the roux to cool a little before you whisk it in. When it is boiling again, cover and cook gently for 15 minutes.*

**Mornay sauce**. *Add 1 oz/30 g grated Parmesan and 1 oz/30 g grated Emmental to 2 cups/4.5 dl béchamel sauce. Use less salt in the béchamel as the cheese is salty. Season with cayenne pepper and a touch of nutmeg. For a particularly good flavor, infuse the milk for 10 minutes with a sliced onion and a bay leaf before making the béchamel.*

## Velouté sauce

3 tablespoons/45 g butter

4 tablespoons/30 g flour

3 cups/7 dl good homemade chicken stock

salt and freshly ground white pepper

pinch of nutmeg

This is a domestic recipe for velouté as made in French households, not the restaurant version which is more complicated. Make a basic velouté sauce in exactly the same way as béchamel, melting the butter, stirring in the flour and gradually adding the liquid. When all the liquid has been incorporated, season, cover and simmer, very gently, for about 25 minutes, skimming from time to time. Velouté sauce can be made richer by adding a little white wine and a bouquet of herbs.

ALTERNATIVE: **Sauce vouvrillonne**. *This special velouté is served with quenelles and made by adding*

*Vouvray or other dry white wine to the liquid. Some lightly cooked onion and mushrooms are added at the end of cooking, together with a little lemon juice and heavy cream.*

---

## Sauce soubise

½ lb/225 g onions

2 tablespoons/30 g butter

4 tablespoons/30 g flour

2 cups/4.5 dl creamy milk or light chicken stock

salt and freshly ground pepper

pinch each of nutmeg and sugar

dash of cayenne

Peel the onions and slice them finely, then sweat them gently in the butter in a small saucepan for 10–15 minutes. Stir in the flour, cook for 2 minutes, then gradually add the milk or stock, stirring as it thickens. Season and simmer for 15–20 minutes, taking care not to let the sauce catch at the bottom. Sieve the mixture or purée it in a blender and taste for seasoning.

Serve this onion sauce hot as an accompaniment for roast lamb and lamb chops.

---

## Béarnaise sauce

2–3 shallots

1 tablespoon tarragon vinegar

2 tablespoons wine vinegar

12 black peppercorns, coarsely crushed

2–3 sprigs fresh tarragon

3 egg yolks

1¼ sticks/140 g unsalted butter, cut into cubes

salt

Peel the shallots and chop them finely, put them in a small saucepan with the vinegar, peppercorns and tarragon and bring to the boil. Reduce rapidly over a brisk heat until you are left with no more than 1 tablespoon of liquid. Allow to cool, then beat in the egg yolks. Place the pan over a larger pan of hot water—a bain-marie—on a gentle heat and slowly increase the heat, whisking all the time. When the mixture has thickened a little and is creamy, start adding the butter, dropping in a piece at a time and whisking it in until it has been fully incorporated into the béarnaise before adding the next piece. When all the butter has been incorporated, season the sauce and keep it warm over the bain-marie—away from the heat so that it does not get too hot and coagulate around the edges. If the sauce gets too thick, add a few drops of cold water to cool it down. If the egg yolks do not seem to be thickening at all, increase the heat slightly. Serve with beef and lamb.

## Hollandaise sauce

*1 tablespoon white wine vinegar or lemon juice*

*2 large egg yolks*

*1–1¼ sticks/115–140 g slightly salted butter, softened and cut into small cubes*

Take a double boiler or bain-marie and heat some water in the bottom. To lessen the risk of the sauce curdling while it is cooking, keep the water well below the boil and make sure it doesn't actually touch the base of whatever contains the sauce.

Using the bowl or pan which is to go over the water, beat the vinegar with the egg yolks. Place over the hot water and, stirring all the time with a wooden spoon, add the cubes of butter one at a time, letting each one melt before you add the next. Push the egg down from the sides of the pan or bowl, and if the sauce shows signs of thickening too fast or curdling, remove it from the water at once and put it in a bowl of cold water, stirring gently all the time. If it is too thick, add a few drops of cold water or creamy milk. If it refuses to thicken, turn up the heat a little. Taste for salt. If salty, add some unsalted butter. Hollandaise should be smooth and fairly thick. Serve warm with poached fish, particularly salmon, salmon trout and shellfish. It is also good with plain cooked vegetables, such as asparagus, broccoli and sea kale.

ALTERNATIVE: **Mustard sauce.** *Stir 1 or 2 teaspoons of freshly made English mustard into the hollandaise at the last moment. Serve with ham, pig's feet, or boiling sausage.*

## Sabayon sauce for fish

*1–2 bay leaves*

*1 bunch parsley*

*the leafy tops of 2 celery sticks*

*⅔ cup/1.5 dl boiling water or clear pale chicken stock*

*salt*

*3 egg yolks*

*1 tablespoon fresh lemon juice*

Put the bay leaves, parsley and celery tops into a measuring cup and pour in the stock or boiling water. Let it infuse and cool, then season lightly and strain. Half-fill the bottom of a double boiler with hot water and put the egg yolks in the top. Put it on a gentle heat and add the herb infusion. Whisk over a moderate heat until the egg yolks foam and thicken to a light sauce, then add the lemon juice and serve.

The sauce will keep well in the top of a double boiler for up to half an hour. Whisk again just before serving. Based on a recipe by Michel Guérard, it is suitable for delicate fish.

## English butter sauce

*1 stick/115 g unsalted butter*

*2 tablespoons/15 g flour*

*⅔ cup/1.5 dl milk*

*1 squeeze fresh lemon juice*

*salt*

Put the butter and flour into a small saucepan, whisk them together over a very low heat and simmer for a few minutes. Gradually add the milk, whisking after each addition. It will separate and look very odd at first, but persevere until all the liquid has been incorporated and the sauce will become smooth and creamy. Add a few drops of lemon juice, taste and add salt rather sparingly. Cook gently for 5 minutes, whisking all the time. This light sauce is not as rich as hollandaise but just as delicious. Serve very hot with vegetables, such as asparagus, sea kale, broccoli and leeks.

## Mustard sauce for fish

*1 tablespoon Dijon mustard*

*½ stick/55 g butter*

*1 teaspoon flour*

*1 tablespoon chicken stock or milk*

*salt*

# Sauces

Melt the butter in a small saucepan, stir in the flour, then add the chicken stock or milk and the mustard. Stir vigorously over a gentle heat. If it looks as if it is separating, add a little more stock or milk and whisk. When it has combined to make a smooth sauce, season lightly with salt. Serve with broiled fish, particularly herrings.

## Beurre blanc

| |
|---|
| *1 stick/115 g unsalted butter* |
| *3–4 shallots* |
| *3 tablespoons white wine vinegar* |
| *3 tablespoons dry white wine* |
| *salt and freshly ground pepper* |
| *few drops of lemon juice* |

Peel and finely chop the shallots and put them in a small saucepan with the vinegar and the wine. Bring to the boil and reduce until you have 1–2 tablespoons of the liquid left. Remove the pan from heat to cool a little while you cut the butter into small dice, each about the size of a walnut. Add them to the shallot mixture one at a time, whisking well, until it becomes creamy. After you have added 2–3 pieces, place the pan over a low heat and continue whisking and adding pieces of butter until it is all incorporated. Season the sauce, add a few drops of lemon juice and serve hot. If you are not ready to serve the sauce immediately, keep it warm over hot water in a double boiler away from the heat.

For a more refined sauce, sieve before serving.

## Maître d'hôtel butter

| |
|---|
| *1 stick/115 g unsalted butter, softened* |
| *4 large sprigs parsley* |
| *juice of ½ lemon* |

Chop the parsley finely. Put all the ingredients in a bowl, work them together with a fork and when thoroughly combined place in the refrigerator.

Serve a teaspoon of this butter on top of piping hot broiled or fried fish, or on broiled kidneys, steaks and chops.

ALTERNATIVES: **Garlic and herb butter.** *Add a shallot and 2 cloves garlic, pounded, to the butter with finely chopped parsley or tarragon.*

**Horseradish butter.** *Add grated horseradish, and a little Dijon mustard and wine vinegar to the butter.*

## Sauce grelette

| |
|---|
| *4 tomatoes, skinned and seeded* |
| *1½ tablespoons fromage blanc* |
| *2 tablespoons heavy cream* |
| *1 teaspoon Dijon mustard* |
| *juice of ½ lemon* |
| *4 sprigs parsley and 6 fresh tarragon leaves, chopped* |
| *salt and freshly ground pepper* |
| *few drops of Tabasco* |

Cut the tomatoes in small cubes and put them in a colander to drain. Put the *fromage blanc* in a bowl with the cream and mustard and whisk them together. Gradually add the lemon juice, whisking all the time, and finally the tomato, herbs and seasoning. Serve this *nouvelle cuisine* sauce with plainly cooked cold fish, shellfish or with fish pâté.

## Delicate tomato sauce

| |
|---|
| *1 lb/450 g tomatoes* |
| *2 tablespoons/30 g butter* |
| *salt* |
| *1 teaspoon chopped fresh basil or ½ teaspoon dried basil* |
| *½ teaspoon chopped fresh tarragon or ¼ teaspoon dried tarragon* |

Skin the tomatoes and chop them coarsely. Melt the butter in a pan over a gentle heat and add the tomatoes. Cook very gently for 10 minutes, purée them, using the fine blade of a food mill, then season and stir in the herbs. Allow to stand for at least 10 minutes so that the flavor of the herbs can permeate the sauce.

Serve with broiled meat or fish, gnocchi and pasta.

## Bread sauce

| |
|---|
| *2 slices/55 g white bread, crusts removed* |
| *2 small onions* |
| *2 cloves* |
| *1 blade mace and 1 bay leaf* |

1¼ cups/3 dl milk

salt and freshly ground white pepper

2 tablespoons/30 g butter

Peel the onions, stick a clove in each and put them in a small saucepan with the mace, bay leaf and milk. Place on a low heat and simmer without boiling for 10 minutes. Crumble the bread fairly finely and add it to the milk. Season the mixture and cook very gently in the top of a double boiler for 30 minutes to an hour, stirring occasionally. Remove the onions, mace and bay leaf. Beat in the butter and season with more salt and pepper if necessary. The longer you cook it, the smoother it becomes, but lumpy bread sauce is quite nice. The French make it with cream which isn't nearly so good—it becomes far too bland and rich.

If you like you can chop the onions or sieve them and add them to the sauce, but to complement the subtlety of grouse or partridge, bread sauce should not be too highly flavored.

---

## Rouille

1 red chili pepper, dried or fresh, and 1 red sweet pepper

3–4 cloves garlic

1 slice white bread, crusts removed

1 egg yolk

salt

⅔ cup/1.5 dl olive oil

Chop the peppers, removing the seeds, and peel and chop the garlic. Soak the bread in water and squeeze it dry. Put the peppers, bread, garlic and egg yolk into a blender, with a pinch of salt, and blend to a paste, or work them together with a pestle and mortar. Gradually add the oil in a thin stream, beating it in as if you were making mayonnaise. The consistency should be like mayonnaise. Serve with fish soup or bouillabaisse.

---

## Lobster sauce

shell, tomalley and coral of 1 cooked lobster

¾ stick/85 g butter, softened

1 teaspoon flour

1 small onion or 2 shallots

1 carrot

1 tablespoon peanut oil

bouquet garni of tarragon, parsley and thyme

3 tomatoes

1 tablespoon brandy

1 glass white wine

⅔ cup/1.5 dl fish fumet

salt

pinch of cayenne pepper

3 tablespoons heavy cream

Preheat the oven to 300°F/160°C.

Dry the lobster shell in the oven for 20 minutes. Crush and pound the shell using a pestle and mortar and keep it on one side. Put the tomalley and coral in a bowl and mix them with two-thirds of the softened butter and the flour. Peel and chop the onion or shallots and the carrot and put them in a frying pan with the oil and remaining butter. Add the bouquet garni and stew gently for 10 minutes. Remove the vegetables and bouquet garni and add the pounded lobster shell to the pan. Let it simmer for 5 minutes. Skin and chop the tomatoes.

Strain the contents of the pan into another saucepan, mashing the shells in the sieve to extract all the butter and juices. Add the brandy to these juices, let it bubble up, then add the tomatoes, white wine and fish fumet. Pour the fumet over the shells in the sieve. Simmer for 30 minutes, sieve the sauce using the fine blade of a food mill or else purée it in a food processor, and season with salt and cayenne pepper. Stir in the tomalley and coral mixture, let it bubble gently for 2 minutes, then add the cream and serve.

---

## Barbecue sauce

1 clove garlic

5 tablespoons/140 g tomato paste

1¼ cups/3 dl cider

1 teaspoon soy sauce

3 large drops Tabasco

2 tablespoons brown sugar

2 tablespoons cider vinegar

scant teaspoon of salt

Peel and crush the garlic and put it into a small saucepan with the rest of the ingredients. Simmer for 20 minutes.

Eat with chops and hamburgers or spread it over spareribs or kebabs before cooking them.

# Sauces

## Horseradish sauce

| |
|---|
| 3 tablespoons grated horseradish |
| ⅔ cup/1.5 dl whipping cream |
| 1 teaspoon Dijon mustard |
| 1 tablespoon white wine vinegar |
| pinch of sugar |

Whisk all the ingredients together in a bowl. Taste and add more vinegar or an extra pinch of sugar if you think it needs it. Eat with hot or cold roast beef. For a mild horseradish sauce omit the vinegar and add a little more sugar.

---

## Mint sauce

| |
|---|
| 3 tablespoons fresh mint, finely chopped |
| 2 tablespoons boiling water |
| 4 tablespoons vinegar |
| 1–2 teaspoons sugar, according to taste |

Put the chopped mint in a bowl and add the boiling water to moisten it. Let it get cold, then add the vinegar and sugar—malt vinegar is traditional, but white wine or cider vinegar will give a much better, mellower flavor. Allow to stand at least 1 hour before serving to give it time to develop its flavor. Eat with hot or cold roast lamb.

---

## Mayonnaise

| |
|---|
| 2 egg yolks |
| ½–1 teaspoon Dijon mustard |
| salt |
| 1¼ cups/3 dl olive oil |
| 1–2 tablespoons lemon juice or white wine vinegar |

Put the egg yolks, mustard and a generous pinch of salt into a bowl and beat them together with a wire whisk, a fork or a wooden spoon—the whisk gives the quickest results, but some people prefer the feeling of working the yolks with a wooden spoon. When they are well beaten, start adding the oil, pouring it in slowly at first, about half a teaspoon at a time. Work each half teaspoon of oil thoroughly with the egg yolks before adding more. Increase the amount of oil added until, as the mayonnaise thickens, you are adding about 2 teaspoons at a time. When thick, add enough wine vinegar or lemon juice to thin it a little, then continue adding the oil. By this stage it is virtually impossible to curdle mayonnaise and you can finish it quite fast. Taste the mayonnaise for vinegar and salt and eat immediately, or keep in a cool place, not the refrigerator, and revive at the last minute with a whisk. It should be eaten within a couple of days.

Serve with cold vegetables, shellfish, hard-boiled eggs, chicken and cold fish.

ALTERNATIVES: *for a lighter mayonnaise, use sunflower oil, peanut oil, or a mixture of olive oil and peanut oil.*

**Sauce tartare.** *Make the mayonnaise as usual, and stir in a good bunch of parsley, finely chopped, 1 small shallot, finely chopped, 2 tablespoons chopped sweet gherkins, 2 chopped hard-boiled eggs and 2 tablespoons capers, chopped.*

**Aïoli.** *Make the mayonnaise as usual, using half peanut and half olive oil, but mix 3 crushed garlic cloves with the yolks before adding the oil.*

---

## Salsa verde

| |
|---|
| 1–2 cloves garlic |
| 8 canned anchovies, finely chopped |
| 2 tablespoons each of finely chopped capers and parsley |
| ½ tablespoon wine vinegar or juice of ½ lemon |
| 6 tablespoons olive oil |
| salt |

Peel the garlic, chop it finely and put it in a bowl together with all the other chopped ingredients. Mix in the wine vinegar or lemon juice, add the oil in a thin stream, beating all the time, and season. This Italian sauce is extremely good with all boiled meat, particularly tongue, or with boiled or poached chicken or fish.

---

## Vinaigrette

| |
|---|
| 1 large clove garlic, sprinkled with salt and crushed |
| ½ tablespoon each of Orléans white wine vinegar or tarragon vinegar and dry white wine |
| 1 small teaspoon Dijon mustard |
| 5 tablespoons virgin olive oil |
| salt and freshly ground pepper |

Put the wine vinegar (or the tarragon vinegar and

wine) into a small bowl, then stir in the mustard and garlic. Add the oil gradually, beating it in with a teaspoon or fork, so that it makes a nice emulsion with the vinegar, mustard and garlic. When you have added all the oil, season with more salt, if necessary, and pepper. (Some people like to add a pinch of sugar.)

---

## Cumberland sauce

| |
|---|
| *1 orange* |
| *½ lemon* |
| *2 shallots* |
| *4 tablespoons red currant jelly* |
| *1 glass port* |
| *1 teaspoon Dijon or hot mustard* |
| *large pinch of powdered ginger* |
| *salt* |

Pare the orange and lemon as thinly as possible with a citrus peeler or a potato peeler, and slice the peel into fine strips. Drop the peel into a pan of boiling water for a couple of minutes and then drain. Peel and finely chop the shallots, pour boiling water over them and drain, pressing out the water. Melt the red currant jelly in a small saucepan, add the port,

*Cumberland sauce*

shallots and peel. Squeeze the juice from the flesh of the orange and the halved lemon into the pan and add the mustard and ginger. Simmer for a few minutes, season to taste and serve either hot or cold with cold ham and with game. This is a recipe from cookery writer Ambrose Heath.

---

## Applesauce

| |
|---|
| *1 lb/450 g cooking apples* |
| *1 teaspoon sugar* |
| *2 tablespoons/30 g butter* |

Peel, quarter and core the apples and put them with the sugar, butter and 2–3 tablespoons of water—just enough to start them off—in a small saucepan. Cover and cook gently until the apples are a soft fluff, then beat until smooth with a wooden spoon.

---

## Gooseberry sauce

| |
|---|
| *1 lb/450 g plump green gooseberries* |
| *1 tablespoon sugar* |

Put the gooseberries and 2–3 tablespoons of water in a saucepan, cover and cook over a gentle heat until the fruit has burst and softened. Add the sugar, using less or more according to how sharp you would like the sauce to be, and beat with a wooden spoon until smooth.

This fresh, sharp, green sauce is the one to eat with mackerel. It is also excellent with goose. You could cook the gooseberries in a covered pie dish in the oven at the same time as the mackerel or goose.

---

## Cranberry sauce

| |
|---|
| *1½ cups/170 g cranberries* |
| *3 tablespoons brown sugar* |

Pick over the cranberries, discarding any that are soft. Put all the ingredients in a small saucepan with 3 tablespoons of water and bring to the boil. Simmer for 15 minutes until the berries burst. Allow to cool, then mix to a ruby-colored mush. Cranberries have a sweet-acid, slightly spicy taste that is very good with turkey, pheasant and hare.

## Cooking fish

Heat is applied to a fish to develop its flavor, not to make it tender, and cooking beyond the moment when the flesh has just turned from transparent to opaque will make the fish tough and dry. A fish is cooked the moment the flesh flakes when a skewer is inserted into the fleshiest part. Start testing halfway through the recommended cooking time—if the moment passes, your succulent fish will be spoiled.

**Poaching**: boiling extracts flavor from the fish, which is fine for soups and stocks but ruinous for a poached salmon. Fish must never be allowed to boil. The poaching liquid, which must be well salted, should barely shiver, never bubble.

**Steaming**: only steam fish that is absolutely fresh. Season it well, otherwise it will have the bland flavor of hospital food, and place the fish, covered, on a buttered plate over a pan of simmering water.

**Baking**: the important thing to remember is that the fish must not dry out, so always put the fish into an oven that is preheated to about 400°F/200°C, and either wrap the fish in foil, bake it in a sauce or stuff with a moist buttery mixture. Leave the head and tail on if you are baking a whole fish; the fish looks better and will retain more moisture.

**Frying**: for the best flavor, fish should be fried as quickly as possible. Shallow fry in clarified butter, but only just enough to stop the fish sticking to the pan, and be especially frugal with fat when frying oily fish such as herrings. Deep fry fast at 375°F/190°C. Large pieces of fish should be sealed in a coating of batter or egg and bread crumbs. Little fish, such as whitebait, only need a quick dip in milk and seasoned flour.

**Broiling**: always preheat the broiler because fish should be broiled as fast as possible without burning to charcoal. To speed up the process even further, make diagonal cuts in the thickest part of the fish to allow heat to penetrate. Brush the fish with oil or clarified butter (steaks or fillets without skin will need more lubrication than whole fish complete with skin). Broil whole fish with head and bones—they will remain juicy and moist. Fillets do not need to be turned over halfway through broiling, but whole fish and cutlets do.

**Marinating**: marinate well-flavored, very fresh fish in fresh lemon or lime juice to eat raw, and always marinate fish in a glass or ceramic dish, never in metal, as the marinade will pick up a tinny flavor.

## Sole meunière

one 7–8 oz Dover sole or similar flat fish per person
flour for coating
salt
½ stick/55 g butter
sprig of parsley
juice of ¼ lemon

Skin the fish and pat with flour and salt. Heat half the butter or a bit less in a large frying pan. When it turns brown, slide in the fish and let it sizzle for 5 minutes on each side, then a further minute or two on each side if it is a large, thick fish. If it sticks to the pan, slide a palette knife very slowly underneath to detach the browned layer with the fish. The fish should be a good dark brown along the center, paling to the sides, with the white flesh showing here and there. Drain it and put it on a hot plate. Chop the parsley and sprinkle it into the pan together with the lemon juice. Add the remaining butter and swirl it around. When it has melted, pour everything over the fish and serve.

If you are cooking several fish, fry each one in turn, adding a little more butter for each. Keep them hot and add the juice of a whole lemon and a generous nut or two of butter to the pan at the end.
ALTERNATIVES: *dab, plaice, flounder.*

## Halibut in cider

4 fillets halibut about 1 in/2.5 cm thick
1 small shallot or ¼ onion
2 tablespoons/30 g butter
salt and freshly ground pepper
1¼ cups/3 dl hard cider
2 egg yolks
⅔ cup/1.5 dl heavy cream
juice of ½ lemon
1 tablespoon chopped parsley

SERVES 4

Peel and finely chop the shallot or onion. Melt the butter in a frying pan and gently sweat the chopped shallot or onion. Remove the pan from the heat and put in the fillets of fish, seasoned with salt and pepper, turning them in the butter until they are well coated. Pour in the cider and put back over a gentle heat. Poach at a slow simmer for 10–15 minutes. Remove the fish to a serving dish and reduce the cooking liquid by half. Whisk the egg yolks and cream together in a small saucepan, add the reduced cider and whisk over a gentle heat until slightly thickened, then add the lemon juice and parsley. Taste for seasoning. Spoon over the pieces of fish and serve with small, plainly steamed new potatoes.

ALTERNATIVE: *turbot, flounder.*

---

# Seviche

| |
|---|
| 1½ lb/700 g any firm white fish, completely free of skin and bone |
| juice of 2 lemons |
| salt |
| 1 dried red chili pepper |
| 1 teaspoon olive oil |

SERVES 4

The fish in this dish is "cooked" only by the action of the lemon juice. Whatever fish you choose, it must be very fresh and in perfect condition.

With a very sharp, flexible knife, cut the fish in thin slices, then cut the slices into strips the size of your little finger. Put them into a bowl, squeeze the lemon juice over them and leave for 45 minutes. Then season with salt. Add the chili pepper, finely chopped or flaked, with the seeds removed. Leave to marinate for a further 15 minutes.

To serve the seviche, divide the fish between four plates and sprinkle with a few drops of olive oil. Serve with a plain tomato salad, simply dressed with oil and lemon juice.

ALTERNATIVE: *use salmon and the juice of two limes.*

---

# Halibut au gratin

| |
|---|
| 2½ lb/1 kg chicken halibut |
| 3–4 shallots |
| ¼ lb/115 g button mushrooms |
| ½ stick/55 g butter |
| glass of white wine |
| salt and freshly ground pepper |
| 2 tablespoons heavy cream (optional) |

SERVES 6

Preheat the oven to 350°F/180°C.

Slice the shallots and mushrooms. Melt half the butter in a gratin dish, add some of the shallots and a few sliced mushrooms and let them absorb the butter for a minute. Lay the halibut on top and pour over the white wine. Lay the rest of the sliced mushrooms and shallots on top, sprinkle with salt and pepper and dot with thin slices of butter. Bake for 15 minutes per 1 lb/450 g but for not less than 20 minutes. Take out the halibut and, if you would like a rich dish, strain the cooking liquid, add the cream to it and simmer for 2–3 minutes until slightly thickened. Serve the halibut, skinned and taken off the bone, putting a nice piece on each plate and pouring the sauce over and around the fish. Accompany with boiled new or mashed potatoes and some colorful vegetables, such as young peas, baby carrots and green beans.

ALTERNATIVES: *haddock, cod, hake, striped bass.*

---

# Halibut salad

| |
|---|
| 1½ lb/700 g chicken halibut |
| salt |
| few sprigs of parsley |
| ⅔ cup/1.5 dl thick mayonnaise |
| jar of Italian capers in wine vinegar |

SERVES 4 AS A FIRST COURSE

Preheat the oven to 350°F/180°C.

Lay the halibut on a large piece of kitchen foil, sprinkle with salt and lay the parsley on top. Wrap closely in the foil, place on a baking tray and bake for 20–25 minutes. Open up the parcel and make sure the flesh comes away from the bones easily. Test the fish with the point of a sharp knife to see if the flesh flakes apart—if not, put it back into the oven for a further 5–10 minutes.

Remove the parsley, close the foil around the fish again and, when cooled, put it in the refrigerator until chilled through. It will set in its own lovely jelly. Flake the halibut onto a dish, together with the jelly.

Make a thick mayonnaise and stir into it a handful of capers together with 2 teaspoons of their vinegar. Mix the mayonnaise with the flaked fish and serve in individual dishes.

ALTERNATIVES: *instead of capers, you could add a few well-rinsed green peppercorns, chopped hard-boiled eggs and black olives, a handful of shrimps, or a mixture of fresh chopped parsley, chervil and tarragon.*

## *Fried flounder*

| |
|---|
| *4 flounder* |
| *¼ cup/30 g flour* |
| *1 egg, beaten* |
| *6 tablespoons/55 g fine homemade dried bread crumbs* |
| *salt and freshly ground pepper* |
| *2 tablespoons/30 g clarified butter, or 1 tablespoon/15 g each of butter and peanut or sunflower oil* |

SERVES 4

Put the flour, beaten egg and bread crumbs in three separate plates or pie dishes.

Season the fish with salt and pepper and dip each one first in flour, then in beaten egg and lastly in bread crumbs, patting them in well and coating the fish all over. Use one hand for the flour and crumbs and the other for the egg, so that you do not get crumbs stuck to your fingers.

Heat the clarified butter or oil and butter in a frying pan, and when it is hot but not smoking fry each fish for 5 minutes on each side. Serve with hollandaise or tartare sauce.

ALTERNATIVES: *sand dab, silver hake, sole, sea robin or fillets of haddock.*

## *Matelote normande*

| |
|---|
| *2 lb/900 g brill, flounder or sole* |
| *5 cups/900 g mussels* |
| *3 onions* |
| *¾ stick/85 g butter* |
| *1¼ cups/3 dl dry white wine* |
| *¼ cup/30 g flour* |
| *2 tablespoons chopped parsley* |
| *a few shelled shrimps* |
| *juice of ½ lemon, if needed* |
| *salt and freshly ground pepper* |

SERVES 4

Skin the fish and cut it in large slices. Wash and scrub the mussels and put them in a large saucepan with 3 tablespoons of water. Cover the pan and shake it over a fierce heat until all the mussels have opened.

Strain the liquid into a bowl and allow the mussels to cool, then shell them.

Chop the onions finely and sweat them gently in one-third of the butter in a large saucepan until they are tender and translucent, but not brown. Add the liquid from the mussels and the wine and put in the pieces of fish, which should be just covered by the liquid (add water if necessary). Simmer gently for 5–8 minutes until the fish is just cooked.

Work the flour into the remaining butter and add it to the simmering liquid, letting it dissolve and thicken the liquid—it takes 3–4 minutes. Add the parsley, shrimps, shelled mussels and, if you think it needs it, the lemon juice and a seasoning of salt and pepper. Simmer for a few more seconds, just long enough to get the shellfish piping hot without cooking them any longer or they will be tough. Serve in a big tureen with plenty of bread or with croûtons fried in butter.

ALTERNATIVES: *this rich stew can also be made with a mixture of either sea fish or freshwater fish, or with a single kind of fish such as carp, goosefish or eel. In most recipes the fish is cooked in either red or white wine, with onions, and thickened with beurre manié.*

*Matelote normande*

# Cod poached whole

*1 cod, about 7 lb/3 kg*

*few strands of saffron (optional)*

**for the court bouillon:**

*fish bones*

*1 onion*

*4 carrots*

*few sprigs of parsley and a sprig of thyme*

*1 bay leaf*

*2 tablespoons salt*

SERVES 8–10

To make the court bouillon, put the fish bones, the peeled onion, carrots, parsley, thyme and bay leaf into a large saucepan with 5 quarts/4.5 liters very well-salted water and bring to the boil. Simmer for 20 minutes. Remove from the heat and allow to cool to room temperature.

If you are using saffron, put a few strands into the cod's belly. Make two straps of silver foil by folding two 18 in/45 cm square sheets into 2 in/5 cm strips. Place the straps in the pan of court bouillon, lay the fish on top of them and join the strap ends at the top. These are for helping to lift the fish out in one piece when cooked.

Bring the court bouillon slowly to boiling point, turn down the heat until the water is merely swirling, not bubbling at all, and cook at the barest simmer for about 25 minutes. A knife inserted at the thickest part of the fish behind the head should show that there is no trace of pink next to the bone. Serve with new potatoes, young carrots, small beets, green beans and aïoli, or with hard-boiled eggs, potatoes, carrots and butter.

---

# Fish cakes

*¾ lb/340 g cooked cod fish, flaked*

*3 tablespoons/45 g butter*

*⅜ cup/45 g flour*

*scant ⅔ cup/1.5 dl milk*

*2 hard-boiled eggs, chopped*

*juice of ¼ lemon*

*salt and freshly ground pepper*

*egg, bread crumbs and oil for frying*

SERVES 4

Make a very thick sauce with the butter, flour and milk, or milk and cooking liquid from the fish. Stir into it the flaked fish and chopped hard-boiled eggs and add a good squeeze of lemon juice. The mixture must be thick enough to be formed into shapes when it is cold. Season with salt and pepper, spread the mixture about ½ in/1 cm thick on an oiled plate and allow it to get cold.

When it is set, cut in 1 in/2.5 cm squares and form these into the shape you like the best—either small flat cakes or cork shapes are the most traditional—and egg and crumb them. Heat ½ in/1 cm of oil in a large frying pan and fry the fish cakes, turning them once, until a deep golden brown all over. Drain briefly on paper towels and serve very hot with a delicate tomato sauce, or without sauce if they are for breakfast.

ALTERNATIVES: *haddock, or any cooked white fish.*

---

# Fish pie

*¾ lb/340 g fillet of fresh haddock*

*1 small whole smoked haddock, about 1 lb/450 g*

*⅔ cup/1.5 dl milk*

*1 bay leaf*

*2 lb/900 g potatoes*

*butter and milk for mashing*

*4 hard-boiled eggs*

*½ stick/55 g butter*

*2 tablespoons/15 g flour*

*3–4 sprigs fresh tarragon or parsley, chopped*

*salt and freshly ground pepper*

SERVES 4–6

Preheat the oven to 325°F/170°C.

Put both kinds of fish into a baking dish or roasting pan with the milk, ½ cup/1.5 dl water and bay leaf and poach in the oven for 15 minutes. The fish should be just cooked, with a creamy liquid coming to the surface.

Meanwhile, peel the potatoes and start them cooking in salted water.

Turn the oven up to 425°F/220°C, alternatively, heat the broiler.

Flake the fish, taking care to remove the skin and all the bones. Melt half of the butter in a small pan, stir in the flour and make a sauce with the liquid in which the fish was cooked. Drain the potatoes, using some of their liquid to make the sauce the consistency of thick cream. Taste it to see if it needs more salt—it probably won't. Put the fish and the hard-boiled eggs, peeled and chopped, and the tarragon or parsley into the sauce. Mash the potatoes and season well.

Put the fish mixture into a pie dish or gratin dish, cover it with a nice even layer of mashed potatoes, dot the top with thin slivers of butter and either bake for 15–20 minutes until nicely browned, or brown it under the broiler.

ALTERNATIVES: *cod, hake, halibut.*

## Baked sea bass

| |
|---|
| *1 sea bass, about 2 lb/900 g* |
| *3 cloves garlic* |
| *½ lemon or few sprigs of parsley* |
| *2 small onions* |
| *2–3 tomatoes* |
| *4 tablespoons olive oil* |
| *salt and freshly ground pepper* |
| *few sticks and leaves of fennel* |

SERVES 4

Preheat the oven to 325°F/170°C.

Clean, trim and scale the fish, and pat dry. With a sharp, pointed knife make 2 or 3 deep diagonal slashes on either side of the fish. In each slash wedge half a clove of garlic and either half a slice of lemon, peel side outwards, or a sprig of parsley. Put another half clove of garlic in the head and another in the belly. Peel and slice the onions and skin and quarter the tomatoes.

In a buttered ovenproof dish, surround the prepared fish with the tomatoes and onions. Sprinkle with oil, salt and pepper and bake near the bottom of a gentle oven for half an hour. Scatter sticks and leaves of fennel over the fish and bake for a further 15 minutes, or until cooked through. Serve hot with steamed young vegetables, or cold with a garlicky homemade tomato sauce.

ALTERNATIVES: *red or striped mullet, red snapper, porgy or grouper.*

## Fish pipérade

| |
|---|
| *4 small fillets or slices of porgy, each weighing about 4–6 oz/115–170 g* |
| *2 onions* |
| *3 tablespoons olive oil* |
| *2 red or yellow sweet peppers* |
| *2 cloves garlic* |
| *2–3 tomatoes* |
| *salt and freshly ground pepper* |
| *12 black olives* |

SERVES 4

Preheat the oven to 350°F/180°C.

Peel and slice the onions and sweat them in 2 tablespoons of the olive oil in a saucepan. Slice the peppers into strips, removing the seeds, peel and chop the cloves of garlic and skin and roughly chop the tomatoes. When the onions are tender, add the peppers and garlic and let them cook gently with the onions for 10 minutes. Add the tomatoes and season with salt and pepper, and simmer the mixture until the liquid from the tomatoes has evaporated enough to give a good thick sauce.

Meanwhile, heat the remaining tablespoon of oil in a frying pan and fry the pieces of fish, seasoned with salt and pepper, until they are lightly browned all over. Transfer them to an oval gratin dish. When the pipérade is ready, spoon it over the top of the fish and bake for 15 minutes or until it is heated right through.

Put the olives on top a few minutes before the dish is cooked and sprinkle a little fresh olive oil over the onions, peppers and tomatoes.

ALTERNATIVES: *turbot, cod, haddock, hake, sea bass, grouper.*

## Broiled mackerel

| |
|---|
| *4 mackerel, 8–10 in/20–25 cm long* |
| *2 tablespoons olive oil* |

SERVES 4

Heat the broiler for 10 minutes.

Carefully open out the mackerel and remove their backbones. Brush them lightly with oil and lay them on the hot grill rack, opened side upwards. Broil for 10–15 minutes until the flesh is a nice golden brown and the mackerel are cooked right through. Remove carefully to a heated serving dish and serve the mackerel immediately, very hot, with mustard sauce.

ALTERNATIVES: *bluefish. Instead of the mustard sauce, serve the broiled bluefish or the mackerel with maître d'hôtel butter or gooseberry sauce.*

## Herrings in oatmeal

| |
|---|
| 4 boned herrings |
| 1 egg |
| oatmeal for coating, either fine oatmeal or rolled oats |
| salt |
| lard or butter for frying |
| 1 lemon/(optional) |

SERVES 4

Beat the egg, mix the oats with salt and dip the herrings, joined at the stomach like kippers, first in the egg and then in the lightly salted oatmeal. Pat this on to make a good coating. Fry in hot lard or butter for about 8 minutes on each side. Herrings are much nicer overcooked than undercooked, so fry them until they are very crisp and brown. Keep them hot in the oven on paper towels if you need to, and serve them with lemon quarters, mustard or mustard sauce.

Traditionally, herrings in oatmeal are prepared without the egg so that the oatmeal absorbs the oil from the fish, but the egg makes them crisper and a little more delicate in flavor.

ALTERNATIVES: *mackerel, porgy.*

## Fried sardines with lemon

| |
|---|
| 1½ lb/700 g small sardines |
| 2 lemons |
| fine salt |
| 4–5 tablespoons olive oil |
| 1 loaf fresh bread |

SERVES 4 AS A FIRST COURSE

Scale and gut the sardines. Quarter one lemon and put it on a plate. Cut the other lemon in half and squeeze the juice all over both sides of the sardines. Allow to dry out for half an hour. Sprinkle with salt. Heat the oil in a large frying pan until it starts to smoke, and throw in the sardines. Stand well back and wear an apron as the fat will spit. After 2–3 minutes, turn the sardines carefully with a spatula and cook for another 2 minutes.

Remove the sardines to a dish lined with paper towels, then remove the paper and serve the sardines with the quartered lemon and chunks of fresh bread.

ALTERNATIVES: *fresh anchovies, sprats, smelts, young herrings, silversides.*

## Whitebait

| |
|---|
| 1 lb/450 g whitebait, fresh or frozen |
| oil for frying |
| ⅔ cup/1.5 dl milk |
| ¾ cup/85 g seasoned flour |
| 2 lemons |

SERVES 4

If the whitebait are frozen, let them thaw out. Heat the oil in a deep-frying pan. Dip the fish in milk, drain and then shake them, a few at a time, in a paper bag with flour in it. Deep fry, still a few at a time, until golden and crisp—they take about 2–3 minutes. Drain well and serve immediately in a rustling mound with halved lemons and fresh bread and butter.

ALTERNATIVE: *any small fry under 2 in/5 cm long.*

## Broiled tuna

| |
|---|
| 2 lb/900 g fresh tuna steak |
| 4 anchovy fillets in oil |
| 6 tablespoons olive oil |
| 6 tablespoons lemon juice |
| 1 teaspoon chopped marjoram |
| salt |

SERVES 4

Lard the tuna by cutting a few slits in the flesh and pushing anchovies into the slits. Marinate for about an hour, or longer if you have the time, in oil and lemon juice, which helps prevent the tuna drying out during cooking.

Heat the broiler.

When ready to cook, shake the tuna to remove most of the marinade and sprinkle it with marjoram and salt. Broil on kitchen foil under high heat for 7–8 minutes each side, basting with oil and lemon juice from time to time. A very thick piece will need longer. Serve very hot with hot, fresh tomato sauce.

ALTERNATIVES: *bonito, swordfish, sailfish, marlin.*

## Skate au beurre noir

| |
|---|
| 4 wings of skate |
| 2½ quarts/2.25 liters court bouillon |
| ½ stick/55 g butter |

*1 teaspoon wine vinegar*

*salt and freshly ground pepper*

*1 teaspoon chopped parsley*

SERVES 4

Blanch the wings of skate by dropping them into a pan of boiling water and letting them cook for 7 minutes. Remove the fish carefully, drain well and take off the skin.

Bring the court bouillon to simmering point, put in the pieces of skate and bring back to simmering point. Cover the pan, turn off the heat and leave the skate to cook in the retained heat for 15 minutes. Remove, drain and keep hot on a serving dish.

Heat the butter in a small frying pan until it stops sizzling and turns a hazelnut brown. Pour in the vinegar and season with salt and pepper. Add the parsley and pour the mixture over the skate.

ALTERNATIVE: *add capers to the browned butter.*

---

## *Striped mullet with fennel*

*2 medium-size striped mullet*

*salt*

*½ lemon*

*handful of dried fennel twigs*

*a little olive oil*

*4 tablespoons Pernod or anis (optional)*

SERVES 4

Heat the broiler to moderate heat.

Clean the fish, leaving their heads on. Season them inside and out with salt and slash their sides in 2 or 3 places. Slice the lemon, cut each slice into 4 pieces and push a piece into each of the cuts in the fish. Put the remaining pieces of lemon and a few of the twigs inside the fish.

Put the rest of the fennel in an earthenware baking dish, lay the fish on top and sprinkle all over with olive oil. Broil for 5 minutes.

Preheat the oven to 375°F/190°C.

Bake the fish for 20 minutes, after which they should be white and succulent under their slightly crisp skin, with a wonderful ozone flavor. You can cook them entirely in the broiler if you prefer, but the top becomes a little dry and the underneath wet. Some people like to flame the fish in a little heated Pernod or anis after they have been in the broiler. This increases the fennel flavor.

ALTERNATIVES: *red mullet, red snapper.*

## *Red mullet en papillote*

*4 small mullet, about ½ lb/225 g each (the livers can be left in)*

*salt and freshly ground pepper*

*2–3 shallots*

*¼ lb/115 g button mushrooms*

*squeeze of lemon juice*

*2 tablespoons/30 g butter*

*1 tablespoon chopped parsley*

SERVES 4

Preheat the oven to 350°F/180°C.

Season the fish both inside and out with salt and pepper to taste.

Make a duxelles: chop the shallots and mushrooms finely and sprinkle the mushrooms with a little lemon juice to keep them white. Melt the butter in a small pan, add the shallots and mushrooms and stir over a moderate heat until the liquid which exudes from the mushrooms has evaporated and the mixture is rather dry. Season with salt and pepper and stir in the chopped parsley.

Keep on one side.

Cut four large (about 10 in/25 cm) rounds of foil or cooking parchment—place the fish on the paper to

*Red mullet en papillote*

get the right size. Brush the paper with butter, leaving the borders unbuttered. Slash the sides of the fish to help them cook quickly. Place some of the duxelles on half the buttered side of each round of paper, place a fish on top and cover with more duxelles. Fold the paper over the fish and pleat the edges together twice to seal them. Place on a baking sheet and cook for 10–15 minutes, or longer if the fish are large. Serve the fish unadorned, or with velouté sauce into which you can stir any duxelles which may be left over.

---

# Baked stuffed pompano

| | |
|---|---|
| 1 pompano, about 2 lb/900 g | |
| ¾ stick/85 g butter | |
| 6–8 tablespoons/55 g white bread crumbs | |
| 2 tablespoons milk | |
| 2 egg yolks | |
| 1 tablespoon chopped tarragon and chives | |
| salt and freshly ground pepper | |
| ⅔ cup/1.5 dl white wine | |
| 3 tablespoons heavy cream | |
| 2 teaspoons chopped parsley | |

SERVES 4

Preheat the oven to 325°F/170°C.
Without removing the head, carefully cut the fish along the backbone and remove the backbone. To make the stuffing, soften two-thirds of the butter, soak the bread crumbs in the milk and squeeze them dry, and combine them with the butter, egg yolks, tarragon and chives and a seasoning of salt and pepper. Stuff the fish along the back where the bone has been taken out and carefully sew it up.
Put the fish in a very well-oiled baking dish, pour the wine over it, sprinkle with salt and pepper, dot with the remaining butter and bake for 25–30 minutes. Test to see if it is cooked by pushing the tip of your finger into the thickest part of the fish. If it yields, it is cooked. Transfer it carefully to a serving dish and keep it hot while you make the sauce.
Bring the fish cooking juices to the boil and let them reduce to about half. Add the cream, parsley and a little salt, and boil until slightly thick and syrupy. Pour the sauce around and over the fish and serve at once.
ALTERNATIVES: *sea bass or porgy, grouper, red snapper, trout, or any whole non-oily fish.*

# Mediterranean swordfish

| | |
|---|---|
| 1½–2 lb/700–900 g swordfish | |
| 4 onions | |
| 1 lb/450 g tomatoes | |
| 2 cloves garlic | |
| 4–5 tablespoons olive oil | |
| ½ teaspoon dried or 1 teaspoon fresh chopped oregano | |
| salt and freshly ground pepper | |
| 4 slices white bread | |

**for the marinade:**
| | |
|---|---|
| 2 tablespoons olive oil | |
| 1 tablespoon white wine | |
| few sprigs of thyme | |

SERVES 4

Trim the fish of any skin and cut it into pieces about 2 in/5 cm long. Put the pieces in a bowl with the oil, wine and thyme and let them absorb the marinade for 1–2 hours, turning the pieces from time to time. Preheat the oven to 375°F/190°C.
Peel and slice or chop the onions, skin and chop the tomatoes and chop and crush the garlic. Heat a little of the oil in a pan and soften the onions, then add the tomatoes, garlic and oregano, and season with salt and pepper. Put the pieces of fish, together with the marinade, in an ovenproof dish, pour the sauce over them, mix it around and bake for half an hour.
Cut the sliced bread into triangles and fry them in the remaining oil, arrange them around the cooked fish and serve.
ALTERNATIVES: *sea robin or Northern pike.*

---

# Coulibiac

| | |
|---|---|
| 1½ lb/700 g fresh salmon | |
| 1 stick/115 g butter | |
| ⅓ cup/55 g very fine Chinese rice vermicelli (use rice if you cannot obtain the vermicelli) | |
| 1 large onion | |
| ½ lb/225 g very white button mushrooms | |
| 3 hard-boiled eggs | |
| handful of chopped parsley | |
| flaky pastry made with 4 cups/450 g flour | |
| egg for brushing the pastry | |

SERVES 6–8

Skin, trim and bone the salmon and cut it into cubes. Melt three-quarters of the butter and coat the salmon with it. Put aside to cool and set. Cook the

217

vermicelli in boiling salted water until tender, drain and chop it and set aside to cool. Chop the onion finely and sauté gently in the remaining butter until soft. Chop the mushrooms and add them to the onion (peel the mushrooms if their skins are not very white—this onion and mushroom mixture should be as pale as possible). Allow the mixture to cool while you chop the hard-boiled eggs and mix them with the chopped parsley. Season well. Preheat the oven to 400°F/200°C.

Roll out the pastry into a large oblong about 16 × 12 in/40 × 30 cm. Trim off the thick edges and roll out a small oblong from the trimmings. Lay the large piece on a greased baking sheet, spread the salmon pieces down the middle, put the chopped vermicelli on top, then the mushroom and onion mixture and finally the egg and parsley mixture. Brush one side of the small oblong of pastry with beaten egg and lay it egg side down on top of the filling, bringing the sides of the large piece of pastry up and pinching them together to form an oblong case. Decorate with fish shapes made from pastry trimmings, make a small hole in the center and brush with egg. Bake for 30–35 minutes.

Pour a couple of tablespoons of melted butter into the hole in the top of the pie and serve hot, or set aside to cool—this very grand Russian dish is as delicious cold as hot. Serve coulibiac with a fresh green salad.

ALTERNATIVES: *sturgeon or freshwater salmon trout.*

---

## Salmon scallops

| |
|---|
| ¾ lb/340 g tail of salmon |
| salt and freshly ground white pepper |
| ½ lb/225 g white button mushrooms |
| juice of ½ lemon |
| 2 tablespoons/30 g butter |
| ⅔ cup/1.5 dl heavy cream |
| 12 fresh tarragon leaves (optional) |

SERVES 4

Cut the salmon into 4 scallops and season on both sides with salt and pepper. Wash the mushrooms, slice them very finely and then sprinkle with the lemon juice.

Melt the butter in a frying pan large enough to take all the scallops side by side. Put in the mushrooms and let them cook gently without browning

for 4–5 minutes, stirring them from time to time. Pour in the cream, season with salt and pepper, add the tarragon, if using, and allow to cook gently for 2–3 minutes. Place the seasoned scallops on top and let them cook extremely gently for about 2 minutes on each side. Lift them out carefully and put them on a heated plate. Taste the sauce for seasoning, spoon it delicately over the salmon and serve with boiled new potatoes.

---

## Poached salmon

| |
|---|
| 1 salmon, about 3–3½ lb/1.5–2 kg |
| 5 quarts/4.5 liters court bouillon |
| 2 glasses white wine |

SERVES 6–8

Clean the salmon, remove the gills and wipe with a paper towel to remove any blood. With the court bouillon at a lukewarm temperature, add the white wine. Slide in the fish and bring the liquid, which should just cover the fish, up to simmering point. From this point it should simmer gently for 5–6 minutes per 1 lb/450 g (a smaller fish needs a shorter cooking time). Never let the liquid boil.

Lift the fish out and let it stand on a rack, covered with a clean cloth, over the hot liquid for 5 minutes to drain and set. Serve hot with hollandaise, new potatoes and peas, or cold with mayonnaise.

ALTERNATIVES: *salmon trout, char, pike, perch.*

---

## Truite au bleu

| |
|---|
| 4 fresh trout |
| 6 tablespoons wine vinegar |
| 1 tablespoon salt |

SERVES 4

Bring 2½ quarts/2.25 liters of water to the boil with the vinegar and salt.

Meanwhile, if the trout are alive bang them on the head with a knife-sharpening steel or other heavy implement. Clean them carefully and remove their gills, but do not wash or wipe them, and handle them as gently and carefully as possible so that the natural coating on the skin is not disturbed. Slip them into the boiling water and simmer for 5–10 minutes, according to their size, until cooked. Drain well and place on a folded white napkin. Serve with melted butter or beurre blanc.

This recipe is most valuable to those who can obtain freshly caught trout with their skin still covered with a smooth natural slime, which turns a delicate cloudy blue in the cooking process. However, ordinary store-bought trout are also excellent cooked this way, although they will not be the same lovely color.

# Trout in white wine aspic

6 trout
2 onions
¼ lb/115 g carrots
2 sticks celery
a bottle of dry white wine
24 black peppercorns
bunch of parsley
salt
1 egg white
1 tablespoon/7 g gelatine
sliced cucumber, sliced carrot, or fresh tarragon for garnish

SERVES 6

Peel and slice the onions and carrots and chop the celery. In a wide, covered pan bring to the boil the wine, 1¼ cups/3 dl water, vegetables, peppercorns, parsley and a reasonable amount of salt (bearing in mind that this liquid will be reduced later). Simmer for 20 minutes.

Put in the cleaned trout, their tails neatly trimmed with scissors, and poach them gently for 10 minutes. Turn them over and allow them to cool in their liquid. At this point you can serve them straight from the liquid, or put them in the refrigerator to get very cold and then serve them in their own gelatine, which makes an extremely pretty party dish.

To make the aspic, strain the cooking liquid, bring it to the boil and let it reduce to about 2½ cups/6 dl. Clarify it with an egg white. Soften the gelatine in 2 tablespoons cold water and stir it in—it will now be a beautiful pale topaz color. Let it cool, and when it is syrupy but not set, glaze the trout with it. Keep chilled, and when the remaining aspic has set, chop it, and place it around the trout. Garnish with sliced cucumber, carrot or fresh tarragon.

# Carp with thyme stuffing

1 carp, about 2–2½ lb/900 g–1 kg
2 tablespoons/30 g butter for basting
4 tablespoons heavy cream

**for the stuffing:**

1 onion
½ stick/55 g butter
½ cup/55 g fresh white bread crumbs
½ teaspoon chopped thyme
1 teaspoon chopped parsley
1 teaspoon grated lemon rind
salt and freshly ground pepper

SERVES 4

Ask the fish seller to scale the carp and cut off its head so that it can be gutted without opening the stomach. Keep the head. Make certain that the inside is very well cleaned and washed out.

Preheat the oven to 350°F/180°C.

To prepare the stuffing, chop the onion finely and sweat it in the butter in a small frying pan, without letting it brown. Stir in the bread crumbs, thyme, parsley and lemon rind and season with salt and pepper. Stuff the fish with this mixture and put it in a buttered baking dish. Put the head back in place, dot the carp with butter and bake for 20 minutes, basting it from time to time. Add the cream and bake for another 10 minutes. Serve with buttered potatoes and quarters of lemon.

ALTERNATIVES: *shad, grayling or bluegill.*

# Pike quenelles or mousselines

¾ lb/340 g pike
3 slices day-old white bread, crusts removed
4 tablespoons light cream
1¼ sticks/140 g butter
2 eggs and 1 extra egg white
salt and freshly ground white pepper
pinch of nutmeg
1¼ cups/3 dl velouté sauce, delicate tomato sauce or sauce vouvrillonne

SERVES 4

Skin and bone the fish and cut it into small cubes. Soak the bread in the cream, drain it and squeeze out most of the liquid. Crumble it into a small saucepan, add a nut of the butter and stir over a low heat until it forms a smooth mixture which leaves the sides of the pan. Remove from the heat and cool. Put the fish, eggs and the bread mixture (*panade*) into a blender and reduce to a smooth purée, or grind the ingredients and pound them together using a pestle and mortar. Melt the remaining butter and, if you are using a blender, pour it into the other ingredients in a thin stream, letting the machine run slowly until you have a soft, fine, white purée. If you are using a pestle and mortar, pound the butter into the fish mixture a little at a time. Season with salt, pepper and a little nutmeg.

The mixture can now be either chilled in the refrigerator for at least an hour and then shaped for poaching or, for mousselines, cooked in the oven in little ovenproof cocottes. Quenelles are bothersome but give a slightly lighter result; mousselines are decidedly quicker but nonetheless extremely good.

FOR QUENELLES: Use two spoons to mold the mixture, which is very soft, into little torpedo shapes about 3 in/8 cm long. Put these onto a very lightly floured plate and chill thoroughly, or freeze them briefly to firm them up.

Preheat the oven to 375°F/190°C, or, if you are in a hurry, heat the broiler.

Meanwhile, bring a broad, shallow pan, ideally a sauté pan, of salted water to the boil. Turn down the heat until the water is gently simmering and poach the quenelles for 6 minutes, turning them over halfway through. Remove them carefully with a slotted spoon into a heated gratin dish, cover with velouté sauce and bake in the oven until lightly glazed, or glaze to a golden brown in the broiler.

FOR MOUSSELINES: Preheat the oven to 325°F/170°C. Brush the insides of 8 individual cocottes with butter and fill them two-thirds full with the fish purée. Put the cocottes in a bain-marie or stand them in a roasting pan half-filled with boiling water, cover loosely with a sheet of foil and bake for about 30 minutes. The mousselines are ready when they are just set in the center. To serve, fill each cocotte to the brim with velouté or delicate tomato sauce.

ALTERNATIVES: *whiting, goosefish, halibut, turbot, red mullet, hake, flounder, sole.*

---

# Soused herrings

| |
|---|
| 6 plump herrings, each about ½ lb/225 g |
| 1¼–2 cups/3–4.5 dl each cider vinegar and hard cider |
| 2 bay leaves |
| 4 sprigs thyme |
| 12 black peppercorns |
| 6 allspice berries |
| 4 cloves |
| 2 blades mace |

*Soused herrings*

*salt and cayenne pepper*

*fresh fennel for garnish*

**SERVES 6**

Preheat the oven to 350°F/180°C.

Scale and gut the herrings, cut off the heads and fins and trim the tails. If they have roes with them, put them back inside the fish.

Lay the herrings in an earthenware or enamelled iron pie dish or gratin dish and cover with the vinegar and cider (the amount of liquid needed depends on the size and shape of the dish used). Push the herbs and spices in among the fish and season with salt and cayenne. Cover the dish with a sheet of foil and stand it in a bain-marie or a large roasting pan. Pour in enough boiling water to come halfway up the gratin or pie dish and bake for 30 minutes. Allow to cool and garnish with fresh fennel. Eat soused herrings within a day or two.

---

# Bacalao con patatas

*1 lb/450 g salt cod, soaked for 24 hours in 2–3 changes of cold water*

*flour for coating*

*2–3 tablespoons olive oil*

*1 lb/450 g onions*

*2 lb/900 g potatoes*

*4 tomatoes*

*1 clove garlic*

*1 tablespoon chopped parsley*

*salt and freshly ground white pepper*

*good pinch of saffron*

**SERVES 4**

Put the cod into fresh cold water in a frying pan or saucepan and bring it slowly to the boil. Remove it from the heat and allow to cool in its cooking liquid. Cut it into squares, roll the squares in flour and fry them in olive oil in a flameproof casserole. Remove them to a hot plate.

Peel and slice the onions and potatoes, skin the tomatoes, peel and chop the garlic and put them all into the same oil in which the fish was cooked. Stir them over a gentle heat for a minute or two, then add the parsley and enough boiling water to cover. Add a pinch of salt, if needed, cover the dish and simmer until the potatoes are almost cooked. Put in the pieces of cod and the saffron, season with white pepper and simmer for another 10 minutes.

# Creamed finnan haddie

*¾ lb/340 g smoked haddock, preferably on the bone*

*2 tablespoons/30 g butter*

*2 tablespoons/15 g flour*

*⅔ cup/1.5 dl milk*

*1 hard-boiled egg*

*⅔ cup/1.5 dl light cream*

*salt, if needed*

*cayenne pepper*

**SERVES 4**

Preheat the oven to 350°F/180°C.

Poach the haddock in water in a baking dish or an oval gratin dish for 15 minutes. Meanwhile, melt the butter in a saucepan and stir in the flour. Let it cook for 2 minutes over a low heat, then gradually add the milk, stirring all the time, to make a smooth sauce. Let it simmer, covered, while you strip all the flesh from the skin and bones of the haddock and chop the hard-boiled egg. Add the flaked fish, the chopped egg and the cream to the sauce. Heat through, taste the mixture, add salt if necessary and a sprinkling of cayenne.

Serve the creamed finnan haddie on hot toast.

# Taramasalata

*6 oz/170 g salted grey mullet roe or smoked cod's roe, preferably fresh*

*2 thick slices white bread, crusts removed*

*1 large clove garlic*

*juice of 1½ lemons*

*8 tablespoons olive oil*

*cayenne pepper*

**SERVES 4**

If using fresh roes, split them open down one side and scrape out the soft pink part inside. Soak the bread in a little water so that it is moist but not wet and crumble it. Peel and chop the garlic.

Liquidize the roe, bread, garlic and lemon juice in a food processor and reduce to a purée.

Add all but half a tablespoon of the oil alternately with 2–3 tablespoons of cold water. When you have a smooth, light purée, taste and add more garlic or lemon juice if necessary. Transfer the mixture to a bowl and pour the remaining olive oil on top. Sprinkle with cayenne and serve with hot pita bread and radishes or black olives.

## Dressed crab

*1 large crab weighing 3 lb/1.5 kg or 2 small crabs*
*weighing 2 lb/900 g each*

*salt and freshly ground pepper*

*1 teaspoon dried bread crumbs*

*½ teaspoon hot mustard*

*cayenne pepper*

*1 lemon or ⅔ cup/1.5 dl mayonnaise*

SERVES 4

Pick the crab, putting the white meat and the brown into separate bowls. Season the white meat lightly with salt and pepper. Mix the brown meat with the bread crumbs, mashing it well with a fork. Add the mustard, a little salt and cayenne pepper and mix well. Arrange the white meat around the brown and serve with quarters of lemon or, for a richer dish, with mayonnaise, and dark bread and butter.

## Broiled lobster with butter

*2 live lobsters, each weighing about 1½–2 lb/700–900 g*

*3 tablespoons olive oil*

*salt*

*pinch of cayenne pepper*

*1 stick/115 g butter*

SERVES 4

Heat the broiler.

Cut the lobsters in half, clean them and lay them, cut side up, in a roasting pan. Brush liberally with oil, season with salt and cayenne pepper and broil for 5 minutes, then turn the halves and broil on the shell side for 5 minutes more. Meanwhile, melt the butter. Turn the halves of the lobsters over again and spoon some of the butter over the top. Broil for a further 8–10 minutes, pouring on more butter every 2–3 minutes.

Serve immediately with the melted butter from the pan poured over the top.

## Boiled lobster

*1 live lobster, weighing about 1½–2 lb/700–900 g*

*1 onion, finely sliced*

*1 or 2 carrots, finely sliced*

*4–5 parsley stalks*

*1 large glass white wine*

*1 tablespoon salt*

*6 black peppercorns*

SERVES 2

Put everything except the lobster into a large pan. Bring 2 quarts/1.75 liters of water to the boil and let it boil rapidly for 10 minutes, then plunge in the lobster head first. Cover the pan and hold the lid on tightly. Return the water to the boil as rapidly as possible and then turn down the heat and simmer the lobster for 15 minutes, by which time it will be a marvellous brick red, then lift it out and split it in half. Discard the gills and intestinal canal. Serve with melted butter.

## Crayfish cooked with dill

*24 live crayfish*

*12 large sprigs fresh dill and ½ tablespoon dill seeds*

*1 tablespoon/15 g salt*

SERVES 2

Leave the crayfish in a bowl under cold running water for 1 hour.

Put 5 cups/1 liter of water, 6 sprigs of dill, the dill seeds and salt into a saucepan and bring them to the boil. Simmer for 10 minutes, then turn up the heat until the water is boiling rapidly. Drop in the crayfish, bring the water back to the boil, cover and cook gently for 4 minutes. Remove the crayfish, which will have turned a brilliant cardinal red, with a slotted spoon and strain the liquid into a bowl. Let it cool, then put in 4 of the remaining sprigs of dill and the cooked crayfish. Let them soak in this liquid overnight. Remove, drain and serve the crayfish piled up in a pyramid, decorating the top with fresh dill.

## Broiled butterfly shrimp

*2 lb/900 g large raw shrimps or Dublin Bay prawns*
*in their shells*

*salt and freshly ground pepper*

*juice of 1 lemon and 4 tablespoons olive oil*

SERVES 4

Heat the broiler.

Lay the shrimps in their shells on their backs and

slice them in half, cutting from head to tail, but avoid piercing the shell along the back. Open each shrimp out like a butterfly. They can then be de-veined—the dark thread of the intestine is easily pulled away with the fingers. Season the exposed flesh with a little salt and pepper. Whisk the lemon juice and oil together with a fork and brush the shrimps all over with half this mixture. Thread them onto skewers, keeping them flat, and broil for 3 minutes on each side, brushing each side with more oil and lemon after 2 minutes. Serve very hot and eat with your fingers, not forgetting to eat the soft tomalley in their heads.

For a barbecue, grill the shrimps over wood embers or charcoal.

---

## Scampi en brochette

*1 lb/450 g large shrimps or Dublin Bay prawns*
*handful of fresh mint leaves*
*1 stick/115 g butter*
*juice of ½ lemon*
*large pinch of cayenne pepper*
*salt*

SERVES 2

Heat the broiler.

Shell the shrimps and thread them onto skewers, alternating them with the mint leaves and finishing with a shrimp. Put them in a broiler pan without the rack. Melt the butter in a small pan with the lemon juice, cayenne and salt. Pour some of the butter over the brochettes and broil for a few minutes. basting well with the juices and turning once or twice. Remove the brochettes. Add a little chopped mint and a sprinkling of cayenne to the remaining butter, pour this flavored butter over the brochettes and serve immediately.

---

## Scampi in cream and wine

*1 lb/450 g shelled large shrimps or Dublin Bay prawns*
*½ lb/225 g button mushrooms*
*few drops of lemon juice*
*¾ stick/85 g butter*
*sprinkling of flour*
*salt and freshly ground pepper*
*1 small glass dry white wine, preferably Meursault*
*3 tablespoons light cream*

SERVES 4

Drain any water off the shrimps and pat them dry. Wash and dry the mushrooms and sprinkle them with a few drops of lemon juice. Melt half the butter in a frying pan. When it is hot, sprinkle the shrimps very lightly with flour and fry them a few at a time until they are just beginning to brown—they only take a minute or so—turning them once. Remove them to a dish and keep hot. Add the remaining butter to the pan and sauté the mushrooms without letting them get too brown—they should be light golden. Remove them to the same dish as the shrimps, season with salt and pepper and keep hot. Add the wine to the frying pan and reduce it to two tablespoons, then add the cream and swill it around. Let it boil until it starts to thicken. Pour this mixture over the shrimps and mushrooms and shake the dish to blend it with the other juices, which will make a thin and delicate sauce. Serve with plain boiled rice.

---

## Potted shrimps

*1¾ lb/800 g shrimps or prawns in their shells or*
*1 lb/450 g shelled shrimps or prawns*
*½ teaspoon ground mace*
*¼ teaspoon cayenne pepper*
*½ teaspoon grated nutmeg*
*salt*
*clarified butter made with 2 sticks/225 g unsalted butter*

SERVES 4

Shell the shrimps or prawns, or if they are already shelled and seem at all wet, drain well and pat them dry with paper towels. Season them lightly with a little of the spices and a pinch of salt. Put two-thirds of the clarified butter in a saucepan with the rest of the spices, add the shrimps or prawns, drained of any liquid they have given off, and heat very gently for a few minutes. Taste for salt and transfer the shrimps or prawns, with their butter, into small cocotte dishes, dividing them equally and packing them in quite tightly. The butter should just come level with the shrimps or prawns, but not entirely obscure them.

When they have set, heat the remaining clarified butter until just melted and pour it over the prawns or shrimps to make an airtight seal. Cover and keep for at least two days before eating to allow the flavor of the shrimps to develop. Serve cool—do not chill—and eat on hot toast as an hors d'oeuvre.

## Grilled prawns in bacon

*16 raw prawns or large shrimps*

*large pinch of cayenne pepper*

*juice of ½ lemon*

*8 slices bacon*

*olive oil for brushing*

*1 lemon, quartered*

SERVES 4

Shell the prawns or shrimps and season with cayenne and a few drops of lemon juice. Light a charcoal grill or barbecue. Flatten and stretch the bacon slices with the flat side of a knife blade so that they are as thin and long as possible. Cut each slice in half across the middle. Wrap half a slice of bacon around each prawn or shrimp, thread 4 at a time onto skewers and brush all over with oil. Grill for 5 minutes, turning frequently. Serve with the lemon.

## Prawn and cucumber curry

*¾ lb/340 g large raw shrimps, or prawns in their shells or ½ lb/225 g fresh or frozen shelled shrimps*

*1 large cucumber*

*5 tablespoons/70 g butter*

*3 cloves garlic*

*1½ in/4 cm piece of fresh ginger*

*1 large onion*

*1 teaspoon turmeric*

*2 teaspoons garam masala*

*1 teaspoon ground cloves and cinnamon, mixed*

*1 teaspoon sugar*

*½ teaspoon salt*

*1 tablespoon flour*

*1¼ cups/3 dl thick coconut milk*

*1¼ cups/3 dl broth made with shrimp heads and shells and a few vegetables, or use chicken stock*

*3 green chili peppers*

*1 tablespoon lemon juice*

SERVES 4

Peel and quarter the cucumber, cut the quarters lengthwise into quarters and then into 2 in/5 cm pieces. Put them into a pan with plenty of salted water and 1 tablespoon/15 g of butter. Simmer for

*Grilled prawns in bacon*

about 5 minutes until half cooked. Strain the cucumber and keep it on one side. If the shrimps are raw, peel them and cook for just a minute in plenty of simmering salted water. Cut each one in half lengthwise.

Peel the garlic and ginger and chop them finely and skin and slice the onion. Put them into a saucepan with the remaining butter and fry them lightly without browning, then stir in the ground spices—the turmeric, garam masala, ground cloves and cinnamon—together with the sugar, salt and, two minutes later, the flour. Then add slowly half the coconut milk and half the stock and toss in the chili peppers, cut in thin strips. Add the shrimps and cucumber and let them marinate in the mixture for half an hour. Then simmer for 10–15 minutes. Add the remaining coconut milk and stock and the lemon juice, simmer 5 minutes and serve with rice.

---

# Prawn or shrimp mayonnaise

| |
|---|
| *1 lb/450 g shelled prawns or shrimps* |
| *2 ripe tomatoes* |
| *large pinch of cayenne pepper* |
| *1 teaspoon finely chopped herbs: parsley, chervil and chives* |
| *1¼ cups/3 dl homemade mayonnaise* |
| *⅔ cup/1.5 dl heavy cream* |
| *salt (optional)* |
| *squeeze of lemon juice (optional)* |
| *few drops of Worcestershire sauce (optional)* |
| *1 teaspoon tomato paste (optional)* |
| *few slices of lemon or few sprigs of chervil* |

SERVES 4

Skin the tomatoes and chop them finely and purée them in a blender or through a wire sieve. If the result is very liquid, cook for 10 minutes in a small saucepan to evaporate some of the liquid, then allow to become completely cold.

Mix the tomatoes, cayenne and herbs into the mayonnaise. Whisk the cream in a chilled bowl until it is a light, soft snow, then fold it carefully into the mayonnaise. Fold in the prawns or shrimps and taste for seasoning—add salt and more cayenne if necessary. For extra flavor add a little lemon juice and Worcestershire sauce. If the sauce is not a good color, mix in a teaspoon of tomato paste diluted with a few drops of water. Pile the mixture into bowls or glasses or serve on plain white plates, decorating each helping with a small slice of lemon or with a little tuft of chervil sprigs, and serve as an hors d'oeuvre.

---

# Oysters Rockefeller

| |
|---|
| *24 oysters, opened and on the half shell* |
| *few handfuls of rock salt* |
| *3 shallots* |
| *1 stick celery* |
| *½ lb/225 g spinach* |
| *1 stick/115 g butter, softened* |
| *1 tablespoon chopped parsley* |
| *½ tablespoon chopped chervil or tarragon* |
| *2 tablespoons fresh white bread crumbs* |
| *1 tablespoon Pernod or pastis* |
| *dash of Tabasco* |
| *dash of Worcestershire sauce* |
| *salt and freshly ground pepper* |

SERVES 4

Preheat the oven to 425°F/220°C.

Scatter a generous layer of rock salt over the bottom of two large roasting pans, making a steady bed on which to set the oysters. Peel and chop the shallots and chop the celery and spinach finely.

Melt a quarter of the butter in a frying pan and stir in the shallots, celery, parsley and chervil or tarragon. Sweat for 3–4 minutes without browning, then add the spinach and let it wilt down. Purée this mixture in a blender or food processor. Add the remaining butter, the bread crumbs, Pernod or pastis, Tabasco and Worcestershire sauce, blend to a smooth purée, then taste and season. Put a tablespoon of the spinach mixture on each oyster, place them firmly on their salt beds and bake for 4–5 minutes until they are just beginning to turn golden brown. Serve on their salt beds.

ALTERNATIVE: *substitute 12 large mussels per person and halve the amount of spinach mixture.*

---

# Fried scallops

| |
|---|
| *8 large or 12 medium-size fresh scallops* |
| *2 cloves garlic* |
| *2 tablespoons/30 g butter* |
| *sprinkling of flour* |

*1 tablespoon chopped parsley*

*juice of ½ lemon*

*salt and freshly ground pepper*

SERVES 4

Prepare the scallops by removing them from their shells if necessary and dry on paper towels. Peel and chop the garlic. Heat the butter in a heavy frying pan and when it turns nut brown dust the scallops quickly with flour and put half of them into the pan. (If you put them all in at once they lower the heat too much and instead of frying they will boil in their own juices.) Add half the garlic and half the parsley and fry briskly for about 2 minutes, turning the scallops over in the butter. When they are brown remove them to a heated dish. Add more butter to the pan if necessary, heat it and fry the rest of the scallops with the remainder of the garlic and parsley. Remove them to the dish, add the lemon juice to the pan, swish it around and pour it over the scallops. Season with salt and pepper and serve very hot.

## *Scallop and mushroom pie*

*12 large scallops*

*½ lb/225 g firm white mushrooms*

*1 lb/450 g potatoes*

*¾ stick/85 g butter*

*salt and freshly ground pepper*

*1 heaping tablespoon flour*

*⅔ cup/1.5 dl milk*

*milk and butter for mashing*

*pinch of nutmeg*

*2–3 tablespoons heavy cream*

SERVES 4

Preheat the oven to 375°F/190°C.

Prepare the scallops if necessary, and dry them. Peel and boil the potatoes. Meanwhile, melt one-third of the butter in a frying pan. Put in the scallops, seasoned with salt and pepper, and sauté them for 2 minutes. In another pan, melt another third of the butter and gently fry the mushrooms, sprinkled with salt and pepper, for 5 minutes. When the scallops and mushrooms are cooked through, put the remaining butter in a separate pan, stir in the flour and make a sauce with the scallop juices and milk. Let the sauce cook while you mash the potatoes with plenty of milk and butter.

Season the sauce with salt, pepper and nutmeg, stir in the cream and add the scallops and mushrooms. Put the mixture in a small pie dish, cover with mashed potatoes, dot with butter and bake for 30 minutes or until lightly browned on top.

## *Moules à la marinière*

*2½ quarts (4 lb)/2 kg mussels*

*3–4 shallots*

*1 onion*

*1¼ cups/3 dl dry white wine or vermouth*

*⅔ cup/1.5 dl heavy cream (optional)*

*salt and freshly ground pepper*

*2 tablespoons finely chopped parsley*

SERVES 4

Clean the mussels carefully. Peel and chop the shallots and onion and put them in a large pan with the wine or vermouth. Boil for 8 minutes, add the mussels, cover the pan and place over a high heat. Allow all the mussels to steam, stirring and turning them over until they have all opened. There will usually be one or two recalcitrant ones that stay firmly shut—discard them if you feel doubtful about them.

Spoon the mussels into a deep bowl. The counsel of perfection is to strain the cooking liquid through a sieve lined with a cloth and placed over a bowl. This is to eliminate sand and grit. However, if the liquid doesn't look particularly sandy, pour it carefully into another pan, leaving any sand and grit behind at the bottom of the first pan. Heat to boiling point, add the cream, if you are using it, heat through, season and then pour over the mussels. Scatter with parsley and serve with spoons for eating the delicious soup in which the mussels were cooked.

ALTERNATIVE: *to make a simpler version use half wine and half water and leave out the cream.*

## *Seafood salad*

*36 mussels*

*8–10 baby squid*

*24 large shrimps, fresh or frozen*

*½ lb/225 g prawns, shelled*

*1 tablespoon lemon juice*

*6–7 tablespoons olive oil*

*½ dried red chili pepper, finely chopped*

*salt and freshly ground pepper*

SERVES 6

Scrub and wash the mussels, put them in a large pan with 1¼ cups/3 dl boiling water and shake them over a moderate heat until they have opened. Scoop the mussels out of the pan with a slotted spoon, reserving their liquid. Clean and wash the squid and cut them into rings, keeping the tentacles whole.

Bring the mussel liquid to the boil, adding a little boiling water if it becomes too scant. Drop in the pieces of squid and let them cook gently for about 1–2 minutes. Remove them quickly, and if you are using raw shrimps or prawns drop them into the same liquid and poach for 3–4 minutes, until tender. Shell the mussels and arrange them, the shrimps and the prawns on a plate with the squid rings and tentacles. Squeeze the lemon juice over the shellfish, then pour on the oil. Scatter the chopped chili pepper over the top and season with salt and pepper.

ALTERNATIVES: *substitute raw mushrooms, finely sliced, for the squid and let the salad marinate for at least 2 hours before serving, add chopped parsley to the salad, or add small clams.*

---

# Squid risotto

*1 lb/450 g small squid*

*2 tomatoes*

*3 cloves garlic*

*1 large onion*

*3 tablespoons olive oil*

*1 tablespoon chopped parsley*

*1 glass white wine*

*1 cup/170 g round Italian rice*

*1 teaspoon tomato paste*

*salt and freshly ground pepper*

SERVES 4

Skin, seed and chop the tomatoes and peel and chop the garlic and onion. Clean the squid, cut it into thick rings and then cut the rings in pieces.

Heat the olive oil in a fairly wide, shallow pan or sauté pan. Sweat the onion in the oil, without browning, then add the garlic and parsley. Fry gently for 1 minute and then add the squid and the tomatoes, turning them over in the oil. Add the wine and a ladleful of water and stew the squid for

30 minutes, covered. Add the rice, another ladleful of water and the tomato paste. Season with salt and pepper. Keep stirring the rice, adding more water as it becomes absorbed. The rice takes about 30 minutes to swell and cook, by which time it is creamy and a marvellous pink-brown color.

---

# Stuffed squid

*12 small squid*

**for the stuffing:**

*1 large onion*

*1–2 tablespoons olive oil*

*2 cloves garlic*

*3 large or 4–5 small tomatoes, skinned*

*salt and freshly ground pepper*

*chunk of bread, the size of a fist, soaked in milk*

*few sprigs of parsley, chopped*

*2 egg yolks*

**for the sauce:**

*1 onion*

*3 tablespoons olive oil*

*1 bay leaf*

*1 clove garlic*

*1 tablespoon flour*

*1 glass of white wine*

*salt and freshly ground pepper*

SERVES 4

Preheat the oven to 325°F/170°C.

Clean the squid, remove the tentacles and put the bodies to drain on paper towels.

To make the stuffing, peel the onion, chop it finely and sweat it in the olive oil. Peel and chop the garlic. Chop the tentacles rather small and add them to the onions. Chop the tomatoes and add them to the mixture, together with salt and pepper. Add the bread, squeezed dry, and the garlic and parsley. Stir well, take off the heat and add the water and egg yolks, to make a thickish stuffing. Taste for seasoning. Stuff the bodies, and skewer the ends shut with toothpicks. Put them in an oiled gratin dish. For the sauce, peel and chop the onion and sweat it in olive oil with the bay leaf and garlic, peeled and crushed. Add the flour and moisten with the white wine and an equal amount of hot water. Season, simmer for 15 minutes and pour it over the stuffed squid. Bake for an hour, basting occasionally.

ALTERNATIVES: *cuttlefish or small octopus.*

# Meat Pies

## Chicken and ham pie

| |
|---|
| *1 chicken weighing 3–3½ lb/1.5–1.75 kg* |
| *1 carrot* |
| *1 onion* |
| *1 stick celery* |
| *bouquet garni of thyme, parsley and a bay leaf* |
| *1 glass white wine* |
| *salt and freshly ground pepper* |
| *1 tablespoon/15 g gelatine* |
| *2 tablespoons chopped parsley* |
| *1 tablespoon chopped chives* |
| *¼ teaspoon grated nutmeg* |
| *grated rind of ¼ lemon* |
| *¾ lb/340 g sliced ham, preferably carved off the bone* |
| *flaky or rough puff pastry made with 2 cups/225 g flour* |
| *1 egg yolk* |

SERVES 6

Put the chicken in a saucepan with the carrot, peeled onion, celery and bouquet garni. Add the glass of wine, cover with water and bring to the boil. Turn down the heat at once, skim the surface and add 1 teaspoon salt. Simmer for 50 minutes until the chicken is just cooked. Allow to cool in the pan. If you don't have time it doesn't matter too much, but it will be more succulent if it cools in its liquid.

When it is cold, remove the meat from the chicken and throw away the bones. Strain the stock and simmer to reduce it to 2½ cups/6 dl, then dissolve the gelatine in about ½ cup of the stock. If necessary stand the cup in a saucepan of simmering water to dissolve the gelatine completely. Add it to the rest of the stock and taste for seasoning.

Put a layer of chicken in a deep pie dish and sprinkle it with some of the herbs, nutmeg and grated lemon rind. Then put in a layer of ham, and fill the dish with alternate layers of chicken and ham, sprinkling each layer with the remaining flavorings and finishing with a layer of ham. Pour in half the warm stock and leave to cool.

Preheat the oven to 425°F/220°C.

Roll the pastry out to about ¼ in/5 mm thick. Brush the edge of the pie dish with a little water and lay a strip of pastry all around the edge. Brush this strip with water and then cover the whole pie with pastry. Brush the top with the egg yolk beaten with a little salt and a tablespoon of water, decorate with leaves and flowers cut from the trimmings and brush again with egg. Make a hole in the center large enough to take the end of a funnel, for when you add more stock to the pie. Bake for 15 minutes then turn the temperature down to 350°F/180°C and bake for a further 25–30 minutes.

When the top of the pie is nicely browned, cover it with foil or dampened wax paper to help prevent it from burning. When the pie is ready, remove it from the oven and pour into it the remaining stock, using a funnel and pitcher. Stop when you can see that the pie is full of liquid. Allow to set in the refrigerator overnight before cutting. The flavor improves if the pie, which is eaten cold, is kept 24 hours before serving.

---

## Pork pie

| |
|---|
| *1½ lb/700 g pork—half belly, half blade or boned shoulder* |
| *3 oz/85 g unsmoked bacon, or salt pork* |
| *salt and freshly ground pepper* |
| *3 chopped sage leaves or ½ teaspoon dried sage* |

**for the jellied stock:**

| |
|---|
| *1 onion* |
| *1 pig's foot* |
| *trimmings from the pork* |
| *1 carrot* |
| *1 stick celery* |
| *salt* |

**for the pastry:**

| |
|---|
| *5 tablespoons/70 g lard* |
| *1 tablespoon/15 g butter* |
| *salt* |
| *⅔ cup/1.5 dl boiling water* |
| *3 cups/340 g flour* |
| *1 egg, separated* |

SERVES 6

First start the jelly. Peel the onion and put it with the pig's foot, pork trimmings, carrot and stick of celery into a saucepan, together with 2 quarts/1.75 liters water; bring it to the boil, skim, and simmer for 2–3 hours. Strain the resulting liquid— you will need 2½ cups/6 dl. If it is too much, reduce it by boiling to approximately the right quantity and then season with salt.

Chop the pork and bacon, or salt pork, either by hand or in a food processor, into little pieces the size of peas. The meat should be chopped rather than ground to keep its succulence. Season generously with salt, pepper and the sage.

Preheat the oven to 350°F/180°C.

To make the pastry, stir the lard and butter and a pinch of salt into the boiling water and boil, stirring, until the fat dissolves. Put the flour in a large bowl and pour in the boiling hot mixture. Mix it with a wooden spoon at first, as it is very hot, and then knead it to a stiff dough with your hands, adding a little more water if necessary. The pastry must be worked while it is hot. It is easiest to make the pie in a mold—a small soufflé dish or cake pan is ideal. Reserve a lump of the pastry to make the lid of the pie, wrapping it in a cloth to keep it warm. Roll out the rest into a large disc and line the mold with it, working it into place with your fingers. Trim the edge, leaving the pastry just hanging over the edge of the mold. Fill the pie with the pork mixture and then roll out the pastry lid. Lightly beat the egg white and use it to stick the lid in place. Decorate the top with flowers and leaves cut from the pastry trimmings and make a small hole in the center.

Bake for an hour, covering the top loosely with kitchen foil when it has turned a nice golden color. When it is cooked, take the pie very carefully out of the mold, brush the top and side with the egg yolk beaten with a few drops of water, and put it back in the oven for 10 minutes or so, to give it a golden glaze. Lastly, insert a small funnel in the hole in the top and pour in enough of the stock to fill the pie. Allow the pie to cool and the jelly to set for 24 hours before eating.

---

## Sausage and mushroom pie

| |
|---|
| 1 lb/450 g sausage meat |
| 1 clove garlic |
| 3–4 sprigs parsley, chopped |
| generous pinch of dried thyme |
| 2 sage leaves, chopped |
| grating of lemon rind |
| salt and freshly ground pepper |
| grating of nutmeg |
| ½ onion |
| ¾ lb/340 g mushrooms |
| 3 tablespoons/45 g butter |
| flaky pastry made with 2 cups/225 g flour |
| 1 egg, beaten |

SERVES 4–5

Peel and crush the garlic and mix it, together with the chopped herbs and lemon rind, into the sausage meat. Season with salt, pepper and nutmeg. Peel and chop the onion finely and slice the mushrooms thinly. Melt the butter in a frying pan and sweat the onion. Add the mushrooms, season, and cook gently until soft. Allow to cool.

Preheat the oven to 425°F/220°C.

Roll out about two-thirds or rather less of the pastry into a rectangle, 12–14 × 8 in/30–35 × 20 cm, and lay it on a greased baking sheet. Take one-third of the sausage meat and pat it out in the middle of the pastry, leaving a margin of about 2½ in/6 cm all around. Place a layer of mushrooms on this and press them in lightly. Spread more sausage meat, more mushrooms and finish with a layer of the sausage mixture. Pat it into a nice even rectangular shape. Bring up the sides of the pastry, folding it over the sausage meat. Cut off any excess at the corners. There should still be a rectangle of sausage meat visible at the top.

Roll out the remaining pastry into a rectangular lid for the pie; cut even parallel slashes in it at ½ in/1 cm intervals, leaving a margin of ½ in/1 cm uncut all the way around. Brush lightly with water, and place it, moist side down, on top of the pie— the filling should just be visible through the slashes. Brush the pie all over with beaten egg. Allow to dry for 10 minutes, then brush a second time. (Forget this if in a hurry, but it helps to stop the pastry breaking up while the pie is in the oven.) Dry for a further 5–10 minutes.

Bake for 15 minutes, then turn down the temperature to 350°F/180°C and continue to bake for a further 30 minutes. The pie will be golden, and the top will have opened out and risen to show the filling. Allow to cool—if possible overnight— before eating, and serve in thickish slices.

---

## Cornish pasties

| |
|---|
| ¾ lb/340 g chuck steak |
| 2 small potatoes |
| 1 small onion |
| salt and freshly ground pepper |
| shortcrust pastry made with 3 cups/340 g flour |

MAKES 8

Trim the steak of all fat and sinews and cut it into

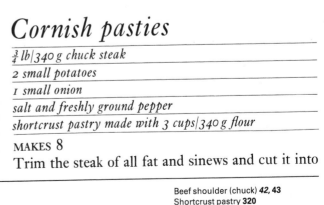

# Game Pie and Pâtés

small pieces, about ¼ in/5 mm across or even a little less. You will need a small very sharp knife to do this with any pleasure. Peel and cut the potatoes into very fine small flakes and peel and chop the onion fairly finely. Mix all these ingredients in a bowl with salt, lots of pepper and a teaspoon or two of water to moisten the mixture.

Preheat the oven to 425°F/220°C.

Roll the pastry fairly thinly, and cut 6 in/15 cm rounds with a saucer and a blunt knife. Put some of the mixture in an oval shape onto the middle of each round, dampen the edges, fold each pasty over and, starting at one end, roll the edges together, pinching them at ½ in/1 cm intervals, to give a rope effect. Pinch the ends to a point. Place the pasties on a greased baking tray and bake for 15 to 20 minutes until nicely browned, then reduce the temperature to 350°F/180°C and continue to bake for 30 minutes more.

---

## Game pie

| 2 pigeons |
| --- |
| 1 pheasant—an older bird will do |
| the legs of a hare or 1 grouse |
| ½ lb/225 g fresh pork belly |
| ¼ lb/115 g salt pork or unsmoked bacon |
| 2 shallots |
| 1 small strip orange peel, blanched in boiling water for 3–4 minutes |
| 6 juniper berries, crushed |
| ½ teaspoon ground allspice |
| ½ teaspoon ground mace |
| 1 small glass port |
| 1 tablespoon brandy |
| salt and coarsely crushed pepper |
| hot-water crust pastry made with 4 cups/450 g flour |

**for the jellied stock:**
*the bones and trimmings of the pheasant, pigeons and hare or grouse*

| 2 pig's feet |
| --- |
| 1 onion |
| 1 carrot |
| 1 stick celery |
| 1 bay leaf |
| 4 peppercorns |
| a little salt |
| 1 tablespoon/15 g gelatine |

SERVES 8–10

Cut the breasts from the pigeons, remove the meatiest parts of the pheasant and cut the meat off the bones of the hare or grouse. Put the carcasses into a large saucepan with all the other ingredients for the jellied stock except the gelatine. Cover with cold water, bring to the boil, skim well, season very lightly and leave to simmer for about 3 hours—until there is no more than about 2½ cups/6 dl of liquid left. Strain it off, dissolve the gelatine in it, and allow to cool.

Meanwhile, cut the pheasant breast meat into fairly large cubes, about ¾ in/2 cm across. Chop the remaining meat—hare or grouse, pheasant and pigeon, but not too fine—the pieces should be no smaller than large peas. Grind or chop the fresh and salt pork, and mix with the chopped game and cubed pheasant breasts in a bowl. Peel and chop the shallots and finely chop the orange peel. Add these to the bowl with the crushed juniper berries, spices, port and brandy, and about a tablespoon of salt and plenty of coarsely crushed black pepper, and leave in a cool place to mellow for 2 to 3 hours or overnight.

When you are ready to make up the pie, make the hot-water crust pastry and preheat the oven to 425°F/220°C.

Grease a 10 in/25 cm spring pan or a cake pan with a removable base, and use two-thirds of the pastry to line it smoothly, making quite sure there are no holes. Put in the meat mixture, brush the edges of the pastry with water, cover with the remaining pastry and trim. Decorate with the trimmings formed into geometric shapes or oak leaves overlapping like scales. Make a hole in the center of the pie and brush with the egg yolk, beaten with a little salt and a few drops of water. Bake for 20 minutes, then turn the oven down to 350°F/180°C and bake for a further hour and 40 minutes, covering the pie loosely with foil when it is well browned to prevent it from burning.

Allow the pie to cool a little and then pour in the just-liquid stock through a funnel inserted into the hole in the top of the pie, filling it almost to the top. Sometimes it is difficult to pour the jellied stock into the middle of the pie. In this case, make a neat hole near the edge if it is round, or at each end if it is a long pie.

Allow the pie to become cool and to set in the pan for at least 24 hours before serving.

# Making pâtés

Remember, when making pâtés, that it is the depth of the terrine rather than the surface that determines cooking time, and that when recipes specify more seasoning than seems reasonable it is because their taste becomes muted once the pâté is cold. Make your pâté at least one day, and preferably two or three days, before it is wanted, to give the flavors time to mature. Keep pâté, covered, in the refrigerator, but do not freeze it—the texture will be hopelessly spoiled.

A distinction is often made between pâtés and terrines, although nowadays they are considered to be the same thing, the word terrine referring to the type of dish used.

— ◆ —

# Pâté en croûte

*hot-water crust pastry made with 4 cups/450 g flour*

*1 egg yolk*

**for the filling:**
*1 lb/450 g chicken livers*

*small glass of dry white vermouth or dry white wine*

*½ lb/225 g ground pork*

*¼ lb/115 g salt pork, soaked to freshen and chopped fine*

*1 lb/450 g chicken hearts*

*3 slices bacon*

*1 shallot*

*1 clove garlic*

*1 egg, lightly beaten*

*¼ teaspoon each of ground mace and ground allspice*

*salt and freshly ground pepper*

**for the jellied stock:**
*2 large onions*

*2 pig's feet*

*2–3 lb/900 g–1.5 kg veal or pork bones and trimmings*

*1 large carrot*

*1 stick celery*

*1 bay leaf*

*½ wine glass medium dry sherry*

*1 teaspoon salt and ½ teaspoon coarsely ground pepper*

*1 tablespoon sugar*

SERVES 8–10

The day before you make the pâté, clean the chicken livers, cut them in half, put them in an earthenware dish and pour the dry white vermouth or the white wine over them.

Mix the pork, salt pork and chicken hearts together in a large mixing bowl. Finely chop the bacon—this makes the pâté a good pink—and add this to the pork and chicken hearts. Add the shallot, peeled and finely chopped, the garlic, peeled, chopped and crushed, and the egg. Season the mixture with the ground spices and salt and pepper, and stir well.

Let the two mixtures stand overnight in a cool place so that the flavors can mellow.

The following day, line a 9 in/23 cm spring pan with two-thirds of the pastry and let it chill in the refrigerator.

Preheat the oven to 425°F/220°C.

Take the chicken livers out of the vermouth, and mix the vermouth into the meat mixture. Put a layer of this forcemeat into the lined pan, lay the chicken livers on top, pressing them into the mixture, put the remaining forcemeat on top, trying not to leave air gaps between the two ingredients. Cover the pie with the rest of the pastry, sealing the edges with water. Brush with the egg yolk—beaten with a pinch of salt and a few drops of water—form the pastry trimmings into lozenges or other shapes to decorate the top, glaze these too, then in the middle of the pie make a hole large enough to take the end of a funnel—you will be adding the liquid after the pâté is cooked. Bake for an hour and 30 minutes, covering the top with foil when the pastry is nicely browned. Allow to cool in the pan.

Meanwhile, make the jellied stock. Peel the onions and put all the ingredients except the salt, pepper and sugar in a pan and simmer for 2 hours. Strain, season and reduce to about 3¼ cups/7.5 dl. Skim off the fat and clarify if you want perfection, then caramelize the sugar and add it to the clear stock to give it a good color. Allow to cool and then put it into the cooled pie, pouring through a funnel. Let the pie stand in a cool place or the refrigerator overnight before taking it out of the pan. Cut into wedges and serve with a salad.

— ◆ —

# Fish pâté

*1 lb/450 g each of fresh salmon and hake or sole, boned and skinned*

*1 glass white wine*

231

# Pâtés and Galantines

salt and freshly ground white pepper

2 small bunches watercress

1 shallot

2 sticks/225 g softened butter

2 eggs

SERVES 6–8

Cut the salmon into long strips, put it in a small dish with the white wine and season lightly with salt and white pepper. Allow to marinate in the wine for an hour or so.

Meanwhile, trim away the rooty parts of the watercress stalks and wash the sprigs. Bring a pan of lightly salted water to the boil and drop in the watercress. Let it blanch for a minute, remove, refresh under cold water and then press dry. Peel and chop the shallot and sweat it, without browning, in a tablespoon of the butter. Cut the hake into cubes and put into a food processor with the softened shallot. Blend for 3–4 minutes until completely smooth. Add the eggs and season with salt and white pepper. Blend for a minute, then add the remaining butter and blend for 30 seconds. Take two-thirds of the mixture out of the food processor, add the watercress to the remaining third and purée briefly until it is a beautiful bright green. Chill both mixtures for 30 minutes.

Preheat the oven to 275°F/140°C.

Put a layer of half the white mixture into a lightly oiled oblong terrine—a long, narrow, enamelled iron terrine 10 × 3½ in/25 × 9 cm is the best. Put in a layer of half the salmon strips, then a layer of all the green purée. Then put in the remaining salmon strips and the rest of the white purée. Cover with foil and the lid and cook for 2½–3 hours. Allow to cool and then chill overnight in the refrigerator. Serve this fish pâté with sauce grelette.

## Pâté de campagne

¾ lb/340 g chicken livers

½ lb/225 g unsmoked bacon or salt pork

½ lb/225 g neck of veal

2 cloves garlic

8 juniper berries, crushed

15 peppercorns

1 wine glass dry white wine

dash of brandy

1 large egg

½ cup/55 g fresh white bread crumbs

1 level teaspoon each of dried sage and thyme

½ teaspoon quatre épices or ground allspice

½ onion or 2 shallots

½ stick/55 g butter, softened

1½ teaspoons salt

¼ lb/115 g pork fatback

SERVES 8

Pick over the chicken livers, removing strings and any greenish parts. Grind the bacon and veal coarsely or chop in a food processor. Transfer to a bowl. Chop the livers fairly finely, and add them to the bacon and veal. Peel and crush the cloves of garlic and mix them into the meat together with the crushed juniper berries and peppercorns, wine, brandy, egg, bread crumbs, herbs and spices. Mix everything together well and leave to mature for 2–3 hours. Peel and chop the onion or shallots and sauté in the butter in a small pan until tender and translucent. Add this to the meat together with the salt. Put the mixture into a terrine.

Preheat the oven to 350°F/180°C.

Beat the pork fatback flat, with the side of a cleaver, and cut into strips. Arrange them in a lattice over the top of the pâté, cover the terrine and cook for an hour. Then remove the lid and cook for a further 30 minutes uncovered. Allow to stand overnight, or longer, before cutting.

## Rillettes of pork

¼ lb/115 g fatback or salt pork, soaked to freshen

2 lb/900 g boned pork shoulder

salt and freshly ground pepper

grating of nutmeg

SERVES 8

Preheat the oven to 275°F/140°C.

Cut the fat and pork into 1½ in/4 cm cubes and put them into a heavy pan or casserole with 3 table-spoons water, and season. Cover and cook in a very low oven for 4 hours.

Strain off and reserve the fat and liquid. Purée the meat briefly in a food processor, or wait until cool but not cold, and shred it with your fingers, removing any cartilages. (This is a lengthy job but there is no better way; you are aiming at fine, soft threads of meat in a creamy, spicy base.) Season very well with salt, pepper and nutmeg and return the fat and liquid to the meat. Reheat until it bubbles then put in stoneware jars or china or earthenware dishes. It will keep for weeks in the refrigerator. This is good for a cold lunch or snack. Serve just below room temperature, not chilled.

ALTERNATIVES: *you can add pieces of rabbit or pigeon at the beginning, but it should be mainly pork.*

## Pheasant pâté

| |
|---|
| *1 pheasant weighing 2 lb/900 g* |
| *2 tablespoons peanut oil* |
| *1¼ lb/565 g pork belly or boned shoulder* |
| *4 slices bacon* |
| *1 small onion or 2 shallots* |
| *½ teaspoon dried thyme* |
| *1 teaspoon finely chopped parsley* |
| *3 crushed juniper berries* |
| *2 teaspoons salt and ½ teaspoon coarsely crushed pepper* |
| *1 small glass white wine* |
| *dash of brandy* |
| *¼ lb/115 g pork fatback, in a piece* |

**for the jellied stock:**

| |
|---|
| *2 leeks* |
| *2 sticks celery* |
| *the pheasant giblets or chicken giblets* |
| *1 bunch parsley* |
| *salt and freshly ground pepper* |
| *1½ teaspoons/7.5 g gelatine* |

SERVES 8

Slice the leeks and celery and put them in a pan with the pheasant or chicken giblets and the bunch of parsley, season lightly and cover with 5 cups/1 liter water. Simmer uncovered for 3 hours, skimming once or twice, until reduced to about 1¼ cups/3 dl. Strain and allow to cool.

Preheat the oven to 450°F/230°C.

Brush the pheasant with the oil, place it in a roasting pan and roast in a hot oven for 15 minutes, then allow to cool. This makes handling it very much easier. Remove the flesh from the pheasant with a small sharp knife; keep the breasts on one side and discard the skin. Grind or chop the pork belly, bacon and all the pheasant meat except the breasts. Peel and chop the onion or shallots very finely indeed. Mix together in a bowl the minced pheasant meat, bacon and pork, the shallot or onion, the herbs, juniper berries, the salt and coarsely crushed pepper, the wine and brandy; allow to stand for 30 minutes or longer, so that the flavors can blend together.

Preheat the oven to 325°F/170°C.

Place half the pheasant forcemeat in the bottom of a 5 cup/1 liter terrine. Cut the pork fatback into ¼ in/5 mm dice and the pheasant breasts into dice of ½ in/1 cm. Place a layer of half the dice on top of the forcemeat, then another thin layer of forcemeat, then the rest of the dice and finish with the remaining forcemeat. Let the terrine rest for a further 30 minutes, then cover it and let it cook in the oven for an hour and 30 minutes, taking the cover off for the last 30 minutes, and then allow to become completely cool.

When the terrine is cold, make the jelly. Dissolve the gelatine in 2 tablespoons hot water in a bowl. If it won't completely dissolve, stand the bowl in a pan of hot water and place it on a moderate heat. Stir the gelatine until it dissolves, then mix it with the strained stock and season with salt and pepper. Remove any fat that has accumulated around the sides of the pâté during cooking and then pour on the jellied stock. Allow to mature for at least 24 hours—preferably longer—before eating, and serve with hot toast.

ALTERNATIVE: *you can decorate the top of the terrine with a fan of bay leaves or sprigs of tarragon before covering it with jelly.*

## Galantine of chicken

| |
|---|
| *1 chicken weighing 4 lb/2 kg* |
| *black olives, tarragon leaves, flat parsley or chervil to decorate* |

**for the jellied stock:**

| |
|---|
| *2 pig's feet* |
| *salt* |
| *3 carrots* |
| *3 sticks celery* |
| *2 onions* |
| *bouquet garni of thyme, parsley and a bay leaf* |
| *the giblets of the chicken* |
| *1 glass white wine* |
| *12 peppercorns* |
| *1 tablespoon/15 g gelatine* |

**for the forcemeat:**

| |
|---|
| *1½ lb/700 g pork belly or boned shoulder* |

# Galantines

½ lb/225 g tenderloin of pork
½ lb/225 g chicken livers
⅓ cup/115 g pistachio nuts, shelled
1 clove garlic
2 tablespoons brandy
salt and freshly ground black pepper
1 tablespoon/15 g butter

SERVES 10–12

Start work 2 days before you want the pâté. First make the stock (which has to be simmered for an hour and 30 minutes before the chicken bones are added to it).

Put the pig's feet to soak for an hour in a bowl of warm water with 1 tablespoon salt. Wash the carrots and celery, peel the onions and put the vegetables in a large pan with 3 quarts/2.75 liters water. Add the herbs, chicken giblets—except the liver, which goes into the forcemeat—and the white wine and peppercorns. Then add the soaked pig's feet, bring slowly to the boil and skim. When you have thoroughly skimmed the stock, cover the pan and simmer the contents over a gentle heat for an hour and 30 minutes.

Meanwhile, bone the chicken very carefully, keeping the skin intact and leaving in the drumstick bones. Put the bones you have removed into the stock and let it simmer on.

Next make the forcemeat. Remove the bones and skin from the belly of pork (if you're using belly) and put them in with the stock (pig's skin is very gelatinous). If you're using pork shoulder, remove any sinews or fat from the shoulder. Reserve one small (2–3 oz/55–85 g) piece of fat. Remove the sinews from the pork tenderloin. Trim all the livers, removing the strings and any greenish patches, put them into a strainer and run cold water over them. Leave them to drain over a bowl. Put the pistachio nuts into a bowl, pour boiling water over them and leave them to cool. Peel and crush the garlic. Put both kinds of pork and the chicken livers (but not the one reserved from the chicken you are using) through the finest blade of a grinder, or chop them finely in a food processor. Put the ground meat in a bowl with the garlic, brandy, a tablespoon of salt and plenty of pepper. Skin the pistachio nuts and stir them into the meat. It will start to smell very good. Sauté the liver saved from the chicken in the butter in a small frying pan. Chop it and stir it into the forcemeat. Carefully fillet off the breast meat from the inside of

the boned chicken and put it on one side. Cut away the thigh meat and grind it coarsely or chop it briefly in the food processor, together with the bit of fat you have reserved. Mix this into the forcemeat. Cut the breast meat into strips the width of a finger. Spread the boned chicken out on a clean cloth large enough to completely surround the chicken. Spread the whole chicken with a layer of forcemeat, using slightly over half of it. Arrange the pieces of chicken breast over the top lengthwise, then pile the rest of the forcemeat down the middle. Roll the chicken to enclose the stuffing, getting the legs and wings in the right place. It will be shaped something like a bolster. Sew up the skin with a trussing needle and twine. Then fold the cloth firmly around it and tie it at each end with a piece of string.

Preheat the oven to 300°F/160°C.

Put the bundle into the hot stock, bedding it down among the bones and vegetables—if there isn't room, remove some of the bones. Bring to the boil, then transfer it to the oven and simmer for an hour and 45 minutes. When it is done, lift the chicken out of the pot and put it in a dish, breast upwards and still in its cloth. Put in a cool place overnight. Strain the stock into a bowl and leave in the refrigerator overnight.

The following day, peel the cloth away from the galantine of chicken and wipe away any fat that is clinging to it. Put the chicken in the refrigerator. Next make the jellied stock. Skim all the fat off the top of the stock. Measure off 2½ cups/6 dl and clarify it with 2 egg whites. Dissolve the gelatine in a little hot water, add it to the stock and put it in the refrigerator until it turns syrupy.

Spoon the just-liquid jelly over the chicken, decorate with very thinly sliced pitted black olives, tarragon leaves and flat parsley or chervil. Spoon some more of the jelly over the top. Just before serving, cut any remaining jelly into cubes and arrange around the galantine on the dish.

To serve, remove the drumsticks and then cut the galantine into ¼–½ in/5 mm–1 cm slices. A slice looks most appetizing and attractive when it is studded with green pistachio nuts and marbled with little bits of fat and small pieces of white breast meat.

ALTERNATIVE: *add a chopped canned truffle and its juice to the forcemeat for an even more rich and luxurious dish.*

234

# Galantine of duck

*1 duck weighing 3½–4 lb/1.5–2 kg*
*small glass of brandy*
*tarragon leaves, parsley, hard-boiled egg*
*and cucumber to decorate*

### for the jellied stock:
*2 onions*
*bones of the duck and giblets except for the liver*
*strip of orange peel*
*1 carrot*
*1 stick celery*
*1 bay leaf*
*salt*
*6 peppercorns*

### for the stuffing:
*1 shallot*
*2 tablespoons/30 g pistachio nuts, shelled*
*½ lb/225 g ground pork with plenty of fat—about one-third fat to two-thirds lean*
*½ lb/225 g ground veal*
*1 slice ham, about 1 oz/30 g, cut into ¼ in/5 mm cubes*
*1 egg*
*1 strip orange peel, blanched for 5 minutes and finely chopped*
*1 small glass white wine*
*2 very generous pinches mace*
*2½ rounded teaspoons salt and 15 white or black peppercorns, pounded coarsely*
*hazelnut-size lump or 1 teaspoon saltpeter (optional)*
*3 chicken livers or duck livers*

### for the braising liquid:
*2 onions*
*4 carrots*
*3 sticks celery*
*2 tablespoons/30 g butter*

SERVES 6–8

Bone the duck, sprinkle the inside with a little brandy, and put it on one side. Peel the onions and put them with all the rest of the ingredients for the stock in a pan, cover with 5–8 cups/1–2 liters water, bring to the boil and skim. Season lightly with salt, add the 6 peppercorns and simmer for about 2 hours.

Meanwhile, take some leg and breast meat from the inside of the duck and chop this and the duck's liver into cubes. Peel the shallot and chop it finely. Put the pistachio nuts in a bowl, pour boiling water over them and leave until cool. Skin the nuts and mix them into the ground meat with all the rest of the ingredients for the stuffing except for the livers. (The saltpeter is optional but it does make the stuffing a beautiful rose-pink.) Add the remaining brandy. Take a little piece of this mixture and fry it and taste it so that you can see if the seasoning is right. Put a layer of this farce on the boned duck, lay the chicken or duck livers down the middle, and cover with the remaining stuffing. Roll up the duck and sew it into a long sausage. Tie it with string in two places to keep it in a nice rounded shape.

Preheat the oven to 340°F/175°C.

For the braising liquid, peel and chop the vegetables, and cook them in the butter in a heavy pan for 10 minutes. Lay the duck on top, pour on the strained stock and cover the pan.

Braise for 2 hours, leaving the pan uncovered for the last 30 minutes of cooking so that the duck becomes an appetizing brown. If it bursts along the top don't worry too much—it means you have put in a bit too much stuffing; simply cook it uncovered until the burst place has healed, basting it from time to time. (You can hide the bursts with decorations before you put on the jellied stock.)

Let the duck cool in its liquid, then remove it and put it to chill in the refrigerator so that it becomes firm. Strain the liquid and allow it to get completely cold. It should set into a nice jelly with a layer of fat on top. Remove the fat and then clarify the jelly and let it cool, but do not allow it to set completely.

Remove the string from the duck, place the bird on a white oval serving dish and decorate it with geometric shapes or flowers made from tarragon leaves, parsley, pieces of hard-boiled egg, pieces of cucumber peel and so forth. Pour the half-set rather syrupy jelly over the duck—it is probably best to pour it through a tea-strainer so that you can guide it to where you want it to go. Give the duck two layers of jelly—experience is the only way to make this an easy operation; it is hard to catch the jelly at the crucial moment as it is turning from a liquid to a solid. It helps if you have the duck very cold and do the operation in a cold place. Any jelly that runs off, or is left over, can be chilled and chopped and put on either side of the duck on its serving dish. Chill before serving.

Make the first cut right across the middle of the galantine as the ends are not so impressive. Give everyone a generous slice.

## *Filet de boeuf en croûte*

*2 lb/900 g beef tenderloin in one piece preferably from the middle*

*salt and freshly ground pepper*

*2–4 tablespoons/30–55 g butter*

*3 shallots or 1 small onion*

*½ lb/225 g tiny white button mushrooms*

*1 tablespoon chopped parsley*

*2 tablespoons port*

*1 tablespoon brandy*

*flaky pastry made with 2 cups/225 g flour*

*1 egg, separated*

SERVES 8

Season the well-trimmed fillet with pepper. Heat a knob of the butter in a frying pan until it foams and then brown the fillet carefully—taking about 10 minutes altogether. Set it on one side to cool. Peel and chop the shallots or onion finely and sauté in the same butter until transparent. Slice the mushrooms finely and add them to the pan. Season them with salt and pepper, sprinkle with the chopped parsley and cook until soft, adding a little more butter if necessary, and turning them gently with a spatula so that they do not break. Add the port and brandy and reduce until the mixture is just moist. Allow to cool.

Preheat the oven to 425°F/220°C.

Roll three-quarters of the pastry into a large oblong and brush it all over with the white of the egg, beaten with a pinch of salt. Place the fillet on top and cover it with the mushroom mixture. Bring up the sides of the pastry, cutting off the corners and brushing the seams lightly with water to make them stick. Roll out the remaining pastry and trim it into an oblong lid that will just fit over the top of the pastry case, enclosing the fillet completely. Brush the under edges with water and stick them down firmly. Roll out the remaining pastry trimmings very thinly, and cut them into decorative leaves. Stick these on top of the pie with water. Beat the yolk of the egg with half a teaspoon of water and some salt and brush it all over the pie. Leave the glaze to dry and then give the pastry a second coat.

Pierce three holes in the top of the pie, to allow steam to escape, and bake for 12 minutes. Lower the heat to 375°F/190°C, and bake for a further 15–20 minutes—timing depends on the thickness of the fillet. Cover the pie loosely with kitchen foil if it looks as though it is getting too brown. Serve hot or cold with a horseradish sauce, mixed with a few tablespoons of light cream.

---

## *Blade steaks with shallots*

*4 blade steaks weighing about ½ lb/225 g each*

*7–8 shallots*

*1 stick/115 g butter*

*2 tablespoons olive oil*

*1 glass white wine*

*salt and freshly ground pepper*

*1 tablespoon chopped parsley*

SERVES 4

To tenderize the steaks, take a very sharp heavy knife and score each steak in both directions, cutting almost through to the middle. Make the cuts very close together so that the surface is finely divided, and all the fine tough connecting tissues are cut through in both directions.

Peel and chop the shallots, and put them in a small pan with a quarter of the butter and a tablespoon of the oil. Let them simmer gently until tender and then pour in the white wine, season lightly with salt and pepper and boil quite rapidly until the liquid has reduced to 2 tablespoons and become a little syrupy. Set it on one side, but keep it hot.

Next cook the steaks. Heat another quarter of the butter and the remaining oil in a large frying pan, and cook the steaks to your liking over a brisk heat. When they are ready, put them on four hot plates. Stir the remaining butter and the parsley into the shallot mixture, and divide it up between the steaks, spreading a generous tablespoonful over the top of each one. Serve immediately with very moist mashed potatoes or with French fries.

ALTERNATIVES: *use rump steaks or entrecôtes but do not score them. This shallot sauce is delicious with any broiled or fried beef steak.*

---

## *Steak au poivre*

*4 entrecôte steaks*

*2 scant teaspoons black peppercorns*

*a little olive oil*

*2 tablespoons/30 g butter*

*⅔ cup/1.5 dl chicken stock*

*salt*

*2 teaspoons brandy*

SERVES 4

Crush the peppercorns coarsely using a pestle and mortar, until they are the texture of fine bread crumbs. This is a mignonette pepper and the flavor is best if the peppercorns are freshly crushed. Rub the steaks on both sides with a very little olive oil and then press the crushed pepper on to the surfaces with your fingers.

Heat half the butter in an iron frying pan and, when it browns, put in the steaks and fry them fairly rapidly but without allowing the butter to blacken, turning them over now and then. When the steaks are cooked the way you like them, transfer them to a heated dish, sprinkle with salt and keep warm. Put the remaining butter in the frying pan and let it melt, but not brown. Add the stock and let it boil, scraping up the juices from the bottom of the pan. Season with a little salt. Allow the stock to reduce to half its volume and then add the brandy. Boil for half a minute more, then pour over the steaks and serve immediately.

# Boeuf en daube

*2½ lb/1 kg top round or tip roast of beef*

*¼ lb/115 g bacon in a piece*

*1 large onion*

*3–4 large cloves garlic*

*3–4 tablespoons olive oil*

*⅓ bottle red wine*

*small glass dry white vermouth*

*bouquet garni of 3 sprigs thyme, 1 bay leaf and a strip of orange peel*

*1 tablespoon tomato paste*

*⅔ cup/1.5 dl beef stock*

*salt and freshly ground pepper*

*½ cup/115 g pitted black olives*

SERVES 6

Preheat the oven to 290°F/150°C.

Trim the meat and cut it into large pieces. Dice the bacon, rind removed, and blanch it for 4–5 minutes in boiling water. Peel and chop the onion and garlic.

Heat the olive oil in a flameproof casserole and fry the drained dried bacon, the garlic and the onion for 5–10 minutes. Remove them to a plate, then brown the meat rapidly on all sides. It is best to do this in two batches. Bring the wine to the boil in a separate pan. Return the onion and bacon to the casserole, pour the vermouth over the meat and then the boiling wine. Add the bouquet garni, tomato paste, a little stock—as necessary—and some pepper. Do not add much salt yet as the bacon and subsequently the olives will probably make it salty enough. Cover, and cook in the oven for about 2 hours or until tender. Add the olives and cook for a further 30 minutes. Taste the sauce for seasoning and serve.

ALTERNATIVE: *you can add a nice ripe tomato or two to the stew instead of the stock—this makes it a little thicker and richer.*

# Boeuf bourguignonne

*3 lb/1.5 kg top round or tip roast of beef*

*¼ lb/115 g bacon in a piece*

*½ cup/30 g seasoned flour*

*4 tablespoons olive oil*

*½ bottle red burgundy*

*about 1¼ cups/3 dl beef stock or water*

*bouquet garni of thyme, parsley and a bay leaf*

*salt and freshly ground pepper*

*about 20 button onions*

*½ lb/225 g button mushrooms*

*2 tablespoons/30 g butter*

*1 teaspoon sugar*

SERVES 6

Preheat the oven to 350°F/180°C.

Cut the bacon into little sticks and blanch them in boiling water for 5 minutes—this makes the flavor milder. Meanwhile cut the beef into large cubes, about 1½ in/4 cm across; if you make the pieces smaller than this, they seem to lose some of their succulence before they are tender. Coat the pieces thoroughly with seasoned flour.

Dry the bacon and brown it in half the olive oil in a flameproof casserole. Remove the bacon and brown the meat in the same fat, adding a little more oil if necessary and putting in enough pieces to cover the bottom of the pan—you can then make sure they are all evenly browned. Keep the heat very brisk for this. If there is any fat left at the end, pour it out and return the meat to the pan together with the bacon. Add the wine and bring it to the boil. Add just enough of the stock or water to leave the top halves of the uppermost pieces of meat showing above the liquid. Add the bouquet garni, stir the meat around, season with salt and pepper and simmer in the oven for 2 hours.

While the meat is cooking, peel the onions and simmer them in the remaining stock or water for 5 minutes. Then brown the onions and mushrooms in the remaining oil and the butter, with a teaspoon of sugar, and stir them in with the meat. Heat through gently, taste for seasoning, and serve.

This is an extremely rich stew that makes a substantial and delicious dish.

## Steak and kidney pudding

| |
|---|
| *1½ lb/700 g beef—two-thirds chuck, one-third skirt steak* |
| *½ lb/225 g beef kidney* |
| *1–2 tablespoons flour, seasoned with salt and pepper* |
| *2 shallots* |
| *¼ lb/115 g button mushrooms, washed and trimmed* |
| *1 teaspoon each of anchovy essence, Worcestershire sauce, mushroom ketchup and tomato paste* |
| *small glass of red wine* |
| *salt and freshly ground pepper* |
| **for the suet crust:** |
| *2 cups/225 g self-rising flour* |
| *¼ lb/115 g shredded suet* |
| *salt and freshly ground pepper* |

SERVES 6

Cut the beef into pieces about ½ in/1 cm across, trimming away fat and sinews. Remove the central core from the kidney and cut it into pieces about the same size. Roll the meat thoroughly in the seasoned flour. Peel and chop the shallots. Mix the meat, mushrooms and shallots in a bowl.

Next make the suet crust. Mix the flour, suet, salt and pepper in a bowl and add 7–8 tablespoons cold water to make a pliable dough. Roll out two-thirds of the dough on a floured board, and use it to line a greased pudding bowl.

Pile the beef, mushrooms, kidney and chopped shallots into the lined bowl. Mix the anchovy essence, Worcestershire sauce, mushroom ketchup, tomato paste, wine, salt and pepper, and 1¼ cups/3 dl water in a jug. Pour it into the pudding, adding enough extra cold water to come just below the top

of the meat. Roll out the remaining pastry into a round. Brush one side of it with water, and put it loosely over the top of the meat, damp side down, pressing well around the edges with your fingers to seal it to the lower half of the pastry. Trim away any excess pastry from the edges. Take a large round of aluminum foil, grease it on one side, and place it loosely over the pudding. Put an even larger round of foil loosely over this, and tie tightly with string just below the rim of the pudding bowl. Tie a string handle across the top of the bowl so that it can be removed easily at the end.

Take a large pan with a well-fitting lid, and half fill it with water (to which you can add a dash of vinegar to prevent staining the pan with long boiling).

Bring the water to the boil and lower in the pudding —the water should come about 1 in/2.5 cm below the string. Cover the pan—this is most important— and boil gently for 4 hours 30 minutes, replenishing the pan with more boiling water as necessary.

To serve the pudding, lift it out of the pan, remove the foil and pin a neatly folded white napkin around the bowl. Put it on a plate, place it on the table, and plunge in the serving spoon to release a cloud of scented steam.

## Carbonnade de boeuf

| |
|---|
| *3 lb/1.5 kg bottom round of beef* |
| *3 onions* |
| *1 clove garlic* |
| *¼ lb/115 g bacon* |
| *4–5 tablespoons lard or oil* |
| *2 tablespoons flour* |
| *2½ cups/6 dl pale ale* |
| *1 teaspoon sugar* |
| *2 bay leaves* |
| *salt and freshly ground pepper* |
| *1 tablespoon wine vinegar* |

SERVES 6–8

Cut the beef into cubes about 1 in/2.5 cm across or a bit less. Peel and slice the onion and garlic, and cut the bacon into little sticks. Heat the oil in a flameproof casserole, fry the meat—a few pieces at a time—and, as the pieces become well browned, put them on a large plate. When all the meat is browned, turn down the heat, add a little more oil or lard if you need it, and start to fry the sliced onions and the bacon.

Preheat the oven to 300°F/160°C.

When the onions and bacon have started to brown, stir in the flour, let it bubble for a minute or two, then gradually add the beer, stirring to keep the liquid smooth while it thickens. Add the meat and its juices. Throw in the sugar, sliced garlic, bay leaves, salt, plenty of pepper and the vinegar, bring to the boil and simmer in the oven for 2 hours, or until the meat is tender.

Serve this hearty beef stew with plain boiled potatoes and a green salad.

---

# Veal with apples and cream

6 veal scallops

4 green eating apples

3 shallots

salt and freshly ground pepper

4–6 tablespoons/55–85 g butter

small glass of brandy or, even better, Calvados

1¼ cups/3 dl light cream

SERVES 6

Peel and core the apples and cut them into very small neat cubes. Put them in a covered pan with a little water and cook gently while you peel and chop the shallots. Season the scallops on both sides with salt and pepper. Heat a nut of butter in a frying pan and when it begins to brown, put the scallops in the pan and cook them for about 2 minutes on each side and then for a further 3 minutes on each side.

Put the cooked scallops on a hot dish while you fry the shallots in the same pan. Add the brandy or Calvados and stir. Add the apples when they are tender, stir in the cream—enough to make a smooth sauce. Taste for seasoning.

Pour the rich creamy sauce over the scallops and serve with a crisp endive salad.

---

# Scaloppine al Marsala

4 veal scallops, each weighing about ¼ lb/115 g

2 tablespoons olive oil

½ stick/55 g butter

2 tablespoons flour

salt and freshly ground pepper

1 wine glass dry Marsala

SERVES 4

Trim the edges of the scallops of any fat, skin or connective tissue. Heat the olive oil and half the butter in a large frying pan. Dip the scallops lightly into the flour, shake off any excess, and when the oil is very hot, slide them into the pan. Fry for about a minute on each side. Remove them to a heated dish, and season lightly.

Pour the Marsala into the cooking juices, let it bubble and reduce for 1 minute. Add the remaining butter and swirl it around in the pan until it has dissolved and amalgamated with the Marsala. Slip the veal scallops back into the pan, together with any juice that may have run out, turning them over so that they are well coated with the sauce. Serve very hot.

---

# Involtini di vitello

1 lb/450 g small, thin veal scallops

flour for dusting

¼ lb/115 g prosciutto, thinly sliced

½ lb/225 g mozzarella

1 sage leaf or a good sprinkling of dried sage for each slice of veal

salt and freshly ground pepper

about ½ stick/55 g butter

freshly grated Parmesan

SERVES 6

Preheat the oven to 375°F/190°C.

Sprinkle each slice of veal with flour, flatten it, and on each piece put a thin slice of prosciutto, several thin slices of mozzarella, a crushed leaf of fresh sage (or a sprinkling of dried sage), and salt and pepper. Roll up each scallop and fasten with a toothpick.

In a flameproof dish, melt enough butter to cover the bottom generously, then add the rolled scallops and sauté them until brown. Sprinkle the meat generously with freshly grated Parmesan and melted butter and bake in a moderately hot oven for 10 minutes.

Involtini di vitello is a rich and extravagant dish. It should be served at once with a simple fresh green salad.

## Veal with mushrooms

| |
|---|
| *3 lb/1.5 kg rolled and tied loin or boned shoulder of veal* |
| *3 thick slices bacon* |
| *¾ stick/85 g butter* |
| *salt and freshly ground pepper* |
| *sprinkling of dried thyme or 2 sprigs fresh thyme* |
| *¾ lb/340 g firm white button mushrooms* |
| *20 white button onions* |
| *2–3 tablespoons veal or light beef stock, white wine or water* |

SERVES 6

Preheat the oven to 325°F/170°C.

Cut the bacon into little sticks (lardons). Melt a little of the butter in a lidded flameproof casserole into which the veal will fit nicely. Fry the pieces of bacon gently in this butter until they have given up all their fat, then put in the veal, rubbed with salt and pepper and thyme. Brown it on the ends and on all sides, without letting the butter get too brown. Cover the casserole and cook gently in the oven for approximately 2 hours, turning the meat over from time to time. Test by piercing the meat with a skewer to see if it is tender.

Meanwhile, sauté the mushrooms in the remaining butter. Peel the onions and blanch them in boiling salted water for 5 minutes. Drain them and put them into the casserole 30 minutes before the veal is ready. (If you are using ordinary small onions, brown them in the fat with the meat and cook for the same length of time as the meat.) Add the mushrooms 15 minutes later.

When the veal is cooked, put it on a serving dish with the onions, mushrooms and bacon. Keep it hot. Skim the gravy a little and, if you like, add a spoonful or two of stock, white wine or water. Taste for seasoning, allow to bubble for a minute or two and serve separately. This gravy is thin and of a most delicious flavor. If you prefer it thick, thicken with a little beurre manié.

This method is a perfect way of keeping a piece of veal succulent.

## Costolette milanese

| |
|---|
| *4 veal chops on the bone, taken from the loin* |
| *1 egg* |
| *¾ cup/85 g fresh white bread crumbs* |
| *3–4 tablespoons/45–55 g butter* |
| *salt* |
| *1 lemon, quartered* |

SERVES 4

Trim the meat and beat it with a cutlet beater or rolling pin, but do not season it. Beat the egg and have ready a plate of fresh white bread crumbs. Sit the chops in the beaten egg, coating them on both sides. Heat the butter in a wide frying pan, large enough to hold all four chops. When the butter has started to brown, pick up the chops, shake off any excess egg, dip them in the crumbs, patting them in well all over. Fry the chops rather fast on each side for a minute, then when they have browned and sealed, turn the heat right down, so they are just sizzling, and let them cook further for about 6–10 minutes on each side, depending on the thickness of the chops, until they are cooked through. Drain the chops well, serve sprinkled with salt and accompany with wedges of lemon. The butter at the end will be dark and ruined, but the chops—if you have not let them burn—will be perfectly crisp outside, delicate and juicy within.

## Osso bucco milanese

| |
|---|
| *2 lb/900 g osso bucco (slices of veal knuckle, each about 1½ in/4 cm thick and enclosing a piece of bone)* |
| *few strands of saffron* |
| *1 glass white wine* |
| *1 onion* |
| *1 large clove garlic* |
| *1 stick celery* |
| *1 carrot* |
| *1 lb/450 g tomatoes* |
| *½ stick/55 g butter* |
| *2 tablespoons flour* |
| *1 tablespoon tomato paste* |
| *peel of ½ lemon* |
| *salt and freshly ground pepper* |
| *2 teaspoons chopped parsley* |
| *2 canned anchovies, chopped* |
| *½ cup veal or light beef stock (optional)* |

SERVES 3–4

Soak the saffron in the white wine. Peel the onion and garlic. Chop the onion, garlic, celery and carrot finely. Skin and chop the tomatoes.

Melt half the butter, or a little more, in a heavy

pan or casserole. Roll the slices of veal in flour and brown them all over in the butter. Remove them, and fry the very finely chopped onion, celery and carrot in the same pan, adding more fat if necessary; return the meat. Add the wine, let it sizzle until it has evaporated almost completely, then add the tomatoes, tomato paste, 2 strips of the lemon peel, salt and pepper, and cover the pan. Simmer, adding a little water if necessary but keeping the mixture fairly dry.

When the meat is tender—an hour and 30 minutes to 2 hours—sprinkle in the chopped parsley, garlic, anchovies and lemon peel, and cook for 2 or 3 minutes, turning the pieces of meat over once. Put the veal on a dish, add the remaining butter to the sauce and, if necessary, half a cup of water or stock, heat through and pour it over the veal.

---

## Edward VII lamb cutlets

| |
|---|
| 8 rib chops |
| 2 thin slices ham |
| salt and freshly ground pepper |
| 1 egg, beaten with 1 tablespoon water |
| $\frac{1}{3}$ cup/85 g dry bread crumbs |
| 2 tablespoons/30 g butter |
| 1 tablespoon olive oil |

SERVES 4

Trim the chops neatly, if the butcher has not already done so, cutting off any excess fat. Cut the slices of ham in quarters and put a piece on each chop. Season with pepper and a little salt. Paint the chops with the beaten egg, using a pastry brush. Dip them into the bread crumbs.

Heat the butter and oil in a frying pan. When the butter starts to brown, swirl it around to mix with the oil, and put in the chops, ham side up. Fry them for about 4–5 minutes, then turn them carefully and fry for a further 4–5 minutes.

Serve at once with freshly made mayonnaise.

---

## Gigot d'agneau

| |
|---|
| 1 leg of lamb, weighing 4 lb/2 kg, boned |
| 2 cups/340 g dried navy beans or green flageolets, soaked overnight |
| 1 ham bone or a 1 lb/450 g piece of bacon or salt pork |
| 3 cloves garlic |
| handful of parsley, chopped |
| $\frac{3}{4}$ stick/85 g butter |
| salt and freshly ground pepper |
| 1 large onion |
| 1 tablespoon pork drippings, or butter and oil mixed |
| 2 tablespoons tomato paste or 3–4 tomatoes |
| 1 glass white wine |

SERVES 6–8

Put the dried navy beans or flageolets in a heavy pan together with the ham bone or whatever piece of pork or bacon you have. Cover with plenty of cold water, bring to the boil and simmer gently for an hour to an hour and 30 minutes.

Preheat the oven to 425°F/220°C.

Peel and chop the cloves of garlic and cook gently with the parsley in a little of the butter, without browning. Allow this mixture to cool and then push it into the cavity in the leg of lamb. Add salt, pepper and a lump of the remaining butter. Roll up the leg and tie it at $1\frac{1}{2}$ in/4 cm intervals with string. Rub the outside with the last of the butter and some salt, and roast for 30 minutes, basting and turning from time to time.

Turn down the heat to 350°F/180°C and cook for a further 40 minutes to an hour, depending on how you like your lamb.

Peel and chop the onion fairly finely and sauté gently in the pork drippings or butter and oil. Stir in the tomato paste and let it reduce. (If you are using fresh tomatoes instead of tomato paste, skin and chop them, and reduce them considerably before adding them to the softened onions.) Add the white wine to the onion and tomato and a cupful of the beans' cooking liquid, simmer a minute or two, then stir in the strained cooked beans. Let them simmer very gently until the meat is ready.

When the lamb is done, remove it from the pan and keep it hot. Spoon all the fat off the juices in the roasting pan, then stir these juices into the beans. Season the beans and transfer them to a heated dish. Carve the lamb and lay the slices down the middle of the dish of beans.

ALTERNATIVES: *you can serve this dish sprinkled with finely chopped garlic and parsley mixed with bread crumbs—which you quickly brown in the broiler. You can also add little sausages, well fried, to the beans. But perhaps best of all is plain gigot and beans bathed in their own excellent sauce.*

## Lamb korma

| | |
|---|---|
| 3 lb/1.5 kg shoulder or neck of lamb | |
| 2 in/5 cm piece of fresh ginger | |
| 1 large onion | |
| 2 cloves garlic | |
| 3 tablespoons/45 g butter | |
| 1 tablespoon ground coriander seeds | |
| 1 teaspoon ground turmeric | |
| ½ teaspoon each of ground cardamom pods and ground cloves | |
| salt and ½ teaspoon freshly ground black pepper | |
| ⅔ cup/1.5 dl natural yogurt | |
| juice of ½ lemon | |
| handful of cashew nuts, lightly toasted | |

SERVES 6–8

Remove the meat from the bones and cut it into large pieces. Peel the ginger and slice it in fine slivers and mix into the meat. Peel and chop the onion and garlic finely and sweat them in the butter. Add the spices and a generous measure of black pepper and let them fry for a minute, stirring well, then add the meat and fry it, turning the pieces around until they are colored on all sides.

Add the yogurt and a little salt and cover the pan. Let the curry simmer, covered, for an hour and 30 minutes until it is tender and almost dry. Add the lemon juice and cashew nuts, cut in pieces, and let it cook on for a further 15 minutes.

This rich, mild and very delicious curry was a firm favorite with the Madras Club in the nineteenth century.

## Navarin aux pommes

| | |
|---|---|
| 2 lb/900 g each of boned shoulder and rib of lamb | |
| 1 large onion | |
| 3 cloves garlic | |
| 2 tablespoons oil | |
| 3 tablespoons/23 g flour | |
| 2 tablespoons tomato paste | |
| salt and freshly ground pepper | |
| bouquet garni | |
| 2 cups/4.5 dl dry white wine | |
| 2 cups/4.5 dl chicken stock | |
| 1½ lb/700 g potatoes | |

SERVES 6–8

Trim the meat and cut into large pieces, eliminating most of the fat. Peel and chop the onion, and peel and crush the cloves of garlic. Brown the meat in hot oil in a large flameproof casserole. Remove the pieces as they are browned and brown the sliced onion in the same oil, together with the cloves of garlic. Stir in the flour and let it cook for a minute before adding the tomato paste, salt and pepper and bouquet garni.

Preheat the oven to 325°F/170°C.

Return the meat to the pan, add the wine and stock and bring to the boil. Cover and simmer in the oven for an hour and 30 minutes.

Meanwhile, slice the potatoes. Halfway through the cooking of the meat, skim off the fat from the top, add salt and push the sliced potatoes into the stew, covering the surface with a thick layer. Continue to cook, with the lid on, until the potatoes are almost tender, then remove the lid, turn the oven up to 375°F/190°C, and cook for a further 20–30 minutes. The potatoes will absorb all the remaining fat from the top of the navarin, and turn an appetizing golden brown.

ALTERNATIVE: *cast a handful of peas into the navarin just before you cover it with the sliced potatoes.*

## Lamb masala

| | |
|---|---|
| leg or shoulder of lamb, weighing 3 lb/1.5 kg, boned | |
| 1 onion | |
| 2 cloves garlic | |
| 1 teaspoon ground ginger or a 1 in/2.5 cm piece of fresh ginger | |
| 1 teaspoon ground dried red chili peppers | |
| 1¼ cups/3 dl natural yogurt plus an extra 1–2 tablespoons | |
| juice of 1 lemon | |
| salt | |
| 2 tablespoons/30 g shelled pistachio nuts | |
| ⅓ cup/55 g blanched almonds | |
| ¼ lb/115 g lamb's liver | |
| 2 lamb's kidneys | |
| ⅔ cup/115 g raisins | |
| ½–¾ stick/55–85 g butter | |
| 1 tablespoon clear honey | |

SERVES 6

Start a day ahead.

Peel and chop the onion finely. Peel the garlic and, if you are using it, the fresh ginger. Mash the garlic, ginger and ground chili with a little salt.

Mix them with the onion, the $1\frac{1}{4}$ cups/3 dl yogurt and the lemon juice. Prick the boned lamb here and there with a skewer, to allow the flavors of the marinade to penetrate the meat. Spread the yogurt paste over the lamb, inside and out. Leave it in the refrigerator overnight.

The next day before you commence preparations preheat the oven to 325°F/170°C.

Chop all the nuts. Boil the liver and kidneys in salted water until they are firm, and then chop finely; mix them with the nuts and the raisins. Add salt and a tablespoon or two of natural yogurt and spread the inside of the lamb with this mixture. Press it well down on to the meat with your hands. Roll the lamb and put skewers in to hold it while you tie it with string at 1–2 in/2.5–5 cm intervals to keep the stuffing in. Sprinkle it with salt and put it into a deep ovenproof casserole with the butter and the marinade. Cover the pot and roast for an hour,

then turn the meat over. Add a tablespoon of honey and roast for a further 2 hours, basting with the honey and juices and turning the meat every 30 minutes. Take the lid off for the last 30 minutes. Put the lamb on a heated dish and serve surrounded with boiled rice, which has been cooked in salted water with 4 cardamom pods and 2 cinnamon sticks. Skim the fat off the cooking juices and serve them separately; they are rather rich with all the honey, yogurt and onion, but taste good on the rice.

This is a really fine dish for a dinner party, and looks as beautiful as it tastes. Take off the string and carve into fairly thick slices.

---

# Pork scallops with juniper

2 whole pork tenderloins

juice of 1 lemon

20 juniper berries, crushed

salt and freshly ground pepper

2 cloves garlic

2 tablespoons/30 g butter

1 tablespoon sunflower or olive oil

1 glass red wine

SERVES 6

Cut the pork into little round slices $\frac{3}{4}$ in/2 cm thick and beat these flat between two pieces of cellophane or damp parchment paper. Sprinkle them with lemon juice. Mix the juniper berries with salt and freshly ground pepper. Pat this mixture into the little scallops. Peel and slice the garlic.

Heat the butter and oil in a heavy frying pan, and fry the pieces of pork quickly, not more than 2–3 minutes on each side; halfway through, add the sliced cloves of garlic.

When the scallops are done, put them on a hot dish and keep hot. Pour the glass of wine into the frying pan. Let it bubble, scrape the sediment off the bottom of the pan and pour it all over the pork. Serve immediately.

---

# Roast loin of pork

1 loin of pork, weighing about $3\frac{1}{2}$ lb/1.75 kg, skin on

2 cloves garlic

a little wine vinegar or lemon juice

Lamb masala

*2 nice sprigs rosemary*

*1 glass white wine or cider*

*2 teaspoons flour*

*⅔–1¼ cups/1.5–3 dl chicken stock*

*salt and freshly ground pepper*

SERVES 6–8

Preheat the oven to 350°F/180°C.

The loin should be on the bone, but chined by the butcher. Score the skin well to make crisp, manageable crackling.

Place the loin, skin side up, on a rack in a roasting pan. Tuck the rosemary under the pork and push the unpeeled garlic cloves between the meat and the fat or next to the bone. Rub the surface with lemon juice or vinegar and fine salt but no oil or other fat.

Roast the pork, without basting, for 2 hours, putting it low in the oven if the crackling is getting too dark on the top. Remove the meat to a heated dish and keep it hot for at least 15–20 minutes, covered loosely with foil or an old-fashioned meat cover, so that it can relax. This makes the meat juicier and easier to carve.

Meanwhile, make the gravy; spoon most of the fat from the roasting pan and remove the rosemary. Retrieve the cloves of garlic and crush them, then add the glass of wine or cider and stir and scrape the roasting pan over a rapid heat, to dissolve all the meat juices from the sides and bottom. When the wine has reduced considerably, add the flour to the pan, stir it around and break up the lumps, then add the stock, stirring all the time. Let the gravy cook for a few minutes, season it and then strain through a conical strainer into a gravy boat or pitcher. Serve the loin of pork with this gravy, applesauce and roast potatoes.

———◆———

# *Fried pork chops*

*4 pork chops*

*2 cloves garlic*

*1 tablespoon sunflower or olive oil*

*salt and coarsely ground pepper*

*2–3 sprigs thyme*

SERVES 4

Preheat the oven to 350°F/180°C.

Peel and crush the cloves of garlic. Trim the excess fat from the chops and then rub them well with oil and with the crushed garlic. Season them with coarsely ground black pepper and a few thyme leaves but no salt yet.

Heat a frying pan large enough to hold all the chops side by side and coat the bottom with a light layer of oil. When the oil is really hot, put the chops in the pan and sear them quickly, then fry at a slightly lower temperature until they are just resilient but still slightly soft to the touch. Transfer the chops to a dish, stacking them one on top of the other, and cover lightly with foil. Put them in the oven for 10 minutes, keeping the door slightly open.

The trouble with cooking pork chops is that very often, by the time they are thoroughly done right through, which of course they must be, they have become dry. Cooked this way, however, they should be perfectly done, tender and juicy. Season with salt just before serving.

———◆———

# *Tongue with nuts and raisins*

*1 beef tongue*

*2 onions*

*2 carrots*

*1 stick celery*

*bouquet garni of parsley, thyme and a bay leaf*

*2 tablespoons/30 g butter*

*2 tablespoons raisins*

*⅓ cup/55 g blanched almonds*

*3 tablespoons white wine vinegar*

*1 tablespoon tomato paste*

*2 tablespoons white wine*

*⅔ cup/1.5 dl veal or light beef stock*

*salt*

SERVES 4

It is important to find out from the butcher if the tongue needs soaking—if it has not been in the brine tub for long it will be ready to cook without soaking. If it is heavily salted—a good indication of this is that it will be tough and hard—soak it overnight in a quantity of cold water.

Put the prepared tongue in a casserole, cover it with water and add one of the onions, peeled, the carrots and stick of celery. Throw in the bouquet garni, cover the pan, bring to the boil and simmer very gently for 2 hours 30 minutes to 3 hours. When the tongue is tender, peel and slice the remaining onion. Sweat it in the butter in a small frying pan, add the raisins and almonds and fry them until the raisins are plump and the almonds starting to brown. Add the vinegar and the tomato paste, stir the mixture over the heat for a minute, then add the white wine and stock and let it bubble. Allow the sauce to reduce for a few minutes, then season with a little salt.

Meanwhile, remove the tongue from the cooking liquid, peel off the skin in big strips starting from the tip—always a finger-burning operation—and slice as much of the tongue as you think you will need. Arrange the slices on a hot dish, pour the raisin and almond sauce over the top and serve very hot with plainly cooked vegetables such as boiled potatoes and young carrots.

---

# Tuscan tripe

2 lb/900 g fine-grained very white fresh tripe, dressed and prepared

1 onion

2 cloves garlic

1 stick celery

2 carrots

3–4 tablespoons olive oil

3–4 tomatoes

1¼ cups/3 dl dry white wine

salt and freshly ground pepper

2½ cups/6 dl homemade chicken broth or beef stock

1 small glass brandy

SERVES 6

Cut the tripe into strips about the size of your little finger, peel the onion and peel and chop the garlic. Chop the onion, celery and carrots finely and put them in a heavy iron casserole with the olive oil. Sweat them, stirring from time to time, until they are golden. Add the tripe and garlic and let them cook for a few minutes while you skin, seed and chop the tomatoes. Add the tomatoes to the tripe together with the wine. Season and leave to simmer gently, uncovered, for 2 hours. Add a ladle of the stock or broth from time to time—just enough to keep the tripe bathed in a nice sauce.

When the tripe is cooked, taste for seasoning and add a small glass of brandy. Serve very hot.

This traditional recipe for Tuscan tripe is always served with an accompaniment of tender boiled pinto or cannellini beans.

# Fried calves' brains

4 calves' brains

1 onion

1 carrot

1 stick celery

1 bay leaf

1 tablespoon wine vinegar

salt and freshly ground pepper

2 tablespoons oil, preferably olive oil

2 tablespoons/30 g butter

1 egg

2 tablespoons/30 g dried bread crumbs

1 lemon, quartered

SERVES 4

Wash the brains thoroughly and let them soak in cold water for 30 minutes. Peel and slice the onion and carrot and chop the celery. Put the prepared vegetables in a pan with 2½ quarts/2.25 liters water, the bay leaf, vinegar and 1 teaspoon salt. Bring it to the boil and then slip the calves' brains into the pan. Simmer for 20 minutes until the brains are set and firm. Drain and allow to cool. Refrigerate for 30 minutes, then peel away the outer skin very carefully, removing all blood vessels and membranes.

Heat the oil and butter in a frying pan and dip the brains first in the egg—beaten with a tablespoon of water and a little salt and pepper (this gives a lighter coating than undiluted egg)—and then in bread crumbs. Fry the brains to a golden brown, turning them carefully so that they brown evenly all over. Drain on paper towels and serve very hot with quarters of lemon.

Fried calves' brains should have a crisp, tender crust on the outside, and be hot, creamy and melting in the middle.

ALTERNATIVE: *fried brains are also delicious if they are cut into pieces the size of a walnut before being egg-and-crumbed and fried.*

---

# Foie de veau lyonnaise

1 lb/450 g calves' liver, thinly sliced

4–6 onions

2 tablespoons/30 g butter

1 teaspoon olive oil or lard

salt and freshly ground pepper

½–1 tablespoon wine vinegar

# Meat *Variety meats*

SERVES 6

Peel and slice the onions and fry them in the butter and oil or lard over a fairly gentle heat until they start to brown. Cover the pan, turn down the heat and cook them gently for 10–15 minutes until they are very soft. Push them to one side of the pan or remove them to a plate. Season the slices of liver with pepper and fry them in the same pan over a moderate heat for about 3 minutes on each side. Put the onions on top of the slices of liver, throw the vinegar into the pan, let it sizzle, season with salt and more pepper and serve straightaway.

## *Braised liver with bacon*

| |
|---|
| *1 pork liver, in one piece weighing 2–2½ lb/900 g–1 kg* |
| *3 carrots* |
| *2 onions* |
| *1 stick celery* |
| *10 slices bacon* |
| *2 cloves garlic* |
| *salt and coarsely ground pepper* |
| *2 tablespoons olive oil* |
| *bunch of parsley and thyme* |
| *1 large glass red wine* |

SERVES 6

Peel the carrots and onions. Cut the carrots, onions and celery into coarse julienne strips about the size of your little finger. Cut four of the slices of bacon into pieces 1½ × ¾ in/4 × 2 cm.

Peel, chop and crush the garlic and press it into the pieces of bacon. Season them liberally with coarsely ground pepper and roll up the pieces—one at a time—into little rolls. Make rows of deep short cuts in the liver and insert the rolls of bacon with your finger.

Preheat the oven to 350°F/180°C.

Heat the oil in an ovenproof casserole and add the vegetables. Cover the pan and sweat the vegetables gently for 5–10 minutes. Put the liver on top of the vegetables and the remaining slices of bacon on top of that. Add the herbs, tied in a bundle, the wine, a little salt and pepper and any leftover garlic. Cook in a slow oven for an hour. Take out the herbs. Remove the liver and bacon from the pan and keep them hot in a deep serving dish. Reduce the sauce over a high heat until it is slightly syrupy and then pour it over the meat.

## *Sautéed chicken livers*

| |
|---|
| *1 lb/450 g chicken livers* |
| *2 onions* |
| *1 teaspoon olive oil* |
| *2 tablespoons/30 g butter* |
| *1 glass Marsala* |
| *a little sage, fresh or dried* |
| *salt and freshly ground pepper* |

SERVES 4

Peel and chop the onions and sweat them in a mixture of the olive oil and butter. When they are tender and starting to brown, pour the Marsala into the pan and let it evaporate. Add the carefully trimmed chicken livers and the sage, salt and pepper. Sauté over a medium heat—it should be hot enough to prevent the juices from running out of the livers, but not so hot that the onions are burned —until the livers are firm but still moist inside. Serve very hot with rice, a fresh salad or perhaps with well-drained spinach. The chicken livers will be very savory and fragrant.

## *Kidneys with mustard*

| |
|---|
| *2 veal kidneys each weighing about ¾ lb/340 g* |
| *1 tablespoon Dijon mustard* |
| *4 tablespoons heavy cream* |
| *6 juniper berries, crushed* |
| *salt and freshly ground pepper* |
| *3 tablespoons/45 g butter* |
| *1 tablespoon olive oil* |
| *1 tablespoon brandy* |

SERVES 4

Mix the mustard into the cream. Remove the fat from the kidneys and strip off the thin transparent membrane that covers them. Cut them in half lengthwise, trim away the cores and slice each half thinly. Scatter the juniper berries over the kidneys and press them in well. Season with salt and freshly ground pepper.

Heat the butter and oil in a frying pan and throw in the sliced kidneys. Let them brown rapidly, turning them so that they cook evenly. After about 4 minutes, pour in the brandy and let it bubble up for a few seconds. Add the cream mixture and stir well until the kidneys are nicely coated with hot sauce. Serve at once with fresh spinach.

# Kidneys with red wine sauce

| |
|---|
| *8 lambs' kidneys or 4 pork kidneys* |
| *1 tablespoon flour* |
| *2 onions* |
| *¼ lb/115 g button mushrooms* |
| *2 tablespoons/30 g butter* |
| *1 tablespoon olive oil* |
| *salt and freshly ground pepper* |
| *bouquet garni of parsley, thyme and a bay leaf* |
| *4 juniper berries, crushed* |
| *1¼ cups/3 dl red wine, or half and half wine and chicken stock* |

SERVES 4

Free the kidneys of their transparent skins, cut away the central core and slice them across into pieces the size of a small walnut. Roll them in a little flour. Peel the onions. Cut the onions and mushrooms into thin slices.

Heat the butter and oil in a sauté pan and throw in the kidneys. Brown them fairly briskly then transfer them to a dish while you sauté the onions to a golden brown in the same pan. Add the mushrooms and turn them over with the onions on a moderate heat for a minute or two. Return the kidneys to the pan and season with salt and pepper. Add the bouquet garni, juniper berries and red wine or wine and stock and cover the pan.

Bring to simmering point over a very low heat and cook for an hour to an hour and 15 minutes, adding a little water or stock if the sauce evaporates and seems to be becoming dry. Taste for seasoning, and test to see if the kidneys are tender.

*Kidneys with red wine sauce*

# Braised sweetbreads

| |
|---|
| *2–3 veal sweetbreads* |
| *3 carrots* |
| *2 onions* |
| *2 sticks celery* |
| *1 leek* |
| *2 tablespoons/30 g butter* |
| *bouquet garni of thyme, parsley and a bay leaf* |
| *2 tablespoons dry white vermouth* |
| *1¼ cups/3 dl homemade chicken stock* |
| *salt and freshly ground pepper* |
| *1 heaping teaspoon arrowroot* |

SERVES 4

Prepare the sweetbreads. Clean and slice the vegetables into coarse julienne strips.

Preheat the oven to 350°F/180°C.

Melt the butter in a casserole and put in the sweetbreads. Allow them to brown gently all over, then remove them to a dish and put the vegetables into the casserole. Turn them over in the butter and let them sweat for 5 minutes without browning. Put in the bouquet garni, place the sweetbreads on top and pour in the vermouth and stock. Season with salt and pepper and cover the casserole. Bring the liquid to the boil, then transfer the pan to a moderate oven and simmer for 30–40 minutes.

Remove the sweetbreads to a board, slice them, arrange the slices on a heated dish and keep them hot. Take the bouquet of herbs out of the pan, bring the juices and vegetables to the boil on top of the stove and reduce for 5 minutes. Mix the arrowroot to a thin cream with 2 tablespoons of water and stir this into the juices. Boil to thicken the sauce slightly, taste for seasoning, then pour the entire contents of the pan over the sweetbreads. Serve with new or small plain steamed potatoes.

## *Charcoal grilled venison*

*1 venison steak from the leg or loin, weighing*
*2–3 lb/900 g–1.5 kg*

*1 teaspoon salt and ½ teaspoon coarsely crushed pepper*

*½ glass red wine*

*2–3 fresh rosemary or juniper branches (optional)*

SERVES 6

Make up the fire so that it is glowing nicely—if you do not have a charcoal grill, an open fire in a fireplace will do equally well.

Heat the grill rack. Rub the meat all over with the salt and pepper and put it over the fire on the rack. After 5 minutes, brush the steak with red wine and turn it over. After another 5 minutes, brush it with wine and turn again. Brush and turn frequently, cooking it for about 25 minutes altogether.

Remove the meat from the grill and wrap it in foil. Let it rest for 7–8 minutes. Freshen the charcoal fire and put the rosemary or juniper on the coals to smoulder and smoke. Unwrap the meat and put it back on the fire and let it cook and smoke for 5 minutes to give the outside a nice smoky flavor. The meat should be rosy red but not rare.

Carve the steak at the table, cutting it into fairly thick slices.

Serve with a salad, baked potatoes filled with sour cream and chopped chives or dill, and bread.

## *Braised venison*

*2 lb/900 g shoulder of venison in a piece*

*2 onions*

*2 tablespoons/30 g butter and 1 tablespoon olive oil*

*salt and coarsely ground pepper*

*1 teaspoon juniper berries, coarsely crushed*

*1¼ cups/3 dl beer*

*⅔ cup/1.5 dl chicken or beef stock*

*8 allspice berries*

*4 cloves*

*2 tablespoons heavy cream*

*nut of beurre manié, if needed*

SERVES 6–8

Peel and chop the onions. Trim the venison. Heat the butter and oil in an enamelled casserole and brown the shoulder on both sides. Season with half a teaspoon of salt, coarsely ground pepper and the crushed juniper berries. Add the beer and stock, chopped onions, allspice and cloves and let it simmer for 45 minutes or until tender. Remove the venison from the pan and keep it hot. Add the cream to the juices, which should be much reduced. Thicken the sauce lightly with a walnut of beurre manié if it seems too thin.

Carve the shoulder into slices and serve with small potatoes cooked in their skins, red currant jelly, and puréed celeriac. Serve the sauce separately.

ALTERNATIVE: *if using moose, braise it in exactly the same way, but serve it with black currant jelly or jam instead of red currant jelly.*

## *Roast haunch of venison*

*1 small haunch of venison*

*2 tablespoons/30 g lard*

*1 cup chicken or beef stock, or water*

*2 sticks celery, chopped*

*2 teaspoons flour*

*1 teaspoon green peppercorns or 1 teaspoon coarsely crushed black pepper*

*salt*

**for the marinade:**
*2 onions*

*1–2 tablespoons olive or peanut oil*

*2 bay leaves*

*bunch of parsley*

*2 glasses red wine*

*2 teaspoons black peppercorns*

SERVES 6–10

Start 2–3 days ahead.

Before you cook the venison, marinate it for a few days to help keep it moist. To make the marinade, peel and slice the onions, fry them in the oil until they start to brown and add the bay leaves, parsley, wine and peppercorns. Boil for 5 minutes, then add 2½ cups/6 dl water and boil the mixture, covered, for 15 minutes. Let it cool before use. Put the liquid into a flat earthenware dish, then put in the venison and let it marinate for 2–3 days. Turn the meat from time to time. This marinade, which has no vinegar, gives the venison a delicious rich flavor. When you are ready to roast the venison, preheat the oven to 375°F/190°C.

Remove the meat from the marinade—which you keep for the sauce—and wipe it dry. Wrap it completely in oiled foil and place it in a roasting pan. Put the haunch in the oven and let it roast for 25 minutes per 1 lb/450 g, or 20 minutes per 1 lb/450 g for a haunch weighing over 10 lb/4 kg. Then remove the foil, reserving the juices, rub the meat with lard, and roast it for a further 30 minutes. Meanwhile, boil the marinade together with the stock or water and the celery.

When you are ready to make the gravy, remove the meat from the roasting pan, stir in and brown the flour, and strain the marinade and juices into the pan, stirring to make a nice gravy. Add the green peppercorns or pepper and reduce the gravy to a syrupy consistency and serve separately. Sprinkle the meat with salt just before serving.

ALTERNATIVES: *you may add a little heavy cream to this gravy, and thereby make an even richer sauce. This recipe is also suitable for hare.*

---

## Jugged hare

1 large hare (with its blood if possible), skinned, gutted and jointed

12 small onions

¼ lb/115 g bacon, in a piece

flour for dusting

½ stick/55 g butter

2 tablespoons olive oil

4 sticks celery

4 large stout carrots

2 tablespoons/30 g lard

2 glasses red wine

stock made with the heart, liver and kidneys of the hare, a few vegetables and a bunch of herbs

salt and freshly ground pepper

pinch each of ground cloves, ground cinnamon and ground nutmeg

2–3 cloves

1 tablespoon beurre manié

SERVES 6

Peel the onions and cut the bacon into cubes. Dust the joints of hare with seasoned flour and fry them in a heavy iron casserole in the butter and oil. When they are a rich mahogany brown, transfer them to a large plate.

Preheat the oven to 325°F/170°C.

Slice the celery into crescents and the carrots into rounds, and sauté them with the onions and bacon in the butter and oil remaining in the casserole,

together with the lard, until the onions are nicely browned and glazed.

Pour off any excess fat. Return the pieces of hare, pour on the wine, let it bubble up and then add the strained stock, to come two-thirds of the way up the meat, and season with salt, pepper and the spices. Let the sauce come to the boil, then put the casserole in a low oven for an hour or until the hare is tender.

Put the casserole over a low heat on top of the cooker. Transfer the pieces of hare, bacon and vegetables to a heated serving dish and keep them hot. Add the beurre manié to the gravy in little pieces and stir it in. Let it simmer and when it has thickened a little, take the pan off the heat, let it cool a moment, then stir in the blood of the hare. Allow to stand for a few minutes, then pour the gravy over the hare and serve with boiled potatoes, and triangles of fried bread.

ALTERNATIVE: *if you feel the gravy needs a sweet note, add 1–2 tablespoons red currant jelly, beaten smooth with a fork, before you add the beurre manié.*

---

## Hare in sour cream

1 saddle of hare—use the rest for pappardelle alle lepre

1 onion

1 carrot

1 stick celery

small bouquet garni of thyme, parsley and a bay leaf

6 black peppercorns

1 wine glass red wine

4 thin slices bacon

1 teaspoon flour

⅔ cup/1.5 dl sour cream

salt and freshly ground pepper

SERVES 2

Start a day ahead.

Ask the game merchant to trim the saddle, removing the thick outer membrane and the flaps. Put it in a small earthenware dish. Peel and slice the onion and carrot thinly, and cut the celery into crescents. Put them in a small saucepan together with the bouquet garni and peppercorns. Add ½ cup/1.5 dl cold water and the red wine, bring to the boil and simmer for 5 minutes.

Pour the hot marinade over the saddle and allow to marinate for 24 hours.

When you are ready to cook the saddle, preheat the oven to 375°F/190°C.

Take the hare out of the marinade and wipe it dry. To prevent the saddle from curling up while it cooks, puncture the spinal column in several places with the point of a sharp knife before wrapping it in bacon. Wrap it in the slices of bacon, put it in a small roasting pan or gratin dish, and roast for 20 minutes, basting frequently with a tablespoon or two of the strained marinade. (You should add a wine glass of liquid altogether.)

Mix the flour with the sour cream, and add it to the juices in the roasting pan, stir it in, season with salt and pepper and cook for a further 10 minutes. Put the saddle on a heated serving dish, arrange the bacon around it and keep hot. Bring the sauce to the boil, add more marinade if it is too thick, or boil it for a minute or two if it is too thin. When it is the consistency of cream, pour it through a strainer over the saddle.

Serve with small, whole, steamed or boiled potatoes and red currant jelly.

heat and, when the hare starts to brown, sprinkle in the flour. Stir it in, then gradually add the wine, stirring well all the time. When this comes to the boil, add the tomato paste, cover the pan and simmer for 2 hours over a gentle heat, stirring occasionally and adding more liquid if it is becoming too dry.

At the end of this time put a large pan of well-salted water on to boil for the pasta.

Take the sauce off the heat, remove the bones from the hare and put the meat back into the pan. Simmer for about 15 minutes longer, seasoning if necessary. Meanwhile, put the pappardelle into the boiling water to cook. When they are just tender, drain and put into a heated bowl. Dress the pasta with the remaining butter and the Parmesan, pour the hare sauce over the top and serve at once.

This Italian sauce is only served with the little fluted pasta strips known as pappardelle, which by tradition must be yellow and not green.

## *Pappardelle alle lepre*

| |
|---|
| *1¼ lb/565 g hare on the bone—you can use the pieces left after cooking a saddle of hare* |
| *1 stick celery* |
| *1 onion* |
| *1 carrot* |
| *2 slices bacon or pancetta* |
| *5 tablespoons olive oil* |
| *¼ lb/115 g butter* |
| *salt and freshly ground pepper* |
| *1 bay leaf* |
| *1 tablespoon flour* |
| *2 cups/4.5 dl dry red wine* |
| *1 tablespoon tomato paste* |
| *1 lb/450 g fresh pappardelle* |
| *¾ cup/85 g Parmesan, freshly grated* |

SERVES 4

Wash and dry the pieces of hare and chop them into small pieces with a cleaver. Clean the vegetables and chop them finely. Cut the bacon or pancetta in strips. Heat the oil and half the butter in a saucepan and put in the chopped vegetables, bacon and chopped hare, together with a seasoning of salt and pepper and the bay leaf. Stir over a brisk

*Rabbit with prunes*

# Rabbit with prunes

*1 plump rabbit, skinned and cleaned*

*flour for dusting*

*1 onion*

*2–4 tablespoons/30–55 g butter*

*1 cup/2 dl red wine*

*½ lb/225 g dried prunes, soaked overnight in just enough water to cover them*

*salt and freshly ground pepper*

*a little stock (optional)*

**for the marinade:**

*1¾ cups/4 dl red wine*

*1 cup/2 dl wine vinegar*

*salt*

*6 black peppercorns*

*6 juniper berries*

*sprig of thyme*

*1 bay leaf*

*a few fennel twigs*

SERVES 4

Mix the ingredients for the marinade and place the rabbit in it, together with its liver and kidneys. Turn it once or twice and let it soak for a few hours, but not more than 12 hours.

Take the rabbit out, wipe it dry, and cut it into joints. Sprinkle them well with flour. Peel and chop the onion. Melt the butter in a sauté pan and brown the pieces of rabbit. Remove them to a plate and gently sauté the onion in the same butter. Return the pieces of rabbit and add the red wine, the prunes in their liquid, and season with salt and pepper. Cover the pan and simmer for 30 minutes, turning the pieces of rabbit from time to time. Then simmer, uncovered, for 15–40 minutes or until the rabbit is very tender (this will depend on the quality of the rabbit).

Taste the sauce, and if it is too rich, add a little stock or water. It should be fairly strong, not too sweet, and very well flavored. Season it if necessary and serve with small, whole, steamed or boiled potatoes. This is a Belgian recipe.

# Sautéed rabbit with mustard

*1 nice fat rabbit, skinned, cleaned and jointed*

*flour for dusting*

*2 tablespoons/30 g butter*

*1 tablespoon olive oil*

*1 onion*

*2–3 sprigs fresh thyme or ½ teaspoon dried thyme*

*1–2 glasses white wine*

*1 cup stock, preferably chicken*

*3 teaspoons each of Dijon mustard and hot mustard*

*salt and freshly ground pepper*

*2–3 tablespoons heavy cream*

SERVES 4

Keep the liver of the rabbit for a pâté. Dry the pieces of rabbit and pat them lightly with flour and salt. Heat the butter and oil in a large sauté pan or heavy flameproof casserole, and sauté the pieces until they are nicely browned. Meanwhile, peel the onion, cut it in half from top to tail, and slice each half downwards into slivers. Add the onion to the pan and let it just start to brown. Add thyme, wine and stock, a teaspoon of each mustard and a little salt and pepper. Bring the liquid to the boil and then turn down the heat.

Simmer the rabbit, uncovered, for 20 minutes, turning the pieces from time to time before adding the remaining Dijon mustard. Simmer on until the rabbit is tender. (A very plump young rabbit will take from 45 minutes to an hour altogether, a tough rabbit may take 2 hours or more.) Just before serving, stir in the remainder of the hot mustard. Taste for seasoning, and lastly add the cream. Serve with plain boiled potatoes.

ALTERNATIVE: *the rabbit's liver can be fried in butter, cut in thin slices and added to the sauce at the last moment for a richer flavor.*

# Braised rabbit and tomatoes

*1 rabbit, skinned, cleaned and jointed*

*1 onion*

*1 lb/450 g tomatoes*

*1–2 carrots*

*2 sticks celery*

*1 clove garlic*

*3–4 tablespoons olive oil*

*flour for dusting*

*salt and freshly ground pepper*

*1 small glass red wine*

*bouquet garni of parsley, thyme, marjoram and a bay leaf*

SERVES 4

Peel and chop the onion and tomatoes. Chop the

carrots and celery finely and peel and crush the garlic. Heat the oil in a flameproof casserole and fry the onion, carrots and celery together with the clove of garlic until they are beginning to soften and brown.

Dry the pieces of rabbit, dust them with flour, and put them in with the vegetables, turning up the heat. Try to get them in contact with the bottom of the pan to brown them. Frying the rabbit with the vegetables rather than before, gives it a more intense flavor.

When the pieces of rabbit are more or less brown all over, season them with salt and pepper, and add the red wine. Let it bubble until the smell of wine has disappeared and then add the tomatoes and the bouquet garni. Cover the pot and let it simmer for 45 minutes to an hour—or longer for a tough rabbit.

## Rabbit stew

| |
|---|
| *2 rabbits, skinned, cleaned and jointed* |
| *flour for dusting* |
| *20 shallots or button onions* |
| *2 cloves garlic* |
| *3 tablespoons olive oil* |
| *½ stick/55 g butter* |
| *sprig each of parsley and thyme, chopped* |
| *a few chives, chopped* |
| *1 large glass white wine or dry vermouth* |
| *1¼–2 cups/3–4.5 dl chicken stock or water* |
| *salt and freshly ground pepper* |
| *¾ lb/340 g button mushrooms* |
| *¾ lb/340 g tiny new potatoes, no larger than walnuts* |
| *1 tablespoon beurre manié* |

SERVES 6

Trim and dry the pieces of rabbit and pat them with flour. Peel the shallots or onions and the garlic. Sauté the whole shallots or onions in the oil and half the butter in a wide heavy casserole, until they are lightly browned. Spoon them out onto a plate. Brown the pieces of rabbit all over in the same oil and butter, return the shallots or onions and add the herbs, wine and half the garlic. Add enough stock or water to bathe the rabbit without covering it and season with salt and pepper. Bring to the boil, and simmer gently until the rabbit is tender. Even with young rabbits this can vary radically from 40 minutes to 2 hours, but a fine, fat rabbit should

come meltingly away from the bone after an hour. Meanwhile, lightly sauté the mushrooms in the remaining butter with the rest of the garlic, some salt and plenty of pepper, and scrape and boil the new potatoes. When the rabbit is tender, reduce the cooking liquid if it is too copious by straining it off and boiling it in a separate pan. Thicken the liquid with the beurre manié and pour it over the rabbit, which, if you are a perfectionist, you will have transferred to a clean casserole. Throw in the mushrooms and potatoes, heat through and serve.

## Pheasant with celery

| |
|---|
| *2 plump hen pheasants, plucked and cleaned, and their giblets* |
| *1 onion* |
| *6 black peppercorns* |
| *salt and freshly ground pepper* |
| *¾–1 stick/85–115 g butter* |
| *flour for dusting* |
| *1 tablespoon sunflower oil* |
| *4 thick slices bacon* |
| *1 head celery* |
| *⅔ cup/1.5 dl heavy cream* |
| *2 tablespoons Calvados, brandy or whisky* |

SERVES 4

Peel and slice the onion and put it in a small pan with all the giblets—except the livers—some salt and peppercorns. Cover with water and simmer gently for about an hour.

Preheat the oven to 425°F/220°C.

Season the pheasants inside and out, put a nut of the butter in each, dust the breasts with flour and brown them all over in 2 tablespoons/30 g of the butter and the oil in a frying pan. Transfer the birds to a roasting pan, lay 2 slices of fatty bacon over the breast of each, and roast for 35 minutes, basting frequently with half the remaining butter. Meanwhile chop the celery finely, so that it makes little crescents; wash these in a colander. Melt the remaining butter in a pan with half a glass of water, add salt and the celery and simmer, covered, turning the celery over with a wooden fork from time to time. It should gradually absorb the liquid. Ten minutes before the birds are done, remove the bacon and put it in the roasting pan beside the pheasants, adding the livers, turning them once to moisten them with fat all over, then return the pan to the oven. Strain the by now much-reduced giblet gravy, and add it to the celery, reducing it rapidly again. Just before you dish up the birds, add the cream to the celery, and the Calvados or brandy—or even whisky. Let it boil rapidly and reduce while you put the pheasants on a carving plate, together with the bacon and the cooked livers. Put them back in the oven and turn it off. Keeping the pheasants warm for a few minutes makes them easier to carve, as the meat sets.

Pour off all the fat from the juices in the roasting pan, scooping off the last bit with a teaspoon, and add the juices to the celery mixture. Let it bubble again for a few minutes, stir it thoroughly and serve in a hot bowl with a ladle. It is not a thick sauce and needs frequent stirring, but tastes wonderful, and is much better with this dish than anything thick and bland.

---

## Pheasant with raisin sauce

| |
|---|
| *1 young hen pheasant, plucked and cleaned, and its giblets* |
| *½ cup/85 g seedless Malaga raisins* |
| *1 shallot or small onion* |
| *½ stick/55 g butter* |
| *1 chicken liver (optional)* |
| *salt* |
| *1 small slice white bread, crusts removed* |
| *flour for dusting* |
| *1 tablespoon sunflower oil* |
| *4 slices bacon* |
| *⅓ cup sherry* |
| *about ⅔ cup/1.5 dl stock made with the pheasant's neck and heart, 1 onion, 2 carrots and 1 bay leaf* |

SERVES 2–3

Put the raisins in a small saucepan and just cover with cold water. Bring to the boil and simmer 3–4 minutes. Drain, rinse with cold water and drain again. (This removes any preservative mineral oil, which can really spoil the flavor of raisins, and softens them a little.) Set them on one side. Peel and chop the shallot or onion finely. Melt a walnut of the butter in a small frying pan, put in the chopped shallot and let it soften. Chop the pheasant's liver finely (if this has not been reserved use a chicken liver) and add it to the pan. Season with a little salt and let it cook gently for 2–3 minutes, mashing it with the back of a wooden spoon. Let the mixture cool, then spread half on the piece of bread, roll it up and put it inside the pheasant. Keep the rest of the liver mixture to one side. Preheat the oven to 400°F/200°C.

Dust the outside of the pheasant with flour, melt the remaining butter with the sunflower oil in a roasting pan and brown the pheasant all over, then tie the bacon over the breast and roast for 35 minutes, basting occasionally. Take off the bacon for the last 5 minutes of the cooking time. Remove the pheasant to a serving dish, cover it with foil and let it sit in the oven, which should be turned off, with the door slightly open. Remove most of the fat from the roasting pan with a spoon, and add the raisins and the rest of the liver mixture to the juices left in the pan. Heat through, then add the sherry; let it bubble for a minute, then add the stock and a little salt. Simmer until reduced by half.

Carve the pheasant and serve accompanied by the raisin sauce in a separate bowl or sauce boat and a spoonful of the bread stuffing on each plate. Braised endive is good with this dish—another combination of bitter and sweet.

---

## Pheasant with chestnuts

| |
|---|
| *1 pheasant, plucked and cleaned, and its giblets* |
| *2 Spanish onions* |
| *2 shallots* |
| *6 small carrots* |
| *6 thick slices bacon* |
| *2 tablespoons/30 g butter* |
| *flour for dusting* |
| *⅓ cup red wine* |
| *1¼ cups/3 dl stock, made with the pheasant's neck, heart and liver, 1 onion, 2 carrots and a bay leaf* |
| *salt and freshly ground pepper* |
| *bouquet garni of 1 bay leaf and a sprig each of thyme and parsley* |
| *½ lb/225 g chestnuts* |
| *1 teaspoon arrowroot* |

SERVES 2–3

Preheat the oven to 325°F/170°C.

Peel and slice the onions, shallots and carrots. Cut the bacon into little sticks, and fry them in the butter in a flameproof casserole. Dust the pheasant with flour and fry it gently in the same butter on all sides, until it is nicely browned. Remove the pheasant and the pieces of bacon, and fry the vegetables lightly in the fat remaining in the casserole without browning them. Pour in the red wine and let it bubble for a few minutes; return the bacon to the casserole, and put the pheasant on its side on top of the vegetables. Pour on the stock, season with salt and pepper and add the bouquet garni. Cover the pan and put the casserole in a low oven for 30 minutes.

Meanwhile, peel the chestnuts. Put them into the casserole around the pheasant, turn the bird over, and replace the lid. Cook for a further 30 minutes. Remove the pheasant, chestnuts and vegetables with a slotted spoon and keep them hot. Skim the braising juices, tipping the casserole to make it easier. Dissolve the arrowroot in 3 tablespoons of water in a cup and stir it into the juices. Taste for seasoning. Allow to simmer for 5 minutes, stirring from time to time.

Carve the pheasant. Arrange it with the vegetables and chestnuts on a deep serving dish and pour on the lightly thickened sauce.

## *Normandy pheasant*

*1 plump young pheasant, plucked and cleaned*

*½ stick/55 g butter*

*1 tablespoon peanut oil*

*⅓ cup Calvados*

*3–4 tablespoons chicken stock*

*⅔ cup/1.5 dl heavy cream*

*3 apples—Golden Delicious or green eating apples are best*

*salt and freshly ground pepper*

SERVES 4

Heat half the butter and the oil in a flameproof casserole and brown the pheasant all over. Then cover the casserole and cook the pheasant gently for 40 minutes, turning it over from time to time. Remove the pheasant from the casserole and carve it into four pieces on a board. Arrange the pieces on a dish and keep them hot while you skim about half the fat from the casserole with a tablespoon. Pour the Calvados into the casserole and let it boil for a minute, then add the stock—and a little later the cream. Let it bubble, stirring, until it thickens.

Meanwhile, peel, quarter and core the apples and fry them to a golden brown in the remaining butter in a separate pan. Season the sauce, pour it over the pheasant, arrange the fried apples around the edge and serve very hot.

## *Roast partridge*

*4 plump young partridges, plucked and cleaned, and their livers*

*8 thin slices bacon*

*salt and freshly ground pepper*

*1 chicken liver*

*4 small slices white bread, crusts removed*

*1 clove garlic, peeled and cut in half*

*¾ stick/85 g butter*

*½ tablespoon sunflower oil*

*6 tablespoons white wine*

*1 bunch watercress*

SERVES 4

Preheat the oven to 425°F/220°C.

Truss the birds neatly, covering each carefully with 2 slices of bacon, and season them inside and out with salt and freshly ground pepper. Crush the partridge livers and the chicken liver, mashing them well with a fork and removing any fibers. Rub the slices of bread with the halved clove of garlic and then spread them with butter and then the crushed livers. Season lightly with salt and pepper, roll up the pieces of bread, liver side inwards, and push one inside each partridge.

Heat the remaining butter and oil in a roasting pan and brown the birds all over for 5 minutes. Then transfer them to the oven and roast for 10 minutes. Remove the covering of bacon, and roast for a further 5 minutes to finish browning the birds. Take them out, remove the trussing strings and put the birds on a serving dish. Turn down the oven temperature to 300°F/160°C.

Put the birds in the oven to keep hot while you make the gravy. To do this, add the wine and 3–4 tablespoons of water to the roasting pan, from which you have removed most of the fat with a teaspoon, and let it boil over a moderate heat while you stir and scrape up the juices. When the liquid has reduced by half, pour it into a small gravy boat. Serve the partridges with sprigs of watercress arranged around them on their serving dish.

# Partridge with celeriac

*4 plump young partridges, plucked and cleaned*

*4 shallots*

*8 juniper berries, crushed*

*1½ sticks/170 g butter*

*salt and freshly ground pepper*

*4 slices bacon*

*1 medium celeriac—about 1 lb/450 g*

*1 small potato*

*4 tablespoons white wine*

*juice of ½ lemon*

SERVES 4

Preheat the oven to 400°F/200°C.

Put a peeled shallot, 2 crushed juniper berries and a little butter, salt and pepper inside each partridge and lay a slice of bacon over the breast of each. Spread ½ stick/55 g of the remaining butter over the birds and put them in a roasting pan. Roast for 15 minutes, then turn down the oven temperature to 325°F/170°C.

Remove the bacon and roast the birds for a further 10 minutes, basting occasionally.

Meanwhile, peel the celeriac and potato, cut them into pieces, put them in a pan of cold salted water. Bring to the boil and simmer for about 25 minutes until completely tender. Drain, mash, and whisk to a purée with the rest of the butter and season lightly with salt and pepper.

When the partridges are tender, take them out of the oven and put them on a board. Do not turn the oven off. Carve the birds into breasts and legs and put the pieces on a dish. Sprinkle them with the white wine and lemon juice. Discard the other bones—or reserve them for making stock. Skim most of the fat from the roasting pan and mix the remaining juices into the celeriac purée. Transfer this to an oval gratin dish. Put the pieces of partridge on top, season with salt and pepper, then put the gratin dish into the oven to cook for a further 10–15 minutes, until heated right through.

ALTERNATIVE: *make the same dish with squabs, allowing an extra 10 minutes' roasting time.*

---

*Partridge with celeriac*

# Roast grouse

*4 young grouse, plucked and cleaned*

*1 stick/115 g butter*

*salt and freshly ground pepper*

*few sprigs of lovage (optional)*

*flour for dusting*

*1–2 slices bacon*

*⅔ cup/1.5 dl game or chicken stock for gravy*

SERVES 4

Preheat the oven to 425°F/220°C.

Put a lump of butter, rolled in salt and pepper, inside each bird—you can also add a sprig of lovage. Dust the outside of the birds with flour. Put ½ stick/55 g of the butter and a slice or two of bacon into the roasting pan (the bacon fat will mix with the butter and prevent it from burning). Put the pan into the oven and when the fat is very hot, put in the grouse and baste. Roast them very fast for 10 minutes, baste again and then put them back in the oven.

Turn down the oven temperature to 350°F/180°C, and leave the birds to roast for a further 10–15 minutes if you like them pink and juicy, 20–25 minutes if you like them well cooked.

Serve the grouse with fried bread crumbs and clear gravy, made with game or chicken stock and the juices from the pan. Watercress tastes particularly good with these juices.

ALTERNATIVES: *if they are available, a few ripe rowanberries or raspberries may be pushed into the grouse before roasting, to keep them moist and improve the gravy. If there isn't any gravy—no game stock, rowanberries or pan juices—serve the grouse simply with plain melted butter.*

---

## Roast woodcock

4 woodcock, plucked but not cleaned
$\frac{3}{4}$ stick/85 g butter
4 slices white bread
salt and freshly ground pepper
$\frac{1}{2}$ tablespoon brandy
4 tablespoons white wine or dry vermouth

SERVES 4

Preheat the oven to 425°F/220°C.

Skin the birds' necks and heads and remove the crop and the eyes. Truss the birds by passing their long beaks through their bodies beneath the wing, and tying the legs close in to the body. Cover the birds with two-thirds of the butter, and put them in a roasting pan. Roast for 15–25 minutes, according to how pink you like them, basting once or twice.

Meanwhile, cut four circles from the slices of bread, and fry them gently to a pale golden color in the remaining butter. Drain them on paper towels and keep them hot.

When the woodcock are done, carefully scrape out their insides with a teaspoon, discard the seed-shaped gizzard, season the rest of the entrails with a little salt and pepper, and chop them on a board. Remove half the fat from the roasting pan with a spoon, add the chopped "trail" and pour the brandy into the remaining roasting juices. Add the wine, stirring and scraping up the juices from the bottom of the pan. When it has reduced somewhat, rub the sauce through a sieve into a heated sauce boat.

To serve the woodcock, remove the beaks from the bodies, and cut the heads in half, so that you can eat the brains. If you can't face this, simply remove the heads and necks before serving. Put the pieces

of fried bread underneath the birds and hand the gravy separately.

ALTERNATIVE: *roast snipe can be cooked in exactly the same way, but for 12–15 minutes only.*

---

## Quails with juniper

8 quails, plucked and cleaned
16 juniper berries, crushed
8 sprigs thyme
$\frac{1}{2}$ stick/55 g butter
4 strips orange peel
salt and freshly ground pepper
juice of 1 orange
small glass of eau-de-vie, marc or brandy

SERVES 4

Preheat the oven to 375°F/190°C.

Push a couple of crushed juniper berries and a sprig of thyme into each bird, together with its liver if possible. Melt the butter in a large casserole, and when it starts to brown, put in the birds and brown them all over. Add the orange peel, season the birds, then cover the casserole and put in the oven for 10 minutes. Add the juice of the orange, cover the casserole again and cook for a further 10 minutes, then turn the oven temperature up to 425°F/220°C.

Pour on the eau-de-vie, marc or brandy (or fundador or other grape liquor), baste the birds, return to the oven and let them cook, uncovered, for 5–10 minutes. This will emulsify the juices into a fragrant, smooth gravy instead of separate layers of sediment, juices and fat.

This is a superlative way of cooking quail—they need the sweet, bitter and sour of the orange, juniper berries and the spirits.

---

## Quails poached in consommé

4 quails, plucked and cleaned (or use 8 quails for a more substantial dish)
1 stick celery
4 carrots
$\frac{1}{4}$ lb/115 g white button mushrooms
juice of $\frac{1}{2}$ lemon
$\frac{1}{4}$ lb/115 g green beans

*5 cups/1 liter homemade chicken consommé*

*1 small head lettuce*

*salt*

SERVES 4

Preheat the oven to 425°F/220°C.

Cut the celery into small delicate crescents, peel the carrots and slice them lengthwise into narrow julienne strips. Slice the mushrooms rather thinly and sprinkle them with the lemon juice. Top and tail the green beans. Cook the celery, carrots and beans separately in plenty of boiling, salted water, taking them out before they are quite cooked. Keep the carrot cooking water, and bring it just to simmering point. Drop in the quails and poach them gently for 10 minutes. Take them out and carve them into breasts and legs. Divide them between four deep ovenproof soup bowls. Scatter the cooked vegetables and the mushrooms on top, sharing them out evenly between the bowls. Pour on the consommé and place a few small inner lettuce leaves over the top of each bowl. Put the bowls in a large roasting pan and slide them into the oven for 10–15 minutes. Serve very hot.

---

# Roast mallard

*1 mallard duck, plucked and cleaned*

*½ an orange*

*½ stick/55 g butter*

*salt*

*1 shallot, peeled*

*1 in/2.5 cm piece of celery*

*½ glass red wine*

*squeeze of lemon juice*

*few drops of Tabasco*

SERVES 2

Rub the mallard with a quarter of an orange, peel and all, then put this inside the bird with a nut of the butter, salt, the shallot and celery. Spread a little more of the butter over the breast of the bird. Preheat the oven to 400°F/200°C.

Pour a dash of red wine into the inside of the bird, put it in a roasting pan, and roast for 30 minutes, basting from time to time.

When the duck is cooked, keep it warm while you make the gravy. Pour the juices from the inside of the duck into a small saucepan. Add the juice of the remaining quarter of orange, a squeeze of lemon

juice, and a few drops of Tabasco. Add a walnut-size piece of butter and swish it around over a gentle heat until the butter has amalgamated with the juices. Taste the gravy, add a little salt if needed, and serve.

Carve the slices from the breast of the duck—the legs are very often too rare and too tough to eat when the breast is perfect. Use them together with the bones (but not the skin) for making soup. The skin is, generally speaking, not worth eating, but serve the slices of duck with the skin on and let people choose.

---

# Salmis of wild duck

*2 wild ducks, plucked and cleaned*

*1 onion or 6 shallots*

*2 anchovy fillets*

*½ stick/55 g butter*

*1 large glass red wine*

*⅔–1¼ cups/1.5–3 dl chicken, beef or game stock*

*3 cloves*

*bouquet garni of thyme, parsley and a bay leaf*

*pinch each of cayenne pepper, ground nutmeg and ground allspice*

*salt and freshly ground pepper*

*4 tablespoons port*

*nut of beurre manié*

*squeeze of lemon juice*

SERVES 6

Preheat the oven to 425°F/220°C.

Put the ducks in a roasting pan and roast them for 15 minutes. Put them on a board, allow to cool and cut them into legs and breasts. Peel and chop the onion or shallots and chop the anchovy fillets. Melt the butter in a casserole and sauté the chopped onion or shallots without letting them brown. Add the legs, but not the breasts of the ducks, and the red wine. Let it come to the boil, simmer for 2–3 minutes, then add enough stock to moisten the pieces of duck without covering them. Add the cloves, chopped anchovies, bouquet garni, cayenne pepper, nutmeg, allspice and a little salt and simmer until tender—this can take from 25 minutes to an hour depending on the age of the ducks.

Remove the bunch of herbs and take out the pieces of duck, putting them on one side. Stir in the port and beurre manié, broken into small pieces, and simmer until the liquid thickens. Slice the breast fillets into long strips and put them, together with the legs, into the sauce. Add lemon juice, season with salt and pepper, and heat through.

---

## Roast moorhen

| |
|---|
| 2 moorhens |
| ½ stick/55 g butter |
| salt and freshly ground pepper |
| 1 small glass red wine |
| 4 tablespoons game or chicken stock |

SERVES 2

Pluck the birds after dipping for an instant into boiling water, and remove the down by scraping it with a knife. Gut them and remove their crops. Preheat the oven to 425°F/220°C.

Put a nut of the butter and a seasoning of salt and pepper inside each bird. Spread the rest of the butter over the breasts and put the birds in a roasting pan. Roast for 20 minutes, basting.

Put the birds on a serving dish and keep them hot; remove the fat from the roasting pan and pour the red wine into the remaining juices. Let this simmer and reduce to a couple of tablespoons, add the stock, season lightly with salt and pepper, and simmer a few minutes more. Serve the moorhens with this gravy and a watercress and sliced orange salad.

---

## Braised squabs and cabbage

| |
|---|
| 4 squabs, plucked and cleaned |
| flour for dusting |
| salt and freshly ground pepper |
| 2 onions |
| 3 tablespoons/45 g butter |
| 1 tablespoon sunflower or other oil |
| 1 cabbage, white or green |
| 2–3 slices bacon |
| 2 tablespoons cider vinegar |
| 1 small glass white wine |
| ⅔ cup/1.5 dl chicken stock |
| 4 allspice berries |
| 6 juniper berries, crushed |
| 1 bay leaf |
| 2 teaspoons sugar |

SERVES 4

Dust the birds with flour and season with salt and pepper, inside and out, and peel and slice the onions. Melt a third of the butter, together with the oil, in a flameproof casserole, large and deep enough to hold the birds on their layer of cabbage. When it is sizzling, brown the birds all over rather gently and then put them on one side. Preheat the oven to 325°F/170°C.

Add the rest of the butter to the casserole and put in the sliced onions, letting them soften and brown very lightly. Finely slice the cabbage, removing the stalk, and cut the bacon into squares. Add the cabbage and bacon to the onions, stir them around and let them sweat, covered, for about 5 minutes. Add the vinegar, wine, stock, allspice, juniper berries, bay leaf and sugar. Season with salt and pepper, put the squabs on top and cover tightly. Bring the liquid to the boil, then braise in the oven for an hour to an hour and 30 minutes.

---

## Sugo di carne Toscano

| |
|---|
| 2 squabs about 1–1¼ lb each |
| 2 chicken livers |
| 1 onion |
| 2 carrots |
| 1 stick celery or a piece of peeled celeriac |
| 6 basil leaves, chopped |
| 4 tablespoons olive or peanut oil |
| salt and freshly ground pepper |
| 1 large glass red wine |
| 1¼ cups/3 dl chicken stock or water |
| ½ oz/15 g dried ceps |
| 3 fresh or canned tomatoes, peeled and chopped |

SERVES 4

Cut the squabs into pieces about the size of a large nut, leaving the bones in—these are removed later. Roughly chop the chicken livers. Peel and chop the onion and carrots and chop the celery or celeriac. Put the meat in a medium-size saucepan with the onion, carrots, celery and basil. With the pan still away from the heat, add the oil and a little salt and pepper. Put the pan, uncovered, over a brisk heat, stirring from time to time with a wooden spoon. If the vegetables stick to the bottom so much the better, but don't let them burn. When they are browning nicely, pour in the wine. Keep the heat very brisk. Scrape the bottom of the pan carefully to mix in the pieces that have caramelized on the bottom, and blend them with the wine. This is very important. Continue cooking so that the wine reduces and loses its smell but doesn't totally evaporate. Add the chicken stock or water. Lower the flame and simmer for 1½ hours, or until tender. Meanwhile soak the dried mushrooms in a little lukewarm water. When the meat is cooked, scoop it out and remove the bones. Chop the meat coarsely —this texture gives the sauce its character. When the mushrooms have softened, chop them roughly. Add meat, mushrooms and mushroom liquid to the pan, together with the tomatoes. Simmer gently for 15 minutes, stirring frequently and adding stock a little at a time if necessary, to obtain a nice rich sauce. If the sauce seems too thin, cook it slowly until it has reached a rich, thick consistency.

This exquisite meat sauce, fundamental to the Tuscan kitchen, makes a delicious change from Bolognese sauce. It is ideal with spaghetti and tagliatelle, for stuffing ravioli and cannelloni and with gnocchi. ALTERNATIVES: *instead of squabs use 8–10 oz/225–280 g rabbit, lean beef, or half beef and half chicken.*

# Squab pie

| |
|---|
| *2 squabs, 1–1¼ lb each, plucked and cleaned* |
| *1 large onion* |
| *¾ lb/340 g chuck steak* |
| *flour for dusting* |
| *3 tablespoons sunflower oil* |
| *1 teaspoon Worcestershire sauce* |
| *salt and freshly ground pepper* |
| *1 bay leaf* |
| *shortcrust pastry made with 1½ cups/170 g flour* |
| *1 egg yolk* |

**for the stock:**

| |
|---|
| *the squab bones* |
| *1 onion* |
| *1 carrot* |
| *1 stick celery* |
| *bouquet garni of parsley, thyme and a bay leaf* |
| *¼ cup red wine* |

SERVES 4–6

Joint the squabs so that each makes four joints—keeping the rib cage for the stock. To make the stock, peel and slice the onion and carrot, and wash and chop the celery. Put the stock bones in a saucepan with the onion, carrot and celery, the bouquet of herbs and the red wine. Add 1¼ cups/3 dl cold water, bring to the boil, skim, and simmer, covered, for an hour or more.

Peel and chop the large onion, and cut the beef into smallish cubes. Dust the beef and squabs generously with flour and brown them—a few pieces at a time—in the oil. Transfer to a deep pie dish, and place a funnel in the center. Brown the chopped onion lightly in the same oil, and then transfer it to the pie dish with the squabs and beef. Strain the stock, mix it with the Worcestershire sauce and pour it over the meat and onions. Allow to cool, season with salt and pepper, and put in the bay leaf. Preheat the oven to 425°F/220°C.

Roll out the pastry, cut a long strip and moisten it with a pastry brush dipped in water. Stick the strip around the edge of the pie dish. Brush again with a pastry brush moistened with water, put the remaining pastry over the top and trim around the edge with a small knife. Decorate the pie, crimp the edge and brush with an egg yolk beaten with a teaspoon of water.

Bake for 15 minutes until the crust is set, then turn down the oven to 300°F/160°C, and continue to bake it for a further hour and 30 minutes, covering the pie with foil as soon as it has turned a nice brown color.

# Chicken with marjoram

| |
|---|
| *1 chicken weighing about 3½ lb/1.75 kg* |
| *½ stick/55 g butter* |

**for the stuffing:**

| |
|---|
| *½ onion* |
| *3 tablespoons butter, softened* |
| *2 thick slices day-old white bread, crusts removed* |
| *1½ teaspoons dried or 3 teaspoons chopped fresh marjoram* |
| *salt* |

SERVES 4–6

Preheat the oven to 375°F/190°C.

Peel and finely chop the half onion and sauté gently in a tablespoon of the butter until transparent but not browned. Grate the bread to make fairly coarse crumbs. Mix these with the onion and its butter, the marjoram, a little salt and the remaining softened butter. Stuff the bird with this mixture,

put it in a roasting pan, cover it with butter and roast for an hour, basting often. Don't press the stuffing too firmly as it should be very light.
ALTERNATIVE: *in France this recipe is often used with guinea fowl.*

---

## Chicken on a bed of garlic

*1 chicken weighing 3½–4 lb/1.75–2 kg*

*1, 2 or even 3 large heads garlic (not cloves but whole heads containing 15–20 cloves each)*

*¼ stick/55 g butter*

*salt and freshly ground pepper*

SERVES 4–6

Preheat the oven to 375°F/190°C.
Peel each clove of garlic one by one. Put a couple of cloves of garlic and a lump of the butter inside the chicken and season it inside and out with salt and pepper. Put the other peeled cloves of garlic in an oval gratin dish. Put half the remaining butter in the dish, spreading the rest over the chicken.
Roast the chicken for an hour—basting it often. The basting is important, as the butter is permeated with the flavor of the garlic and by basting you will transfer it to the chicken.
The garlic cloves will become mild, soft and tasty and delicious to eat. Serve the chicken in the dish with the garlic and cooking juices. It is wise to serve beautifully mashed potatoes to sop up the butter. This is a simple way of improving a dull bird.

---

## Devilled chicken legs

*4 chicken legs or 8 drumsticks*

*1 small glass sherry*

*1 tablespoon tarragon vinegar*

*2 teaspoons Worcestershire sauce*

*2 teaspoons hot mustard*

*salt and freshly ground black pepper*

*2–3 tablespoons olive oil*

SERVES 4

Make the devil sauce: mix the sherry, vinegar, Worcestershire sauce and mustard in a bowl. Season with salt and half a teaspoon of pepper.
Make a few neat cuts in the chicken legs or drumsticks, parallel with the bone. Put them in an earthenware dish just large enough to hold them side by side and pour the devil mixture over them, rubbing it into the cuts with your fingers. Let them marinate in the mixture for an hour so that they absorb the flavors.
Heat the broiler or make sure the barbecue has a nice bed of glowing embers, and heat a wire grill or grilling rack.
Drain the legs or drumsticks well and then paint them with the olive oil. Put them on the grill rack, close to the source of heat, searing the outside of the legs on all sides. Then move them farther away from the heat and finish cooking, basting alternately with the devil mixture and olive oil. When they are cooked through but still moist inside, after about 15 minutes, serve very hot.
Salad and rice are good with this if the chicken pieces are to be eaten at the table, but for an outside party simply eat them with the fingers, with bread—pita bread is excellent.

---

## Chicken pie

*1 boiling fowl weighing 3–3½ lb/1.5–1.75 kg*

*2 onions*

*3 carrots*

*2 sticks celery*

*3 sprigs parsley, tied together*

*1 bay leaf*

*3 tablespoons/45 g butter*

*⅜ cup/45 g flour*

*salt and freshly ground pepper*

*¼ lb/115 g button mushrooms*

*¼ lb/115 g lean sausage meat rolled into marble-size balls*

*⅔ cup/1.5 dl heavy cream*

*shortcrust or puff pastry made with 6 oz/170 g flour*

*1 egg, beaten (optional)*

SERVES 4–6

Peel and slice the onions and carrots; wash the celery and cut it into crescents. Put the chicken into a large saucepan with the sliced vegetables and the herbs. Cover with cold water, bring slowly to the boil, skim and simmer for 30 minutes. Add salt, and simmer on until the chicken is cooked—this takes about 45 minutes to an hour in all. Let it cool in its liquid if there is time, then remove and take the meat off the bones. (Some people leave wing and leg bones in to make a more substantial pie.) Make a sauce with the butter, flour and 2 cups/4.5 dl of the strained chicken broth. Season it well, stir in the mushrooms and cook gently while you lightly fry the sausage meatballs for a few minutes. Drain them on paper towels. Stir the cream, the meatballs and the chicken very gently into the sauce. Place a funnel in a deep pie dish, then pour in the mixture and allow to cool.

Preheat the oven to 400°F/200°C.

Cover the chicken mixture with pastry, brush with beaten egg or the last few drops in the cream pot, and bake for 12–15 minutes. Then turn the oven down to 350°F/180°C, and bake for a further 15–20 minutes.

---

stirring but adding more of the stock as necessary. When the rice is cooked and has absorbed all the stock, add the saffron and vermouth or wine, cook for a few minutes, mix in the parsley and then put it into a hot bowl. Take the chicken out of the oven and put it on a heated dish. Pour all the juices, including the butter, from the roasting pan over the rice, stir it well and serve immediately with the chicken.

ALTERNATIVES: *this is a very happy combination, often found in Middle Eastern cooking—meat with fruit and nuts. If you prefer to use either cashew nuts or pine nuts, the result will still be very pleasing. You could also fry 2–3 cloves and a piece of cinnamon stick with the shallots and rice for a spicier dish.*

---

## Chicken with almonds

| |
|---|
| *1 chicken weighing 3 lb/1.5 kg* |
| *1 small onion* |
| *salt and freshly ground pepper* |
| *$\frac{1}{2}$–$\frac{3}{4}$ stick/55–85 g butter* |
| *$\frac{1}{2}$ lemon* |
| *3 shallots* |
| *$\frac{2}{3}$ cup/115 g almonds* |
| *$\frac{1}{2}$ cup/85 g raisins* |
| *3 tablespoons olive oil* |
| *generous 1$\frac{3}{4}$ cups/340 g long-grain rice* |
| *5 cups/1 liter chicken stock, made with the chicken giblets, 1 glass dry vermouth or white wine, some parsley and 1 onion* |
| *1 pinch saffron strands, soaked in 1 glass dry vermouth or white wine* |
| *1 heaped tablespoon chopped parsley* |

SERVES 4

Preheat the oven to 375°F/190°C.

Peel the onion. Season the chicken, inside and out, with salt and pepper, and place a large lump of the butter and the onion inside. Rub the chicken's skin with lemon juice and butter, and roast for an hour, basting from time to time.

Meanwhile, peel and finely chop the shallots. Blanch the almonds, slice them in half lengthwise and toast them, with the raisins, in a dry frying pan. Heat the olive oil in a sauté pan and add the finely chopped shallots; cook gently without browning, stirring continuously. Add the rice, and after 3–4 minutes add the raisins, almonds and enough stock to cover the rice. Simmer for 25 minutes without

## Poulet à la provençale

| |
|---|
| *1 chicken weighing 3 lb/1.5 kg, cut into four pieces* |
| *salt and freshly ground pepper* |
| *1–2 cloves garlic* |
| *6 tomatoes* |
| *3–4 tablespoons olive oil* |
| *1 glass white wine* |
| *12 black olives* |
| *few sprigs of fresh basil, or some dried basil or oregano* |

SERVES 4

Season the pieces of chicken with salt and pepper. Peel and chop the garlic and tomatoes. Heat the olive oil in a large frying pan, brown the pieces of chicken on all sides and when they are golden and well sealed, turn down the heat. Let the chicken cook gently for 30 minutes, turning the pieces frequently, then remove them to a hot dish.

Meanwhile, pour the white wine into the frying pan, stirring and scraping it with a spoon to collect all the bits. Add the chopped garlic, the tomatoes, the olives and the basil or oregano. Let the sauce simmer for 15 minutes, season, pour over the chicken and serve.

---

## Coq au vin

| |
|---|
| *1 plump young chicken weighing 3 lb/1.5 kg* |
| *$\frac{1}{4}$ lb/115 g unsmoked bacon, in a piece* |
| *$\frac{1}{2}$ stick/55 g butter* |

*1 tablespoon oil*

*flour for dusting*

*2 cloves garlic*

*bouquet garni of thyme and parsley*

*½ bottle red wine*

*salt and freshly ground pepper*

*12 button onions*

*12 white button mushrooms*

SERVES 4

Preheat the oven to 350°F/180°C.

Cut the chicken into six pieces, and the bacon into little sticks about ¼ in/5 mm across and 1½ in/4 cm long. Heat half the butter and the oil in an oven-proof casserole and put in the pieces of bacon. When they are starting to brown, flour the pieces of chicken lightly, add them to the bacon and sauté until they are nicely browned all over.

Peel and crush the cloves of garlic and add them to the casserole with the bouquet of herbs and the wine. Season with salt and pepper, bring to the boil and transfer to the oven for about an hour, until the chicken is almost tender when pricked with a fork or skewer.

Meanwhile, peel the onions and cook them in a saucepan of boiling salted water for 10 minutes. Drain, and sauté them in the remaining butter until slightly brown. Remove them with a slotted spoon, and transfer them to the casserole with the chicken. Trim the mushrooms and sauté them in the same butter. When they are lightly cooked, transfer them to the casserole, remove the bouquet garni and heat through. Serve with plain boiled potatoes or turnips, and a green salad.

ALTERNATIVE: *if you like a thicker sauce, strain the liquid into a saucepan before you add the vegetables. Reduce it by boiling for 5 minutes and then thicken it with a teaspoon or two of beurre manié. Pour it over the chicken, bacon and vegetables and simmer for 10 minutes or so before serving.*

---

## Poularde Brillat-Savarin

*1 chicken weighing 3½ lb/1.75 kg*

*small bunch of tarragon or parsley*

*½ stick/55 g butter*

*½ lb/225 g button mushrooms*

*a little stock made from chicken giblets, 1 carrot and*

*2 shallots or 1 onion*

*1–2 tablespoons sherry*

*⅔ cup/1.5 dl heavy cream*

*salt and freshly ground pepper*

SERVES 6

Preheat the oven to 375°F/190°C.

Put the herbs inside the chicken and put it into a casserole with the butter. Cover and cook in the oven for an hour, turning it from time to time. Then add the cleaned mushrooms, stir them into the cooking juices and cook for a further 10 minutes. Remove the chicken and mushrooms to a dish and keep them hot. Reduce the juices a little and then add the sherry and a wine glass of stock. Let it simmer for 2 or 3 minutes, then moisten with the cream, tipping the pan back and forth to mix the cream and juices. Simmer for 5 minutes and season. Either carve the chicken into six pieces and pour the sauce over, or serve the chicken whole and the sauce separately. This is an excellent recipe—both simple to make and very luxurious.

---

## Poulet paysanne

*1 chicken weighing 3 lb/1.5 kg*

*18 small new potatoes, a bit larger than a walnut*

*¼ lb/115 g mushrooms*

*2 cloves garlic*

*½ stick/55 g butter*

*3 tablespoons peanut oil*

*salt and freshly ground pepper*

*1 tablespoon chopped parsley*

*⅔ cup/1.5 dl chicken stock made with the giblets*

SERVES 4–6

Scrape or scrub the potatoes. Slice the mushrooms thinly, and peel and chop the garlic. Cut the chicken into six pieces. In a wide shallow pan, heat half the butter and 2 tablespoons of the oil, and put in the pieces of chicken, side by side. Let them cook gently, uncovered, for about 15 minutes, turning them from time to time until they are golden.

Meanwhile, heat the remaining butter and oil in a smaller pan and add the potatoes, first dried in a cloth. Let them brown, shaking the pan occasionally, and turning them over. When the potatoes are evenly colored, add the sliced mushrooms and mix them in. Let them cook together for a minute or two, then add them together with their butter to the chicken. Season with salt and pepper, cover the pan and simmer gently for about 30 minutes until the chicken is tender and the potatoes are cooked through.

Remove the lid, and sprinkle in the chopped parsley and garlic. Stir around and cook on for a further 3–4 minutes. Remove the pieces of chicken, potatoes and mushrooms to a deep serving dish and keep them hot. Spoon the fat off the cooking juices and pour the chicken stock into the pan. Scrape and stir to dislodge any cooking juices caramelized on the bottom of the pan and allow the liquid to reduce to about half its volume. Pour it over the chicken, and serve very hot.

---

## Chicken paprika

| |
|---|
| *1 chicken weighing about 3 lb/1.5 kg* |
| *2–3 onions* |
| *2 tablespoons/30 g butter* |
| *1 tablespoon sunflower oil* |
| *2 tablespoons paprika* |
| *salt* |
| *1 lb/450 g tomatoes* |
| *⅔ cup/1.5 dl sour cream* |

SERVES 4

Preheat the oven to 300°F/160°C.

Cut the chicken into six pieces. Peel and chop the onions. Heat the butter and oil in an ovenproof casserole and brown the pieces of chicken evenly all over.

Transfer the pieces to a dish while you fry the chopped onions in the same fat. When they are lightly browned, stir in most of the paprika, let it cook for a minute or two, then return the pieces of chicken. Turn down the heat, season with salt, and cover the casserole first with a sheet of foil or greaseproof paper and then with the lid. Put it into the oven and let it simmer for an hour. It will make its own juice.

Meanwhile, skin the tomatoes, cut them in half, squeeze them to press out the seeds, then chop them coarsely. Put them into a saucepan and let them simmer, uncovered, until they start to thicken. Just before serving, stir this very plain tomato purée into the chicken juices, heat through and serve.

Put a tablespoon of sour cream and a sprinkling of paprika on each helping.

## Chicken with mustard sauce

| |
|---|
| *1 chicken weighing about 3 lb/1.5 kg* |
| *1 onion* |
| *2 thick slices bacon* |
| *2 tablespoons/30 g butter* |
| *1 tablespoon peanut oil* |
| *1 glass white wine or cider* |
| *1 tablespoon Dijon mustard* |
| *2 sprigs fresh thyme or ½ teaspoon dried thyme* |
| *salt and freshly ground pepper* |
| *⅔ cup/1.5 dl light cream* |

SERVES 4–6

Cut the chicken into six pieces. Peel and slice the onion, and cut the bacon into pieces the size of your little finger. Melt the butter with the oil in a casserole and fry the dry chicken pieces until they are golden brown on all sides. Remove them and fry the onion and bacon until they, too, have turned a good brown color.

Return the pieces of chicken, add the wine or cider, the mustard, thyme and seasoning. Let it bubble up, then turn down the heat very low. Simmer, uncovered, for 45 minutes, turning the pieces occasionally.

When the chicken is tender, stir in the cream, scraping up all the juices from the bottom of the pan. Taste the sauce and if you like it stronger add a little more mustard. Boil and tip the casserole to thicken and blend the sauce to a good consistency. Serve with mashed potato.

---

## Fried chicken

| |
|---|
| *2 small chickens (better than one large one)* |
| *salt* |
| *dried bread crumbs and flour for coating* |
| *2 eggs* |
| *8 tablespoons peanut oil* |
| *1 stick/115 g butter* |

SERVES 6–8

Cut each of the chickens into six pieces. Remove the skin and pat each piece with salt.

Put the crumbs on a plate. (If you don't have any dried crumbs, freshly grated crumbs will do.) Pat each piece of chicken with a little flour. Beat the eggs in a wide, flat-bottomed bowl. With one hand dip a piece of chicken into the egg, turning it around and giving it as thin a coat as possible; shake off any extra egg. Take the piece of chicken in the other hand and coat it with crumbs, turning it around so it is evenly coated. Repeat with each piece of chicken. Use one hand for egg and the other for crumbs, or you will end up with great lumps of egg-and-crumb everywhere.

Heat the oil and butter in a wide-bottomed frying pan, until it is sizzling. Slide in the pieces of chicken, brown them nicely all over, cover with a lid and leave on a very low heat for 20–25 minutes. Remove the pan lid, turn the heat up to make the crumbs crisp again and then remove the pieces of chicken to drain on crumpled paper towels. You may have to do two batches, in which case keep the first lot hot in a low oven. They should be very juicy inside, crisp and chestnut-brown outside and very well flavored. Serve with a green salad and perhaps French fries and sauce tartare.

ALTERNATIVE: *the leftover bones and skin, together with the giblets, can be used to make a traditional gravy for the chicken, but it must be planned ahead and the chickens cut up an hour before cooking. Simmer bones, skin and giblets with an onion, a carrot, salt and peppercorns for 45 minutes. Strain the stock. When you have fried the chicken and removed the pieces, pour off most of the fat from the pan, stir a tablespoon of flour into the remaining fat and make a thickish sauce with the giblet stock. Add a few tablespoons of cream, season to taste with salt, pepper and nutmeg, and serve piping hot.*

**Fried frogs' legs.** *Substitute large frogs' legs for the chicken pieces.*

## Wyvern's chicken curry

| |
|---|
| *1 nice young chicken, jointed and skinned* |
| *2 small onions* |
| *4 tablespoons/55 g clarified butter* |
| *1 clove garlic* |
| *1–2 cups/3–4.5 dl thick coconut milk* |
| *⅔ cup/1.5 dl chicken stock made from the giblets (optional)* |
| *2 teaspoons lemon juice* |
| *salt* |
| **for the paste:** |
| *2 cloves garlic, peeled* |
| *piece of fresh ginger the size of a hazelnut, peeled* |

| |
|---|
| *¼ teaspoon each of ground cloves, ground cinnamon, ground mace and ground cardamom seeds* |
| *few sprigs of fresh coriander* |
| *3 or 4 blanched almonds* |
| **for the powder:** *(enough to use on two occasions)* |
| *2 teaspoons ground turmeric* |
| *4 teaspoons ground coriander seeds* |
| *1 teaspoon ground cumin* |
| *½ teaspoon poppy seeds* |
| *1 teaspoon ground fenugreek* |
| *½ teaspoon ground ginger* |
| *¼ teaspoon mustard seed* |
| *½ teaspoon chili powder* |
| *½ teaspoon freshly ground pepper* |

SERVES 4

Put the ingredients for the paste in a food processor and reduce to a purée. Peel and slice the onions and let them fry gently in half the butter, without browning, for a few minutes. Peel and finely crush the clove of garlic and add it to the onions, together with the paste and a heaping tablespoon of the curry powder. Fry the mixture for 2 or 3 minutes and then slowly add half the coconut milk and simmer for 15 minutes.

In a separate pan, fry the pieces of chicken very lightly in the remaining butter until they are brown all over. Put them into a heavy saucepan with the curry sauce and let them marinate in this for half an hour. Then start simmering it very slowly, adding a little chicken stock if necessary; it will take from 45 minutes to an hour. When it is cooked, add a little lemon juice, the remaining coconut milk and season with salt.

This is an Anglo–Indian recipe from 1878.

## White devil

| |
|---|
| *12–18 slices cold roast turkey* |
| *2 cups/4.5 dl heavy cream* |
| *2 tablespoons Worcestershire sauce* |
| *2 teaspoons hot mustard* |
| *2 tablespoons sherry* |
| *generous dash of Tabasco* |
| *salt and freshly ground pepper* |

SERVES 6

Preheat the oven to 350°F/180°C.

Lay the slices of turkey in the bottom of an oval earthenware gratin dish. Mix all the rest of the ingredients in a saucepan and heat to boiling point. Pour the mixture over the turkey and heat in the oven for 20 minutes. If necessary put the dish quickly under a hot grill until brown, glazed and bubbling.

Serve with a refreshing salad of lettuce, crisped in the refrigerator, which is excellent for mopping up the juices left on the plate.

---

# Roast turkey

| |
|---|
| *1 turkey weighing 8–10 lb/3.5–4.5 kg* |
| *¾ stick/85 g butter* |
| *3 tablespoons olive oil or peanut oil* |

**for the chestnut stuffing:**

| |
|---|
| *1 lb/450 g chestnuts* |
| *2 sticks celery* |
| *1 tablespoon/15 g butter* |
| *1 slice onion* |
| *8 prunes, soaked in warm water for 2–3 hours* |
| *salt and freshly ground pepper* |
| *1 egg* |

**for the sausage meat stuffing:**

| |
|---|
| *1½ lb/700 g sausage meat* |
| *1 onion* |
| *2 tablespoons/30 g butter* |
| *the turkey liver* |
| *½ cup/55 g fresh white bread crumbs* |
| *1 egg* |
| *2 heaping tablespoons chopped parsley* |
| *2–3 tablespoons dry white wine* |
| *finely grated rind of 1 lemon* |
| *¼ teaspoon grated nutmeg* |
| *salt and freshly ground pepper* |

**for the gravy:**

| |
|---|
| *3 cups/7 dl good stock, made with the turkey giblets except the liver, or 2½ cups/6 dl stock and ⅔–1¼ cups/ 1.5–3 dl heavy cream* |
| *1 tablespoon flour (optional)* |
| *1–2 glasses white wine or 1 glass dry sherry* |
| *salt* |

SERVES 8

Make the two stuffings, starting with the chestnut stuffing. Remove the shells of the chestnuts with a sharp knife. Put the shelled chestnuts in a saucepan, just cover them with the turkey stock—later to be used for the gravy—and boil until just tender, about 15–20 minutes, and then drain. Remove the skins,

and put the skinned and slightly broken chestnuts into a bowl. Slice the celery finely into crescents; heat the butter in a frying pan with a scrap of chopped onion, add the celery and let it cook in the butter for 5 minutes. Then mix the celery into the chestnuts. Cut the prunes in half and remove the pits. Roughly chop the halved prunes and mix them with the celery and chestnuts. Season with salt and pepper, break in an egg, mix it in thoroughly and stuff the neck cavity, skewering the neck flap underneath the bird to secure it.

Preheat the oven to 325°F/170°C.

Next make the sausage meat stuffing. Peel and chop the onion fairly finely and cook it gently in the butter in a small frying pan until tender and transparent. Mix it into the sausage meat in a bowl. Chop the turkey liver and mix this in too, then add all the rest of the ingredients and work them together thoroughly. Stuff the body of the turkey with this mixture, and skewer the rear opening closed.

Spread the butter all over the turkey—breasts, legs and wings should all get their share. Put it into a roasting pan and pour on the oil. Place the pan fair and square in the center of the oven, and roast for about 20 minutes per 1 lb/450 g. It will take about 3 hours, depending on your oven. The bird is roasted rather slowly so that it cooks evenly. Baste it frequently and when it is an even golden brown all over, cover it loosely with foil to prevent it going too dark. To test the bird, stick a skewer deep into the thigh; a bead of clear or cloudy, pale pink or colorless liquid will emerge. (If it is a reddish color the bird is not cooked.) Turn off the oven, leave the door slightly open and let the bird rest for 20 minutes to firm and set. This will make it easier to carve.

To make the gravy, take the turkey out of the roasting pan, transfer it to a heated platter and keep it hot. Spoon most of the fat from the roasting pan (you can use it for frying potatoes on some other occasion), stir in the flour—if you like a slightly thickened gravy—and pour in a glass or two of wine. Let it boil for a few minutes over a medium heat, scraping up all the brown sediment and caramelized juices from the pan. Then add the stock and let it boil for about 10 minutes. Taste the gravy and season it with salt. For a cream gravy, substitute sherry for wine and use stock and cream instead of all stock.

A traditional roast turkey should be a really splendid

dish. Two kinds of stuffing keep the bird succulent and give it an interesting flavor. Serve the turkey with bread sauce or cranberry sauce (or both), roast potatoes, creamed onions and brussels sprouts with chestnuts.

TIMING A ROAST TURKEY: *an unstuffed turkey takes 20–30 minutes less than a stuffed bird. The following chart is for stuffed turkeys, and is only a rough guide, since ovens vary considerably. To prevent disaster— and the margin for error increases with larger birds and longer cooking times—check frequently during the last part of the cooking.*

*At an oven temperature of 325°F/170°C the following times are recommended:*

| | |
|---|---|
| 6–8 lb/2.5–3.5 kg | 2½–3 hours |
| 8–10 lb/3.5–4.5 kg | 3–3½ hours |
| 10–12 lb/4.5–5.5 kg | 3½–4 hours |
| 12–14 lb/5.5–6 kg | 4–4½ hours |
| 14–16 lb/6–7 kg | 4½–5 hours |
| 16–18 lb/7–8 kg | 5–5½ hours |
| 18–20 lb/8–9 kg | 5½–6 hours |

## Roast duck

| |
|---|
| *1 duck with its giblets* |
| *1 orange* |
| *2 carrots* |
| *1 onion* |
| *large bunch of thyme* |
| *3 shallots or button onions* |
| *2 oz/55 g salt pork or bacon, in a piece* |
| *sprinkling of olive oil* |
| *1 glass white wine* |
| *a very little flour* |
| *salt and freshly ground pepper* |

SERVES 4

Preheat the oven to 425°F/220°C.

Put the duck's giblets, except the liver, into a small pan together with half the orange, the peeled and chopped carrots and onion, the thyme and a little salt. Cover with 5 cups/1 liter water and bring to the boil. Skim well and turn the heat right down. Let the stock simmer gently, covered, while you cook the duck.

Peel the shallots and chop them finely, together with the duck's liver and salt pork. Score the skin of the remaining half of the orange and rub it over the outside of the duck, then rub the inside and outside of the orange with salt. Push the piece of orange inside the duck, together with the salt pork, shallot and liver stuffing. Sprinkle the duck with olive oil and put it on a rack in a roasting pan. Roast it fast for 15 minutes, then turn down the oven to 350°F/180°C, and roast for an hour and 15 minutes to an hour and a half, according to the size of the duck, basting alternately with white wine and its own fat.

Remove the duck to a dish and keep it hot while you spoon all the fat from the roasting pan. Sprinkle into the juices a teaspoon or so of flour— just enough to take up any remaining fat. Strain in the stock, stirring all the time over a medium heat. Taste for seasoning, put into a gravy boat and serve, putting a little of the stuffing on each plate. (The duck fat is good for frying potatoes.)

## Duck with green olives

| |
|---|
| *1 duck weighing 3½–4 lb/1.75–2 kg* |
| *2 cups/4.5 dl chicken stock* |
| *1 teaspoon tomato paste* |
| *bouquet garni of parsley, thyme and a bay leaf* |
| *salt and freshly ground pepper* |
| *1¾ cups/170 g pitted green olives* |
| *2 teaspoons potato flour* |
| *½ glass Madeira or dry sherry* |

SERVES 4

Preheat the oven to 450°F/230°C.

Prick the duck here and there in order to allow the fat to escape during cooking. Put the bird into a casserole and brown it on all sides in the oven for about 15 minutes. Pour off the fat and add the stock, tomato paste, the bouquet garni and a generous seasoning of salt and pepper. Cover the casserole and cook the duck for a further hour and 10 minutes; test to see if it is tender by piercing the thickest part of the thigh with a skewer.

Meanwhile, blanch the olives in a large pan of unsalted boiling water for 5 minutes. Drain them. Take the duck out of the casserole, put it on a heated serving dish and keep it hot. Remove most of the fat from the top of the sauce with a tablespoon and add the olives. Put it over a gentle heat, dissolve the potato flour in the Madeira or sherry and add it to the sauce. Remove the bouquet garni and simmer the sauce over a gentle heat, stirring constantly, until it thickens and coats the back of the spoon.

Taste for seasoning, add salt and pepper if necessary and then pour the sauce over the duck. Serve with plain boiled potatoes.

---◆---

# Goose with apple stuffing

| |
|---|
| *1 goose weighing about 11–12 lb/5–5.5 kg* |
| *2 lb/900 g russet or Golden Delicious apples* |
| *1 onion* |
| *2½ cups/6 dl stock made with goose giblets, or chicken stock* |
| *1 glass sweet white wine* |
| *1 tablespoon dried sage* |
| *1½ tablespoons flour* |
| *salt and freshly ground pepper* |

SERVES 8–10

Preheat the oven to 425°F/220°C.

Salt the goose inside and out, removing any stray quills. Remove the stalks of the apples, core the apples but leave them whole and unpeeled, and fill the goose with them. Sew up or skewer closed the bird's rear cavity and neck flap.

Peel and slice the onion. Cover the bottom of a roasting pan with the stock and white wine. Add the onion and sage, put the goose in the pan, breast downwards, and roast in a fast oven for an hour, basting with the liquid and pricking the skin with a fork to let the fat run out. Then turn the bird over and roast for a further 2 hours at 350°F/180°C, continuing to baste and prod it with a fork, but not too deeply or you will make the juice run out of the meat. When the goose is done, remove it to a hot dish and put it back in the oven while you pour off most of the copious fat from the roasting pan. Add the flour to the juices remaining in the pan, stirring it around until it is cooked. Taste the gravy for seasoning. Add boiling water if it is too concentrated. Strain into a gravy dish.

Serve the goose with this sauce and the apples from the inside of the bird—they will have collapsed into a delicious stuffing.

(The goose fat that runs out copiously during roasting of the bird is an excellent medium for cooking fried potatoes.)

In Germany it is traditional to eat potato dumplings and braised celery with this dish.

# Roast guinea fowl

| |
|---|
| *1 guinea fowl* |
| *2 shallots or ½ small onion* |
| *2 oz/55 g button mushrooms* |
| *4 Petits Suisses or 4 tablespoons cream cheese* |
| *1 tablespoon chopped chives or very small scallions* |
| *1 teaspoon dried tarragon* |
| *3 heaping tablespoons chopped parsley* |
| *salt and freshly ground pepper* |
| *½ stick/55 g butter* |
| *1 glass white wine* |
| *⅔ cup/1.5 dl chicken stock* |

SERVES 2

Peel the shallots or half onion and clean the button mushrooms. Chop both the onion and mushrooms finely. Mix them in a bowl together with the Petit Suisse or cream cheese. Blend in the finely chopped chives or scallions, the dried tarragon and the chopped parsley. Season this stuffing to taste with salt and pepper.

Preheat the oven to 425°F/220°C.

Slip your hand under the skin covering the breast of the bird, working it loose from the breast and legs. Then take some of the mixture in your hand, and pat it in place on the breast of the bird, between skin and flesh. Coat the whole breast and both legs with the stuffing, and then wash your hands and press the skin lightly back into place. Spread the skin with a little butter, put a nut of the butter inside the bird and place in a roasting pan together with the remaining butter. Roast for 30 minutes, basting several times with the melted butter and juices surrounding the guinea fowl. Then turn down the oven temperature to 350°F/180°C, and give the bird another 15 minutes.

Tip the juices out of the bird into the pan, put the guinea fowl on a heated serving dish and leave in a warm place to relax for 10–15 minutes while you make the gravy.

To make the gravy, pour the white wine into the roasting pan and simmer for 3–4 minutes, then add the stock and simmer a few minutes more, stirring well to scrape up any sediment from the bottom of the pan. Taste the gravy for seasoning, add salt and pepper if necessary, and serve in a gravy boat.

This recipe for roast guinea fowl is adapted from a *nouvelle cuisine* recipe by Michel Guérard.

## *Boiled eggs*

**Soft-boiled eggs**: the remark about not being able to boil an egg is really no joke. Often the egg cracks and the white pours out, and often the yolk somehow gets overcooked. Many people do not know that eggs should be simmered, not boiled, to prevent the white toughening. Soft-boiled eggs take 3–5 minutes from the time they are lowered into the simmering water, new-laid eggs taking perhaps a minute longer to cook than store-bought eggs.

A foolproof way to boil an egg is to coddle it. Put the egg in a pan of cold water, bring to the boil, take it off the heat, cover, and leave for 5 minutes.

**Hard-boiled eggs** take 10–12 minutes; simmering longer will give a dark grey ring around the yolk, since the iron in the yolk and the sulfur compounds in the white are released to form ferrous sulfide. Plunge the eggs into cold water or run them under the cold tap as soon as the time is up, whether you are going to peel them at once or not. If you are, it helps to cool them enough to handle and if you are not, it prevents them continuing to cook in their heat. And it makes them easier to shell.

## *Oeufs mollets aux fines herbes*

*1 or 2 eggs per person*

*1 stick/115 g butter*

*1 teaspoon each of finely chopped fresh chives, parsley and tarragon*

*salt and freshly ground pepper*

SERVES 4

Bring a pan of water to a simmer, place the eggs in the water and cook for 5 minutes if they are store-bought, 6–7 if they are newly laid. Melt the butter in a small saucepan and add the herbs—do not allow the butter to brown. As soon as the eggs are cooked, put them into a bowl of cold water until they are cool enough to handle, then shell them quickly but with care. Season the butter and herb mixture with salt and pepper. Put the eggs in little individual egg dishes and pour a little of the butter over each one. Serve immediately.

ALTERNATIVE: **Oeufs mollets with cream and bacon.** *Instead of melted butter and herbs, pour a hot mixture of fried bacon strips and light cream over the eggs and sprinkle with chopped chives.*

## *Egg mayonnaise*

*4 eggs*

*1¼ cups/3 dl mayonnaise, made with peanut oil or half peanut, half olive oil*

*2 tablespoons light cream*

*sprinkling of cayenne pepper*

SERVES 4

Boil the eggs for exactly 12 minutes, then cool them under cold running water and shell them carefully. Cut them in half and put them rounded sides up in an oval dish. Stir the cream into the mayonnaise, to make it more liquid, taste it to make sure it is well flavored and spoon it over the eggs. Sprinkle lightly with cayenne pepper and serve.

ALTERNATIVE: *instead of cayenne pepper, decorate the tops of the eggs with anchovy fillets.*

## *Curried eggs*

*8 eggs*

*1 large onion*

*½ stick/55 g butter*

*3 tablespoons curry powder*

*1¼ cups/3 dl good chicken stock*

*salt and freshly ground pepper*

*1 teaspoon arrowroot*

*⅔ cup/1.5 dl heavy cream*

*⅔ cup/1.5 dl boiling water*

*3 tablespoons shredded coconut or fresh grated coconut*

*juice of ½ lemon*

SERVES 4

Preheat the oven to 350°F/180°C.

Boil the eggs for 12 minutes, then cool them under cold running water. Shell carefully and put to one side. Peel the onion and chop finely. Melt the butter in a small saucepan and add the onion and curry powder. Let the onion fry, stirring, until tender and transparent, then add the stock. Season with salt and pepper and allow to simmer for 10 minutes. Mix the arrowroot into the cream, stir it into the curry sauce and simmer for a few minutes more. Meanwhile, pour ¼ pint/1.5 dl boiling water onto the coconut. When it has cooled, pour it through a wire sieve into the curry sauce, pressing the coconut with a spoon to extract all the liquid. Add the lemon juice to the sauce and taste for seasoning.

Slice the eggs into rounds or halve them, put them

in an ovenproof dish, pour the sauce over them, cover the dish loosely with kitchen foil and put in the oven to heat through.

———◆———

# Scotch eggs

6 eggs

1 tablespoon finely chopped parsley or fresh sage

finely grated rind of 1 small lemon

salt and freshly ground pepper

pinch of grated nutmeg

$\frac{1}{2}$ lb/225 g sausage meat

egg for coating

$\frac{3}{4}$ cup/115 g dried white bread crumbs

peanut or sunflower oil for deep frying

SERVES 6

Boil the eggs for 12 minutes, cool them under cold running water and shell them carefully. Work the parsley or sage and the lemon rind into the sausage meat, adding a little salt, pepper and grated nutmeg. Any other seasoning you choose to add, such as marjoram or basil, should be worked in at the same time. Make a coating for each whole hard-boiled egg out of the sausage meat, working it around the egg with wet hands to form an even layer. Roll each in beaten egg and then in bread crumbs.

Heat the oil, put in three of the eggs carefully and let them fry until a deep golden color; turn them as they cook, so that they brown evenly. Drain them on paper towels and repeat with the remaining eggs. Halve them lengthwise and eat hot or cold.

———◆———

# Oeufs meulemeester

8 eggs

1 tablespoon/15 g butter

$\frac{1}{2}$ teaspoon each of chopped chervil and parsley

$\frac{1}{2}$ teaspoon Dijon mustard

$\frac{1}{4}$ lb/115 g shelled shrimps

$1\frac{1}{4}$ cups/3 dl heavy cream

salt and freshly ground pepper

pinch of grated nugmeg

$\frac{1}{2}$ cup/55 g grated cheese

SERVES 4

Preheat the oven to 400°F/200°C.

Boil the eggs for 6–7 minutes, cool them under cold running water and shell them. Put the butter, chervil, parsley, mustard, shrimps, cream, salt, pepper and nutmeg into a pan. Chop the eggs coarsely and stir them into the mixture. Heat through and pour into a buttered ovenproof dish—an oval gratin dish is ideal. Sprinkle with the grated cheese and bake in the top of the oven until the surface is golden. Serve very hot.

This is an old recipe from Bruges, taken from Countess Morphy's invaluable book, *Recipes of All Nations*, first published in 1935.

———◆———

# Poached eggs

Use either a shallow sauté pan or a heavy frying pan, rather than a saucepan, which is difficult to get the eggs in and out of.

Fill the pan with enough water to cover the eggs. You can add a little vinegar to hasten the setting, but no salt, as this will toughen the white. Bring the water to the boil, turn down the heat a little so the water is just rolling and break the eggs in one at a time, keeping your hands very close to the pan. Let them poach until the whites have lost their transparent look. If the yolks are not quite covered, spoon the water over them to cook the tops.

When they are done, lift the eggs out one at a time with a slotted spoon, taking care as you slide it under each egg that you do not break the yolk. Let the eggs drain on the spoon for a few moments before putting them on a warm dish. If you are not ready to serve them immediately, they will keep hot in a bowl of warm water.

For a neat egg, trim off the untidy edges. A fresh egg has a definite rounded shape with a few trailing bits around the outside which are easily trimmed away with a knife or scissors. Fresh eggs poach best; eggs that are not fresh will spread out and disintegrate.

———◆———

# Eggs in overcoats

6 eggs plus 2 extra egg whites

6 large potatoes

hot milk for mashing

6 tablespoons chopped ham

2 tablespoons chopped parsley

½ stick/55 g butter

2 tablespoons heavy cream

salt and freshly ground pepper

1 tablespoon vinegar (optional)

2 tablespoons Cheddar cheese, grated

SERVES 6

Preheat the oven to 400°F/200°C.

Scrub the potatoes and put them in the oven to bake. When they are cooked, lay them flat and cut the top off each with a sharp knife. Scoop the insides into a bowl, reserving the skins, and mash to a smooth fluff with a little hot milk. Add the ham, parsley, butter, cream and salt and pepper.

Heat the broiler.

In a separate bowl, beat the two whites until stiff and mix them into the potato mixture. Taste for seasoning and keep it hot. Lightly poach the eggs in water that is barely simmering, to which you may add a tablespoon of vinegar but no salt. Drain the eggs carefully. Half fill the potato skins with a layer of the mashed potato mixture, then place a poached egg in each and cover with the remaining mixture. Sprinkle the tops with grated cheese and brown briefly under the broiler.

This is a straightforward but far from cloddish English country dish from Mrs. Leyel, famous herbalist and author of several delightful cook books published in the 1930s.

ALTERNATIVE: **Oeufs Suzette.** *The Ritz Hotel, London, used to serve a similar dish in the 1920s rather grandly called Oeufs Suzette, in which the potato was mashed more simply with butter and cream only. Poached eggs were tremendously popular at that time; quite rightly so, they are delicious.*

# Eggs Benedict

4 eggs

4 slices white bread

½ stick/55 g butter

1 teaspoon oil

4 slices ham

hollandaise sauce made with lemon juice

SERVES 4

Heat the broiler.

Trim the crusts off the slices of bread or cut them in rounds and fry them in a mixture of the butter and oil until crisp and golden brown. Keep them hot while you poach the eggs lightly. When they are ready, a cup of cold water added to the water in which they were poached will stop them from cooking any further. The eggs can be left in the water for a moment or two.

Trim the ham and lay a slice on each piece of fried bread. Drain the eggs well, trim any uneven edges with a pair of kitchen scissors and lay one on each piece of ham. Spoon the hollandaise over the eggs so that it completely covers eggs, ham and bread. Brown for a minute under a hot broiler and serve as soon as possible.

ALTERNATIVES: *the Savoy Hotel, London, uses a toasted crumpet instead of fried bread, and in America a split and toasted English muffin is used, but this is a matter of choice.*

# Eggs Florentine

4 eggs

1½–2 lb/700–900 g spinach

salt

2 tablespoons/15 g flour

grated nutmeg

2–3 tablespoons heavy cream

scant 2 cups/4.5 dl mornay sauce

SERVES 4

Wash the spinach and shake it gently. Put it into a pan, making sure that there is still a little water clinging to the leaves, cover with a lid and start cooking over a gentle heat. As it becomes wetter and wilts down, add a pinch of salt and turn the heat up. Cook until it is just tender, drain very thoroughly and return to the pan.

Mix the flour and a pinch of nutmeg into the cream and mix both into the spinach. Simmer over a low heat, stirring from time to time, until the mixture has thickened and the flour has absorbed any water which is still running from the spinach. Keep hot. Heat the broiler.

Make the mornay sauce and keep it hot. Poach the eggs and keep them warm in a bowl of hot water. A cup of cold water added to the water in which the eggs were poached will stop them cooking any further. Put the spinach in an oval gratin dish, drain the eggs, lay them on top of the spinach and pour the mornay sauce over them. Brown the dish quickly under the broiler.

# Ham and eggs

*8 eggs*

*4 slices ham*

*½ stick/55 g butter*

*salt and freshly ground pepper*

SERVES 4

Preheat the oven to 180°C/350°F, gas mark 4. Divide the butter between 4 individual enamel gratin dishes or flameproof earthenware dishes or, failing those, saucers. Heat the butter over a gentle heat, then put a slice of ham into each dish and break 2 eggs on top. Sprinkle with a little salt and plenty of pepper and bake for 10–15 minutes, until the whites of the eggs are set. You can finish cooking the tops of the eggs under the grill.

ALTERNATIVES: *instead of ham, put slices of chorizo salami in the dishes, or finely sliced, lightly fried zucchini, or a thin layer of ratatouille.*

---

# Chakchouka

*4 eggs*

*1 or 2 green or red sweet peppers*

*½ lb/225 g tomatoes*

*1 clove garlic*

*2 tablespoons oil*

*salt and freshly ground pepper*

SERVES 2–4

Cut the peppers in half, remove the pith and seeds and cut them into strips. Skin the tomatoes, chop them fairly finely and peel the garlic. Heat the oil in a frying pan and fry the clove of garlic, whole, until it is brown. Put in the pieces of pepper and let them stew gently in the oil until soft. Add the tomatoes, season with salt and pepper and allow to simmer for 15 minutes, covered with a tilted lid.

Taste the mixture and add salt and pepper if you think it is needed. Break the eggs on top, cover the pan and cook until the eggs are just set. Serve straight from the dish in which they have been cooked, as soon as possible.

Chakchouka is originally a Tunisian dish, now widely eaten in most Middle Eastern countries. It is also found in the South of France where it is known as *pipérade basquaise*, but in the Basque version the eggs are scrambled rather than cooked whole as in this recipe.

# Scrambled eggs

To make scrambled eggs that are creamy and rich, you need patience, butter and, if possible, a non-stick pan (to help the dishwasher).

Away from the heat, break the eggs into the pan, season with salt and freshly ground pepper. Add a good lump of butter—about 1 tablespoon for every 2 eggs. Put the pan over a low heat, take a wooden spoon to the mixture and stir it with intelligence—that is, moving every bit of egg around, not just following a clockwise track. Gradually the eggs will thicken, and while they are still just runny, remove the pan from the heat and continue to stir until they become a soft, creamy mass.

Serve scrambled eggs straightaway, on hot buttered toast, or they will harden at the bottom. If you don't possess a nonstick pan it is better to melt the butter a bit before breaking in the eggs.

ALTERNATIVES: *add chopped parsley or chives to the eggs before you start to scramble them, or flaked cooked haddock, finely grated black or white truffles, finely chopped ham or prosciutto, or, when the eggs are cooked, put them onto hot buttered toast and place two fillets of smoked eel on top.*

---

# Pipérade

*4 eggs*

*2 onions*

*2 tablespoons olive oil*

*1 green sweet pepper*

*1 red sweet pepper*

*2 cloves garlic*

*4 tomatoes*

*salt and freshly ground pepper*

SERVES 4

Slice the onions finely and sweat them in the oil in a heavy pan. Cut the peppers in thin strips, removing the seeds, and add them to the onions. Crush the cloves of garlic in salt and add these, too. When all the vegetables are tender, skin the tomatoes, chop them roughly and put them into the stew. Season well and simmer for 15 minutes.

Break the eggs into the pan and stir as you would if you were making scrambled eggs. When the eggs begin to thicken, the pipérade is cooked. Serve these Provençal scrambled eggs in an earthenware dish.

## Oeufs en cocotte à la crème

4 fresh eggs

1 tablespoon/15 g butter

salt and freshly ground pepper

4 tablespoons heavy cream

SERVES 4

Preheat the oven to 400°F/200°C.

Put a sliver of butter and a pinch of salt and pepper in the bottom of each of 4 small ovenproof cocotte dishes. Break an egg into each and season with more salt and pepper. Pour a tablespoon of cream over each egg and add a further sliver of butter.

Put the cocotte dishes in a bain-marie or a roasting pan and pour enough boiling water around them to come halfway up the sides of the dishes. Place in the oven and bake for 7–8 minutes. Test the eggs by gently shaking the cocotte dishes—the whites should be just set and the yolks still runny.

ALTERNATIVES: **Oeufs en cocotte aux champignons**. *Simply fry ¼ lb/115 g mushrooms in the butter and then divide these between the cocotte dishes before adding the eggs and cream. Season with salt, pepper and a grating of nutmeg.*

**Oeufs en cocotte aux crevettes**. *Put a few small shrimps into each cocotte dish with a little butter before adding the eggs.*

## Omelet fines herbes

2–3 eggs

salt and freshly ground pepper

1 teaspoon each of chopped fresh chives, parsley, tarragon and chervil

½ tablespoon Parmesan, freshly grated

1 tablespoon/15 g butter for frying

SERVES 1

Whisk the eggs lightly in a bowl, just enough to break them down. Season with salt and pepper, add the herbs and cheese and whisk lightly once again to spread the herbs evenly through the mixture. Heat the butter in an omelet pan. When it starts to brown, pour in the egg mixture. Stir it around for a minute, tipping the pan and lifting the edges as they set, so that the liquid can run underneath.

When the egg is set and brown underneath, but still creamy and runny on top, flick one half over towards the middle of the omelet and then roll the

omelet onto a heated plate so that it is folded in three. It should look like a plump golden cushion. Eat at once: speed is essential for both the cooking and the eating of omelets.

## Omelet fillings

Omelets can be filled with almost any cheese, shellfish, vegetable or herb as well as with some meats such as bacon, ham and kidneys. Among the nicest omelets are:

**Cheese omelet** made with a handful of grated Emmental or Emmental and Parmesan mixed.

**Mushroom omelet** made with a few button mushrooms, sliced and lightly fried in butter with parsley and a little garlic.

**Shrimp omelet** made with a few shrimps or prawns, lightly cooked in a little cream and flavored with chives.

**Spinach and cheese omelet** made with spinach first cooked in butter and then stirred into the eggs with a little grated Parmesan.

**Ham or bacon omelet**, made with the ham in little strips sizzled in butter, or bacon diced and fried, stirred into the eggs with grated cheese.

**Portuguese omelet** is filled with croûtons that have been shaken in a paper bag with grated Parmesan, parsley and cayenne pepper.

## Omelet Arnold Bennett

8 eggs

1 medium-size smoked haddock, weighing about 1½ lb/700 g

generous ⅔ cup/1.5 dl milk

1 bay leaf

½ stick/55 g butter

¼ cup/30 g flour

½ cup/55 g grated Gruyère or Emmental

salt and freshly ground pepper

SERVES 4

Preheat the oven to 325°F/170°C.

Put the smoked haddock with the milk, ½ cup/1.5 dl water and the bay leaf into a baking pan and put it in the oven. After 15 minutes the fish should be just cooked through. Make a roux with half the butter and the flour. Drain the fish and use 1¼ cups/

3 dl of the liquid to make a béchamel sauce. Flake the haddock into the sauce. Break the eggs into a bowl, add the haddock mixture and half the cheese and beat well until the eggs are frothing and the sauce has combined with them. Season with salt and pepper.

Heat the broiler.

Brown the remaining butter in a large heavy frying pan and pour in the egg mixture. Let it fry and cook, shaking to keep the omelet loose. When it is half cooked, sprinkle the remaining cheese over the top and put the pan under the broiler. Remove from the heat after 1–2 minutes, when the omelet should be brown on top but still creamy and runny in the middle. Serve in wedges like a cake.

# Flat omelets

**A frittata** is a sort of cake made of eggs and lightly cooked vegetables. It is cut like a cake, too, and eaten hot, cold or warm—a temperature Italians quite like for certain dishes. It should be a fairly solid golden disc, nicely crusted on top.

**A tortilla** is the Spanish version of the frittata, containing a mixture of sliced, fried onions and potatoes. It can also contain little slices of hot paprika sausage, green or red peppers and garlic. It is eaten hot or cold—wedges of cold tortilla are an essential part of the *tapas*, or appetizers, available in every bar in Spain.

# Spinach frittata

| 6 eggs |
| --- |
| *½–¾ lb/225–340 g spinach* |
| *2 cloves garlic* |
| *2 tablespoons olive oil* |
| *salt and freshly ground pepper* |
| *pinch of grated nutmeg* |
| *2 tablespoons heavy cream* |
| *¾ cup/85 g finely grated Emmental* |

SERVES 4

Preheat the oven to 350°F/180°C.

Wash and thoroughly drain the spinach and, unless it is very young and tender, remove the stalks. Peel and crush the garlic. Heat half the olive oil in a large frying pan and throw in the garlic. Let it brown slightly, crushing it into the oil, then add the spinach. Scatter a pinch of salt over it and stir it around, letting it wilt down and cook until most of the moisture has evaporated (about 10–15 minutes). Let the spinach cool, drain and then chop it roughly. Put into a bowl and keep on one side.

Beat the eggs in a bowl, season with salt, pepper and nutmeg and whisk in the cream, cheese and spinach. Heat the remaining olive oil in an enamelled iron gratin dish or a small roasting pan. Pour in the egg mixture and put it in the oven for 15–20 minutes according to its thickness. When it is set and cooked through, either eat it hot or allow to cool for 15 minutes, then turn it over onto a board or dish and allow to get completely cold. Cut in slices or wedges according to the shape of the frittata you have made and serve with small juicy black olives passed around separately.

# Tortilla

| 8 eggs |
| --- |
| *2–3 waxy potatoes* |
| *2 onions* |
| *8 tablespoons olive oil* |
| *salt and freshly ground pepper* |

SERVES 6

Peel the potatoes, cut them into quarters and slice thinly so that you have small triangular pieces. Peel the onions and slice them thinly, downwards. Heat most of the olive oil in your best large frying pan and put in the potatoes and onions. Season them with salt and pepper and cook gently until tender, covering the pan but removing the lid to turn and stir the vegetables from time to time.

Meanwhile, beat the eggs in a bowl and season them with salt and pepper. When the vegetables are tender, turn up the heat, take off the lid and pour the eggs into the pan. Let them cook for a minute, then turn down the heat a little and cook for 3–4 minutes, loosening the edges and keeping the tortilla loose. To turn the tortilla, put a large plate over the frying pan and turn the whole thing upside down, then return the pan to the stove, add the remaining oil and, when it is hot, slide the tortilla back into the pan, cooked side up. Cook for 2–3 minutes more and serve.

## Omelet cake

A very pretty omelet cake can be made with three thin omelets of different colors: one green with spinach, one pink with freshly made tomato purée and one yellow with cheese, piled one on top of the other, with mornay sauce or cream in between.

---

## Egg mousse

6 eggs
¼ lb/115 g white button mushrooms
juice of ½ lemon
½ stick/55 g butter
2 tablespoons Worcestershire sauce
or 3 tablespoons dry sherry
2 teaspoons of gelatine dissolved in ⅔ cup/1.5 dl of hot consommé, canned or homemade
1¼ cups/3 dl heavy cream, chilled
salt and freshly ground pepper
6 fresh leaves tarragon or 6 sprigs parsley

SERVES 4 AS A MAIN COURSE OR 6 AS A FIRST COURSE
Boil the eggs for 12 minutes, then cool them under cold running water. Shell and chop or slice.
Cut the mushrooms in small dice ¼ in/5 mm across and squeeze the lemon juice over them to prevent them browning. Melt the butter in a small frying pan and cook the mushrooms gently for 3–4 minutes. Transfer to a wire sieve to drain. Add the Worcestershire sauce or sherry to the gelatine and consommé mixture. Whisk the cream until it is a soft snow—do not over-whisk or it will turn to butter. Mix together the cream, consommé (reserving 3 tablespoons), eggs and mushrooms. Taste for seasoning. Pour the mixture into a soufflé dish and allow to set in the refrigerator.
Place the tarragon leaves or parsley on top of the mousse, pour on the remaining consommé, just melted, and allow to set. Serve with mayonnaise made green with chopped and pounded parsley.

---

## Crêpes

1 egg
1¼ cups/140 g flour
pinch of salt
1¼ cups/3 dl milk and water mixed
2 tablespoons/30 g butter, melted
peanut oil for frying

SERVES 4
Put the flour and salt in a bowl, break in the egg and add a little of the milk and water mixture. Beat to a smooth paste, then pour in the rest of the milk and water mixture and the melted butter. Beat well for a smooth, creamy batter. Allow to rest for half an hour or so.
Heat the frying pan, brush the inside with oil or clarified butter and then add just enough batter to cover the bottom of the pan. When the underside of the crêpe is browned, turn it over to allow the other side to cook. When each crêpe is cooked, place it flat on a plate and keep warm.
These crêpes can be simply eaten with lemon juice and sugar as a dessert, or they can be stuffed with all sorts of fillings and then quickly baked.

---

## Mushroom filling for crêpes

½ lb/225 g mushrooms
3 tablespoons/45 g butter
squeeze of lemon juice
salt and freshly ground pepper
pinch of grated nutmeg
2 tablespoons/15 g flour
⅔ cup/1.5 dl milk
2 tablespoons heavy cream

SERVES 4
Wash the mushrooms, cut them in quarters if small or chop coarsely if large. Melt 2 tablespoons/30 g butter in a small pan, add the mushrooms with a squeeze of lemon juice and a generous sprinkling of salt, pepper and nutmeg. Cover and simmer gently for 7–8 minutes.
Melt the remaining butter in a small pan, stir in the flour and let it bubble for a minute. Add the milk, stirring it in gradually to keep the mixture smooth. Allow it to cook for 5 minutes over a low heat, stirring from time to time. Add the mushrooms, their liquid and the cream. Keep hot.
Preheat the oven to 425°F/220°C.
Fry the crêpes in a little oil. Place one flat on a plate, pour some of the sauce over the top, roll it up and repeat with the remaining crêpes. Put them into a buttered gratin dish, then heat in the oven.

# Bacon and egg quiche

*2 eggs*

*4–5 slices bacon*

*⅔ cup/1.5 dl milk*

*½ cup/55 g grated cheese*

*salt and freshly ground pepper*

*pinch of grated nutmeg*

*shortcrust pastry made with 1½ cups/170 g flour*

SERVES 4

Preheat the oven to 400°F/200°C.

Cut the bacon in little strips about 1 in/2.5 cm long and ½ in/1 cm wide and fry in a small pan until the fat runs and the pieces start to brown.

Break the eggs into a bowl, add the milk and beat well. Add the cheese and a little salt, pepper and nutmeg. Roll out the pastry to a large round. Butter a 7 in/17.5 cm fluted quiche pan. Lift the pastry carefully on the rolling pin and drape it over the pan, and make it fit snugly against the sides, without stretching it at all or it will shrink while cooking. Trim the extra pastry, holding the blade of your knife flat against the rim of the pan. (A problem with quiches and flans is that quite frequently the pastry at the bottom seems soggy and undercooked. One answer is to bake the shell blind for 10–15 minutes before putting in the filling, another is to place the quiche on a preheated baking sheet while it cooks.)

Arrange the pieces of bacon on the bottom of the pastry shell. Put the quiche in the middle of the oven and bake for 10 minutes before lowering the heat to 375°F/190°C. Bake it for a further 25–30 minutes until it is nicely puffy and brown.

This very simple but extremely good dish, something like a quiche Lorraine, is delicious hot or cold, and very good for picnics.

---

# Quiche fillings

With some imagination, quiches, can, like omelets, be filled with a great variety of ingredients. Here is a selection of some of the more interesting types of quiche, all made in the same way as the basic egg and bacon quiche with 2 eggs and ½ cup/1.5 dl milk.

**Cheese:** the kinds that can be used are innumerable. Practically any unprocessed cheese will be strong enough to make an interesting taste, provided it is neither blue nor just plain moldy. Gruyère and Emmental are both good, and grated Parmesan is an excellent addition to any other cheese—it seems to give a more pungent flavor. But perhaps best of all is a mixture of Parmesan and fontina which melts into a delicious light and gooey mass.

**Cottage cheese:** mix ½ lb/225 g cottage cheese with ½ cup/1.5 dl heavy cream, 1 egg and 3 extra egg yolks and a few slices of bacon, fried until brown and crisp.

**Potatoes:** fry boiled potatoes, cut in cubes, with thick slices of bacon; add plenty of grated cheese and season with nutmeg and perhaps some chives if they are available.

**Spanish onion:** add a thick mass of sliced Spanish onions, cooked first in butter and oil.

**Watercress:** chop a bunch of watercress and mix with some grated cheese and a little cream.

**Chives:** simply add a bunch of chopped chives to the basic egg, milk and cheese mixture.

**Scallions:** chop a few scallions and add them to the basic mixture.

**Spinach:** add a few leaves of spinach, washed and finely chopped and sweated in butter until limp.

**Leeks:** sweat a couple of chopped leeks in butter before adding to the mixture.

**Ham:** add a few thick strips of ham sizzled in their own fat with chopped garlic.

---

# Asparagus soufflé

*4 eggs*

*½ lb/225 g fresh or frozen asparagus*

*¼ stick/55 g butter*

*6 tablespoons/45 g flour*

*1¼ cups/3 dl milk*

*6 tablespoons/45 g freshly grated Parmesan*

*salt and freshly ground pepper*

SERVES 4

Cook the asparagus in boiling salted water until tender. Fresh asparagus will need up to 18 minutes according to thickness while frozen asparagus will take 8–10 minutes. Drain and keep on one side.

Preheat the oven to 400°F/200°C.

Melt the butter in a saucepan and stir in the flour. Cook gently for a minute or two, then gradually add the milk, stirring all the time, until you have a smooth, thickish sauce. Simmer gently for 5 minutes, stirring frequently to prevent it sticking to the bottom of the pan. Add the cheese, let it melt, season the sauce with salt and pepper and put the bowl on one side.

Separate the eggs, cut the tips off the asparagus and put the stalks with the yolks in the blender or a food processor. Reduce to a light, golden-green purée and mix this into the cheese sauce.

Butter a soufflé dish. Whisk the egg whites to a soft peak and stir a tablespoon or two into the asparagus mixture, then fold in the rest lightly and thoroughly. Put half the mixture into the soufflé dish, scatter in the asparagus tips, cover with the rest of the mixture and bake in the oven for about 20 minutes until well risen but still moist. Serve by itself or with a little melted butter.

## Stilton soufflé

| |
|---|
| *5 oz/140 g Stilton or other blue cheese* |
| *½ stick/55 g butter* |
| *6 tablespoons/45 g flour* |
| *1¼ cups/3 dl milk* |
| *pinch of salt* |
| *cayenne pepper* |
| *4 eggs and 1 extra egg white* |

SERVES 4

Preheat the oven to 400°F/200°C.

Melt the butter in a saucepan. Stir in the flour and let it cook gently for a minute or two, then add the milk gradually, stirring gently until you have a smooth, thick sauce. Let it cook over a low heat for several minutes, stirring frequently to prevent it sticking to the bottom of the pan.

Crumble the Stilton into the sauce and let it melt. Stilton is often quite salty so taste the sauce before adding salt. Season quite highly with cayenne pepper and allow to cool slightly. Separate the eggs and beat the yolks into the sauce one at a time.

Butter a 2 quart/1.75 liter soufflé dish. Whisk the egg whites until they hold their shape and stand up stiffly on the end of the whisk. Stir a tablespoon of beaten egg white into the sauce to make it a little lighter, then fold the mixture thoroughly into the rest of the egg whites. Spoon the mixture lightly into the soufflé dish and cook for 20–25 minutes until well risen but still moist. Serve immediately.

## Swiss fondue

| |
|---|
| *1¼ lb/565 g Emmental or Emmental and Gruyère mixed, grated* |
| *2 cloves garlic* |
| *1 glass dry white wine* |
| *1 teaspoon flour, preferably potato flour* |
| *freshly ground black pepper* |
| *pinch of nutmeg* |
| *1 small glass kirsch* |
| *1 drop corn oil* |
| *plenty of French bread cut in quarters lengthwise and then cut in 1 in/2.5 cm cubes* |

SERVES 6

Peel and crush a clove of garlic and rub the chafing dish with it. Pour the wine into the dish and add the remaining clove of garlic, peeled. Heat the wine gently and add the grated cheese, sprinkled with the teaspoon of potato flour to ensure a smooth finish. Stir with a wooden spoon and add a little more wine if it seems too thick. When the cheese has melted to a cream, add a pinch of pepper, the nutmeg and the kirsch with the corn oil in it.

Carry the dish to the table and place it over a gentle burner. When the fondue begins to bubble, the guests can start dipping their bread into it on the end of their forks. Twist the forks around to prevent the cheese dropping off in long strings. When the bottom starts to make a crust, those who like it can scrape this up with their spoons. Turn the heat down to prevent it burning.

Special fondue sets include long-handled forks, a stoneware or enamelled iron chafing dish to hold the cheese and a little burner to keep the cheese hot and bubbling. If you don't have one of these, you might improvise with a candle warmer. Traditionally white wine is drunk with fondue, or hot, unsweetened tea as an aid to digestion—never cold water.

## Toasted blue cheese

| |
|---|
| *½ lb/225 g Stilton or other blue cheese* |
| *4 thick slices very fresh white or dark bread, crusts removed (walnut bread is delicious)* |
| *butter for spreading* |
| *1 large teaspoon hot mustard* |
| *freshly ground pepper* |
| *2 teaspoons red wine or ale (optional)* |

SERVES 4

Heat the broiler.

Make 4 rounds of thick, tender toast, butter them well, spread with mustard and season with pepper. Place them in an ovenproof dish. Slice the cheese thinly and distribute it over the toast. If you like, sprinkle the cheese with red wine or ale. Place under a moderate broiler until the cheese has melted and is piping hot. Serve at once.

The old-fashioned Welsh way of serving this dish was to put a layer of cold roast beef, spread with mustard and horseradish, under Stilton cheese and to sprinkle, or rather saturate, the cheese with ale and shallot vinegar, which sounds like heavy eating but must have been delicious.

ALTERNATIVES: *Monterey Jack can be used in this recipe instead of Stilton, or, if you can get them, Leicester or Cheshire. Emmental and fontina also toast particularly well.*

## Croque monsieur

| |
|---|
| ¼ lb/115 g Emmental cheese, in 4 slices |
| 8 thinly cut slices light white bread |
| butter for spreading |
| 4 thin slices best ham |

SERVES 4

Heat the broiler.

Butter the bread, cover 4 of the slices with ham, then cover the ham with a layer of cheese. Make sandwiches by covering with the remaining pieces of bread and toast both sides under a hot broiler.

ALTERNATIVE: *fry the sandwiches on both sides until golden, in a mixture of oil and butter. Croque monsieur makes a splendid quick lunch or supper.*

## Mozzarella in carrozza

| |
|---|
| 6 oz/170 g Mozzarella cheese, in 4 slices |
| 8 slices white bread, crusts removed |
| 8 anchovy fillets (optional) |
| 3 eggs |
| salt |
| oil for frying |

SERVES 4

Cut each slice of cheese and each slice of bread in half. Make eight sandwiches with the bread and cheese, and you can add an anchovy fillet to each. Beat the eggs in a bowl with a pinch of salt. Heat the oil. Dip each sandwich into the beaten egg, immerse in the hot oil and fry until golden, turning them over as they fry so that they brown on both sides. Drain on a paper towel and sprinkle with salt. Serve very hot.

## Cheese straws

| |
|---|
| ¼ lb/115 g Cheddar cheese, finely grated |
| puff pastry made with 2 cups/115 g flour |
| 1 teaspoon curry powder |

MAKES 20

Preheat the oven to 375°F/190°C.

Roll out the pastry fairly thinly into a square. Scatter half of the square lavishly with the cheese and season with half the curry powder. Fold the other half of the pastry over the top and roll out lightly. Scatter with the rest of the cheese and curry powder, fold and roll again and cut in strips. Twist the strips and bake for 15–20 minutes until well risen and golden brown. Serve hot.

This is a good way of using up any trimmings of puff pastry left from making pies.

## Potted cheese

| |
|---|
| ½ lb/225 g Stilton or other blue cheese, or Cheddar |
| ½ stick/55 g unsalted butter, softened |
| ¼ teaspoon ground mace |
| 1 teaspoon hot mustard |

Mash the cheese with the butter, season with mace and mustard and work to a cream. Pack into small earthenware or china pots, making sure that it is well pressed down. If you want to keep it for any length of time, cover the cheese with clarified unsalted butter.

ALTERNATIVES: *potted cheese is good made with a mixture of leftover cheeses. If the mixture seems somewhat on the dry side, a small glass of dry sherry can be mixed in to moisten it, or port if Stilton is being used. To vary the flavor, add a little curry powder or cayenne pepper to the mashed cheese and butter, in place of the mustard.*

# Pasta

## Making fresh pasta

$2\frac{1}{4}$–$2\frac{1}{2}$ cups/225–280 g all-purpose flour

3 eggs, preferably free-range

SERVES 4

Put the flour on a board or in a bowl, make a well in the center and break the eggs into it. Using the fingers of your right hand like a fork, break up the eggs and gradually mix in the flour until you have a thick mass that you can start kneading, drawing in more flour so that you end up with a moist, pliable —but not sticky—dough. There may be some flour left over, since eggs vary tremendously in the amount they will absorb. Free-range eggs are best for pasta making; battery eggs don't seem to have the right sticky texture or the golden yolks that give the pasta its lovely yellow color.

ALTERNATIVE: *whizz the eggs for 30 seconds in a food processor, add the flour and whizz for 30 seconds more.*

### Rolling pasta by hand

Wash your hands, if you have made the dough by hand, and clean the work surface. Using both hands, start kneading the dough, sprinkling on a little more flour if it gets too sticky. After five minutes or so, when the dough is really smooth and silky, wrap it in a sheet of plastic wrap and let it rest for half an hour, but not in the refrigerator— pasta does not like to get too cold.

When you roll pasta dough, there is a special technique for rolling and stretching it at the same time. Always roll away from you, rolling only the half that is farthest from you. Keep turning the sheet, lifting it on your rolling pin and rotating it by $45°$. As it gets larger, let the part nearest to you hang down over the edge of the table—this helps to stretch it. Work as fast as you can; you must finish before it gets too dry and becomes unmanageable. As the dough begins to look thin, like a sheet of suede, increase the stretching action, rolling the far edge up around the rolling pin and pushing it away from you, running your hands from side to side over the dough on the rolling pin as you do so. Keep turning, rolling and stretching until the sheet is so fine that you can see your fingers through it when you slip your hand underneath. The surface should be faintly textured like fine leather—this is what makes it superior to machine-made pasta, which has a smooth, slippery surface that doesn't hold the sauce so well or feel so sympathetic to the palate.

If you are using the dough to make tagliatelle or tagliarini, spread it out and cover it lightly with a dry dish towel. Let it dry for half an hour, turning it over after 15 minutes, before starting to cut it. If you are making stuffed pasta, start cutting it immediately, keeping everything, except the piece you are working on, well covered with a slightly damp cloth so that it does not dry out, otherwise the edges of the pasta will not stick together properly.

### Rolling pasta in a machine

Rolling out pasta dough with the help of a pasta machine is quick and easy and gives excellent results, even if not as authentic as handmade pasta. The best mixture to put through a machine is the one below.

## Tuscan pasta dough

$2\frac{1}{4}$ cups/225 g all-purpose flour

3–4 teaspoons olive oil

pinch of salt

2 eggs

SERVES 4

Mix the ingredients in exactly the same way as in the previous recipe.

Make sure the machine is very clean and set the rollers at their widest. Cut the dough into as many pieces as there are eggs in the mixture. Flatten one piece into an oblong shape and feed it through the machine (keep the rest of the dough covered to prevent it drying out). Fold it in three lengthwise and feed it through again. Keep folding it and feeding it through. Do this 8–10 times—this has the effect of kneading the dough.

Now move the rollers one notch closer together and feed the dough through again. Move the machine up another notch and feed it through again, holding it up in your hand above the rollers. As you keep setting the rollers closer together, the pasta ribbon will get longer and longer and thinner and thinner. Take it to the finest setting on the machine—it is now thin enough.

If you are making tagliatelle or tagliarini, spread the dough strips out, lightly covered with a cloth, to dry for 15–20 minutes. For stuffed pasta keep it well covered with a slightly damp cloth and use as quickly as possible before it becomes dry.

# Making pasta shapes

**Tagliatelle** is pasta cut in narrow ribbons and is eaten with all sorts of sauces, creamy, tomato or meat based. To make tagliatelle by hand, roll up the sheet of pasta and then slice it across at $\frac{1}{4}$ in/5 mm intervals all the way along the roll. You will now have dozens of little spirals of dough. Unroll them and hang them on a cloth placed over the back of a chair. Lo and behold, perfect tagliatelle.

**Tagliarini** is pasta cut in very narrow strands, a third the width of tagliatelle. It is usually eaten in soup or sometimes with a creamy sauce. It is not usually made without a machine as it is a bothersome job. Put the handle of the machine into the section with narrow teeth and turn, feeding in the dough. Use short lengths or they may stick together.

**Pappardelle**: roll out fresh plain pasta and with a fluted cutter, divide it into strips, $\frac{3}{4}$ in/2 cm wide and about 12 in/30 cm long.

**Farfalle**, or butterflies, are eaten with the same sauces as tagliatelle. They are made by hand with a fluted pastry wheel: cut the sheet of dough into 2 in/5 cm squares, and with the forefinger and thumb of your right hand pinch each square together across the middle in an even fold, to give a sort of butterfly or bow-tie effect.

**Lasagne**: cut the dough with a fluted pastry wheel into 4 × 10 in/10 × 25 cm strips. These are cooked briefly in boiling salted water, then dipped in a bowl of cold water containing a teaspoon of oil, drained on a damp cloth and layered with meat sauce, cheese and béchamel sauce. The lasagne is then baked until it is bubbling and browned.

**Cannelloni**: cut the pasta dough into rectangles 4 × 5 in/10 × 12 cm. Boil them a few at a time for a minute or two in boiling salted water, dip into a bowl of cold water containing a teaspoon of oil and drain on a damp cloth. Put the pieces on a board, spread 2–3 tablespoons of stuffing along the short side of each piece and roll them up loosely. Lay the cannelloni in a shallow earthenware dish, dot with butter and bake. Serve with tomato sauce.

**Maltagliate** (literally, badly cut) are triangular pieces, about half the size of postage stamps, cut from a sheet of dough with a knife and used in soups.

# To cook pasta

Allow $\frac{1}{2}$ lb/115 g of pasta per person and 1 gallon/3.25 liters of water for every 1 lb/450 g of pasta. Add 2 level tablespoons of salt to each gallon. Bring the water to a rapid boil, drop in a small nut of butter and put in the pasta all at once. Long spaghetti should be pushed down as it softens until only a little is left sticking out of the water. This is then pushed under the water with a wooden spoon. Stir the pasta for 1–2 minutes to keep it separate. Boil spaghetti and other dried pastas for about 12 minutes and fresh pastas for about 4 minutes, uncovered, until the pasta is *al dente*, that is, tender but resilient when you bite it.

Take it off the heat and either scoop out the pasta with salad servers and transfer it to a heated white earthenware bowl, or pour it into a large colander, shake it around and then turn it immediately into a heated bowl. Leave a tiny amount of water in the pasta—if it is too well drained it will stick together. Add a large piece of butter or, if you are having an oily sauce, 2 tablespoons of olive oil, and mix it around. You can add some grated Parmesan at this point if you want to. Now add the sauce or half the sauce, mix it in briefly and serve immediately in broad heated soup bowls. Serve any remaining sauce and a bowl of grated Parmesan separately.

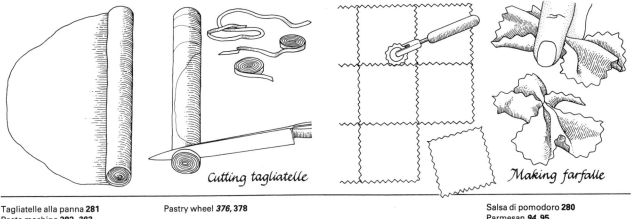

*Cutting tagliatelle*

*Making farfalle*

## Salsa di Pomodoro

| |
|---|
| 2 onions |
| 3 cloves garlic |
| 4 carrots |
| 4 sticks celery |
| 4 tablespoons olive oil |
| 1½ lb/700 g fresh tomatoes or a 1 lb/450 g can tomatoes |
| salt and freshly ground pepper |
| ⅔–1¼ cups/1.5–3 dl chicken stock (optional) |
| 3 tablespoons/45 g butter |
| freshly grated Parmesan |

SERVES 6

Peel the onions and garlic and chop them finely, together with the carrots and celery, and fry in the olive oil in a heavy saucepan until soft and starting to color. Add the tomatoes, if necessary peeled and roughly chopped, and the salt and pepper and simmer for an hour, adding stock or water if the mixture becomes too dry. Put the sauce through the medium mesh of a food mill, or blend in a food processor, and add the butter. Put the Parmesan in a bowl and serve separately.

This is a domestic everyday sauce of northern Italy, where every day means once or even twice every single day. Italians make enough to last a week and eat it with all kinds of pasta, with semolina gnocchi and with polenta.

ALTERNATIVE: *in Italy this sauce is very often heated in a frying pan until it bubbles. Drained pasta is then stirred around in it for a few minutes before serving.*

## Pesto alla genovese

| |
|---|
| 12 large healthy basil leaves |
| 2 large cloves garlic |
| 1 teaspoon coarse salt or pinch fine salt |
| 1 tablespoon pine nuts |
| 2 tablespoons Parmesan, freshly grated |
| 3 tablespoons olive oil |
| 2 tablespoons/30 g butter |
| freshly ground pepper |

SERVES 4

Tear up the basil leaves and put them into a mortar. Peel and chop the garlic and pound it with the basil leaves and the salt until you have a moist purée. Shake the pine nuts over a high flame in an iron frying pan until they are toasted to a pale brown.

Pound them with the basil, then throw in the cheese and start adding the oil drip by drip. Stir all the time until you have a thick green sauce, glistening with oil, from which rises the most incredibly delicious smell, pungent and aromatic.

Serve the fragrant pesto stirred into just-cooked and well-drained tagliatelle or spaghetti, dot with little slips of butter and sprinkle with Parmesan and coarse pepper. This is a memorable dish.

## Ragú alla bolognese

| |
|---|
| ½ lb/225 g each of ground veal or beef and ground pork |
| 1 onion |
| 2 cloves garlic |
| 1 large carrot |
| 3 tablespoons olive oil |
| 3 chicken livers |
| 3 large ripe tomatoes |
| 1 large sprig thyme, chopped |
| salt and freshly ground pepper |
| ⅔ cup/1.5 dl chicken stock |
| 1 glass red wine |
| 2 tablespoons heavy cream |
| freshly grated Parmesan |

SERVES 6

Peel the onions, garlic and carrot, chop them finely and sauté them in the oil in a heavy pan. Add the ground meat, turn up the heat to brown it, then add the chicken livers, chopped into small pieces. Skin and chop the tomatoes and add them to the meat, together with the thyme, and season with salt and pepper. Cook fairly fast until most of the liquid from the tomatoes has been absorbed. Add a little of the stock and red wine and simmer the sauce slowly, adding more stock and wine as it is needed, using water if you run out of these. After about an hour and 30 minutes the sauce should be rich and smooth. Add the cream, away from the heat, and serve with grated Parmesan on any kind of pasta.

## Spaghetti alla rustica

| |
|---|
| 1 lb/450 g spaghetti |
| 2 cloves garlic |
| 6 tablespoons olive oil |

*1 can anchovy fillets in oil*

*2 teaspoons oregano*

*salt and freshly ground pepper*

*2–3 tablespoons coarsely chopped parsley*

*freshly grated Parmesan*

SERVES 4

Peel and crush the garlic and fry in the oil in a small saucepan. When the garlic has browned and smells nutty, remove it and turn the heat down as far as it will go. Chop the anchovies, add them to the oil and let them melt down to a mush. Add the oregano. Cook the spaghetti in a large pan of boiling, well-salted water until it is *al dente*—this is particularly important for this type of spaghetti dish, which does not have a thick disguising sauce. Put the drained spaghetti into a heated dish, stir in the anchovies and olive oil, season and sprinkle with the parsley. Serve with plenty of Parmesan—this is a particularly fine way of eating spaghetti.

------◆------

# Spaghetti all'amatriciana

*1 lb/450 g spaghetti*

*1 small onion*

*¼ lb/115 g bacon or pancetta*

*1½ tablespoons olive oil*

*sprinkling of cayenne pepper*

*1½ cups/280 g canned tomatoes*

*salt*

*freshly grated pecorino or Parmesan*

SERVES 4

Peel the onion and chop it finely. Cut the bacon in little dice and cook over a brisk heat. When lightly browned, remove with a slotted spoon and keep hot. Add the oil and cook the onion in the same pan with the oil and bacon fat, adding a good sprinkling of cayenne pepper. Meanwhile cut the tomatoes in half, drain them in a sieve, remove their seeds and chop. When the onions start to brown, put the chopped tomato flesh into the saucepan. Season with salt and cook for 10 minutes. Add the bacon to the sauce. Bring a large pan of salted water to the boil and cook the spaghetti. When it is cooked—it must be *al dente*—drain it and put into a heated bowl. Stir in the sauce and then add the cheese, mixing it in well. The spaghetti should be a delicate pink—not bright red. Serve immediately with more freshly grated pecorino or Parmesan cheese.

# Spaghetti alla carbonara

*¾ lb/340 g spaghetti*

*¼ lb/115 g bacon, unsmoked if possible, or pancetta*

*2 tablespoons/30 g butter*

*5 eggs*

*2 tablespoons finely chopped parsley*

*salt and freshly ground black pepper*

*½ cup/55 g freshly grated Parmesan*

SERVES 4

Cut the bacon into tiny sticks or dice and fry it over a gentle heat until crisp and brown. Drain the bacon and keep it hot. Add the butter to the pan to melt; keep the fat hot. Meanwhile break the eggs into a bowl and beat them together with the parsley and a generous quantity of black pepper. Bring a large pan of salted water to the boil. Cook the spaghetti until it is just tender. As soon as the spaghetti is cooked, drain it and put it into a heated bowl or return it to the hot pan in which it cooked and stir in the bacon and the fat. Next add the beaten egg mixture and turn the spaghetti over several times with a wooden spoon and fork until it is well coated. Lastly mix in the grated Parmesan. All these steps must be done extremely fast so that the pasta can be served very hot.

------◆------

# Tagliatelle alla panna

*¾ lb/340 g dried tagliatelle, or sufficient freshly made tagliatelle for 4*

*4–5 tablespoons heavy cream*

*3 tablespoons/45 g butter*

*salt and freshly ground pepper*

*grating of nutmeg*

*¼ lb/115 g raw or cooked ham, thinly cut*

*freshly grated Parmesan*

SERVES 4

Bring a large pan of salted water to the boil and cook the tagliatelle until just *al dente*. Meanwhile put the cream and butter into a large saucepan, season with salt, pepper and grated nutmeg and heat through. Cut the ham into tiny, delicate strips.

When the pasta is cooked, drain it well and put it in with the cream and butter mixture, turning it over until well coated. Add the ham, stir it and cook over a gentle heat for 2 minutes.

Serve in a large dish accompanied by freshly grated

Parmesan. This recipe is extremely rapid and simple to make and is quite extraordinarily good.

ALTERNATIVE: *add a tablespoon of meat glaze or consommé to the cream and butter mixture. The brown jelly that can be separated from cold beef drippings is perfect for this and helps to prevent the sauce from becoming too bland.*

---

## Macaroni and cheese

| |
|---|
| ¼ lb/115 g macaroni |
| 2 tablespoons/30 g butter |
| ¼ cup/30 g flour |
| scant 2 cups/4.5 dl creamy milk |
| salt and freshly ground pepper |
| pinch of grated nutmeg |
| ¼ lb/115 g Cheddar, grated |
| 2 oz/55 g lean ham, chopped |
| 3 tablespoons/30 g fine homemade bread crumbs |
| 1 tablespoon/15 g butter |

SERVES 4

Preheat the oven to 375°F/190°C.

Bring a pan of well-salted water to the boil and toss in the macaroni. Cook until just tender. Don't overcook it or it will go flat and will not absorb the sauce. Meanwhile, make a strongly flavored cheese sauce: melt the butter in a saucepan, stir in the flour and allow it to cook for 2 minutes. Gradually add the milk, stirring all the time to obtain a smooth, velvety sauce. Season with salt, pepper and grated nutmeg. Let it cook gently for 10–15 minutes, then stir in the cheese and ham. When the cheese has melted, stir in the macaroni, taste for seasoning and pour the mixture into a buttered pie dish. Sprinkle the top with bread crumbs, dot all over with butter and bake for about 20 minutes until golden brown. The point with this dish is to make plenty of sauce and not to put in too much macaroni, so that it is moist and succulent.

---

## Bucatini alla marchigiana

| |
|---|
| ¾ lb/340 g bucatini (ribbed elbow macaroni) |
| 1 small onion |
| 1 stick celery |
| 1 carrot |
| 2 tablespoons olive oil or 1 tablespoon/15 g lard |
| 3 oz/85 g ham, cut in little strips |
| 1 small glass red wine |
| 1 lb/450 g ripe tomatoes or a 1 lb/450 g can of tomatoes |
| 2 tablespoons tomato paste |
| pinch each of marjoram and thyme |
| salt and freshly ground pepper |
| ¾ cup/85 g freshly grated Parmesan |

SERVES 4

Peel the onion and then chop all the vegetables, except the tomatoes, together finely to make a battuto (a mixture of chopped vegetables). Brown them in a saucepan in the oil or lard.

Add the ham and stir it around for a few minutes. Add the wine and let it reduce until it has almost evaporated. Chop the tomatoes and add them to the pan with the tomato paste, herbs and seasoning and bring to the boil. Turn down the heat and simmer for half an hour.

Drop the macaroni into a large pan of boiling salted water and cook for 15 minutes or until just tender. Drain, put into a heated bowl, mix in 3 or 4 tablespoons of Parmesan and stir in half the sauce. Serve the remaining sauce and cheese separately.

---

## Lasagne

| |
|---|
| ½ lb/225 g lasagne |
| 2 onions |
| 4 tablespoons olive oil |
| 1 lb/450 g ground beef |
| ½ lb/225 g ground pork |
| ¾ lb/340 g fresh tomatoes, skinned, or 2 cups/400 g canned tomatoes |
| 3 cloves garlic |
| 1 heaping teaspoon each of dried oregano and basil |
| ⅔–1¼ cup/1.5–3 dl chicken or light beef stock (optional) |
| salt and freshly ground pepper |
| 1 scant quart/9 dl milk |
| 1 bay leaf |
| ¾ stick/85 g butter |
| 6 tablespoons/85 g flour |
| pinch of grated nutmeg |
| 4 cups/450 g grated mozzarella |
| ¾ cup/85 g freshly grated Parmesan |

SERVES 6

Peel and chop the onions and sweat them in the oil in a large pan. Add the meat and fry until crumbly. Roughly chop the tomatoes and peel and crush the garlic. Add tomatoes, garlic and herbs to the pan and let them soften. If they do not make enough liquid to cook the meat in, gradually add a little stock, but always a bit less than you think you might need—you can add more later if necessary. Season with salt and pepper and cook gently in the pan for about an hour.

Preheat the oven to 350°F/180°C.

Meanwhile cook the lasagne and leave it to drain. Put the milk in a small saucepan on a gentle heat and infuse the bay leaf in it for a few minutes. Make a béchamel sauce with the butter, flour and warmed milk and season with nutmeg, salt and pepper.

When everything is ready, put a layer of meat in a long buttered gratin dish or casserole, then a layer of béchamel, a layer of half the mozzarella and half the Parmesan, then a layer of lasagne. Add more meat, more béchamel, more lasagne, then another layer of meat and béchamel, finally topping the dish with the rest of the grated cheeses. Bake for about 45 minutes until browned on top.

ALTERNATIVE: *if you are in a hurry, you can brown it under the broiler.*

---

# Ravioli

*fresh pasta made with 3 eggs*

**for the filling:**

*10 fresh basil leaves*

*1 lb/450 g spinach*

*5 oz/140 g ricotta or cottage cheese*

*4 tablespoons Parmesan, freshly grated*

*¼ teaspoon grated nutmeg*

*salt and freshly ground pepper*

**for the sauce:**

*⅔ cup/1.5 dl light cream*

*2 tablespoons/30 g butter*

*salt and freshly ground pepper*

*freshly grated Parmesan*

SERVES 4

To make the filling, chop the basil finely. Wash the spinach thoroughly, put it into a large pan and cook in the water that clings to the leaves until just tender. Drain, chop it finely and mix with the cheese, basil and nutmeg. Season with salt and pepper. Roll out the pasta as thinly as possible—this is important with ravioli, as it has a double

thickness along the edges of each little square. Cut it with a fluted pastry wheel into strips about 3 in/8 cm wide. Put dabs of filling 1½ in/4 cm apart all down one side of each strip, ¾ in/2 cm in from the edge. Fold the other side of pasta over the top, so that the two long edges meet. Press down all around and in between the dabs of filling, sealing the long edge carefully. Cut between the little parcel with the fluted cutter. Bring a large pan of salted water to the boil.

Meanwhile, heat the cream and butter together and season lightly with salt and pepper.

When the water boils, drop a few of the ravioli into the pan, let them cook for 3–4 minutes and transfer them to a hot dish, using a slotted spoon. Keep them warm in a bowl and sprinkle each layer with the cream sauce before putting another layer on top. When all the ravioli are cooked, pour the remaining sauce over the top and serve with a sprinkling of freshly grated Parmesan.

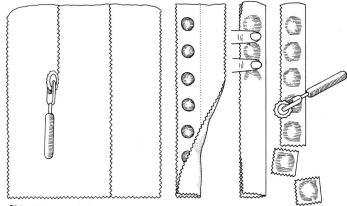

*Making ravioli*

---

# Crespolini

**for the meat sauce:**

*½ lb/225 g each of pork and veal, finely ground*

*1 onion*

*1–2 tablespoons olive oil*

*2 cloves garlic*

*⅔ cup/1.5 dl red wine*

*1 heaping teaspoon fresh chopped thyme*

*¾ lb/340 g fresh tomatoes, skinned, or*

*2 cups/400 g canned tomatoes*

*salt and freshly ground pepper*

**for the batter:**

*2 eggs*

*1¼ cups/140 g flour*

# Pasta and Gnocchi

pinch of salt

1¼ cups/3 dl milk

1 tablespoon brandy

1 tablespoon/15 g butter, melted

olive oil for frying

**for the cheese sauce:**

¼ cup/30 g each of grated Parmesan and mozzarella

1–1½ tablespoon/15–20 g butter

2 tablespoons/15 g flour

scant 2 cups/4.5 dl milk, heated

1 large or 2 small bay leaves

1 blade mace

salt and freshly ground pepper

SERVES 4

Start by making the meat sauce. Peel and finely chop the onion and fry in the olive oil. Add the meat, turn up the heat as high as it will go and let it fry for 1–2 minutes. Stir it well, then let it fry again. Repeat this until the meat is well browned and there is a good brown crust forming on the bottom of the pan. Peel and slice the garlic and add to the pan with the wine and thyme. Stir well and let it bubble up. Chop the tomatoes, add them to the pan and season with salt and pepper. Simmer, uncovered, for about an hour, adding more liquid if it becomes dry.

To make the crespolini crêpe batter, beat the eggs into the flour and salt. Gradually add the milk, beating well to get rid of the lumps before the mixture gets too thick. You can do this with an electric beater on a low speed. Add the brandy and melted butter, beat well and stand for 30 minutes to an hour. While the batter is resting, make the cheese sauce. Melt the butter in a thick-bottomed pan, stir in the flour and when it begins to seethe around the edges, gradually stir in the heated milk. (This is a very thin béchamel, the consistency of pouring cream.) Drop in the bay leaves and blade of mace, season with salt and pepper and let it cook, stirring from time to time, for about 5 minutes. Add the cheese, stir until it melts and keep the sauce warm until you need it. Preheat the oven to 425°F/220°C.

Fry 2–3 small, thin crêpes in olive oil for each person and keep them warm. It is best to leave the making of the crêpes to the last, so they will not have time to become soggy. They should be tender and light. Put a crêpe into a buttered oval gratin dish, lay a line of meat sauce along the middle, roll up the crêpe and lay it at one end of the dish. Stuff all the crêpes in this way, laying them side by side. Ten 7 in/18 cm crêpes will fit into a

gratin dish 12 × 8 in/30 × 20 cm. When the dish is full, pour the cheese sauce all over the top and bake, uncovered, for about 30 minutes until the top is brown and bubbling.

This dish is troublesome to make with its three separate recipes, but the light and delicate results make the effort well worthwhile.

ALTERNATIVE: *use the meat sauce to stuff cannelloni and the cheese sauce to cover.*

---

# Gnocchi romana

5 oz/140 g semolina

2½ cups/6 dl milk

1 bay leaf

1 onion, peeled

pinch of grated nutmeg or 1 blade mace

1 egg yolk

½ cup/55 g freshly grated Parmesan

½ stick/55 g butter

salt and freshly ground pepper

SERVES 4–6

Heat the milk very slowly, infused with the bay leaf, onion and nutmeg or mace. Scoop the bits out of the pan as the milk comes to the boil and pour in the semolina. Stir it well for 2–3 minutes until it is really thick, then turn the heat right down, cover the pan and cook gently for about 15 minutes, stirring often. Take the pan off the heat and stir in the egg yolk, half the cheese and half the butter, and add salt and pepper to taste. Moisten a large plate with cold water and spread the mixture over it evenly with the palm of your hand to about ½ in/1 cm thick or less. Preheat the oven to 325°F/170°C.

When the gnocchi mixture has cooled, cut it into 1½ in/4 cm rounds with a wine glass, re-forming the leftover bits with your hands and cutting more rounds until it is all used up. Lay the little gnocchi overlapping in a buttered gratin dish. Dot with the remaining butter, sprinkle with the cheese and bake for half an hour or until nicely browned.

In Italy this is eaten just as it is, without sauce, because the flavor of these gnocchi is rather delicate and easily overpowered. If you do feel it needs an accompaniment, serve with a light tomato sauce.

ALTERNATIVE: *gnocchi can also be made from a dough of mashed potatoes and flour, poached, then baked in the oven with butter and cheese.*

# Plain boiled rice

*½ cup/55 g long-grain rice per person*

*salt*

If you soften the rice grains and remove some of their surface starch before cooking, it helps to prevent them sticking together. You can do this by soaking the rice for half an hour before you cook it, by washing it in a sieve under cold running water for several minutes, or by pouring a kettle of boiling water over it, in a sieve, before lightly washing it.

Prepared in any of these ways, rice cooks very quickly and very well. Simply throw it into a large pan of boiling, well-salted water, stir it and then let it boil for 10 minutes, testing after 8 minutes to make sure that it is not already cooked. Drain it well and serve very hot.

---

# Brown rice

*2 cups/225 g brown rice, soaked for 2 hours in cold water*

*½ stick/55 g butter*

*2 tablespoons olive oil*

*1 quart/9 dl chicken stock*

*salt*

SERVES 4

Drain the soaked rice thoroughly in a wire sieve. Heat the butter and oil in a shallow saucepan or sauté pan. Put in the rice and stir it around for a minute or so until it is glistening and thoroughly coated in butter and oil. Start adding the chicken stock, a little at a time, stirring the rice around so that it absorbs the stock gradually and remains separate. Add more stock as it is absorbed and cook fairly gently, uncovered, for about 40 minutes, stirring frequently and keeping it just moist. When tender, remove from the heat and let it steam for 5 minutes before serving.

Brown rice is much denser than white rice and so takes longer to cook. Plainly boiled it is rather stodgy, but if treated like Italian rice, as here, it is very good, with an interesting nutty flavor.

ALTERNATIVES: *soften an onion and some mushrooms in the oil before adding the rice.*

*A number of other vegetables can be added to brown rice to make it into a meal. Particularly good are sweet peppers, eggplant, zucchini and tomatoes.*

# Risotto alla milanese

*1½ cups/170 g Italian rice*

*1 small onion*

*2–3 tablespoons olive oil and butter, mixed*

*2 or 3 generous pinches powdered saffron*

*3¾–4½ cups/9 dl–1 liter chicken or beef stock*

*¼ cup/30 g Parmesan, freshly grated*

*2 tablespoons/30 g butter*

*salt and freshly ground pepper*

SERVES 4

Peel the onion, chop it finely and put it in a frying pan or sauté pan with the oil and butter. Let it cook until it is just tender, then add the rice, stirring it around until it becomes transparent, but do not allow it to brown.

Meanwhile dissolve the saffron in the stock in a saucepan and bring it just to the boil. When it boils, add a ladleful of the stock to the rice. It will hiss and bubble violently, but let it bubble and simmer fairly quietly after this initial boiling has died down. Keep stirring all the time—this is an important part of making good risotto. When the rice has absorbed almost all the stock, add another ladleful of stock and when this, too, has been absorbed add another and so on, stirring continuously. The rice should never be really wet; adding the stock slowly means the rice swells and cooks slowly and the liquid becomes creamy.

When the rice is tender, after about 25–30 minutes, stir in the Parmesan and a good nut of butter. Taste for seasoning and add a little salt and freshly ground pepper. Let it settle for 2–3 minutes away from the heat before serving.

ALTERNATIVE: **Chicken liver risotto**. *Fry a few chopped chicken livers with the onion, adding also a glass of Marsala or vermouth. Throw some chopped sage leaves into the stock and omit the saffron.*

---

# Mushroom risotto

*1½ cups/170 g Italian rice*

*1 oz/30 g dried ceps*

*½ lb/225 g button mushrooms*

*2 cloves garlic*

*3 tablespoons olive oil*

*½ stick/55 g butter*

*2 tablespoons chopped parsley*

*1 glass dry white wine*

*1¼ cups/3 dl chicken stock*

*¼ cup/30 g freshly grated Parmesan*

*salt and freshly ground pepper*

SERVES 4

Soak the ceps for half an hour in 2 cups/4.5 dl of hot water. Squeeze them dry, keeping the liquid to use when cooking the rice.

Slice the fresh mushrooms, and peel and chop the garlic. Heat the oil and half the butter in a large frying pan and fry the ceps and sliced fresh mushrooms, together with the garlic and chopped parsley. When the mushrooms have exuded some of their juice, add the rice and fry it for a minute or so, stirring it around until it becomes slightly transparent. Add the white wine and let it bubble until it has almost all evaporated, then add a ladleful of the stock and stir the rice until the liquid is almost all absorbed and becoming creamy. Keep adding first the stock and then the liquid in which the ceps were soaked, leaving a little at the bottom of the bowl as there may be some grit in it left over from the ceps.

When all the liquid has been absorbed and the rice is tender and bathed in a creamy sauce, stir in the grated cheese and a good knob of butter. Taste for seasoning, add a little salt and freshly ground pepper if necessary, and serve.

—◆—

# Pilau rice

*1¼ cups/225 g long-grain rice*

*4 cloves*

*8 cardamom pods*

*2 in/5 cm piece of cinnamon stick*

*1 onion*

*½ stick/55 g butter, clarified*

*2 bay leaves*

*scant ¼ cup/30 g blanched almonds*

*⅓ cup/55 g raisins*

*salt*

SERVES 4

Wash the rice thoroughly under cold running water and leave to drain. Bruise the cloves, cardamom pods and cinnamon stick. Peel the onion and cut it into the thinnest of rings. Heat about a quarter of the butter and fry the onion rings, without stirring, until they are a cinnamon

brown. Lift them out of the pan with a fork and keep them hot.

Add the remaining butter to the pan and stir in the spices and bay leaves and then the rice. Cook gently for 7–8 minutes, stirring the rice around until it becomes translucent. Add about 2 cups/4.5 dl water, stir it in and add the almonds and raisins. Season with salt, bring to the boil, cover and simmer for about 25 minutes over a gentle heat until the rice is tender, adding a little more water if it is necessary.

Serve, scattered with the browned onion rings, as an accompaniment to curries or with spiced chicken.

—◆—

# Paella

*2 cups/340 g arborio rice*

*1 small chicken, about 2 lb/900 g*

*1 onion*

*2 cloves garlic*

*½ lb/225 g tomatoes*

*1 lb/450 g mussels*

*½ lb/225 g small squid*

*2 pinches saffron*

*5 cups/1 liter chicken stock*

*1 red sweet pepper*

*3–4 tablespoons olive oil*

*salt and freshly ground pepper*

*1 bay leaf*

*½ cup/115 g shelled peas*

*12 large cooked shrimps in their shells*

*12 black olives*

*1 lemon, sliced*

SERVES 4–6

Take the meat off the raw chicken with a sharp knife. Peel and chop the onion and garlic finely and skin, seed and chop the tomatoes. Scrub the mussels and put them in a heavy saucepan with ½ cup/1.5 dl boiling water. Shake them over a rapid heat until they have all opened, then drain them, put them to one side and reserve the liquid. Clean the squid and cut the body into rings and the tentacles and flaps into pieces. Soak the saffron in the chicken stock. Turn the red sweet pepper close to a flame until it blisters and then peel off the thin skin. Cut the flesh into strips, discarding the core and seeds. Heat the olive oil in a paella pan or broad, deep frying pan and sauté the pieces of chicken over a brisk heat until browned. Add the onion, garlic, tomatoes and squid, the chicken stock with its saffron and the red sweet pepper. Bring the liquid to the boil and add salt, pepper and the rice. When it returns to the boil, add the bay leaf, turn down the heat and simmer very gently, with the lid on, for 20 minutes.

When the rice is becoming swollen and tender, stir in the peas and place the shrimps and mussels on top and the black olives all around the edge. Add the mussel cooking liquid, cover again and cook for a further 5 minutes until the rice is completely tender and separated. Serve with a slice of lemon on each plate to add a touch of tartness to this traditional Spanish dish.

---

# Burghul pilaf

| |
|---|
| 1½ cups/225 g burghul |
| 1 small onion |
| 2 cloves garlic |
| 2–3 tablespoons olive oil |
| 3 cups/7 dl chicken stock |
| salt |
| pinch of cayenne pepper |
| 4 tablespoons chopped parsley |
| juice of 1–2 lemons |
| ⅔ cup/1.5 dl natural yogurt |

SERVES 4

Peel and chop the onion and garlic. Sweat the onion in the olive oil in a large frying pan, and when it is tender and a pale golden color add the garlic and cook for a few minutes more. Stir in the burghul, and when it is well coated with oil add half the chicken stock and a little salt and cayenne pepper. Cover the pan and cook gently for 10 minutes, then add the rest of the stock, cover again and continue to simmer gently for a further 10 minutes or so.

Taste for seasoning, stir and let the burghul steam over a very low heat for 10 minutes longer, until it becomes light and separated. Stir in the chopped parsley and season well with lemon juice. Serve, hot or cold, with the yogurt.

One good way to eat this excellent pilaf is to put a pile of crisp lettuce leaves on the table and to scoop up the cracked wheat with the leaves, eating them both together.

# Tabbouleh

| |
|---|
| generous ½ cup/170 g fine burghul |
| 1 bunch scallions |
| 2 tomatoes |
| 4 tablespoons freshly chopped parsley |
| 2 tablespoons freshly chopped mint |
| 3 tablespoons olive oil |
| juice of 2 lemons |
| salt and freshly ground pepper |

SERVES 4

Chop the scallions finely and skin and chop the tomatoes. Put the burghul in a bowl, cover it with cold water and allow to soak for 15 minutes. Take it out by the handful, squeezing out the water as you do so.

Put the burghul in a clean, dry bowl, stir in the onions, tomatoes, parsley and mint. Add the olive oil and lemon juice, stir it in, taste the salad and add more oil or lemon juice if it is needed. Season with salt and pepper and serve with crisp lettuce leaves with which to scoop up the salad.

---

# Veneto polenta

| |
|---|
| 3¼ cups/450 g coarse yellow cornmeal (polenta) |
| 1½ teaspoons salt |

SERVES 6

Bring 2 quarts/1.75 liters of salted water to the boil and turn down the heat until it is simmering steadily. Take a handful of cornmeal at a time, and pour it into the pot in a thin stream, letting it trickle out between your fingers. At the same time keep stirring it continuously with a wooden spoon. The stream of cornmeal should be so thin that you can see the individual grains as they fall. Keep stirring all the time or lumps may form. If they do, you can crush and dissolve them against the side of the pan with a wooden spoon. Keep stirring over a low heat for 20 minutes—the polenta is done when it pulls away from the sides of the pot.

Serve it piping hot, with melted butter, or wet a large clean board or wooden platter and pour the polenta onto it in a large golden pool. It will spread and set. Let it cool and slice it for frying or broiling to eat like bread or to serve with game and stews. Slices of polenta are especially good fried in butter and serve topped with Gorgonzola cheese.

Burghul **104**
Chicken stock **194**
Yogurt **91, 92**

Cornmeal **104–105**, *105*
Gorgonzola **99–100**, *100*

# Grains and Dried Peas and Beans

## Muesli

| |
|---|
| 2 cups/170 g rolled oats |
| 2 tablespoons hazelnuts, walnuts, cashew nuts or almonds |
| 2 tablespoons bran |
| 2 tablespoons each of raisins and sultanas |
| 1–2 tablespoons brown sugar |
| pinch of coarse salt |

SERVES 4

Chop the nuts coarsely and if using hazelnuts, cashews or almonds, put them in a dry frying pan over a gentle heat and toast them lightly. You can also toast the oats in the same way for a particularly nutty flavor. Mix all the ingredients together and serve with milk and freshly sliced banana or apple, or with blackberries.

---

## Kasha

| |
|---|
| 1⅓ cups/255 g toasted buckwheat (kasha) |
| salt |
| 2 tablespoons goose or duck drippings, or ½ stick/55 g butter |

SERVES 4

Put the kasha in a saucepan together with a pinch of salt. Add 2½ cups/6 dl of boiling water, stir it around, add half a teaspoon of salt and cover the pan. Bring to the boil over a gentle heat and simmer for a few minutes. It will become like porridge. Stir in the goose drippings, duck drippings or butter and cook, covered. After about 10 minutes, remove the lid and fork up the kasha, tossing and turning it to separate the grains. Now leave it over a very low heat, uncovered, tossing and turning it over lightly with a fork every 5 minutes. After about an hour the kasha will be light, separated and cooked. Serve with all meat dishes, especially pork and goose; it has an elusive almond flavor.

---

## Indian millet

| |
|---|
| 1⅓ cups/225 g millet |
| 2 onions |
| ½ stick/55 g butter |
| ½ cauliflower |
| 2 zucchini |
| 4 cardamom pods |
| 1 teaspoon cumin seeds |
| 4 cloves |
| 2 cloves garlic |
| salt and freshly ground pepper |

SERVES 6

Peel one of the onions and slice it very finely into rings. Heat half the butter in a large frying pan and fry the onion over a medium heat without stirring until the rings are dry and a nice deep cinnamon brown. Remove them to a plate and keep them in a warm place.

Chop the remaining onion, the cauliflower and the zucchini into small pieces and sauté them in the same frying pan with the rest of the butter until lightly browned. Add the millet, spices and the garlic, peeled and chopped, and stir everything around for 3–5 minutes. Add enough water to cover, season with salt and pepper and simmer for about 20–25 minutes, until just cooked through, stirring and forking up the millet from time to time to help keep it light and separated.

Allow to steam, off the heat, for 5 minutes, fork up again and serve with the brown onion rings scattered over the top.

This dish makes a delicious and extremely healthy lunch course.

---

## Boston baked beans

| |
|---|
| ¾ cup/340 g navy or pea beans, soaked overnight |
| ¼ lb/115 g salt pork, or slab bacon, rind removed |
| 2 tablespoons/30 g butter |
| 1 onion |
| 2 tablespoons molasses |
| 2 tablespoons tomato paste |
| 1 tablespoon hot mustard |
| 1 teaspoon cider vinegar |
| salt |

SERVES 4

Put the beans into a large saucepan and cover with fresh cold water, which should come 1 in/2.5 cm above the level of the beans. Simmer for about an hour, until tender. To see if they are cooked, take out a spoonful of beans, pour off the liquid and blow lightly on the beans. The outer skin will curl if they are ready. Drain them, reserving the cooking liquid, and put them in a special bean pot or, if you do not have a bean pot, a heavy, deep casserole. Preheat the oven to 300°F/160°C.

Cut the pork or bacon into thickish slices. Melt the butter in a frying pan and fry the slices on both sides. Transfer them to the casserole or bean pot, together with their fat, and half bury them in the beans. Peel the onion and push it into the middle of the beans. Mix the cooking liquid from the beans with the molasses, tomato paste, mustard, vinegar and a teaspoon of salt and pour it all over the beans. Cover the pot and bake in a very slow oven for 2–3 hours, adding more water if necessary. Remove the lid for the last 30 minutes to brown the top.

---

# Black beans and rice

| |
|---|
| _1 generous cup/170 g black beans, soaked overnight_ |
| _1 large onion_ |
| _2 tablespoons olive oil_ |
| _1–2 dried or fresh red chili peppers_ |
| _1 small green sweet pepper_ |
| _1 clove garlic_ |
| _⅔ cup/115 g rice_ |
| _2 tomatoes_ |
| _salt_ |

SERVES 6

Put the drained beans into a saucepan, cover them with 1 in/2.5 cm of fresh water and bring them slowly to the boil. When they start boiling, turn down the heat and simmer until tender—it will take about 1½ hours.

Peel and chop the onion and fry it in the olive oil until nicely browned. Remove pith and seeds from the chili peppers (take care not to touch your face while you do it) and the green sweet pepper. Chop them coarsely and add them to the onions, together with the garlic, peeled and chopped, and allow to sweat gently for 5 minutes. Add the rice and stir it around for a minute or two, and lastly add the tomatoes, skinned and chopped, and the beans with the water in which they were cooked, plus enough fresh water to cover everything. Season with salt and simmer for 15–20 minutes until the rice is just tender. Add a little more water if necessary; the beans should be moist and bathed in a light sauce. Rice and beans are a daily food of most of the peoples of Latin America.

This is a Cuban recipe.

# Israeli falafels

| |
|---|
| _2⅔ cups/450 g chick-peas, soaked overnight_ |
| _1 clove garlic_ |
| _½ onion or 2 shallots_ |
| _½ teaspoon baking powder_ |
| _4 eggs_ |
| _large handful of parsley, finely chopped_ |
| _2 teaspoons salt_ |
| _4 teaspoons cumin seeds_ |
| _½ teaspoon coriander seeds_ |
| _oil for deep frying_ |

SERVES 6

Peel and chop the garlic and the onion or shallots and put them together with the other ingredients in a food mill or in a food processor. Process until everything is well chopped—the texture should be like moist, very fine bread crumbs. Allow the mixture to stand for about half an hour. Form into small flat or round cakes about the size of a walnut—the mixture is rather crumbly but it will make cakes if handled carefully. Transfer them with a spatula to a pan of hot oil and fry to a deep brown. Eat hot as an appetizer.

These are much enjoyed in the Middle East. They are sometimes served with tahina made into a light sauce with crushed garlic and enough water to make a smooth cream.

ALTERNATIVE: **Egyptian falafels, or ta'amia.** _Use dried white fava beans (ful nabed)._

---

# Hummus bi tahina

| |
|---|
| _1⅓ cups/225 g chick-peas, soaked overnight_ |
| _salt_ |
| _2 cloves garlic_ |
| _8 tablespoons tahina paste_ |
| _juice of 2 lemons_ |
| _1 tablespoon olive oil_ |
| _sprinkling of cayenne pepper_ |
| _1 tablespoon chopped parsley_ |

SERVES 4

Put the drained chick-peas into a large saucepan of cold water, bring them to the boil and simmer for an hour. Then add ½ teaspoon salt and simmer on, until the chick-peas are soft. This will take a further 1½–2 hours or more. Strain the chick-peas and purée them through the fine blade of a food mill or pressing them through a sieve. This removes the skins. Peel and crush the garlic.

Beat in the garlic and about 8 tablespoons of tahina paste, the lemon juice and up to 10 tablespoons of cold water. The aim is to make a fairly smooth cream, the consistency of thick mayonnaise. Add salt if necessary, put the mixture into a serving bowl and flatten the top. Pour a tablespoon of olive oil over the top, sprinkle a patch of cayenne pepper onto the middle and scatter chopped parsley all over the top.

## Magedra

| |
|---|
| ⅔ cup/115 g brown lentils, soaked for 2 hours in cold water |
| 2 large onions |
| 3 tablespoons olive oil |
| 1¼ cups/225 g long-grain rice |
| salt |

SERVES 4

Put the drained lentils into 5 cups/1 liter of fresh cold water, bring them to the boil and simmer for half an hour, or a little longer, until tender. Meanwhile, peel and slice the onions in rings and fry them gently in half the oil without stirring until they are a deep cinnamon brown. Drain and keep them warm. When the lentils are cooked, strain off their cooking liquid and reserve it.

Rinse the rice in a sieve. Bring the lentil cooking liquid to the boil in a saucepan and add the rest of the oil, a little salt and the rice. Cook gently with a half-tilted lid for about 15 minutes. When the rice has absorbed the liquid, take off the lid and allow the rice to steam for a few minutes, then, when it is dry and fluffy, stir in the lentils and heat through.

Serve this Baghdadian dish, also known as "the food of the poor," with the fried onion rings scattered on top, and eat with fresh plain yogurt or tomato sauce.

## Dhal

| |
|---|
| ¾ cup/115 g dhal |
| 2½ cups/6 dl chicken stock or water |
| salt |
| ¼ teaspoon turmeric |
| 1 onion |
| 3 cloves garlic |
| 1–2 tablespoons oil or melted butter |
| 1 green chili pepper, sliced |
| ¼ teaspoon chili powder |
| ¼ teaspoon cumin seeds |
| handful of fresh coriander, chopped |

SERVES 4

Pick over the dhal to remove bad ones, husks and any small stones and wash it in several waters to free it of dust and starch. Put it in a pan with the stock or water, a pinch of salt and the turmeric and cook until tender. The time varies according to how you like the dhal—dry like rice or smooth and moist—and on the type of dhal you are cooking.

When it is almost cooked, peel and slice the onion and cloves of garlic and fry them in the oil or butter together with the chili pepper pieces, chili powder and cumin seeds. When the onion is a golden brown, add the dhal and the chopped coriander. Cook, stirring, over a low heat for 5 minutes.

This reheats very well; if it gets too dry, add a little more chicken stock or water. Dhal is a practically indispensable companion for curry but is also a main dish, served with plainly boiled rice.

## Pease pudding

| |
|---|
| 2¼ cups/450 g split green peas, soaked for 3–4 hours |
| salt and freshly ground pepper |
| 3 tablespoons/45 g butter |
| 1 egg plus 2 extra yolks |

SERVES 6

Put the drained peas in a saucepan, cover them with 1 in/2.5 cm cold water and simmer for about 2 hours until tender. Season the peas with salt and pepper and purée them using the medium blade of a food mill or in a food processor. Mix in the butter, egg and the extra yolks, turn the mixture into a greased pudding bowl and cover. Boil in a covered saucepan half filled with boiling water for an hour, turn out onto a plate and serve with boiled ham or with pork.

It is easier to make pease pudding in a bowl than in a linen bag as it was originally done. It was usually served with boiled fresh pork, boiled pickled pork or boiled bacon and was sometimes cooked in the same pot with the meat.

## Baking bread

Baking bread is a craft—once you have learned it, nothing could possibly be easier or more enjoyable. If you have never baked before, start with a loaf made primarily with whole wheat flour, as making a good white loaf only comes with practice.

**Using yeast**: fresh yeast is becoming increasingly difficult to obtain, and although these recipes all call for it, dried yeast can always be substituted. Remember that, weight for weight, dried yeast is twice as potent as fresh, and the directions on the packet should be carefully followed. When using dried yeast, reactivate it by dissolving it in a little tepid water with a pinch of sugar. Add any more liquid called for in the recipe at the same time as you add the frothy yeast.

**Kneading**: to develop the gluten and distribute the yeast evenly, put the dough on a floured board and with a rhythmic, regular action, pull it towards you with bent fingers, and push it away with the palm of your hand and fingers closed. Continue until the dough is smooth and elastic.

**Rising and knocking down**: after kneading, the dough is left to rise in a covered bowl, in a warm place such as over a pilot light or near a heater or radiator. When it has roughly doubled in size it should be punched down with the fist to expel the air, until it is roughly its original size.

**Rising**: for the final stage before baking, the dough is shaped if necessary or put into pans ready for baking, then allowed to stand again in a warm place until it is taut, puffy and well risen.

---

## Whole wheat bread

| |
|---|
| *10 cups/1.1 kg whole wheat flour* |
| *2 cups/225 g cracked wheat, lightly toasted* |
| *1 tablespoon molasses* |
| *3 cakes fresh yeast* |
| *1 heaping tablespoon salt* |

MAKES 3 LOAVES

Mix the flour and the toasted cracked wheat together in a large bowl and allow the mixture to warm slightly for a few moments in a low oven. Mix the molasses into a scant quart/9 dl water—slightly warmer than lukewarm—in a measuring pitcher. Put the yeast in a bowl with a few tablespoons of the molasses and water and mix it to a thin cream. Leave in a warm place until it froths. Mix the salt into the remaining molasses and water and pour it into a well in the middle of the flour. Add the yeast mixture and mix thoroughly to a dough. Knead briefly, until the dough is smooth, then cover the bowl with a sheet of wax paper and a cloth and leave it in a warm place to rise for about 1–1½ hours, when the dough will have doubled in size. Prepare three loaf pans, greasing them sparingly with sunflower oil or butter.

Take the dough out of the bowl, knead it for a minute on a floured work surface and cut it into three pieces. Form the loaves by kneading each piece of dough into a ball, then flattening the ball into a thick disc. Roll up the disc, tuck the two ends of the roll underneath and drop into a greased loaf pan. Fill all three pans in the same way, then cover them lightly with the wax paper and a cloth and leave them in a warm place to rise.

Preheat the oven to 425°F/220°C.

When the loaves are puffy and have risen almost to the top of the pans, put them into the oven and bake for 15–20 minutes, then turn down the heat to 350°F/180°C and bake them for another 40 minutes. After 20 minutes of this time, look at the loaves and if they are becoming too brown cover them loosely with foil.

At the end of the cooking time, if the loaves do not seem crisp and the bottom does not sound hollow when tapped, take them out of their pans and put them back in the oven on their sides for 5 minutes more. When they are cooked, allow them to cool on a wire rack.

This bread is delicious, wholesome and nutty.

ALTERNATIVE: **Walnut bread**. *Make in exactly the same way but substitute coarsely crushed walnuts for some of the flour, mixing them well before adding the yeast and the liquid.*

---

## Plain white loaf

| |
|---|
| *4 cups/450 g all-purpose flour* |
| *½ oz/15 g fresh yeast* |
| *pinch of sugar* |
| *1 tablespoon salt* |

MAKES 1 LARGE LOAF

Dissolve the yeast and sugar in 3 tablespoons of

warm water taken from 1¼ cups/3 dl in a small bowl. Put the flour in a warm bowl, mix in the salt, then make a well in the center and pour in the yeast mixture. Flick a little flour over the yeast and leave in a warm place. When the yeast has frothed and the flour has cracked, add the remaining warm water and mix everything together to a rough dough. Turn it out onto a board and knead it well for several minutes until it is smooth, adding a little more flour if it seems sticky. Form it into a ball and leave it to rise on the board, covered with a sheet of plastic wrap and a cloth. After about 1½ hours knead it again and leave it to rise once more —until it has almost doubled in size.

Preheat the oven to 425°F/220°C.

Knead the dough and flatten it into a thick disc. Roll it up to fit the pan, tucking the two ends of the roll underneath. Drop it into a buttered loaf pan and push around the sides of the pan to give the top of the loaf a good shape. Dust the top with flour, then cover loosely and leave to rise for half an hour or so, until well risen and puffy. Bake for 10–15 minutes, then turn down the oven to 350°F/180°C and cook for a further 30 minutes. Take the loaf out of the pan and test by tapping the bottom with your knuckles. If it sounds hollow, it is done; if not, put it back on the oven rack, on its side, for 5–10 minutes to finish cooking in the still-warm oven. Cool on a rack and eat the same day.

## Saffron bread

7 cups/800 g all-purpose flour
1 cake fresh yeast
½ teaspoon sugar
1 generous pinch whole saffron strands
1 generous pinch saffron powder
salt
1 egg, beaten
3 tablespoons olive oil

MAKES 1 LOAF

Make a sponge with the yeast, ¼ cup/1.5 dl warm water, the sugar and 7 tablespoons of the flour. Leave the sponge in a warm place to start working. Meanwhile, soak all the saffron in 1¼ cups/3 dl warm water. Warm the flour and put it in a large bowl, scatter on 2 heaping teaspoons of salt and make a well in the center. Keep the flour warm.

When the sponge is well risen, pour it into the well in the flour, add the beaten egg, the warm saffron-flavored water and the olive oil, and mix with a wooden spoon. Turn the mixture out onto a board and knead thoroughly until smooth and elastic. Cover the bowl loosely with a sheet of oiled plastic wrap and a folded cloth, and leave to rise in a warm place. When it has doubled in size, knock it down, and knead it again. Form into a large round loaf, put it on a greased and floured baking sheet and cover as before—with a sheet of plastic wrap and a cloth. Leave to rise.

Preheat the oven to 425°F/220°C.

When the loaf has risen well and is puffy and taut, make a cross-cut in the middle with a sharp knife and put it in the oven. Bake for 10–15 minutes, then turn down the heat and cook for a further 30–40 minutes at 350°F/180°C. When the loaf sounds hollow when it is tapped on the bottom, take it out of the oven, and let it cool on a rack.

Saffron bread is particularly good with fish soup and with other seafood dishes but it can be eaten at any meal, and makes delicate toast.

## Kilkenny brown bread

4 cups/450 g whole wheat flour
2 cups/225 g all-purpose flour
2 teaspoons bicarbonate of soda
3 teaspoons salt
½ stick/55 g butter
1 egg, beaten
2 cups/4.5 dl milk mixed with 1 tablespoon molasses

MAKES 1 LARGE LOAF

Preheat the oven to 375°F/190°C.

Put the flour in a large bowl, sift the soda and salt and mix them in. Rub in the butter and add the beaten egg, keeping back a little to brush the top of the loaf if a shiny top is wanted.

Add the milk. It may take less or more, depending on the flour, but make the mixture wet and quite slack or the loaf will be hard. Knead the bread lightly on a floured board until it is smooth. Quickly shape the bread into a round flattish loaf, handling it lightly. Put it on a baking sheet and cut almost through in quarters. Brush the top with egg or sprinkle with more flour, rest 5 minutes and put in the oven. Bake for 45 minutes to an hour, lowering the heat to 350°F/180°C after ten minutes. Cover the loaf with foil if it becomes too dark. It can be wrapped in a cloth when you take it out of the oven to prevent the crust becoming too tough. Eat this soda bread on the day it is made as it is best when very fresh.

ALTERNATIVE: **White soda bread.** *This can be made by using only all-purpose white flour instead of two different flours.*

# Corn bread

| |
|---|
| *generous ¾ cup/115 g cornmeal* |
| *1½ cups/170 g all-purpose flour* |
| *2 teaspoons sugar* |
| *1 teaspoon salt* |
| *1 teaspoon baking powder* |
| *1 egg* |
| *1½ cups/3.5 dl milk* |
| *½ stick/55 g butter, melted* |

MAKES 1 LOAF

Preheat the oven to 425°F/220°C.
Sieve the cornmeal, flour, sugar, salt and baking powder together into a mixing bowl. Beat the egg and milk together in another bowl and pour them into the cornmeal and flour, together with the melted butter, and mix thoroughly. Transfer the mixture into a buttered round or 8 in/20 cm square baking pan, and bake for 30–35 minutes. Test with a skewer, and if it still has not set in the middle, give it another 5–10 minutes. Allow to cool on a rack. Serve warm or cold, cut in slices and buttered.

# Rye bread

| |
|---|
| *5¾ cups/450 g rye flour* |
| *3 cups/340 g all-purpose flour* |
| *2–3 tablespoons whole wheat flour* |
| *2 cakes fresh yeast* |
| *1 teaspoon sugar* |
| *1 tablespoon salt* |
| *1 tablespoon yogurt* |
| *1½ tablespoons/15 g caraway seeds (optional)* |

MAKES 1 LARGE OR 2 SMALL LOAVES

Mix the flours together thoroughly in a large bowl. To set the sponge, dissolve the yeast in ¼ cup/1.5 dl of warm water in a mixing bowl, add a pinch of sugar and stir in 4–5 tablespoons of the flour. Cover and leave to rise for about 2 hours.

Dissolve the salt, yogurt and the rest of the sugar in a further 1¼ cups/3 dl warm water. Make a well in the bowl of flour, add the caraway seeds if you are using them, and pour in the foamy, well risen sponge and the yogurt mixture, mixing well with a wooden spoon. If the mixture seems too sticky, add a little more flour. Turn out onto a floured board and knead well for several minutes, then form into a ball and put back in the cleaned bowl. Cover with a sheet of oiled plastic wrap and a cloth and leave for 3–4 hours to rise—or even better, leave it overnight. When well risen, knock the dough down and shape it into 1 large or 2 small loaves. Put them on well-floured baking sheets, and dust the tops with flour. Allow to rise for about 1 hour, lightly covered with a sheet of plastic wrap.
Preheat the oven to 425°F/220°C.
Put the loaves in the oven and bake for 15 minutes, then turn down the heat to 350°F/180°C and bake for a further 40–45 minutes. Cover the loaves lightly with foil if they are becoming too brown, and give them a final 5 minutes in the oven off the baking sheets, before cooling them on a rack.

# Malt loaf

| |
|---|
| *2 cups/225 g all-purpose flour* |
| *4 cups/450 g stone-ground whole wheat flour* |
| *2 cakes fresh yeast* |
| *large pinch of salt* |
| *¼ lb/115 g raisins* |
| *½ stick/55 g butter, melted* |
| *3 tablespoons malt extract* |
| *1 tablespoon molasses* |
| *sugar and milk for glazing* |

MAKES 2 MEDIUM-SIZE LOAVES

Cream the yeast with a little warm water and leave it in a warm place to froth up. Mix the flour, salt and raisins in a large warmed bowl, make a well in the center and pour in the creamed yeast. Add the butter, malt, molasses and a scant 2 cups/4.5 dl warm water, kneading to make a somewhat slack dough.
Cover with a sheet of oiled plastic wrap and allow to rise for 2 hours or until the dough has doubled in

size. Cut the mixture into two pieces, then form into loaves by kneading each piece of dough into a ball, then flattening the ball into a thick disc. Roll up the disc, tuck the two ends of the roll underneath and drop into a greased loaf pan. Press down well, shaping the top so that it is nicely rounded, cover, and allow to rise for 45 minutes until puffy. Preheat the oven to 375°F/190°C.

Bake the loaves for 50 minutes or longer, turning the pans round halfway through and covering the loaves with foil if they start to look too black. Boil a little sugar and milk together and glaze the loaves with the mixture 5 minutes before the end of the cooking time.

Children love this excellent tea bread.

## Croissants

| |
|---|
| *2 cups/225 g all-purpose flour* |
| *1 cake fresh yeast* |
| *1 teaspoon sugar* |
| *⅔ cup/1.5 dl milk* |
| *salt* |
| *1 tablespoon sunflower oil* |
| *1 stick/115 g unsalted butter, chilled* |
| *1 egg yolk, beaten* |

MAKES 8–10 CROISSANTS

Dissolve the yeast in 3 tablespoons warm water with the sugar and leave in a warm place for 10–15 minutes until it froths up. Put the flour in a warmed bowl. Warm the milk in a small saucepan—it should be little more than hand hot. Stir in a level teaspoon of salt and the oil and pour the mixture into the flour, together with the yeast. Mix it in with a wooden spoon, let it rest for 5 minutes and then knead the mixture until it is smooth and elastic. Add a little more flour if the mixture is too sticky. Leave it to rise, covered, in a warm place until it has doubled in size and is light and springy, then put the bowl in the refrigerator for 20 minutes. Take the chilled dough out of the bowl, put it on a lightly floured board and knead it for a minute or two, then roll it out with a floured rolling pin into a rectangle about 12 × 6 in/30 × 15 cm. Cut about a third of the chilled butter into thin flakes and lay them in a layer over half the dough, leaving a margin around the edge. Fold the other half of the dough over to enclose the butter neatly

in an envelope of dough. Press the edges lightly with the rolling pin to seal them. Turn the dough by 90 degrees, roll it out into a long oblong about 15 × 5 in/38 × 12.5 cm, keeping the rolling pin and board lightly dusted with flour. Fold the oblong in three, slip it into a plastic bag and chill for 10–15 minutes. Repeat this buttering, turning, rolling and folding, twice more, using an equal amount of butter each time, and chilling after each operation. Finally chill for an hour or longer.

Take out the dough and flatten it slightly with your hands. Roll it out on a floured surface into a 12–14 in/30–35 cm square. It is best to roll it out only once, and to do it quickly and in a fairly cool place. Cut it into four squares, trimming the edges carefully. Cut each square in half diagonally to make two triangles. Roll up each triangle starting at the wide edge, and place on a buttered baking sheet. Bend them into the familiar crescent shape. Leave in a very warm place, lightly covered with a sheet of plastic wrap, for 30 minutes to an hour until they are well plumped up, light and springy. Heat the oven to 375°F/190°C.

Brush the tops of the croissants with the egg yolk, beaten with a little salt and a few drops of water, and bake for 15 minutes or a little more, until nicely risen and golden.

Risen, uncooked croissants can be left, covered, in the refrigerator overnight. Give them about 30 minutes to recover at room temperature before baking. They can also be frozen in their risen, uncooked state for a few days and then baked while still frozen.

## Brioche loaf

| |
|---|
| *5 cups/565 g all-purpose flour* |
| *2 cakes fresh yeast* |
| *2 tablespoons sugar* |
| *4 eggs* |
| *5 tablespoons warm milk* |
| *1 tablespoon salt* |
| *1 stick/115 g butter* |

MAKES 2 LOAVES

Cream the yeast with 5 tablespoons of warm water, add ½ teaspoon of the sugar and leave in a warm place to start working. Beat the eggs in a bowl with the milk, salt and the rest of the sugar and leave in a warm place. Warm a bowl and put the flour in it.

When the yeast is frothy, pour it and the egg mixture into a well in the center of the flour and mix thoroughly. Knead until smooth on a clean work surface, sprinkling on a little more flour if the dough becomes too sticky and unmanageable. When you have a smooth ball, let it rest for a few minutes and then start incorporating the butter—this is a messy business, but it will all go in eventually. First flatten the dough and put a few dabs of butter over the surface (using about 1 tablespoon/15 g of it). Then fold up the dough and knead it well until the butter is smoothly worked in. Let the dough rest for a minute, then repeat; keep on adding butter, kneading and resting the dough until all the butter has been mixed in. Let the dough rest again, knead to a smooth ball, put in a bowl in a warm place, cover with a sheet of plastic wrap and a cloth, and leave for 1½ hours until puffy and risen. Knock back the dough, kneading it for a minute, then re-form it into a ball and return it to the bowl to rise for a second time, covered with some plastic wrap and a cloth as before. Leave it for 1½–2 hours more and butter two clean loaf pans.

Preheat the oven to 400°F/200°C.

When the dough has risen a second time, divide it in two. Knead each piece into a round disc, roll up each disc into a sausage shape, tuck the two ends underneath and put into the buttered tins. Cover again and leave to rise until they are well risen and rounded, then bake for 30–35 minutes. Allow to cool on a rack and eat warm or cold.

Brioche is the lightest, richest bread imaginable, is exquisite for breakfast and makes very good toast.

## Scones

| |
|---|
| 2¼ cups/255 g self-rising flour |
| ¼ teaspoon bicarbonate of soda |
| salt |
| 3 tablespoons/45 g butter |
| ⅔ cup/1.5 dl buttermilk, or ⅔ cup/1.5 dl sour milk and 2 tablespoons cream |

MAKES 12

Preheat the oven to 375°F/190°C.

Sieve the flour, bicarbonate of soda and salt into a bowl and rub in the butter with your fingertips until the mixture is the texture of very coarse bread crumbs. Add the buttermilk, or milk and cream, and mix to a dough.

Turn onto a floured board and roll out until about ½ in/1 cm thick. This should be done quickly, and with a light touch. Cut the dough with a cutter into 2 in/5 cm rounds, dust the tops with flour and put them on a baking sheet. Bake for 10–15 minutes until puffed and golden brown. Cool on a rack and eat warm, split in half, with plenty of butter, or cool with cream and raspberry or strawberry jam. The lightest scones are those made with buttermilk.

## Crumbs, croûtons, toasts

**Fresh bread crumbs**: cut thick slices of white bread, remove the crusts, cut the slices into cubes and reduce them to crumbs in a food processor. Alternatively, you can use a grater, but this is a much slower process.

**Dried bread crumbs**: put all your leftover ends of bread in a very low oven until dry, golden and biscuity. Wrap the dried pieces in a clean cloth and pound them with a rolling pin, using a rolling motion once they begin to break down. Sieve the resulting crumbs—any lingering bits and pieces should be pounded again.

**Croûtons**: cut crustless slices of white bread into small neat cubes and fry them in a mixture of hot butter and oil, tossing them frequently, until they are an even golden brown. Remove them with a slotted spoon and drain them on kitchen paper. Croûtons can be reheated in a low oven.

**Melba toast**: toast slices of white bread, with their crusts on, and when brown on both sides, slice each piece horizontally in half. Scrape away the soft untoasted inside, cut off the crusts and dry the wafer-thin pieces for a few minutes in a low oven until they begin to curl and brown. Serve with hors d'oeuvre, caviar, pâté.

**Pain perdu** soak slices of white or dark bread in beaten egg, shallow fry in butter until brown on both sides and serve hot, sprinkled with sugar and cinnamon, or with a spoonful of maple syrup and crisp slices of bacon.

Pain perdu is also known as French toast and makes an excellent breakfast dish.

## Salade niçoise

*1 head of Romaine lettuce*

*1 lb/450 g fresh green beans, trimmed*

*3 hard-boiled eggs*

*3–4 tomatoes*

*3–4 small freshly boiled new potatoes*

*small can of tuna*

*small can of anchovies*

*1 tablespoon wine vinegar*

*6 tablespoons olive oil*

*1 clove garlic*

*salt and freshly ground pepper*

*handful of black olives*

*sprinkling of chopped parsley*

SERVES 4

Wash and dry the lettuce, discard the outer leaves and cut the heart into quarters. Cook the beans and cool them rapidly under cold water. Peel and slice the eggs and slice the tomatoes and potatoes. Flake the tuna and drain the anchovies. Make a good dressing with the wine vinegar and olive oil, together with the garlic crushed with salt, season with black pepper and mix it into the beans, the tomatoes and the potatoes in a salad bowl. Lay the flaked tuna over them and put the eggs, anchovies and black olives on top. Arrange the quarters of lettuce heart around the edge, standing them on end, and serve sprinkled with parsley.

ALTERNATIVES: *add to the salad sliced cooked artichoke hearts, green or red sweet peppers, cucumber, capers, radishes, or raw Florence fennel. Cold cooked peas and Belgian endive are also sometimes included, and cold cooked white beans are quite good too.*

## Endive in butter and cream

*4 plump fresh heads Belgian endive*

*2 tablespoons/30 g butter*

*juice of ½ lemon*

*few tablespoons chicken stock*

*salt*

*6 tablespoons heavy cream*

SERVES 4

Cut the heads of endive lengthwise into strips ½ in/1 cm wide and cut each strip in half across the middle to give you little ribbons of endive about 2–2½ in/5–6 cm long. Put them in a wide pan with the butter, lemon juice, just enough stock to cover and a pinch of salt. Bring to the boil and cook until the stock has almost evaporated.

Add the cream and boil gently, shaking the pan from time to time, until the liquid thickens and clings to the endive, bathing it in a little light sauce. Serve very hot.

If you are not ready to serve the endive immediately, it can be reheated at the last moment.

## Crudités with aïoli

*1 cucumber*

*bunch of radishes*

*2 sticks celery*

*2–3 carrots*

*2–3 zucchini*

*½ lb/225 g green beans, trimmed*

*2 heads Belgian endive*

*1 red sweet pepper*

*2–3 firm tomatoes*

*¼ lb/115 g black olives*

*1¼ cups/3 dl aïoli*

SERVES 6–8

Peel the cucumber, slice into 2 in/5 cm pieces and cut these into sticks, removing the seeds. Clean and trim the radishes. Cut the celery and carrots into 2 in/5 cm strips about the width of green beans. Cook the zucchini, but only just, cool and slice lengthwise. Cook the beans, refresh under cold water and drain. Slice the endive. Cut the pepper into narrow strips and put into boiling water for 2 minutes, then drain well. Slice the tomatoes. Put all the prepared vegetables and the olives into separate little dishes, or lay them in groups side by side on a large platter, and chill.

The vegetables should be eaten with the fingers and dipped into the rich aïoli. Coarse dark bread and butter is good with this. This is a delicious and simple dish eaten in the south of France before a whole baked fish, or even as a main course.

It can be casual and quick to make or delicate and fiddly, according to how the vegetables are sliced.

ALTERNATIVES: *use any vegetables in season: cold small new potatoes, fresh boiled beets, small leeks, tiny raw globe artichokes the size of walnuts, celeriac, young raw lima beans, quartered lettuce hearts and small boiled turnips are all beautiful on a white plate.*

# Radis au beurre

*1–2 bunches best radishes, preferably French Breakfast radishes*
*½–¾ stick/55–85 g fresh butter, the best you can buy*
*coarse salt*

SERVES 4–6
Wash the radishes, trim off the roots and the leaves, leaving a tuft about ½ in/1 cm long. Wrap them up in a damp dish towel and leave them in the refrigerator for at least an hour to become crisp and cold. Just before serving, take them out of the refrigerator, put them in a bowl and serve them just as they are. Eat the radishes with a dab of butter and a little sprinkling of salt as an hors d'oeuvre.

# Spinach and bacon salad

*1 lb/450 g fresh young spinach leaves*
*1 avocado*
*6 thick slices bacon*
*1 teaspoon olive oil*

**for the dressing:**
*4 tablespoons olive oil*
*1 tablespoon white wine vinegar or sherry vinegar*
*small pinch of sugar*
*salt and freshly ground pepper*

SERVES 4–6
Make the dressing first, mixing the ingredients together with a fork. Wash, drain and dry the spinach, shaking it well in a cloth, a third at a time, to get all the moisture off the leaves without bruising them too much—spinach leaves are very fragile.
Halve the avocado, remove the seed, skin the halves and cut them into either thin slices or fairly small dice. Toss them in a bowl with about 2 teaspoons of the dressing to keep them a fresh green. Cut the bacon into strips and fry them in the olive oil. While they fry to a crisp brown, put the spinach into the bowl with the avocado and dress it lightly with the remaining salad dressing. When the bacon is brown, pour it—still sizzling—with all its fat, over the salad and serve at once.
ALTERNATIVES: **Pissenlits au lard.** *Make the salad with cultivated dandelion leaves—this is a classic French dish.*
**Salade frisée au lard.** *Use curly endive instead of spinach and avocado.*

# Spinach and walnut salad

*10 oz/280 g fresh young spinach leaves*
*1 cup/115 g freshly shelled walnuts*
*vinaigrette dressing, preferably made with 4 tablespoons walnut oil and 1 tablespoon olive oil*

SERVES 4
Wash and drain the spinach leaves and shake them dry in a cloth, a third at a time, so that they do not get crushed. Put them into a bowl. Scatter the walnuts over the spinach. Dress lightly with the walnut oil dressing just before serving.
ALTERNATIVE: *add a chopped hard-boiled egg to the salad after you have tossed it in the dressing.*

# Spinach and chick-peas

*1 lb/450 g spinach*
*½ lb/225 g chick-peas, soaked overnight*
*1 slice bread*
*4 tablespoons olive oil*
*3–4 tomatoes*
*1 onion*
*salt*
*1 tablespoon paprika*
*1 clove garlic*

SERVES 4–6
Cook the chick-peas in a pan of fresh water until tender. Drain and return them to the pan.
Fry the slice of bread in half the oil until golden and peel and chop the tomatoes and onion. Keep the fried bread warm while you fry the onion in the same oil, then add the tomatoes. Wash the spinach, shake well and sprinkle with salt.
Heat the rest of the oil in a large pan, add the paprika and stir it in. Add the spinach and when it has sweated down turn the mixture into the pan with the drained chick-peas.
Peel the garlic and pound it using a pestle and mortar, add the fried bread and pound again. Add this mixture to the chick-peas, together with the tomatoes and onion and a scant half cup of water. Cover the pan and simmer for about 30 minutes, adding a little more water if it becomes too dry.
You should end up with a fragrant vegetable stew, extremely meaty in flavor and substantial enough to make a whole meal. It is very good for a cold day.
ALTERNATIVE: *use spinach and black-eyed peas.*

## Colcannon

| |
|---|
| *1 small green cabbage* |
| *1 lb/450 g potatoes* |
| *2 small leeks, or the green tops from a bunch of scallions* |
| *¾ cup/2 dl milk or light cream* |
| *salt and freshly ground pepper* |
| *pinch of mace* |
| *½ stick/55 g butter, melted* |

SERVES 4

Wash and quarter the cabbage and cook it in boiling salted water until just tender, then drain. Peel and boil the potatoes until tender, drain well and mash them.

Chop the leeks or onion tops and simmer them in the milk or cream until tender. Add the leeks or onion tops and milk to the mashed potato, beat until smooth, then add the cabbage cut in shreds. Beat the mixture further over a low heat until fluffy, and add the seasoning.

Pile into a heated serving dish, make a well in the centre and pour in the melted butter. Serve very hot; it should be a delicate green. (If you have any left over, fry it in bacon fat until crisp and brown.)

## Buttered cabbage

| |
|---|
| *1 small Savoy or other green cabbage* |
| *½ stick/55 g butter* |
| *salt and freshly ground pepper* |

SERVES 4

Remove all the unattractive outside leaves. Cut the cabbage in strips and remove the core. To clean the cabbage, leave the strips in cold water with a tablespoon of salt for 10 minutes or so. Drop the drained cabbage into enough boiling salted water to float it, and cook fast for 7–8 minutes, until just tender when stuck with the point of a knife. Drain very thoroughly in a colander, cutting any large pieces through here and there with a knife. Melt half the butter in the pan in which the cabbage was cooked, return the cabbage to the pan and stir over a very low heat. Add a great deal of pepper and a little salt. As the liquid from the cabbage is produced and re-absorbed, add the remaining butter a bit at a time, stirring gently to separate the strips of cabbage. When there is no

extra liquid in the pan and the butter has thoroughly coated the cabbage—it takes 10–15 minutes—serve at once. The cabbage does not lose its beautiful green color, but it does become considerably reduced in volume.

This is quite delicious, not at all like the overcooked cabbage so often associated with England.

## Stuffed cabbage

| |
|---|
| *1 Savoy or other green cabbage* |
| *12 chestnuts, peeled* |
| *2½ cups/6 dl stock* |
| *1 onion* |
| *2 sticks celery* |
| *2 tablespoons/30 g butter* |
| *⅓ cup/55 g long-grain rice* |
| *1 egg* |
| *¼ lb/115 g each of veal and pork, finely ground* |
| *large pinch of mace* |
| *salt and freshly ground pepper* |
| *1 lb/450 g can of tomatoes* |
| *¼ cup brandy or kirsch* |

SERVES 4

Cook the peeled chestnuts in the stock until tender, adding more liquid if needed. Drain them and mash roughly, keeping the stock on one side. Wash the cabbage carefully and drop it into a pan of boiling salted water. Boil it for 5 minutes and drain in a colander.

Peel and chop the onion and slice the celery fairly finely. Melt the butter in a frying pan and soften the onion and celery. Add the rice and stir it around until it is well coated with butter. In a bowl, mix the vegetables and rice, egg, minced pork and veal, chestnuts, mace, salt and pepper, and a little stock. Preheat the oven to 275°F/140°C.

When the drained cabbage is cool enough to handle, open it out like a flower, turning back each leaf like a petal. Put a spoonful of the stuffing into an inner leaf, pat it back into its original shape and fill all the leaves with stuffing, one by one, patting them back into place as you do so. Tie up the cabbage with gauze strips like a parcel. If you haven't any gauze, use folded strips of kitchen foil. Put the cabbage in a deep earthenware pot or casserole, add the stock from the chestnuts and then the tomatoes. Taste for seasoning, cover the pot

tightly and bake for 2½ hours, basting occasionally.
Add more stock if necessary.
Just before serving, remove the tapes or strips and
pour the brandy or kirsch over the cabbage.

# Coleslaw

| |
|---|
| ¼ small cabbage |
| 1 stick celery |
| 1 apple |
| 12 walnut halves |
| 1 tablespoon wine vinegar |
| 1 teaspoon Dijon mustard |
| 1¼ cups/3 dl mayonnaise |
| 3 tablespoons light cream |
| salt |

SERVES 6

Remove the coarse outer leaves of the cabbage, cut
it in quarters and take out the core. Shred the
cabbage very finely. Put the shreds in a bowl, cover
with a damp cloth and chill in the coldest part of
the refrigerator for several hours or overnight.
Cut the celery and peeled apple into matchstick
strips and coarsely chop the walnuts. Mix all these
into the cabbage. Blend the vinegar and mustard
in a bowl, stir in the mayonnaise and cream, taste
for seasoning and mix the dressing into the cabbage.
Serve right away.

# Braised red cabbage

| |
|---|
| 1 red cabbage |
| 1 tablespoon pork drippings or butter |
| 1 onion |
| 2 apples |
| 1 strip orange peel |
| ¼ cup wine vinegar |
| 1 wine glass red wine |
| 2–3 tablespoons brown sugar |
| 3–4 juniper berries, crushed |
| 2 bay leaves |
| salt and freshly ground pepper |

SERVES 4

Melt the pork drippings or butter in a fireproof
casserole—earthenware or enamelled iron is better
than enamel, which is a bit too thin. Peel and chop
the onion finely and sauté it in the fat until soft.
Preheat the oven to 325°F/170°C.
Meanwhile, cut the cabbage in half, cut out the
core and slice it vertically from top to bottom into
¼ in/5 mm slices. Cut the slices across in a few
places. Put the cabbage into the pot with the onion
and stir it around to coat it with the pork drippings.
Add the apples, peeled, quartered and cored, the
orange peel, vinegar, red wine, sugar, crushed
juniper berries, bay leaves, salt and pepper.
Cover the pot with foil or cooking parchment and a
lid. Put it into the oven and cook for 1½–2 hours.
If the dish is properly sealed, there is enough
liquid to cook it in without adding any extra. Stir
it around from time to time, and if it does seem to
be getting too dry add a little more red wine or
water. Taste it about 30 minutes before you are
going to eat it, and if it seems too bland, add more
vinegar and sugar—this depends very much on the
quality of the cabbage. Some are pale and insipid,
others are dark and have a wonderful rich flavor.
This is excellent with roast pork and game stew.

# Cauliflower au gratin

| |
|---|
| 1 large cauliflower, broken into flowerets |
| ½ stick/55 g butter |
| ¼ cup/30 g flour |
| 2 cups/4.5 dl milk |
| ½ cup/1.5 dl light cream |
| ¾ cup/85 g Emmental, Gruyère or Parmesan, freshly grated |
| salt and freshly ground pepper |
| ½ cup/55 g fresh white bread crumbs |

SERVES 4–6

Cook the cauliflower in boiling salted water for
8–10 minutes, drain and keep hot. Make a good
mornay sauce with half the butter, the flour, milk,
cream and most of the cheese—it should be fairly
thin but creamy. Season with salt and pepper.
Heat the broiler.
Fry the bread crumbs, sprinkled with a little salt,
in the remaining butter until they are nicely
browned and crisp. Add the cauliflower, mix it
around until every piece is coated with the fried
bread crumbs, and put it all in a gratin dish. Pour
the sauce around the cauliflower, sprinkle with the
rest of the cheese and brown under the broiler.

## Sprouts with chestnuts

| |
|---|
| *1 lb/450 g brussels sprouts* |
| *½ lb/225 g fresh chestnuts, peeled* |
| *½ stick/55 g butter* |
| *salt* |

SERVES 4

Trim the outside leaves from the brussels sprouts, and if they are very large, you can cut a cross in the stem, but otherwise do not bother.

In two separate pans of boiling water, cook the sprouts for about 12 minutes and the chestnuts for 12–15 minutes. Both must be just tender, but not soft and mushy. Drain them thoroughly and return them to a clean saucepan. Add the butter, and toss over a low heat for a few minutes until well coated with butter. Season with salt.

Serve with roast turkey or with game.

ALTERNATIVE: *Cook the peeled chestnuts in chicken stock instead of water for a more interesting and stronger flavor.*

## Celery and Parmesan salad

| |
|---|
| *1 head fresh celery* |
| *½ cup/55 g fresh softish Parmesan in a piece* |
| *4 tablespoons olive oil* |
| *juice of ½ lemon (optional)* |
| *salt and freshly ground pepper* |

SERVES 6

Wash the celery and cut it into fine crescents. Slice the Parmesan into the thinnest possible flakes—if they are very large, break them up a bit. Mix the celery and Parmesan in a bowl, dress with olive oil only, or with olive oil and a squeeze of lemon juice. Season lightly with salt, add plenty of pepper and serve as a separate course after roast veal or pork, or as an hors d'oeuvre.

## Fennel salad

| |
|---|
| *2–3 heads fresh Florence fennel* |
| *4 tablespoons best olive oil* |
| *salt and freshly ground pepper* |

SERVES 4–6

Remove any brown or shrivelled parts from the fennel and then slice it as thinly as possible across the bulb, so that you get a cross-section with a round piece of stalk in the middle—do not discard this, the stalk has a good flavor and texture. Lay the slices of fennel on a white dish and sprinkle them with a good fruity olive oil. Season with salt and freshly ground pepper. Do not add lemon juice or vinegar—the sweet, nutty flavor of fennel is best with olive oil on its own.

## Fennel au gratin

| |
|---|
| *3 plump heads Florence fennel* |
| *salt* |
| *½ cup/55 g Parmesan, freshly grated* |
| *½ stick/55 g butter* |

SERVES 6

Slice the fennel across into thick slices, or alternatively cut it into quarters. Bring a large pan of salted water to the boil and plunge in the fennel. Cook for 10 minutes, until tender but still slightly resistant. Drain thoroughly in a colander.

Preheat the oven to 375°F/190°C.

Butter an oval gratin dish and put in a layer of fennel. Sprinkle with a little of the Parmesan and dot with a little of the butter. Continue putting in layers of fennel, cheese and butter until all the ingredients are used up, finishing with a generous layer of Parmesan and plenty of butter. Bake for 20–25 minutes until golden.

## Artichokes alla romana

| |
|---|
| *8–12 very small globe artichokes* |
| *juice of 1 lemon* |
| *4 cloves garlic* |
| *3–4 sprigs mint, chopped* |
| *½–¾ cup olive oil* |
| *salt and freshly ground pepper* |

SERVES 4 AS A STARTER

For this recipe, the stalks of the artichokes are left on. Peel the stalks and lower parts of each artichoke with a small stainless knife, cutting away the outer layer of leaves. If the artichokes are more than 2 in/5 cm across, they will contain spiny chokes which should be removed in the same way as when preparing artichoke hearts. Put each prepared artichoke immediately into a bowl of water acidulated with the juice of a lemon.

When you have prepared all the artichokes, peel and chop the garlic and fry it gently with the mint in a tablespoonful of the olive oil for 2–3 minutes. Remove the artichokes from the water, shake them and push some of the mint and garlic mixture either into the middle of each one, if you have scooped out the chokes, or, if the artichokes are still whole, stuff the mixture in among the leaves. Put them, stalks upwards, in a heavy pan into which they will just fit. Pour on the oil and add about a cup of water. Season lightly with salt and pepper and cook, covered, over a low heat for about 45 minutes. Remove the lid and finish cooking over a brisk heat for 15 minutes, or until the cooking juices are well reduced. Spoon the oil over the artichokes and serve hot or cold with plenty of fresh bread to soak up the juice.

# Peas with ham

| 2–3 lb/900 g–1.5 kg peas, unshelled, or 1 lb/450 g frozen |
| 1 small onion |
| 2 tablespoons/30 g butter |
| 6 slices ham carved off the bone |
| 2/3 cup/1.5 dl heavy cream |
| salt and freshly ground pepper |

SERVES 4–6

Shell the peas and peel and chop the onion. Melt the butter and soften the onion. Add the peas and 3 tablespoons water, season with a pinch of salt and boil for 10 minutes. Add the ham cut in strips and lower the heat. Simmer until the peas are tender and the liquid is absorbed. Stir in the cream, season with pepper, heat through and serve.
This makes a good summer lunch.

# Petits pois à la française

| 3/4 lb/340 g shelled peas |
| few sprigs of savory or thyme |
| 2 lettuce hearts |
| 1/2 stick/55 g butter |
| salt and a pinch of sugar |

SERVES 4

Tuck the savory or thyme into the lettuce hearts and put them in a pan with the peas, butter and about half a cup of water. Season with a little salt and sugar. Bring to the boil and simmer for 15 minutes. Drain well and serve hot.

# Peas—an Indian way

| 3/4 lb/340 g shelled peas |
| 1 large onion |
| 1 green chili pepper |
| 3 tablespoons ghee, clarified butter |
| or 1 tablespoon/15 g butter and 2 tablespoons oil |
| 1/2 teaspoon cumin |
| small bunch of green coriander, washed and chopped, or a few crushed coriander seeds |
| salt |

SERVES 4

Peel and chop the onion and chop the chili pepper. Heat the butter or butter and oil in a shallow pan with a lid. Fry the onion in the hot fat with the cumin until soft and golden, but not brown. Add the peas, chili and coriander leaves or seeds and stir them around in the fat for 1–2 minutes, then add 4 tablespoons water and a little salt and cover the pan. Cook until the peas are tender, which will be from 10 to 20 minutes, depending on their age. Do not strain them.

ALTERNATIVE: *in India peas are often cooked without any water at all—they come out deep green and rather strongly flavored.*

# Green beans with cream

| 1 lb/450 g small green beans |
| salt and freshly ground pepper |
| 4 tablespoons heavy cream |
| 1 tablespoon/15 g butter |
| pinch of grated nutmeg |
| 1 tablespoon chopped chives |

SERVES 4

Wash and top and tail the beans. Bring a large pan of water—about 2½ quarts/2.25 liters—to the boil. Throw in 2 tablespoons salt, or 3 if you are using coarse salt. (The very large amount of salt helps to keep the beans green.) Plunge the beans into the boiling water and let them cook for 8 minutes, then start testing to see if they are done. Test them frequently by trying one between your teeth—when they are only just tender, even still a little crisp, drain them well in a colander.

Splash them lightly with cold water to prevent them cooking further, then put them back in the saucepan with the cream, butter, nutmeg and pepper and heat through. Swish the beans around in the cream, letting it bubble until slightly thickened. Stir in the chives and serve while still hot. It is very good with plainly cooked meat—chicken or steak—or a baked fish.

## Fava beans with their pods

| 3 lb/1.5 kg young fava beans in their pods |
|---|
| salt |
| 2 tablespoons/30 g butter |

SERVES 6

Shell the beans, reserving the most tender pods. Break the reserved pods into pieces about the size of an ordinary postage stamp. Bring a large pan of salted water to the boil and throw in the pods. Let them cook for 5 minutes, and then add the beans and cook them both for about 8–10 minutes until they are tender. Drain the beans and pods thoroughly, return them to the pan with a lump of butter, and stir them around until they are well coated. Serve at once.

## Lima beans and bacon

| 3 lb/1.5 kg lima beans |
|---|
| salt |
| 6 slices bacon |
| nut of butter |

SERVES 6

Shell the lima beans and cook them in boiling salted water until tender. Just before the beans are ready, cut the bacon in small strips and fry it, starting it off in a little butter to stop it sticking to the pan. When the beans are ready, drain well, put them into a heated bowl and mix in the bacon with all its drippings. This is particularly good when there are so many lima beans you don't know what to do with them—the bacon fat makes a very delicious change from butter.

## Fava beans à la paysanne

| 3–4 lb/1½–2 kg small young fava beans |
|---|
| 2 heads lettuce |
| 3 fresh or canned artichoke hearts (optional) |
| 1 onion |
| ¼ lb/115 g lean ham in a thick slice |
| 2 tablespoons olive oil or butter |
| salt and freshly ground pepper |
| nutmeg |

SERVES 4

Shell the beans and chop the hearts of the lettuces, throwing away or saving the outer leaves for the guinea-pig. Cut the artichoke hearts, if you are using them, into four or six pieces, depending on how large they are. Put them into a bowl of water acidulated with lemon juice to prevent them blackening. Peel and chop the onion.

Cut the slice of ham into dice and put them into a flameproof casserole or heavy saucepan with the oil or butter and let them cook a little. Add the chopped onion and let it soften for several minutes without browning. Add the beans, artichoke hearts and lettuce and cook gently for 5–10 minutes, shaking the pan from time to time. Season with salt, pepper and nutmeg and add a few spoonfuls of water or stock to make a little sauce to bathe them in. Cover the pan and cook them slowly and gently for 20–30 minutes. If the juice is too liquid, stir in a little beurre manié and go on adding little pieces of it until the sauce is smooth and velvety. Stir the vegetables very gently so that beans and artichokes are not broken.

This makes a delicious accompaniment to an omelet or lamb chops, or is a good lunch on its own.

## Corn on the cob

| 4 ears of fresh corn, husks and silk removed |
|---|
| 1¼ cups/3 dl milk |
| 1 teaspoon sugar |
| salt |

SERVES 4

Put the milk and 2½ cups/6 dl of water into a saucepan—the liquid should be at least 1 in/2.5 cm deep. Bring to the boil and drop in the ears of corn, one at a time so that the liquid continues to boil. Boil for 5 minutes, add the sugar and a teaspoon salt and boil for a further 3–5 minutes, according to the age of the corn.

---

# Glazed onions

| 1½ lb/700 g button onions |
| --- |
| ⅔ cup/1.5 dl clear, preferably jellied, chicken or beef stock |
| 1–2 teaspoons sugar |
| salt |

SERVES 4

Peel the onions and drop them into boiling salted water in a pan in which the onions will lie neatly side by side. After 5 minutes, strain away all but 2–3 tablespoons of the cooking liquid and add the stock, sugar and, remembering that the juices will become very concentrated, just a little salt.

Let the onions cook very gently, shaking them in the pan from time to time so that they become evenly coated with their glaze. When the glaze is reduced to a varnish-like syrup, the onions are ready. They should be just soft all the way through and bathed in a golden glaze.

Glazed onions can be kept hot for some time without spoiling.

---

# Onions in cream sauce

| 24 button onions |
| --- |
| 2 tablespoons/30 g butter |
| ¼ cup/30 g flour |
| 1¼ cups/3 dl milk |
| ⅔ cup/1.5 dl heavy cream |
| salt and freshly ground pepper |
| pinch of ground cloves or grated nutmeg |

SERVES 4–6

Peel the onions and drop them into a pan of boiling salted water. Cook for 5–10 minutes, according to how young and tender they are—new onions cook very quickly. Meanwhile, melt the butter in a saucepan, stir in the flour and let it cook for a minute or two. Then gradually add the milk, a little at a time, stirring after each addition. Lastly add the cream and a seasoning of salt, pepper and cloves or nutmeg.

Drain the onions thoroughly, drop them into the sauce and heat through.

Serve with roast turkey or roast lamb.

---

# Leeks in cream

| 6 fat leeks |
| --- |
| ½ stick/55 g butter |
| salt and freshly ground pepper |
| grating of nutmeg |
| 4 tablespoons heavy cream |

SERVES 4

Trim the leeks and split them in half. Wash them thoroughly and then cut them into pieces about ½ in/1 cm long. Melt the butter in a heavy saucepan and add the leeks. Season them with salt, pepper and nutmeg, stir them around and cover the pan. Let them cook gently for 15 minutes. Add the cream, stir it in and cook for a minute or two more, until the cream thickens slightly.

This is a rich and delicate way of cooking leeks.

ALTERNATIVE: **Leeks with truffles.** *Add a small, very thinly sliced truffle to the leeks with the cream.*

---

# Roast potatoes

| 8 medium or 4 large floury potatoes |
| --- |
| salt |
| ¾ stick/85 g butter and 4 tablespoons sunflower oil, or the drippings from a large roast that is cooking at the same time |

SERVES 4–6

Preheat the oven to 400°F/200°C.

Peel the potatoes and, if they are large, cut them in half. Put them into a saucepan of cold, salted water, bring to the boil and let them simmer, covered, for 5 minutes. Drain them, return them to the pan and dry them over a low heat, uncovered, for a minute or two. Now shake the pan to give the potatoes a rough surface.

Heat the fat in a roasting pan—if you are not using drippings—and put the potatoes either in the pan or around the roast. Baste them with the hot fat and roast for 45 minutes to an hour, turning them over from time to time. Remove them from the fat with a slotted spoon and serve with the roast.

ALTERNATIVES: *1. Parboil the potatoes and sprinkle them with flour before putting them in the hot fat. Baste well and roast for 45 minutes to an hour, turning from time to time.*

*2. Put the peeled raw potatoes straight into the hot fat and roast them for an hour, basting and turning them from time to time.*

---

## Pommes rissolées

| |
|---|
| *1½ lb/700 g new potatoes—the size of walnuts* |
| *½ stick/85 g butter* |
| *salt* |

SERVES 4

Wash, scrub or scrape the potatoes, but don't peel them; dry them well in a cloth. Melt the butter in a wide-bottomed pan—it should be large enough for every potato to touch the bottom. Throw in the potatoes and let them brown fairly rapidly, shaking the pan to turn them. When they are browned all over, sprinkle with salt and cover with a lid. Turn down the heat and cook gently for 30 minutes until they are tender. Test with the point of a knife. Remove the lid and turn up the heat to crisp them a little. Scoop them out with a perforated spoon and serve very hot.

Eat them with veal, or almost any roast meat with which you would normally serve plain new potatoes. The best pan for cooking these delicious little potatoes is a sauté pan with a lid.

---

## Pommes dauphinoise

| |
|---|
| *2 lb/900 g good waxy potatoes* |
| *¼ cup/30 g Parmesan, freshly grated* |
| *½ stick/55 g butter* |
| *salt and freshly ground pepper* |
| *1 large clove garlic* |
| *⅔–1¼ cups/1.5–3 dl light cream* |

SERVES 4–6

Preheat the oven to 350°F/180°C.

Peel the potatoes and slice them finely, either with a mandoline or in a food processor, and peel, chop and crush the garlic. Butter a wide, shallow oven-proof dish. Cover the bottom of the dish with a layer of potatoes, sprinkle with a little of the grated cheese, dot with some of the butter, season, add a tiny sprinkling of the crushed garlic and pour on a little cream. Repeat these alternate layers until the ingredients are almost finished. Arrange the top layer neatly with the remaining slices of potato, overlapping like fish scales. Pour the last of the cream over the top and sprinkle with the rest of the cheese. Dot well with butter and cook in a moderate oven for an hour and 15 minutes.

Serve on a separate plate from the meat, as the juices from the meat are better not mixed with the cream and cheese. Pommes dauphinoise should be very moist—it should not be allowed to dry out during cooking so, if necessary, cover the dish.

ALTERNATIVE: *leave out the cheese for a slightly plainer dish.*

---

## Scalloped potatoes

| |
|---|
| *3 lb/1.5 kg potatoes* |
| *½ stick/55 g butter* |
| *½ cup/55 g flour* |
| *1 quart/9 dl milk* |
| *grating of nutmeg* |
| *salt and freshly ground pepper* |
| *1 bay leaf* |
| *½ lb/225 g bacon* |
| *3 onions* |

SERVES 6–8

Preheat the oven to 350°F/180°C.

Peel the potatoes, slice them in ¼ in/5 mm slices and put them to soak in a large bowl of cold water. Make a béchamel sauce with the butter, flour and milk, flavor it well with the nutmeg, salt and plenty of pepper and add the bay leaf. Allow the sauce to simmer while you cut the bacon in small pieces and peel and slice the onions thinly.

Drain the potatoes and layer them with the bacon and onions in a large buttered casserole, finishing up with a layer of potatoes. Pour on the béchamel and shake the pot so that the sauce is spread evenly throughout the dish. Cover the casserole and bake for an hour, then remove the lid and bake for another hour so that the top becomes brown.

# Baked stuffed potatoes

| |
|---|
| 4 large unblemished potatoes of equal size |
| salt and cayenne pepper |
| $\frac{2}{3}$ cup/1.5 dl creamy milk |
| 1 egg |
| 1$\frac{1}{2}$ cups/170 g Cheddar, freshly grated |
| $\frac{1}{2}$ stick/55 g butter |

SERVES 6

Preheat the oven to 350°F/180°C, or 400°F/200°C, depending on how much time you have.
Scrub and prick the potatoes, roll them in salt and bake them for an hour and 30 minutes at the lower setting or an hour at the higher setting.
Turn the oven up to 425°F/220°C.
Take out the potatoes, cut them in half lengthwise and turn out the middles into a bowl, forking them out lightly rather than scooping them out with a spoon. Keep the skins. Bring the milk to the boil and pour it into the potato flesh, whisking it in with a fork until you have a smooth purée. Beat in the egg, cheese and butter and season with salt and cayenne pepper. Pile the mixture back into the skins, and bake for 15 minutes until they become a golden brown.

ALTERNATIVES: *sour cream and chives, bacon pieces, chopped ham or broiled mushrooms can all be added to the potato filling in place of the cheese. For a crispy finish, sprinkle the stuffed potatoes with bread crumbs before returning them to the oven.*

---

# Glazed carrots

| |
|---|
| 1$\frac{1}{2}$ lb/700 g young carrots |
| salt |
| 2 teaspoons sugar |
| $\frac{1}{2}$ stick/55 g butter |

SERVES 6

Scrape the carrots or peel thinly with a potato peeler and cook in boiling salted water until just tender. Drain off all but about 2 tablespoons of the cooking water. Add the sugar and let it dissolve over a gentle heat. Add the butter and let the sugar and butter mixture cook fast until it starts to brown, rolling the carrots and shaking them until they are nicely coated. They will be sweet and succulent and have a very good flavor.

ALTERNATIVES: **Glazed turnips.** *Prepare and cook young turnips in the same way as glazed carrots.*
**Glazed salsify.** *Treat in the same way but drop each one as it is peeled into a bowl of water acidulated with vinegar. Salsify is best cooked in a blanc— 1 tablespoon of flour dissolved in 2 quarts/1.75 liters water and a teaspoon of salt. Watch it carefully—it will boil over if left on too high a heat.*

---

# Céleri rémoulade

| |
|---|
| 1 lb/450 g celeriac—2 heads |

**for the sauce:**

| |
|---|
| 1 generous teaspoon Dijon mustard |
| 1 egg yolk |
| generous $\frac{1}{2}$ cup/1.5 dl peanut or sunflower oil |
| squeeze of lemon juice |
| salt and freshly ground pepper |
| 2–3 tablespoons light cream |

SERVES 4

Make the sauce in exactly the same way as you make mayonnaise, mixing the mustard and egg yolk together vigorously with a pinch of salt before starting to add the oil. Stir in the cream at the end and taste for seasoning.
Peel the celeriac and grate it coarsely, either on the wavy blade of a mandoline or on a grater. Drop the shreds into a bowl of water acidulated with lemon juice as you grate them, to keep them nice and white. Bring a saucepan of salted water to a vigorous boil. Drop in the grated celeriac and drain it immediately in a colander, splashing it with cold water to cool it down. This short blanching keeps the celeriac white but some prefer it raw. When it has drained thoroughly and is completely cold, mix it with the mayonnaise and serve the same day, either as a dish on its own or as part of an hors d'oeuvre.

---

# Hot beet salad

| |
|---|
| 4–5 beets |
| 1 tablespoon olive oil |
| $\frac{1}{2}$ stick/55 g butter |
| salt and freshly ground pepper |
| juice of 1 lemon |
| handful of parsley, chopped |

SERVES 4–6

Cook the beets whole in boiling salted water for 1½–2 hours; then rub off their skins while they are still hot.

Preheat the oven to 375°F/190°C.

Put the oil in the bottom of an ovenproof dish. Slice the cooked beets, lay them in the dish, dot each layer with butter and season with salt and pepper. Squeeze the lemon juice over the beets, dot the top with more butter and bake in a moderate oven for 15 minutes. Spoon the juice over the top of the beets, sprinkle with the chopped parsley and serve hot.

---

## Mashed rutabaga

| |
|---|
| *1 rutabaga* |
| *2 potatoes* |
| *2 tablespoons/30 g butter* |
| *3–4 tablespoons heavy cream* |
| *salt and freshly ground pepper* |

SERVES 4

Peel the rutabaga and potatoes and cut them into chunks. Put them in a saucepan of cold salted water, bring to the boil and boil until completely tender. Drain the vegetables in a colander, mash them and then make a fine purée by sieving them through the medium blade of a food mill or using a food processor. Return the purée to the cleaned saucepan and beat in the butter and cream; season with salt and plenty of pepper. Serve very hot.

---

## Jerusalem artichokes

| |
|---|
| *2 lb/900 g Jerusalem artichokes* |
| *2 tablespoons/30 g butter* |
| *salt and freshly ground pepper* |
| *5 cups/1 liter chicken stock or water* |
| *2 tablespoons chopped parsley* |
| *⅔ cup/1.5 dl heavy cream* |
| *grating of nutmeg* |
| *squeeze of lemon juice* |

SERVES 4

Peel the artichokes and slice them thinly, a little thicker than a coin. Melt the butter in a large heavy frying pan and put in the artichokes. Season with salt and pepper and cook gently for 5–6 minutes until each slice is well coated in butter. Add enough stock or water to come just to the top of the artichokes and simmer, uncovered, until just tender. Add the parsley and the cream and continue to cook gently until the artichokes are bathed in a creamy sauce. Taste and add salt, pepper, nutmeg and a squeeze of lemon juice. Serve hot with game or roast pork.

---

## Ratatouille

| |
|---|
| *scant ¾ cup/1.5 dl olive oil* |
| *2 lb/900 g tomatoes* |
| *salt and freshly ground pepper* |
| *2 pinches sugar (optional)* |
| *2–3 onions* |
| *3 cloves garlic* |
| *2 red or green sweet peppers* |
| *1 lb/450 g zucchini* |
| *1 large eggplant* |

SERVES 6

Heat half the olive oil in a small pan. Skin and chop the tomatoes and simmer them in the oil with a seasoning of salt, pepper and, if they are not very ripe and sweet, 2 good pinches of sugar, for 10–15 minutes.

Meanwhile, peel the onions and slice them downwards, fairly coarsely. Peel and slice the garlic, cut the peppers in strips or squares, discarding the core and seeds, and cut the zucchini into ¼ in/5 mm slices or quarter them lengthwise. Finally, cut the eggplant into slices and quarter each slice. Heat the remaining oil in a heavy-bottomed pan, throw in the onions and garlic and fry gently. When the onions are soft, throw in the peppers, then the zucchini and finally the slices of eggplant. Add salt and pepper and continue to cook slowly.

When the vegetables are shining and beginning to soften, add the tomatoes, which will have collapsed to a fairly moist sauce. Gently stir the vegetables around at all stages of cooking this dish, otherwise they will cook unevenly and stick to the bottom of the pan. When all the vegetables are soft and tender, the ratatouille is done. It reheats very well.

Ratatouille comes from the south of France where the dish varies from a delicate mixture of lightly cooked vegetables to a really dark brown stew,

floating with oil and exhaling garlic. Ideally it should be rich and moist with different vegetables just distinguishable in a smooth, aromatic tomato sauce. Frying the vegetables and tomatoes separately, as here, helps them to remain intact.
ALTERNATIVES: *add sprigs of thyme or basil, some black olives, or extra garlic.*

# Sweet pepper salad

| |
|---|
| 2 red, yellow, or green sweet peppers |
| 2–3 tablespoons olive oil |
| salt |

SERVES 2–4 AS AN HORS D'OEUVRE OR SALAD
Heat the broiler.
Remove the stalks from the peppers with a small sharp knife, pulling out the cores with them, and shake out any loose seeds. Put the peppers whole under the hot broiler and let them blister and blacken, turning them frequently so that they become black all over. Take them from under the broiler and wrap them in a clean cloth and leave them to cool. When cooled in this way, the peppers will be perfectly easy to skin.
The broiling makes them sweet and mellow.
Cut them into large 1 in/2.5 cm wide strips and lay them all facing the same way on a rough plate—this is simple food and does not need smart

*Sweet pepper salad*

serving. Pour the oil over the peppers, sprinkle with salt, turn the pieces over in this dressing and serve lukewarm or cold.
ALTERNATIVE: *add some lemon juice to the dressing.*

# Stuffed tomatoes

| |
|---|
| 6 large tomatoes |
| 1 large clove garlic |
| 8 green olives |
| 6 anchovy fillets |
| ½ cup/55 g fresh white bread crumbs |
| ½ stick/55 g butter, melted |
| 1 teaspoon chopped basil or marjoram |
| salt |

SERVES 4–6
Preheat the oven to 325°F/170°C.
Cut the tomatoes in half across the middle, scoop out the insides and discard the seeds. Peel and chop the garlic and chop the olives and anchovies.
To make the stuffing, mix together the tomato flesh, garlic, olives, anchovies and bread crumbs, moisten the mixture with the melted butter and add the basil or marjoram and a little salt. Stuff the mixture into the tomato halves, put them in an oiled roasting pan and bake in the top of the oven for 40 minutes until tender.
Serve on their own as an hors d'oeuvre or with a simple salad as a delicious lunch.
ALTERNATIVES: *stuff the tomatoes with a lamb, rice and herb stuffing; or with onions, garlic, ham and bread crumbs; or simply with garlic, parsley and bread crumbs doused in olive oil.*

# Guacamole

| |
|---|
| 3 ripe avocados |
| juice of 1 lime |
| 1 tomato |
| 4–6 green chili peppers |
| 1 scallion (optional) |
| ⅔ cup/0.75 dl olive oil |
| salt and freshly ground pepper |
| dash of Tabasco (optional) |

SERVES 6–8
Remove the flesh from the avocados and mash it

together with the lime juice, mixing well. Skin and chop the tomato. Chop the chili peppers and scallion finely and pound them to a paste using a pestle and mortar or food processor.

Add the mashed avocados and the tomato. Slowly incorporate as much of the olive oil as you can, drop by drop, whisking with a fork or blending in the food processor. Add salt and pepper and a little Tabasco. Chill briefly and serve with toast.

Guacamole should taste both hot and cool at the same time.

## Eggplant purée

| 2–3 eggplants |
| --- |
| ½ small onion (optional) |
| 2 small tomatoes |
| 1–2 cloves garlic |
| 6 tablespoons olive oil, or more if needed |
| squeeze of lemon juice |
| salt and freshly ground pepper |

SERVES 4 AS AN HORS D'OEUVRE

Heat the broiler, or alternatively preheat the oven to 425°F/220°C.

Wash the eggplants and put them either under the heated broiler or in the hot oven. Leave them until the skins have blackened and the insides are becoming soft—about 20 minutes depending on their size—then turn them over and finish cooking until they are completely soft inside.

Meanwhile, peel the onion (if you are using it) and chop it finely, skin and chop the tomatoes, peel 1 clove garlic and crush it to a fine pulp.

Once the eggplants are done and have cooled a little, open them up and scoop out all the flesh onto a board, using a spoon to scrape the skins. Chop the flesh finely and put it into a bowl. Mix in the onion, tomatoes and garlic and then gradually add the oil, as if you were making mayonnaise. Taste the mixture and add a few drops of lemon juice, more garlic, and salt and pepper as necessary. Eggplant purée, known as poor man's caviar, has a very good and interesting smoky flavor. Serve it cold with dark bread and butter or hot toast, or as a salad with other quick salads, such as tomato salad or cucumber salad. It also makes a good lunch together with some slices of salami and a few black olives, or with stuffed vine leaves.

## Melanzane alla parmigiana

| 2 lb/900 g eggplants |
| --- |
| flour for coating |
| generous ¾ cup/1.5 dl sunflower oil |
| 2 lb/900 g tomatoes |
| 1 onion |
| 2 cloves garlic |
| 12 leaves fresh basil |
| 5–6 tablespoons olive oil |
| 2 tablespoons chopped parsley |
| salt and freshly ground pepper |
| ¾ lb/340 g mozzarella |
| 1 teaspoon dried oregano |
| ¼ cup/30 g Parmesan, freshly grated |

SERVES 4–6

Cut the eggplants lengthwise in slices about ¼ in/5 mm thick and dust them with flour. Brown them on both sides in the sunflower oil in a large frying pan, cooking a few at a time, draining them well and transferring them to a separate dish as they turn brown.

Skin and chop the tomatoes, onion and garlic and tear the basil in shreds. Heat the olive oil in a saucepan, throw in the chopped onion and garlic and when they have sweated add the tomatoes, half the basil and half the parsley. Season with salt and pepper and simmer for about 30 minutes, until the sauce has thickened.

Preheat the oven to 350°F/180°C.

While the sauce is cooking, cut the mozzarella in small cubes. When everything is ready, fill a buttered oval gratin dish, starting with a layer of half the eggplants, followed by half the sauce and then a scattering of half the mozzarella cubes. Sprinkle most of the remaining basil and parsley and some of the dried oregano into the dish and then repeat the layers of eggplants, sauce and mozzarella. Scatter the Parmesan and the rest of the herbs over the top. Bake for 25–30 minutes until heated through and beginning to brown on top. Serve hot.

## Buttered summer squash

| 2 lb/900 g summer squash |
| --- |
| salt |
| ½ stick/55 g butter |

SERVES 4–6

Peel the squash and cut it in half. Remove the seeds and cut the flesh into pieces about 2 in/5 cm long and 1 in/2.5 cm thick. Bring a large pan of salted water to the boil and drop in the pieces of squash. Let them cook for about 10 minutes until just becoming tender. Drain very well—this is important as squash can easily become soggy.

Melt the butter in the same pan and return the pieces of squash. Toss them quickly in the butter over a low heat until they are well coated. Serve for lunch with chicken or steak and kidney pie.

---

## Squash provençale

| |
|---|
| 1 lb/450 g summer squash |
| 1 onion |
| 2 cloves garlic |
| 2 tablespoons olive oil |
| ½ stick/55 g butter |
| 1½ lb/700 g ripe tomatoes |
| 3–4 sprigs thyme |
| 1 tablespoon chopped parsley |
| salt and freshly ground pepper |
| 1 teaspoon sugar |

SERVES 4

Peel and chop the onion and garlic and sauté them in the oil and half the butter. Skin and chop the tomatoes and add them to the onion and garlic with the thyme, parsley, salt, pepper and sugar. Simmer to a thickish sauce. Meanwhile, cut the marrow into rectangular pieces, 2 x 1 in/5 x 2.5 cm, removing the seeds. Drop the pieces into boiling salted water, cook until just tender and drain well. Heat the broiler.

Mix the cooked squash into the sauce and pour the whole glorious mixture into a large oval gratin dish. Dot the top with the remaining butter and put under a fierce broiler until brown and bubbling. This really glorifies a common squash.

---

## Stuffed summer squash

| |
|---|
| 1 large summer squash |
| **for the stuffing:** |
| 2 small onions |
| 2 tomatoes |
| 2 tablespoons olive oil or butter |
| ½ lb/225 g ground beef |
| salt and freshly ground pepper |
| 1 cup/115 g Emmental or Cheddar, freshly grated |
| **for the sauce:** |
| 1 large onion |
| 2 cloves garlic |
| 2–3 tablespoons/30–45 g butter |
| 1 lb/450 g tomatoes |
| salt and freshly ground pepper |

SERVES 4

Peel the squash and cut it in half lengthwise. Scoop out the seeds and sprinkle the cut surfaces with salt. Drain upside down for 30 minutes.

Meanwhile, make the stuffing. Peel and chop the onions and skin and chop the tomatoes. Sauté the onions in the oil or butter until soft and add the meat, stirring and crushing it to break up any lumps. When the meat starts to stick to the pan and sizzle, add the tomatoes, salt and pepper and 2 tablespoons water. Cook for 30 minutes until the stuffing has the consistency of a thick sauce. Stir in the cheese; let it melt into the stuffing and then remove the pan from the heat.

Preheat the oven to 350°F/180°C.

Next make the sauce. Peel and chop the onion and garlic and melt the butter in a saucepan. Sauté the chopped onion in the butter, add the garlic and fry until golden. Meanwhile, skin and chop the tomatoes. Add them to the onions, season with salt and pepper and simmer to a sauce.

Fill each half of the squash with stuffing, pour the sauce into a gratin dish or roasting pan, place the stuffed squash halves in the sauce and bake for 45 minutes to an hour until done.

ALTERNATIVE: *zucchini, cut in half, can be substituted for large summer squash.*

---

## Zucchini au gratin

| |
|---|
| 1½ lb/700 g zucchini |
| salt |
| 2 tablespoons/30 g butter |
| ½ cup/55 g Parmesan, freshly grated |

SERVES 4

Preheat the oven to 425°F/220°C.

Peel the zucchini in strips with a potato peeler,

then slice them into rounds $\frac{1}{4}$ in/5 mm thick. Put them in a colander, sprinkle lightly with salt and leave them to drain for 30 minutes. Dry the zucchini slices on paper towels and drop them into a pan of boiling salted water. Bring them back to the boil, boil for 1 minute, then drain them again really thoroughly.

Butter an oval gratin dish, put in a layer of zucchini, season with salt and pepper, dot them with half the butter and sprinkle generously with some of the cheese. Repeat the layers, ending up with a layer of cheese.

Put the dish in the oven and cook for about 15–20 minutes until the zucchini and cheese are bubbling and the top is a pale golden brown. Serve piping hot.

## Stuffed zucchini

2 lb/900 g zucchini

1¼ cups/3 dl thick béchamel sauce

½ cup/55 g Parmesan, freshly grated

2 oz/55 g prosciutto crudo or cooked ham, sliced thinly and cut into ½ in/1 cm squares, about ½ cup

salt and freshly ground pepper

pinch of grated nutmeg (optional)

SERVES 4

Cut the zucchini in half lengthwise and scoop out the seeds with a teaspoon. Drop the halved zucchini into boiling salted water and let them cook for about 8–10 minutes. Drain very thoroughly in a colander.

Preheat the oven to 425°F/220°C.

Make a thick béchamel sauce, stir in most of the Parmesan and all the ham. Taste for seasoning, add a little nutmeg if you like and allow to bubble for 15 minutes. Put the drained zucchini into an earthenware gratin dish and then, using a spoon, fill them with the mixture. Bake for 15 minutes. Heat the broiler.

Sprinkle the stuffed zucchini with the remaining cheese and brown quickly under the broiler.

Serve as an appetizing hors d'oeuvre or a very light summer lunch.

They are eaten, in Italy, before a beef steak or a baked fish. (The only other vegetables would be in the form of a mixed salad of lettuce, little leaves of rocket and a few finely sliced rounds of radish.)

## Mushrooms à la grecque

¾ lb/340 g button mushrooms

4 tablespoons each of olive oil and red wine

bunch of thyme, parsley and marjoram

2 bay leaves

1 teaspoon coriander seeds, lightly crushed

salt and freshly ground pepper

SERVES 4–6

Slice the mushrooms across into rounds or cut them into quarters. Put the oil, red wine, 4 tablespoons of water, the herbs and the coriander seeds together in a pan and boil for 5 minutes. Add the sliced mushrooms and salt and pepper and cook, uncovered, for 10 minutes. Allow to cool and serve with dark or French bread, or homemade white bread, butter and a glass of wine.

These mushrooms shrink alarmingly, but when you come to eat them you will find that a very little is enough—they are extremely rich.

ALTERNATIVE: **Zucchini à la grecque** *are very good but may need to cook a little longer than mushrooms.*

## Mushrooms and peppers

½ lb/225 g mushrooms

2 red or yellow sweet peppers

1 clove garlic

3 tablespoons olive oil

3 tablespoons red wine

squeeze of lemon juice

bunch of thyme

12 crushed coriander seeds, or a handful of chopped basil

2 tablespoons chopped parsley

salt and freshly ground pepper

SERVES 4

Slice the mushrooms fairly thinly (you can leave them whole if you prefer) and slice the peppers in small strips. Peel and slice the garlic.

Sauté the peppers in the oil in a small pan, add the mushrooms and garlic, the wine, lemon juice and 3 tablespoons water. Throw in the thyme, the coriander or basil and parsley, and season with salt and pepper. Simmer for 10–15 minutes until the mushrooms are cooked through. Allow to cool, and eat cold with bread and butter. This makes a good, rich start to a summer lunch.

# Garlic mushrooms

*1 lb/450 g large button mushrooms*

*a little lemon juice*

*3 cloves garlic*

*¾ stick/85 g butter*

*1 tablespoon olive oil*

*2 tablespoons chopped parsley*

*salt and freshly ground pepper*

**SERVES 4**

Clean the mushrooms and cut them in quarters. Sprinkle them with a few drops of lemon juice to keep them white. Peel the cloves of garlic and chop them coarsely. Melt the butter with the oil in a large frying pan and throw in the mushrooms, garlic and parsley. Fry until the mushrooms exude their juices, stirring them around all the time with a wooden spoon. Season them with salt and pepper and leave over a moderate heat for about 5 minutes more, stirring from time to time.

Serve the mushrooms with garlic and parsley very hot, with a roast chicken, broiled chops, broiled steak or roast beef.

*Garlic mushrooms*

# Dolmades

*20–30 fresh young vine leaves*

*3 large ripe tomatoes or 1 tablespoon tomato paste*

*1 onion*

*4–5 tablespoons olive oil*

*½ lb/225 g raw ground lamb, or ground left-over roast lamb*

*⅔ cup/115 g long-grain rice*

*3–4 sprigs marjoram, chopped, or 1 teaspoon dried oregano*

*2 tablespoons pine nuts (optional)*

*salt and freshly ground pepper*

*squeeze of lemon juice*

*pinch of cinnamon*

**SERVES 4–6**

Choose young leaves with no holes. Bring a pot of salted water to the boil. Drop the leaves in, a few at a time, and let them darken, grow limp and cook for a minute before taking them out to drain. Skin and chop the tomatoes. Peel and chop the onion finely and sauté it in 2–3 tablespoons of the olive oil; add the lamb and when it has started to brown, add the rice and pine nuts. Stir it until the rice glistens. Add two of the skinned and chopped tomatoes, the marjoram or oregano, salt, pepper, lemon juice and cinnamon and simmer gently.

When the tomatoes have reduced to make a sauce for the other ingredients, take the pan off the heat. (If you are using tomato paste, mix it first with a little water before adding it to the stuffing and let this reduce to a sauce.)

Lay each vine leaf flat on a board, put a teaspoonful of the stuffing in the middle at the stalk end. Half enclose the stuffing by rolling it away from you, starting at the stalk end. Fold the sides in and then finish rolling the leaf up to make a little parcel. Give it a gentle squeeze in the palm of your hand to stick the whole thing together. The aim is to enclose the stuffing neatly in the leaf for cooking. Fill all but a few of the leaves.

Line a small sauté pan with half the spare cooked vine leaves, sprinkle with 1 tablespoon of the remaining oil and place all the stuffed vine leaves side by side in the pan. Scatter on the remaining skinned and chopped tomato (or some lemon juice, if you have used tomato paste), the last of the oil and ½ cup/1.5 dl water. Cover with the remaining unfilled vine leaves and a lid and simmer for 25–30 minutes, making certain that they do not become dry; if this should happen, add a little more water. Eat dolmades cold with drinks or hot with kebabs.

## *Impromptu fruit salad*

| |
|---|
| *1 kiwi fruit* |
| *2 oranges* |
| *1 large slice very red watermelon* |
| *2 ripe peaches* |
| *juice of 1 lemon* |
| *1 tablespoon/15 g sugar, preferably superfine* |
| *a few black grapes* |
| *scant 2 cups/225 g strawberries* |

SERVES 4

Peel the kiwi fruit and slice it thinly. Peel and segment the oranges with a sharp knife. Cut the flesh from the watermelon and slice it into 8 thin slices. Dip the peaches in boiling water, peel them carefully, cut into halves and remove the stones, then slice them and sprinkle with lemon juice and sugar. Halve the grapes and remove their seeds, and hull the strawberries.

Divide the fruits between four plates, placing them in groups and arranging them prettily, so that the colors are delicately balanced. Serve chilled.

ALTERNATIVES: *any pretty fruits such as figs, pears, cantaloupe or other melons, mulberries, loganberries and wild strawberries may be included in this salad, depending on what is in season. If you like, you can serve sieved raspberries, sweetened with sugar, as a sauce to go with these fruits.*

## *Apple fritters*

| |
|---|
| *8 cooking apples* |
| *1 cup/115 g flour* |
| *3 tablespoons butter, melted* |
| *¼ cup/55 g sugar, preferably superfine* |
| *large pinch each of ground cinnamon and ground cloves* |
| *salt* |
| *beaten white of 1 egg* |
| *oil for deep frying* |

SERVES 4–6

Make the batter about an hour before it is needed. Mix together the flour and melted butter and gradually add 1 cup/2.5 dl lukewarm water. Let it stand in a cool place.

Peel and core the apples and cut into slices. Dust them with the sugar mixed with the cinnamon, cloves and a pinch of salt.

Fold the beaten egg white into the batter and dip the apple rings in it. Deep fry them in hot oil and drain on paper towels. Sprinkle the fritters with leftover spiced sugar and serve with cream.

## *Apple crumble*

| |
|---|
| *1 lb/450 g cooking apples* |
| *2 strips lemon peel* |
| *½ cup/115 g sugar* |
| *1 stick/115 g butter* |
| *¾ cup/85 g flour* |
| *1 teaspoon ground cinnamon* |
| *salt* |

SERVES 4

Preheat the oven to 350°F/180°C.

Peel, quarter and core the apples, and put them in a small baking dish with 1–2 tablespoons of water, the lemon peel and 2 tablespoons/30 g sugar. Dot with a nut of the butter.

Mix the remaining sugar with the flour, cinnamon and a pinch of salt and add the remaining butter, rubbing it in with your fingertips until the mixture is the texture of fine bread crumbs. Sprinkle the mixture in a thick layer over the top of the apples and bake for 40 minutes until well browned.

## *Quinces in lemon syrup*

| |
|---|
| *1 lb/450 g quinces* |
| *¾ cup/170 g sugar* |
| *2 strips lemon peel* |
| *3 cooking apples* |

SERVES 4

Put the sugar, ½ cup/1.5 dl of water and the lemon peel in a saucepan. Dissolve the sugar over a gentle heat and then boil the syrup for 5 minutes.

Remove from the heat and let it cool a little while you peel and core the quinces and cut them into pieces, each the size of a large sugar lump. Put them into the syrup and simmer gently for an hour, covered at first and then, when tender, uncovered. Peel and core the apples and cut them into pieces the same size as the pieces of quince. Add them to the quinces and simmer further until the apples are cooked and all is bathed in a golden-pink syrup. Remove the lemon peel and serve warm or cold.

# Pears in red wine

4 large juicy pears
2½ cups/6 dl red wine
¼ cup/55 g sugar, preferably vanilla sugar
6 cloves
1 cinnamon stick
2 strips orange peel
½ lemon

SERVES 4

Put the wine in a small saucepan with the sugar, cloves, cinnamon and orange peel. Bring it to the boil and simmer for 5 minutes.

Peel the pears carefully, leaving their stalks on and rubbing them with half a lemon as you peel to prevent them browning. Arrange them on their sides in a saucepan or casserole that will just hold them, pour the spiced wine over them, put the pan over a very gentle heat and poach the pears for an hour, covered, turning them over half-way through so that they are evenly colored a nice reddish brown.

# Fresh orange gelatine

about 6 large juicy oranges
6 tablespoons/85 g sugar
1 tablespoon/15 g gelatine

SERVES 4

Dissolve the sugar in 1¼ cups/3 dl of water and add the rind of an orange, pared thinly in strips. Bring to the boil and simmer for 5 minutes. Remove from the heat and dissolve the gelatine in the hot syrup—return the pan to a gentle heat, if necessary, and stir without boiling until it has completely dissolved. Allow to cool. Meanwhile squeeze the oranges into a measuring pitcher, using as many as it takes to make about 2½ cups/6 dl of juice. Strain in the cooled syrup and then pour into a mold. Set in the refrigerator.

# Clafoutis

1½ lb/700 g cherries, preferably black ones
3 tablespoons flour
salt

3 eggs
3 cups/7 dl milk
small glass of kirsch
3 tablespoons sugar

SERVES 6

Preheat the oven to 375°F/190°C.

Pit the cherries. Put the flour in a bowl with a pinch of salt and break in the eggs. Stir and beat well, then add the milk slowly, stirring with a wooden spoon to make a batter. Then stir in the kirsch and sugar and beat the mixture well for several minutes.

Butter a gratin dish and put the pitted cherries in the bottom. The blacker they are the better. Strain the batter over them and bake for 50 minutes. Sprinkle with sugar and serve with cream.

This French specialty is very rich and is delicious hot or cold.

# Strawberry fool

3½ cups/450 g strawberries
¾ cup/170 g sugar, preferably superfine
1¼ cups/3 dl heavy cream

SERVES 4

Keep 2–3 of the best strawberries on one side. Hull and chop the rest and put them in a bowl with half the sugar. Leave them to steep and exude their juices for half an hour, then crush them finely in their syrup with a fork.

Whip the cream with a balloon whisk until soft and thick, gradually adding the rest of the sugar. Do not overbeat or the cream will separate.

Stir the crushed strawberries into the cream. Put the mixture into a nice bowl and top with a few whole or halved strawberries.

ALTERNATIVES: **Raspberry fool.** *Substitute raspberries for strawberries.*

**Gooseberry fool.** *Use cooked sweetened gooseberry purée instead of the strawberries.*

# Pavlova

4 cups/450 g fresh raspberries
4 egg whites
salt

*1¼ cups/280 g sugar, preferably superfine*

*flour for dusting*

*1 teaspoon eau-de-vie framboise (optional)*

*1¼ cups/3 dl heavy cream*

SERVES 4–6

Whisk the egg whites, together with a pinch of salt, in a spotlessly clean bowl, using a balloon whisk which must also be extremely clean, since any trace of grease will prevent the whites rising properly. An electric beater is not quite so good.

When the whites form very firm peaks, add about ½ cup/115 g of the sugar and whisk until firm again. Fold in another ½ cup/115 g sugar very lightly but thoroughly with a spatula.

Preheat the oven to 250°F/130°C.

Now comes the tricky part. Take a large clean plastic bag, such as a freezer bag, and cut off one corner to make a hole about ½ in/1 cm across, or better still, use a pastry bag with a ½ in/1 cm nozzle. Fill the bag with the meringue mixture.

Dust a nonstick baking sheet with flour and use a 10 in/25 cm diameter plate to make a circular imprint on the flour. Starting in the middle and coiling the meringue around on itself like a snail shell, pipe out a flat disc of meringue on the marked baking sheet, squeezing the meringue gently through the hole in the bag. Put a second layer of meringue around the edge of the disc to make a wall so that you have a circular meringue shell. Bake for 2 hours, until the meringue is just cooked enough to handle. It will still be very delicate, so take care with it: leave it on the baking sheet to cool and crisp before you move it to a plate.

Fill the meringue shell with raspberries and sprinkle them with the remaining sugar and—if you are using it—the eau-de-vie framboise. Whip the cream to a light snow, cover the raspberries with a nice thick layer, and serve this extravagant Australian concoction at once.

---

## Raspberries and peaches

*3 cups/340 g raspberries*

*3 peaches*

*sugar to taste, preferably superfine*

*juice of ½ lemon*

SERVES 4

Put the raspberries in a bowl, sprinkle them with plenty of the sugar and put them in the refrigerator for 2–3 hours, until their juice has run into the sugar.

Dip the peaches in boiling water, skin them, cut them away from their stones in thin slices and arrange them over and around the raspberries. Squeeze the lemon juice over the top and sprinkle with more sugar. Put them back in the refrigerator to chill for an hour or two. Serve the fruit plain, without cream.

This is a delicate dessert with a pleasant sharpness.

## Summer pudding

*4 cups/450 g raspberries and 2 cups/225 g red currants and 2 cups/225 g black currants or blueberries*

*1¾ cups/400 g sugar*

*1 small loaf white bread*

SERVES 4–6

Cook the raspberries as lightly as possible with ¾ cup/170 g of the sugar, and the red and black currants in separate pans with ½ cup/115 g of sugar each. Try not to stir the fruit, nor to let it become too mushy. You need some juice but not too much. (These fruits cook very quickly and masses of juice floods out.) A teaspoon of water in the bottom of each pan before it is put on the heat prevents burning and sticking.

Cut the loaf of bread lengthwise into large slices, remove the crusts and use these large slices to line a 5 cup/1 liter pudding bowl, cutting them to size and leaving no gaps. Put in a layer of currants, then a thick layer of raspberries, more currants and then fill with raspberries. Do not add much juice—this should be put in a jar in the refrigerator.

Cover the top with more bread and put a weighted plate on top. Allow to stand for 24 hours. The bread should all be pink. If there are white patches, add more juice. Turn out and serve with the juice and with cream. This is a prince among puddings.

---

## Sherry trifle

*5 slices sponge cake*

*1 small glass sherry*

*⅔ cup/115 g blanched almonds*

*raspberry or strawberry jam*

*scant 2 cups/4.5 dl milk*

*2 tablespoons vanilla sugar or 2 tablespoons sugar
and a large strip of lemon peel*

*1 bay leaf (optional)*

*4 eggs*

*⅔ cup/1.5 dl heavy cream*

*1 tablespoon/15 g sugar*

*a few crystallized violets or glacé cherries and angelica,
or fresh raspberries or strawberries for the decoration*

SERVES 6

Put the slices of sponge cake in a beautiful bowl (cut glass is traditional). Pour the sherry over and allow it to soak in. Sprinkle with half the almonds, cut into slivers, and spread with the jam.

Next make the custard. Heat the milk to boiling point with vanilla sugar, or with plain sugar and lemon peel. Let it stand for 10 minutes to absorb the flavors—some people add a bay leaf to their custard, which gives it a very good but somewhat unexpected taste. Beat the eggs and pour onto them the now slightly cooled milk in a thin stream, beating all the time. Strain the mixture back into the pan and heat over a saucepan of hot, not boiling, water, stirring from time to time, until it coats the back of the spoon. Allow it to become fairly cool before pouring it into the bowl on top of the sponge cake. When it is cold, it should set fairly firm but by no means solid.

Whisk the cream together with the 1 tablespoon/ 15 g sugar to a soft snow and pile it on top of the cold custard. Decorate the top with the remaining almonds, cut in slivers and stuck into the cream like a hedgehog's prickles, and with crystallized violets, or glacé cherries and angelica, or fresh strawberries or, best of all, raspberries. Serve chilled, but do not leave it too long after the cream is added as it sinks a bit after an hour or so. It can be made up to the point of adding the custard, and then the cream piled on top, and decorated at the last moment.

# Crème brûlée

*scant 2 cups/4.5 dl heavy cream*

*4 egg yolks*

*1 tablespoon sugar and a vanilla bean, or*

*1 tablespoon vanilla sugar*

*superfine sugar for the top of the pudding*

SERVES 4–6

Heat the cream to scalding point, together with the bruised vanilla bean, if you are using one. Take it off the heat just before it comes to the boil. Meanwhile, beat the egg yolks with the sugar until they become light and a little thickened. Pour the cream onto the egg yolks in a thin stream, stirring all the time until they are well mixed.

Boil some water in the bottom of a double boiler and then turn the heat down, so that the water is just below boiling point. Put the mixture into the top saucepan and stir over the hot, almost boiling water until it coats the back of the spoon thickly. Pour into ramekins or a gratin dish and chill. Heat the broiler.

When the cream is cold and set, sprinkle with a layer of superfine sugar a little less than $\frac{1}{4}$ in/5 mm thick and place the dish under very high heat to caramelize the sugar. It will color unevenly, making it like tortoiseshell, ranging prettily from golden to almost black. Serve chilled.

ALTERNATIVE: **Trinity cream.** *The Cambridge University college, Trinity, invented this dish and they still make it in the same way as crème brûlée, but without sweetening the cream.*

*Crème brûlée*

## Crème caramel

| |
|---|
| *¾ cup/170 g sugar, preferably superfine* |
| *2½ cups/6 dl milk* |
| *sliver of lemon peel* |
| *1 in/2.5 cm piece of cinnamon stick or a piece of vanilla bean* |
| *2 eggs plus 1 extra yolk* |

SERVES 6

First make the caramel: dissolve half the sugar in ½ cup/115 ml of water, then bring it to a rapid boil. Do not stir it after it boils. When it starts to brown, watch it carefully and tip the pan gently to make the caramel an even gold. Pour it quickly into a shallow serving bowl, a china pie dish or some other round or oval dish with sloping sides and swirl it a little to coat the sides.

Preheat the oven to 325°F/170°C.

Heat the milk in a saucepan to scalding point (just below boiling point, when the milk shows small bubbles around the edge of the pan) with the lemon peel, the rest of the sugar, the cinnamon or vanilla and let it infuse over a very gentle heat for 5 minutes. Beat the eggs and the extra yolk together and add to the milk, beating all the time. Strain the mixture into the dish on top of the caramel and bake for at least an hour with the dish set in a bain-marie or a large roasting pan half filled with water. Test the custard to see if it is cooked by sliding in the point of a knife. If it makes a clean cut, the custard is ready; it should be shivery and tender and not a solid mass. Cooked in this way, crème caramel has a beautiful velvety texture.

ALTERNATIVE: **Individual crème caramels.** *The above ingredients will also make 5–6 small crème caramels, which will cook in 15–20 minutes.*

## Zabaglione

| |
|---|
| *1 egg yolk* |
| *2 tablespoons Marsala* |
| *1 tablespoon superfine sugar* |
| *grating of lemon peel* |

SERVES 1

Put all the ingredients in the top of a double boiler. Beat them together well with a wire whisk. Start heating the water in the lower pan, but don't let it boil. Keep whisking with the wire whisk until the whole thing has trebled in volume and is light and frothy all the way through. It takes less time if you start with hot water in the pan.

Pour into a warmed glass and eat immediately.

To make it for several people, just multiply the ingredients by the number of people.

## Syllabub

| |
|---|
| *2 lemons* |
| *3 tablespoons sugar, superfine if possible* |
| *1 glass dry white wine or sherry* |
| *2½ cups/6 dl heavy cream* |

SERVES 6–8

Grate the peel of the lemons on the fine side of the grater and marinate it overnight with the juice of one of the lemons, the sugar and the wine or sherry. Next day, put the mixture into a large bowl and whip in the cream until it stands up in soft peaks. Do not overbeat or the cream will separate. Serve chilled in small glasses, with macaroons.

Syllabub should be very light in texture and just lemony enough to avoid being over-rich.

## Chocolate mousse

| |
|---|
| *3½ oz/100 g unsweetened baking chocolate* |
| *3 eggs* |
| *4 tablespoons/55 g superfine sugar* |
| *⅔ cup/1.5 dl plus 1 tablespoon heavy cream* |
| *salt* |

SERVES 4–6

Grate the chocolate. Separate the egg yolks from the whites and put the yolks in the top of a double boiler with the chocolate, sugar and ½ cup/1.5 dl of cream. Whisk until light, then thicken over hot but not boiling water, stirring from time to time. When it is thick and creamy, let it cool and add the remaining cream and a tiny pinch of salt. Whisk the egg whites in a clean bowl until stiff. Stir a tablespoon of the whites into the chocolate mixture to lighten it, then fold in the rest lightly, but very thoroughly, with a metal spoon or a spatula. Turn the mixture into little pots and chill.

ALTERNATIVES: **Rich chocolate mousse.** *Leave out the egg whites and incorporate 1¼ cups/3 dl of*

whipped cream into the lukewarm chocolate mixture.
**Chocolate orange mousse.** *Add the grated rind
of half an orange to the chocolate mixture before
adding the egg whites.*

---

# Orange sherbet

*6 oranges*

*1 lemon*

*generous ⅔ cup/115 g confectioners' sugar*

**SERVES 4**

Squeeze the oranges and lemon to make just over
2½ cups/6 dl juice. Add the confectioners' sugar,
mixing it in thoroughly so that it dissolves. Transfer to an ice cream maker or a freezer tray and freeze
to a slush, then purée it in a food processor so that
it becomes very light and fine grained. Transfer to
a soufflé dish or a mold and freeze.

Take the sherbet out of the freezer about 30–45
minutes before eating and soften in the refrigerator.

---

# Grapefruit sherbet

*4 grapefruit (use pink grapefruit if you like)*

*6 tablespoons/85 g sugar, preferably superfine*

**SERVES 4–6**

Dissolve the sugar in 3 tablespoons of water in a
small saucepan. Bring to the boil and boil for 5
minutes, then allow to cool. Meanwhile squeeze
the grapefruit. Add the cooled syrup to the grapefruit juice and strain it into an ice cream maker or
a freezer tray and freeze.

When it is a frozen slush, transfer to a food processor and whizz to a fine snow. Transfer to a
suitable white china dish and freeze until needed.
Take it out at least half an hour before it is needed
and let it soften in the refrigerator.

---

# Melon sherbet

*2 cantaloupes or small honeydew melons weighing
about 1 lb/450 g each*

*juice of 2 lemons*

*⅔ cup/225 g confectioners' sugar*

**SERVES 4**

Cut the melons in half through the middle and
scoop out the soft flesh with a sharp tablespoon
discarding all the seeds and fibers from the middle.
Keep the rinds on one side. Put the melon flesh in a
food processor together with the lemon juice and
the confectioners' sugar and blend to a smooth
purée. Spoon into an ice cream maker or a freezer
tray and freeze. Turn out into the food processor
again, blend to a light, smooth slush and pile it into
the melon rinds before refreezing.

Served in their shells, these sherbets should be all
covered in frost and look very pretty.

---

# Elderflower sherbet

*3 large sprays fresh elderflowers*

*½ cup/115 g sugar, preferably superfine*

*2 large grapefruits*

*1 lemon*

**SERVES 4**

Wash the elderflowers briefly. Melt the sugar in
1¼ cups/3 dl of water in a small saucepan, bring to
the boil and boil for 5 minutes. Remove the pan
from the heat, plunge in the elderflowers, stalks
upwards, and leave, uncovered to infuse and cool.
Squeeze the juice from the grapefruits and lemon
and pour it into the cold elderflower infusion. Pour
through a wire sieve into an ice cream maker or a
freezer tray and freeze. If not using an ice cream
maker, whisk once as the sherbet freezes to a slush
to prevent large ice crystals forming.

This sherbet has a delicate, summery flavor.

---

# Rich vanilla ice cream

*6 egg yolks*

*6 tablespoons/85 g sugar, superfine if possible*

*2½ cups/6 dl milk or 1¼ cups/3 dl each of milk
and light cream*

*1 vanilla bean, bruised*

*slice of lemon peel*

*15 coriander seeds, coarsely crushed*

*⅔ cup/1.5 dl heavy cream, lightly beaten*

**SERVES 4–6**

Beat the egg yolks and sugar together for 5–10

minutes, or until the sugar dissolves and the mixture becomes pale and frothy.

Heat the milk or milk and cream in the top of a double boiler, together with the vanilla bean, but do not boil. Remove the vanilla bean and pour the liquid in a fine stream into the egg yolks, beating all the time. Transfer the mixture to the top of the double boiler, together with the vanilla bean, lemon peel and coriander seeds, and keep stirring over very hot but not boiling water until the mixture thickens enough to coat the back of a wooden spoon. Allow the mixture to cool, then strain it into the lightly beaten heavy cream and whisk them together. Stir again and freeze in an ice cream maker or freezer tray in the refrigerator set at its coldest setting.

If you are not using an ice cream maker, remove your ice cream from the freezer tray after about an hour, put it in a bowl and beat it until all the ice crystals have disappeared, or blend it in a food processor. Freeze again. Repeat the beating or blending twice more, or once if you are not fussy; the ice cream takes about 3 hours or longer to set. This ice cream is a beautiful creamy yellow and soft and smooth, just the way ice cream is supposed to be. The lemon and coriander are very ancient and traditional additions to vanilla ice cream.

## *Coffee ice cream*

*3 egg yolks*
*$\frac{1}{4}$ cup/55 g vanilla sugar*
*$\frac{2}{3}$ cup/1.5 dl milk or light cream*
*$1\frac{1}{4}$ cups/3 dl strong black coffee*
*1 teaspoon good instant coffee powder*
*$\frac{2}{3}$ cup/1.5 dl heavy cream*

SERVES 4

Beat the egg yolks with the sugar until pale and frothy. Add all the remaining ingredients and whisk well. Transfer the mixture to an ice cream making machine or a freezer tray and freeze to a slush. Blend to a fine-textured snow in a food processor. Spoon into a soufflé dish or mold and freeze again. Take the ice cream out of the freezer or ice compartment of the refrigerator 20 minutes before serving to allow time for it to soften.

Eat this ice cream within 2–3 days of making it.

ALTERNATIVE: **Chocolate ice cream.** *Use a scant 2 cups/4.5 dl milk or light cream, replace coffee with $\frac{1}{4}$ lb/115 g grated chocolate. Heat the milk and chocolate together until the chocolate melts, cool a little and then whisk into the egg and sugar mixture. When cool, add the cream and freeze, blend and freeze again, as for coffee ice cream.*

## *Cassata*

*$1\frac{1}{4}$ pints/6 dl good vanilla ice cream*
*1 pint/4.5 dl chocolate ice cream*
*$\frac{2}{3}$ cup/1.5 dl heavy cream*
*generous $\frac{1}{3}$ cup/55 g confectioners' sugar*
*$\frac{3}{4}$ cup/115 g mixed candied fruit, cut into small dice*
*1 egg white*

SERVES 6–8

Use a stainless steel or enamelled bowl as a mold —it should be large enough to hold the two ice creams and the fruit mixture which goes in the middle. A 2 quart/1.75 liter bowl should do.

With a metal spoon dipped in hot water, line the inside of the mold with a layer of the vanilla ice cream. Freeze solid. Cover with a layer of chocolate ice cream, leaving a well in the center for the cream. Freeze again.

Meanwhile make the light, foamy filling. Whip the cream to a soft snow and stir in the confectioners' sugar and the candied fruit. Whip the egg white to a fairly firm peak and fold it into the cream thoroughly. Pile the mixture into the mold, tapping the mold to avoid air bubbles. Smooth off the top, cover with foil and freeze for several hours until the whole cassata is firm.

Unmold the cassata by dipping it briefly in hot water and serve cut in wedges.

## *Strawberry ice cream*

*$3\frac{1}{2}$ cups/450 g ripe strawberries*
*3 egg yolks*
*$\frac{2}{3}$–$\frac{3}{4}$ cup/140–170 g sugar, superfine if possible*
*$\frac{2}{3}$ cup/1.5 dl milk*
*$\frac{2}{3}$ cup/1.5 dl heavy cream*

SERVES 4–6

Put the egg yolks and $\frac{1}{2}$ cup/140 g sugar in a bowl and whisk them together with either an electric



Eggs **89**
Milk, cream and butter **90–92**
Sugars **183**
Ice cream maker **380, *381***
Vanilla sugar **183**
Coffee **186–188**
Molds **365**
Chocolate **189, *189***
Rich vanilla ice cream **317**
Candied fruit **160, *161***
Bowls **363–364**
Strawberries **150, *151***

beater or a hand whisk until the mixture becomes light and pale. Set the bowl aside.

Heat the milk and cream to just below boiling point and pour it in a thin stream into the egg and sugar mixture, beating all the time. Transfer the mixture to the top of a double boiler and thicken over hot water on a gentle heat, stirring from time to time, until you have a nice thick custard that smoothly coats the back of the spoon. Allow to stand until it becomes completely cool.

Hull the strawberries and purée them in a food processor or put them through the medium blade of a food mill. When the custard is cool, fold in the strawberry purée, taste the mixture and add more sugar if necessary. Ice cream tastes less sweet after freezing, so the mixture should be fairly sweet when it goes into the freezer. Transfer it to an ice cream maker or freezer tray and freeze. If you don't have an ice cream maker, blend the mixture once or twice in a food processor as it sets to prevent the formation of large ice crystals.

ALTERNATIVE: **Raspberry ice cream**. *Substitute the same amount of raspberries for the strawberries, and add a teaspoon of eau-de-vie framboise if you like, although it is not necessary.*

*Strawberry ice cream*

# Peanut chip ice cream

**for the basic ice cream:**

| |
|---|
| *3 egg yolks* |
| *¼ cup/55 g vanilla sugar* |
| *1¼ cups/3 dl creamy milk* |
| *2 tablespoons heavy cream* |

**for the peanut chip:**

| |
|---|
| *¼ lb/115 g dry roasted peanuts* |
| *½ cup/115 g sugar* |

SERVES 4

First make the ice cream mixture. Whisk the egg yolks and sugar together, either in a food processor or by hand, until they are pale and frothy. Add the milk and the cream, whisk together thoroughly and strain the mixture into a bowl. Chill thoroughly in the refrigerator.

To make the peanut chip, wash the peanuts and dry them with paper towels. Spread them in a non-stick cake pan. Dissolve the sugar slowly in 4 table-spoons of water in a small, heavy pan. Do not boil until the sugar has melted, then boil fast until the syrup caramelizes and colors evenly to a deep golden brown. Pour the caramel immediately over the peanuts and quickly stir it around so that the peanuts are well coated, then allow to cool and set. Put the peanut brittle you have made into a tough plastic bag and bang it with a rolling pin, banging it into chips the size of grains of rice. Some of the caramel will become completely pulverized. Stir it all into the ice cream mixture, and freeze in an ice cream maker or in a freezer tray.

If you are not using an ice cream maker, freeze to a slush and then put into a bowl and whisk with a wire whisk. (Don't forget this step or the caramel may sink to the bottom.) Then freeze again.

ALTERNATIVE: **Toasted almond ice cream**. *Use toasted almonds instead of the peanuts.*

# Bread and butter pudding

| |
|---|
| *6 slices well-buttered bread—white, raisin or currant loaf—with the crusts cut off* |
| *handful of raisins or sultanas* |
| *2 eggs* |
| *1½ tablespoons sugar* |
| *large pinch of cinnamon* |
| *generous 1¼ cups/3 dl creamy milk* |

# Puddings and Pastry

SERVES 4

Lay the bread in layers, buttered side up, in a buttered pie dish, sprinkling the fruit between the slices. Beat together the eggs, 1 tablespoon of the sugar and the cinnamon, then beat in the milk. Pour over the bread and leave to soak for an hour. Preheat the oven to 275°F/140°C.

Just before putting the pudding in the oven, sprinkle it with the remaining sugar and bake for 1–1½ hours (at the bottom of the oven if you are cooking something else). It will puff up and the top will become a delicious golden brown crust.

---

## Rice pudding

| |
|---|
| 2½ cups/6 dl milk |
| 2 tablespoons heavy cream |
| scant ½ cup/85 g short-grain rice |
| 2 tablespoons/30 g vanilla sugar |
| pinch of grated nutmeg |

SERVES 4–6

Preheat the oven to 300°F/160°C.

Heat the milk and cream. Butter a large pie dish, put the rice in it and pour on the hot milk and cream. Allow to stand for 15 minutes. Stir in the sugar, sprinkle the top with grated nutmeg and bake for 2 hours.

ALTERNATIVE: *infuse the milk with a bay leaf for 5 minutes before pouring it onto the rice.*

---

## Cheesecake

**for the crust:**

| |
|---|
| 1½ cups/225 g graham cracker crumbs |
| 1 stick/115 g butter, melted |
| ¼ teaspoon each nutmeg and cinnamon |
| 3 tablespoons/45 g sugar |

**for the filling:**

| |
|---|
| ½ lb/225 g cream cheese |
| 2 tablespoons sour cream or heavy cream |
| 2 tablespoons sugar, vanilla sugar if possible |
| 2 eggs |
| juice of ½ lemon |
| ⅓ cup/55 g sultanas |

SERVES 4–6

Pound the graham cracker crumbs to powder and mix with the melted butter, spices and sugar. Line a well-buttered 8 in/20 cm spring-sided pan by patting this mixture over the bottom and up the sides into a firm layer. Chill in the refrigerator until the butter is set.

Preheat the oven to 350°F/180°C.

Beat the cream cheese, add the sour or heavy cream and the sugar, then the eggs one at a time, beating continually. Finally add the lemon juice and sultanas. Pour the mixture into the firm crust and bake for 20 minutes.

Allow to cool and then chill for 1–2 hours in the refrigerator before carefully removing the cheesecake from the pan.

---

## Shortcrust pastry

| |
|---|
| 1¼ cups/170 g all-purpose flour |
| salt |
| ¾ stick/85 g cold butter |
| 2 tablespoons/30 g cold lard |

SERVES 4

Put the flour and a pinch of salt into a bowl. Add the butter and the lard and cut it up with a knife. Keep cutting and stirring the pieces of fat into the flour until they are about the size of peas.

Very briefly rub these pieces between thumbs and fingertips, raising your hands well above the bowl as you do so, so that the pieces fall back in a shower. Do not try to get the mixture to look like fine bread crumbs as this makes the pastry dense rather than leafy, as it should be. Stop rubbing as soon as the fat looks more or less like cornflakes.

Add just enough very cold water to bind the mixture—about 3–4 tablespoons—and mix it in with a knife blade until it starts to bind together. Quickly make the mixture into a ball with your hands and put it in a plastic bag. Chill in the refrigerator—if possible for three hours or, better still, overnight.

Roll it out lightly, sprinkling it with flour where the pieces of fat get sticky, and use for such dishes as pies, flans and tarts.

The secret of this pastry is to touch it as little as possible with your hands while you are making it. The result should be very crisp and golden.

ALTERNATIVE: *for sweet pastry dishes, add 1–2 teaspoons of superfine sugar to the flour.*

# Pâte brisée

*1½ cups/170 g plain flour*

*1 teaspoon sugar, preferably superfine*

*2½ tablespoons/15 g dried milk powder*

*salt*

*1 stick/115 g butter*

*1 tablespoon brandy or lemon juice*

*1 egg*

Mix the flour in a bowl with the fine sugar, dried milk powder and a pinch of salt. Cut the butter into small cubes and put them into a well in the center of the flour, with the brandy or lemon juice and egg. Mix well with your fingers until the mixture sticks together, crushing the butter and incorporating it thoroughly with the other ingredients.

Put the sticky mixture onto a floured board, sprinkle it with flour and smear it across the board with the heel of your hand. Do this two or three times until the butter is completely worked into the other ingredients. Then roll the mixture into a ball, with floured hands, put it in a plastic bag and chill in the refrigerator for about 2–3 hours, or until it is required.

This pastry is used for sweet tarts and flans.

---

# Rough puff pastry

*¾ stick/85 g butter, chilled*

*6 tablespoons/85 g lard, chilled*

*2 cups/225 g all-purpose flour*

*salt*

*about 8 tablespoons ice water*

Cut the butter and lard into cubes the size of small hazelnuts on a floured board. Sieve the flour and a pinch of salt into a bowl and add the cubed fat. Mix in ice water with a knife, adding a little at a time until the mixture is just holding together—it may not need 8 tablespoons. Chill for 15 minutes in the refrigerator.

On a well-floured board roll the dough out into a rectangle, fold over in thirds and press the sides together with the rolling pin to contain the air. Chill for 15 minutes, then roll out again into a rectangle, fold over, press edges together and chill as before. Roll out once more and you will have 27 layers of paper-thin crust.

Chill for the last time, then fold into thirds again, pinch the sides together and roll out. You will now have 81 thin layers of crust with air in between. Use as an alternative to flaky pastry.

---

# Flaky pastry

*2 cups/225 g all-purpose flour*

*2½ sticks/280 g butter*

*salt*

Put the flour, ½ stick/55 g of the butter, 1 level teaspoon of salt and about ⅔ cup/1.5 dl of cold water into a food processor and work it until it clings together and can be formed into a ball. Place the ball of dough in a plastic bag and put it to rest and chill in the refrigerator for an hour or two. At the same time chill the remaining butter next to the dough—they should be at the same temperature.

Take the chilled dough and butter out of the refrigerator; put the butter into a loose plastic bag and beat it with a rolling pin into a rectangle about ¾ in/2 cm thick. Roll out the dough, which is rather elastic and difficult to roll, into a rectangle large enough to envelop the flattened butter completely. Place the butter in the middle of the rectangle of dough and fold the edges over to enclose the butter. Roll out this parcel on a well-floured surface into a rectangle about $8 \times 16$ in/$20 \times 40$ cm, scattering flour on any places where the dough breaks or the butter seeps out.

Fold this rectangle into three, turn it around by 90° so that it faces the opposite direction and repeat the rolling and folding twice more—three times altogether. Put the folded dough back into the refrigerator in the plastic bag and chill for an hour, then repeat the three rollings and foldings and return it to the refrigerator for another hour. It is now ready to use, or you can roll and fold it again if you like, to make nine times altogether.

This pastry, which is also known as pâte feuilletée, is used for light tarts, pies and pastries.

---

# Choux pastry

*5 tablespoons/70 g butter*

*¼ teaspoon salt*

*¼ teaspoon sugar*

Superfine sugar **183**, *183*
Lard **101**

*¾ cup/85 g flour*

*3–4 eggs*

Put the butter, salt and sugar into a heavy saucepan, add ⅔ cup/1.5 dl of water and bring to the boil. Simmer until the butter has melted, remove the pan from the heat, allow it to cool a little, sift the flour into the mixture and beat with a wooden spoon until it is completely smooth. Return the saucepan to the heat and beat the mixture for a further 1–2 minutes until it starts to leave the sides of the pan and forms a mass. Remove the pan from the heat again and break in an egg, beating it in until it is absorbed. Add the second and third eggs in the same way. Break the fourth egg into a cup, whisk it with a fork and add just enough of it to make a soft mixture that holds its shape—3 eggs may have been enough if they were large ones.

Use for cream puffs, éclairs, profiteroles and so forth, and use the rest of the fourth egg, beaten with a little salt, to glaze them.

## Hot-water crust pastry

*4 cups/450 g flour*

*salt*

*¾ cup/170 g good quality lard*

*⅔ cup/1.5 dl milk*

Put the flour and a generous pinch of salt into a bowl. Bring the lard, milk and ⅔ cup/1.5 dl water to the boil in a saucepan, and pour into the flour. Mix the ingredients well with a wooden spoon and then work them together lightly and quickly to a smooth dough.

When the dough is cool enough to handle, knead it lightly and evenly with your hands—don't over-handle, or it will become tough. This type of pastry is traditionally used for making such dishes as raised pies.

## Baking blind

To prevent the bottom crust being rather under-cooked and soggy when making tarts and quiches, it is a good idea, if time is on your side, to bake the pastry "blind" before you put in the filling. To do this, line the quiche pan or pie dish with the pastry, prick the bottom with a fork and cover the bottom of the pastry shell with foil, bringing it up the sides as well. Then fill the pastry shell with dried beans, to weight the pastry. It is a good idea to keep a jar of beans for this purpose. Bake for 12–15 minutes at 425°F/220°C. Remove the beans and foil and cook a few minutes more until the bottom crust has lost its transparent look. You can now add the filling.

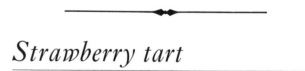

## Rhubarb and raisin pie

*2 lb/900 g rhubarb*

*⅓ cup/55 g raisins soaked in a little red wine*

*shortcrust pastry made with 1½ cups/170 g flour*

*2 teaspoons flour*

*6 tablespoons/85 g sugar*

*a little creamy milk*

SERVES 6

Preheat the oven to 425°F/220°C.

Trim and wash the rhubarb and cut into 1 in/2.5 cm pieces. Line a pie plate with half the pastry, put in the rhubarb and sprinkle with the flour and most of the sugar. Spread the raisins over the top and pour the red wine over them. Cover with the rest of the pastry and decorate with oblique cuts. Brush with the creamy milk, sprinkle with the remaining sugar and bake for 12–15 minutes, then lower the temperature to 350°F/180°C and bake for a further 20–25 minutes, covering loosely with foil if the pastry looks as if it might otherwise become too brown.

Serve this excellent pie hot with fresh cream.

## Strawberry tart

*3 cups/450 g strawberries*

*pâte brisée made with ¾ cup/85 g flour*

*2–3 tablespoons crabapple jelly*

*grated rind of ½ orange*

SERVES 4

Preheat the oven to 350°F/180°C.

Roll out the pastry and cut a 10 in/25 cm round, using a plate as a guide. Transfer it to a buttered baking sheet and bake for 15–20 minutes until cooked and a nice pale biscuit color. Whisk the crabapple jelly in a small bowl, with a fork, and mix in the grated orange rind. Brush the jelly over the pastry, leaving a $\frac{1}{2}$ in/1 cm margin all around the edge of the tart.

Hull the strawberries, cut them in half and arrange them carefully on the jelly in concentric circles. Eat while still warm, if possible, but it is still delicious cold.

ALTERNATIVE: **Lemon tart.** *Spread the pastry with freshly made, warm lemon curd.*

---

## Blackberry and apple pie

$2\frac{1}{2}$ cups/450 g fresh plump blackberries

3 cooking apples

6 tablespoons/85 g granulated or light brown sugar

3 cloves

shortcrust pastry made with $1\frac{1}{4}$ cups/170 g flour

1 egg yolk beaten with $\frac{1}{2}$ teaspoon water, or a little water and a sprinkling of sugar

SERVES 6

Preheat the oven to 425°F/220°C.

Pick over and wash the blackberries and peel, core and slice the apples. Put a pie funnel in the middle of a pie dish, put in the fruit in layers, sprinkling the sugar over the layers as you go. Drop in the cloves. Cover the top with pastry, decorating it with leftover pieces, and then glaze the pie with the egg-wash, brushed on with a pastry brush. If you prefer, you can leave off the egg-wash and brush the pie with water and sprinkle it with a little sugar instead.

Bake the pie for 12–15 minutes, then turn the heat down to 350°F/180°C and bake for a further half an hour. If the top of the pie is becoming too brown, cover it loosely with foil.

Serve the pie hot with plenty of fresh cream.

---

## Apricot tart

1 lb/450 g apricots, fresh or canned

flaky pastry made with 1 cup/115 g flour

$\frac{1}{4}$ cup/55 g sugar, preferably superfine

$\frac{1}{2}$ stick/55 g butter

SERVES 4

Preheat the oven to 425°F/220°C.

Cut the apricots in half and remove the stones. If using canned apricots, drain them very thoroughly in a sieve. Roll out the pastry into an oblong shape about $8 \times 12$ in/$20 \times 30$ cm and trim the edges very neatly with a sharp knife—if it is not cleanly cut the pastry won't rise properly.

Put the pastry onto a moistened baking sheet. Press the apricot halves, cut side up, into the pastry in rows, leaving a $\frac{1}{2}$ in/1 cm margin all the way around. Sprinkle them with the sugar and dot the butter all over the top. Bake for 10 minutes, then turn down the heat to 400°F/200°C for a further 20–30 minutes until the pastry and apricots are glazed with melted butter and sugar, and starting to blacken on the very tips. Eat hot or cold.

ALTERNATIVE: **Apple tart.** *Place neatly arranged rows of thinly sliced apples on the oblong of pastry instead of the apricots.*

---

## Pumpkin pie

shortcrust pastry made with $1\frac{1}{2}$ cups/170 g flour

$1\frac{1}{2}$ lb/700 g pumpkin

6 tablespoons/85 g sugar, preferably superfine

$\frac{1}{4}$ teaspoon ground allspice

1 teaspoon ground ginger

3 eggs

$\frac{2}{3}$ cup/1.5 dl creamy milk or light cream

$\frac{1}{2}$ teaspoon ground nutmeg

SERVES 4

Line an 8 in/20 cm pie dish with the pastry and bake it blind.

Peel the pumpkin, cut it in cubes and put the pieces in a large shallow saucepan or sauté pan with 3 tablespoons of water. Cook gently, stirring from time to time, until the liquid starts to run out of the pumpkin. Let it soften over a low heat for about 40 minutes, stirring occasionally. The liquid should run out quite liberally. When the pumpkin is soft and translucent, put it in a wire sieve and drain. Preheat the oven to 375°F/190°C.

Purée the drained pumpkin with the fine blade of a food mill, a blender or a food processor, then add the sugar, allspice and ginger, the eggs and the milk or cream and blend to a creamy purée. Put the mixture into the prepared piecrust, sprinkle the top with nutmeg and bake for an hour. Cover with foil, loosely, if the pastry becomes too brown.

## Pecan pie

| shortcrust pastry made with $1\frac{1}{2}$ cups/170 g flour |
| --- |
| $\frac{3}{4}$ stick/85 g butter, softened |
| scant $\frac{1}{2}$ cup/85 g soft light brown sugar |
| 1 tablespoon vanilla sugar |
| 3 eggs |
| 4 tablespoons corn syrup |
| $1\frac{1}{2}$ cups/170 g pecans |
| salt |

SERVES 4–6

Preheat the oven to 425°F/220°C.

Line an 8 in/20 cm pie dish with the pastry and bake it blind. Cream the butter and the sugars together, either in a food processor or by hand, and then beat in the eggs one at a time. Stir in the honey, the nuts and a pinch of salt. Fill the cooked pie shell with the mixture and bake for 30 minutes. To test the filling, insert the point of a knife into the middle of the pie—if it comes out clean, the pie is ready. Eat it warm—not really hot or cold.

## Almond tart

| 1 stick/115 g unsalted butter, softened |
| --- |
| $\frac{1}{2}$ cup/115 g sugar, preferably superfine |
| 3 egg yolks |
| 2 cups/225 g ground almonds |
| 5 tablespoons/70 ml heavy cream, whipped |
| 2 teaspoons dark rum or $\frac{1}{2}$ teaspoon grated lemon peel |
| flaky pastry made with 2 cups/225 g flour |
| egg and milk for glazing |

SERVES 4–6

Cream the butter and sugar together until pale and light, add the egg yolks and beat for 2 minutes, then lightly mix in the almonds, cream and rum. If you prefer, add grated lemon peel instead of the rum. Preheat the oven to 400°F/200°C.

Divide the pastry in two, one part slightly larger than the other. Form the smaller of the two pieces into a ball and roll it out into a round the thickness of a penny, leaving it untrimmed. Moisten a baking sheet. Transfer the rolled-out pastry onto it. Spread the almond mixture evenly over it, leaving a margin of about 1 in/2.5 cm around the edge.

Form the second piece of the pastry into a ball and roll it out slightly larger and thicker than the first piece. Dampen the edges of the bottom layer of pastry, lay the cover over the top and press the two together lightly. Trim and notch the edge. Glaze the top with egg and milk, make a pattern of lines over it with a knife and bake for 35–40 minutes. When it is cooked, take it out and sprinkle the top with a little sugar.

This tart is often seen in French pastry shops, a shining brown puff, the top decorated with one of a thousand different geometric designs, the middle varying from a smooth honey-colored paste made with confectioners' sugar to a solid, granular marzipan made with whole eggs. It makes a delicious dessert and is equally good for tea.

## Golden sponge

| 1 stick/115 g butter |
| --- |
| $\frac{1}{2}$ cup/115 g sugar, preferably superfine |
| 2 eggs |
| 1 cup/115 g self-rising flour |
| 2–3 tablespoons milk |
| 6–8 tablespoons Golden Syrup or maple syrup |

SERVES 4–6

Cream the butter and sugar together, beat in the eggs one at a time, alternating with a little flour. Stir in the rest of the flour, then add 2–3 tablespoons milk to lighten the mixture, which should be soft and drop lightly from the spoon. Butter a pudding bowl and put the syrup in the bottom. Turn the mixture into the bowl, cover and steam for 2 hours. Turn out onto a dish to serve it and, if you wish, pass syrup around separately.

## Christmas pudding

| 2 cups/225 g shredded suet |
| --- |
| $1\frac{1}{4}$ cups/225 g light brown sugar |
| $1\frac{1}{3}$ cups/225 g raisins |
| $1\frac{1}{3}$ cups/225 g sultanas |
| $\frac{1}{2}$ cup/115 g candied peel |
| $\frac{1}{2}$ teaspoon mixed spice |
| $\frac{1}{4}$ teaspoon ground nutmeg |
| 2 cups/225 g fresh white bread crumbs |
| 1 cup/115 g flour |
| $\frac{2}{3}$ cup/115 g blanched almonds, cut in halves |
| $\frac{3}{4}$ cup/115 g glacé cherries |

4 eggs

$\frac{2}{3}$ cup/1.5 dl milk

$\frac{1}{2}$ wine glass brandy

MAKES 2 PUDDINGS, EACH SERVING 8 OR MORE

Prepare all the dry ingredients and mix them together. Whisk the eggs well, add the milk and mix thoroughly with the dry ingredients. Let the mixture stand for 12 hours in a cool place, add the brandy, put into well-greased pudding bowls and cover tightly with foil or muslin.

Boil for 8 hours or longer. Before serving, reboil for 2–3 hours. Like all Christmas puddings, these are best made a month or so before, and improve with keeping.

This recipe is based on the English royal family's Christmas pudding.

---

## Arlettes

puff pastry made with 2 cups/225 g flour (you can use leftover pastry but it must be in a thickish piece)

confectioners' sugar

MAKES ABOUT 16

Preheat the oven to 350°F/180°C.

Cut a rectangular block of puff pastry across the grain into $\frac{1}{2}$ in/1 cm strips. Put each one down flat on a pastry board dusted with confectioners' sugar; roll it out as thinly as possible. Dust the top lavishly with more sugar sprinkled through a sieve, and place on a dampened baking sheet. Fill the baking sheet with more slices rolled out and dusted with confectioners' sugar in the same way. Bake at the bottom of the oven for 6 minutes, then take them out and turn up the heat to 425°F/220°C.

Dust the arlettes with more of the sifted sugar and put them back at the top of the oven for 2–3 minutes until they are beautifully shiny and brown. Place them on a rack to cool.

These crisp, feathery, shiny biscuits are the very simplest thing to make; eat them with strawberries or raspberries and cream or with ice cream.

---

## Madeleines

2 eggs

$\frac{1}{2}$ cup/55 g self-rising flour

$\frac{1}{4}$ cup/55 g sugar, preferably superfine

5 tablespoons unsalted butter, softened

squeeze of lemon juice or a little grated lemon or orange peel

MAKES ABOUT 24

Preheat the oven to 375°F/190°C.

Separate the eggs and add the sugar to the yolks, beat well (at a slow speed if you are using an electric mixer) until the sugar is dissolved and the mixture is very pale and fine. Add a good squeeze of fresh lemon juice or some grated lemon or orange peel, the butter and then the flour, beating the mixture all the time.

When it is light and well beaten, stir and break up the egg whites with a fork and beat them in briefly (using a slightly higher speed if using a mixer) until they are well mixed.

Butter shell-shaped madeleine pans and put a teaspoon of the mixture in each shell. Bake for about 20 minutes until they are golden brown. Take out and let them set for 2–3 minutes before you remove them to cool on a wire rack. They are best eaten while still warm.

---

## Cream puffs

choux pastry made with $\frac{3}{4}$ cup/85 g flour

1 egg beaten with a pinch of salt for glazing

$1\frac{1}{4}$ cups/3 dl heavy cream

1 teaspoon vanilla sugar

**for the icing:**

$\frac{1}{4}$ lb/115 g semisweet baking chocolate

2 teaspoons rum

1 stick/115 g butter, softened

MAKES 8–10 PUFFS

Preheat the oven to 350°F/180°C.

Moisten two baking sheets. Put rounded tablespoons of the choux pastry, well spaced out, on the baking sheets or, better still, put the dough in a pastry bag with a $\frac{1}{2}$ in/1 cm nozzle and pipe out rounds of dough about $1\frac{1}{2}$ in/4 cm across and 1 in/2.5 cm high. Brush the tops with the beaten egg and flatten the puffs lightly with the pastry brush.

Bake for 20 minutes, or until they are firm and golden. Put them on a wire rack to cool, and while they are still warm prick a small hole in the bottom of each to let the steam escape.

Whip the cream lightly with the vanilla sugar and

when the puffs are cool and crisp open them a little and fill them with whipped cream. Alternatively pipe it in through the hole in the bottom.

To make the icing, melt the chocolate in the top of a double boiler, together with the rum. Remove from the heat and add the butter, a little at a time, stirring in each addition. Put the saucepan in cold water and beat until the icing is thick enough to spread on top of the puffs. Allow the icing to cool and set before serving.

---

## Hazelnut cakes

| |
|---|
| 3 egg whites |
| ¾ cup/170 g sugar, preferably superfine |
| 1½ cups/170 g ground hazelnuts |

MAKES 12–18

Preheat the oven to 350°F/180°C.

Whisk the egg whites to a stiff peak and fold in the sugar and ground hazelnuts lightly but thoroughly. Spread the mixture ½–¾ in/1–2 cm thick on a sheet of foil dusted with flour in a baking pan and bake for about 20 minutes or until brown and crisp on top. Cut into squares, turn them over carefully and put them back in the oven at 275°F/140°C to dry off for 10–15 minutes.

Hazelnut cakes have a delicious rich flavor and should be soft in the center but with a slight crunch to them.

---

## Rolled oat cakes

| |
|---|
| ¾ stick/85 g butter |
| 6 tablespoons/85 g sugar, preferably superfine |
| 2 tablespoons Golden Syrup |
| 2½ cups/170 g rolled oats |

MAKES APPROXIMATELY 20

Preheat the oven to 350°F/180°C.

Melt the butter, sugar and syrup together in a small saucepan over a gentle heat. Stir in the oats, mixing them in well. Spread the mixture about ¼ in/5 mm thick in a greased baking pan and bake for 15 minutes until golden.

Allow to cool a little, then mark out into rectangles with a knife and break into pieces. Allow to cool completely before eating or storing.

## Gingerbread men

| |
|---|
| ½ stick/55 g butter |
| ½ cup/115 g sugar |
| 4 tablespoons molasses |
| 3 cups/340 g self-rising flour |
| 2 teaspoons ground ginger |
| ½ teaspoon each of ground cinnamon and ground cloves |
| salt |

**for the icing**:

| |
|---|
| 2–3 tablespoons confectioners' sugar |
| few drops lemon juice or water |

MAKES 15–20

Preheat the oven to 350°F/180°C.

Cream the butter and sugar thoroughly, add the molasses and 4 tablespoons of water, and blend. Mix the flour, spices and a pinch of salt in a bowl, pour into the butter, sugar and molasses mixture and blend quickly until the mixture is like fine crumbs. Turn it out into a bowl and work to a dough with your hands. Add a little more water if it feels too dry.

Roll out half the mixture on a floured board and cut out gingerbread-men shapes with a knife or a cutter. Transfer them carefully to a greased baking sheet with a spatula and bake for 8–10 minutes. Allow to cool on a rack, then decorate with white icing made from the confectioners' sugar mixed to a paste with a few drops of lemon juice or water. It can be put on with a toothpick.

ALTERNATIVE: *the gingerbread men can be decorated before they are cooked with currants, raisins and bits of candied peel to provide them with little eyes, coats, buttons and hair.*

---

## Brownies

| |
|---|
| 6 tablespoons/85 g shortening or butter |
| 3 tablespoons/45 g cocoa powder |
| 1 cup/225 g sugar, preferably vanilla sugar |
| 2 large eggs |
| ½ cup/55 g all-purpose flour |
| ½ teaspoon baking powder |
| salt |

MAKES 16

Preheat the oven to 350°F/180°C.

Melt the shortening in a pan, remove from the heat

and stir in the cocoa and sugar. Add the eggs one at a time, beating them in thoroughly. Add the flour and baking powder sieved together and $\frac{1}{4}$ teaspoon salt. Beat gently but thoroughly and then pour the mixture into an 8 in/20 cm square pan. Bake for 30 minutes and cut in 2 in/5 cm squares when cool.

━━━━━━◆━━━━━━

# Summer sponge cake

| 4 eggs |
| --- |
| $\frac{1}{2}$ teaspoon cream of tartar |
| $1\frac{1}{2}$ cups/340 g sugar, preferably superfine, including |
| 2 teaspoons vanilla sugar |
| $\frac{2}{3}$ cup/1.5 dl boiling water |
| 2 cups/225 g self-rising flour |
| salt |

**for the filling:**

| 4 tablespoons homemade jam |
| --- |
| $\frac{1}{2}$ cup/115 ml heavy cream, whipped |

Preheat the oven to 300°F/160°C.

Butter and flour a deep 10 in/25 cm round pan. Separate the eggs and beat the whites with the cream of tartar, preferably with a hand-held electric mixer, until they are stiff. In a separate bowl, beat the yolks with 3 tablespoons of cold water for at least 3 minutes with the mixer until the yolks start to turn pale, gradually adding the sugar and then the boiling water in a thin stream.

Sieve the flour with a pinch of salt, then, using a spatula or large metal spoon, gradually fold the flour into the egg-yolk mixture, followed by the beaten egg whites. Turn the mixture into the cake pan and bake for 2 hours.

Allow to cool, then cut the cake in half and spread one half with jam and the other with whipped cream. Sandwich the two halves of this white, light, fluffy cake together and sift the top with a little confectioners' sugar.

ALTERNATIVES: *put chocolate or coffee butter icing inside and white, pink or chocolate icing outside.*

━━━━━━◆━━━━━━

# Madeira cake

| large piece of candied citron peel or a large slice of candied lemon or orange peel |
| --- |
| 1 stick/115 g butter |
| $\frac{5}{8}$ cup/140 g sugar |
| $1\frac{1}{4}$ cups/140 g self-rising flour |
| $\frac{1}{4}$ cup/30 g cornstarch |
| salt |
| 2 eggs |
| 2 tablespoons milk |

Preheat the oven to 350°F/180°C.

Soften the citron peel, if using, by soaking it in a little warm water. Cream the butter and sugar together until they are pale and creamy. Sieve the flour and cornstarch together and add a pinch of salt. Add one egg to the creamed butter and sugar, beat it in, then add half the flour and stir it in; add the remaining egg and flour alternately. Finally stir in the milk. Turn the mixture into a deep, buttered and floured 6 in/15 cm cake pan and bake in the center of the oven for $1\frac{1}{4}$ hours. After half an hour, decorate the top of the cake with strips of peel arranged in a star in the center.

This good, plain, moist cake is excellent in the middle of the morning with a glass of wine or a cup of coffee or tea.

ALTERNATIVE: **Cherry cake.** *This can be made using the same recipe, but add $1\frac{1}{2}$ cups/225 g glacé cherries, lightly tossed in flour, at the end of the mixing. Decorate with white frosting and stud the top with a few halved glacé cherries. It is a real children's treat and is not too rich.*

━━━━━━◆━━━━━━

# Angel food cake

| 4 egg whites |
| --- |
| $\frac{1}{4}$ teaspoon cream of tartar |
| $\frac{5}{8}$ cup/140 g sugar, preferably superfine, including |
| 2 tablespoons/30 g vanilla sugar |
| 7 tablespoons/50 g flour |
| 2 tablespoons/15 g cornstarch |
| salt |

Preheat the oven to 325°F/170°C.

Dust a tube pan with flour, but do not grease it or the cake will become too brown. Beat the egg whites until foamy, add the cream of tartar and beat again to a soft peak. Sieve the sugars and flours together four times and add a pinch of salt. Fold carefully into the egg whites, two tablespoons at a time, until the mixture is even. Spoon the mixture into the tube pan. Bake for 30 minutes and leave the cake in the pan until cool. Then turn this airy, sugary sponge out of the pan and coat with whipped cream or a thin white glacé icing, lightly flavored with vanilla.

---

## Devil's food cake

*3 oz/85 g semisweet baking chocolate*

*1½ cups/310 g dark brown sugar*

*1 teaspoon vanilla sugar*

*2 tablespoons dark rum*

*1 stick/115 g butter, softened*

*2 eggs*

*2 cups/225 g self-rising flour*

*4 tablespoons milk*

Put the chocolate, about half of the brown sugar, the vanilla sugar and rum into a small saucepan, add 2 tablespoons of water and heat gently, stirring until the mixture becomes smooth. Allow to cool. Preheat the oven to 350°F/180°C.
Cream the butter and remaining sugar and beat until light and fluffy. Beat in the eggs, one at a time. Add the cold chocolate and rum mixture and beat again. Add the flour and milk and mix them in thoroughly with a wooden spoon. Grease three 8 in/20 cm layer cake pans and divide the mixture between them. Bake for 20–25 minutes and allow to cool in the pans for 5–10 minutes before turning out onto racks. When completely cold, fill with two layers of chocolate cream filling.

---

## Walnut cake

*1½ sticks/170 g butter*

*¾ cup/170 g sugar, preferably superfine*

*3 eggs*

*1½ cups/170 g self-rising flour*

*salt*

*½ cup/85 g coarsely chopped walnuts, plus a few whole nuts*

**for the filling:**

*5 tablespoons/70 g butter, softened*

*scant 1¼ cups/170 g confectioners' sugar*

*3 tablespoons strong black coffee*

Preheat the oven to 325°F/170°C.
Grease a deep 6 in/15 cm cake pan. Cream the butter and sugar until light and pale, then beat in the eggs one at a time, adding a tablespoon of the flour after you have beaten in the second egg to prevent the mixture curdling. Lightly stir in the flour and a pinch of salt, using a wooden spoon or spatula. Do not use a mixer as too much beating toughens the flour. Stir in the chopped walnuts, turn the mixture into the greased cake pan and bake for an hour. Cool, halve, and put in the filling. To make the filling, put all the ingredients into a bowl or food processor and beat them to a smooth cream. When the cake is cold, pour white frosting over it and smooth it with a spatula. Decorate with halved walnuts. Leave to set for several hours.

---

## Dundee cake

*1½ cups/170 g flour*

*salt*

*1 teaspoon mixed spices*

*1½ sticks/170 g butter*

*generous ¾ cup/170 g brown sugar*

*4 eggs*

*⅔ cup/115 g blanched almonds and 1 cup/115 ground almonds*

*¾ cup/115 g each glacé cherries and chopped candied peel*

*1⅓ cups/225 g each of currants, sultanas and raisins*

Preheat the oven to 325°F/170°C.
Mix the flour, a pinch of salt and the mixed spices and sieve them together. Cream the butter and sugar, beat the eggs and add the flour and eggs alternately to the creamed mixture, beating before each addition. Cut all but about 8 of the blanched almonds into slivers. Add the slivered almonds, ground almonds, cherries and candied peel to the mixture. Shake the currants, sultanas and raisins in a little extra flour and stir them in. Turn the mixture into a lined, greased 8 in/20 cm cake pan, decorate the top with a star of whole almonds, and bake for 2½–3 hours, covering the top lightly with foil about halfway through. Test with the point of a skewer: if it comes out clean the cake is cooked. Allow to cool in the pan.

---

## Twelfth Day cake

*4 cups/450 g self-rising flour*

*1 teaspoon each mixed spices, ground ginger and nutmeg*

| |
|---|
| *1 lb/450 g butter* |
| *2¼ cups/450 g dark brown sugar* |
| *6 eggs* |
| *1½ cups/225 g candied peel, chopped* |
| *2 cups/340 g each of currants, sultanas and raisins—large seedless ones if possible* |
| *1½ cups/225 g halved glacé cherries* |
| *1 cup/115 g ground almonds* |
| *⅔ cup/115 g blanched almonds, cut in slivers* |
| *1 large glass Madeira or brandy* |

MAKES 2 LARGE CAKES

Preheat the oven to 350°F/180°C.

Sieve the flour and spices together. Soften the butter, but do not let it become oily. Cream the butter and sugar until light and pale, and beat in the eggs one at a time, adding a tablespoon of the flour and spices after each egg. Add the remaining flour, mix it in with a wooden spoon and then stir in the peel, fruit, almonds and Madeira or brandy. Turn the mixture into two lined and buttered pans and bake for 2½–3 hours. Look at the cakes from time to time and turn them around if they are rising unevenly. Cover them with a sheet of foil when they are starting to brown and before they start to blacken. Twelfth Day is 6 January and is, according to old custom, a day of kings, cakes and wassailing. A Twelfth Day cake was traditionally lavishly decorated with colored confectionery designed as stars, palaces and dragons, and should have a bean and a pea inside; the person who receives the bean is king for the night and the one who receives the pea is queen.

ALTERNATIVE: **Christmas cake.** *Cover the entire cake with marzipan and royal icing*

# White frosting

| |
|---|
| *2 tablespoons/30 g vanilla sugar* |
| *scant 1 cup/200 g sugar* |
| *1 egg white* |

Put the sugars with 5 tablespoons/70 ml of water into a small saucepan and stir over a low heat until the sugar has dissolved completely. Bring to the boil and continue to boil until the syrup reaches a temperature of 240°F/120°C, at which point a drop of the syrup makes a soft ball when dropped into a cup of cold water.

Remove from the heat and set the pan aside.

Whisk the egg white in a clean bowl until it is stiff, then pour in the syrup in a thin stream, whisking all the time and continuing to whisk until the mixture is very thick.

Pour or spread the frosting over the cold cake and tidy it up with a spatula.

This icing should be very white and light.

# Royal icing

| |
|---|
| *3¾ cups/450 g confectioners' sugar* |
| *2 egg whites* |
| *salt* |
| *2 teaspoons lemon juice* |

MAKES ENOUGH TO COVER 1 LARGE CAKE

Sieve the confectioners' sugar. Whisk the egg whites with a pinch of salt until thick and soft. Add the lemon juice and then gradually whisk in the sugar until the mixture is smooth and thick.

Use the icing straightaway, spreading it on with a spatula. Leave it to dry overnight before cutting the cake. This is the icing to use for covering Christmas cake.

# Orange glacé icing

| |
|---|
| *generous 1¾ cups/225 g confectioners' sugar* |
| *juice of ½–1 orange* |

MAKES ENOUGH TO COVER AN 8 in/20 cm CAKE

Sieve the confectioners' sugar into a bowl and add the juice of half an orange, stirring it in well until the confectioners' sugar has completely blended in the juice. If you want a thin, translucent glaze add more orange juice. Spread the mixture over the cake with a spatula. Use for sponge cakes.

ALTERNATIVE: **Lemon glacé icing**. *Use lemon juice instead of the orange juice.*

# Butter icing

| |
|---|
| *1½ sticks/170 g butter* |
| *1 heaping cup/170 g confectioners' sugar* |
| *1 teaspoon orange or lemon juice, or very strong coffee or cocoa powder* |

# Cakes and Preserves

MAKES ENOUGH FOR I LARGE CAKE

Beat the butter and sugar together to a cream and beat in the flavor you have chosen. If using orange or lemon, a little grated peel can be added for a stronger flavor.

## Chocolate cream filling

| |
|---|
| 3 oz/85 g semisweet baking chocolate |
| 2 tablespoons/30 g butter |
| ⅔ cup/1.5 dl heavy cream |
| 1 cup/140 g confectioners' sugar |
| salt |

Melt the chocolate and butter together in a bowl over a pan of hot water. Allow to cool. Mix in the cream, confectioners' sugar and a tiny pinch of salt, and beat with an electric mixer or by hand with a balloon whisk until thick.

Allow 8–10 minutes for beating with an electric mixer and a little longer when whisking the mixture by hand.

## Marzipan

| |
|---|
| generous 1¾ cups/225 g confectioners' sugar, sieved |
| 1 cup/225 g sugar, preferably superfine |
| 3 cups/340 g ground almonds |
| 2 eggs |
| 1 teaspoon rum or brandy |

COVERS I LARGE CAKE

Mix the dry ingredients thoroughly in a bowl. Beat the eggs in a small bowl with the rum or brandy and add most of this mixture to the dry ingredients. Work everything together thoroughly to make a paste, using a wooden spoon at first and then your hands. Add more of the egg mixture if the paste is too crumbly—it should be firm enough to handle but pliable enough to roll out.

Scatter some confectioners' sugar on the board so that the marzipan doesn't stick too much and roll out the mixture to ¼ in/5 mm thick with a rolling pin.

ALTERNATIVES: *if you like a very pronounced almond flavor, add a few drops of almond essence to the mixture; and instead of rum or brandy, marzipan can be flavored with a few drops of rosewater or orange-flower water.*

## Making jam

Making good jam does not necessarily mean an afternoon's devotion to the preserving pan. Making small quantities is perfectly practical and does not take long. But before you start, it is as well to know a few golden rules.

**Preparation:** have everything ready and scrupulously clean. You can warm the sugar slightly in a low oven before adding it to the fruit; this helps it to dissolve quickly.

**Pectin:** this is the substance, present in certain fruits, which together and in balance with sugar and fruit-acid ensures a good set in jams. Fruit that is slightly unripe contains more pectin than ripe fruit; and fruits that are tart even when ripe, such as apples, quinces, red currants, black currants, gooseberries, Seville oranges and lemons, are particularly rich in pectin. When making jam with fruit that is low in pectin, such as strawberries, the setting can be helped along with the addition of lemon juice or fresh red currant juice. For a really firm but less good result, commercial pectin made from apple pulp can be added.

**Setting point:** test the jam frequently after it has boiled for 10 minutes. To see if setting point has been reached, cool a little of the hot jam on a cold plate and then nudge it with your finger: if it wrinkles and clings to the spot, the jam is ready. Skim it at this point, to remove scum and froth.

**The jars:** when setting point has been reached, allow the jam to cool a little to prevent the fruit rising to the top of the jars, before pouring it into clean heated jars. If using cellophane covers with rubber bands, put a layer of melted paraffin wax on top of the hot jam to seal it from the air. To ensure a tight fit, moisten the cellophane on the outside before putting the covers onto the cool jars.

**Storing:** store homemade jams in a cool, dark, dry place: this way they will keep better.

## Seville orange marmalade

| |
|---|
| 3 lb/1.5 kg Seville oranges |
| 2 lemons |
| about 6 lb/2.5 kg sugar |

MAKES ABOUT 3 QUARTS/1.5 KG

Scrub the oranges and lemons with a vegetable

brush, peel them and cut the peel into fairly coarse strips. Chop the orange and lemon pulp and remove the seeds and any pith. Tie the pith and seeds in a muslin bag—they contain the pectin that sets the marmalade, so don't leave out this step. Put the peel and flesh in a preserving pan with the bag of seeds, add $3\frac{1}{2}$ quarts/3 liters of water and simmer gently until the volume has reduced by about one-third.

Squeeze the bag of seeds to press out all the juice, and discard it. Measure the cooked pulp and return it to the preserving pan together with 1 lb/450 g sugar for each $2\frac{1}{2}$ cups/6 dl of pulp. Stir over a gentle heat until the sugar has dissolved and then boil until setting point is reached; for this test in the same way as for jam.

Allow the marmalade to cool a little to prevent the peel rising to the top of the jars, and then ladle into hot, dry jam jars. Keep a week or two, or longer, before eating.

## Clear quince jelly

2 lb/900 g ripe golden quinces

about 4 cups/900 g sugar

MAKES 3–4 QUARTS/1.5–2 KG

Wash the quinces, cut them up into coarse pieces and put them into a saucepan with about 2 quarts/ 1.75 liters of water. Bring to the boil and simmer gently until the fruit is completely soft.

Strain the liquid from the cooked quinces by pouring it into a jelly bag to drip into a bowl. Don't squeeze the bag at all—just let it drip, so that the liquid runs out a clear pale pink. When it has stopped dripping, throw away the quince pulp and measure the strained juice into a large preserving pan. Add 2 cups/450 g of sugar for every $2\frac{1}{2}$ cups/ 6 dl of juice. Bring to the boil slowly, stirring to dissolve the sugar completely before the liquid starts to boil, then boil rapidly until the jelly sets when dropped on a cold plate.

Skim and pour the jelly into warm clean jars and then cover.

This delicate jelly is an exquisite clear red and is delicious both on bread and with pork.

ALTERNATIVES: **Crabapple jelly**. *Make in exactly the same way and eat with cold meats and poultry.*
**Medlar jelly**. *This also is made in the same way but*

*the equivalent amount of medlars will yield much less juice, so the result is about $1\frac{1}{2}$–2 quarts/700–900 g of jelly. Eat medlar jelly, which is a clear pink and has a slightly tart flavor, with game or lamb.*

## Red currant jelly

2 cups/450 g sugar for every $2\frac{1}{4}$ cups/6 dl red currant juice

This method is very extravagant, but makes such superb jelly that if you have plenty of red currants it is well worthwhile. Choose some slightly unripe ones as these have more acid and help set the jelly. To extract the juice, push the currants into large canning jars, cover them and put the jars in a large pan of water. Bring the water to the boil and let it seethe until the currants have sunk in the jars and their juice has run out. This will take perhaps 2–3 hours.

Hang the fruit in a jelly bag or in fine muslin cloth over a bowl and let the juice drip through overnight. Measure the juice and put it in a preserving pan with the correct amount of sugar, stir over a low heat until the sugar dissolves completely and bring to the boil. Boil rapidly until setting point is reached. Skim well and pour very quickly into hot clean jars. Cover when cool, and do not tip or shake the jars while the jelly is cooling.

If this method seems too wasteful, mash the berries to extract more juice before putting them into the jelly bag, but this slightly darkens the color.

## Peach conserve

1 quart/9 dl cooked peaches (about $2\frac{1}{2}$ lb/1 kg fresh ones)

juice of 1 lemon

2 cups/450 g sugar

small glass of brandy

MAKES ABOUT 3 QUARTS/1.5 KG

This is an excellent way of using up bruised peaches.

To skin the fruit, dip each peach for half a minute into boiling water, then peel off the skin with a blunt knife. Cut the peaches in half and take out the stones, cutting away any bruised flesh. Put the fruit into a large pan and simmer very gently for 45 minutes with a tablespoon of water. Remove the pan from the heat and measure the cooked peaches in a measuring pitcher, then return them to the preserving pan together with the lemon juice and sugar. Put the pan over a gentle heat and stir until the sugar has dissolved, then turn up the heat and boil for 6 minutes. Remove the pan from the heat, cover it and leave in a cool place overnight.

The next morning return the peach pulp to the stove, bring to the boil, stir in the brandy and pour into warm clean jars. Allow to cool and then cover in the usual way.

## Strawberry jam

| 3 quarts/2 kg firm strawberries |
| 8 cups/2 kg sugar |
| juice of 2 lemons |

MAKES ABOUT 6 QUARTS/2.5 KG

Warm the sugar in a low oven. Put the firm strawberries and the lemon juice in a preserving pan and let them soften over a very gentle heat. The juice will gradually run out of the fruit—stir the pan from time to time to help it along.

When the strawberries are floating in their own juice, which may take 20–30 minutes, add the warmed sugar and stir until it dissolves. Bring to a rapid boil, stirring frequently, and boil until the jam reaches setting point. Take the pan off the heat, draw the scum to the sides and skim it off carefully. Allow the jam to cool a little before ladling it into heated clean jars.

Strawberry jam never sets quite as well as other jams unless, as here, you add some form of acid- and pectin-forming fruit such as lemon.

## Gooseberry jam

| 2 cups/450 g sugar for every 1 pint/450 g gooseberries |

Top and tail the gooseberries. Put them in a preserving pan with ⅔ cup/1.5 dl of water for every 1 lb/450 g of fruit and bring to the boil. Let the fruit soften for about 15 minutes over a low heat, then add the sugar, stirring to dissolve it before the liquid returns to the boil. Let it boil steadily and rather fast for 10 minutes.

Gooseberry jam, because it gets very thick, has a tendency to burn. To avoid this, stir it with a wooden spoon while it boils, or stand the preserving pan on an asbestos pad.

By the time it has boiled 11–12 minutes—depending on the quantity of gooseberries—it should have reached setting point. Skim quickly and carefully, pour into heated clean jars and cover immediately.

Gooseberry jam has a particularly beautiful color.

## Black currant jam

| 2½ quarts/2 kg black currants |
| 8 cups/2 kg sugar |

MAKES 7–8 QUARTS/3–3.5 KG

With a fork, pick the stalks from the currants and remove any green fruit. Put the currants in a preserving pan with 1 cup/225 g of the sugar and 2½ cups/6 dl of water, bring slowly to the boil and simmer for 10–15 minutes. Add the remaining sugar and stir until it has dissolved before starting the simmering again, then simmer for 15 minutes or until the jam sets firmly. Skim well, stir, pour into heated clean jars and cover.

This makes a soft and thick jam. So often black currant jam is hard, or has little chewy currants that feel disagreeable between the teeth, but simmering before the bulk of the sugar goes in softens the fruit completely.

## Lemon curd

| 2–3 lemons |
| 1 stick/115 g butter |
| 1 cup/225 g sugar, preferably superfine |
| 2–3 eggs, beaten |

MAKES ABOUT 2 QUARTS/900 KG

Pare the rind from the lemons very thinly. Squeeze the juice from the lemons and strain it. Melt the butter, add sugar, lemon juice, lemon peel and beaten eggs, mix and thicken gently in the top half of a double boiler, or an earthenware jar standing in a pan of hot, but not boiling, water. Stir from time to time until the mixture coats the back of the spoon. Strain the curd through a wire sieve and bottle it in heated clean jars.

# Mincemeat

| |
|---|
| 1⅓ cups/225 g each of currants, raisins and sultanas |
| ⅓ cup/55 g blanched almonds |
| ¾ cup/115 g candied peel |
| 1 carrot |
| 6 firm hard green apples |
| 1 lemon |
| 2 cups/225 g shredded suet |
| scant 1¼ cups/225 g dark brown sugar |
| 1 teaspoon ground cinnamon and ground cloves, mixed |
| good grating of nutmeg |
| ½ teaspoon ground mace |
| 1 glass each of whisky and sherry |

MAKES 3–4 QUARTS/1.5–2 KG

Chop the currants, raisins, almonds and the candied peel. Wash, scrape and grate the carrot coarsely. Peel, core and chop the apples finely, wash the lemon, grate its rind and squeeze the juice.

Mix all the ingredients except the whisky and sherry in a large bowl and keep covered in the kitchen for three days, stirring daily. Add the alcohol, pack into clean jars and cover. Store in a cool, dry place.

This mincemeat will keep for about two months. If you want to keep it longer, put the mixture in the oven at 250°F/130°C for 3 hours before adding the alcohol.

---

# Green tomato sour

| |
|---|
| 6 lb/2.5 kg small green tomatoes |
| 2 lb/900 g onions |
| salt |
| 3 green sweet peppers |
| 3½ cups/700 g light brown sugar |
| 3 tablespoons mustard seed |
| 1 tablespoon coriander seed |
| ½ teaspoon celery seed |
| 2 teaspoons turmeric |
| 5 cups/1 liter distilled vinegar |

MAKES ABOUT 8 QUARTS/3.5 KG

Slice the tomatoes thinly and peel and chop the onions. Put them in layers in a large earthenware bowl, sprinkling each layer with plenty of salt. Let them stand overnight. Drain off the liquid and put the tomatoes and onions together with the green peppers, deseeded and chopped, the sugar, spices and vinegar in a preserving pan—the vinegar should barely cover the vegetables. Simmer for 2 hours, return the mixture to the bowl and allow to stand overnight.

Simmer the chutney further for about half an hour until there is just enough liquid—it should be thickish—to cover the vegetables when they are packed together. Pour the chutney into hot clean jars and keep for at least three weeks before opening and eating.

Despite its name, green tomato sour is in fact not at all sour but is a very sweet chutney with an interesting mellow flavor.

---

# Pimento chutney

| |
|---|
| 2 red sweet peppers |
| 2 green sweet peppers |
| 3 onions |
| 4 tablespoons olive oil |
| 1 clove garlic |
| 1 lb/450 g tomatoes |
| salt |
| ½ teaspoon ground ginger |
| 1 teaspoon mixed spices |
| 12 allspice berries, coarsely crushed |
| ¼ lb/115 g raisins |
| ¾ cup/170 g sugar |
| ⅔ cup/1.5 dl white wine vinegar |

MAKES ABOUT 2 QUARTS/900 G

Peel the onions, chop them coarsely and sweat them in the olive oil over low heat. Meanwhile remove the pith and seeds from the peppers and cut them in large flat pieces each about the size of a postage stamp. Peel and chop the garlic and skin and chop the tomatoes.

When the onions are tender, add the peppers, a little salt, ginger, mixed spice, the coarsely crushed allspice and chopped clove of garlic. Let them cook gently for 10 minutes, then add the tomatoes and raisins. Cook for 10 minutes more, then add the sugar and wine vinegar and simmer for 2 hours or until the chutney is rather thick and a beautiful bronze color. Pour into clean jars, seal them and keep in a cool, dry place for at least two weeks before opening and eating.

This excellent chutney is a good accompaniment for all cold meats and game.

# Drinks

## Iced tea

4 tea bags
5 cups/1 liter cold water
1–2 teaspoons sugar
4 sprigs mint or 4 slices lemon, or both

SERVES 4
Put the tea bags in a pitcher, add the cold water, and leave to steep overnight in the refrigerator. Strain, stir in the sugar and serve with a sprig of mint or a slice of lemon—or both—in each glass.

## Lemonade

4 lemons
3 cups/700 g sugar
2 tablespoons/30 g citric acid powder
1 teaspoon cream of tartar
5 cups/1 liter water

MAKES ABOUT 5 CUPS/1 LITER OF CONCENTRATE
Pare the skin of 1 lemon and squeeze the juice of all of them. Put the lemon skin and juice into a bowl with the sugar, citric acid powder and cream of tartar. Bring the water to the boil and pour it over the mixture. Allow to cool and store in clean bottles. Dilute with water, soda or Perrier water.

## Ginger beer

about ½ cup/30 g ginger root, in pieces
5 quarts/4.5 liters water
1 lemon, sliced
1 teaspoon cream of tartar
2 cups/450 g sugar
2 tablespoons/15 g brewer's yeast
1 egg white

MAKES 5 QUARTS/4.5 LITERS
Bruise the ginger and put it into a large saucepan with the water. Bring to the boil and simmer for 30 minutes. Remove the ginger, pour into a large bowl and add the sliced lemon, rind and all, the cream of tartar and the sugar. Stir until the sugar has dissolved and leave to cool.
When the liquid is lukewarm, stir in the yeast, cover the bowl with a cloth and leave to ferment for two days. Skim off all the scum and strain the beer

into another bowl. Whisk the egg white into it and transfer it all into clean bottles. You must use thick bottles for ginger beer, preferably with screw tops, because it has a tendency to explode.
Keep for at least three weeks before drinking.

## Sangria

1 bottle red wine, chilled
ice cubes
1 orange, sliced
1 lemon, sliced
small sherry glass of Spanish brandy
⅔ cup/1.5 dl Perrier water
2 teaspoons sugar (optional)
sprig of mint

SERVES 6–10
Half fill a pitcher with ice cubes, add the sliced orange and lemon, pour in the brandy, the bottle of red wine and the Perrier water. Taste and, if needed, add sugar. Top with the mint and serve.

## Glögg

5 cups/1 liter red wine
1¼ cups/6 dl muscatel
⅔ cup/115 g raisins
3 strips orange peel
5 cloves
5 cardamom pods
1 cinnamon stick
2 tablespoons brown sugar
⅔ cup/1.5 dl akvavit
⅓ cup/55 g blanched almonds

SERVES 6–10
Put the red wine, muscatel, raisins, orange peel, slightly bruised spices and sugar into a large earthenware bowl and allow to stand overnight— this draws the flavor out of the spices.
Put the mixture into a large heavy pan or preserving pan and bring it to boiling point. Add all but one tablespoon of the akvavit and the almonds. Just before serving the glögg, heat the remaining akvavit, pour it over the top and light it. Serve immediately in mugs or tumblers, giving each person a spoon with which to eat the raisins and almonds.

# PART THREE

## Presentation

*A sense of style*

# The Pleasures of the Table

As I hope this book amply demonstrates, food in its natural state is beautiful and requires little help from man to enhance its inherent beauty.

Cooking does sometimes alter the look of food, but rarely does it need the sort of persnickety decoration and attention that some cooks, bristling with red and blue ribbons, have advocated over the years. Their ideas seem to me to be the very antithesis of good food and to demonstrate the sort of Victorian primness that caused the legs of chairs to be covered with skirts. If some of the time and energy that they and their followers put into decoration went instead into improving the quality of the food they cook, I for one would be a happier man.

Good, fresh food radiates beauty: when it is growing or living in its natural environment; when it is gathered and presented for sale in the market; and when it is brought into your kitchen ready for preparation.

Food, and the cooking utensils you use to prepare it, should be an endless source of pleasure to the senses, and when the food is finally ready to be eaten you should present it in a simple, fresh and natural way.

## The pleasures of the marketplace
Man seems to have done all he can over the last century to remove the pleasure from buying food. The bustling marketplaces, the specialist fish dealers, butchers and grocers with exquisite displays of good fresh food, rapidly gave way to supermarkets and other such temples of convenience foods. All in the name of progress some would say, but in my opinion these megastores demonstrate a decline into a sad lack of interest in the quality and pleasures of life.

Mercifully there seems to be a renewed concern over the qualities of food and the pleasure of buying it. There seems to be a resurgence of markets and small specialist shops. Some of the brighter supermarkets have noticed this trend, and small areas within their otherwise sterile acres are sprouting proper butchery, fresh fish, bakery and greengrocery departments.

To me a good meal begins in the marketplace. Despite all the preplanning and consultation of cook books that may have gone on before the shopping trip, all plans can be turned upside down when a particularly beautiful pair of crabs or a basket of freshly gathered mushrooms catches your eye and your imagination—I have learned now to go out without a shopping list but with a fairly firm idea of how much I want to spend, and also the number of meals I am marketing for, and to let the quality and freshness of the available food dictate my purchases.

When I return from marketing, I spread out my purchases in bowls, baskets and on platters. Cooking utensils seem to be so sympathetic to raw materials that the whole assembly looks like a seventeenth-century still life and almost too good to eat.

## The pleasures of cooking
Cooking a meal should always be enjoyable. It is quite hard to tell this to an overworked housewife with snivelling children around her skirts and an unappreciative husband to feed day in, day out, but the preparation of food, however simply it is done, can always be a pleasure if you are prepared to make it one. Lowering a brown egg in a perforated steel spoon into a pan of boiling water, timing it for four minutes 15 seconds, scooping it out, carefully placing it into a white eggcup standing on a flower-sprigged plate, adding a slice of brown toast, some yellow butter and a pinch of coarse salt—all such tasks are pleasurable if you are in the mood for them to be so, but if in your mind the whole thing is a chore, then it will be so.

## The pleasures of presentation
Many good pots, pans, casseroles and terrines which normally live in the kitchen are quite handsome enough to bring to the table, unless of course you are giving a stylish and elegant dinner party with sophisticated food to match.

The simple shapes of traditional European stoneware and earthenware cooking pots are perfectly complementary to the food they were designed to cook, and there is no earthly reason why their contents should be decanted into some serving dish for the sake of unity on the dinner table.

Equally, the fine heavy white porcelain bowls, dishes and tureens which have been made through the centuries in France always present food in a way that enhances the quality or beauty of the food itself. Whatever the dish, it is better to choose a simple and elegant frame for it rather than a mess of gilded rococo that detracts from the masterpiece within. What could look finer than a salmon trout lying on a perfectly plain white oval dish, or a green salad sprinkled with chives in a white porcelain bowl?

Elizabeth David, the famous cookery writer, who just after World War II opened our minds to the pleasures of cooking and eating, also opened our eyes to the tawdriness of much contemporary tableware. In her book *French Provincial Cooking*, first published in 1960, she wrote: "Before you buy sets of eccentrically shaped and busily ornamented serving dishes, do just give a thought, which the designers have omitted to do, to the food which is to be served upon them. If you are going to cook a fine big fish, is it necessary to indicate to your guests that

it is a fish by serving it on a dish clumsily devised in the same shape? When you cook a good old-fashioned dish of beans and sausages you do not need a fancy casserole got up to match your dining room wallpaper —a good sturdy brown or dark blue earthenware pot will please you much more in the long run."

You might imagine I am suggesting that all decoration is taboo when it comes to the preparation and presentation of food—this is certainly not the case, but when you are a beginner, keep it simple and rely on classically simple pots, pans and serving dishes, and scrubbed wooden boards for presenting cheese and bread, starched white cloths to cover the table and a jug or vase of simple flowers to decorate it.

But when you have gained confidence, and especially if you have a genuine flair, then this is a most rewarding area for experiment. You should begin to put a few patterned or colored plates or dishes with your plain ones, then gradually you can start to build complex schemes of pattern on pattern and even evoke atmospheres and memories with almost theatrical settings. This is all terrific fun for you and your guests, but you should never lose sight of the fact that it is the food that is the important thing, and that your table setting and decoration should complement rather than submerge it.

## The ground rules
There are one or two simple rules that make the preparation and serving of food a pleasure. In the kitchen always keep your pots, pans and preparation surfaces scrupulously clean and your knives razor sharp. One of the ways of doing this is to clean up as you go along; in a professional restaurant there are young apprentices to see that the chef always has clean utensils to hand, and in your own kitchen you will find that during the preparation of most meals there is plenty of time to clean up as you cook. Really good food never comes out of a dirty, messy kitchen, and the thought of a great stack of dirty dishes dulls one's appetite. From a practical point of view it is usually much easier to wash pots that come straight from the stove, but above all the pleasure you get from working in a clean and tidy kitchen makes the effort more than worth while.

Much the same rules apply to setting the table. The cloth and napkins should be ironed and crisp, and if you are eating at a wooden table see that it is polished or scrubbed—no greasy smears. The silver, if you have it, should shine, the glass should be polished and twinkling, and above all the plates should be hot. The trouble that you take in presentation will be amply repaid by the even greater enjoyment of your food, I promise you.
*Terence Conran*

# Farmhouse Supper

## *Menu*
Baked field mushrooms
Chicken pie
Buttered summer squash
Cheese
Cottage loaf
Blackberries and cream
*To drink*
Ale

---

This appetizing spread is based entirely on the simple natural ingredients that abound in the English countryside—some free and wild like the field mushrooms and blackberries from the hedgerows, some of them cultivated like the squash and the old hen for the chicken pie, all of them simple and honest with a real country flavor.

The surroundings are as appropriately traditional as the food—nothing is false, nothing contrived. An old oak settle, a handwoven linen cloth, pewter dishes, mugs and candlesticks, unpretentious earthenware pie dishes, bowls and pitchers, all of them working as well today as they ever did.

We enjoyed the mushrooms, the pie and the squash, finishing the feast with a selection of cheeses—an English Cheddar truckle, an old Dutch Farmhouse Edam and a black-skinned *alt* Gouda, all washed down with ale drawn from an oak cask.

This traditional farmhouse supper was brought to a close with a bowlful of juicy blackberries, freshly picked from the hedgerows, and topped with dairy cream.

*Field mushrooms look and taste quite different from the cultivated kind. You have to get up early to gather them—they grow best in fields where horses graze.*

## *Menu*
Cucumber sandwiches
Fresh bread and butter
Black currant jam
Summer sponge
Frosted red currants
and black currants
*To drink*
A choice of tisanes

Although afternoon tea is a British custom that has not crossed the Atlantic, the following could provide an original setting for an afternoon's entertainment—the terrace or the conservatory would be the ideal spot.

Of course, a teatime spread such as this is a rare sight these days, but this theatrical

*The "back stage" preparations—a pan full of bubbling fruit soon to become delicious jam.*

*Freshly picked tresses of red currants and black currants, painted with egg white then rolled in sugar, make elegant sweets that burst deliciously with flavor on the palate.*

scene is not difficult to put together, and it would make a marvellous birthday surprise, especially for a fan of the mannered comedies of Oscar Wilde. The trick is to give a light-hearted, witty touch to what would otherwise be an overelaborate anachronism, and here, this has been achieved by the choice of a charming, slightly rustic, old-fashioned tea service of the type you might easily find when burrowing about in junk shops or antique markets. The tablecloth, too, has an essential part to play in setting the scene: it must be white and crisp and prettily decorated with embroidery or lace.

The artistry does not stop at the choice of setting, tablecloth and china—the food is a carefully staged celebration of the fruits of summer. The sponge cake, set on a simple cake stand of fine white porcelain, is filled with whipped cream and raspberry jam; the black currant jam has been freshly made to accompany the bread and butter, and the red currants and black currants, piled into a pretty glass dish, sparkle with a frosting of egg white and fine white sugar. A plate of crustless, triangular, cucumber sandwiches is, of course, an essential prop, and the sandwiches, simply decorated with cress, taste just as good as they look.

The drink is a complete departure from convention. Instead of the expected China or Indian tea, the teapot contains a delicate summery tisane—an infusion made from dried lime flowers. But, as at every good tea party, there is a choice of beverage—a difficult choice between marigold, lemon balm, camomile and mint.

*The tisanes are as pretty as potpourri—bring them to the tea table in an assortment of china bowls. Tisanes made from camomile flowers, lemon balm, mint, lime or marigold petals infused in boiling water make a delicious alternative to conventional teas.*

# Romantic Supper

## Menu
Plateau des fruits de mer
Roast pheasant with raisin sauce
Braised Belgian endive
Grapefruit sherbet
*Wines*
Bollinger champagne
Chambolle Musigny 1969

A romantic, candlelit supper like this should happen at least once in everyone's lifetime. In this case the setting was idyllic—the beautiful marble wall glowed in the candlelight, reminiscent of the seas and rock pools from which the langoustines, mussels, clams, oysters, whelks, cockles and crabs had been freshly gathered. The plates for the first course were shaped like Botticelli's fragile scallop shell and suffused with pink; the glasses were as romantic as the champagne, generous of measure and delicately hand painted; and the silver cutlery and candlesticks were of a classic Edwardian design.

A plateau des fruits de mer is a perfect dish to share with a very good friend—succulent pieces can be offered across the table: a taste of this, a mouthful of that, a sip of wine, an exchange of confidences. The next course was a roasted pheasant carved at the table, the breast in fine slices and the legs left whole to be eaten with the fingers. Finally, a cooling grapefruit sherbet to clear the palate and refresh the body.

The Japanese well understand how to present food so that every bite is filled with symbolism, and something of that art should be reflected in a meal such as this.

*To set the mood, a chilled bottle of Bollinger is delicious with shellfish.*

*The plateau des fruits de mer is a beautiful cornucopia of seafood, heaped on a plain white dish over a bed of crushed ice and seaweed.*

*This scallop-shell plate is perfect for the seafood. The little forks and silver picks are necessary to get at every last vestige of meat.*

*Whole endives, lightly poached in stock and braised in butter.*

*A simple white platter shows off the roast pheasant, which was served with pommes rissolées and liberally garnished with dark green watercress.*

*A fine ending—the grapefruit sherbet served in irresistible hand-painted wine glasses.*

# Sunday Lunch

## Menu
Egg mayonnaise
Roast leg of lamb
Spring vegetables
New potatoes
Summer pudding with cream
*Wines*
Sauvignon blanc
Château Figeac 1970

The setting for a leisurely Sunday lunch in a country house should be simple yet civilized. This midsummer meal began simply with an egg mayonnaise—the white and gold of the eggs and the mayonnaise contrasting deliciously with the crisp, fresh green of a lettuce leaf.

The young vegetables that accompanied the roast leg of spring lamb were freshly picked in the morning, so by the time they were cooked they had lost none of their fugitive flavor. Carefully arranged on a large serving dish, the bright orange of the tiny carrots became the focal point of the table for the main course. A selection of lightly cooked vegetables served on a platter like this has an immediate, mouth-watering appeal, and is much easier to deal with and much more attractive than a clutter of serving dishes with lids.

The fitting finale was a lovely purpley-red summer pudding—a colorful fruit-filled mold of white bread steeped in the rich juices of raspberries and red currants.

One of the reasons why this meal is a success is because it is a visual feast—the subtle and interesting colors of the food are enhanced by the pale and pretty china

plates and the highly polished silver and glass. The table, polished with sweet-smelling beeswax, gleams in the sunlight. A jug of richly colored sweet peas permeates the whole dining room with a distinctly summery scent.

The flavor and freshness of the food are equally important. Although there is nothing unconventional on the menu, the meal has a refreshing lightness—quite unlike those traditional, heavy Sunday lunches of roast meat and potatoes under a thick gravy that induce the equally traditional Sunday afternoon feeling of overfed ennui.

*It is worth decanting a good bottle of old wine—pour gently through a funnel lined with a paper towel, leaving the lees, or sediment, in the bottle. Allow the wine to settle in the decanter for an hour or two.*

*The first course—egg mayonnaise—arranged appetizingly on a pretty patterned plate.*

*Summer pudding—that particularly English combination of soft fruits and bread—provides a colorful ending.*

*To make glasses sparkle, first wash them, then rinse in really hot, clean water and polish with a clean linen cloth.*

*Transfer the vegetables carefully from the serving dish to avoid a muddle.*

*A slice of summer pudding looks delicious on the pale plate.*

# Riverside Picnic

## *Menu*
Potted shrimps and saffron bread
Spinach frittata
Sausage and mushroom pie
Salade niçoise
Cheese
Dundee cake
*Wine*
Lirac Rosé 1977

A good picnic is a meal that is planned but which still allows for some things to be done and some dishes to be assembled when you finally find your perfect site and spread yourselves and the food out on the grass.

Paper plates and plastic mugs are certainly practical, and obviously if the picnic is mainly for the benefit of children, then these unbreakable accoutrements are advisable. But choose plastic and paper in cool colors and simple patterns, as the garishness of most picnic ware is as indigestible as most prepackaged picnic food.

The best picnic sites are often beside water, sometimes at the lakeside or the seaside, but best of all by fast-running rivers or streams. Apart from the pleasing sights and soothing sounds, running water is a practical bonus for picnickers—for cooling wine, beer and butter, cleaning vegetables and fruit, and at the end of the meal for washing the plates, glasses and hands.

The meal pictured here is not a children's outing but a civilized picnic for adults. The food is real food, the plates real china, the glasses real glass, all spread out on a real cotton gingham cloth.

This picnic was planned as a very special occasion and a delicious and rather elaborate menu was arranged. The food, wine, plates and glasses were wrapped in gingham napkins and in the tablecloth, and everything was carried to the river's edge in large handwoven willow baskets.

On arrival at the chosen spot, the first task was to tie the bottles of wine to a stick and lower them into the river to cool. We then settled down to the pleasurable preparation of the salade niçoise: slicing tomatoes and boiled new potatoes, cutting the crisp lettuce hearts and the hard-boiled eggs in quarters, and finally opening cans of anchovy fillets and tuna fish and a jar of black olives, and mixing all these ingredients together with olive oil, wine vinegar, salt, pepper and a little French mustard. Obviously if this had all been prepared before we set off, the salad would have lost its essential freshness and during the journey would have become a limp and somewhat unattractive sludge.

Everything else had been prepared in the kitchen before we set out, even the spinach frittata—which as you might guess is a flat omelet with fried spinach and garlic, and is at its best when eaten cold, in slices. The potted shrimps, prepared simply by pouring clarified butter spiced with mace and nutmeg over freshly peeled shrimps, made a delicious first course, followed by a cold pie of sausage meat and sliced button mushrooms wrapped in a flaky pastry case and accompanied by the salade niçoise.

Finally we enjoyed a marvellous selection of cheeses: a rare and costly natural blue Cheshire; *pithiviers au foin*, which is covered in hay so it doesn't matter too much if it rolls off into the grass; a *chèvre* cheese, *banon d'or*, covered in chestnut leaves, another ideal packaging for a picnic cheese, and finally an oozing Brie de Melun. With all this wonderful food we ate home-baked whole wheat bread and saffron bread, which was especially good with the potted shrimps. After the feast we all had a snooze in the long grass and awoke at teatime—refreshed and just hungry enough to enjoy a slice of rich Dundee cake.

*To be appetizing, a salad must be freshly prepared at the picnic site. This salade niçoise looks good in a simple olivewood bowl.*

*The plates were washed in the river between courses—the beautiful fish pattern is just the thing for a picnic at the water's edge.*

*The cheese arrived from the supplier in this simple wooden tray lined with reed mats—it made a natural presentation case for our marvellous selection of unusual French and English cheeses.*

*An improvised wine-cooling system: tie the necks of the bottles firmly to a stake, and lower the wine into a fast-moving stream.*

*Packed and ready to go at the end of the day.*

# Hallowe'en Party

## Menu

Pumpkin soup
Corn on the cob
Boston baked beans
Devilled chicken legs
Devil's food cake
Pecan pie
Brownies
Popcorn
Gingerbread men
Peanut chip ice cream
*To drink*
Glögg
Apple juice
Lemonade

All-Hallows Eve falls on the last day of October and is a great excuse to throw a spooky Hallowe'en party—a party to be hugely enjoyed by children and adults alike, to celebrate appropriately all that is ghostly, ghastly and ghoulish.

Traditionally, this is a fancy-dress party and everyone should come suitably dressed—as ghosts, witches, devils, bats or cats. An old barn or garage is the ideal place to hold such a party, so that the children can creep around in the gloom, shriek and swoop about on broomsticks indoors and out, scaring each other without being frightened of tripping over the furniture.

This party was held in an old barn in the country in a scary atmosphere of flickering candlelight and smoky wood fires. Night lights glowed inside paper lanterns and hollowed-out pumpkins and the table groaned beneath a delicious Hallowe'en meal—the dishes kept simple to appeal to adults and children.

The orange pumpkin is really the symbol of Hallowe'en and it was the centerpiece of this party menu, its flesh scooped out to make the soup, the shell used as a natural soup tureen. There was a dish of golden corn on the cob, glistening with butter, a pot of rich brown Boston baked beans with delicious cubes of salt pork, devilled chicken legs and plenty of other food to nibble at as the evening wore on.

After a lot of frenzied activity bobbing for apples, untangling sprawling spiderwebs of string with prizes tied to the end of each strand and eating sticky buns on strings, generous helpings of peanut chip ice cream cooled everybody down—an appropriately nutty end to a nutty night.

*A selection of pumpkins, gourds and squashes —some became lanterns, one a soup tureen.*

*To make a Hallowe'en lantern, carve a face in the shell of a hollowed-out pumpkin.*

*Cheerful, brightly patterned party plates reflect the designs on the paper lanterns. They are teamed with practical, plastic-handled cutlery and paper napkins.*

346

*Gingerbread people have always been popular with children—these have been decorated with cheeky icing faces.*

*For the kids: peanut chip ice cream in a pretty glass dish, washed down with lemonade from a dotty glass.*

*Devil's food cake—a wickedly tempting chocolate layer cake displayed on a dark, white-rimmed plate.*

# Formal Dinner Party

## Menu
Fish pâté with sauce grelette
Filet de boeuf en croûte
Horseradish sauce
Snow peas
Parmesan cheese
Syllabub with Amaretti
*Wines*
Meursault 1976
Magnum of Château Latour 1970
Coffee
Liqueurs

It is a great pleasure to give or to go to a really grand and formal dinner party every once in a while. This party was held in the London apartment of art dealer John Kasmin, and the occasion lived up to all expectations.

Kasmin's dining room admirably combines all the best qualities of traditional and modern design in an effortless way. The plain white oval-topped "Tulip" table on its slender, tapering center pedestal is by the Finnish architect Eero Saarinen and is the perfect companion for the antique chairs and the carved fireplace *circa* 1815. Anything more ornate than this classic modern table would have drawn attention away from the chairs and the fireplace and one would not have noticed their qualities so clearly. The room is painted white and the floor is covered with white tiles, which allow the quality of the ceiling moldings and the huge Helen Frankenthaler painting, which acts as a backdrop to the table, to be totally appreciated.

For this evening party, the candlelight had an important part to play in transforming what might otherwise have been a rather clinical room into a stage bathed in shadow and sparkle. The plain, hard white table top was subtly complemented by the china, an English design called "Concept," which I consider to be the most interesting modern tableware in the world today. The cutlery is a contemporary adaptation in stainless steel of the traditional English "pistol grip"

*The fish pâté, striped with salmon and watercress, is subtly framed by the finely sculptured plate.*

*The creamy, lemon syllabub was served in delicate bowls of the thinnest possible glass with tiny macaroons.*

*An appetizing prospect for the eye and the palate: a slice of boeuf en croûte, a jug full of horseradish sauce, and a magnum of Château Latour.*

*The coffee came in plentiful supply from a beautiful French cafetière and was served in handsome cups from the "Concept" range, "the most interesting modern tableware in the world today."*

*A simple vase of Madonna lilies—an elegant complement to the surroundings.*

style. The fine, modern glasses for the white wine are made by Orrefors of Sweden —the slight fluting of the trumpet refracts the light and increases the sparkle.

In this restrained setting the food, the wines, the guests and their hosts were shown off to advantage. Neither the furnishings, china, cutlery nor glass were so remarkable that they competed for attention —the food was the important thing and nothing detracted from it.

The well-balanced menu was as refined as the surroundings, and the food looked as good as it tasted. The subtle colors of the delicious fish pâté and sauce grelette looked almost too good to eat, and the intense green of the little snow peas positively sang out from the plain dish. The glazed pastry case of the *boeuf en croûte* lent a serious and solid note, ensuring that nobody left the table feeling hungry. Between the main course and the dessert, a huge chunk of

Parmesan cheese appeared on the table on a cool white marble slab. Small nuggets were cracked off and eaten with the fingers —just what was needed before the rich and subtle flavor of the creamy syllabub. Amaretti di Saronno are tiny macaroons, each wrapped in fine tissue paper. If you roll this into a tube, place the tube upright on a side plate and set fire to the top, it will float to the ceiling like a hot-air balloon: an elegant end to an elegant evening.

# Lunch in the Garden

## Menu
Crudités with aïoli
Pâté de campagne
Bread and cheese
Fruit salad
*To drink*
Kir

Very often the most enjoyable meals are completely unplanned. It can so easily happen that friends telephone and, on the spur of the moment, you invite them to lunch. Then a rapid visit to the vegetable garden and the market is in order; and with no fixed menu in mind, the produce itself inspires you to compose a meal from the best that is available.

On this occasion, the fresh young vegetables in the garden were so delicious that it would have been a shame to cook them, so crudités with a good garlicky mayonnaise seemed the most natural choice.

At the market there was an abundance of fresh fruit, some of it quite exotic, which inspired the colorful fruit salad—a sweet counterpart to the crudités. The robust middle course was a pâté de campagne

from the larder and some cheeses—sage Derby, double Gloucester and *pipo crème*—with freshly baked bread.

Instead of preparing this meal alone in the kitchen, everything was taken outside and hosts and guests prepared the meal together, sitting around in the spring sunshine, sipping glasses of Kir (chilled white Burgundy and cassis) and chatting while scraping, slicing and stirring.

The plates and glasses were chosen in the same *ad hoc* way as the meal had been conceived. Nothing matched but, of course, each item reflected the personal and particular taste of an individual with a discerning eye, so they all looked good together.

The simple backdrop for this eclectic collection was the bleached top of an old wooden garden table and the silver-grey of

the French woven chestnut chairs, the perfect foil for such a colorful display.

It was the impromptu nature of this lunch that made it such a pleasure. The meal was designed around all that was good, fresh and available, and the table setting was improvised accordingly. The fruit salad looked at its very best laid out, almost geometrically, on a creamy white platter; the sliced raw vegetables were neatly arranged on a plate of duck-egg blue; the pâté was served on interesting hand-painted plates in appetizing hues of green.

One of the more delightful aspects of meals with no formal structure is that they can so easily stretch langorously over several hours, developing with the addition of tea and cakes into a tea party and on, via some more bottles of wine, into the night.

*Vegetables and fruit from the garden and the market are assembled ready for preparation.*

*Trimmed and finely sliced, the raw vegetables look colorful and appetizing. They are eaten with aïoli—a golden mayonnaise well flavored with garlic.*

*The robust pâté de campagne is served on hand-painted plates and eaten with old bone-handled cutlery.*

*The fruit salad is a work of art in itself, as carefully and as artfully composed as any abstract picture.*

*These pompoms are from leeks that have gone to seed.*

# Country Breakfast

## Menu
Muesli and cold milk
Ham and eggs with fried bread
Croissants with strawberry jam
Whole wheat bread and butter
*To drink*
Fresh orange juice
Coffee with hot milk

The breakfast illustrated here would make a wonderful start to the day. It is a meal for weekend and holiday mornings when there is plenty of time to enjoy good things at leisure. It is substantial enough to be a substitute for lunch, and it certainly makes a good preface to a day of energetic activity.

The best breakfasts are cheerful and informal. People will probably arrive unpunctually, so there is no point in serving food that is liable to deteriorate if kept warm. Serve food that will not suffer from such treatment or something so simple that latecomers can cook it themselves when they eventually make an appearance. You shouldn't have to wait long, as there is nothing like the smell of warm bread and freshly ground coffee to drag the most recalcitrant of snoozers from their beds.

The color of the breakfast table is important: keep it bright, fresh and cheerful—nothing too subtle or rich. A gingham tablecloth and a jug of daffodils with simple, chunky white porcelain seem just right. Keep the mahogany, the lace tablecloths and shining silver for later in the day.

*Muesli is a wonderful mixture of rolled oats, bran, toasted nuts and dried fruit—just add slices of apple and creamy milk.*

# PART FOUR

## Equipment

*How to choose it and use it*

# Knives and Cleavers

A good sharp knife that is comfortable to hold is the most essential tool in the kitchen—one which makes the preparation of food a keen pleasure, rather than a troublesome chore.

## Quality and materials

Before selecting the right shape of knife for the particular tasks you have in mind, it is important to know what factors raise a kitchen knife into the top-quality class.

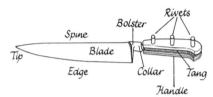

*The anatomy of a knife*

**Balance** It is critical that the weight of a knife should be evenly distributed along the blade and handle, as an unbalanced knife is tiring to use. Heavy-bladed knives should be balanced by a tang that runs the full length of the handle. A full tang will also lend extra strength to a knife designed for tough tasks. Light or heavy bladed, the tang should be securely fixed inside the handle, preferably with rivets.

**Machine-ground edge** Grinding gives a blade both keenness and strength, and knife grinding is a craftsman's job. The best knives are "taper" ground with grinding marks at right angles to the cutting edge.

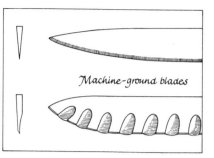

*Machine-ground blades*

**Hollow-ground blades** are recognizable by their profile—a thick blade abruptly pinched in at the cutting edge. The blade is machined so it cannot be sharpened, and it does not make a good edge for a chopping knife, but hollow grinding does make the hardest, most durable serrated edge.

**Handles** on the best-quality kitchen knives will be either of close-grained hardwood (usually Brazilian rosewood or boxwood) which will not split or warp, the slight texture of which gives a secure grip, or of plastics-impregnated wood, which combines extreme toughness with the natural properties of wood. High-quality plastic handles are practical, as they can withstand the heat of a dishwasher, but they are inclined to be slippery in wet hands.

**Stainless steel** is a rust-resisting alloy of iron and chromium. Many people are disparaging of stainless steel, claiming that it is impossible to give it a really keen edge. This is certainly true of inferior-quality knives stamped out of a flat piece of metal, but those forged from tempered stainless steel with a high carbon content are among the best knives you can buy and they hold a very fine edge indeed.

**Carbon steel** has the advantage of being cheaper than stainless steel and it will sharpen to a razor edge. The disadvantage is its susceptibility to rusting and staining, especially from foods with a high acid content, such as lemons and tomatoes. Knives made of carbon steel must be cleaned and dried immediately after use—never left to soak or to lie around on wet drain boards. If the blades do become stained, burnish with a cork sprinkled with an abrasive cleaning powder.

## Shape and size

There are dozens of different knives designed for all the specialist tasks a professional chef may have to perform, but a carefully chosen collection of six or seven will equip most kitchens admirably.

### Chopping

To chop vegetables, herbs, garlic, nuts and so on finely, you will need a tough, well-balanced knife with a deep, smoothly curved blade that tapers towards a pointed tip. The handle should be shaped to the grip with a down-turned curve at the end to prevent the hand slipping backwards. It should have a full tang to balance the weight of the blade and absorb the chopping vibrations.

The bolster must be thick and deep to shield the hand and to allow the full length of the cutting edge to be used without crushing the knuckles against the chopping surface. The correct way to use this type of knife for fine chopping is to rest one hand lightly on the spine at the tip to keep the blade in contact with the chopping board, while the other hand rocks the handle up

a   b   c   d   e   f   g   h   i

and down, gradually moving the knife across the food. For rougher chopping, raise and lower the whole blade.

For tough chopping jobs a cleaver should be used. This tool relies for its strength on a wide, really hefty blade, and is one of the few instances where an imbalance between handle and blade is desirable. Butchers may be seen wielding this implement with considerable force and accuracy, but ferocious hacking can chip and blunt the cutting edge very quickly. To chop through bones, rest the cleaver in position and knock the back of the blade with a mallet.

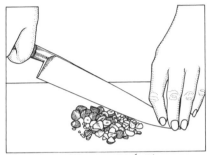

*Chopping with a cook's knife*

Cleavers are traditionally used for all the endless chopping and shredding that goes into the preparation of Chinese and Japanese dishes. Using the knuckles of one hand the blade is guided across the food, then with a final flourish the pieces are scooped on to the blade and deftly transferred to the pot. Chinese and Japanese chefs are able to cut a thin scallop of meat or fish by placing it under their palm and passing the cleaver through it—their palm acting as a sort of radar device.

## Slicing

The type of knife you use will depend entirely on what you are slicing.

**Cold meats** The compact, tender fibers of cooked cold meats offer little resistance to a sharp knife and can be sliced very thinly. Choose a knife with a long narrow blade, which should be flexible and strong. Sometimes meat slicers have a rounded tip to prevent accidental slashes to the meat, and a serrated edge which gives a little purchase to the first stroke and reduces friction.

**Fruit and vegetables** A small, serrated, stainless steel blade is wonderfully efficient for slicing lemons, tomatoes, cucumbers, peppers and all those other fruits with tough or slippery outer skins. The serration pierces the skin so easily that the flesh beneath is not bruised or squashed and each slice will keep all its juice.

**Bread** A long serrated edge is good for cleanly penetrating the rough outer crust. Choose a straight, firm knife with hollow-ground serrations.

## Boning

This operation is carried out in a series of small cutting movements, frequently using the tip of the knife to follow the contours of the bone, so good blade control is important.

For lightweight cuts of meat or poultry, a short knife is best with a broad handle and a slim, pointed blade. The blade should be flexible enough to go around the bone. The larger the piece of meat to be boned, the larger and more rigid the blade should be.

## Filleting fish

Choose a pointed, straight-edged knife with a flexible blade which will feel its way around the soft cartilaginous fish bones—this is a task requiring precision and dexterity. The blade should be protected by a bolster and have a full-tanged handle.

## Paring, peeling and scraping

Everyone has a favorite little knife which tucks under the forefinger and can be used almost as an extension of the hand. As the hand should be in close contact with the food, use only a light knife with a comfortable,

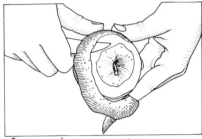

*A paring knife in action*

**a, b, c, d** *Carbon steel general purpose cook's knives in a good range of sizes* **e** *High-carbon stainless steel carving knife with a riveted handle* **f** *Heavy-duty stainless steel meat cleaver* **g** *Chinese carbon steel cleaver holds a fine, sharp edge for precise slicing and chopping* **h** *Round-tipped ham slicing knife in high-carbon stainless steel* **i** *Serrated slicing knife with a hollow-ground blade* **j** *Stainless steel paring knife with a serrated edge* **k** *Chinese slicing knife has a wide, sharp blade of carbon steel and a wooden handle* **l** *Stainless steel bread knife* **m, n** *Boning knives* **o** *Stainless steel filleting knife* **p, q** *Stainless steel paring knives* **r** *Stainless steel mezzaluna*

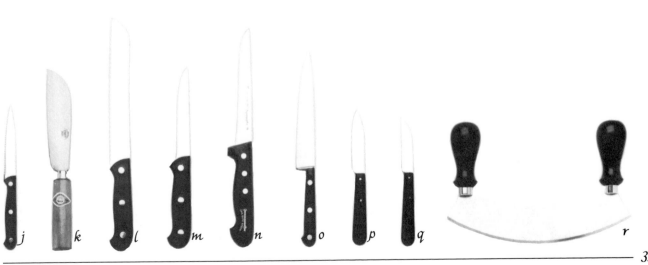

*j* *k* *l* *m* *n* *o* *p* *q* *r*

# Knives and Cleavers

preferably wooden, handle and a short blade of good-quality stainless steel capable of holding a really sharp edge.

## Mincing

The Italians have a very practical instrument called a *mezzaluna* (renamed in France the *demi-lune*). It is a double-handled knife with a crescent-shaped blade that is rocked over herbs, peppers, strips of meat, garlic and sliced vegetables, mincing them to fine shreds.

## Carving

Happily the days are past when a good performance with a carving knife was deemed to be the test of a gentleman, but a good sharp knife is still a reassuring ally on these occasions. Bulky hot roasts with a bone require a straight, sharply pointed knife, and it helps when carving the meat around the bone if the blade curves slightly upwards towards the tip. Like the cook's knife the handle should be shaped to the hand, preferably have a full tang, and a bolster to prevent the hand slipping onto the blade. A slim blade that is slightly flexible will enable the carver to slice the meat thinly.

---

## Care and storage

Dishwashers are very unkind to knives. The high temperature and harsh detergents loosen, warp and split the handles, so it is better to wash them by hand unless they are guaranteed machine-proof.

Knives should be quickly washed in hot, soapy water and dried immediately. You should always chop on a wooden or polypropylene board to preserve the edge.

If by any chance a knife gets put in the dishwasher you may find that its handle turns out of alignment with the blade. This will be because the tang is fixed to the handle not with rivets but with resin that softens with heat. To realign the knife put the handle in boiling water for a few minutes, then twist it straight, and don't do it again.

## Sharpening

Knives should always be kept in razor-sharp condition. A blunt knife is frustrating and dangerous to use—it performs badly, needing a great deal of force, and it can all too easily slip out of control.

Many of the stone window sills in our village have deeply worn hollows where knives (and perhaps even swords) have been sharpened for many years, but with the advent of high-carbon stainless steel and hollow-ground edges this method has dropped into disuse.

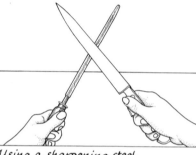

*Using a sharpening steel*

The best method is to use a hand-held steel, and draw the blade lightly down the steel at a shallow angle. Repeat, putting the knife first to the front of the steel, then

the back. Make sure the steel you buy has a small guard or hilt to protect the hand.

Stainless steel is harder than carbon steel and will therefore require a harder sharpening steel. Hardness is measured in degrees on the Rockwell scale and most reputable suppliers will sell a steel to suit the knives in their range.

There are many special devices on the market for sharpening knives, but these usually grind down the blade very quickly and are not to be recommended.

## Storage

Kitchen knives should not be stored in drawers or jars where the blades will clash together, bending the tips and dulling the fine edges. Each knife should be separated from its neighbors and clearly visible to the cook, who can then easily select the right knife for the job.

The best solution is to slot the knives in a knife box or in a wall-fixed rack within easy reach of the work surface, but inaccessible to children. Magnetic racks are good, but they may not be strong enough to hold very heavy knives or cleavers.

Carbon steel knives will need a light coating of vegetable oil to protect them from the steamy atmosphere of the kitchen.

a *Sharpening stone* b *Sharpening steel* c *High-carbon stainless steel carving knife* d *Bread knife with a hollow-ground, serrated blade* e *Oyster knife with a wooden handle* f *Clam knife has a blunt blade and a rounded tip* g *Swedish sandwich spatula for spreading and cutting* h *Grapefruit knife* i *Steak knife* j *Cheese knife* k *Skinning knife* l *Knife rack* m *Magnetic rack* n *Knife box*

# Other Cutting Implements

There are some cutting tasks that are quite difficult to carry out with a straight-bladed knife, however sharp, and over the centuries a wide variety of special tools has been invented to do these jobs more quickly, safely and efficiently.

Some, like scissors, are strokes of genius, invaluable in the kitchen and elsewhere. Others are so specialized that it is advisable to examine your needs quite dispassionately before acquiring them, as they might well spend more time collecting dust than attracting compliments.

The following tools, used in conjunction with a basic collection of knives, should equip the cook to deal with most cutting tasks in the kitchen.

## Graters

**Hand-held graters** are one of the most difficult tools to operate—unless you are careful you will grate your knuckles as well as the food. Choose a sturdy, stainless box-shaped grater that will sit firmly in a bowl or on a flat surface without slipping or sliding. Each face should offer a different grating surface, and the box should be large enough for the food to collect neatly inside without being squashed.

Hand-held graters have two kinds of surfaces—the abrading variety, consisting of a series of jagged puncture holes for rasping tough or brittle foods (e.g., lemon rind, Parmesan, nutmeg); and the smoother

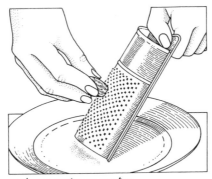

*Using a nutmeg grater*

directional type, which cuts smooth slices or slivers from softer cheeses and vegetables. The texture of the grated food is controlled by the size of the cutting holes.

**A conical abrading grater** is useful for holding over dishes to add a dash of nutmeg or lemon zest at a stroke.

**Hand-operated rotary graters** are speedy and pleasant to use, keeping the fingers at a safe handle's length from the grating surface. A plate holds the food tightly against the grating drum, which is turned by hand. Choose a model with a selection of drums of fine and coarse gauges.

## Peelers and corers

**Potato peeler** It is perfectly possible to peel a potato quickly and easily with a small, sharp knife, but the chances are that the discarded peel will contain far more nourishment and flavor than the potato that ends up on the table. The *raison d'être* of a good potato peeler is to shave the skin so finely that nothing of value is lost.

Fixed-blade peelers are used in the same way as knives, but left-handed people should make sure they buy a left-handed version. The swivel-action peeler is moved quickly to and fro over the potato; its sharp steel blade will cut equally well in either direction. Both types have a pointed end for digging out eyes.

**Citrus peelers or zesters** There are several types of peeler available which will remove only the zest—the outer top layer of citrus skin—in ribbons ranging in width from the slenderest filaments to generous martini twists. The object of these specialist peelers is to leave behind the bitter pith, which is hard to avoid when using a knife.

**Apple corer** The top of this tool should be

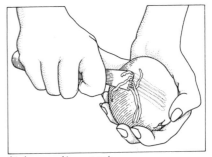

*Using a citrus zester*

**a** *Stainless steel box grater* **b** *Nutmeg grater* **c** *Conical nutmeg grater* **d** *Rotary grater* **e** *Fixed-blade potato peeler* **f** *Potato peeler-cum-corer* **g** *Swivel-action potato peeler with a built-in bean shredder* **h** *Swivel-action peeler* **i, j** *Citrus peelers which remove a shallow strip of peel* **k** *Citrus zester removes slivers of peel with no pith* **l** *Apple corer* **m** *Cherry pitter* **n** *Plum pitter*

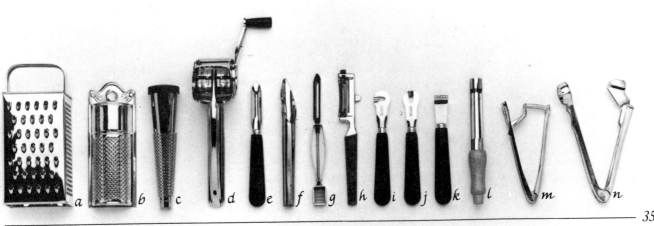

# Other Cutting Implements

placed over the target area and pushed firmly through the apple; when it is withdrawn the core will be retained in the center of the corer. It is a most useful gadget for preparing baked apples, the only drawback being that not every apple has an obligingly straight core of a standard size. Choose a corer with a sharp bottom edge.

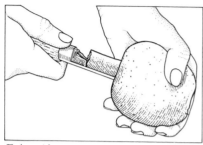

*Extracting an apple core*

**Cherry or olive pitter** This little gadget looks as if it would be more at home punching eyeholes in leather belts. But its real function is to eject pits from cherries and olives, and a sturdy stainless steel pitter will do the job very efficiently—a boon if you make a great deal of cherry jam.

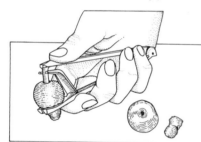

*Using a cherry pitter*

## Slicers

**Mandoline** This instrument is used for high-speed slicing of firm, crisp foods such as potatoes, onions, carrots, cucumbers or celeriac in a variety of thicknesses from hefty slices to transparent wafers. Two adjustable blades (preferably of high-carbon stainless steel), one rippled for producing thin sticks, the other straight, are set on opposite faces of a smooth wooden board. The mandoline is held firmly in place with one hand while the other, guided by the board, moves the food over the blade with a regular strumming movement.

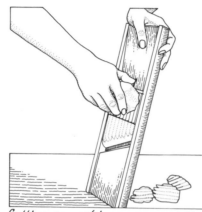

*Cutting game chips on a mandoline*

**Rotary slicers** These machines are perfect for cutting very fine, even slices of soft food such as cooked meats, salamis, sausages and bread. It is an invaluable aid for those faced with making sandwiches for the local football team, or for any other large-scale slicing job. A good-quality slicer will have clamps to fasten it securely to the work

surface, a stainless steel circular blade with a calibrated dial to control the thickness of the slices and a heavy, enamelled metal body.

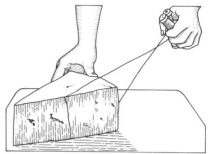

*Using a cheese wire*

**Cheese wire** This is only useful if you buy cheese in large pieces. However hard or crumbly the cheese, a stainless steel cutting wire, drawn taut, will melt through it leaving a clean, straight cut.

**Egg slicers** Wire slicers are the best way of cutting hard-boiled eggs without displacing or crumbling the yolk. Some kinds cut wedges, some flat slices. The shapes are a matter of personal preference, but do ensure that the wires are of stainless steel.

**French-fry cutter** If you eat a lot of French

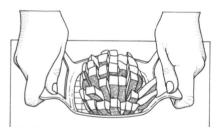

*Using a French-fry cutter*

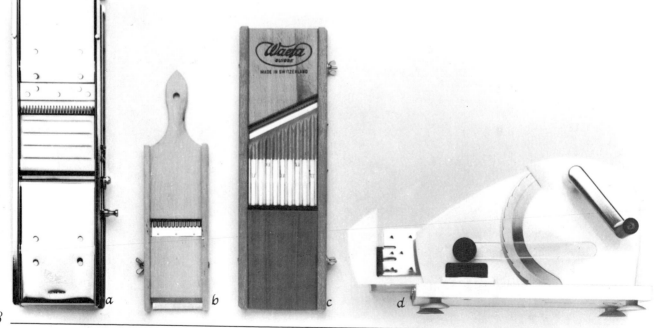

fries then this gadget is quite useful. The whole peeled potato is placed under it, the checkered stainless steel cutter pushed down, and within a few minutes you have a bowl of neatly cut potato sticks ready for frying. Instruments for cutting raw potatoes must be sturdy, so be prepared to pay for a heavy-duty steel model. A flimsy cheap cutter is worse than useless.

**Scissors** Kitchen scissors should be very sharp, strong and made of stainless steel because they are constantly in water and must be impervious to rust. For tough jobs their power will be strengthened if the lower handle is large enough to take the last three fingers of the cutting hand, and a serrated edge is sometimes useful for giving an extra bite to the first cut.

The blades should cut evenly right down to their tips, in fact especially at the tips because snipping is an important function of this tool. Scissors should be professionally sharpened when they become blunt.

**Shears** Like a gardener's cutters this tool gains its strength from the tension in the coiled spring that is to be found just below the pivot point of the blades.

Usually one blade is serrated to give a sound grip when tackling tough assignments such as small bones, cartilage, poultry, etc., and the pointed tips enable the shears to reach and operate effectively in small, awkward places.

Some versions are very handsome, and as well as being invaluable in the kitchen they can be used at the table for dividing a roast duck (or a small game bird) into neat and manageable portions. This is an especially good way to serve duck, as its bony carcass makes carving most unrewarding.

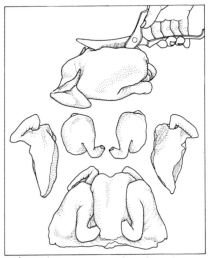

*Dissecting with poultry shears*

**Kitchen saw** A lightweight saw is ideal for all home butchery tasks. Bones, especially the big fat ones, make wonderfully nutritious stock and this tool will quickly cut them into pot-size pieces.

## Cleaning and storage

It is an unpleasant fact that behind every meal there looms the inevitable stack of dirty dishes. Even if there is a dishwashing machine in the kitchen, there will still be a hard core of gadgets, knives and pots that has to be hand washed. Some of the items listed in this section come into this rather unfortunate category.

Mandolines should be cleaned with a brush, rinsed and dried quickly—the wood will warp if it is left to soak. Brushing is also

the best way to clean graters, although the larger, box-shaped ones will clean perfectly well in a dishwashing machine.

Some rotary slicers can be dismantled for easy cleaning, but take care not to cut yourself when the guard is removed from the sharp, circular blade.

Most of these implements have sharp cutting edges, so do not jumble them all into a drawer as this will ruin the blades and you will most probably cut your fingers as you root about, searching for the appropriate gadget. Some can be hung from a rack or a rail on butcher's hooks and larger items can be kept on a shelf, but in all cases the cook must be able to see and reach them easily.

**a** *Stainless steel mandoline, both beautiful and expensive, is the choice of professional cooks* **b** *Small wooden mandoline has just one stainless steel blade for slicing* **c** *Standard wooden mandoline with two high-carbon stainless steel blades* **d** *Efficient rotary slicer with a heavy, enamelled metal body and a razor-sharp blade* **e** *Simple stainless steel cheese wire with wooden handles* **f** *Egg slicer with stainless steel cutting wires will divide a hard-boiled egg into perfect, even slices* **g** *Aluminum egg wedger with wires of stainless steel* **h, i** *French-fry cutters, one with wires, one with blades—the model with blades is the sturdier and therefore easier to use* **j, k** *Kitchen scissors, one pair coated with Teflon, the other made of stainless steel with a comfortable plastic grip. Scissors are useful for all kinds of jobs—snipping herbs, degristling meat, trimming fish fillets, and opening vacuum-sealed plastic packs* **l** *Stainless steel poultry shears* **m** *Lightweight butcher's saw*

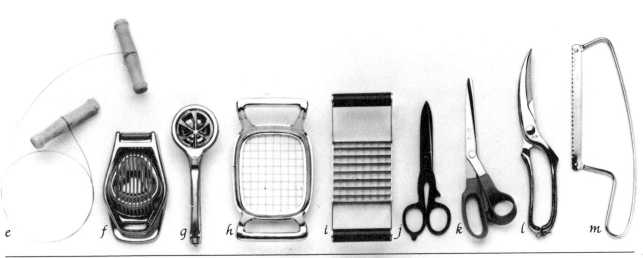

# Grinders and Mashers

When you look at a collection of modern kitchen tools, efficient, easy to use, simple to clean, light and comfortable in the hand, it is easy to believe that they are all twentieth-century inventions. But most of them have a long and interesting lineage, and this is certainly true of the diverse group of tools in this section designed to refine or change the texture of food.

Even before the advent of bread our ancestors had realized that seeds and grains could be made more digestible or aromatic by pounding and grinding; pieces of cloth filled with berries and wrung tightly were the first juice extractors, and loosely woven cloths suspended on wooden frames were the predecessors of modern sieves.

## Crushers

**Pestle and mortar** This elegant descendant of the primitive pounding pole is still the most effective tool for pulverizing nuts, garlic, berries, seeds and herbs.

The mortar should have a smooth, regularly curved bowl and a compatibly shaped pestle made of the same material—this is important because if the hardness of the pestle and the mortar are not equal, one will wear away the other. The grinding surfaces should be slightly rough to provide the necessary friction and prevent the food sliding away from the pestle.

Pestles and mortars are available in wood, glass, tough unglazed porcelain, stone and marble (which is lovely but very expensive). The wooden ones are excellent for crushing dry food, but should not be used for anything that exudes moisture because the pungent juices will impregnate the wood.

The white vitrified porcelain versions are probably the most handsome and best all-around performers at a reasonable price.

Another version of the pestle and mortar consists of a wooden bowl used with a curved blade so that herbs and spices can be finely chopped rather than crushed.

**Pepper mills** Peppercorns should be ground when and where they are needed so that their fugitive pungency can be enjoyed before it fades.

The mealtime musings of many designers have resulted in an enormous variety of pepper mills to choose from, but perhaps the favorite is still the classic wooden mill with a removable top for easy filling and a highly efficient steel grinding mechanism.

**Salt mills** Where the pepper goes salt goes too, so most manufacturers make a salt mill to match their pepper mills. They are, strictly speaking, superfluous, but they will reduce coarse sea salt lumps to small grains.

**Coffee grinders** Freshness is the essence of good coffee, and the only way to ensure it is to grind your own. Hand-operated mills are preferred by some purists as the beans are ground rather than cut.

## Beaters and pounders

**Cutlet beater** Any thin slices of uncooked meat, such as scallops of veal, which are to be cooked quickly should be cut across the grain of the meat and then flattened to half their original thickness. This is best done by stroking with a smooth heavy beater to homogenize the texture of the flesh and break down the fibers, which contract when cooked causing shrinkage and toughness.

**Meat tenderizer** These pounders have many small spiky protuberances in wood, plastic or steel which cut through the fibrous tissue and in effect partially prechew the meat before it is cooked.

## Grinders

A mechanical grinder should be very strong and have clamps or suction feet for fixing it rigidly to the working surface. The handle turns a small Archimedean screw, which inexorably pushes the food from the hopper onto the rotating stainless steel grinding plates, which will process almost anything except bones. Ensure that the machine has been designed to come apart completely so that every part can be easily cleaned.

## Sieves

There are sieves for sifting, sieves for straining and sieves for puréeing: versatility breeds variation, and the sieve family is no exception.

Round-framed wire- or nylon-mesh sieves are best suited to sifting tasks, but the wire-mesh ones can also be used for puréeing with the aid of a wooden mushroom-shaped pestle called (unsurprisingly) a champignon. In time, though, there is a danger that constant pushing will cause the mesh to part from the frame.

Sieves should not be filled too full for sifting—simply knock the side of the frame gently against the palm of the free hand to help the contents pass through the mesh.

Sieves can be very difficult to clean, and for this reason the wood-framed sieves are best avoided for puréeing—metal-framed drum sieves are better suited as they are stronger and can be immersed in really hot and soapy water, or better still left for the dishwasher to cope with.

**Chinois** For heavy puréeing jobs a chinois or cone-shaped sieve is preferable. When buying, check that the frame and the perforations are formed from one piece of metal with no seams or welds. The food is forced through the perforations by a long narrow pestle, which fits right into the tip.

*Using a chinois*

360

Wire-mesh chinois are also excellent for straining, the tapering point channelling the liquid neatly down in a single trickle.

**Food mill** This rotary sieve produces a whole range of purées from the most delicate tomato sauce to a robust vegetable soup. An electric food processor, of course, would do the same, but a food mill often gives better results as it does not rob the food entirely of its intrinsic texture. The whole machine can be easily dismantled for cleaning or to change the base for a coarser or finer finish. The best food mills have bodies of tinned steel.

### Juice extractors

A citrus fruit squeezer must be able to deliver up the maximum amount of juice free from seeds, pith and other solids. If you are not averse to plastic, there are good models available where the reamer and strainer are molded in one piece, which fits onto a container with a lip for pouring.

More traditional but not so efficient is the familiar glass version with teeth which only halfheartedly trap the seeds and pieces, and a moat which barely holds the juice of one lemon.

For extracting just a few drops of juice without sacrificing a whole lemon or lime there is a very clever little gadget which, when plugged into the fruit, will produce the required number of drops.

### Mashers

Choose a strong four-square masher that deals severely with the food and will not collapse under pressure. Avoid painted wooden handles because the paint will eventually rub off and flake into the food.

**Garlic press** The slippery garlic clove is streamlined for easy escape from anyone hoping to crush it between two spoons, and for those who are wary about impregnating a pestle and mortar with its all-pervading flavor, the garlic press is the answer. Select a sturdy aluminum press with a fairly coarse mesh—then there is no need to peel the clove of garlic before you squeeze. Beware—crushed garlic is more overpowering than chopped.

**a, b** *Pestle and mortar sets in wood and porcelain* **c** *Mortar and curved blade* **d** *Rotary herb grinder* **e, f, g** *Pepper mills* **h, i** *Coffee grinders* **j, k** *Meat tenderizers* **l** *Heavy metal cutlet beater* **m** *Tinned steel grinder* **n** *Wood-framed drum sieve* **o** *Wire-mesh sieve* **p** *Metal chinois* **q** *Food mill* **r, s** *Lemon squeezers* **t** *Juice extractor* **u** *Garlic press*

# Small Utensils and Bowls

Some tools are never far from the cook's hand—usually tucked into a jar by the stove ready in an instant to tend those dishes that need stirring, whisking or skimming while they cook. Billowy sauces and soufflés, plump omelets or luxurious soups can be produced by any cook who has a good sense of timing and the right tools, which will respond instantly and efficiently.

### Whisks and beaters

Substances are whisked to lighten their texture by the introduction of air, or to emulsify and blend ingredients, or to thicken those substances which contain fat. Egg whites for instance have an almost infinite capacity for trapping air when they are whipped; gently folded into sponges, soufflés or meringues, the air bubbles expand when heated to give the food a texture of honeycombed lightness.

A brisk whisking will rescue a lumpy sauce and transform egg yolks and oil into a golden mayonnaise.

The gregarious behavior of agitated fat particles is well known—they clump together and thicken up—but take care not to get overenthusiastic when whisking cream or the result will be coarse and grainy, like curdled butter.

There are many varieties of whisks but the most reliable and effective types are:

**Balloon whisks** made of several loops of wire bound together around a central handle. They are simple and effective instruments with no moving parts to go wrong, but they do need a good strong arm to keep up the whisking motion for some minutes without flagging. Sizes range from large heavy-duty models for egg whites to small, dainty ones for light sauces and delicate dressings.

**Rotary beaters** can be heaven or hell depending on the quality of manufacture. A cheap version is really a waste of money; unless the gear mechanism is carefully made of high-quality materials, the beater will not operate smoothly at high speed. The best types work very well indeed and are less tiring to use than wire whisks, but they do occupy both hands, which is sometimes a disadvantage.

**The flat whisk** is a neat, efficient spoon-shaped tool that can get right into the sides of a pan, or control one or two egg whites so well that they can be whisked on a plate.

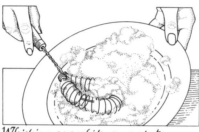

*Whisking egg white on a plate*

### Spoons

**The wooden spoon** is regarded by most people with affection, not only because it is associated with childhood treats like scraping the mixing bowl, but also because it is one of the most useful tools in the kitchen.

A wooden spoon is invaluable for beating, mixing and stirring, it will never burn your hand because wood is a very bad conductor of heat, it will not scratch or wear away saucepans, and it is quiet and strong in use.

Choose a spoon of close-grained wood like beech or box which is not likely to split and whose bowl has a fairly thin edge that can get right to the bottom corner of steep-sided saucepans—some spoons are specially shaped to help you do this.

**Metal spoons** Although wooden and metal spoons share the same shape, their functions do not overlap in any way. While wooden spoons are good for stirring and beating, metal ones excel at transferring food quickly from pan to dish, and gently folding together delicate mixtures. A metal spoon should always be used for last-minute taste checks on soups and sauces, as wood can hold a tiny bit of the flavor from its last use.

**Perforated metal spoons** are excellent for removing and serving solid food that has been cooked in liquid. The excess drains through the holes leaving the food whole, undamaged and pleasantly moist.

**Ladles** The familiar shape of the ladle has remained unchanged since very ancient times, and like most classics ladles are both satisfying to use because of their geometric balance and pleasing to the eye.

Soups and stews can be dexterously served without fear of a drop missing the mark; just the right quantity of batter can be poured into the crêpe pan for feather-light pancakes; and lipped ladles will transfer punches from mixing bowl to glasses.

### Skimmers

**Wire skimmers** These shallow lightweight wire baskets on long handles will scour the surface of a bubbling soup or stock, gathering up any unwanted pieces of skin or fat that may rise to the surface, or scoop a bobbing doughnut from a pan of hot oil at exactly the right moment to be rolled crisp and hot in the sugar.

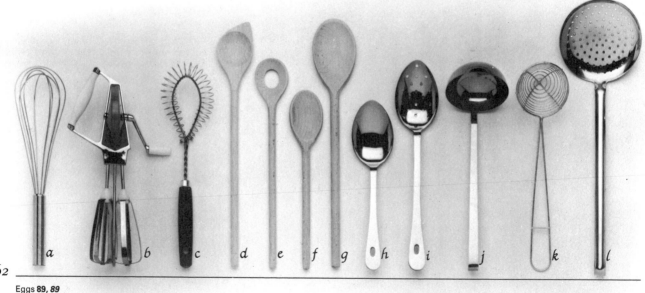

a  b  c  d  e  f  g  h  i  j  k  l

Solid perforated disc skimmers skim liquids more finely than their wire relatives, but are not so good in the deep-frying department, where their bulk will lower the temperature of the oil and the perforations are not large enough to allow the oil to drain freely from the food.

## Turners, spatulas and tongs

**Metal turners** The flexibility of a good turner must be finely judged: slim and whippy enough to slide under the food without causing damage, and broad and firm enough to support it as it is turned or lifted from the pan. Perforations in the blade will allow excess fat or oil to escape and a stout wooden handle insulates the hand from the heat of the pan.

**Wooden spatulas** It is strange that this archaic tool should be the perfect companion to the nonstick pan—that culinary spin-off from space-age technology—and although as a turner it is somewhat lacking in flexibility, nothing harsher than wood should be used on this vulnerable finish.

Spatulas are available in rounded spoon shapes, or with a flat blade and a slanted straight end, which fits snugly against the sides of pans and bowls, gathering up everything in its path.

**Rubber or plastic scrapers** These tools are the delight of a frugal cook's heart. Nothing else can scrape a bowl so clean that washing it becomes almost a formality. Their plastic or rubber heads have a rounded side and an angular edge so they will fit a wide variety of pots, pans and surfaces. Never put a rubber spatula into the dishwasher or hot liquids—it will perish.

**Palette knife or spatula** The long, thin, flexible blade of the palette knife is ideally suited to those large-scale spreading jobs—like professionally smoothing a layer of icing on a cake or deftly distributing its filling. It is also a handy tool for turning scones or muffins on a griddle and lifting a slice of tart from a baking pan.

**Tongs** These reach like a pair of heatproof fingers into sizzling pots and pans to grip small awkwardly shaped items.

**Spaghetti tongs** are invaluable for serving slippery pasta.

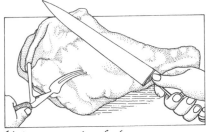

*Using a carving fork*

## Forks

**Metal forks** A strong fork with two long tines is necessary for holding meat firmly while it is carved. The best forks have a full tang riveted to a wooden or plastic handle and a guard to protect the hand.

**A toasting fork** looks a bit like Neptune's trident and has an extendable handle so that bread can be safely toasted over an open fire.

**Wooden fork** This friendly giant is ideal for gently swirling spaghetti while it cooks in the pot. Many cooks also find its light touch useful when adding the liquid to pastry or dough mixtures.

## Bowls

Bowls, like clothes, reflect their owner's activities—the more varied these are the more choice is needed. Those who merely reconstitute precooked or premixed convenience food could probably manage with one or two bowls, but cooks with an exciting repertoire will need a well-furnished wardrobe of bowls.

Bowls must be suited to the job in hand—too large and the ingredients spread themselves in a film around the sides, too small and the contents overflow.

Bowls are used for cooking, storing and serving and are available in a huge variety of materials and sizes, each having qualities suited more to one purpose than another.

Every serious kitchen needs at least one huge bowl, suitable for soaking tongues and hams and steeping oxtails; it will also come in handy for serving salads for large parties.

As for the number of smaller bowls you will need, there are, of course, seasonal fluctuations to take into consideration (during holiday periods like Christmas, a number of bowls can be out of action—occupied by puddings for several weeks).

### Ceramic bowls

The traditional, solid Gripstand mixing bowl is still standard equipment for every kitchen and the cornerstone of the bowl collection. It is wide enough to allow an unrestricted mixing action and deep enough to contain the mixture that is being stirred, beaten or rubbed, and it is also the ideal bowl for dough making. At the bottom of one side there is a small flat area that acts as a base for holding the bowl steady when it is tilted for beating or creaming.

**China pudding bowls** The sides of a pudding bowl are steeper and more tapered than those of a mixing bowl because this shape gives support to the center of the pudding and prevents it collapsing or sagging when it is turned out. The tough glazed finish will withstand even the high temperatures of a pressure cooker, and its raised rim holds the string firmly in place.

But containing steamed puddings is not the only destiny for this versatile bowl; it is indispensable for all small beating, whipping and mixing tasks and for storing food in the refrigerator or larder.

**Other small bowls** There are of course quantities of small porcelain, earthenware, terra-cotta, stoneware and salt-glaze bowls

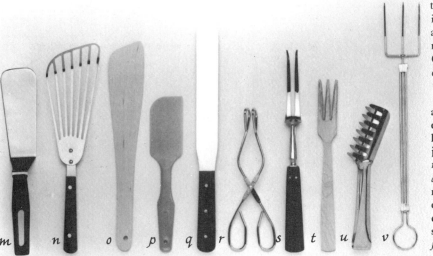

a *Tinned steel balloon whisk* b *Rotary beater* c *Flat whisk* d, e, f, g *Boxwood spoons* h *Metal spoon* i *Perforated metal spoon* j *Stainless steel ladle* k *Wire skimmer with a lightweight wire basket* l *Perforated disc skimmer* m *Flexible metal turner* n *Metal turner with slits for draining* o *Beechwood spatula* p *Plastic scraper* q *Metal palette knife* r *Metal tongs* s *Carving fork with guard* t *Beechwood fork* u *Spaghetti tongs* v *Toasting fork*

# Bowls

of both ancient and modern design that are endlessly useful. Handmade bowls with slightly rough interiors are good for making mayonnaise and vinaigrette—the surface helps the mixture to emulsify.

## Plastics

When plastics first arrived on the domestic scene their qualities were greeted with such enthusiasm that they were indiscriminately adopted for many products. Manufacturers produced plastic goods using existing or traditional designs which did not necessarily suit the properties of the new material, and consequently the kitchen was flooded with cheap plastic tools and gadgets which neither worked well nor looked good. Thankfully the tide has receded and the survivors are now valued in the kitchen.

Plastic bowls are quiet, non-porous, virtually unbreakable and are good insulators, but they have to be treated carefully because they are vulnerable to scratching and to distortion through heat, and of course they cannot be used in the oven or for steaming chores. A rubber-ringed base will keep the bowl anchored safely in place. Melamine is the best plastic for mixing bowls and can be put in the dishwashing machine.

## Stainless steel

Generations of china pudding bowls come and go, but the immortal stainless steel body will outlive them all. It is not surprising that restaurant kitchens use stainless steel bowls almost to the exclusion of all others. The conductivity of metal makes these bowls ideal for ingredients that need to be cooled or heated over water. Whenever possible use wooden utensils to avoid the clash of metal on metal.

## Copper

An unlined copper bowl is a non-essential but beautiful piece of kitchen equipment. Unfortunately its sole culinary use is to contain egg whites while they are being whipped—some say it is the chemical reaction between the copper and the egg whites that enables them, when whipped, to reach Himalayan proportions; others say that the copper absorbs all the heat generated by whipping, leaving the egg whites to rise spectacularly in the cool.

Clean the bowl thoroughly before use by scrubbing the inside with salt and lemon quarters until the copper is gleaming and free from any traces of verdigris or discoloration, wash it in hot water and dry carefully. Never use an unlined copper bowl for mixing, cooking or storing food.

## Wood

A handsome wooden bowl is the perfect setting for fresh green leaves. It should be wide and deep enough to contain an exuberant curly salad while it is being tossed.

Wooden bowls need to be washed as soon as possible after use as they absorb the flavor of food. They should be dried away from direct heat. An occasional coating of vegetable oil will keep the color rich and help to prevent the wood from absorbing too much moisture.

a *Gripstand ceramic mixing bowl* b, c, d *White china pudding bowls in a range of sizes* e *Plain white porcelain salad bowl* f *Pyrex mixing bowl* g *Small white French porcelain bowl* h *Danish melamine bowl* i *Copper bowl for beating egg whites* j *Wooden salad bowl* k *Aluminum colander* l *White enamelled colander* m *Collapsible salad shaker* n *Plastic spin-dryer*

## Colanders

For the speedy separation of food from water, a rounded, double-handled metal bowl standing on a firm base and laced with a pattern of perforations is the most effective instrument. Choose the most roomy colander you can find so that when you are washing fruit, vegetables or salad there is plenty of space to swish them around.

Enamel, stainless steel or aluminum are all well suited to the duties of a colander and will not be harmed by heat.

## Salad baskets

These airy balloons of wire will contain a leafy salad with the minimum of restriction while they are whirled around out in the garden by energetic arms to extract the water by centrifugal force.

If you don't have revolving arm sockets, or don't like the open-air exercise in mid-December, there are some ingenious salad spin-dryers, which are operated by handle. These should be used in the sink if they have no container to catch the water.

# Molds

The form of food is an important part of the preparation process and should not be dismissed as a last-minute detail. The link between the eye and the appetite is very strong, so a carefully and sensitively presented meal that is also a mouthwatering sight will put the diners' palates in a receptive mood before they have even tasted the first mouthful.

Food that has little form of its own, like an aspic or a mousse, can look rather dull and uninteresting if left to its own devices in a simple bowl. One way of overcoming this for a special occasion is to shape the food in a decorative mold which will translate a shapeless form into a glamorous centerpiece suitable for a party.

Foods that have to be cooked in their molds, such as pâtés and some mousses, must obviously be cooked in suitable containers made of either heavy-duty tinned steel or ovenproof porcelain. Molds specifically for cold foods—ice creams, gelatines or chocolate—are likely to be made of a thin metal that is easily impressed into complicated, convoluted forms. Such molds often have soldered seams that cannot withstand even moderate heat, so check what a mold is made of before you buy.

All molds should be shaped so that they are able to relinquish their contents without damaging the pattern. Something that has been cooked should be allowed to cool before it is wrested from the container, and a cold mold should be heated briefly in warm water up to the rim so that the food surface melts slightly and the food makes a clean exit. A gentle shaking will help to dislodge blancmanges, creams and mousses.

*a, b, c Copper fish molds lined with tin in a variety of shapes and sizes d Thin hardwood thistle butter print for stamping out butter pats e White coeur à fromage cream-cheese mold with perforated base for draining f French stone-colored earthenware curd-cheese drainer g Large, deep, white ceramic mold h Delicate copper mousse or gelatine mold with a scalloped rim i Tortoise-shaped mold of toughened glass j, k Tinned rice ring molds also turn out cakes that never sag in the middle l, m Thin metal molds with intricate patterns n Square, tinned steel ice cream bombe with patterned top o, p Stainless steel Easter-egg molds both plain and patterned q, r, s Copper molds lined with tin t, u Tinned steel chocolate or cake molds in various shapes and sizes held together by clips v, w The dismantled parts of a rabbit-shaped mold x Tinned steel star mold y Rubber fondant mold*

# Measuring

The Art of Cooking is a familiar phrase which conjures up images of cooks, rather like temperamental prima donnas, tossing the odd handful of herbs or spices into the pot and instinctively producing a splendid masterpiece. In reality the art of cooking for most people is concerned with mastering the basic culinary techniques and then finding recipes that please them.

It is obvious from just a cursory glance at any cook book that artistry needs to be underpinned by a solid foundation of science. Ingredients must often be measured in exact amounts, assembled and prepared in an ordered sequence, and cooked at precise temperatures for a predetermined length of time.

Measuring equipment is therefore an important component of the batterie de cuisine, enabling recipes to be perfectly balanced not just once but every time.

In these days of international recipe exchanges, measuring is complicated by the different systems used in Europe and America. Americans mete out their ingredients in a cup, which is a misleadingly vague term for what is in fact a precise volume, whereas Europeans measure their dry ingredients by weight. The English Imperial pints and gallons are quite different from the American measures, which share the same names, while on the Continent everything from milk to oil is measured in fractions of the liter. So whenever possible buy measuring devices that are marked with both metric and Imperial or American calibrations to save duplication.

## Scales

Balancing quantities of goods against weights of constant or standard size is a very ancient practice that began in the marketplace as a fair method of trading. In these days of high technology, scales are more important than ever, not least in the kitchen, where they are one of the keys to successful cooking.

**Balance scales** A strong pair of balance scales will last a lifetime because they operate on a simple seesaw principle and there is no complicated mechanism to wear out. The weight is not indicated on a register, but when the weights on the two sides exactly match, a pointer lines up with a central marker on the fulcrum. These scales are usually so sensitive that two or three crumbs added to either side is enough to tip the balance.

Imperial or metric weights may be used according to the recipe instructions, and these are available in brass or, less expensively, in cast iron for the heavier weights over 1 oz or 25 g. The pan for containing the food should ideally be a pear-shaped stainless steel or enamel bowl which, when tipped, will channel its contents neatly into a mixing bowl or saucepan.

**Spring-balance scales** In this type of scale the weights have been replaced by a metal coil or spring. The ingredients are balanced against the tension stored in the spring and the weight is registered on a calibrated scale, usually marked with both metric and Imperial measures.

This principle lends itself to compact and streamlined designs such as those where the plastic dish is inverted and used as a cover for the scales when they are not in use. The capacity is of course limited by the power of the spring, so these scales are more suited to weighing light loads. There is also a tendency for spring balance scales to wander out of true, but accuracy can usually be restored by means of an adjustment screw when the scales are at rest.

**Beam scales** are a neat, domestic-size adaptation of those angular giants that used to stand like gallows in the corner of pharmacies before the days of the penny weighing machines. Weights are moved along a beam marked with grams or pounds which will hang suspended in a central position when the weight in the tray is equal to the weight marked on the beam. These scales have a good capacity and are more accurate than spring-balance scales.

**Pocket balances** These small tools are for the biggest jobs and will handle those weighing tasks that are beyond the scope of ordinary kitchen scales. Hung from a secure hook, this balance will weigh the Christmas turkey, sacks of fruit or vegetables, or even excess baggage. There is of course an upper weight limit determined

by the strength of the spring, which stretches downwards as the weight is applied, and the attached marker converts the extent of the stretch to pounds or kilograms on a calibrated scale.

## Measuring pitchers and cups

For cooking purposes liquids are measured in units of cups, pints or liters.

**A Pyrex measuring pitcher** is perhaps the most useful; the glass, which can withstand the impact of boiling liquids, enables the cook to see exactly how much is in the pitcher, and because it is such a poor conductor of heat the handle always remains cool.

**Clear plastic measuring pitchers** are cheaper, but must be treated more carefully; heat can craze or distort the plastic, and if the shape of the pitcher alters it may no longer be an accurate measure.

**China or stainless steel pitchers** have the measure printed or etched on their inner surface, but the cook will often have to peer into their steamy depths to see if the correct level has been reached.

**Measuring cups** The variety in American cooking reflects the diversity of its origins with contributions from almost every country in the Old World, but the ingredients are always measured in cups. This does not mean any old cup picked at random from the shelf—it means exactly eight fluid ounces, so a special measure is practical and necessary. Cup measures are also available in fractions or multiples of one cup and the whole set of cups will nest neatly inside one another.

## Measuring spoons

Many recipes call for spicy or highly flavored ingredients to be added by the spoonful. It is often left to the whim of the cook to decide whether these are administered, heaped or unheaped, in mammoth

Victorian teaspoons or measured out in coffee spoons, and the resulting balance of flavors may thus be spoiled by a disproportionate amount of one over the other.

A set of measuring spoons is therefore useful and will accurately dispense small amounts ranging from $\frac{1}{4}$ teaspoon to one tablespoon, but the ingredients should be levelled off with a knife unless the recipe specifies a heaping measure.

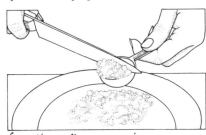

*Levelling off a measuring spoon*

## Thermometers

A well-fitted kitchen will have a variety of thermometers to cope with the whole gamut of culinary needs, from monitoring the coldest depths of the deep freeze to recognizing the six stages of sugar boiling.

**Freezer thermometers** There are two enemies to be faced when preserving food by freezing: first the bacteria that cause the food to decay, and second the enzymes that break down its structure and impair the flavor. Food frozen to $0°F/-18°C$ will be safe from bacteriological activity. You should check that this temperature is constantly maintained, as the enzymes will begin to function at $14°F/-10°C$.

Refrigerators occasionally need to be run at a specific temperature (when chilling white wine for instance) so buy a thermometer that registers cool temperatures as well as those way down in the minus range.

**Middle-range thermometers** will measure temperatures up to approximately $250°F/121°C$ and are available with either metal or glass sensors. Precise temperature control is essential for the safety and success of many recipes such as bottled fruit and vegetables and for keeping custards, junkets, and creamy sauces under boiling point.

**Sugar or deep-fat thermometers** register the highest temperatures that are encountered in cooking. The secret of successful deep-fat frying lies in preheating the oil to about $375°F/190°C$ before adding the food. At this temperature the oil will seal the food instantly, preventing the escape of any juices or flavor, and conversely the oil will not impregnate the food.

When sugar is heated it passes through various stages of crystallization at certain critical temperatures until at $356°F/180°C$ it becomes caramel. Each of these stages is valuable to the cook, but without a thermometer it is difficult to catch the sugar at just the right moment before it passes to the next stage. High-temperature thermometers are made of glass, so warm them in hot water before use.

**Oven thermometers** In a perfect world these would be superfluous equipment, but ovens are notorious for their idiosyncrasies (usually the result of a sluggish thermostat) and wide temperature variations between the top and bottom shelves. The cook can discover the temperature pattern inside a difficult oven by standing a mercury-filled thermometer in various positions and noting the differences.

**Meat thermometers** enable you to detect that narrow band of perfection when meat has reached a high enough temperature to kill any dangerous bacteria without losing any of its succulent juices. This is sometimes a very hit-or-miss affair, particularly when cooking an unfamiliarly large roast.

Some types of meat thermometer are just used for spot checks, while others are inserted into the meat before cooking begins, and left until the hand points to the appropriate place on the dial.

**Wine thermometers** Wine has an optimum temperature at which its flavor is most fully developed. A wine thermometer has a register showing the correct serving temperatures of various types of wine attached to a sensor, which is dipped into the bottle after the cork is drawn.

## Salometer

This instrument is only useful if you regularly pickle meat, fish or vegetables. The salometer measures the density of brine, which varies according to the amount of salt it contains.

## Clocks

Meal preparation is a temporal juggling act, and the cook always has one eye on the clock to ensure that the differing cooking times for the various elements will be completed simultaneously at the appointed hour. Choose a clock with a clearly marked face that can be read at a glance—a hand for marking seconds is also useful.

**Automatic timers** Very often it is the sense of smell which tells a busy or forgetful person that something is not only cooked but overcooked. An automatic timer that can be preset to ring at a certain time will attract the attention of the whole household.

**Sand timers** Egg timers and hourglasses have been largely superseded by automatic timers, but they are quiet, accurate and cost a fraction of the price of their mechanical usurpers.

*a Balance scales and weights b Spring balance scales c Beam scales d Pocket balance e, f, g Measuring pitchers in stainless steel, plastic and Pyrex h Set of measuring cups i Measuring spoons j Freezer thermometer k Middle-range thermometer l Brass sugar thermometer m All-purpose cooking thermometer n, o Oven thermometers p Meat thermometer q Wine thermometer r Sand egg timer s, t Automatic minute timers u Battery-operated kitchen clock*

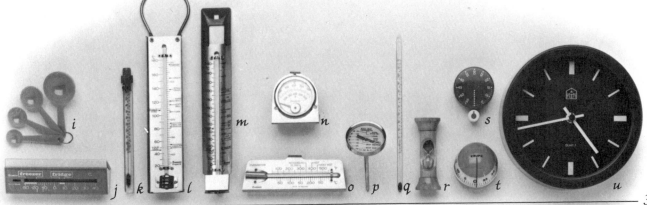

# Preserving

Although homemade preserves are no longer the lifeline for winter survival that they once were, they still merit an important place in the cook's seasonal round of activities.

### Freezing

Preserving by freezing requires little special equipment beyond a selection of tough plastic bags, boxes and foil containers, and of course the freezer itself—and it is here that a small note of warning should be sounded. Huge freezers loom like great white coffins in garages and outbuildings all over the country, many of them chugging away freezing empty air space for six months of the year. This, of course, is a terrible waste of both energy and money, and so is filling up the freezer unnecessarily with cheap bulky items like loaves of bread purely to justify the running costs, so it is important to choose one that is the right size for your needs.

Unless you have access to a garden, thus ensuring plentiful supplies of cheap seasonal food, it will cost a great deal of money to fill a large freezer, and it is a continuing commitment. It is worth remembering that there are fresh vegetables in season all the year round and frozen produce should merely add variety rather than replace the winter crops, and that the texture and taste of most food that has been in a freezer is less good than when it was fresh.

### Jam and pickle making

Cooks rarely have a chance to admire their handiwork for long before it is eaten, which is perhaps why the less transient splendors of a well-stocked cupboard arouse such deep feelings of satisfaction and pride.

**Jam jars** should be carefully hoarded throughout the year because opportunities to make jams and jellies have a habit of cropping up without warning—a kindly friend unexpectedly arrives bearing armfuls of fruit which have to be turned into jam without delay, or you suddenly find yourself driving past an orchard where produce is being sold at bargain prices.

Glass is the best material for jam jars because it is easy to check that they are scrupulously clean and dry and that you have not poured the jam while it is still too hot, causing all the fruit to rise to the surface—and an obvious bonus is that if the label becomes detached, the contents can still be identified without opening the cover.

**Canning jars** Fruits and vegetables preserved in brine, vinegar or alcohol must be put into hermetically sealed jars. These jars are made of heat-resistant glass because they need to be sterilized by heat. They usually have a two-piece screw top, and are available in several sizes. The seal is secured by soft rubber rings, which should be renewed every time the jar is used.

**Tongs** with rubber grippers are useful for maneuvering hot sterilized jars.

**A preserving pan** is a good investment even if you only use it three or four times a year. Large saucepans are not good substitutes, and are likely to cause the cook a good deal of extra work cleaning the burned jam from the pan and stove top.

Preserving pans should have very thick bottoms, which quickly conduct the heat away from the source so that the contents will not burn and stick even at very high temperatures. The pan is deep to allow maximum evaporation and expansion of the contents, and most types have handles for both carrying the pan and steadying it during pouring.

The most practical preserving pans are made of aluminum, which is highly conductive, durable and resistant to high temperatures. Its performance is only equalled by copper, but this metal reacts with acid foods to form poisonous salts so copper pans should be lined with tin or stainless steel.

**Wide-mouthed aluminum funnels** are necessary for pouring jams, jellies or syrups into the jars and keeping the outsides free from sticky, congealed trickles, which are so hard to clean off.

**Paraffin wax** If you are not using screw-top jars, you should seal the preserve with a thin film of melted paraffin wax.

**Jelly bag** Some coarse or seeded fruits are better preserved as jellies by straining the cooked fruit through the close weave of a suspended jelly bag, which keeps back the seeds and lets through all the pectin and flavor to make a clear, smooth jelly.

### Wine and beer making

Real enthusiasts appear to be able to make wine out of practically anything—even tea—but the right equipment is necessary to make this alchemy possible.

**Glass wine-making jars or demijohns** for fermenting the wine are closed with a cork fitted with a water-filled one-way air lock, which cleverly allows the gas to escape from the jar while preventing the entry of air and insects.

**A hydrometer** is necessary to check when fermentation is complete. It measures the specific gravity of the brew. Alcohol being lighter than water, the lower the specific gravity, the more alcoholic the wine.

**Funnels** are needed for pouring liquid into bottles, or, when lined with filter paper, for removing the sediment.

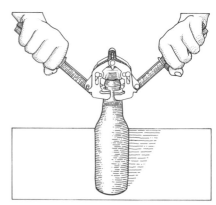

*Fixing a crown cap on a beer bottle*

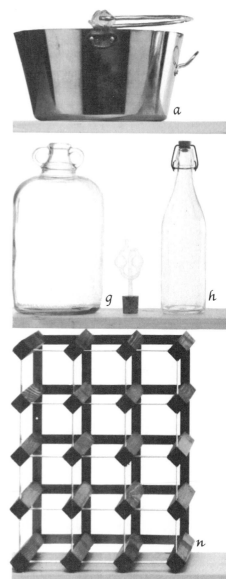

Preserves **330–333**
Making jam **330**

Rubber tubing fitted with a tap is the way to siphon beer or wine into containers.

Curved glass tubing is used for decanting wine from large containers without disturbing the sediment.

Corking machine It is often hard enough to get corks out of bottles, but for the reverse process you really need the help of a corker. It is most important that the cork fits really tightly in the neck of the bottle, and this machine will compress the most unwilling cork into position.

Wine racks Wine bottles should be stored on their sides so that the corks are kept moist and swollen tight in the neck of the bottle. There are many types of racks available—folding, self-assembly, wall hung, or infinitely extendable systems that can be expanded in line with your income.

Beer bottles need to be of thick, strong, dark glass, preferably with screw stoppers that can withstand the pressure of good, foamy beer. You may have to buy your initial supply directly from a manufacturer.

Plastic refuse bins with clip-on lids bought specially for the purpose of brewing beer make ideal vats for the initial fermenting process.

Crown caps If you can't obtain screw-top beer bottles, you will have to seal the bottles with the familiar metal crown caps. These are applied with the aid of an extremely forceful gadget and give a very strong seal.

a *Aluminum preserving pan with a strong galvanized handle and a pouring lip* b *Aluminum jam funnel* c *Self-adhesive labels for jam jars* d *Jelly bag on a stand* e *Muslin jelly bag* f *Glass canning jars* g *Glass demijohn or bell jar with stopper and air lock* h *Bottle with spring-clip closure* i *Glass wine bottle* j *Cast aluminum hand corker forces corks into wine bottles* k *Absorbent paper wine filter* l *Plastic wine funnels in varying sizes* m *Plastic and glass tubing for siphoning wine into bottles* n *Pine and steel wine rack, easily assembled at home* o *Folding wine rack which accommodates ten bottles* p, q *Crown cap gadget comes with a supply of crown caps* r *Large plastic bin with lid*

# Barbecuing and Smoking

Cooking outdoors is one of the greatest pleasures of summertime and, to many, barbecuing is the easiest and the most enjoyable way of preparing food outside the kitchen.

Devotees of barbecuing will not need to be convinced of its benefits, but those who have not tried it should not be put off by the apparently vast selection of tools and equipment available: the rule is—the simpler the better. Food cooked on a piece of chicken wire over a pile of stones on a beach tastes just as good as (some would say better than) food prepared on an elaborate barbecue cart with hot cupboards and a motorized spit.

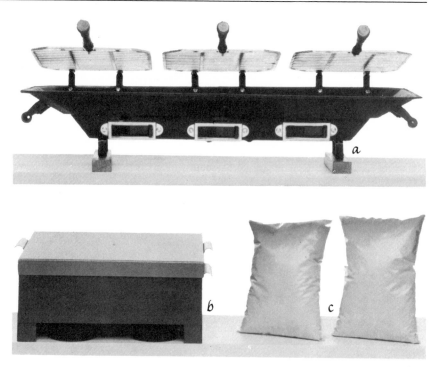

## The barbecue

Before buying or building your barbecue it is a good idea to consider how much the barbecue will be used. Large, complicated and usually expensive grills need to be housed during the winter, and if they are used only once or twice a year they will not justify the outlay. Alternatively, if barbecue parties or cook-outs are a regular feature of your summer, a small hibachi or picnic grill will not be adequate. For those with large gardens, a built-in brick barbecue is worth considering; it allows you to design extra warming cupboards and preparation levels, and it can also be used (where legal) for burning garden trash in winter. The small portable barbecues are, of course, ideal for picnics or camping holidays.

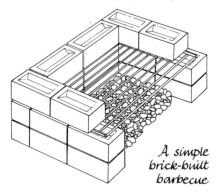

*A simple brick-built barbecue*

### Types of barbecue
Heavy-gauge metals and cast-iron grills are less likely to bend or become misshapen with repeated use than lightweight nickel-plated and chrome-plated grills, which do have the advantage of being rustproof.

The grill rods should be fairly close together for grilling sausages and small hamburgers. Most people find it is convenient to cook at table height and this is certainly safer for the usual barbecuing conditions of outdoor light and uneven ground, so if you buy a small portable barbecue you will need to set it on a table or on a board on two stools. This is also an important consideration when designing your own brick barbecue. Some ready-made brazier barbecues have legs—check that they are high enough to cook on in comfort.

**Hibachis** These are small Japanese-style black cast-iron troughs, rectangular or round, with strong wooden-handled grilling grids. The height of the grids is adjustable and the troughs have vents to adjust the heat. Suitable for tabletop cooking, hibachis come in single, double or triple sizes, but they are not adaptable for spit-roasting.

**Braziers** Often made in unsuitably lightweight materials, braziers are round or square trays on legs, and sometimes on wheels. Hoods and spits can be fitted, but the main drawback of braziers is that they are often too low to cook on comfortably. Some models have legs which screw in or fold up, making them as portable as picnic barbecues.

**Picnic barbecues** This is really only a term applied to the small compact types of brazier which can be easily packed for travel. They may be rectangular or round and are usually made of lightweight metal.

**Kettle barbecues** As the name suggests, kettle barbecues are totally enclosed by means of a hinged lid. This can be raised to the vertical to provide a windbreak, but usually the food is cooked with the lid down, which reflects the heat like an oven. Made from cast aluminum or vitreous-enamelled steel, kettle barbecues are ideal for the windy garden or for smoke-cooking food.

**Barbecue carts** Probably the most elaborate of barbecues, these are usually on wheels and sometimes covered. The larger kinds have all manner of modern cooking aids such as warming cupboards, electric rotisseries, thermometers, cutting tables and equipment racks. They are extremely bulky and need storage room in winter, and somehow they seem to reduce the fun and impromptu pleasures of barbecuing.

**Lateral heat barbecues** For those who like to cook outdoors but dislike the typically smoky, blackened look and taste of barbecued foods, a revolving spit or rotisserie adjacent to a bank of charcoal or gas or electric burners may provide an alternative. In this way natural juices released during the cooking are caught in a tray beneath the food, and there is no danger of flareups from dripping fat catching fire. Steaks and hamburgers are cooked in a basket-like tambour to hold them in place.

## The accessories

There is no real need to assemble a battery of gadgets for the barbecue, but some specialized items will aid the cook considerably and some are essential for safety reasons.

**Heatproof gloves and apron** Protective gloves and an apron are a must when cooking over an open fire to save you from fat splashes and prevent burns from unexpectedly hot handles. Choose really thick ones and avoid plastic.

**Bellows or a fan** Not essential but most fire makers find that they are a boon to encourage a reluctant blaze.

**Basting brush or bulb baster** Succulent barbecued food needs frequent basting. For steaks and chops a basting brush is easiest to use, but for large spit-roasts a bulb baster allows you to baste over the heat.

**Long-handled fork** Useful for lifting and turning food over the heat and for holding food that is being carved. Those with wooden handles are best.

**Tongs** Long-handled tongs are useful both for moving glowing coals and for lifting food without piercing it. Wooden handles are best.

**Stiff wire brush** is ideal for removing burned-on fragments of food.

**Skewers** Long ones are preferable because they enable you to leave the handles outside the heat. Stainless steel skewers will not rust, and those with wooden handles will be easier to use.

**Wire grill grids or baskets** Unless your barbecue has very narrow grill wires to lay tender fish and crumbly hamburgers on, you need a wire grill basket to cradle them gently while cooking and to keep them in one piece. Made usually of tinned steel, grill grids consist of two sides of close-set wires hinged together and two long, flat wire handles. Steaks and hamburgers are cooked in a flat round or square grill which, if heated before use, sears the food with a lovely pattern. Fish grills are curved so that the delicate flesh is not crushed and they are usually shaped in the form of a single large fish. Sardine grills are round with twelve small fish shapes nose to nose. Some fish grills have little wire feet so that they can stand among the coals. All wire grills need to be greased with oil or melted butter before use or the food will stick to them.

**Spit with adjustable tines and motor** The simplest spit is a long stainless steel rod with a plastic or wooden handle, and two or four sharp angled tines which can be adjusted to hold the bird or joint in place.

These simplest of spits are usually made to slot into the hood of a barbecue. A motor-driven spit with either battery or electrical power is essential for roasting evenly.

Make sure the spit is strong enough to take the heaviest roast without bending, and when loading it always test it for balance before cooking or you will wear out the spit motor and the meat will cook most on the heaviest side.

**Frying pans and saucepans** For cooking soups, sauces or vegetables over the barbecue fire, a few heavy cast-iron pans are useful. Choose those with long and preferably wooden or insulated handles. They can also be used to cook steak and chops if you prefer to catch the juices from the food to use for gravy.

**Cast-iron grill plates and racks** are really only necessary if you have built your own barbecue, because most ready-made types have their own grills. Cast iron is the best material, but it must be dried and oiled after use or it will rust. Always oil them before use, too. Solid iron grill plates with ridges are, like frying pans, ideal for steaks or chops if you wish to use the juices for a sauce.

## Smoke cooking

Smoke cooking or hot smoking is a refinement of barbecuing: the food is cooked in a covered barbecue, and sawdust or wood chips are added to cause a fragrant smoke to flavor the food. The temperature in the smoker must be about 350°F/180°C. This method is particularly suitable for eel, trout, herring, buckling and mackerel. Resinous woods of any kind must never be used because they will make the food taste of disinfectant. Favorite woods are apple, hickory and oak.

Smoke cooking is a fast method of cooking, but cold smoking or smoke curing, with which it is often confused, is a long, complicated process which does not cook the food (with the exception of very small fish) but cures it. Before being cold smoked or smoke cured, all foods must be brined. You can make your own cold smoker from a barrel, a few bricks, a slender pole and a piece of wet sacking.

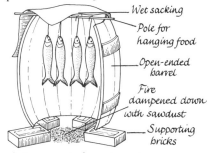

Wet sacking
Pole for hanging food
Open-ended barrel
Fire dampened down with sawdust
Supporting bricks

*A homemade barrel smoker*

There are many kinds of smoke cooker available, all of which come complete with the manufacturer's instructions. It is best to site your smoker outdoors because there will be a fair amount of smoke escaping, and even if you set it by an open window or door you will find that the smell of the smoke will permeate the house. As it cooks, the fish will turn a beautiful light mahogany color.

a *Simple hibachi charcoal-burning barbecue of black cast iron with galvanized aluminum grids complete with wooden handles* b *Aluminum smoke-cooking box* c *Sawdust bags* d *Bulb baster* e *Basting brush* f, g *Chromed steel fork and tongs with wooden handles* h *Stiff wire brush* i *Oriental skewer with a turned wooden handle* j *Set of stainless steel skewers* k *Stainless steel sardine grill* l *Tinned wire grill* m *Cast-iron grill pan with ridged bottom and wooden handles* n *Oblong grill in cast iron with black finish*

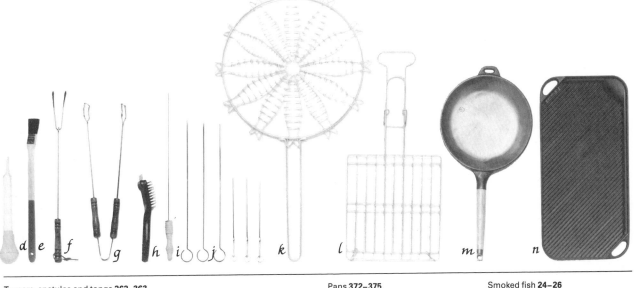

d e f g h i j k l m n

# Pans and Casseroles

The daily relationship between a cook and his or her pans can, like a marriage, be either blissfully happy or a source of aggravation and misery, with many grey shades of dissatisfaction between.

But (unlike marriage) a successful partnership can be guaranteed if, before purchasing, the cook takes care to find out what the qualities of good pans are, and the various properties of the metals they are made from. Equipped with this information it is possible to make a selection which will suit all needs and give a lifetime's reliable service.

Mistakes are expensive, and hang around the kitchen for years, burning, buckling and generally enraging the cook until they are finally thrown out in disgust.

## Copper
The great advantage of copper is that it can transfer heat from one place to another more quickly than any other metal, and its rich golden-red color adds a warm glow to the kitchen. But it is expensive and regrettably promiscuous—combining chemically with food, liquids and air to form a poisonous layer of green verdigris. For this reason copper vessels must always be lined with tin or silver to prevent this reaction from spoiling the food. Copper also needs constant polishing to keep it bright, and for some this is just one chore too many.

**Care** Salt and lemon halves will keep copper pans burnished—commercial cleaners give a light finish which is difficult to maintain. Avoid harsh scouring pads or powder; tin-lined pans should be soaked and then cleaned with soapy water and a brush. Use only wooden utensils for stirring.

## Iron and steel
Steel pans are very susceptible to corrosion and distortion by heat, and although a well-seasoned heavy steel frying pan is a very satisfying thing to use, steel saucepans are only useful if they are covered with a sturdy layer of vitrified enamel.

In spite of its propensity to rust, cast iron is popular for certain types of pan such as steak griddles, paella pans and crêpe pans where cooking the food evenly at high temperatures is important.

**Care** Maintenance is a continual battle against rust. Pans should be thoroughly dried before being stored, and if they are not used very often, coat them with a light layer of cooking oil before putting them away. New steel frying pans should be prepared for use by heating slightly and washing thoroughly in hot soapy water to remove the manufacturer's protective coating. Dry the pan and heat again, with some cooking oil in the pan, to a fairly high temperature; run the oil over the base and up the sides until the whole surface of the pan has been covered, cool, then wipe out surplus oil.

## Enamelled iron and steel
Enamelled cast iron makes very strong, sturdy vessels which are excellent for slow stove-top or oven cookery.

Enamelled steel pans are inexpensive, but

Baking pans and dishes **376–378**

they need to be treated with care—do not allow empty pans to heat over a flame or they will distort and shed their protective enamel coating, and never clean them with an abrasive substance or you will eventually expose the metal.

**Care** This finish needs the same gentle treatment as lined copper pans. Harsh scouring powders or pads will destroy the glassy surface and eventually wear through the enamel; any stains can be easily removed by soaking the pan in a dilute solution of liquid bleach. Be careful not to bang or knock these pans, particularly when they are hot, as the enamel chips very easily.

## Aluminum

This metal is a good all-arounder: tough, an excellent conductor of heat, non-toxic and reasonably priced. Alkaline foods and hard water will leave a black stain inside the pan, but this is easily removed with a steel wool pad. Aluminum is not totally immune from interaction with acid foods such as spinach and wine- or vinegar-based sauces, so do

not allow these substances to linger in the pan longer than necessary.

**Care** Clean as soon as possible after use and remove any black staining with a soap-filled steel pad. Do not expect aluminum pans to retain a mirror polish for long—they soon revert to a matt finish.

## Stainless steel

The most durable metal in the kitchen, stainless steel will retain a highly polished finish throughout its long life, and is completely impervious to acids or alkalis. Alas— this promising metal will only conduct heat reluctantly, which is of course an enormous drawback in a pan.

**Care** Soak pans to loosen food deposits and clean with a gentle bristle or nylon brush and plenty of warm soapy water.

## Nonstick pans

Nonstick surfaces are a gift from modern technology and daily appear in more durable and long-lived forms. They are particularly useful for lining milk saucepans and frying

*a, b, c, d Heavy gauge aluminum pans e, f, g, h Enamelled steel saucepans with heatproof plastic handles and a casserole from the same range i Stainless steel steamer with heatproof handles j Ceramic milk jug can be heated directly on the stove-top and brought piping hot to the table k Nonstick milk pan l Egg poacher m Wire-mesh stove mat n Perforated aluminum rice steamer hangs on the side of a pan o Aluminum trivet turns a combination of pans into a bain-marie p Polished aluminum fish kettle with a steaming platform q Nonstick frying pan r Traditional heavy steel frying pan with riveted handle s Heavy steel omelet pan t Cast-iron skillet u Oval copper frying pan with a brass handle that will remain cool thanks to the reduction of heat conductivity between different metals v Round copper sauté pan with lid w Paella pan is a traditional Spanish cast-iron pan with handles on both sides x Cast-iron griddle which can be heated to very high temperatures*

Oven-going iron skillet **378**
Electric kettle **380, 380**
Electric frying pan **380, 381**
Paella **286**

# Pans and Casseroles

pans, where eggs and fillets of fish will cook happily without any fat and be released completely intact at the end, leaving scarcely a smear in the pan.

**Care** Clean with a cloth in hot soapy water, rinse and dry. Avoid using metal spoons or spatulas, which will scratch the finish and expose the metal beneath.

### Tin

As it is a soft metal with a low melting point, tin is not used for pans where it will come into contact with a direct flame, but it is valuable as a lining for copper because it is completely stable and non-toxic.

### Porcelain and glass

Pans of porcelain or heat-resistant glass are both expensive and beautiful. They need to be treated with great care—always used over a low flame (in the case of glass use a heat-retarding mat) and never placed over heat when empty. Both are eminently suitable for delicate butter sauces, and they travel well from stove-top to table.

### The perfect metal

Unfortunately no one particular metal is capable of providing the perfect pan. In the case of aluminum the shortcomings are not serious, and a set of thick cast pans in this metal will give excellent service, but until a single hybrid alloy can be produced combining the beauty and conductivity of copper, the lightness of aluminum and the stability of stainless steel, the next best thing is to laminate the various metals in such a way as to combine all their best qualities and minimize their negative points. Combinations which give excellent results are: aluminum sandwiched between an outer layer of copper and an inner lining of stainless steel; copper lined with tin or silver; aluminum lined with a nonstick finish; cast iron coated with enamel or stainless steel, with a thick copper or aluminum base.

### Choosing pans

Once you have decided on the best metal or combination of metals, you should then concern yourself with the design and quality of the pan. Look for the following points:

● Thick, heavy-gauge metal, particularly on the base, which will not distort or dent and will spread the heat evenly from the source to all parts of the pan.

● Sides that curve gently in to the base so that no part of the pan will be inaccessible to the spoon. This is a good feature to look for in a frying pan—curved sides enable delicate omelets and crepes to be rolled gently onto a plate without damage.

● Handles should be strong, securely riveted to the pan and preferably insulated from the heat so that they always remain cool enough to hold. They should have comfortable well-rounded contours—thin angular shapes cut into the hand when pouring or lifting heavy pans. Plastic or wooden handles are the best insulators, but may loosen and split if cleaned in a dishwasher. A ring or hole in the end of the handle is useful for hanging the pan on a rack.

● Lids must give a tight seal and be shaped so that condensed water vapor is returned to the pan and does not escape in trickles

Baking pans and dishes **376–378**

down the outside. Lid knobs, like handles, should remain cool enough to touch—again plastic or wood are best.

## Storage

If possible, pans should be kept at eye level, or at least above the waist, either hanging from a rack or lined up on a shelf. Dark, low cupboards infuriate the busy cook, pans get piled together indiscriminately by helpful dish-dryers because nothing has a special place, and eventually they get scratched and chipped, or pushed to inaccessible corners in the general melee.

## Casseroles

After a cold or tiring journey nothing can make the arrival home more welcoming than the warm, savory smell of a casserole that has been simmering gently for several hours. The meat will have reached that stage of perfection where it melts in the mouth, and the vegetables, herbs and stock will have fused and blended their flavors.

All casseroles require slow, lengthy cooking so conservation of moisture is of paramount importance. Lids must fit the cooking pots very closely to prevent the escape of steam, and the seal must be designed so that condensed water vapor is channelled back into the pot. Handles, which are usually made of the same material as the casserole, should be easy to grip, yet small so that the pot will fit into an oven.

Casseroles made of enamelled cast iron, or other suitably heavy-gauge metals, may, of course, also be used on top of the stove both for sealing the meat over a high heat (if this is required), or for lengthy simmering. If the casserole is the only dish to be cooked, it is worth remembering that one ring costs far less to heat than a whole oven. Earthenware or heat-resistant glass dishes should only be used in the oven. It is useful to have a range of casseroles of various sizes because it is important that the contents should fill the pot in the right proportion—a small stew in a large pot will dry out long before it is cooked.

*a Aluminum asparagus pan—a perforated steaming cylinder holds the asparagus heads out of water during cooking b Aluminum pressure cooker c Aluminum deep fryer d Heavy-gauge aluminum sauté pan with a long tinned handle. The base is heavier than the sides for better heat conductivity e Steel wok and accessories for high-speed Chinese stir-frying f Copper and porcelain double boiler g Enamelled cast-iron fondue set h Aluminum couscous steamer i, j, k Enamelled cast-iron casserole dishes —the lids have heatproof knobs, but you will need oven gloves to touch the handles l Enamelled cast-iron oval casserole m Round earthenware casserole n Half-glazed earthenware casserole o, p Earthenware marmite pots are ideal for long, slow cooking—the tall sides slant inwards, thus reducing evaporation q Cast-iron doufeu is a traditional French cooking pot r, s Cooking pot and chicken brick of terra-cotta t, u, v Glazed earthenware casseroles in assorted sizes w, x Dutch pots of glazed earthenware*

# Baking

A baking session is usually heralded by the rustle and clash of pans, and perhaps the odd muttered curse when something is proving particularly difficult to find, for baking pans come in myriad shapes, from crenellated fantasies to the sober loaf tin, and in a diversity of materials, which adds to the confusion of choice.

## Baking pans and dishes

When food is placed in the dry, hot atmosphere of the oven it is cooked equally from all directions, and the containers do not have to withstand and conduct heat from an intense source as saucepans do. The function of a baking pan is to mold and contain, and to respond as fast as possible to the ambient heat of the oven.

The shape of pan you use depends entirely on what you are baking and what you want it to look like; the choice of the material needs to be approached more scientifically.

### The materials

Some baking pans have bright shining surfaces, which deflect the heat away from the contents so that they will not scorch, others have dark finishes, which absorb and hold the heat and need a temperature reduction of 10 degrees to achieve the same results.

**Tin plate** is the cheapest and most widely used material for baking containers. It is really worth spending the extra money on good quality baking pans that have the minimum number of seams, as nooks and crannies are difficult to clean and dry. Corrosion is the chief enemy of tin plate, for underneath the shining exterior lurks a metal that is addicted to oxidation through even the smallest pin hole in the tin coating.

Never use steel wool or other abrasive cleaning materials; wash and dry baking pans as soon as possible after use and then air them thoroughly in a warm dry place.

A good quality well-treated pan will last a lifetime and gradually its surface will acquire a dark patina that acts as a further protection and improves performance. Tin is susceptible to attack from acid foods, so it is not a suitable material for pie dishes.

**a** *Marble slab* **b** *Rolling pins: revolving and straight* **c** *Pastry blender* **d** *Sugar dredger* **e** *Pastry wheels* **f** *Pastry brush* **g** *Pastry board* **h** *Cookie cutters* **i** *Pie funnel* **j** *Flour dredger* **k** *Assorted cutters* **l** *Wire rack* **m** *Pastry bag with nozzles* **n** *Cake pan* **o** *Jelly roll tray* **p** *Baking sheet* **q** *Spring clip pan* **r** *Brioche molds* **s** *Bun sheets* **t** *Icing syringe and nozzles* **u** *Revolving decorating stand* **v** *Tart pan* **w** *Layer-cake pan* **x** *Loaf tin*

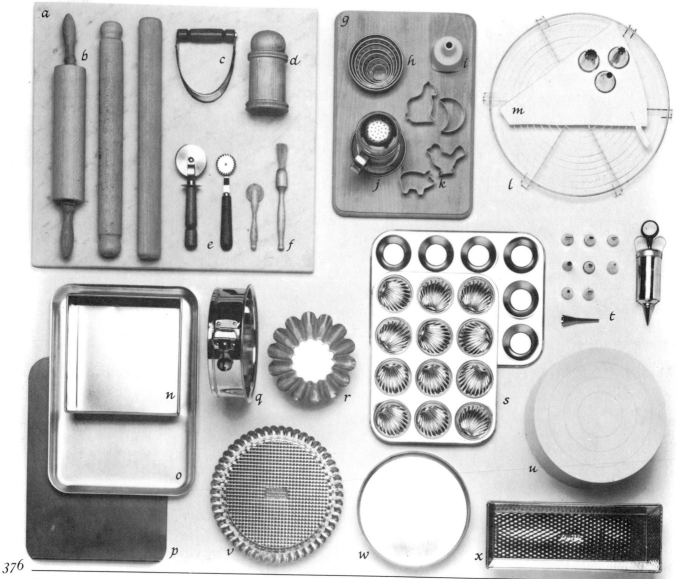

**Aluminum** is of course impervious to atmospheric oxidation but is also a good deal more expensive than tin plate. This light and durable material is an excellent conductor of heat.

**Nonstick silicone** surfaces are a boon and can be applied to either tin plate or aluminum. The surface will not last if metal utensils are used to scoop out the flan or spear the roast. To clean nonstick surfaces, soak for a few minutes, wipe with a soapy cloth and rinse.

**Enamel** High quality porcelain enamel on steel or cast iron is a most durable, hard-wearing combination—the glassy finish will not be affected by even the most corrosive rhubarb pie. Its weakness lies in the different expansion rates of the enamel and base metal, so it is particularly vulnerable to chipping when it is heated or cooled.

**Cast iron** Without an envelope of thick enamel, cast iron needs constant care and vigilance to keep it in good condition. This material is used most frequently for top-of-the-stove griddles and plates for baking on.

**Stainless steel** conducts heat so slowly that its use in the oven is limited to roasting pans and fish poachers.

**Glass** Ovenproof glass behaves in the same way as dark metal surfaces when it is heated, and cooking temperatures should be reduced slightly when using glass baking dishes. The brittleness, however, and sensitivity of glass to temperature changes means that careful handling is essential.

**Porcelain** The beauty and tempered fineness of this material make it especially suitable for those dishes which must be served straight from the oven. Although porcelain is prone to chipping and cracking and must be handled with reverence, the highly vitrified surface is very tough.

**Stoneware** is another tough ceramic with a sturdy homey quality and the ability to withstand high temperatures in the oven.

**Earthenware** has a traditional, rustic simplicity which people find particularly attractive. It is not as highly fired as stoneware and will chip and crack more easily.

**Unglazed terra-cotta pots** for cooking meats or vegetables without fat will be essential for those who are diet conscious or who just enjoy the flavor of meat and vegetables stewed in their own juice.

**Aluminum foil** If you are baking for the

**a** *Quiche pan* **b** *Aluminum meat roasting pan* **c** *Ceramic pie dish* **d** *Soufflé dishes/ramekins/cocottes* **e** *Enamelled steel pie pan* **f** *Earthenware terrine* **g** *Pyrex baking pan* **h** *Iron pizza tray* **i** *Enamelled steel roaster* **j** *Enamelled terrine* **k** *Earthenware gratin dish* **l** *Ceramic terrine* **m** *Earthenware pâté dish* **n** *Custard pots* **o** *Enamelled gratin dish* **p** *Individual pie dish* **q** *Ceramic flan dish* **r** *Earthenware gratin dish*

# Baking

deep freeze, it is a great nuisance to lose the use of baking containers for weeks on end. Variously shaped aluminum foil dishes are cheap and can be used in the oven and thence transferred to the deep freeze.

**Waxed paper cases** can be used for cooking large batches of cupcakes or muffins.

## Baking tools

Of course there is a lot more to baking than the pans. The business of making bread, cakes and pastry turns from a chore to a pleasure if the tools you use are well designed and efficient.

### Rolling pins

Some cooks enjoy handling ingredients and are perfectly happy to be up to their elbows in flour; those who have this direct, tactile approach to baking will probably opt for a rolling pin made from a single cylindrical length of wood, which keeps the palms close to the dough.

The revolving pin is more likely to suit people who prefer to keep food at a distance. The two handles, which remain stationary in the hands, guide the roller.

The best rolling pins of either type are heavy and of a good size, made of hard, close-grained wood such as boxwood that has been smoothed to a fine, silky finish. Ceramic and glass rolling pins are also available, but these break easily and do not roll as well as the wooden ones—the smooth surface will not hold a dusting of flour. Rolling pins with painted handles should be avoided as the paint will inevitably flake off into the pastry after a while.

### Pastry boards and slabs

Pastry can be rolled perfectly well on the smooth tops of kitchen units, provided, of course, they have been scrupulously cleaned.
**Marble slabs** These are satin smooth, impervious to flavors, and keep the pastry cool while it is being worked, but they are also expensive, heavy, breakable and susceptible to damage from acids.
**Wooden boards** are practical and tough and relatively inexpensive. To preserve the smooth surface they should only be used for pastry and not double as bread or chopping boards. The wood should never be saturated as this will warp the board, and they should be kept away from heat.

### Pastry-making equipment

A pastry cook needs a good supply of tools as pastry is not improved by handling.
**Blenders** The shape should be a good deep oval to reach the bottom of the deepest bowl. The wires should be of stainless steel.
**Cutters** A graded set of tinned-steel crinkly edged cutters is basic equipment for cookie

making; the top edge should be rolled for strength, the cutting edge sharp.
**Pastry wheels** These can cut straight or crimped lines through pastry or sheets of ravioli with professional panache, dividing dough with a smooth, even pressure.
**Pie funnels** Little china chimneys are placed in pies to prevent the top crust from collapsing into the contents, and to offer a quick way out for the steam.
**Pastry brushes** Soft natural or nylon bristles will spread glazes, jam, or melted butter without damaging the surface of delicate or uncooked pastry. They are also useful for greasing the awkward grooves and ridges on patterned pans and molds.

### Cake-decorating equipment

Icing enhances the look and the taste of certain cakes, whether it is a dribble of frosting or a full-scale cover-up of royal icing.
**Icing bags** These cone-shaped bags are usually made of flexible plastic or tightly woven cotton fabric which can be easily washed and dried after use. A nozzle is fitted into the opening in the tip of the bag and the contents are forced through by twisting the top of the bag and then applying gentle hand pressure.
**Decorating nozzles** A set of these will contain large, plain round nozzles for shaping cream puffs or éclairs, large rosettes for whipped cream fillings, and a galaxy of smaller tubes for decorating iced cakes.

**a** *Tin cream horn mold* **b** *Porcelain scallop shells* **c** *Tinned mold for cold meat pies* **d** *Aluminum madeleine sheet* **e** *Tin éclair sheet or langues de chat pan* **f** *Cast-iron waffle iron* **g** *Tinned petits fours molds* **h** *Bottomless tart frame for fruit flans* **i** *Charlotte pan* **j** *Dariole molds* **k** *Oven-going iron skillet*

**Decorating syringes** These are rigid metal tubes with a range of screw-on nozzles and a plunger to force the icing out. As a rule these are unsatisfactory because the plunger requires considerable force to push the stiffly mixed icing through the nozzle.
**Revolving turntable** When decorating a cake it is important to have the part you are working on facing you—it is all too easy to trail a sleeve across an intricate pattern of wet icing while adding a finishing touch to the far side. Turntables can be rotated as you work with just a flick of a finger.
**Casters or dredgers** are attractive items, usually made of metal such as aluminum. Flour dredgers should have larger holes than sugar dredgers.

### Cooling racks

Raised wire racks are essential for newly baked pastries and cakes. If the steamy moisture is not allowed to escape soon after cooking, it will condense inside the dough, making it leaden. Choose a large one made of good quality tinned steel.

# Electrical Appliances

Before buying any piece of electrical equipment the first thing you must do is check that it is safe to operate and that its cost will be recovered (if not by a saving in store-bought food, then by its frequent use).

### Blenders/liquidizers

For blending soups, making vegetable purées, pâtés and whisking drinks, a blender is the best tool. Many blenders claim to be able to pulverize nuts, chop vegetables and grate cheese, but few have the power and the capacity to do so, unless they possess an additional (sharper) set of blades. A blender is also useless for whipping cream or egg whites. When buying a blender look for a simple two-speed (high and low) type with blades set low in the container. This way you will be able to blend small quantities such as one or two egg yolks for mayonnaise.

Choose the largest blender you can because the container rarely works when more than half full and it is time-consuming trying to blend a huge pan of soup in a blender that takes about a cupful at a time.

The container should be clear toughened glass or heavyweight plastic to enable you to see how things are getting on; avoid lightweight plastic which may chip or crack. A small trapdoor in the lid allows you to dribble in your oil for mayonnaise without spattering the kitchen.

### Hand mixers

The main advantage of an electric mixer over a rotary hand beater is that it frees one hand to hold the bowl or add ingredients as you beat. It is also faster. A disadvantage is the noise level. Choose a mixer with three speeds (high, medium and low) and a switch that is easy to alter with a flick of the thumb. The beaters should be easy to remove for cleaning. Unless you want, or already have, a mixer on a stand, buy a hand mixer with a heavy-duty motor and a selection of beaters for tough jobs such as mixing dough.

### Mixers with stand and bowl

More substantial than a hand mixer, stand mixers are useful for many kitchen jobs besides cake making. Some have a dough hook attachment and some a separate liquidizer and/or coffee mill, which can be used with the same motor and base.

When a mixer also has such varied attachments as a grinder, a juicer, a potato peeler and a shredder and slicer it has really moved into the next function and price bracket of the all-in-one food processor. Before buying a multi-function appliance, check that the motor is capable of coping with the heavy-duty jobs and is not just a glorified blender/mixer.

Depending upon the model, the mixer bowl may be plastic, toughened glass or stainless steel; obviously for durability toughened glass or stainless steel is best. In some mixers the beaters are simply inserted into the motor housing and rotate on the spot. These often leave a ring of unbeaten ingredients around the bowl. The best machines are those with beaters that travel in a circle as they rotate and thus beat every part of the mixture efficiently. Make sure too, if you can, that the beaters are capable of handling a small quantity such as one egg or a tablespoon of fat—you don't always expect to make large quantities. Mixers with light plastic bases and bowls may be lighter to move around, but a solid base with a rubber pad is more practical and will prevent the machine "creeping" during prolonged activity.

### Food processors

The ultimate in kitchen machines, these chop, slice, shred and grate vegetables, grind meat, whip and beat desserts and cakes, knead dough, and purée soups and pâtés. Some models go even further and, with attachments, squeeze citrus fruit, mill coffee, peel potatoes, open cans, make ice cream and pasta. They will not beat egg whites, however, so a separate egg beater is still essential.

The more compact the design, the better for worktop storage, but you will still have to find room for all the attachments.

Choose a model that has a heavy-duty motor and, if possible, one that has a circuit-breaker to prevent it overheating or burning out. Also buy one with a large-capacity bowl because, like blenders, they work better if they are filled no more than half full. Rubber foot pads will make the machine stay put during any operation and if there is a handy niche in the machine for storing the electric cord when not in use, all the better.

Look for the models that will not operate unless the cover is locked in place over the blades, as they are much safer.

### Coffee mills

The advantage of electric coffee mills over manual is that they are quicker, but they are often noisy. The ideal mill is quiet, efficient and neat, and, of course, safe to use. It is also useful if you can preselect the grind required from powder to coarse ground; if you can't, you will find that you never seem to get the same grind twice. The safest electric coffee mills are those which won't work unless the lid is on.

### Filter coffee makers

The electrical filter coffee maker is an elaborate version of the filter drip method. It first boils the water and then pours it over the ground coffee and a hot plate under the

a *Blender that purées and liquidizes*
b *Hand-held mixer with three speeds*
c *Mixer with stand and bowl* d *All-in-one food processor has an assortment of blades*

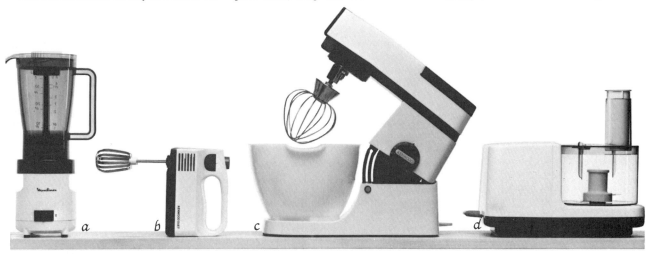

# Electrical Appliances

vessel keeps the coffee warm. As long as you put the correct amount of coffee in the filter, it's a foolproof way to make decent coffee.

## Kettles

Many electrical items are luxurious, but for many people an electric kettle is an essential. The range of styles and capacities is large and depends on personal choice, but look for a long guarantee period and a non-corrosive body. An automatic cut-out kettle which prevents you filling the room with steam is worth paying for.

## Toasters

Toasters are very simple electrical gadgets and because most of them do their job efficiently there is a large selection to choose from. Some have a shade control which is useful. Most toasters are now automatic and eject the toast when it has reached the required shade. Some take four slices—a must for the large family—but most take two. Make sure the slots are wide enough to take thick uneven slices of homemade bread without burning them. Look for a long guarantee and a removable crumb tray.

## Infrared grills

A table-top grill is ideal for apartment-dwellers, people out at work all day and those with a taste for English muffins. They are faster and more economical than traditional electric ranges. There are several models on the market: some have preset heat controls so you can't cook anything gently, others have a variable thermostat. Most models have nonstick surfaces, but unless they are detachable they will be difficult to clean. The use of aluminum foil on the plates cuts down excess fat, which otherwise tends to burn and smoke. These grills are particularly useful for toasted sandwiches and steaks, and for cooking small amounts of frozen food.

## Waffle irons

These are very like the infrared grill in appearance and function—indeed, waffle irons can and do double as sandwich toasters. The main difference is that the waffle iron's grill plates usually have shell-like or square hollows to mold the batter into a solid shape. These also serve to seal the edge of the sandwich and to prevent the filling from running all over the grill surfaces. Usually treated with a nonstick coating, it is nevertheless preferable if the grill plates are removable for washing.

## Slow cookers

At the opposite end of the time scale to infrared grills, slow cookers take the longest time to cook stews, casseroles, pot roasts and many other essentially liquid dishes, thus enabling busy people to put meals on to cook in the morning and to eat them some twelve hours later. The electricity used is minimal (supposedly about the same as a light bulb); preparation time, however, is not reduced, because meat for lengthy cooking is usually browned in hot butter or oil and the cooking liquid is heated before it goes into the casserole. They are ideal for cooking cheap, tough cuts of meat because the slow cooking makes them tender. For preference buy one that has an inner stoneware dish which can be removed for cleaning; however if it is not removable, the highly glazed surface makes it extremely easy to clean with a soft brush and soapy water. Never immerse the entire thing in water, or attempt to clean it while it is plugged in—a rule which applies to all electrical equipment.

## Deep fryers

An electric, thermostatically controlled deep fryer with a lid takes the guesswork and the smell out of frying. It brings the fat up to the correct temperature and holds it there, and comes in chromed or stainless steel, round or square and with various capacities.

## Frying pans

Like the deep fryer, the main advantage of electric pans is that they reach the temperature you select for frying and stay there throughout the cooking. They also leave more space on the stove top for other dishes —useful if you have a small range. But their disadvantages seem to outweigh these advantages. It is difficult to adjust the temperature quickly during cooking if you need to. Since it is not possible to shake the pan, it would be useless for sautéing.

If you have decided to buy one, choose a model with a detachable cord and heat control so the unit can be washed at the sink.

## Yogurt makers

If you want to have creamy, natural yogurt constantly available then a yogurt maker is a must. They are extremely simple to use. All you need is milk and some live yogurt culture. You can add fruit or flavorings at the serving stage if you wish. Some machines have a thermometer to tell you when the milk is at the correct temperature for adding the culture. The mixture is then left gently warming for the required time.

## Ice cream makers

Old methods of ice cream making involved a great deal of stirring over buckets of crushed ice and rock salt. The latest machines can be put into the freezer, where they will achieve the same results in a quarter of the time and with none of the effort. There are two basic shapes: round and rectangular. The rectangular versions tend to be shallower (about 4 in/10 cm high) although they still have a 2 qt/1.5 liter capacity; the round models may be anything from 4 in/10 cm to 8 in/20 cm high and usually hold about 1 qt/1 liter.

Choose an electric ice cream maker that switches itself off and lifts out the paddles when the ice cream becomes thick, or the motor might burn itself out.

## Microwave ovens

The basic advantage of microwave cooking is its amazing speed, but the larger the pieces of food cooked in it, the more slowly it cooks them; and the more pieces cooked, the longer it will take.

The main drawback of microwave is that it cooks by vibrating the molecules in the food, and the energy created cooks it from the center outwards. This means that food does not brown and may look unattractive when cooked. Some ovens do have additional

*a*

*e*

*h*

elements or infrared rays to brown the food, but they consume a vast amount of electricity and are as complicated as (if not more than) simply popping the food in the oven or under the broiler. It is also impossible to cook meat so that it is brown on the outside and rare on the inside.

So why buy a microwave? They do defrost frozen food evenly and speedily. They are also a boon to households full of children hungry for snacks of fish sticks or frozen pies, which can be heated quickly and do not need browning.

But, and this is a big but, the long-term effects of possible microwave radiation have been questioned by some authorities.

## Convection ovens

For fast tabletop cooking, convection ovens are ideal. They do what a microwave oven claims to, but not quite as fast. A steady flow of hot air is circulated around the food, which cooks it in about one-third less time than an ordinary oven. The food browns evenly and there is less shrinkage. They will not cook casseroles or liquid dishes, because it is important to use either the slotted dish that comes with the appliance or to place the food straight onto the oven rack. Conventional vessels reduce the air flow and increase the cooking time. Convection ovens are easy to clean because they have a filter unit that cleans the air and the walls have a special coating that prevents stains. The door is usually easily removed for washing too. Most models are quite small (about 15 in/38 cm high maximum), but they can cope with large roasts and some have a rotisserie. They also defrost efficiently.

## Hot trays

If you have ever cooked a delicious meal and had to keep it waiting in the oven for a late arrival, you will have noticed with some despair how dried up it usually becomes. Hot trays are partially the answer to this problem because they keep food hot without drying it up too much. They come in many shapes and sizes, but the most popular kind is a sheet of shatterproof glass with wooden or plastic handles and a heated area that will hold one large or two small casseroles, and a "hot spot" for coffee.

**a** *Kettle with automatic switch-off mechanism* **b** *Yogurt maker with six glass jars* **c** *Coffee mill with a safety mechanism and cord that winds neatly around the base* **d** *Filter coffee maker with a heatproof glass vessel* **e** *Infrared grill with nonstick coated plates* **f** *Ice cream machine with plastic housing and a tinned steel ice cream container* **g** *Glass hot tray* **h** *Deep-fat fryer, thermostatically controlled* **i** *Two-slice toaster* **j** *Electric frying pan with detachable heat control* **k** *Slow cooker*

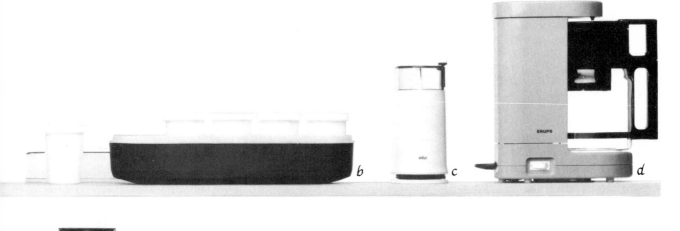

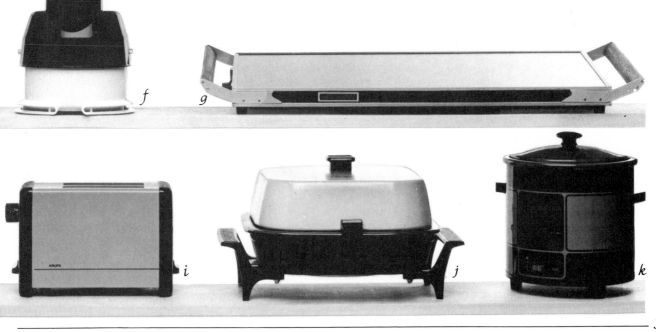

# Miscellanea

When buying kitchen equipment, whether can opener or coffee pot, the rule is quite straightforward. Choose the best, the sturdiest and the simplest.

### Corkscrews
The coil (or worm) should be an extremely sharp, thin spiral, preferably of a triangular section so that it really cuts into the cork. It should have a comfortable, solid handle to pull upon and it should be long enough to penetrate the whole cork.

**The wooden enclosed model** involves no pulling, simply a gentle screwing in and out on the Archimedean screw principle.

**The winged or double-lever version** is easier to use. No pulling is required; the coil is screwed in and the two arms slowly depressed to raise the cork.

**The waiter's friend** (why it's called this is a mystery as it can cut your fingers horribly) only needs a little strength and is quite efficient and reliable.

**The classic corkscrew** with a simple wooden crossbar can need a lot of effort, especially if the cork is a stubborn one.

### Pasta machine
This operates a bit like an old-fashioned clothes mangle with adjustable rollers, and has attachments to produce all shapes and sizes of pasta. The best are made in chrome-plated steel with stainless steel rollers.

### Larding needles and trussing needles
For larding meat you will need a long, hollow needle with a pointed end and a clasp at the other to hold the lardon. For trussing, the needle need not be hollow but it should have a large hole for the twine.

### Bottle openers
Choose the simplest and sturdiest shape you can find. Wooden handles have a nice feel to them; see that the shape fits your hand.

### Nutcrackers
Heavy chromed or silver-plated nutcrackers with a simple squeezing action are probably the most popular and traditional shape, but people with weak wrists may find them difficult to use, so a wooden version like an old linen press is a worthwhile alternative.

### Can openers
**The butterfly-action opener** is not hard to use, but unless it grips the rim of the can firmly it will not move around the can.

**The scythe cutting-action opener** has no moving parts to wear out, but it requires a firm pushing action to cut through the lid.

**A wall-mounted opener** is probably the easiest to use because the can is slotted into the jaws and held there by a lever.

### Coffee makers
**Drip filter** To start with the simplest, the drip filter coffee maker is very quick as you only have to boil the water, then pour it over the finely ground coffee.

**Filter pot** An attractive version of the drip-filter method is the porcelain filter pot. It needs no filter papers, as the top has its own perforations.

**The Neapolitan filter pot** makes hot coffee that is almost as strong as espresso. Made in shiny aluminum, this pot needs to be inverted at one point during its operation, so read the instructions carefully or you could be scalded.

**Moka express** Real dark espresso coffee is easily made with the cast aluminum Junior or Moka espresso pot. When the coffee is made it gurgles up into the upper chamber and the pot must be removed from the heat.

**The cafetière** has an elegant glass container in which the coffee is first infused, then a plunger is pushed to the bottom, which acts as a filter and isolates the grounds.

**Heat-resistant glass coffee makers** The upper and lower sections of glass percolators and filter pots such as the Cona or Chemex are, of course, heatproof but they are also fragile, so be careful when doing the dishes.

a *Pasta machine* b *Filter pot* c *Drip filter*
d *Neapolitan filter* e, f *Moka express*
g *Cona* h *Cafetière* i, j, k, l *Corkscrews*
m *Larding needle* n *Trussing needle*
o *Bottle opener* p *Nutcrackers* q, r, s *Can openers: scythe, butterfly and wall mounted*

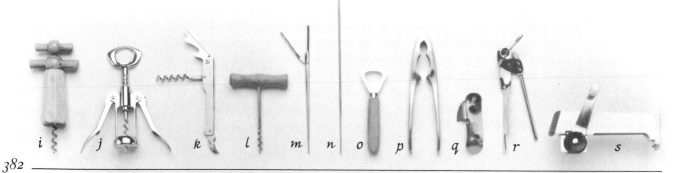

# PART FIVE

## Carving, Glossary & Index

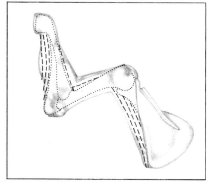

6 *Finish off by carving more vertical slices until you reach the bone*

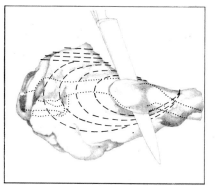

**Leg of lamb** 1 *Start on the rounded, meatier side. Cut slices from the knuckle*

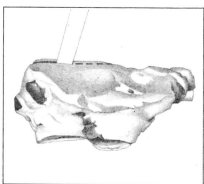

2 *When a small disc of gristle appears in the middle of the lean, turn the leg over*

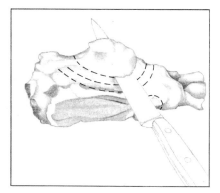

3 *Carve big, flat slices from each surface in turn until you reach the bone*

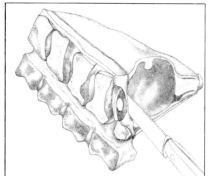

**Rib of beef** 1 *Cut the chined bones away before starting to carve*

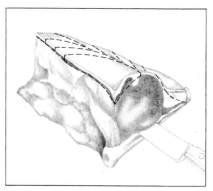

2 *Trim any fat or gristle and run knife carefully between meat and bone*

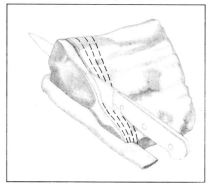

3 *Start carving at the thick end, at a slight angle to the bone*

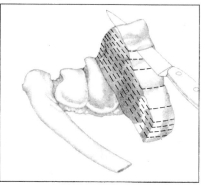

4 *Finish by carving the wedge you are left with, gradually flattening it out*

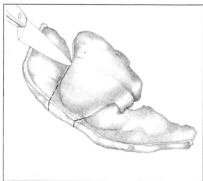

**Steaks** 1 *To carve boneless steak, first divide along the natural seams*

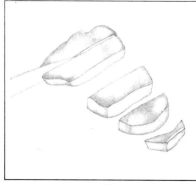

2 *Each muscle tastes different, so share out the meat from each section*

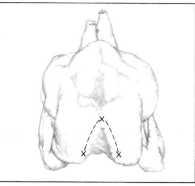

**Large chicken or turkey** 1 *Remove the wishbone by snipping the sinews at either side*

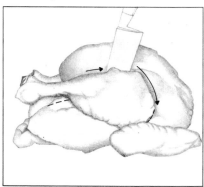

2 *Stick your fork into the drumstick and cut through the ball and socket joint*

Knives **354–356**
Sharpening knives **356,** *356*
Carving knife **356,** *356*
Metal fork **363,** *363*

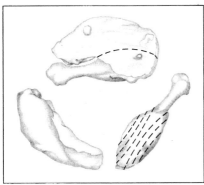

**3** *Cut slices from the thigh and more slices from the drumstick*

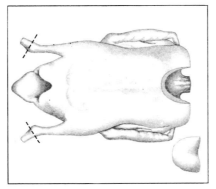

**4** *Starting halfway down the breast, carve careful vertical slices*

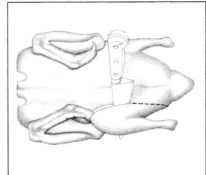

**5** *Remove the wing by levering it away with the fork and cutting through the joint*

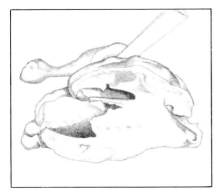

**6** *Carve the other side in the same way, tilting the bird with your fork*

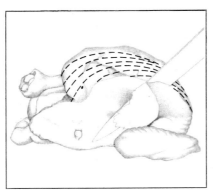

**Large duck 1** *Remove wingtips and cut away the wishbone with a small, sharp knife*

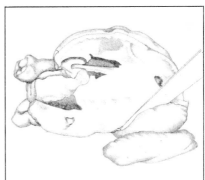

**2** *Turn the bird onto its breast, cut through past the leg, severing the ball joint*

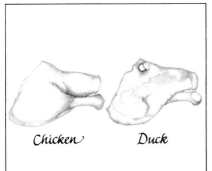

Chicken    Duck

**3** *Divide the leg in two (the leg joint is offset—quite different from a chicken's)*

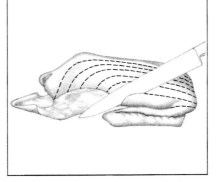

**4** *Turn the bird over and carve vertical slices, working up to the breastbone*

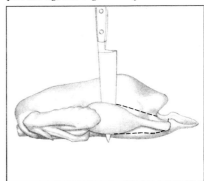

**5** *Now cut the other leg off in the same way as you did the first*

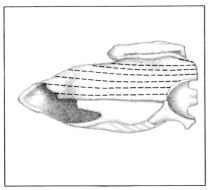

**6** *Carve the other breast—serve the wings whole if the duck is young and tender*

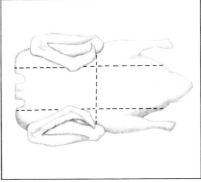

**Small duck 1** *Divide this into portions with blows from a sharp, heavy knife*

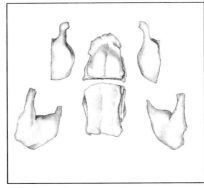

**2** *Sufficient for three—each person gets a meaty bit and a bony bit*

387

# Glossary

## Measurements

In this book, both standard and metric measurements have been given. As the equivalents are not exact (1 ounce in fact equals 28.35 grams, for example), metric measurements have been rounded out. Tablespoons and teaspoons are standard measure – amounts given are for level spoonfuls. In some instances, liquid and butter measurements have been given in non-standard terms because the amount used largely depends on the personal preference of the cook. As a guideline, however, a wine glass traditionally holds 4 fl oz/115 ml, and a nut or knob of butter is about the size of a walnut.

## Cooking terms

### Acidulated water
Water to which lemon juice or vinegar, preferably white wine vinegar, is added, and used to immerse certain vegetables such as celeriac, salsify and globe artichokes to prevent their discoloration. It is also used to purify sweetbreads and brains.

### à la forestière
Food served with morels or other mushrooms sautéed in butter; also refers to diced potatoes fried in butter.

### à la grecque
Vegetables, particularly mushrooms and globe artichokes, cooked in olive oil with coriander seeds and other seasonings and served cold.

### à la lyonnaise
The addition of onion, and sometimes potatoes, as a garnish.

### à la meunière
Literally "in the style of the miller's wife," the phrase refers to browned butter, seasoning, lemon juice and parsley served with food such as fish, sweetbreads and brains.

### à la princesse
Food garnished with asparagus tips.

### à la provençale
Food, especially seafood and vegetables, that is cooked with tomatoes and garlic, usually with the addition of olive oil.

### Al dente
Literally the Italian for "to the tooth." In cooking the phrase is used to describe the texture of food, mainly pasta, when it is properly cooked and just firm to the bite. It can also refer to vegetables.

### Antipasto
Literally meaning "before the pasta," this is the Italian equivalent of hors d'oeuvre and often consists of slices of salami, vegetables marinated in oil and seafood salads.

### Aspic
This is the jelly used to cover or glaze cold foods. Usually the jelly has been clarified so that various decorations such as herb leaves, nuts, olives, or truffles can be seen shining through. An aspic may also refer to a non-sweet jelly served as a salad.

### Au bleu
French term that applies to freshly killed fish, particularly trout, that are poached in a court bouillon until the skin has a bluish tinge. In France, trout can be seen swimming in tanks at the fish dealers—they are killed by a blow on the head at the time of purchase.

### Au gratin
Dishes, usually precooked and topped with a sauce, often containing cheese, that are sprinkled with bread crumbs and broiled or cooked in the oven long enough to brown the top.

### Bain-marie
Also known as a water bath, this consists of a large pan such as a roasting pan filled with water in which saucepans or bowls containing food are set (ideally on a special trivet). The bain-marie may be used to keep prepared foods hot and moist, but its most useful purpose is to ensure that certain delicate foods such as custards and sauces cook at a constant low temperature without drying out or scorching. The advantage of a bain-marie over a double saucepan is that the former ensures that the food remains moist while cooking, due to the surrounding steam caused by water evaporation.

### Bard
Originating from the old French word *barde*, which was a horse's iron armor, this means to wrap thin sheets of fat, usually pork fat (which can be flattened first between two sheets of wax paper), around meat, poultry or game to moisten the flesh while roasting.

### Baste
To spoon juices over food while it cooks to keep it from becoming dry.

### Battuto
The Italian term for a very finely chopped vegetable and bacon or ham mixture which is cooked and then used for flavoring sauces, stews and soups.

### Beurre blanc
A reduced mixture of white wine, wine vinegar and finely chopped shallots into which butter is whisked to make a velvety sauce.

### Beurre manié
Flour and butter worked together to a paste, added as a liaison to thicken soups, sauces and stews.

### Beurre noir
A sauce for skate and other fish, in which butter is cooked until nut brown (not black, despite the name, or it would be burned). Vinegar, parsley and seasoning are then added.

### Beurre noisette
A sauce of butter, cooked until just brown, with lemon juice and seasoning.

### Bind
To add egg or liquid to a mixture to hold it together. Foods such as pâtés, rissoles and stuffings sometimes require binding.

### Bisque
A thick creamy soup based on seafood—especially lobster, crayfish or shrimp—game or poultry.

### Blanch
In cooking terms, this means to immerse food briefly in boiling water to soften it, to remove its skin (as for almonds), or to remove excess salt.

### Braise
To cook food slowly, after it has been browned, in a minimum of liquid under a tight cover.

### Brine
A salt-water solution used to preserve meat, fish or vegetables.

### Canapés
Small cubes or triangles of bread, fresh, fried or toasted, topped with various non-sweet mixtures and served as appetizers.

### Carbonnade
Beef stew in which a large proportion of the cooking liquid is beer.

### Cassoulet
Stew originating from Languedoc and traditionally prepared in an earthenware dish called a *cassolle d'Issel*. Cassoulet consists of dried white beans simmered with meat such as pork, sausages and preserved goose (confit d'oie).

### Charcuterie
This French term refers to the wide assortment of pork products—sausages, pâtés, hams—which are sold in specialist shops called charcuteries.

### Charlotte
The name given to two different desserts that are prepared in a special large round mold. Charlotte russe is a cold, creamy dessert, while a fruit charlotte—usually made with apples—is hot.

### Chiffonade
A garnish for soups consisting of thin ribbons of shredded lettuce, sorrel or other green leafy vegetables, that have usually been lightly cooked in butter.

### Chine
To loosen the backbone from the ribs of a piece of meat to allow easier carving. A butcher will usually do this for you.

### Choucroute garnie
A dish from Alsace of sauerkraut garnished with sausages, pig's ears or feet and similar meats.

### Chowder
A type of soup that takes its name from the French word for pot or cauldron, *chaudière*. The term usually denotes a milk-based seafood soup, such as New England clam chowder.

### Chutney
An Indian relish, cooked or uncooked, of fruits or vegetables and spices mixed together and served with curries and cold meats.

### Clarify
To free fats—particularly butter for cooking—stocks and consommés from impurities.

### Cobbler
This American specialty is a fruit dish—usually made with blueberries, peaches or cherries—baked with a biscuit-like topping and served hot.

### Cocotte
Small ovenproof dish used for baking individual mousses, soufflés or egg dishes.

### Compote
Fruit cooked in a sugar syrup, often seasoned with spices such as cloves and cinnamon.

### Confits
Fruits or vegetables preserved in sugar, often with brandy added. The word is extended to mean meat or poultry preserved in its own fat, the best known of which are confit d'oie and confit de canard—goose and duck.

### Court bouillon
Liquid used for poaching fish, made from water and wine or vinegar with herbs and vegetables for flavoring.

### Crackling
The crisp scored skin of roasted pork.

### Cream
To beat butter or butter and sugar to a light consistency about twice its original volume.

### Croquette
Cork- or oval-shaped mixtures of chopped meat, fish, eggs or vegetables that are egg-and-crumbed and deep fried.

### Croustade
Small pastry or fried bread case in which chopped meat, chicken or game is served.

### Cuisine minceur
The phrase means "slimming cooking" and was developed by the French chef Michel Guérard, who also wrote the book of the same name. His cooking emphasizes the lightness and simplicity of foods and also the use of low fat and dietetic ingredients such as saccharin and *fromage blanc*.

### Curd
The coagulated substance that is produced in milk when milk is soured, usually by the addition of rennet, and used in the making of cheeses.

**Dariole**
Either a small cylindrical mold or the food—usually a pudding, pâté or pastry, such as a custard tart—that is baked in it.

**Daube**
A stew of braised meat and vegetables. *Boeuf en daube* uses red wine as the cooking liquid.

**Deglaze**
To scrape browned solidified cooking juices off the bottom of a roasting or frying pan with the help of a liquid such as wine, brandy or stock. This is used for making sauces and gravies.

**Dégorger**
To soak certain foods, such as sweetbreads, in water to remove too strong a flavor or improve their color. Eggplant and cucumbers are sprinkled with salt and left until their bitter juices are drawn out.

**Devil**
To season foods with spicy ingredients, usually mustard, cayenne and Worcestershire sauce, often in the form of a sauce.

**Dredge**
To coat foods lightly with flour, confectioners' sugar or other fine powder.

**Dress**
When used in connection with poultry or game birds, this means to make them ready for cooking by plucking, cleaning and trussing them. With salads it means to add the vinaigrette.

**Duxelles**
Finely chopped mushrooms, often mixed with chopped shallots or onions, sautéed in butter and used for stuffings and garnishes.

**Emulsion**
A mixture such as mayonnaise in which fat or oil is held in suspension.

**En croûte**
The method of cooking food, particularly pâté and meat, entirely encased in pastry.

**En papillote**
Papillote is literally the French for curl-papers, and food *en papillote* is cooked, and often served, in paper cases (preferably parchment).

**Escabeche**
The word literally means "pickled" and describes a Portuguese and Spanish way of preparing fish, poultry and game. Food is cooked and then pickled in a marinade of vinegar.

**Fabada**
A Spanish stew of beans, usually with sausages, pork and garlic.

**Farce**
Originating as a comic interlude in medieval plays, the farce has since become a type of play in its own right, but its culinary meaning is closely linked to its origin since it is a stuffing that is inserted into meat.

**Flan**
An open pie or tart cooked in a ring. In Spain it means a baked caramel custard.

**Fondue**
Cheese sauce with kirsch and white wine, a specialty of Switzerland. Also vegetables cooked to the consistency of a purée.

**Fool**
An English cold dessert made of puréed fruit and whipped cream.

**Forcemeat**
A mixture of ground meat, vegetables or bread used as a stuffing.

**Forestière, à la,** see *à la forestière*

**Fry, deep-fat**
To immerse food, usually coated with batter or egg and bread crumbs, into very hot deep fat in order to cook it through.

**Fry, shallow**
To cook food in a little fat in a shallow pan.

**Frumenty**
A whole wheat grain porridge popular in medieval England. It was cooked overnight in the ashes of the fire, the lengthy cooking making it set to a jelly.

**Fumet**
A reduced stock, usually made with fish, used to give flavor to other stocks and sauces.

**Galantine**
Boned and stuffed poultry, game or meat, usually glazed with aspic, decorated and served cold.

**Game chips**
Thin rounds of potatoes fried until very crisp and served with roasted game birds.

**Garam masala**
A mixture of ground spices and herbs that is used in making Indian curries.

**Glaze**
To make food shiny by coating it with a sugar syrup, aspic, beaten egg or milk.

**Gluten**
The elastic substance produced by some grains, such as hard or strong wheat, in the presence of water, that helps to trap the air bubbles produced by fermenting yeast, making a light, well-risen bread.

**Granita**
A frozen water ice from Italy flavored with fruit or coffee.

**Grecque, à la,** see *à la grecque*

**Gumbo**
A thick soup, peculiar to Creole cookery, made from shellfish, poultry, tomatoes, okra and filé (powdered sassafras leaves).

**Hang**
To suspend meat or game from hooks for a period of time to make them more tender and allow their flavor to mature.

**Hash**
A fried dish consisting of chopped meat, potatoes and other vegetables, as in corned beef hash. The word is derived from the French *hacher*—to chop.

**Infuse**
To extract flavor from food by steeping in a hot liquid—the resulting liquid is an infusion. This technique is usually applied in making tea, coffee and tisanes. Milk is infused with onion for béchamel sauce.

**Julienne**
Thin match-like strips of vegetables, often used as a garnish, and also a clear soup.

**Kosher**
Food that is prepared according to Jewish dietary laws.

**Langues de chat**
Long narrow pastries which resemble a cat's tongue in appearance, hence their French name. They are often baked in special pans also called langues de chat.

**Lardons** or **lardoons**
Strips of fat which are inserted into meat, using a special needle, to make it more succulent during roasting.

**Liaison**
A thickening for a sauce or soup, either an emulsion such as oil and egg yolk in mayonnaise, or a starch such as flour or cornstarch in a liquid.

**Macedoine**
A mixture, cooked or uncooked, of fruits or vegetables cut into small cubes.

**Macerate**
To steep in sugar, liquor or liqueurs.

**Marc**
The substance left after the pressing of vegetables and fruits, especially applied to grapes in wine-making. Also a clear alcohol made from the pressed grapes after wine-making.

**Marinate**
To soak raw foods in a liquid to make them more tender and flavorful; a typical marinade for meat would include vinegar, herbs and spices, red wine and oil. A marinade also helps to preserve food.

**Matelote**
A fish stew made with wine, onions and sometimes including shellfish, thickened with beurre manié.

**Meunière, à la,** see *à la meunière.*

**Mezzes**
Middle Eastern hors d'oeuvre, often including olives, cheese and sliced sausages, and nuts such as pistachios and almonds.

**Mirepoix**
Diced vegetables such as carrots, onions, parsnips and leeks used as a basis for a braise, or, cooked in butter, as a garnish for cutlet or fish dishes.

**Navarin**
A French lamb or mutton stew made with a large proportion of turnips, carrots, onions and potatoes, and in spring with peas and young vegetables, when it becomes *navarin printemps.*

**Noisette**
A good cut of lamb for party dishes, taken from the rib, that has been trimmed and tied with string into a small boneless round.

**Nouvelle cuisine**
A "new" type of French cooking much in vogue with some of France's great chefs. The message of the *nouvelle cuisine* is simplicity: it rejects the richer aspects of traditional French cooking, while ensuring that the food is still superbly cooked.

**Paella**
Spanish rice dish with a combination of shellfish, ham and chicken, seasoned with saffron and cooked in a round shallow pan, also called a paella.

**Pâté**
A non-sweet mixture of finely chopped meat or game, usually containing a proportion of pork and pork fat, which is baked and served cold, either with or without a casing of pastry. Also mixtures that are not baked, such as fish pâtés.

**Paupiettes**
Thin slices of meat rolled around a non-sweet filling.

**Poach**
To cook gently by immersing food in simmering liquid, frequently a court bouillon.

**Pot-au-feu**
A classic French provincial dish of various meats and vegetables cooked together in water. The resulting broth is eaten first, as a soup, followed by the meat and vegetables.

**Potée**
Thick hearty soup from France cooked in an earthenware pot, often with cabbage; also, by extension, any dish cooked in such a pot.

**Pot-herb**
Any herb used to flavor soups or stews.

**Pot-vegetable**
Any vegetable, but especially the root vegetables,

that is used to give flavor to soups and stews.

**Praline**
Hot caramelized sugar and browned almonds mixed together and left to set into a brittle sheet, which is then broken into pieces or pounded in a mortar to a fine consistency. In America, praline is a type of fudge made of brown sugar and nuts, usually pecans.

**Princesse, à la,** see *à la princesse*

**Provençale, à la,** see *à la provençale*

**Purée**
Cooked food, usually vegetables or fruit, that is mashed and then sieved.

**Quenelles**
Lightly cooked dumplings made of finely chopped fish or meat, such as *quenelles de brochet*, pike dumplings.

**Quiche**
Originally from Lorraine, a baked pastry shell containing a custard of eggs and milk or cream, often mixed with cheese and bacon, or fresh vegetables such as spinach, asparagus or leeks, or fish such as salmon or haddock.

**Ragout**
French stew of meat and vegetables.

**Ragú**
Italian for a meat stew or meat sauce.

**Ramekin**
Small ovenproof dish for individual servings.

**Ratafia**
A tiny macaroon; also a flavoring made from bitter almonds, or from the almond-flavored kernels of certain fruits.

**Reduce**
To concentrate or thicken a liquid by rapid boiling. To reduce by half means to boil until half the liquid has evaporated.

**Render**
To melt animal fat slowly to a liquid. It is then strained to eliminate any residue.

**Ripieno**
Italian word for stuffing: for example, *pera ripiena*, stuffed pear.

**Risotto**
An Italian dish based on rice. Blanched round-grain rice of the Arborio type, which absorbs liquid in large quantities, is used to make the best risottos.

**Rissole**
Small patty made of cooked meat, sometimes with rice or vegetables, bound together and fried.

**Roulades**
French for either rolled slices of meat or pastry stuffed with cheese, or for galantine-like preparations in the form of a long roll. Sometimes also used to describe rolled soufflé omelets.

**Roux**
Fat, usually butter, and flour mixed together and cooked to make the basis for non-sweet sauces.

**Rub in**
To mix flour or other dry ingredients with fat, usually butter or lard, using the fingertips to give a crumbly rather than a smooth result. This technique is especially important in the making of pastry and shortcake.

**Rusk**
Dried and hardened bread.

**Salmi**
Ragout of game cooked in red wine.

**Sambals**
Hot, spiced side dishes, akin to Western hors

d'oeuvre, served as an accompaniment to Indonesian or southern Indian food.

**Sauté**
From the French word "to jump"; brisk cooking in a small amount of fat in a shallow frying pan, shaking the pan to make sure that the pieces being fried are evenly browned. The food is either just browned or cooked through.

**Scald**
To heat liquid, usually milk, to just below boiling point, until bubbles form around the edge of the pan. Fruit and vegetables are also scalded in boiling water to remove their skins.

**Score**
To make shallow cuts, preferably with a heavy knife, over the surface of certain meats such as steaks, to tenderize them by cutting through their fine connecting tissues before they are either broiled or fried.

**Seviche**
Pieces of raw fish marinated in lemon or lime juice, the acidity of which "cooks" them.

**Simmer**
To keep a liquid at just below boiling point so that it remains gently "shivering."

**Smörgåsbord**
Swedish selection of cold buffet-type foods such as sliced meats, crisp breads, pickled fish and cheese.

**Smørrebrød**
Literally Danish "buttered bread": open-faced sandwiches, often with sliced meats and cheese.

**Souse**
To pickle in vinegar or brine; a method particularly applied to oily fish such as herrings.

**Steam**
To cook food in steam in a perforated container set above boiling water.

**Stir-fry**
A method of cooking favored by the Chinese, in which finely chopped ingredients are quickly stirred and tossed in a little oil or lard over a high heat. A wok is the best pan for this as the rounded shape distributes the heat evenly and a lot of food can be fried in a very little fat.

**Stock**
A well-flavored broth in which meat, poultry or vegetables or a combination of these have been cooked. It is used instead of water in the cooking of many dishes, particularly soups and sauces, to enhance their flavor.

**Stufato**
Italian for a meat stew with wine.

**Sweat**
To soften vegetables, particularly onions, by cooking them gently, covered, so that they release their juices but do not brown.

**Tapas**
Snacks traditionally served in Spanish bars, consisting of marinated vegetables, olives, meats and slices of cold Spanish omelet and the like.

**Tart**
Open-faced pie made of pastry filled with fruit or other sweet fillings; in America, any small pie, covered or open faced.

**Terrine**
The earthenware, oblong pot used for cooking pâté; the word is extended to mean the food which is cooked in a terrine. Terrines are usually lined with strips of fat.

**Timbale**
Cup-shaped earthenware or metal mold; also the

dish cooked in such a mold, usually containing rice or pasta.

**Turnover**
A sweet or savory filled pastry folded in a triangle.

**Vol-au-vent**
Light puff pastry case usually filled with chopped hard-boiled eggs, meat, fish or poultry in a sauce.

**Whey**
The watery liquid that separates out when milk or cream curdles.

**Zest**
The oily outer part of citrus skin, used as a flavoring agent.

## Papers, plastics and foils

**Aluminum foil**
An indispensable item of kitchen equipment, foil has two main advantages: it is non-flammable, and it cools immediately it is removed from the heat. Its one disadvantage is that it is thin and tears easily. Its uses are many: as a substitute lid for casseroles and baked dishes; as a cover for cakes, breads and meats that are browning too fast in the oven; as an easy-to-handle wrapper for such things as garlic bread, baked potatoes or pieces of chicken; as a lining for oven, broiler and barbecue racks; and as a freezer and general food wrap. Made of nothing more than a rolled out block of pure aluminum, it can be used shiny or dull side up, and pieces can be folded and reused several times.

**Boiling bags**
These come in handy for people living alone. Small portions of food can be frozen in the bag, then simply taken from the freezer and dropped into boiling water, still in the bag.

**Freezer bags**
These come in all shapes and sizes and should be kept in plentiful supply if you have a freezer, since they are perfect for freezing practically all foods except liquids. Make sure that they are vapor-proof. Ordinary plastic bags are not thick enough to prevent loss of moisture by the contents and should not be used for storing food in the freezer.

**Parchment paper**
This is the traditional type of cooking paper to use when cooking *en papillote*. Aluminum foil often takes its place nowadays, as it is less expensive and easier to obtain. Foods come away easily from parchment paper and it is also used to line pans for foods such as meringues, which tend to stick.

**Plastic wrap**
This is a most useful invention. When covered with plastic wrap refrigerated foods with pervading smells, such as melon, lemons and cheese, are no longer a problem. Stretched over plastic or china bowls (it grips wood and metal less effectively), plastic wrap makes an airtight seal, keeping foods fresh for much longer than usual and staving off discoloration in such dishes as puréed avocado—the plastic wrap in this case must be in contact with the food.

**Roasting bags**
The advantages of these crinkly, transparent bags are that they keep the oven clean, since all the fat and juices from the roast are sealed inside the bag, and they are self-basting. They are mainly used for roasting chicken, but all meat and fish can be cooked in them.

**Wax paper**
This can be used to cover dishes in the refrigerator and to line baking pans. It is coated with paraffin on both sides and does not provide such an airtight seal as plastic wrap.

# Index

# Index

# Index

# Index

# Index

# Acknowledgements

The Publishers would like to thank the following for their invaluable help and advice in compiling this book:

## PARTS ONE & TWO

Chris Sowe (Assistant to Clive Corless)
A–Z Collection/Eric Soothill
Carolyn Brooke (who, with Caroline Conran, tested all the recipes)
Diane Corless
Mary Ann Green
Doreen Messant
Anna Monaghan
Rocco Longo/Bruce Coleman
Marion Starr

Agricultural Attaché, American Embassy, London
W. Baxter & Sons, Leadenhall Market, London EC3
Billington (Edward) (Sugar) Ltd
British Egg Information Service
British Farm Produce Council
British Poultry Federation
Robert Bruce, Covent Garden, London WC2
I. Camisa & Son, 61 Old Compton Street, London W1
Cheese From Switzerland Ltd
Victor A. Shanley and Raymond Sargent of Clifton Nurseries Ltd (Garden Centres), Clifton Villas, Warwick Avenue, London W9
Bryan Simpson, Technical Advisor, ESS-Foods (UK) Ltd Danish Agricultural Producers
W. Fenn Ltd, 27 Frith Street, London W1
German Food Centre, 44 Knightsbridge, London SW1
Harrods Ltd, Knightsbridge, London SW1
International Food Store, 8 Green's Court, London W1
Adrian Cullingford of Justin de Blank, 42 Elizabeth Street, London SW1
Mack & Edwards Ltd, Covent Garden, London WC2
Ministry of Agriculture, Fisheries and Food
Arthur Myall & Sons Ltd, 23 Romilly Street, London W1
National Dairy Council
Natural Sausage Casing Association
Roberto Terzaga of Negroni (Pietro) Ltd
Dr Peter Moore, Department of Plant Sciences, King's College, Half Moon Lane, Herne Hill, London SE24

R. Portwine & Sons, Leadenhall Market, London EC3
Richards (Fishmongers), 11 Brewer Street, London W1
Selfridges, Oxford Street, London W1
Jack Shiells, 11 Billingsgate Market, London EC3
J. O. Sims Ltd, Borough Market, London SE1
E. P. Spackmann, 25 High Street, Hungerford, Berkshire
John Steed, Suffolk
Sunwheel Foods Ltd
Swedish Embassy, London
Wendy Godfrey, Home Economist, Tate & Lyle Refineries Ltd
Van den Berghs & Jurgens Limited
Pat Rance of Wells Stores, Streatley, Berkshire
And many thanks to all stallholders at the Berwick Street and Rupert Street Markets, London W1

## PART THREE

Jean-Luc Bernard (Assistant to Christine Hanscomb)
Antonia Gaunt
Dinah Morrison

## PART FOUR

Jonathan Grey (Assistant to Terry Trott)
Jackie Baker
Keith Hammond

Our very special thanks to the following companies who so kindly loaned us equipment for photography:
Braun
The Conran Shop, 77/79 Fulham Road, London SW3
Elizabeth David, 46 Bourne Street, London SW1
Divertiment, 68/72 Marylebone Lane, London W1
Habitat, 206–222 King's Road, London SW3 & 156 Tottenham Court Road, London W1
Leon Jaeggi, 232 Tottenham Court Road, London W1
Kenwood
Krups (UK) Ltd
David Mellor, 4 Sloane Square, London SW1
Moulinex Ltd

William Page & Co., 87/91 Shaftesbury Avenue, London W1
Prestige
Rima Electric Ltd
Salton Ltd
H. & M. Staines Catering Equipment, 15/19 Brewer Street, London W1
Sunbeam

## INDEX

Anne Hardy